Hasanlu V:
The Late Bronze and Iron I Periods

Robert H. Dyson at the entrance to stone tomb SK49 in Operation X (1958).

HASANLU EXCAVATION REPORTS

Voigt, Mary M. 1983. *Hajji Firuz Tepe, Iran: The Neolithic Settlement.* Hasanlu Excavation Reports, Vol. 1.

Danti, Michael D. 2004. *The Ilkhanid Heartland: Hasanlu Tepe (Iran) Period I.* Hasanlu Excavation Reports, Vol. 2.

HASANLU SPECIAL STUDIES

Winter, Irene J. 1980. *A Decorated Breastplate from Hasanlu, Iran.* Hasanlu Special Studies, Vol. 1.

Muscarella, Oscar White 1980. *The Catalogue of Ivories from Hasanlu, Iran.* Hasanlu Special Studies, Vol. 2.

Marcus, Michelle I. 1996. *Emblems of Identity and Prestige: The Seals and Sealings from Hasanlu, Iran.* Hasanlu Special Studies, Vol. 3.

de Schauensee, Maude, editor. 2011. *Peoples and Crafts in Period IVB at Hasanlu, Iran.* Hasanlu Special Studies, Vol. 4.

Hasanlu Excavation Reports III

Hasanlu V:
The Late Bronze and Iron I Periods

Michael D. Danti

with contributions by
Megan Cifarelli

UNIVERSITY OF PENNSYLVANIA MUSEUM OF ARCHAEOLOGY AND ANTHROPOLOGY
PHILADELPHIA

LIBRARY OF CONGRESS CATALOGING-IN-PUBLICATION DATA

Danti, Michael D.
 Hasanlu V : the Late Bronze and Iron I periods /
 Michael D. Danti ; with contributions by Megan Cifarelli.
     pages   cm
 Includes bibliographical references.
 ISBN-13: 978-1-934536-61-2 (hardcover : acid-free paper)
 ISBN-10: 1-934536-61-X (hardcover : acid-free paper)
 1. Hasanlu Site (Iran) 2. Iran–Antiquities. 3. Hasanlu Site (Iran)–Historiography. I. Title.
 DS262.H37D357 2013
 935'.74--dc23
                                  2013014062

© 2013 by the University of Pennsylvania Museum of Archaeology and Anthropology
Philadelphia, PA
All rights reserved. Published 2013

Published for the University of Pennsylvania Museum of Archaeology and Anthropology by the University of Pennsylvania Press.

Printed in the United States of America on acid-free paper.

This Book is Dedicated to
Professor Gordon D. Young (1936–2012)
Long-Time Professor of Ancient History at Purdue University
Mentor, Scholar, Raconteur, and Friend
So Many of Us Owe You So Much

Contents

List of Figures	ix
List of Plates	xv
List of Tables	xix
Abbreviations	xxi
Acknowledgments	xxiii
Preface	xxv
1. Ušnu-Solduz and the Lake Urmia Region in the Later 2nd Millennium BC	1
2. "Hasanlu V": Definition, Research Questions, and History of Scholarship	25
3. The Reanalysis of "Hasanlu V": Stratigraphy, Architecture, and Radiocarbon Dating	53
4. Overview of the Ceramic Assemblages of Hasanlu VIa–IVc	143
5. The Middle Bronze, Late Bronze, and Iron I Graves of Hasanlu and Dinkha	277
6. The Personal Ornaments of Hasanlu VIb–IVc *by Megan Cifarelli*	313
7. Conclusions	323
Appendix I. Archaeological Survey and Reconnaissance of Ušnu-Solduz	331
Appendix IIa–e. Radiocarbon Dates	353
Appendix III. Concordance of Section Numbers and Stratum Descriptions	367
Appendix IVa. Catalog of Hasanlu Burials of Periods VIb–IVc by Periods	397
Appendix IVb. Catalog of Hasanlu Low Mound Burials	407
Appendix V. Architectural Dimensions	415
Appendix VI. Catalog of Personal Ornaments, Cemetery, Outer Town, Hasanlu Periods VIb–IVc	417
Bibliography	421
Plates	437

Figures

(The color insert and foldout seriation appear between pages 292 and 293)

1.1	Map of the Near East	*color insert*
1.2	The Lake Urmia Basin	*color insert*
1.3	Map of the Solduz Valley showing archaeological sites and modern settlements	*inside back cover*
1.4	Topographic map of Hasanlu Tepe showing excavation areas relevant to the later 2nd millennium BC	18
1.5	The Iron I Citadel of Hasanlu Tepe	20
1.6	The Iron II Citadel of Hasanlu Tepe	21
2.1	Original chronology of Hasanlu Tepe	30
2.2	Revised Bronze and Iron Age chronology of Ušnu-Solduz	30
2.3	Two-sigma radiocarbon date ranges for Hasanlu and Dinkha, Periods VII–IVc	*color insert*
2.4.	Two-sigma radiocarbon date ranges for Hasanlu and Dinkha, Periods VIb–IVb	*color insert*
3.1	Hasanlu Tepe: Operation W28/LXXX in 1960 showing the Well Trench and Well Sounding	58
3.2	Hasanlu Tepe: sherds from the Well Trench and Well Sounding (Op. LXXX/Grid W28)	60
3.3	Hasanlu Tepe: north section of Operation I (T28)	62
3.4	Hasanlu Tepe: east section of Operation I (T28)	62
3.5	Hasanlu Tepe: the northwest citadel in Period IVb	64
3.6	Hasanlu Tepe: north section of Operation QR20 showing IIIb fortification wall and the probable IVb fortification wall	65
3.7	Hasanlu Tepe: Operation II west section showing IIIb fortification wall and the probable IVb fortification wall	65
3.8	Hasanlu Tepe: calibrated one-sigma radiocarbon date ranges and pooled mean from carbonized grain and grape samples found in the Terminal IVb phase of Burned Building III	69
3.9	Hasanlu Tepe: the northwest citadel in Period IVc	70
3.10	Hasanlu Tepe: the northwest citadel in Period V	72
3.11	Hasanlu Tepe: north section of the U22 Sounding	74
3.12	Hasanlu Tepe: east section of the U22 Sounding	76
3.13	Hasanlu Tepe: east section of T22	78
3.14	Dyson's sketch of the U22 north section of 1962	79
3.15	Hasanlu Tepe: east section of S22	80
3.16	Hasanlu Tepe: RS22–23 Period V columned hall	82
3.17	Hasanlu Tepe: RS22–23 Period IVc columned hall	83
3.18	Hasanlu Tepe: east section of R22	84
3.19	Hasanlu Tepe: RS22–23 early Period V architecture	87
3.20	Hasanlu Tepe: the Q24 Area Pre-Burned Building III	90
3.21	Hasanlu Tepe: the entry to Burned Building III of probable Period IVc as excavated in 1962–64	90
3.22	Hasanlu Tepe: section A–A' of the entry area of BBIII	92
3.23	Hasanlu Tepe: section B–B' of the entry area of BBIII	93

3.24	Hasanlu Tepe: the YZ27–29 area as excavated showing remains of Periods V–IVc below Period IVb Burned Building I East	94
3.25	Hasanlu Tepe: east and south sections below BBIE Room 3 of Period IVb	96
3.26	Hasanlu Tepe: west and north sections below BBIE Room 3 of Period IVb	98
3.27	Hasanlu Tepe: east section below BBIE Room 6	100
3.28	Hasanlu Tepe: north section below BBIE Room 6	102
3.29	Hasanlu Tepe: south section below BBIE Room 6	103
3.30	Hasanlu Tepe: west section below BBIE Room 6	104
3.31	Hasanlu Tepe: east section below BBIE Room 5	106
3.32	Hasanlu Tepe: west section below BBIE Room 5	108
3.33	Hasanlu Tepe: north section below BBIE Room 5	110
3.34	Hasanlu Tepe: south section below BBIE Room 5	112
3.35	Hasanlu Tepe: YZ27–29 Phase V:1b	113
3.36	Hasanlu Tepe: YZ27–29 Phase V:1a	114
3.37	Hasanlu Tepe: YZ27–29 Phase IVc:3b	115
3.38	Hasanlu Tepe: YZ27–29 Phase IVc:3a	116
3.39	Hasanlu Tepe: YZ27–29 Phase IVc:2	117
3.40	Hasanlu Tepe: YZ27 west section below the façade of BBIW	118
3.41	Comparison of the YZ27–29 Building and the Lower Court Gate	119
3.42	Hasanlu Tepe: the location of the soundings in the Burned Building II western storerooms	120
3.43	Hasanlu Tepe: pre-Burned Building II remains in BB28–29	121
3.44	Hasanlu Tepe: sections from the soundings in the western storerooms of Burned Building II	121
3.45	Hasanlu Tepe: north section of CC27	122
3.46	Hasanlu Tepe: south section of BB28–29	122
3.47	Hasanlu Tepe: Operation CC27 Period IVc	123
3.48	Hasanlu Tepe: DD30–DD31 Periods IVb and IVc	124
3.49	Hasanlu Tepe: V30–V31 Period V	125
3.50	Hasanlu Tepe: south section of Operation IV	126
3.51	Hasanlu Tepe: west section of Operation IV	127
3.52	Hasanlu Tepe: graves in Operation IV	128
3.53	Hasanlu Tepe: Operation V BBXIII Artisan's House Phase C	129
3.54	Hasanlu Tepe: Operation VI and extensions	130
3.55	Hasanlu Tepe: burials in Operations VI, VIa, VIb, and VIc	131
3.56	Hasanlu Tepe: east and north sections Operation VI	132
3.57	Hasanlu Tepe: south and west sections Operation VI	132
3.58	Hasanlu Tepe: north and west sections Operation VIa	133
3.59	Hasanlu Tepe: vessels from Operations VI and VIa	134
3.60	Hasanlu Tepe: south section Operation VIb	135
3.61	Hasanlu Tepe: select burials in Operations VIe, VIf, VIh, and VIj	136
3.62	Hasanlu Tepe: south section Operation X	137
3.63	Hasanlu Tepe: west section Operation X	138
3.64	Hasanlu Tepe: south section Operation LIII	139
3.65	Key to sections	140
4.1	Hasanlu Tepe: U22 ceramics of Period VIb	148
4.2	Hasanlu Tepe: U22 ceramics of Period VIb	150

4.3	Dinkha IV jars by Ware Types	*color insert*
4.4	Dinkha IV bowls by Ware Types	*color insert*
4.5	Dinkha IV pots by Ware Types	*color insert*
4.6	Frequency of Dinkha IV wares by phases	*color insert*
4.7a	Typical Terminal MBII (Dinkha Period IV Phase D) bowls	156
4.7b	Rare Terminal MBII (Dinkha Period IV Phase D) bowls	156
4.8	Rare Terminal MBII (Dinkha Period IV Phase D) bowls	158
4.9	Terminal MBII (Dinkha Period IV Phase D) pots	160
4.10	Terminal MBII (Dinkha Period IV Phase D) pots	162
4.11	Terminal MBII (Dinkha Period IV Phase D) ceramics	164
4.12	Terminal MBII Dinkha (Period IV Phase D) ceramics from Tomb B10a B27	166
4.13	Terminal MBII Dinkha (Period IV Phase D) ceramics from Tomb B10a B27	168
4.14	Hasanlu Tepe: sherds from Operation I Stratum 6a	170
4.15	Dinkha Tepe: Kramer's ceramic types exclusively in Grey Ware	172
4.16	Dinkha Tepe: Hasanlu VIa ceramics	174
4.17a	Dinkha Tepe: Hasanlu VIa Urmia Ware	176
4.17b	Dinkha Tepe: Urmia Ware from various contexts	176
4.18	Dinkha Tepe: early Hasanlu V "Trash Deposit"	180
4.19	Hasanlu and Dinkha Tepe: bowls from Periods VIa and early V graves	186
4.20	Hasanlu Tepe: early Period V ceramics from the U22 Sounding	188
4.21	Hasanlu Tepe: early Period V ceramics from the U22 Sounding	190
4.22a	Geoy Tepe: lower Tomb K	192
4.22b	Geoy Tepe: upper Tomb K	192
4.23	Hasanlu Tepe: early Period V ceramics from the U22 Sounding	194
4.24	Hasanlu Tepe: early Period V ceramics from the U22 Sounding	196
4.25	Hasanlu and Dinkha Tepe: jars from Periods VIa and early V graves	198
4.26	Hasanlu and Dinkha Tepe: cups and small jars from Periods VIa and early V graves	200
4.27	Hasanlu Tepe: early Period V ceramics from the U22 Sounding	202
4.28	Hasanlu Tepe: late Period V ceramics from the U22 Sounding	206
4.29	Hasanlu Tepe: late Period V ceramics from the U22 Sounding	208
4.30	Hasanlu Tepe: late Period V ceramics from RS22–23	210
4.31	Hasanlu Tepe: late Period V–IVc ceramics from RS22–23	212
4.32	Hajji Firuz and Dinkha Tepe: bowls and cups from late Period V graves	214
4.33	Hasanlu Tepe: late Period V ceramics from the U22 Sounding	216
4.34	Hasanlu Tepe: late Period V ceramics from the U22 Sounding	218
4.35	Hasanlu Tepe: late Period V ceramics from the U22 Sounding	220
4.36	Hajji Firuz, Hasanlu, and Dinkha Tepe: bowls and cups from late V graves	222
4.37	Hasanlu Tepe: Period V ceramics from below the late Hasanlu V columned-hall structure of RS22–23	224
4.38	Hasanlu Tepe: ceramics from Q24 Stratum 10	226
4.39	Hasanlu Tepe: ceramics from Q24 Stratum 10	228
4.40	Hasanlu Tepe: ceramics from Q24 Stratum 10	230
4.41	Hasanlu Tepe: Period IVc bowls from RS22–23	232
4.42	Hasanlu Tepe: Period IVc holemouth jars from RS22–23	234
4.43	Hasanlu Tepe: Period IVc ceramics from RS22–23	236

4.44	Hasanlu Tepe: Period IVc bowls from YZ27–29	238
4.45	Hasanlu Tepe: Period IVc bowls from YZ27–29	240
4.46	Hasanlu Tepe: Period IVc bowls from YZ27–29	242
4.47	Hasanlu Tepe: Period IVc holemouth jars from YZ27–29	244
4.48	Hasanlu Tepe: Period IVc holemouth jars from YZ27–29	246
4.49	Hasanlu Tepe: Period IVc jars from YZ27–29	248
4.50	Hasanlu Tepe: Period IVc cups, holemouth jars, and jars from YZ27–29	250
4.51	Hasanlu and Dinkha Tepe: Period IVc bowls from graves	252
4.52	Hasanlu and Dinkha Tepe: Period IVc vessels from graves	254
4.53	Hasanlu and Dinkha Tepe: Period IVc jars from graves	256
4.54	Hasanlu Tepe: Period IVc ceramics from U22 Stratum 5–6	258
4.55	Hasanlu Tepe: late Period IVc–early Period IVb ceramics from RS22–23	260
4.56	Hasanlu Tepe: late Period IVc–early Period IVb ceramics from RS22–23	262
4.57a	Hasanlu Tepe: Period IVc ceramics from Test Trench A in the northwest storeroom (Room 13) of Burned Building II (Grid BB28)	264
4.57b	Hasanlu Tepe: Period IVc ceramics from Test Trench A in the center west storeroom (Room 14) of Burned Building II (Grid BB28)	264
4.58	Hasanlu Tepe: Period IVc–IVb ceramics from the south storeroom (Room 6) of Burned Building V	266
4.59	Hasanlu Tepe: Period IVc–IVb ceramics from the south storeroom (Room 6) of Burned Building V	268
4.60	Hasanlu Tepe: Period IVc–early IVb ceramics from the west storeroom (Room 4) of Burned Building V	270
4.61	Bowl types in Ušnu-Solduz over time	272
4.62	Cup types in Ušnu-Solduz over time	273
4.63	Holemouth jar types in Ušnu-Solduz over time	274
4.64	Jar types in Ušnu-Solduz over time	275
5.1	Hasanlu Tepe: SK4–5, Operation IV	284
5.2	Hasanlu Tepe: SK45, Operation X	285
5.3	Hasanlu Tepe: SK49, Operation X	287
5.4	Hasanlu Tepe: SK61, Operation VIa	288
5.5	Hasanlu Tepe: SK66, Operation VIa	289
5.6	Hasanlu Tepe: SK112, Operation LIVf	290
5.7	Hasanlu Tepe: SK70, Operation VIa	290
5.8	Hasanlu Tepe: SK25, Operation VI	291
5.9	Hasanlu Tepe: SK29, Operation VI	292
5.10	Hasanlu Tepe: SK504, Operation VIj	294
5.11	Hasanlu Tepe: SK116, Operation LIII	296
5.12	Hasanlu Tepe: SK67, Operation VIb	296
5.13	Hasanlu Tepe: SK445/449, Operation VIc	297
5.14	Hasanlu Tepe: SK459, Operation VIe	298
5.15	Hajji Firuz Tepe: K10 Burial 1	300
5.16	Hasanlu Tepe: SK479, Operation VIf	303
5.17	Hasanlu Tepe: SK494, Operation VIh	304
5.18	Hasanlu Tepe: SK24, Operation VI	305

5.19	Hasanlu Tepe: SK73, Operation VIa	306
5.20	Hasanlu Tepe: SK57, Operation VIa	308
5.21	Hasanlu Tepe: SK6, Operation IV	309
5.22	Hasanlu Tepe: SK53, Operation VIa	309
5.23	Hasanlu Tepe: SK63, Operation VIb	310

Seriation of Periods VIb–Early IVb Graves from Hasanlu, Dinkha, Geoy, Yanik, and Hajji Firuz with Relevant Diagnostics from Hasanlu and Dinkha Occupation Deposits *after page 292*

Plates

3.1	Hasanlu Tepe: The Well Trench and Well Sounding looking east in 1960	438
3.2a	Hasanlu Tepe: The Operation I area in the central depression of the High Mound in 1956, looking southwest	439
3.2b	Hasanlu Tepe: Operation I in 1956 showing the central depression of the High Mound	439
3.3a	Hasanlu Tepe: R24. Victims SK197, SK199, and SK200 of Terminal Period IVb in the court of Burned Building III in 1962	440
3.3b	Hasanlu Tepe: S24. Distribution of objects in the BBIII Room 4 kitchen in 1962	440
3.4	Hasanlu Tepe: S24 and R24. The BBIII Room 4 kitchen in 1962 looking south	441
3.5	Hasanlu Tepe: R24. The north end of the Room 4 kitchen of BBIII in 1962 looking northwest to the doorway of Room 5	442
3.6a	Hasanlu Tepe: S24. The BBIII Room 4 kitchen in 1962 looking southeast	443
3.6b	Hasanlu Tepe: S24. Artifacts in the Room 4 kitchen of BBIII in 1962 looking southeast	443
3.7	Hasanlu Tepe: R24. The interior of BBIII Room 5 showing the level of the floor and the upper portion of the burned deposit in 1962. Bronze in storage jar not *in situ*	444
3.8a	Hasanlu Tepe. Right foreground: Period IVc U22 Building Room 1. Center background: the eastern wall of Period IVB BBVII. Right background: Operation T23. Looking northeast in 1962	445
3.8b	Hasanlu Tepe. Foreground: U22 Stratum 6, U22 IVc Building Room 2. Center middle: U22 IVc Building Room 3. Left background: T23 Stratum 4. Looking north in 1962	445
3.9a	Hasanlu Tepe: The cleaning of the "U22 Period VI test pit" in 1970 looking southeast	446
3.9b	Hasanlu Tepe: U22 Deep Sounding looking north in 1972. The stone footings of the Period V structure are visible in the foreground (Rooms 1 and 2)	446
3.10	Hasanlu Tepe: U22 Deep Sounding Area 7 Stratum 15 looking northwest in 1972	447
3.11a	Hasanlu Tepe: U22 Deep Sounding Strata 37–42 from the west in 1974	448
3.11b	Hasanlu Tepe: U22 Deep Sounding Strata 37–42 from the southwest in 1974	448
3.12a	Hasanlu Tepe: S22 Wall D and Wall E in 1972 from the west	449
3.12b	Hasanlu Tepe: S22 stairwell in 1972 from the southwest	449
3.13	Hasanlu Tepe: S22 stairwell in 1972 looking northwest	450
3.14	Hasanlu Tepe: RS22–23 Period V structure, looking northwest in 1972	451
3.15	Hasanlu Tepe: RS22–23 Period V columned hall, looking northeast in 1972	452
3.16	Hasanlu Tepe: RS22–23 Period V columned hall, looking southeast in 1972	453
3.17	Hasanlu Tepe: RS22 Stratum 11 column base and raised hearth, looking northeast in 1972	454
3.18	Hasanlu Tepe: S22 Wall D looking southeast in 1972	455
3.19	Hasanlu Tepe: S22 Area 15 Stratum 11 reed impressions under Wall D in 1972	456
3.20	Hasanlu Tepe: Burned Building III portico room (Room 6) looking northwest in 1962	457
3.21	Hasanlu Tepe: Burned Building III's main entrance looking northwest in 1962	458
3.22	Hasanlu Tepe: Burned Building III buttresses in Q24 looking northwest in 1962	459

3.23a	Hasanlu Tepe: YZ28 Area 4 and Wall 22, Room 5 on the left and Room 2 on the right; looking west in 1972	460
3.23b	Hasanlu Tepe: Y28 Area 6 and Wall 22, Room 4 on the left and Room 2 on the right; looking west in 1972	460
3.24a	Hasanlu Tepe: Z29 Wall 26 and Area 4 on the right and Area 1/Room 4 on the left; looking east in 1972	461
3.24b	Hasanlu Tepe: Z29 Area 1/Room 4 on the right and Area 4 on the left; looking west in 1972	461
3.25a	Hasanlu Tepe: Y28 Area 6 and Wall 22 looking east in 1972. Stone footings of Walls 21 and 24 in the background; Room 2 on the left and Room 4 on the right	462
3.25b	Hasanlu Tepe: Y28 Area 6 from the north in 1972. Room 4 in the background, Room 2 in the foreground. Stone footings of Walls 21 and 24 on the left	462
3.26a	Hasanlu Tepe: Y28 Area 6/Room 2 looking north in 1972	463
3.26b	Hasanlu Tepe: Y28–29 Area 6/ Room 2 looking northwest in 1972	463
3.27a	Hasanlu Tepe: Burned Building II northeast corner of Room 13	464
3.27b	Hasanlu Tepe: Burned Building II northeast corner of Room 14	464
3.28	Hasanlu Tepe: The "Bead House" on the left and Burned Building II northwestern storeroom on the right in 1960	465
3.29	Hasanlu Tepe: CC27/Operation XVI from the east in 1960	466
3.30	The area of the North Cemetery from the northern perimeter of the Low Mound, looking southeast	467
4.1	Hasanlu Tepe: Two views of the Theriomorphic Vessel from the Period V RS22–23 Building	468
5.1a	SK4–5 objects HAS57-107, -108	469
5.1b	SK4–5 HAS57-109, -219, -130a–b, -131	469
5.2a	SK45–47 Operation X	470
5.2b	SK45–47 Operation X	470
5.3a	SK45–47 objects HAS58-120–131	471
5.3b	SK45–47 objects HAS58-121, -125, -126, -131	471
5.3c	SK45–47 object HAS58-134	471
5.4	Robert H. Dyson at the entrance to stone tomb SK49 in Operation X (1958)	472
5.5a	SK49 objects HAS58-146, -148	473
5.5b	SK49 object HAS58-149	473
5.5c	SK61 object HAS59-91	473
5.5d	SK61 object HAS69-116	473
5.5e	SK66 object HAS59-140, -141	473
5.6a	SK112 object HAS59-224	474
5.6b	SK70 object HAS59-169	474
5.6c	SK70 object HAS59-171	474
5.6d	SK25 objects HAS57-126, -127	474
5.6e	SK116 object HAS59-323	474
5.6f	SK116 object HAS59-325	474
5.7a	SK25 Operation VI Burial 15	475
5.7b	SK29 Operation VI Burial 19	475
5.8a	SK29 Operation VI Burial 19	476
5.8b	SK29 objects HAS57-159 (M), -187(L), -188 (R, intrusive)	476
5.9	SK15 of Operation VI dating to early Period IVb	477
5.10a	SK504 Operation VIj Burial 5	478

5.10b	SK67 Operation VIa Burial 18	478
5.11a	SK67 object HAS59-146, -147	479
5.11b	SK67 object HAS59-147	479
5.11c	SK24 Operation VI Burial 14	479
5.12a	SK445/449 Object HAS64-335	480
5.12b	SK24 object HAS57-121	480
5.12c	SK73 object HAS59-184	480
5.13a	SK459 Operation VIe Burial 10	481
5.13b	SK459 Operation VIe Burial 10	481
5.13c	SK459 object HAS64-90	481
5.13d	SK459 object HAS64-91	481
5.13e	SK479 object HAS64-176	481
5.13f	SK494 object HAS64-299	481
5.13g	SK57 object HAS59-80	481
5.13h	SK53 object HAS59-57	481
5.14a	SK479 Operation VIf Burial 8	482
5.14b	SK479 Operation VIf Burial 8	482
5.15a.	SK57 object HAS59-83	483
5.15b	SK57 object HAS59-83	483
5.15c	SK57 object HAS59-77–80, -83	483
5.15d	SK57 object HAS59-79	483
5.15e	SK57 object HAS59-79	483

Tables

3.1	Radiocarbon Samples from Burned Building III (Room 4 North) North Kitchen and Storeroom (Room 5)	66
3.2	Radiocarbon Samples from Burned Building III Room 4 South	67
3.3	The Periods, Subperiods, Phases, and Strata Designations of the U22 Sounding	73
3.4	Stratigraphic Concordance of Northwest Mound Excavations	75
3.5	The Phasing of the YZ27–29 Building and Burned Building I East	95
4.1	Young's "Period V" Ware Types	183

Abbreviations

BB	Burned Building
BIB-IRAN	Bibliographie analytique de l'archéologie de l'Iran ancien
BM	British Museum
Deco.	Decoration
Dia.	Diameter
Disc.	Discarded
EBA	Early Bronze Age
ETC	Early Transcaucasian
EWGW	Early Western Grey Ware *sensu* Young 1965 (Early MBW)
GW	Middle Bronze Age Grey Ware
H.	Height
HAS	Hasanlu Field Number Prefix
HF	Hajji Firuz Field Number Prefix
KW	Khabur Ware
L.	Length
LBA	Late Bronze Age
LWBW	Late Western Buff Ware
LWGW	Late Western Grey Ware *sensu* Young 1965 (Late MBW)
MBA	Middle Bronze Age
MBW	Monochrome Burnished Ware, previously "Grey Ware"
MMA	Metropolitan Museum (New York, NY) Accession Number
NR	Not Recorded
OW	Orange Ware
PKW	Painted Khabur Ware
POW	Painted Orange Ware
RLA	Reallexikon der Assyriologie und Vorderasiatische Archäologie
ROM	Royal Ontario Museum
SK	Skeleton Number (Hasanlu)
Str.	Stratum
SW	Simple Ware
TM	Tehran Museum
UPM	University of Pennsylvania Museum Registration Number
W.	Width
WBW	Western Buff Ware *sensu* Young 1965

Acknowledgments

I would like to thank the White-Levy Foundation for Archaeological Publication and the Hagop Kevorkian Fund for their extremely generous support of the Hasanlu Publication Project. Their funds provided me with the time and resources to begin the publication of Hasanlu in earnest. My thanks go to Larry Stager and Ralph Minasian for all they have done to support this project. The Iran Heritage Foundation also contributed much-needed financial assistance.

How may I thank Robert H. Dyson, Jr.? Bob opened the doors to Hasanlu and provided me with the chance to work on the dataset freely. While the views expressed in this volume are often at odds with his, and I am occasionally critical of the excavations as I am sure future generations will be of my own fieldwork, the present work is a testament to Bob's pioneering efforts in the archaeology of Iran, as well as his kindness and generosity. We must never lose sight of the difficult conditions under which the Hasanlu Project operated and the magnitude of its contribution to our current understanding of the ancient Near East. In that vein, I would be remiss not to thank the many excavators of Hasanlu.

In many ways, Richard Hodges, the former Williams Director of the University of Pennsylvania Museum of Archaeology and Anthropology, cleared the path for the present work. I owe him a deep debt of gratitude for his guidance, leadership, and collegiality. Richard Zettler, Associate Curator-in-Charge of the Museum's Near East Section, has been an unstinting mentor, friend, and fellow publisher of archival excavations—his obsession being Nippur. Many archaeologists understand the trials and tribulations of publishing "old" excavations, and it does a soul good to have a sympathetic ear. James Mathieu, Director of Publications, has provided additional morale boosting and technical support during the completion of this volume. Katherine Blanchard, the Fowler/Van Santvoord Keeper of the Near East Collections, exhibits the patience of Job with regard to my frequent trips to Iran storage and my research requests.

Archaeological research can often be a solitary endeavor. I have been fortunate in having Stephan Kroll as a fellow researcher and as a model of archaeological practice. In 2004, Stephan made it possible for me to see Hasanlu and Ušnu-Solduz for the first time: I can think of no better guide. Dr. John Curtis, the Keeper of Special Middle East Projects of the British Museum, read and commented on a draft of this volume, and it is much improved as a result. I greatly appreciate his critical eye as well as his encouragement and support.

My friends and colleagues in the Archaeology Department of Boston University have provided a most welcoming and collegial environment: it is a pleasure to work with such a fine group of scholars. Although I produced the majority of the illustrations in this volume myself, several illustrators contributed to this work, including Denise Hoffman, Jana Fisher, Ted Hemmaplardh, Kimberley Leaman Insua, and Nick Chasuk.

I began working on Hasanlu V many years ago, and the project has necessitated sacrifices on several fronts. Most important, I wish to thank my wife Samantha for her assistance on this project and her constant support. My children, Nathaniel, Kersten, and Jacob, have made many sacrifices over the years, as the families of archaeologists so often do. They probably believe that their father is glued to his desk chair when not in Syria, Iran, or Iraq, and at this point they know many of the Hasanlu excavators by name.

Preface

For those versed in Near Eastern archaeology, Hasanlu Tepe usually conjures up images of an Iron Age II (1050–800 BC) sacked and burned citadel with thousands of *in situ* objects, over 250 human victims lying where they originally fell in the final stages of the onslaught, and monumental columned-hall buildings, all unusually well preserved by burning and rapid, often almost immediate, deposition. With its frozen moments in time and rich material record, Hasanlu IVb is often presented as the Pompeii of early Iron Age Iran. I often refer to its Iron II level as the grisly physical evidence of the realities of warfare blithely depicted in Assyrian reliefs and other contemporary art and documented in texts. We can only guess at the identities of the perpetrators of this crime, although Urartu seems a likely suspect.

With its archaeological fame thus firmly established, it is easy to forget that Hasanlu was also instrumental in the development of the archaeological chronology of Iran and the definition of several archaeological horizons, key among them the Early and Late Western Grey Ware horizons (EWGW and LWGW, respectively), which enjoy almost celebrity status (for some, perhaps, infamy) in Iranian archaeological circles. The appearance of the EWGW horizon has held a special fascination in Near Eastern archaeology as one of the premier datasets bearing on possible ancient migrations and the capacity of archaeology as a discipline to cope with such events. The topic is quite an intellectual thicket given the dating of EWGW and its associations. The horizon appeared and thrived during the protohistoric era when we have only tantalizing textual hints regarding happenings in northwestern Iran. Further, EWGW origins have long been entangled with Indo-European and Indo-Iranian migration theory, a veritable scholarly minefield. The origin and development of the EWGW horizon in the southern Lake Urmia Basin are the subjects of this volume, the result of a long-term research project ultimately aimed at the final publication of Hasanlu IVb. The story of Hasanlu IVb begins with Hasanlu V in the 2nd millennium BC—many of the details may come as a surprise.

Perhaps the most recognizable artifact from Hasanlu is the gold bowl (a large beaker, in fact), most often pictured being held aloft by one of its excited discoverers in 1958 as shown in full color in the pages of *Life* magazine in 1959. Were I to choose the poster artifact of the archaeological horizon, however, it would surely be the bridgeless-spouted jar in highly burnished Grey Ware (hereafter called Monochrome Burnished Ware or MBW), or for that matter so-called Late Western Grey Ware more generally (hereafter Late MBW). Understanding the Late MBW horizon and its precursor, the Early MBW horizon (formerly EWGW), is crucial to Iranian archaeology, yet little has been published from the essential sites. Our current view is far too dependent on early, unsystematic, and poorly published excavations, especially chronologically floating cemeteries, and the scrapings left by looters and commercial antiquities dealers. Unlike most other excavated sites, Hasanlu provides occupation deposits. While Late MBW from Iron II Hasanlu is still poorly known, the situation is even less satisfactory for the rarer and even lesser-known MBW levels which precede the burned citadel, originally dated to 1450–1050 BC and designated Hasanlu V/Iron I. This dataset is supplemented by neighboring Dinkha Tepe, where graves and trash deposits of this same period are labeled Dinkha Period III. In the traditional view, Hasanlu V follows on the heels of a strong foreign presence in the southern Lake Urmia Basin (Hasanlu VIb) characterized by a Khabur Ware (KW) assemblage of Mesopotamian inspiration, if not derivation, dating to the early-to-mid 2nd millennium BC. The apparent disjunction between Hasanlu VI and V (Dinkha IV and III) has inspired a great deal of hypothesizing regarding the contributing cultural processes, with consensus gravitating around a complete break with the previous "Bronze Age" cultural traditions precipitated by the arrival of newcomers. A hiatus or gap in occupation has occasionally been inserted between the periods. Such interpretations were often cast in tones of the "Iranianization" of the region, but direct links to specific ethnic groups have since generally been eschewed. Thirty-five years after the close of excavations at Hasanlu Tepe, Hasanlu V still stands as the archetype of the earliest "Iron Age" in western Iran. Yet relative to the amount of generalizing interpretation, the publication record is a virtual *tabula rasa* with regard to data presentation and middle-range theorizing.

Between 1956 and 1977, Robert H. Dyson, Jr., directed the excavations at Hasanlu and at a number of neighboring sites, forever changing our understanding of northwestern Iran in antiquity. The discoveries in the rich Iron II citadel of Hasanlu catapulted Dyson to fame and placed increasing demands on his time, culminating in a stint as the Dean of the College of Arts and Sciences at the University of Pennsylvania and in a long term of service as the Director of the UPM. Bob has always been an active researcher, teacher, and leader in the field of archaeology and, as his career developed, the publication of Hasanlu took a backseat to other tasks. Having worked with Bob on a daily basis for seven years, first as a draftsman as I completed my dissertation at the UPM and later as a young postdoctoral scholar working on Hasanlu, I can attest to his concerns over the course the Hasanlu Project had taken with regard to publication. Probably most troubling to him was the extent to which archaeology had changed since the late 1950s and 1960s. Work at Hasanlu spanned three momentous decades in the history of archaeology in terms of its methodological and theoretical development. The Hasanlu excavations of the 1950s and early 1960s markedly contrast with those conducted in the 1970s, and so too the final seasons of the Hasanlu Project compare somewhat unfavorably with today's standards. This has made writing the Excavation Reports challenging. Moreover, the publication of specialized studies of select bodies of data in advance of detailed examinations of archaeological contexts has compounded these difficulties.

I benefited greatly from my time spent working on the excavation records with Bob. My first work on Hasanlu focused on its earliest extensively excavated level (Danti, Voigt, and Dyson 2000). This task entailed analyzing the entire sequence of the site using the U22 Sounding. I was quickly drawn to the 2nd millennium BC material and questions regarding the origins of the MBW archaeological horizon. I was especially inspired to re-evaluate the chronology and cultural processes of the period by a memorable conversation with Bob in my first year as a draftsman. I had made some comment on the presence of ceramics of Middle Bronze Age (MBA) date at Hasanlu with parallels to Mesopotamia and was promptly corrected that there was no "Middle Bronze Age" in Iran. Bob inculcated the dictum, "Your Mesopotamian Middle Bronze Age is the Late Bronze Age in Iran, and your Late Bronze Age is our early Iron Age." I was intrigued by the prospect of investigating how and why such a singular application of archaeological terminology had emerged in a region of Iran with close ties to northern Mesopotamia, but these interests had to wait. My first solo act was to prepare the Excavation Report on the site's Ilkhanid occupation (Danti 2004).

This re-analysis and excavation report on Hasanlu V has led to a major reassessment of the period, which is better attested in terms of excavated exposures and depth of stratified deposits than has hitherto been reported. Much material previously designated Hasanlu V in fact belongs to Dyson's subperiod Hasanlu IVc/Iron Age IIa (1250–1050 BC) in terms of absolute chronology. Dyson originally defined Period IVc as the period during which the Hasanlu citadel was extensively remodeled, an undertaking which he first identified in the construction sequence of certain monumental columned-hall buildings. While Dyson's subdivision of the unwieldy 450 years of the old period "Hasanlu V" was a crucial step toward improved interpretation, the subperiod has lacked the underpinnings of an extensive re-analysis of the Hasanlu dataset beyond the architectural phasing of the columned halls: previously we have had only a rudimentary understanding of Hasanlu IVc material culture. I argue here that Hasanlu IVc should be re-designated the Iron I, and Hasanlu V (1450–1250 BC) should now be termed the Late Bronze Age (LBA). Previous definitions of "Period V" were heavily weighted toward the latter part of its original time range—that is, Hasanlu IVc. As with most periods at Hasanlu prior to the Urartian (Hasanlu IIIc) and Achaemenid Periods (Hasanlu IIIa), Period IVc exhibits some ties to northern Mesopotamia in terms of both cultural contacts and developmental sequence. The proposed break between Hasanlu V and Hasanlu VI (herein Hasanlu VIb), the "great divide" between the Bronze and Iron Ages, has also proved to be misleading, and the situations at Hasanlu and Dinkha Tepe are far more complex than previously reported. Previous assessments of the MBW horizon have presented it as arriving suddenly in western Iran in a fully developed form; closer inspection, however, has shown the oft-cited marked contrast in material culture between "Hasanlu V" and "Hasanlu VI" is due to the invalid comparison of what were in effect the late LBA and Iron I to the MBII, in the terminology of Mesopotamia. Hasanlu Period VIa or the MBIII (1600–1450 BC), attested at Dinkha and Hasanlu, represents the transition from Period VIb to Period V and exhibits cultural continuity.

This work constitutes the Excavation Report on Periods VIa, V, and IVc and at the same time provides a reappraisal of earlier interpretations. The volume is divided into seven chapters. Chapter One presents an overview of the Ušnu-Solduz region, especially the southern Lake Urmia Basin, located in northwestern Iran. I have attempted to pull together the numerous archaeological surveys and reconnaissance projects conducted by the Hasanlu Project with a comprehensive site catalog and regional map. Chapter Two provides a chronological overview of how we have arrived at the prevailing archaeological chronology of northwestern Iran and how scholars have interpreted the Early MBW horizon set against the story of the Hasanlu Project. I strongly advocate the revision of the terminology and periodization used for the 2nd millennium BC. Chapter Three details for the first time the stratigraphy and architecture of mid-to-late 2nd millennium BC Hasanlu, and Dinkha III–IV are briefly reviewed, as well. The relevant radiocarbon dates are also recalibrated and included. The Early MBW horizon did not arrive in Ušnu-Solduz fully developed in a single event, and the gap proposed between Hasanlu VI and V (Dinkha IV and III) is nonexistent in the region. Chapter Four provides the results of my detailed study of the ceramics of Hasanlu along with some crucial material from Dinkha. Virtually none of this material has been previously published, and in fact some of it of MBIII date had clearly not been examined since it was first brought from Iran to the UPM. The chapter begins with a look at the MBII, with special attention dedicated to the final phase of this period, which I designate the Terminal MBII—essentially the 17th century BC. This period and the newly defined MBIII form the transition to the Early MBW horizon of the LBA or Hasanlu V. Assemblages from Hasanlu Periods VIa, V, and IVc are presented in detail—these were largely lumped together in the former "Hasanlu V." The early stages of the Early MBW horizon in northwestern Iran exhibit a great deal of regional variation in ceramics, followed by inter-assemblage convergence by the Late MBW horizon. The assemblages of the MBIII and LBA testify to strong influences from the southern Caucasus and northern Mesopotamia. I argue that the assemblages of the Early MBW horizon did not arrive in northwestern Iran in a fully developed form in a punctuated manner. Ties to the Caucasus and northern Mesopotamia are far better attested than are links to northeastern Iran and southwestern Central Asia. The graves of Hasanlu VI, V, and IVc form the subject of Chapter Five, which out of necessity reviews the graves of Dinkha III. This is the first time the Hasanlu graves have been presented. The dichotomy between intramural and extramural burial has long been argued to represent the Bronze Age and Early Iron Age, respectively. This distinction is unsupported. In Chapter Six, Megan Cifarelli presents her analysis of the personal ornaments from the Hasanlu graves. Finally, Chapter Seven details my conclusions on the MBW horizon as seen at Hasanlu and the implications of the revisions detailed here on our broader understanding of the later 2nd millennium BC.

1

Ušnu-Solduz and the Lake Urmia Region in the Later 2nd Millennium BC

Iran is a complex geographical area … this diversity of environment led to multiple cultural adaptations in prehistoric times, making cultural generalizations difficult. For this reason, archaeologists working in the area have concentrated on the development of stratified regional sequences before undertaking studies of major time periods as such.

— Voigt and Dyson 1992:122

This chapter presents the environmental and cultural backdrop of the core area of the Early Western Grey Ware (EWGW) archaeological horizon of the later 2nd millennium BC as defined by T. Cuyler Young (1965), which has long been associated with the earliest Iron Age in Iran and wave migration and population replacement theories (Dyson 1977b). The area concerned, broadly construed, is northwestern Iran, but in particular our subject area is found at the heart of this upland zone, the Lake Urmia Basin and its premier excavated site, Hasanlu Tepe, located in the Solduz valley of the southern basin (Fig. 1.1; see color insert). The EWGW horizon was first explored in detail here, and Hasanlu played a profound role in shaping the archaeological chronology of Iran at a time when other archaeological sequences remained rudimentary. The reasons for this are straightforward: Hasanlu was one of the first high, well-stratified mounds (*tepe*) to be extensively excavated using modern techniques and the site provided occupation deposits, a massive destruction level datable to the Iron II period, and vast cemeteries on the Low Mound with abundant grave goods.

Any assessment of the origins and development of the so-called Grey Ware horizon of northwestern Iran must address, in some manner, its environmental context. In northwestern Iran, these contexts consist of relatively isolated mountain valleys with distinct environmental conditions and resources; the region has thus traditionally been typified by marked cultural diversity. This presents certain obstacles to archaeologists seeking to reconstruct larger cultural patterns, since building chronologies can be a daunting task given the limited historical record. One relative constant shared by local populations across time is a heavy emphasis on a form of pastoralism, which follows a pattern of bi-seasonal vertical transhumance. Some regions—such as the Urmia and Ušnu-Solduz valleys—provide ample arable land and irrigation sources. This has contributed to patterns of fairly continuous occupation in these regions and the development of large mounded sites with long archaeological sequences, partly owing to a preference for mudbrick and *chineh* (packed mud) architecture and partly to conditions conducive to the preservation of such materials. Neighboring areas, in contrast, suffer from salinity, higher altitudes, steep slopes, and a scarcity of arable land, and hence have been characterized by a higher degree of pastoral transhumance, a lower density of settlement, and construction techniques which utilize terracing and stone and wooden beam construction, resulting in relatively ephemeral and unstratified archaeological remains.

While the above quote from Dyson and Voigt is apt with regard to the prehistoric periods in Iran, I would contend the exact opposite in fact typifies archaeological research into protohistoric periods. Speculation on the origins and character of the Iranian "Iron Age" followed fast on the heels of the first phase of exploratory, haphazard excavation in widely divergent locales, and it was not until the 1970s that some key regions had archaeological sequences worthy of the moniker—that is, long after theories regarding the origins of the "Grey Ware Culture" had become deeply entrenched. Major lacunae continue to plague archaeologists. Many regions, such as the valley systems immediately south of Ušnu-Solduz and the crucial Sidakan/Mudjesir Valley to the southwest that leads to Assyria, remain largely unexplored (Boehmer 1973, 1979; Boehmer 1993–1997; Boehmer and Fenner 1973; Radner 2012). The field has also suffered from a lack of detailed archaeological reporting. The main objectives of the current volume are to provide the final report on all material of the later 2nd millennium from Hasanlu, as well as a revised assessment of the Hasanlu sequence of Ušnu-Solduz, widely believed to be one of the most complete and considered one of the most influential in the archaeology of Iran. At times the details are not glamorous, but given that so much interpretive superstructure has been built on this (somewhat unstable) foundation, it is high time it be made available.

The "Grey Ware" phenomenon in north-central Iran has recently been broken down spatially and temporally into more discrete units (Piller 2004). This trend will likely continue as data accumulates, and it underscores how we are just beginning to build regional sequences capable of addressing cultural processes such as demic diffusion—arguably the most popular theory explaining Grey Ware's origins in western Iran—although this is certainly not to be taken as an endorsement of any link between "Grey Ware" and Iranians or any other ethnonym. On the contrary, the reanalysis of the archaeological record undertaken for this volume falsifies the punctuated migratory wave model and population replacement model for explaining culture change in Ušnu-Solduz in the 2nd millennium BC. As in other areas of northern and western Iran, the Grey Ware horizon, herein redefined and renamed the Monochrome Burnished Ware (MBW) horizon, developed from the local MBA archaeological cultures and only became a coherent spatial horizon in the late 2nd millennium BC. There is no evidence for a migratory wave or sudden population replacement, as such migrations are historically extremely rare (Anthony 1990, 1992, 1997; Burmeister 2000:540); the possibility of a long-term, gradual infiltration of the region by migrants (a steady migratory stream), however, remains a distinct possibility. After all, migration is a demographic constant in most populations and, with regard to the case at hand, can only be fully addressed after the vast data set attributable to the Hasanlu IVb period has been completely analyzed.

The Lake Urmia Basin

Lake Urmia lies in northwestern Iran, in the Zagros Mountains, which straddle the modern Iranian provinces of Eastern and Western Azerbaijan. The line of demarcation between the modern Iranian provinces of Azerbaijan and Kurdistan, to the south, is artificial; this area has traditionally shared tribal and ethnic groups since antiquity. In archaeological terms, the region of interest with regard to the later 2nd millennium BC extends beyond the northern border of Iran into Nakhichevan, southern Armenia, and the Republic of Azerbaijan, and it is closely affiliated with eastern Anatolia, the southern and western Caspian littoral, and the region stretching from Takab and Qazvin eastward along the southern flanks of the Elburz and southward, skirting the eastern Zagros to the environs of Kashan (Fig. 1.2; see color insert). A number of archaeological surveys have been conducted in the lake region over the last 50 years, but the results have not always been published (Burney and Lang 1971:5) and the methodologies employed have differed markedly (see the annual reports of Kleiss in *Archäologische Mitteilungen aus Iran*; Kroll 1994a, 2005, and sources cited therein; Pecorella and Salvini 1984; Swiny 1975). The Lake Urmia Basin is today one of the most densely settled and agriculturally productive parts of Iran, the preeminent urban center being the city of Tabriz. Lake Urmia and its adjacent valleys are hemmed in by high mountains in most places; the valleys provide important lines of communication through nearby high mountain passes—the lake basin thus forms a hub for a number of overland routes. A number of rivers flow into the lake and water the valleys, and these have been settled fairly continuously from the 6th millennium BC (Voigt 1983).

Geology

The Lake Urmia Basin is an intermontane plateau (1300 m AMSL) situated in the Northwest Zagros geographic zone (Fisher 1968, 1971). The Zagros orogen was created by the opening and closing of the Neo-Tethys Ocean and consists of three parallel tectonic zones (Alavi 1994; Stöcklin and Setudinia 1972); from southwest to northeast, these are the Zagros Simply Folded Belt, the Sanandaj-Sirjan Zone, and the Urmia-Dokhtar Magmatic Arc (Stöcklin and Setudinia 1972). The Zagros in the vicinity of the southern Lake Urmia Basin attains peaks of 2500 m AMSL and, in the east, Mount Sahand (Kuh-i Sahand)—a much-eroded stratovolcano—rises to 3707 m. The area is tectonically active, forming part of a mush zone between the colliding Arabian and Eurasian plates (McKenzie 1972, 1976); the folding and faulting, as well as differential tectonic movement along the fault lines, has produced a table-land of horsts and graben (downthrow basins) and igneous extrusions. The Lake Urmia Basin is the largest of these subsiding tectonic basins, measuring 50,000 km^2 (Berberian and Arshadi 1975). Andesitic and rhyodactic volcanism ranges in date from the Oligocene to Recent,[1] the most noteworthy being the massive calc-alkaline Sahand Complex, as well as several smaller outcroppings along the lake's eastern shore and forming parts of the Shahi Peninsula (Kelts and Shahrabi 1986).

The Lake Urmia Basin exhibits a varied lithology. To the west, in the Zagros-proper, are metamorphic outcrops of the Palaeozoic. In the east, Mesozoic fysch extends up to the shoreline of the lake and makes up some of the islands. The northwest shore has coralline limestones of the Lower Miocene (Qom Formation). The north margins of the basin and the northeast are dominated by the Middle Miocene continental Fars Formation of lower evaporite marl series and upper red bed conglomerate series. Several Miocene salt domes penetrate the surface, contributing to salinity in runoff water. The verticality, varied geology, and volcanism contribute to the mosaic landscape typified by marked environmental and cultural diversity.

Hydrology

Lake Urmia

Lake Urmia is one of the world's largest saline lakes at 5000 km^2—or 140 km long and 15–50 km wide—lying at 1200 m AMSL. The lake is shallow (8–12 m) and hypersaline (>200 g/l, or 22% sodium chloride–sulfate brine) (Fisher 1968:10–12; Kelts and Shahrabi 1986; Sharifi 2002). The streams and rivers that feed the lake collect the salt as they pass through volcanic deposits and catchments of Miocene marine evaporites laden with soluble salts. The absence of an outlet also contributes to the lake's salinity. Due to the high saline content, the lake does not freeze in winter. Lake size has varied markedly over time, ranging between 5000 and 6000 km^2 based on precipitation (Günther 1899). While the saline lake only minimally contributes to the local economy, it does ameliorate the mountain climate in its surrounding littoral.

The lake is supplied by 13 permanent rivers, smaller perennial and seasonal streams, and direct precipitation. Historically, the locations of these rivers have played a profound role in shaping the sociopolitical and economic landscapes and often appear to have constituted discrete territories in antiquity. The main tributaries are the Talkeh Rud, Zarineh Rud, Zola Çay, and Barandüz Çay (Fig. 1.2). A large proportion of the lake's salt content is carried by the Talkeh Rud, which flows through Tabriz. The river has a gentle gradient (3/5000) with high infiltrations and evaporation (Kelts and Shahrabi 1986:110). Large mudflats flank the Talkeh's inlet. At the south end of the lake is the Zarineh Rud, another major tributary, which has the least saline charge of all the rivers that feed into the lake and has its catchment in the highlands of Kurdistan. The south of the lake has a mixture of saltwater and freshwater swamps and lakes.

Due to its salinity, the lake supports nearly no aquatic life with the exception of *Artemia salina* brine shrimp and leafy green algae. Similar to Lake Van in eastern Turkey, Lake Urmia provides paleoclimatologists with a potential source of data on ancient climate, although Lake Urmia has not been studied in such detail. Limnology and lithology studies show lacustrine formation atop a desiccation Playa phase with sedimentation mainly consisting of authigenic aragonite and fecal pellets from shrimp (Kelts and Shahrabi

1986). The shorelines in the north consist in part of coalescing alluvial fan aprons deposited by perennial and seasonal streams and rivers, which merge into salt marshes and extensive mudflats. There are 34 small islands in the lake that have provided botanists with valuable remnant plant communities to study. Some of the larger islands have freshwater springs and were occasionally settled in the past. Despite the salinity of Lake Urmia, the surrounding region has an abundance of freshwater. Wells provide freshwater up to a depth of 30 m thanks to a high hydraulic gradient that forces freshwater toward the lake (Kelts and Shahrabi 1986:111).

Gadar River and Its Tributaries

The Gadar River, the most important water source in Ušnu-Solduz, rises in the western Zagros near the Iran-Iraq-Turkey border. The river was a major focus of settlement in antiquity—the other being the freshwater lake of Šur Gol (Fig. 1.3, see color insert). The Gadar and its tributaries are cut in, especially in the west (Fisher 1968:9–10; 1971:268–69, fig. 13:2). The river flows southeast, eventually discharging into salt flats and marshes south of the lakeshore. It drains an area of roughly 1,900 km^2 (Voigt 1977:307) and has changed its course over time as evidenced by abandoned channels, oxbows, and the siting of linear arrangements of ancient settlements (Fig. 1.3). Voigt has noted "a line of Iron Age sites in association with a fossil riverbed indicates that during the late second and early first millennium B.C. the Gadar flowed near the southern edge of the valley floor" (1983:273). In eastern Solduz the river slows and is not as deeply entrenched; here, irrigation is more feasible, which in part accounts for the historically denser settlement there. The Gadar provided an important line of communication across the southern Lake Urmia Basin linking northeast Mesopotamia and the Iranian Plateau, and this surely influenced cultural development there over the *longue durée*.

Climate

Modern Climate

The Lake Urmia Basin has a Mediterranean pluviseasonal-continental climate regime (Djamali et al. 2008:414; Rivas-Martinez, Sánchez-Mata, and Costa 1999). Temperatures generally range from 0–20°C. The mean annual temperature and precipitation in Urmia from 1951–2000 were 11.2°C and 341 mm, respectively. Mean maximum and minimum temperatures occur in July (23.9°C) and January (-2.5°C). Summer maximum temperatures can reach 40°C and winter minimum temperatures -32°C. The lake mitigates seasonal temperature extremes to some extent. The area is arid, with most precipitation falling in winter and spring. Precipitation is highest in the western Lake Urmia Basin. The rainy season begins in October, with most rainfall occurring in March–May. The lake basin branches into a number of valley systems cut by surrounding rivers and streams that receive their charge from precipitation and snow melt originating in the mountains and uplands. Although precipitation is fairly low throughout much of the region, it falls mainly in the winter and spring rainy seasons in punctuated events, cutting deep valleys and gorges in the mountains and depositing allogenic material in the lake basin and in the lake itself. The region is often cut off from neighboring areas in winter months, as mountain passes are blocked by snowfall. This had a profound impact on populations in antiquity and is most noticeable in historical sources in the prevalence of transhumant pastoralism and the seasonal character of warfare—winter is one of the western Zagros' most formidable bulwarks. Winds prevail from the west during the winter; in the summer, winds are out of the northeast. Spring is characterized by strong southwesterlies.

Proxy Datasets

Cores taken from Lake Urmia have provided an important local proxy dataset on climate and local plant communities stretching back to 13,200 BP. The important cores are numbers 20 and 21 (Bottema 1986; Kelts and Shahrabi 1986). Other datasets on climate and environment include the pollen cores from Lake Zeribar and Lake Mirabad (Wright 1980; van Zeist 1967:304). Core 20 yielded two radiocarbon dates for its upper part. Limnology has shown that the deposition of detrital minerals on the lake bottom, primarily allogenic aragonite, is directly related to the prevalence of *Artemisia* steppe in the area around the lake (Bottema 1986). High occurrences of *Artemisia* mean less grass and thus more erosion. During the last Ice Age (up to 9000 BP), *Artemisia* steppe covered the area. From 9000–8000 BP, with the change to moister and warmer conditions, forest steppe developed and the climate attained conditions similar to those of today by around 7000 BP according to Bottema (1986) or 3500 BC in van Zeist's estimation (1967:310–11). According to Bobek (1968:293), the post-glacial vegetation of western Iran reached a climax in the 3rd millennium BC, after the climate had stabilized in the mid-4th millennium (Bobek 1968:293). This corresponds with the peak period of settlement at Hasanlu known as Hasanlu Period VII or the Early Bronze Age (see below).

Vegetation

Vegetation in the lake basin largely consists of grasses and low bushes. According to both Bobek (1968: fig. 88) and van Zeist (1967: fig. 1), there are three main climax vegetation types known to prevail in western Azerbaijan and Kurdistan:

1. Semi-humid Zagrosian Oak Forest (at elevations of 800–2000 m and average annual precipitation levels of 500–750 mm);
2. Dry Pistachio-Almond-Maple Forest, also called Amygdalus-Pistacia Savanna (elevated areas with annual precipitation of 300–500 mm); and,
3. Artemisia Steppe or Afghano-Anatolian Steppe (primarily composed of *Artemisia fragrans* [Pers. *Dermaneh-e-Moattar*] and located at medium elevations with less than 300 mm annual rainfall).

Relative to neighboring Mesopotamia, timber and stone were available in and near the Lake Urmia Basin and shaped local traditions in architecture and other material culture. The most famous examples of this are the columned hall structures of Hasanlu Period IVb with their abundant use of wooden architectural members, which contributed greatly to the intensity of the fire that destroyed the settlement.

Zohary (1973) has characterized the Lake Urmia Basin vegetation as *Artemisietea fragrantis*, with vegetation on the foothills and plateau consisting of primarily *Artemisia fragrans* and *Artemisia herba-alba* interspersed with remnants of *Quercetea brantii*. At higher elevations, up to 2000 m, there are remnants of xerophilous deciduous steppe forest. The salty marshes and mudflats east and southeast of the lake have halophytic vegetation, especially *Halocnemetea strobilacei*. Lalande (1969) includes *Astragulus, Acantholimon, Acanthophyllum, Onobrychis,* and, at higher elevations, *Quercus pubescens, Betula verrucosa,* and *Zelkova crenata*. The steppe on either side of the lake includes *Festuca, Stiba barbata, Bromus,* and *Artemisia*. There is also more localized, azonal vegetation. Salt marshes and salt flats have halophytic vegetation with *Chenopodiaceae* species (Family *Amaranthacaea* subfamily *Chenopodioideae*; Asri and Ghorbanli 1997) and reeds. Prior to widespread deforestation in the Medieval period, riparian forest was likely to be found along the rivers and halophytic forest possibly grew along the lake shore and in the salt marshes. Although late Holocene vegetation is difficult to reconstruct, refuge stands of vegetation on islands in the lake include *Pistacia atlantica mutica, Rhamnus pallasii,* and *Juniperus excelsa* (Zehzad 1989). Kurdistan Province and the areas along the Iraq-Turkey border have stands of oak (*Quercus infectoria* and *Quercus libnani*). Woodlands of *Rosaceae* species (*Acer, Ficus, Rhamnus, Lonicera,* and *Pistacia*) have been reported just west of the lake (Djamali et al. 2008:414).

Subsistence Economy

There has been no concerted effort to study the subsistence economies of the Lake Urmia Basin of the 2nd millennium BC. Efforts in this vein were directed at the earliest period of settlement in Ušnu-Solduz, Hasanlu Period X, as part of the Hajji Firuz excavations (Voigt 1976, 1977, 1983). The Hajji Firuz excavations explicitly incorporated systematic methods for recovering and recording faunal and botanical remains, whereas at Hasanlu such efforts were haphazard at best. The results of these sporadic zooarchaeological and paleoethnobotanical studies are summarized here and supplemented with other findings, especially the faunal and botanical remains from the Iron II Hasanlu citadel burned around 800 BC and the excavations at Dinkha Tepe (Gilbert and Steinfeld 1977; Orton and Stein n.d.; Stein and Orton n.d.; Tosi 1975). The lack of faunal and botanical studies puts us at a severe disadvantage with regard to understanding the subsistence economy of the later Bronze Age and early Iron Age. This is especially troubling given that pastoral nomadism/horse breeding emerged during this period in the Near East, which must surely have broadly transformed life in the Lake Urmia Basin given its abundant summer pastures.

Settlement patterns in the LBA and Iron I–II make clear the detrimental effects of salinity and the importance of freshwater sources such as the Gadar River, which was used for canal irrigation agriculture in the valley bottom. Modern canals typically run perpendicular to the natural drainage and, in antiquity, their charge would likely have been reserved for wheat crops and gardens, with trees raised along canal banks similar to the modern practice. Surrounding uplands were utilized for the dry farming of more drought-tolerant crops such as barley and other fodder crops, while the uplands and more isolated and confined mountain valleys could be exploited in spring and summer as pasture for herds of sheep, goat, and horses. In winter, pastoralists would return to the lower elevations around the lake for shelter and feed their flocks by means of conserved cold-season fodder. The environmental diversity of the region and the dramatic seasonal climate fluctuations selected for agropastoral economies incorporating a fairly high degree of vertical transhumance in the pastoral component. The introduction of the domesticated horse likely made nomadic pastoralism a viable alternative starting in the LBA and had profound effects on the region in the early Iron Age, both economically and militarily.

Botanical remains from Hasanlu dating from the MBA–Iron II illustrate the importance of cereals in the diet, with einkorn wheat (*Triticum monococcum*), emmer wheat (*Triticum dicoccum*), bread wheat (*Triticum aestivum*), and club wheat (*Triticum compactum*) all well attested. Barley grain and straw served as the primary fodder crop for domesticated animals, but barley grain is also found mixed with wheat for human consumption and was most likely used for brewing. Both two-row barley (*Hordeum sistichum*) and six-row barley (*Hordeum vulgare* and *Hordeum polystichum*) are common. Rye (*Secale cereale*) and millet (*Panicum milliaceum*) were used as fodder, as well. The importance of reeds should not be overlooked. Reeds were readily available in the surrounding marshes and small freshwater lakes and, having been processed into mats, were used in roofing and as floor coverings. Charred reeds were found throughout the burned level of Hasanlu IVb, and the remains of reed mats were often noted in the graves dating to the LBA and early Iron Age (see Chapter 5).

A variety of legumes were raised in irrigated gardens, including chickpeas (*Cicer aerietinum*), lentils (*Lens culinaris*), and horsebeans (*Vicia faba*). Vetch (*Vicia ervilia*) was likely used as animal fodder. As is the case today, the Lake Urmia Basin offered a medley of fruits and nuts, probably both wild and domestic. A wide range of delicacies has been found at Hasanlu, including pistachio (*Pistacia vera*), almond (*Prunus dulcis*), grape (*Vitis vinifera*), fig (*Ficus carica*), apricot (*Prunus armeniaca*), pear (*Pyrus communis*), apple (*Pyrus malus*), and quince (*Cydonia oblonga*).

The Iron II destruction level at Hasanlu provides a rich assortment of charred wood samples from architectural elements and wooden artifacts. Poplar (*Populus alba*) was used for roof beams and columns and was grown along canal banks and near other water sources. Elm (*Ulmus* sp.) was employed for architectural elements and has been cited as likely having been imported from the Caucasus (Bottema 1986:255; Harris 1989:15). The shores of freshwater lakes and the banks of the canals provided habitats for willow (*Salix* sp.) and maple (*Acer* sp.), the latter being used in construction. Oaks (*Quercus* sp.) were available in the surrounding uplands. Other attested species, many imported to the region and found among the charred weapons, implements, furniture, and woodcarvings include: cedar (*Cedrus* sp.), hawthorne (*Crataegus* sp.), ash (*Fraxinus* sp.), cypress (*Cypressus* sp.), hackberry (*Celtis austrlis*), juniper (*Juniperus* sp.), plane tree (*Platanus* sp.), and boxwood (*Buxus sempervirens*). Boxwood was imported from Anatolia, the Caucasus, or the Caspian littoral (Harris 1989:18; Hepper 1996; de Schauenesee 2011).

Faunal remains from Dinkha highlight the critical role of pastoral production in the local subsistence economy with *Ovis aries* and *Capra hircus* found in abundance (Gilbert and Steinfeld 1977:336). Sheep/goat pastoralism provided milk and meat for local consumption, and wool and hair that would have been of broader economic significance in the textile trade. Small ruminant production would have surely been important at Hasanlu, although as yet there has been no systematic study. Textile remains from Hasanlu IVb make clear the importance of both wool and goat hair in textile production (Love 2011). Goat and sheep were the most commonly attested food offerings in the LBA and early Iron Age graves (see Chapter 5). Cattle (*Bos taurus*) provided milk, meat, and traction. Pigs (*Sus scrofa*) were another economically significant species, and canids (*Canis* sp.), almost certainly domestic dogs, were found both at Dinkha, in a LBA grave at Hajji Firuz Tepe (see Chapter 5), and among the victims of the Hasanlu Iron II destruction level (Danti 2011). Faunal remains from Hasanlu and Dinkha also reveal the importance of hunting red deer (*Cervus elaphus*) for meat and antler at Dinkha (Gilbert and Steinfeld 1977:335), and antlers used to ornament important buildings at Iron II Hasanlu (Dyson and Voigt 2003).

The importance of the domestic horse to the people of northwestern Iran cannot be overemphasized. Horses are attested in graves at Dinkha (grave B10a B6; Muscarella 1974) and at Hasanlu (Ghirshman 1964:28–29, fig. 131; Hakemi and Rad 1950:30–31) and as victims in the Hasanlu IVb destruction level (Danti 2011). Equids are frequently depicted in representational art and a wide assortment of horse gear has been found at Hasanlu (de Schauensee 1989; de Schauensee and Dyson 1983). Records of Assyrian campaigns also call attention to the area's reputation as a center for horse-rearing, with large numbers taken as tribute.

Land Routes

Historical sources of the Iron II reveal the strategic importance of the Lake Urmia Basin and such was certainly the case in the LBA and Iron I as well. The location of mountain passes and other features of terrain truly make northwestern Iran a crossroads between Mesopotamia, the southern Caucasus, eastern Anatolia, and the Iranian Plateau. Accordingly, the region's material culture evinces far-flung interconnections and synchronisms but, as in other areas of western Iran, these generally form a superficial, elite veneer over a largely localized material culture. The southern lake region was linked to Assyria via routes through passes at Kel-i Shin and Khaneh/Piranshahr to the expansive catchment of the Upper Zab and the Rowanduz Gorge. The lake basin is connected to the mountains and rolling hills of Kurdistan by the river valleys of the Lower Zab, Tatau Çay, and Zarineh Rud. The other mountain passes in the vicinity of modern Sardasht and Lake Zeribar, near modern Marivan, offer prized east-west routes through the *chaîne magistrale* westward to Erbil and Mosul and to the Diyala River, Suleimaniyeh, and Baghdad. To the south and east, roads led to the caravan city of Hamadan on the Great Khorasan Road via Nausud or Sanandaj. Accordingly, connections and commonalities between Mesopotamia and the Iranian Plateau are manifest in the archaeological record of Kurdistan, as well, particularly in the Iron III.

The archaeology of the Lake Urmia region has typically been subdivided according to river valley systems since they often exhibit marked differences in cultural traditions in antiquity. There has also been a north-south archaeological distinction in the basin for similar reasons.

Urmia Valley

The largest valley in the region takes its name from the modern city of Urmia (formerly Rezaiyeh), the capital of Western Azerbaijan Province. The valley, often referred to as a plain, lies west of the lake, occupying roughly 830 km^2 of arable land today. This figure excludes the neighboring Zeyveh and Mavana valleys to the west and southwest, which form the upper catchments of the rivers that water the plain. The region is separated from the Ušnu valley to the south by the high peaks of the Kuh-i Abrišam (max. elev. 2510 m AMSL). The western shoreline of Lake Urmia has varied considerably over time, as the low and flat plain gently grades into mudflats along the lake's edge. The major rivers are, from north to south, the Nazlu Çay, Ruzeh Çay, Shahar Çay, Berdesur Çay, and the Barandüz-Qasemlu Çay. The littoral plain is interrupted in two places by rocky outcroppings. At the center of the valley, directly east of Urmia, stands the Bezug Dağ, a formation which rises slightly over 1900 m AMSL. Just to the north, near the inlet of the Nazlu Çay, is the smaller *inselberg* of Kuh-e Zanbil (max. elev. 1600 m AMSL).

The area's archaeological sequence is based on excavations conducted in 1948 by Burton-Brown at Geoy Tepe, 7 km south of Urmia (Burton-Brown 1951). This site was looted or commercially excavated prior to Burton-Brown's work (1951:5–6), and some antiquities that reached major museum collections allegedly derive from tombs probably datable to the Middle–Late Bronze and early Iron Age (Lehmann-Haupt 1910:280; Schaeffer 1948:448, fig. 241). Work at Geoy revealed a sequence spanning the Chalcolithic to the Seljuk Period. Both occupation deposits and burials were recovered; however, the site was poorly excavated and recorded. The most difficult obstacle to interpretation today was the collection of archaeological material in arbitrary levels recorded according to depth ranges below surface rather than by strata, which has necessitated later revisions to the Geoy sequence and a great deal of caution in using it in cross-sequence dating. Most important for the current analysis are Geoy Period D (MBII), late D–C (MBIII), B (later LBA and Iron I), and A (Iron I–II).

From 1971–1978, an Austrian team conducted excavations at Kordlar Tepe, 13 km east of Urmia (Dorner, Kromer, and Lippert 1974; Ehringhaus 1994; Heinsch 2004; Lippert 1975, 1977, 1978, 1979). Deep soundings explored levels dating from the Neolithic to the Sasanian periods. This site provides the key late 2nd millennium sequence for the region with coherent architectural remains. Kordlar was occupied fairly continuously from at least the mid-2nd millennium BC (Kordlar V), but little is known of this period since it was revealed only in small soundings. A fortified manor house occupied the mound in the later LBA and Iron I (Kordlar IV–IIb) and was continuously modified and rebuilt through the Iron II (Kordlar IIa–I). Kordlar IV–II provides a primary example of the Early, Middle, and Late MBW horizons underpinned by radiocarbon dates (Felber 1979), but was excavated after the initial formulation of the "Grey Ware" horizon and early "Iron Age" by Young and Dyson and was never adequately incorporated into later reassessments of these constructs. The final early Iron Age levels of Kordlar provide one of our best data sets on the transition from the Iron II to the Iron III.

The Urmia, Mavana-Zeyveh, and Ušnu valleys were intensively surveyed in 1978 by an Italian expedition, which identified sites ranging in date from the Neolithic to the Medieval periods (Pecorella and Salvini 1984). The expedition also conducted excavations at Qal'eh Ismail Aqa, an Urartian fortress (Iron III), and a sounding was made at Tepe Gijlar. Gijlar, one of the largest sites in the Urmia plain and located north of modern Urmia on the Nazlu Çay, provides a sequence similar to that of Geoy, with Chalcolithic (Ubaid), EBA (Early Transcaucasian/Geoy K), and LBA–Iron I–II materials attested (Edwards 1986:67–68; Kroll 1994a; Pecorella and Salvini 1984:186–89, 240–99, figs. 26–27, 56–85). Middle Bronze material appears to be lacking although, as pointed out by Kroll, surface sherds of Transcaucasian Black on Red Ware indicate a MBII level is likely present somewhere on the mound (Kroll 1994a), and Charles Burney purchased 29 ceramic vessels at the site in 1958 that probably came from a 2nd millennium cemetery east of the mound (Edwards 1986:67). Beyond its sheer size and agricultural productivity—the latter reflected by the abundance of ancient settlements—the Urmia plain is especially important since it has often marked the transitional point between northern and southern cultural traditions in the western part of northwestern Iran.

Salmas Plain

The Salmas Plain runs east-west with the Zola Çay, which has its inlet at a small bay in the lake partly defined by a spur of Guverçin Kala (max. elev. 2050 m ASL). The valley is hemmed in by the surrounding mountains. Today approximately 250 km^2 of land is under cultivation. The archaeology of the Salmas region is best known from excavations conducted by Charles Burney at Haftavan Tepe (Burney 1970, 1972, 1973, 1975, 1977; Edwards 1981, 1983, 1986), 5 km south of the modern town of Salmas (formerly Shahpur) in the western valley. The Haftavan sequence spans the EBA to the late Iron Age. While similar to the Hasanlu Sequence, the region was clearly more closely connected to the southern Caucasus and eastern Anatolia in the Bronze and Iron Ages. Haftavan is especially important for its MBII–III sequence, which currently constitutes the fullest assemblage of the highly diagnostic painted wares characteristic of these periods. Regnar Kearton conducted surveys in 1967–1968 (Kearton 1969, n.d.), as did Wolfram Kleiss, the Haftavan Expedition, and the Bastam Expedition (see Kroll 1994a for a summary). From Salmas one can proceed north of the lake region to the intermontane valleys of Marand and Khoy and from there to the Lake Van region and the southern Caucasus. Accordingly, Marand and Khoy exhibit marked regional variations due to these ties (Kroll 1994a).

Tabriz and Sahand

The northern lake littoral in the area of the Salian Rud is quite narrow and thus is sparsely occupied today; the same seems to have been the case in antiquity. On the eastern shore lie the valleys of the Quri

Çay (Meydan Çay) and the alkaline Adji Çay (Talkeh Rud), rising above Sarab and the precipitous slopes of Mount Sahand. The two rivers join to form the Talkeh Rud. Near the confluence of the Quri and Adji lies modern Tabriz, the capital of Eastern Azerbaijan Province. The city's sprawling urban area has largely prevented archaeological excavations, and there appears to have been little ancient settlement in the area west of Tabriz (see Kroll 1984: Maps 3 and 4, and 1994a for a summary of survey results). A lack of fresh water perhaps hindered settlement—surface water is mostly brackish and the rivers are highly saline. Recent salvage excavations in Tabriz at the cemetery of Masjid-e Kabud have uncovered 108 graves of the Iron I–II (Hojabri Nobari 2004) and underscore the fact that our knowledge of 2nd and early 1st millennium BC occupation in the area is incomplete. Ceramics in these graves show links to the Qeytaryeh Group of Western Grey Ware as defined by Piller (2003–2004). Such influences are hardly surprising given the important east-west land routes from Tabriz to the area around Tehran via Miyaneh and Qazvin following the Zanjan valley.

The important site of Yanik Tepe, located 40 km southwest of Tabriz, was the focus of three seasons of excavation by the University of Manchester between 1960 and 1962, under the direction of Charles Burney (1961, 1962, 1964). The site was occupied fairly continuously from the Neolithic to the EBA. Following a break in occupation the site was used as a cemetery in the Late Bronze and early Iron Age, and there is at least one Middle Bronze grave (Burney 1964:60, pl. XV no. 19) and other traces of the MBA, as noted by Edwards (1986:64) and Kroll (1994a). Scattered Iron II sherds suggest an occupation somewhere on the mound.

Maragheh-Bonab Plain

South of the foothills of the Kuh-e Sahand flow the Sufi Çay and Murdi Çay in the area of modern Bonab and Maragheh, the latter famous as a capital city of the Ilkhanid Dynasty. The small, narrow plain is well watered and separated from the lake by a large expanse of salt marsh. While the region has been included within various archaeological surveys, its archaeological record is not especially well known (Kroll 1984, 1994a). The only site that has received specific attention is Gol Tepe, a mound 3 km southeast of the village of Ajabshir (Kroll 1994a; Tala'i 1984). Kroll has dated the ceramics from the site to the Chalcolithic, EBA, and Early Iron Age (1994a); the German survey of the site found no evidence of the MBII Khabur Ware (KW) noted by Tala'i (1984). The presence of Khabur Ware this far to the east would significantly alter its known distribution in northwest Iran which, as of our present understanding, is found only in a narrow stretch of the Ušnu-Solduz valley (Kroll 1994b).

Miyanduab and Mahabad

The large plain of Miyanduab, "between two waters," is generally defined by the courses of the Simineh Rud (Tatau Çay) to the west and the Zarineh Rud (Jaghatu Çay) to the east, both of which run northwest to the southern marshes of Lake Urmia. The area near the rivers has been the focus of archaeological surveys (Kroll 1994a; Swiny 1975).

The Mahabad plain is a north-south running valley at the south end of Lake Urmia lying at an altitude of 1300 m AMSL. The valley, defined by the main channel of the Rud-e Mahabad (formerly the Sanak or Sujbulak Çay), is shaped like a "Y" oriented north-south. At its north end the valley splits, its two branches flanking the east and west slopes of the Kuh-e Siah, a limestone outcropping of Miocene date. Just north of the Kuh-e Siah, the river enters the littoral plain and dissipates in salt marshes and mudflats at the south end of the lake. The valley's main city is Mahabad (formerly Sujbulak, Saujbulaq, Saujbulagh and variants), which has a largely Kurdish population. Just west of the city, the Rud-e Mahabad is controlled by a hydroelectric dam which has formed an impound lake, rendering its upper reaches inaccessible to archaeologists. The Rud-e Mahabad has its catchment in the high mountain ranges of the Kuh-e Chaganlu and the Kuh-e Lowdarvan. The Simineh Rud, which defines the western part of the Miyanduab area, has a larger catchment to the south and east. The western littoral branch of the valley is separated from the Solduz valley to the west by low, rocky hills and marsh. As pointed out by Kroll (1994a), the valley system served as a natural boundary and control point on the south end of the lake and, in the early Iron Age, likely formed the northwest border of Mannea, usually localized in the Miyanduab and Takan areas to the east and in the environs of Qalaychi to the south, near modern Bukan. The archaeological sequences of the Miyanduab and

Mahabad area remain ill defined, as they are largely known from survey materials ordered using excavated sequences from neighboring Ušnu-Solduz (see below), Qalaychi, and Ziwiyeh (Dyson 1963c, 1965; Kargar 2004; Mollazadeh 2008; Motamedi 1997a, 1997b), as well as the Takab region (Thomalsky 2006).

Gadar Plain

At the extreme southern end of the lake is the east-west running Gadar Çay valley, often referred to as Ušnu-Solduz since it can be divided into eastern (Solduz) and western (Ušnu) segments. The names are derived from the principal population centers of the area, Ušnuyeh and Naqadeh (formerly called Solduz). The east-west distinction is somewhat arbitrary and is defined by a topographic bottleneck located at the low mountain spurs of Kuh-e Qal'eh Maran (1725 m AMSL) and Kuh-e Qibleh Daghi (1590 m AMSL) south of the river and Kuh-e Daresur (1640 m AMSL) near the modern villages of Darband and Djashiran to the north (Fig. 1.3). The valley runs for approximately 35 km east–west. The Ušnu valley contains approximately 175 km^2 of arable land, the Solduz an additional 300 km^2. The valley slopes from southwest to northeast and is surrounded by high mountains in the north, south, and west. To the south of Solduz rise the ranges of Kuh-e Mehdi Khan, Darreh-ye Jagher, Darreh-ye Porkani, and Kuh-e Farang with elevations ranging from 1450–2300 m AMSL. Mountain passes lead south into Kurdistan. A range of low hills, the Kuh-e Saral and Kuh-e Qarah Dagh (max. elev. 1659 m AMSL), separates the eastern Solduz valley from the lake and the Mahabad valley to the east, with its easier routes south to Kurdistan and north to Tabriz. At the western end of the Ušnu valley, the Zagros range rises up precipitously. Here, one may proceed westward through the mountains—through the Kel-i Shin Pass and Rowanduz Gorge—to northern Mesopotamia. Western Solduz, the area from Djashiran to a natural bottleneck at the town of Naqadeh, was less densely settled in antiquity, probably due to the narrow dimensions of the valley (7 km north–south, Figs. 1.2, 1.3). There is a narrow north-south branch of the valley in the northwest, the Dilançi Valley, which provides access to the northern upland zone between the Urmia valley and Ušnu-Solduz. Just south of Naqadeh is the hook-shaped Balakchi Valley, which leads south into the high mountains of the Siyah Kuh-Sipan range. This valley route proceeds south to the areas of Piranšar and Pasveh—intermontane valleys that were foci of settlement in antiquity—and to the catchment of the Zab River (Kroll 1994a).

Hasanlu is located in northeastern Solduz, 11 km from the southern shore of Lake Urmia. The site was probably one of at least four political centers located in Solduz in the later 2nd and early 1st millennium BC—the Late Bronze and early Iron Age. Based on site distributions, Hasanlu's territory lay north of the Gadar Çay, where it had no rivals in terms of settlement size. South of the river there appears to have been a line of evenly spaced centers of roughly equal size stretching from Mirabad in western Solduz to Naqadeh, Sakse Tepe, and Mohammadšah Tepe in eastern Solduz. Site catchments measure around 8 km in radius (including Hasanlu). Agricultural territories of 4–5 km are typical given the constraints of cost-distance factors in pre-modern agricultural systems (Chisholm 1970); the smaller sites located around these centers thus were likely situated to extend agricultural territories, functioning as surplus-producing satellites in the agropastoral economy.

The eastern Solduz valley extends much further north than does its western part, providing substantial tracts of agricultural land and grazing. The northeastern quadrant of the Solduz valley is marshy, especially the shoreline of Lake Urmia. The area contains small permanent and seasonal lakes. The largest of these lakes, Šur Gol, lies 2.6 km north of Hasanlu Tepe and today covers 13.4 km^2, although it is quite shallow (maximum depth 80 cm) and varies in extent with seasonal precipitation, even reportedly drying up completely on rare occasions (Voigt 1983:270). The other lakes—the Kheder Hajji and Seyran Goli—are saline. Another seasonal lake/marsh is located just north of the village of Dalma. Šur Gol provides an important source of fresh water and its southern periphery was heavily settled in antiquity. The northeastern valley is partially separated from the Gadar River by the east-west running Dalma range (1300–1350 m AMSL). A pair of higher ranges, the northwest-southeast running Kuh-e Qarah Dagh and Kuh-e Saral, lies between Hasanlu and Lake Urmia (1300–1659 m AMSL) and separates Solduz from the Mahabad valley to the east. In the southeastern corner of eastern Solduz is the north-south running Masu valley and the Masu Çay, a minor affluent of the Gadar. This valley extends the arable land of eastern Solduz significantly and was fairly densely settled in antiquity. The Masu valley allows access south, through the mountains, to the Mahabad Plain via Qazi Gol.

Hasanlu Tepe and Dinkha Tepe

Hasanlu Tepe consists of a High Mound standing 25 m above the surrounding plain and measuring 200 m in diameter surrounded by a Low Mound with 8 m of archaeological deposit and measuring 600 m at its widest observable point (Danti 2004). The modern village of Hasanlu obscures the eastern part of the Low Mound and the village of Aminlu likewise encroaches on the Low Mound in the south. These villages were founded after the second Perso-Russian War (1826–1828) and the signing of the Treaty of Turkomanchay. The peripheries of the High Mound were disturbed by military trenches first documented in aerial photographs taken by Erich Schmidt on July 25, 1937 (Schmidt 1940; Danti 2004: pl. A). These trenches probably date to World War I and were likely dug by the Russian forces occupying this region—they apparently cut trenches into other sites in addition to having excavated for antiquities. The southern Low Mound was never extensively explored due to the presence of a modern Islamic cemetery in the area. An irrigation canal cuts the northern and eastern parts of the Low Mound and has often eroded out ancient burials. Since the close of the Hasanlu Project in 1977, a dirt road located on the eastern Low Mound has been paved and handles quite a bit of local traffic. Overall, the mound and its standing architectural remains of the Iron II are in excellent condition today thanks to the Iranian expedition excavating at the site and undertaking efforts toward its conservation (Khatib Shahidi 2006).

Excavations at Hasanlu and Dinkha in Ušnu have had a profound effect in shaping our understanding of the early Iron Age in northern and western Iran. The first recorded excavations at Hasanlu were conducted in 1934–1935 on the northeastern High Mound by M. Rad and M. Farhadi of the Office of the Tobacco Monopoly in Naqadeh under a commercial excavation permit (Ghirshman 1939:78–79, 253–54, pl. C). Sir M. Aurel Stein was the first to excavate scientifically, doing so for six days in 1936, although he was not especially impressed with the results (Stein 1940). Stein opened four trenches, two on the northern Low Mound, an L-shaped trench near the base of the northern High Mound, and a sounding in a depression located near the center of the High Mound (Stein 1940:389–404, figs. 106, 108–10, pls. XXIV–XXVI, XXX–XXXI). Ali Hakemi and Mahmud Rad resumed commercial excavations on the eastern Low Mound in 1947 and 1949, mainly opening a number of graves (Hakemi and Rad 1950). These early excavations alerted archaeologists to the presence of a "Grey Ware" ceramic assemblage at Hasanlu. This distinctive "Grey Ware" and its correlated vessel forms were known, to a certain extent, from other sites in northern and western Iran, mostly cemeteries. This ceramic tradition had already been dated to the early Iron Age of western Iran, then understood as the late 2nd millennium BC, and was linked by some scholars to Iranian migrations based on extremely limited evidence (Burton-Brown 1951; Contenau and Ghirshman 1935; Ghirshman 1938, 1939, 1954; Hakemi and Rad 1950; Stein 1940). Robert H. Dyson chose the site for excavation in 1956 as part of a four-month survey of sites in northern and western Iran after having briefly excavated at Hamadan (Dyson 1956, 1957).[2] Ten days were spent working on the High Mound. Under Dyson's general direction, the Hasanlu Project subsequently completed ten seasons of excavation at Hasanlu and conducted excavations and regional surveys in the surrounding Solduz and Ušnu valleys until 1977.

The work conducted at Hasanlu and two seasons of excavation at Dinkha Tepe in 1966 and 1968 form the core of our dataset on the EWGW horizon/Iron I of northwestern Iran. While most of the Hasanlu Project's research was focused on the Iron II period, the project collected a large body of data spanning the Pottery Neolithic to the Medieval periods. In all, ten periods—labeled Hasanlu I–X, from latest to earliest—were defined in the Hasanlu sequence (see Chapter 2). Most of these periods are closely linked to cultural developments in northern Mesopotamia, with strong but intermittent influences from the Caucasus. In Dyson's original periodization, the early Iron Age spanned Hasanlu Periods V–IV or his Iron I and Iron II (Dyson 1965:211, table 2). While Hasanlu is particularly important for its early Iron Age sequence in terms of its impact in the development of the archaeology of Iran, the earlier part of this sequence remains obscure. Likewise, perhaps more than any other period at Hasanlu, Period V has been at the center of several important theoretical debates regarding cultural developments in northwestern Iran in the later 2nd millennium BC. The achievements of the Hasanlu Project in the field were unfortunately not matched by an assiduous campaign of publication (see especially Muscarella 2006). Little of the primary data has been published before this, and the following represents a substantial revision of our understanding of the period.

Archaeological Chronology in Ušnu-Solduz

The formulation of the Hasanlu Sequence, an archaeological sequence that spans the Neolithic to the Medieval periods, perhaps represents the most enduring and influential achievement of the Hasanlu Project. This sequence contained two major points of weakness—the mid-to-late 2nd millennium BC and the Iron III–IV. The Iron III–IV periods have been the subject of much recent revision (Dyson 1999a, 1999b; Kroll 2000, 2010, In press b), and correcting the later 2nd millennium chronology has required substantial time, effort, and modifications. The reasons for these inadequacies are both methodological and conceptual.[3] In brief, from 1958 forward the focus of the Hasanlu Project's excavations at Hasanlu was almost exclusively the burned Iron II citadel. Concessions were made to accommodate this research agenda, and the investigation of earlier and later periods was of secondary importance, often being rushed and inadequately recorded (see Chapters 2 and 3).

The Neolithic and Chalcolithic (Hasanlu X–VIII)

The Ušnu-Solduz region was extensively settled in the late Neolithic or Hasanlu Period X—the Hajji Firuz Phase (see Voigt 1983). The beginning of the period may date to as early as the late 7th millennium BC, and settled agricultural populations were well established in Ušnu-Solduz and in the area east of the lake in the 6th millennium (Burney 1964; Voigt 1983; Voigt and Dyson 1992:174). Various scholars have indicated this period is essentially a local variant of the Proto-Hassuna, Hassuna, and possibly Samarran periods of northern Mesopotamia, citing similarities in ceramic assemblages and radiocarbon dates (Voigt and Dyson 1992:174). The Hasanlu Project excavated Hajji Firuz, the type-site for the period, in 1961 and 1968, and this archaeological culture has been documented at other sites by surveys (Voigt 1976, 1983; Young 1962).

The Chalcolithic is likewise well attested in Ušnu-Solduz and is divided into Hasanlu Period IX (Dalma Phase) and Hasanlu Period VIII (Pisdeli Phase). Dalma occupation was documented at the type-site of Dalma, excavated in 1961, as well as at Hajji Firuz, Pisdeli, and at Hasanlu in the Well Sounding on the High Mound (Hamlin 1975; Voigt 1983:7–8, 17–18, figs. 4, 8; Young 1962). Dalma represents a fairly widely distributed archaeological horizon in western Iran (Henrickson 1985, 1986; Kearton n.d.; Solecki and Solecki 1973), and exhibits strong affinities with and connections to the Ubaid archaeological horizon of northern Mesopotamia (Voigt and Dyson 1992:174–75). There is a smooth transition from Period IX to Period VIII. The Pisdeli Period is the local variant of the late Ubaid and early Uruk of Mesopotamia. Aside from the type-site of Pisdeli, which was sounded by the Hasanlu Project in 1961 (Dyson and Young 1960; Young 1962), Pisdeli occupations were documented at Hajji Firuz (Voigt 1983:8, 16–17, figs. 4, 8) and in the Well Sounding at Hasanlu. As noted by Voigt and Dyson (1992:175), the depths of the excavated deposits at Hasanlu and Pisdeli indicate the period was quite long.

The Early Bronze Age (Early-to-Mid 3rd Millennium BC)

The transition from Hasanlu Period VIII to Period VII, the EBA, has not been documented within the limited available dataset. Dyson divided Hasanlu Period VII into three subperiods, previously loosely referred to as phases (Dyson 1973b; Dyson and Pigott 1975). Period VIIc dates to the early 3rd millennium BC and possibly as early as the late 4th millennium BC and is known from deep soundings on the High Mound and Low Mound of Hasanlu (Danti, Voigt, and Dyson 2004). The Low Mound was first settled at this time, and the EBA community is strongly reminiscent of the Kranzhügel of northern Mesopotamia of the mid-3rd millennium. Ceramics indicate that Early Transcaucasian (ETC) influences were especially strong at Hasanlu, contrary to previous assertions (see also Danti, Voigt, and Dyson 2004). The succeeding subperiods Hasanlu VIIb and VIIa are quite different insofar as the ceramics are concerned, with a highly distinctive Painted Orange Ware (POW) component in occupation assemblages and graves at Hasanlu and with only a few ETC sherds. Similar ceramics are known from other sites in the southern Lake Urmia Basin, and a few POW sherds have been found in the Urmia and Salmas regions. Findspots in the south, along the Zarineh Rud and Simineh Rud, provide some indication of the core area of this tradition, and Voigt and Dyson have noted connections between POW and material from Mesopotamia of the mid-3rd millennium BC (1992:175). We see here a division, or "shatter zone," in the Lake Urmia Basin, which runs along a line from the Urmia valley to the purlieu of Tabriz, similar to that which occurred in later periods.

The Middle Bronze I (2100–1900 BC)

We are hindered by a dearth of information regarding regional settlement patterns during the late 3rd–early 2nd millennium BC, the subperiod I now designate Hasanlu VIc; previously, this timespan was lumped within Period VI. Our limited picture of the MBI is due, in part, to a lack of obvious—here meaning painted—ceramic type-fossils following the decline of the POW horizon of the 3rd millennium BC. Excavations at Dinkha Tepe and Hasanlu help to shed some light on the subperiod; Simple Ware (SW) ceramics belonging to Period VIc were found at both sites (on the meaning of this term, see Braidwood and Braidwood 1960). Painted wares are absent, and ceramics tended to be fired at high temperatures, resulting in a greenish-buff appearance indicative of well-developed pyrotechnology. Decoration in appliqué is common and includes rope designs and horizontal ribs. Punctate designs and comb incising in horizontal bands and wavy lines also occur. Typical vessel forms are carinated bowls, large barrel forms, and vats with horizontal ribs and ledge rims or overhanging rims. Overall, the assemblage exhibits close ties to EB–MB transitional and MBI assemblages in northern Mesopotamia of the late 3rd and early 2nd millennium BC. Such assemblages are seen as early manifestations of the Khabur Ware horizon characteristic of the 19th–17th centuries BC, and most of the major vessel forms continue in the MBII. This suggests an in-place development of the succeeding Period VIb ceramic assemblage in Ušnu-Solduz and a late 3rd–early 2nd millennium BC date for the cultural stimuli that resulted in this development, almost certainly of northern Mesopotamian origin/influence.

The Middle Bronze II (1900–1600 BC)

Influences from northern Mesopotamia grew more pronounced in the MBII or Hasanlu Period VIb/Dinkha Period IV. The period is marked by the introduction of Khabur Ware—a cream-slipped buff ware found in painted, incised, and plain varieties (Frane 1996; Hamlin 1971, 1974; Oguchi 1997, 1998). The painted style is readily identifiable in survey collection lots and so we are somewhat better informed on settlement patterns during this period (Kroll 1994b). Excavations at Dinkha Tepe and Hasanlu again provide excavated exposures of this period. The material culture shares strong affinities with northern Mesopotamia. Although it is difficult to prove without written evidence, Dinkha, and perhaps Hasanlu, could have been *kārum* (trading colonies). The implications of this are discussed below (see Chapters 3 and 4).

The final part of the MBII, for now referred to as the Terminal MBII, is known only from excavations at Dinkha, where it is designated Dinkha IV Phase D, and from a few graves at Hasanlu. This subperiod dates to the 17th century BC and is characterized by the rapid decline in the production of Khabur Ware (see Chapter 4). The Terminal MBII and the MBIII constitute an important transitional period during which time the Early MBW horizon emerges. In this regard, the origins of this horizon are similar to other Grey Ware horizons in northern and western Iran of the 2nd millennium BC, as argued by Piller (2003–2004, 2004).

The Middle Bronze III (1600–1450 BC)

I have designated the new subperiod Hasanlu VIa to account for important cultural deposits from small excavated exposures at Dinkha and isolated finds at Hasanlu on the High Mound and in graves from the Low Mound. Previous researchers have nearly all interpreted this timespan in the southern Lake Urmia Basin as a hiatus in the occupational sequence or a time of punctuated, nearly absolute culture change (possibly following the abandonment of the region). The MBIII is much better known in the Urmia and Salmas regions to the north, where it is typified by affinities to the southern Caucasus. We can say little regarding the region's cultures beyond the prevalent styles and distribution of ceramics—painted pottery in particular. This is most unfortunate since this period forms the crucial transition to the Early MBW horizon.

Early MBW (see Chapter 4) and painted wares are the primary markers of the subperiod in northern Iranian Azerbaijan, most notably polychrome painted Urmia Ware (Edwards 1981, 1983, 1986; Rubinson 2004). Many of the diagnostic vessel forms of Dyson and Young's former EWGW horizon are already present in the Early MBW assemblage and most develop from the MBII. Urmia Ware probably develops out of the MBII painted pottery traditions of the northern part of the region, best attested at Haftavan Early VIb and Geoy Tepe early D (Burton-Brown 1951; Edwards 1983). In contrast, the MBII assemblages of the southern Lake Urmia Basin contain an important Khabur Ware component (Hamlin 1971, 1974). Amounts of Painted Khabur Ware (PKW) decline rapidly in the Terminal MBII (17th century). In Phase B (MBII) of the Dinkha Control Sounding, PKW (Kramer's Ware Ie) attains a high of 24% of the assemblage. In Phase D (terminal MBII), PKW makes up a mere 8% (see Chapter 4), and unpainted wares and annular band–painted wares are typical. The MBII KW assemblage is highly localized in northwestern Iran, confined to the area of Dinkha Tepe and Hasanlu and known from surveys at sites running from east to west along the Gadar Çay (Kroll 1994b:165). The southeastern Lake Urmia Basin and the valley of the Zarineh Rud and Simineh Rud were home to a third 2nd millennium BC painted pottery tradition linked to Giyan Tepe III–II and Godin III (Edwards 1986:69; Henrickson 2011; Swiny 1975; Tala'i 1984).

Haftavan, in the Salmas region, provides our best view of the MBIII, where the period is designated Haftavan Late VIB (Burney 1970, 1972, 1973, 1975; Edwards 1981, 1983, 1986). Evidence from Haftavan and other sites in the lake region suggests disruptions occurred during the mid-2nd millennium BC. The Early VIB settlement (MBII) was burned, followed by an ephemeral occupation attested by stake holes and pits. Elsewhere, a mudbrick and timber structure terraced into the slope of the mound was found to be resting on the burned debris of the earlier settlement. MBIII Haftavan has multiple architectural phases of flimsy construction that were repeatedly rebuilt, in addition to rectilinear mudbrick structures on stone footings and an area of large ovens suggesting intensive industrial/residential activities (Edwards 1983:73). The MBIII settlement was also destroyed by fire.

Burton-Brown's excavations at contemporary Geoy Tepe in the Urmia valley yielded one small exposure of MBIII architecture and graves, generally referred to as Geoy late D–C. The division of Geoy D into an earlier and later subperiod stems from an analysis conducted by Dyson (1968:16–17; see also Edwards 1986:58–60). The distinction is necessitated due to the mixing of the two periods, which resulted from the digging of arbitrary levels based on absolute elevations through sloping deposits in Pit [Operation] IV (cf. Burton-Brown 1951: figs. 16, 17b–c). In Pit III, a deposit containing Urmia Ware and Early MBW sealed stone-built tombs initially dated to Geoy Tepe D (MBII; Burton-Brown 1951:110). Dyson (1968:18) dates Tombs A and J to the Period late D–C (MBIII) based on their elevations, and notes Tombs B and H "could belong to the earlier state"—that is, early Period D (MB II; Dyson 1968:18)—while Edwards dates the tombs to the MBIII (Edwards 1986:60–61). Polychrome painted Urmia Ware is not found in MBIII graves, which tend to contain undecorated ceramics. The overlying MBIII deposit was in turn cut by inhumation graves with MBW of early Iron Age date (Burton-Brown 1951:123–26). Poorly preserved architectural remains were recovered in "Pit IV" immediately above structures of Period D (Burton-Brown 1951:72, figs. 17b–c, 18). The situation at Kordlar, in the same valley, is difficult to ascertain. Kordlar V was revealed in limited soundings and produced what might be an intermediate assemblage of ceramics (Heinsch 2004; Lippert 1979: figs. 6:6, 9:2, 10:1–2, 11:2). Edwards (1986:64) dates the period somewhere in the MBIII–early LBA, citing similarities to assemblages recovered at Dinkha (see below) and Kizilvank (Schaeffer 1948: fig. 270, nos. 1–5) as well as radiocarbon dates from overlying Kordlar III–IV (Felber 1979; Lippert 1979:117–18, 137).

Excavations at Dinkha, in the Ušnu valley, show the Terminal MBII settlement (Dinkha IV Phase D) was destroyed by fire. This marks the end of the KW presence in Ušnu-Solduz, with sharply diminishing amounts of annular band–painted buff ware and plain buff ware in later assemblages—others call such material late Khabur Ware. There was no evidence for rebuilding activities during the MBIII in the small excavated area, but the deposit immediately overlying the collapse of the burned MBII structures contained Urmia Ware (Rubinson 2004) and Early MBW. In contrast to other MBIII sites, the Early MBW recovered at Dinkha also occurs in an incised and impressed variant. The MBIII level was overlain by "trash deposits" of the early LBA, and the MBIII and LBA strata were cut by graves of the LBA and Iron I (Muscarella 1974, see below). At nearby Hasanlu, in the Solduz valley, MBIII occupation is suggested by a few sherds from the Well Sounding, a deep sounding dug near the center of the High Mound by a professional well digger. Other stray sherds of Urmia Ware were found on the mound's surface, and MBIII graves were found on the Low Mound. The MBIII is almost certainly present at Hasanlu, but sampling and site formation processes have led some scholars to insert a cultural break and/or hiatus in the Hasanlu sequence—corresponding to my Terminal MBII and MBIII—separating the MBII and early LBA. In Kurdistan, the period is known only from archaeological surveys. Giyan and Godin, in Luristan, provide grave groups and a fragmented occupational sequence for the area to the south, in the environs of Nehevand (Contenau and Ghirshman 1935; Henrickson 1983–1984; 2011:esp. table 6.2; Young 1965). The period is also attested at Sialk in Period A (Ghirshman 1939).

The Late Bronze (1450–1250 BC)

The LBA (Hasanlu V) sees Early MBW become the major ceramic ware in the southern Lake Urmia Basin and in surrounding regions. The period is best attested in graves and occupation deposits at Hasanlu and in "trash deposits" and graves at Dinkha (Muscarella 1974). Graves have also been excavated at Hajji Firuz (Voigt 1976:810–14, fig. 116, pls. LXI–LXII), Dalma (Young 1962:707–8, fig. 8), Haftavan (Burney 1970:165, fig. 8 nos. 1, 7), and Yanik (Burney 1962:136, 146–47, pl. XLIIc nos. 24–29); a tomb of the early LBA was excavated at Geoy Tepe (Burton-Brown 1951:142–45).

The earliest attested columned-hall structure at Hasanlu dates to the latter part of the period. An internal gateway is also known from the late LBA on the southern High Mound (see Chapter 3), and the Hasanlu citadel probably began to take shape at this time. Another columned-hall building of the later LBA–early Iron I is known from Kordlar IV. This fortified manor house had corner towers, a modest columned hall with a single central column and probable side columns, narrow benches, and a central sunken hearth (Lippert 1977: fig. 22). The building's construction can be dated to as early as the late LBA on the basis of radiocarbon samples from Kordlar IV and III (Lippert 1979). The building was destroyed by fire and contained human victims and a fairly large number of artifacts. Comparisons of the artifacts found at Kordlar with those from Hasanlu indicate Kordlar IV was likely destroyed in the early Iron I. At Kordlar we see a concern with fortifying a single structure, while at Hasanlu the later LBA buildings were located within a fortified citadel. Two superimposed residential structures were found on the western low mound of Haftavan V (1450–1000 BC). These are difficult to date precisely (Burney 1973:162–64), and they exhibit new construction techniques. Their low density suggests a decline in the settlement's population. No architecture is known from LBA Dinkha Tepe, although the presence of "trash deposits" in the cemetery area suggests an occupation nearby according to Muscarella (1974:52). Geoy Tepe B might have been occupied and fortified at this time (Burton-Brown 1951:141), but little more is known. I would date Geoy B to the late LBA–Iron I on the basis of ceramic parallels with Hasanlu and Kordlar (see Chapter 4).

The picture we gain from the MBIII and LBA is one of marked regional variations (see Chapter 4) rather than of the homogeneity posited previously by advocates of punctuated demic diffusion theories (see Young 1965). Regional variations subside in the early Iron Age (*pace* Young 1965). The MBIII and LBA previously formed the early portion of Young's EWGW horizon (1965) and the early part of Dyson's Iron I (1965). The material culture of the LBA exhibits ties to northern Mesopotamia, the southern Caucasus, and the region typified by the Gheytaryeh-Group of the EWGW horizon as defined by Piller (2003–2004). The small number of chronologically discrete ceramic diagnostics for the period represents a major obstacle to mapping settlement patterns around Lake Urmia. Only a few vessel forms are diagnostic of the period, and whole vessel forms are often needed to differentiate between the MBIII, LBA, and Iron I. We may assume that the dense and regular settlement pattern of the early Iron Age had its origins in the mid-to-late 2nd millennium BC, but until new archaeological surveys and excavations are conducted in the region this will remain uncertain. The reanalysis of late LBA occupation deposits at Hasanlu shows that a fortified citadel emerged at this time (see Chapter 3). Graves from Hasanlu and Dinkha indicate increasing access to precious goods, heightened status differentiation, and ascribed status. These trends continue in the Iron I (see below) and, taken together with other lines of evidence, suggest a process of secondary state formation.

Iron I (1250–1050 BC)

Hasanlu IVc was formerly lumped within Dyson's Hasanlu V/Iron I and Young's EWGW horizon. I now call this period the Iron I and distinguish its ceramic assemblage as Middle MBW. In the north, regional variations such as painted wares continue at Kordlar, Geoy Tepe, and presumably at Gijlar. While survey data are available, surveys have lacked the chronological resolution necessary to divide the MBW horizon into meaningful temporal units. Previously, the EWGW horizon encompassed roughly the period from 1600–1000 BC. The Late Western Grey Ware (LWGW) horizon, meanwhile, was more temporally discrete, spanning 1000–800 BC, although it should be noted that the 800 BC date rests on the dating of Hasanlu's destruction and not the end of the ceramic horizon in northwestern Iran. Early Western Grey Ware was loosely defined using fairly generic ceramic index fossils and thus not surprisingly has been identified over a broad swathe of northern and western Iran, giving the false impression that it arrived with a wave of migrants bearing burnished bridgeless-spouted jars, tankards, and "worm bowls." Closer inspection has shown these diagnostics and others developed over a long period of time in Ušnu-Solduz, starting in the mid-2nd millennium BC, and that "Iron Age" material culture did not arrive fully developed at a single point in time.

This reanalysis of the Iron I citadel at Hasanlu reveals it was more fully developed than previously interpreted (Dyson 1989a:113–14, fig. 6a). The largest known building of the northwestern citadel was BBIII (Fig. 1.5), a relatively modest columned-hall structure with a niched and buttressed façade, portico room, and antechamber leading to a columned hall. If the internal features of the later Hasanlu IVb BBIII provide any indication of the use of space in the Iron I, the hall had two columns, side benches, and a "throne seat." The side rooms and rear of the building were presumably used as kitchens and storerooms. On the north side of the antechamber, a door led into a stairwell. These internal features of the Iron II period have been reconstructed on the architectural plans of Period IVc used here, with the caveat that we lack evidence of these internal features in secure Iron I contexts. To the southwest of BBIII was a poorly preserved columned-hall structure—the RS22–23 IVc Building. The open space between BBIII and this structure may have been one of the main entrances into the citadel as in the later Period IVb (see below). The RS22–23 Building formed the north end of a line of structures dividing the inner citadel from entry areas to the west. The T22 and U22 Buildings are smaller structures of unknown function (Fig. 1.5). To the south of the U22 Building was an open space, which separated it from the V22 Building. This passageway corresponds to the position of an Iron II gateway, the so-called Foot Gate (see below). Overall, flow patterns in and out of the northwestern citadel seem to have been established by the Iron I and maintained in the Iron II, with added emphasis on controlling access and creating internal fortifications (cf. Fig. 1.6). The southern citadel also took shape during this period and provided the basic blueprint for the well-known Iron II Lower Court area. The main structure was BBII, shown here with its western storerooms (Fig. 1.5) since the available evidence indicates these were original to the structure (see Chapter 3). As with BBIII, the building shown here is reconstructed with internal features attested in the Iron II. BBII was likely a columned-hall temple (Dyson and Voigt 2003). To its southwest was the CC27 Building, the precursor to BBIX and BBX of Period IVb—they seem to have been ancillary structures associated with BBII. To the northwest of BBII stood the YZ27–29 Building, almost certainly a substantial portion of an internal gateway. The building's orientation, with its tower and buttressed façade facing north, seems to indicate that the gateway had been located in Grid YZ27 in late Period V and early Period IVc. Internal modifications reveal this entry was blocked by later Period IVc (see Chapter 3). The location of a gateway in this area is in keeping with the built environment of the Iron II—this was the area of BBIE, the Lower Court Gate, and the entrance to the Upper Court. The orientation and location of the YZ27–29 structure, however, raises the question of what might have been located in the area of Grids VWX28, which were not excavated to the level of Period IVc except in the small Well Trench of Grid W28, where no Period IVc architectural remains were recovered. At least part of the area north of BBII was a courtyard, the western side of which was defined by BBV. This columned hall seems to be aligned to BBII and the YZ27–29 Building, with its main axis running north-south and its main entry on the north side. As was argued by Dyson (1989a:113), columned-hall structure BBIVE to the north probably dates to Period IVc, but it effectively blocked the front façade of BBV, and so may well be a later Iron I addition. The addition of BBIVE had the effect of creating an east-west passageway between it and BBV which, in the Iron II, became BBIV-V: we again see an Iron II emphasis on lowering the permeability of the inner portions of the citadel through the addition of gateways and the narrowing of passageways.

Hasanlu IVc appears to end with a fire and the destruction of major buildings on the High Mound and the Low Mound (Danti 2011), although it is not currently possible to stratigraphically link all these destruction contexts and conclusively attribute them to a single event. The dating of this destruction rests on radiocarbon dates from wooden structural elements used in the rebuilding of the citadel at the start of Period IVb and charred remains from the Period IVc fire (Dyson and Muscarella 1989). The reliance on radiocarbon samples from structural timbers is hardly ideal, and more dates are needed from short-lived samples. We see a pattern of disruption at Kordlar as well. Following the destruction of Kordlar IV, the columned-hall structure was reconstructed using the stubs of the earlier walls as foundations (as at Hasanlu) and the building was provided with a new enclosure wall, with towers. Radiocarbon dates (Felber 1979; Lippert 1979:117–18, 137) and the ceramic assemblages indicate Kordlar IV–III dates to the late LBA–Iron I. The building sequence at Kordlar shows repeated destructions by fire with some human victims. The rebuilt versions of the structure are progressively more fortified, probably in response to external threats or repurposing by a new authority. Other sites such as Geoy Tepe and Haftavan were likely occupied in the Iron I, but little more can be said with certainty at the present time.

Citadel settlements appear to grow in the Iron I period in the Lake Urmia region—our examples are Hasanlu (Fig. 1.5) and Kordlar (Lippert 1977, 1979). The Iron I citadel of Hasanlu likely took shape in the later LBA/Hasanlu V (see Chapter 3), and Kordlar seems to follow a similar, if more modest, developmental trajectory. In Solduz, fortified centers were probably located at Mirabad, Naqadeh, Hasanlu, Sakse, and Mohammadšah (Appendix I). There is evidence of growing external threats, such as destruction levels at Kordlar and Hasanlu, which help contextualize these widespread changes to the built environment. In Ušnu-Solduz, Iron I graves are known from Dinkha, Hasanlu, and probably Dalma, and attest to increasing access to elite goods, acquired status, pronounced status differences, and a higher degree of social heterarchy (see Chapter 5). Iron first appears in the southern Lake Urmia Basin and bronze artifacts are more abundant. Overall, Hasanlu, Dinkha, and Kordlar suggest the continuation of patterns established in the LBA and furnish a view of object types and styles better known for the Iron II (see Chapter 5).

Iron II (1050–800 BC)

The Iron II corresponds to Young's LWGW horizon (1965), defined locally by Hasanlu IVb, which develops from the Iron I. Aside from Hasanlu, which remains largely unpublished (Muscarella 2006), important excavations have been conducted at Dinkha Tepe II, Geoy Tepe A, Kordlar II–I, and Zendan-i Suleiman I. The latter two sites provide our best view of the late part of the period—for lack of a better term, the Iron II–III transition.

The Hasanlu IVb citadel is the best-known Iron II settlement of northwestern Iran, although relative to the size of the dataset it is one of the least published (Fig. 1.6). Moreover, "best known" is not synonymous with "most representative," and our current view of settlement in Ušnu-Solduz is heavily biased (Hasanlu-centric)—other sites in northwestern Iran round out our view somewhat, especially Kordlar, Dinkha, and Zendan-i Suleiman, but we desperately lack excavations at smaller sites in rural hinterlands, lower towns, and even at other citadel centers. Approximately 100

Iron II graves were excavated at Hasanlu's Low Mound and another 68 are known from Dinkha II (Muscarella 1974:58ff.). At Haftavan, 25 graves date to the Iron I–II (Tala'i 2007; Tala'i and Aliyari 2009). In Tabriz, excavations at the important cemetery of Masjid-e Kabud have uncovered 108 graves of the Iron I–II (Hojabri Nobari 2004). Simple inhumations typify Haftavan and Hasanlu, and all graves were located in low mound cemeteries, at what were likely the shifting peripheries of the contemporary settlements. The Hasanlu Low Mound cemetery also contained stone-built hypogea (Danti and Cifarelli n.d.; Hakemi and Rad 1950). Mudbrick and stone tombs and simple inhumations are all attested at Dinkha, along with 19 infant urn burials (Muscarella 1974). The graves of Masjid-e Kabud were of three types: inhumations, stone-covered inhumations, and horseshoe-shaped mudbrick tombs similar to those recorded at Dinkha (Hojabri Nobari 2004).

A detailed description of the Iron II at Hasanlu is well beyond the bounds of the current work, but one cannot interpret the earlier MBW levels of the site without reference to Period IVb. The site is divisible into a fortified citadel (the High Mound) and a Lower

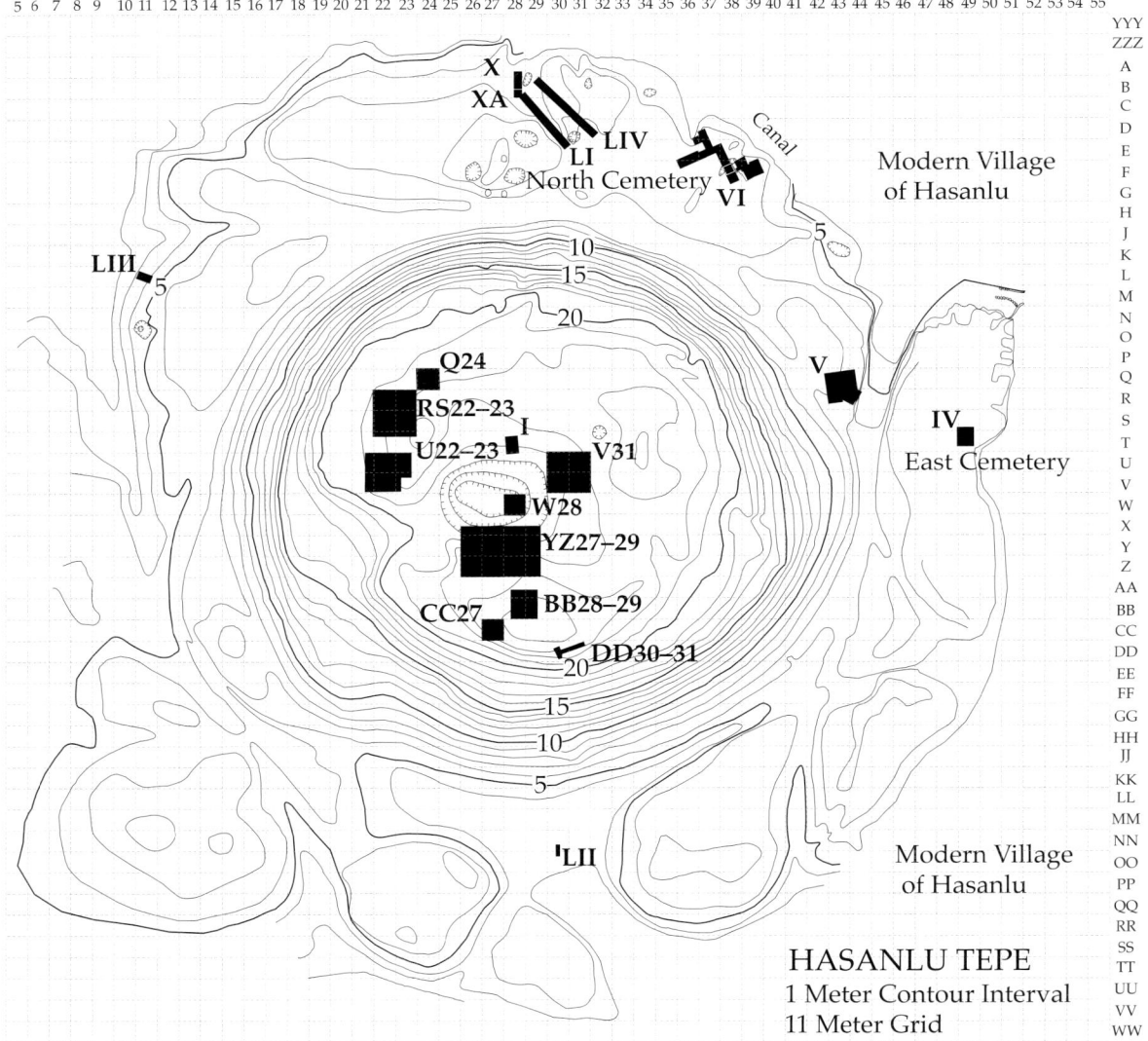

Fig. 1.4 Topographic map of Hasanlu Tepe showing excavation areas relevant to the later 2nd millennium BC.

Town (the Low Mound, Fig. 1.4). Settlement on the Low Mound is poorly understood; only a single Low Mound building, BBXIII, was thoroughly investigated (Danti 2011). Other areas were used as cemeteries, but there are some indications of Iron II architecture in these areas, as well as "burials" that might be interpreted as victims of an attack, possibly the event of ca. 800 BC. The available evidence suggests that the Lower Town was destroyed in the same events as the citadel—in Terminal Hasanlu IVc and Terminal Hasanlu IVb—with human and animal victims, burning, and relatively high numbers of *in situ* artifacts attested in the final Iron II phase of the Lower Town (Danti 2011). Only renewed excavation can resolve such issues. Estimating the size of the Lower Town is difficult. The current site boundaries are set by irrigation canals, a rural highway, and the modern villages of Hasanlu and Aminlu. There is little reason to believe that these modern barriers correspond to the topographically indistinct margins of the *tepe*. Estimates of the density of occupation are similarly problematic, as excavations on the Low Mound were spatially limited and focused mostly in the North Cemetery. Work in Operation V suggests fairly dense occupation (Danti 2011), while other areas show little evidence of Iron II occupation, although the poor quality of excavation and record-keeping prevents greater certitude. Sadly, Hasanlu provides the only moderately detailed picture of a Low Mound settlement in the region for this period.

In contrast, the Iron II citadel of Hasanlu was extensively excavated from 1958–1974 (Fig. 1.6). It provides one of our only views of a citadel, with late Iron II–Iron III Zendan-i Suleiman representing what is likely a unique type of settlement manicured to its inimitable terrain with a strong ritual component in its earliest phases (Boehmer 1961, 1967, 1986; Kleiss 1971; Naumann 1977). Kordlar Tepe IIa continued to serve as a small fortress or fortified manor house. The main entrance to the Hasanlu citadel was located on the southwestern side of the *tepe*. Dyson asserts a triple-road system occupied this area, but Kroll has challenged this interpretation following his thorough re-examination of the excavations in this poorly understood area of the site. I have chosen not to include architecture from this sector on the plans presented here (Figs. 1.4, 1.5), as it would be premature to attempt to reconstruct the gateways and passages leading up to the western citadel. The slopes of the citadel seem to have had glacis, and evidence of a likely Iron II fortification wall was uncovered in small exposures on the High Mound (see Chapter 3). Dyson has also pointed out that the Lower Outer Wall and Upper Outer Wall of the west slope suggest the settlement was fortified (1989a:110). I would add that the Western Enclosure and BBXI formed parts of the fortified entry (see Dyson 1989a:110, fig. 4). The southern end of BBII suggests the existence of a fortification wall to its south. Multiple glacis "layers" were exposed on the slopes of the High Mound in early soundings, but these are difficult to attribute to a specific period since the High Mound was fortified in Periods I, II/IIIa, IIIb/c, IVb and likely in IVc. The presence of an Iron I–II circumvallation protecting the citadel is also indicated by internal gateways and patterns of controlled access within the citadel. In the Iron II, two fortified access points are known on the western side of the citadel. These are the so-called Double Gate (BBVIIE) and the Chariot Gate (BBVIS) and adjacent Foot Gate (BBVIN; Fig. 1.6). Similar spatial patterns are reflected in the architecture of the late LBA and Iron I (see Chapter 3). The area of the Western Enclosure (cf. Dyson 1989a: fig. 6b) and BBXI likely controlled access to an open area to the north that led to the so-called Double Gate and the northwestern citadel. As in the Iron I, the northwestern citadel was dominated by BBIII. This columned-hall structure was an elite residence in the Iron I–II. In the Iron II, an enclosed courtyard with a gate structure was added to the building. To the east, BBVIII was only partially investigated. The small architectural exposure resembles BBVII to the southwest which, in light of its architectural form and contents, likely served a military function. BBVI–BBVIII defined the northwest corner of a large open space, at the south end of which were fortified gateways controlling access to the Upper Court and Lower Court. The Lower Court Gate was an imposing structure with a buttressed façade and towers flanking a stone-paved gateway, which provided access to the large, stone-paved Lower Court,[4] the heart of the citadel. The Upper Court likely also had a gateway south of the stone steps leading to it. At this point, one could proceed to the portico entry of BBIW, which I interpret as another elite residence akin to BBIII, only larger. The exact function of this monumental columned-hall structure is difficult to ascertain since

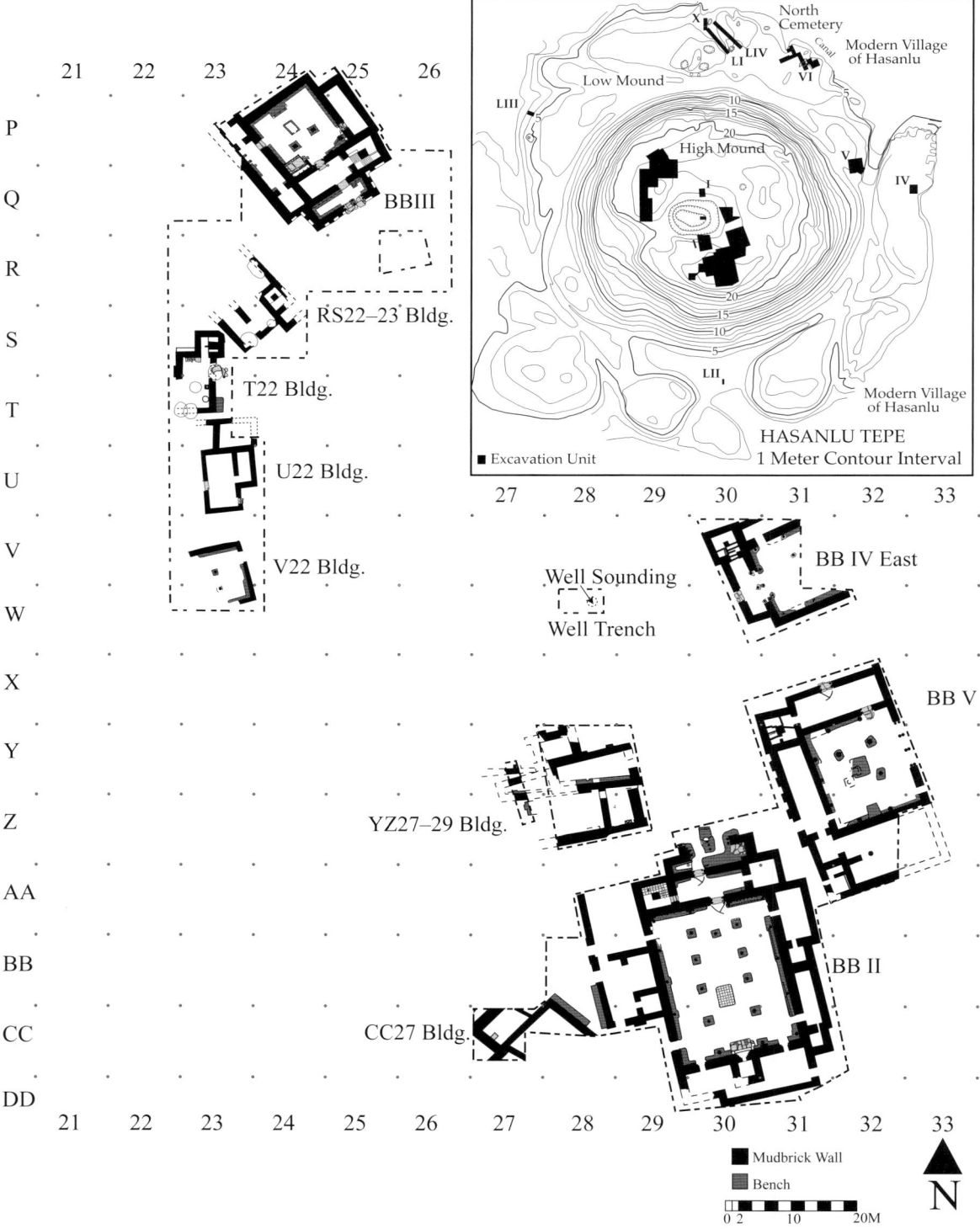

Fig. 1.5 The Iron I Citadel of Hasanlu Tepe.

Fig. 1.6 The Iron II Citadel of Hasanlu Tepe.

the construction of the Urartian wall of Hasanlu IIIC obliterated its western end. The building was entered through a portico room and antechamber. To the south of the antechamber was a stairwell leading to the upper stories/roof. In the Burned Buildings of the Hasanlu citadel, structures with stairwells contained upper and lower burned deposits deriving from the ground floor and upper stories/roof. The types of objects in the upper deposits and the manner of their deposition and proveniences strongly suggest these buildings had upper stories, as does the sheer intensity of the fire, the amounts of ash and burned debris, and the number of carbonized timbers found in the wreckage. Objects from the upper deposits of BBIW and BBII show that these areas were used to store valuables. The upper stories were also the main residential spaces, since the lower levels contained public meeting areas, kitchens, storerooms, and waste disposal chambers.

On the east side of the Upper Court one could pass through a small portico into BBIE and the Lower Court beyond or continue south through a doorway to the east-west running South Street leading to BBIX and BBX, dubbed the Bead House and Square House, respectively. The former dates to late in the Iron II and was named for the mass of beads found inside. The south end of the Lower Court was dominated by BBII, a large columned hall entered through a portico and antechamber. Aniconic stone stelae stood before its entry and sat opposite others erected across the court, in front of BBIV. In the columned hall of BBII, a rabbeted cult target occupied the south wall on the central north-south axis, and artifactual finds from the building indicate BBII was a temple, as do other architectural features of the building (Dyson and Voigt 2003). The vast majority of the Assyrian style artifacts and assyrianizing local copies were found in this building. The western and eastern ends of the building's ground floor contained storerooms, as did the extreme southern end. A stairway east of the antechamber provided access to the upper stories/roof. BBV stood to the east of BBII. This building had been extensively modified over time: its orientation and entries reflect a layout dating to the Iron I. The building's main entrance, to the north, was subsumed within a new structure, BBIV–V, which was apparently constructed to control access to the Lower Court to/from the east. A similar concern with controlling east-west access is reflected in modifications made to BBV's columned hall, where a portico-like window in the east wall (Fig. 1.5) was walled in during the Iron II (Fig. 1.6). At the time of the Terminal Iron II destruction, the columned hall was being used as a stable. The structure contained storerooms and a stairwell. Like BBV, BBIVE to the north showed signs of extensive modification, and the building's alignment—with its main entrance facing west—reflects the Iron I built environment. The main entrance was blocked by the construction of BBIV in Period IVb, and the portico entry to the columned hall was filled in, leaving a narrow doorway. The addition of BBIV created a new façade for the BBIV-IVE complex, with an elaborate portico and aniconic stelae. Architectural parallels with BBII indicate the BBIV-IVE complex served a ritual function, but the rear (eastern) part of BBIVE's columned hall was never excavated—we might expect another cult target here as opposed to a "throne seat."

While impressive, we must remember that Hasanlu IVb was the product of at least 600 years of development. To truly understand the Iron II citadel one must trace its evolution back to the 2nd millennium BC, to its Iron I and LBA precursors. The archaeological culture of Hasanlu IVb has its roots in the mid-2nd millennium, arriving not through punctuated culture change or wave migration, but rather through a gradual development rooted in indigenous traditions. The archaeological culture did not arrive suddenly in a fully developed form, but took shape during the late MBII, MBIII, and LBA, specifically the latter part of this period or the late 14th–early 13th centuries BC. The archaeological culture(s) of the southern Lake Urmia region differ from neighboring regions in northwestern Iran in terms of scale and complexity. The timing and nature of developments in Ušnu-Solduz cannot be divorced from its neighbor, Assyria, and the area's emergence as an urbanized, affluent enclave parallels the rise of Assyria and presumably the intervening buffer state of Musasir/Ardini. In the late LBA and Iron I, I believe we can discern rapid secondary state formation in the Lake Urmia Basin with the emergence of citadel centers, increasing monumentality in architecture, the markedly increasing prosperity evidenced in material culture, enhanced status differentiation attested in architecture and mortuary contexts, and the militarization of the region suggested by fortifications and the ubiquity of weaponry, to name but a few factors. The pace of this development quickened in the early 1st millennium as the area was wedged between a rebounding Assyrian power and Urartu, which evinced close ties with northwestern Iran (Fuchs 2012; Piller 2012). Hasanlu, along with other centers in the region, ultimately fell victim to this volatile political climate. The site was destroyed during a period of Assyrian weakness and of unbridled expansion by Urartu, making the latter seem a prime suspect in Hasanlu's demise: we can certainly establish motive, means, opportunity, and subsequent benefit.

NOTES

1.1. Recent potassium-argon dates have placed the last volcanic activity between 1.2–0.8 mya (Innocenti et al. 1982), but a subsequent study (Karakhian et al. 2002) has argued for a Holocene date.

1.2. The University of Pennsylvania Museum, the Metropolitan Museum of Art of New York, and the Iranian Antiquities Authority jointly sponsored the Hasanlu Project.

1.3. For a review of the methods of the Hasanlu Project, see Danti 2004:8–10; 2011.

1.4. Figure 1.6 does not show the entirety of the stone paving of the Lower Court, although it was recorded by the excavators.

2

"Hasanlu V": Definition, Research Questions, and History of Scholarship

Parvis imbutus tentabis grandia tutus.

Since its initial definition by Robert H. Dyson, our understanding of "Hasanlu V" has been slowly and sporadically constructed through a rather unsystematic, accretive process. The mid-to-late 2nd millennium BC was not the primary focus of the Hasanlu Project given the expedience of excavating Period IVb on Hasanlu's High Mound, yet through Dyson and Young's writings, "Hasanlu V" played an inordinately central role in theories concerning the Iranian "Iron Age"—or, more precisely, the northwestern Iranian Late Bronze Age and Iron I. The period in Ušnu-Solduz is of fundamental importance, as it is the best-attested component of Young's EWGW archaeological horizon. "Hasanlu V" had a profound effect in shaping Young's early thinking on the concerned archaeological culture(s), horizon, and chronological period, Iron I (1965). Young's EWGW, occasionally confused and conflated with the chronological period "Iron I," appears in different regions of northern and western Iran in the mid-2nd millennium BC and is typically identified by the appearance of "Grey Ware," herein referred to as MBW. Various other archaeological diagnostics have been identified and are discussed later. Whether one agrees with Young's designation or not, since it is heavily weighted toward the meaning of spatio-temporal distributions of ceramic wares and forms, interpretations of "Hasanlu V" are still deeply embedded in conceptualizations of the Iranian Iron Age and theories on Iranian migrations into the Zagros. Most scholars have stepped back from such high-level theorizing, and we must begin anew with a reappraisal of "Hasanlu V" and the southern Lake Urmia Basin. It is useful, nevertheless, to briefly retrace the paths that have led to our current state of knowledge.

Scholarship on "Hasanlu V" can be ordered according to three related themes: the elucidation of the period's archaeological correlates, the refinement of the periodization and absolute chronology of the 2nd millennium BC, and the reconstruction of the cultural setting and cultural processes of this period. In terms of timing, these themes roughly correspond to the three phases of the Hasanlu Project. From 1956–1964, the project was conducting pioneering archaeological work in northwestern Iran, albeit under difficult field conditions and with fairly casual methods by today's standards. Excavations at Hasanlu Tepe ceased from 1965–1969, and the focus was on sites in the surrounding region: excavations at Dinkha Tepe clarified "Period V" and Period VI, which had come to be conceptually entangled with the former. From 1970–1977, the focus was again on Hasanlu, with improved excavation and recording methods having been introduced and, with regard to the 2nd millennium BC, research subsequently guided by refined, discrete objectives. This latter period corresponds with a peak in archaeological activity in Iran, and excavations in the northern Lake Urmia Basin and the central western Zagros helped reshape views of the MBW horizon and the 2nd millennium BC, more broadly (cf. Dyson 1971). The Hasanlu

Project's evolution is fairly typical of long-term expeditions that began during this period of Near Eastern archaeology, evincing a shift from inductive data collection and chronology building through cross-sequence comparisons to deductive hypothesis testing with broader theoretical foci. Dyson was methodologically influenced by the Wheeler-Kenyon method combined with Taylor's Conjunctive Approach (Taylor 1948) and Braidwood's multidisciplinary and multiscalar research model employed at Jarmo in 1954–1955. Gradually, the Hasanlu Project incorporated some of the primary tenets of the "New Archaeology" as a new generation of graduate students shaped the project.

In the early phase (1956–1964), the definition and published presentation of finds from Hasanlu—ceramics in particular—prioritized the identification of forms and styles that linked Ušnu-Solduz to other archaeological sequences rather than a more representative type-series exposition or selection based on statistical frequency. No preliminary or interim reports were written; rather, publication entailed syntheses of results and popular accounts written for a general audience. In and of itself, this is neither surprising nor unique for the time; what is unique is that this has largely remained the status quo since 1956 with regard to presenting the data from Hasanlu. In many ways, the publication effort took a top-down approach, producing works focused on specific artifact categories or addressing theoretical issues supported by minimal data presentation. Northwestern Iran was poorly known when the Hasanlu Project began, with only Stein's hurried work in Ušnu-Solduz in 1936 (1940), scant publications of the excavations conducted by Hakemi and Rad at Hasanlu (1950), and Burton-Brown's 1948 season at Geoy Tepe (1951). Radiocarbon dating was in its infancy. Looking farther afield, Dyson drew on the excavations at Tureng Tepe in 1931 (Wulsin 1932), Hissar in 1931 (Schmidt 1933, 1937), Shah Tepe in 1933 (Arne 1935, 1945), Giyan in 1931–1932 (Contenau and Ghirshman 1935), Sialk in 1933–1934 and 1937 (Ghirshman 1938, 1939), and the renewed work at Susa begun in 1946 (Ghirshman 1954). Sialk and Giyan provided a number of graves of the 2nd and early 1st millennia, but were of somewhat limited use given their flexible internal chronologies and floating absolute dating.

With regard to ceramics, the Hasanlu excavators were predisposed to collecting, recording, saving, and publishing highly distinctive forms and styles, particularly decorated wares that were useful for cross-sequence dating—with Nuzi and Assur in the early years, in particular. Over time, the definition of "Period V" shifted from one which emphasized forms and styles that linked Hasanlu to well-defined sequences underpinned by absolute dates derived from inscriptional evidence (especially from northern Mesopotamia) to one that fit Hasanlu within the early "Iron Age" of western Iran and that was predisposed to material attributes that potentially correlated with demic diffusion. This can be attributed to an important paradigm shift: one perceives the advent of an archaeology of northwestern Iran initially rooted, in terms of training and cultural-historical orientation, in Mesopotamia (Abdi 2001).

From 1956–1964, definitions of the "Iron I" were hobbled by the dataset (see below), and problematic links were drawn with northern Mesopotamia. Great interpretive weight was vested in the often tenuous connections between Hasanlu and other sites in Iran, particularly Tepe Hissar IIIc, Giyan Tepe I, Geoy Tepe B–A, Khurvin-Chandar, and especially Tepe Sialk A–B. This introduced further inaccuracies since these sequences/assemblages were problematic. Before these mistakes were corrected in practice or print, the main theoretical current in the fledgling archaeology of Iran of the 1960s shifted full force to models of cultural and demic diffusion that—whether explicitly or implicitly—sought to link the Medes and Persians to the archaeological cultures of the early "Iron Age" and to populate the political landscape of the Zagros—reconstructed from the records of Assyria, Babylonia, and Urartu—with Hurrians, Mannaeans, and other ethnonyms and toponyms. "Iron I" Hasanlu represented one of the few protohistoric sites able to bridge the chasm between historically attested western Iranian populations of the post mid-9th century BC and their protohistoric immigrant forebears. Hasanlu evinced both (1) early, western Zagros attestations of certain archaeological correlates (e.g., "Early Western Grey Ware"), possibly linking the region to earlier 2nd millennium BC putative population movements reconstructed from linguistic studies and the archaeology of northeastern Iran and Transcaucasia; and, (2) possible connections to later, historically attested Iranian populations, especially early columned-hall architecture and, as a more general example, an affinity for horses. At the time, there was a general consensus, ultimately based on Sayce's late-19th century decipherment of the Urartian language, that Parsua—the supposed land of the Persians—lay in the southern Lake Urmia region (Sayce 1882:389). Historic texts linked the region to the Mannaeans, and artifact styles and ceramics pointed to possible Hurrian and Assyrian influences. Hasanlu's propinquity to Mesopotamia afforded the number and type of datable imports needed to further develop an absolute chronology. Such links with Mesopotamia were now reconceptualized.

In the 1960s, most scholars emphasized the cultural break between the "later" or "late" Bronze Age of western Iran—2000–1200 BC, later revised to 2000–1450 BC, with its strong Mesopotamian orientation—and the decidedly unwieldy "Iron I"—which gradually expanded from 1200–1000 BC to 1450–1050 BC, allegedly arriving from the east and/or north according to the then-in vogue cultural-diffusionist and migrationist reconstructions. This had implications both for general theory and at the rudimentary level of defining archaeological horizons. The most obvious manifestation of this was Dyson's use of the term "Iron I," starting in 1965, in referring to Hasanlu V. It was not a valid technological distinction given the lack of iron (Pigott 2004). Shortly after Dyson applied the term, new data and the calibration of radiocarbon dates steadily pushed its starting date back deeper into the 2nd millennium. I would argue the continued adherence to the term's use instead *connoted* the time depth some scholars allotted to the process of "Iranianization" in the region. Mesopotamia, as a source of chronological terminology and cultural influence, was eschewed for the period after 1500 BC, and the later Medes and Persians became key points on the interpretive horizon with decreasing attention given to the Mannaeans and Hurrians (cf. Dyson 1968). This shift was followed by a marked increase in the quantity and quality of archaeological data for the later 2nd millennium BC from Hasanlu and Dinkha Tepe (see below), heightening the importance of these two sites as the best known, earliest attestations of "Iron I" in western Iran at a time when, in the blink of an eye, Iran was closed to foreign archaeological expeditions in the late 1970s.

The latter phase of the Hasanlu Project and the subsequent post-excavation years were characterized by the occasional revisiting of topics concerning the later 2nd millennium BC, yet it is crucial to point out that the archaeological definitions of the "Late Bronze" and "Iron I" periods have languished in a nascent state. The designations were perfunctorily formulated in the pioneering years of archaeology in northwestern Iran, when many mistakes were made, were superficially revised within the diffusionist/Iranian-origin theoretical movements of the mid-1960s and early 1970s, and were cursorily revisited or tacitly employed by the original researchers in subsequent writing with minor nuances. While our understanding of "Iron I" Hasanlu has changed somewhat since the 1970s, no previous definition of the period is underpinned by a thorough and systematic assessment of the excavation results, particularly the occupation deposits. Dyson, Young, and others supported their definitions with a few distinctive vessel forms and selections of small finds from grave groups supplemented by anecdotal references to occupation deposits. While views on "Hasanlu V" and Hasanlu VI shifted markedly from the 1950s to the 1970s, the existing archaeological dataset remained largely unanalyzed and unpublished. Likewise, there was virtually no revision of the primary researchers' views or redaction of the Hasanlu Project's published output on "Hasanlu V." The most pertinent to the current study are a coda to T. Cuyler Young's groundbreaking work (1985), which intentionally raised more questions than it answered, and a critical and informative response by Muscarella (1994a) to the understandable doubts of Medvedskaya (1977, 1991), who had challenged the conceptual validity of the EWGW horizon and its purported links to later Iranian populations.

The "Hasanlu V" Dataset

The "Iron I" was best attested at Hasanlu, where it was recovered from excavations on the High and Low Mounds (Fig. 1.4). On the High Mound, three soundings—Operation I, U22, and the Well Sounding—reached levels of "Hasanlu V" and Hasanlu VI (see Chapter 3). Eight additional areas associated with "Period V" remains were recovered from horizontal clearances. Such exposures were rare on the High Mound, as the excavators were naturally concerned with preserving the impressive standing remains of the burned Hasanlu Terminal IVb citadel. According to Dyson (1977b) and a thorough examination of the project archives, a range of architectural forms were attested on the High Mound in the following exposures (Hasanlu Grid References are provided in parentheses):

1. a columned-hall structure (Grids RS22–23);
2. at least two superimposed structures of unknown functions (Grids U22–23);
3. a lustration room (Grids BB28–29);
4. a kitchen (Grid DD30–31);
5. two adjacent structures separated by an alley (Grid V31);
6. a monumental structure with projecting tower and buttressed façade (Grids YZ27–29);
7. a retaining wall and associated walls (Grid Q24); and,
8. a structure of unknown function (Grid CC27).

These architectural remains will be referred to by their Grid References. Dyson cites similarities in the construction techniques and attested architectural forms between "Hasanlu V" and IVb as indicative of a high degree of cultural continuity between the two periods (1977b:166). I would argue that this line of reasoning is bolstered by continuities in the use of space on the High Mound in four areas—BB28–29, DD30–31, RS22–23, and YZ28–29. As is discussed below, however, "Hasanlu V" as previously applied represented a pastiche of different time periods, and cultural continuity is more precisely between late Hasanlu V and IVc, as redefined herein, and IVb. The scant evidence on early Period V suggests discontinuity in the built environment between the early LBA and the later LBA.

On the Low Mound, seven soundings reached deposits of "Hasanlu V."[1] The main objective of these Low Mound operations was to recover graves, and most operations contained burials of "Period V," especially in the area of the North Cemetery (Fig. 1.4). In total, the Hasanlu Project originally designated 23 graves as "Hasanlu V" and "IV–V"; the excavators employed the latter designation for MBW graves that were difficult to precisely date. These graves were heretofore unpublished (see Chapter 5), and in this re-analysis discussion is largely confined to those with ceramic vessels.[2] Graves of Period VI were also excavated in Operations VIa, X, and LIVf in the North Cemetery: 4 graves are attributable to the period using grave goods (multiple burial SK45–47, tomb SK49, and single inhumations SK66 and SK112). The Hasanlu Project also encountered "Period V" remains during excavations at surrounding sites and identified others in regional surveys. By far the most important work was conducted at Dinkha Tepe in the Ušnu valley in 1966 and 1968, and reference is made to this work throughout this volume. "Period V" graves were also excavated at Dalma Tepe and one grave was excavated at Hajji Firuz. The graves from Dalma have not been included here.

History of Scholarship

In approaching "Hasanlu V" it is useful to examine how conceptions of the period have developed over time against the backdrop of the activities of both the Hasanlu Project and other expeditions. Prior to the Hasanlu Project, Roman Ghirshman had excavated 15 tombs in Sialk Cemetery A (Sialk Period V) containing a monochrome grey-to-black burnished ware; in Tomb 4, he found an iron dagger and "punch" (Ghirshman 1935:240; 1939:9, 20, pls. V:1, XXXIX:S. 458, S. 459)—these stand out from the ubiquitous bronze items. The graves at Tepe Giyan I (as originally defined, Graves 1–63) had already yielded burnished grey and dark red ceramics similar to those recovered from Sialk A, which were associated with copper/bronze artifacts and three iron daggers, from Tombs 3, 5, and 23, respectively (Contenau and Ghirshman 1935:18–22, 44, pls. 8, 19, 12). Ghirshman reasoned that the scarcity of iron indicated that this ceramic "horizon," typified by burnished grey-black ware, dated to the end of the Bronze Age (Ghirshman 1935:245). Sialk Cemetery B (Sialk Period VI), located some distance from Cemetery A and possibly separated temporally by a hiatus of unknown duration, provided evidence of a significantly different material culture, with painted ceramics, little burnished grey-black ware, and a higher incidence of iron artifacts. Ghirshman originally dated Sialk A to 1400–1200 BC and Sialk B no earlier than 1200–1100 BC (1935:245). He later revised his dating of Sialk A to 1200–1000 BC, linking the phase to the graves of Giyan I[4] and I[3] (superscript subperiod designations *sensu* Young 1965), which in turn were compared to graves at Babylon dated to the 12th–11th centuries (Ghirshman 1939:20–21; 1964:277–78). He noted similarities between Sialk A grey-black burnished vessels with white in-filled incised designs and similar wares from the Caucasus, where such material was at that time erroneously dated to around 1000 BC (Ghirshman 1939: pl. XXXVIII s. 431, s. 432; 1964:277–78). Ghirshman thus revised the start of Sialk B, assigning to it a date of 1000 BC (1964:280) in light of the dating of the earlier Sialk A, a Neoassyrian cylinder seal found in one Sialk B tomb, and his belief that this archaeological culture represented the Medes, who are first mentioned in the records of Assyria in 834 BC. Ghirshman therefore asserted that the start of Sialk B must predate this mention. As early as 1948, Schaeffer had questioned the logic of Ghirshman's dating (Schaeffer 1948:469–70, 477), preferring a range from 1400–1200 BC for Sialk A and 1250–1100 BC for Sialk B; this early date for Sialk B, however, cannot be maintained (see Dyson 1965:200–201; Medvedskaya 1983; Young 1963). The earlier graves of Sialk A and Giyan I would thus be more properly assigned to the MBIII, LBA, and possibly Iron I (see also Dittmann 1990; Helwing 2005:40–41; Piller 2004; Tourovetz 1989). The association of grey-to-black monochrome burnished pottery with early iron objects as well as Ghirshman's grouping of the Sialk A graves into a single period would influence later scholars, as would his migrationist theories of culture change driven by multiple waves of immigrants (1954:71, 74–5; 1964:3, 277–78). Ghirshman, building on the work of Arne, issued a statement that would reverberate in Iranian archaeology for decades to come:

> What are the reasons that caused the displacement of the civilization represented by Necropolis A and its appearance at Sialk, at Rey and at Giyan? Arne believes it is the Indo-European invasion which ended the age of grey-black pottery, which had flowered in the Turcoman Plain, which is possible, but with the condition of lowering the date that he gives to the layer of Shah Tepe. At Tureng Tepe, the most recent level (III) shows a radical change in burial practices: on Mound C, at the end of its occupation, the dead were no longer buried under the dwellings but, as at Sialk (Necropolis A), in a necropolis apart from the houses. Two of these tombs contained small iron objects, which makes it possible to believe they are contemporary to Necropolis A. At Damghan [Hissar], one does not note similar changes, but Level IIIB there underwent a violent destruction, and the most recent installation, IIIC, presents several characteristics that link it to the civilization of the Cicaucasus and southern Russia. (Ghirshman 1939:103–4, author's translation)

Ghirshman thus highlighted certain archaeological correlates of putative early Iron Age migrations, whether directly or indirectly linked: "Grey Ware," small amounts of iron, and extramural cemeteries. The field would subsequently be dominated by theories attempting to "connect the dots" of Iranian migrations (see Mousavi 2005)—the primary data often consisted of material salvaged from looted cemeteries, such as at Hasanlu and Khurvin, which proved difficult to date (Hakemi and Rad 1950; vanden Berghe 1964). The area of the Elburz and southern Caspian littoral proved sparse territory for archaeologists in search of a "Grey Ware" horizon, resulting in a stubborn spatio-temporal gap for those attempting to link eastern Grey Ware to its supposed western cousin.

1956–1957

At Hasanlu on the High Mound and at Dinkha, Khabur Ware assemblages precede the main deposits of "Period V."[3] This was verified at Hasanlu in the first season, 1956: in Operation I, sited within the High Mound's central depression (Fig. 1.4), the lower excavated strata contained Khabur Ware and MBA Grey Ware (Figs. 3.3, 3.4, Stratum 6a)—albeit with some MBW—with no apparent stratigraphic break (Fig. 4.14). I strongly believe this overlap exerted some influence on Dyson's conceptions of the 2nd millennium BC in subsequent years, though this was not disclosed in publication. The appearance of painted Khabur Ware in Ušnu-Solduz now marks the beginning of Period VIb, or the MBII (Figs. 2.1, 2.2). In Operation I, this material was preceded by a deposit (Stratum 6c) characterized by plain and incised Simple Ware—a similar assemblage, diagnostic of the newly designated Period VIc, or MBI, was recovered from the U22 Deep Sounding in the 1970s (see Chapter 3). The vessel forms—particularly the ledge rims and barrel shapes—as well as the methods of decoration, including wavy-line incision, ribbing, and rope appliqué, are hallmarks of the late 3rd and early 2nd millennia BC in northern Mesopota-

Hasanlu Period	
I	Islamic
II	Mystery Period
III	Triangle Ware
IVa	Squatter Occupation
IVb	Grey Ware
V	Button Base
VI	Painted Buff Ware/Ring Ware
VII	Painted Orange Ware
VIII	Pisdeli
IX	Dalma
X	Hajji Firuz

Fig. 2.1 Original chronology of Hasanlu Tepe.

Hasanlu Period	
I	Ilkhanid
———Break———	
II	Seleuco-Parthian
IIIa	Iron IV–Achaemenid
———Break———	
IIIb	Iron III
IIIc	Urartian Fortress
———Break———	
IVa	Iron III
IVb	Iron II (Dinkha II)
IVc	Iron I (Dinkha III)
V	Late Bronze (Dinkha III)
VIa	Middle Bronze III (Dinkha III-IV)
VIb	Middle Bronze II (Dinkha IV)
VIc	Middle Bronze I
———Potential Break———	
VIIa	Early Bronze III
VIIb	Early Bronze II
———Potential Break———	
VIIc	Early Bronze I

Fig. 2.2 Revised Bronze and Iron Age chronology of Ušnu-Solduz.

mia. The perceived co-occurrence of painted Khabur Ware and MBW in Operation I was reinforced by the chance discovery in 1957 of a grave in the North Cemetery in Operation VI (see Chapter 5, Burial SK25, Fig. 5.8) which *seemingly* contained both ceramic wares (Dyson 1958:30–31). In retrospect, such graves are known to be rare.

Deep soundings were also conducted on the Low Mound in the initial seasons of the Hasanlu Project. There is little evidence, however, that major occupation deposits containing PKW or KW were excavated there, as only stray sherds and a small number of whole vessels of PKW were recorded, and the latter might be attributable to disturbed graves found nearby. The excavators encountered deposits overlying Period VII in most operations that were in turn cut through by Period IVb-c graves—these deposits must date to the early-to-mid 2nd millennium BC. Unfortunately, these contexts were incompletely recorded and little material was saved from them.

1958–1959

Dyson first designated "Hasanlu V" the "Button Base Phase" (1958:31), following the 1956–1957 excavation seasons (Fig. 2.1). The use of the term "phase" seems meant to denote the provisional nature of the term—in contrast, I employ phase designations to signify groupings of strata, loci, and lots that are temporally and behaviorally meaningful (see Chapter 3). Dyson defined his phase, unknown at the time, using a ceramic assemblage that contained material from Period VI, V, and IVc contexts. On the Low Mound, the most heavily excavated area at that point, Dyson at first thought this phase followed the "Painted Orange Ware Phase" (Hasanlu VII, EBA). His "Button Base Phase" was characterized by "cups with button bases and loop handles, and by small vases with button bases" (Dyson 1958:27). These button-base vessels came in two different wares; the cups (tankards) were burnished grey (MBW) and the vases (beakers) were yellowish-white with bands of reddish-brown paint (PKW) (1958:27). The choice of the terms "button base" and "vase" stemmed from cross-sequence comparisons with Nuzi, Assur, and other sites in northern Mesopotamia where such terms were already in use. The beakers ("vases") found in the North Cemetery graves as well as another type of small beaker found at Hasanlu—the so-called *istikhan*—were well known in northern Mesopotamia. One group of vessels from Nuzi proved particularly influential, although this is somewhat conjectural since exact comparanda were almost never cited in early Hasanlu publications. A fine burnished grey ware (*sensu* Starr 1939) category of vessels dated to the LBA occurs rarely in PKW at Hasanlu. Starr provides a detailed description of the Nuzi vessels:

> The gray-ware vases form a distinct class and are perhaps less like the other Nuzi pottery than any other separate group. They have certain definite characteristics which they all share more or less. All, without exception, are of an unusually fine, dark gray ware, in which fine sand is used as a *dégraissant*. In their essentials, all have the same shape. All have a tool-burnished surface, made by horizontal strokes on the body and vertical ones on the neck. All but two have a rounded button base, useless as a stand except when forced into a depression in the earth floor. The occurrence of gray-ware vases at Nuzi is so comparatively rare, and their treatment in shape, foot, and surface so unlike the usual pottery of Nuzi, that the impression given is that of an imported ware. Its use in bowls and tripod bowls is such as to strengthen this belief. (1939:390–91)

We see Late Bronze Age Nuzi represented an obvious site to examine for comparanda with "Hasanlu V": Starr had published small amounts of painted Khabur Ware and incised KW, a type of burnished Grey Ware, as well as drinking vessels with Hasanlu attributes, particularly button bases. *Istikhans* virtually identical to those from Hasanlu are also known from the same general level at Nuzi (Starr 1939:392, see esp. pl. 76: j, k, m), with at least one attestation in a grey ware (1939: fig. 76:c). According to Starr, these cups gradually developed into footed drinking vessels (1939:392; pl. 76: s–u, w–ee); similar forms are attested in "Hasanlu V," where they were generally referred to as "pedestal-base goblets"—likely a terminological influence from Giyan I—although they are more properly referred to as "tankards" since they have handles. Along with the grave groups from Tepe Giyan, the LBA ceramics from Nuzi almost certainly influenced Dyson to combine Hasanlu North Cemetery grave assemblages with completely unassociated occupation deposits in his definition of the "Button Base Phase"/"Period V." He compared (1958:29–30) "Button Base Phase" assemblages of the Low Mound to the assemblage from Stratum 6 (more precisely 6a) of High Mound Operation I that included painted Khabur Ware (he does not mention the MBW and Middle Bronze Age Grey Ware in the same assemblage). Dyson suggested the painted ware of the "Button Base Phase" was contemporaneous and comparable to painted wares found at Tepe Giyan, and to the "Khabur Ware" assemblages of northern Syria and Iraq, then dated 1800–1500 BC (Dyson 1958:30). The similarities shared with Tepe Giyan led Dyson to date the "Button Base Phase" to around 1400 BC or later. This "phase" was followed by "a period of burnished red and grey wares and local bronze casting dating in part around 1200 BC" (Dyson 1958:32). Dyson distinguished this early MBW period from a later MBW period known at the time only from Low Mound graves (Hasanlu IVb/Iron II). In effect, Dyson had defined my Hasanlu VIa–V as a single period and had delineated Hasanlu IVc and IVb. Overall, this was an accurate start to developing a site chronology, but this approach would not endure.

The year 1958 was a great turning point for the Hasanlu Project; in many ways I feel it was not a positive one. The discovery of the famous "Gold Bowl" in BBIW and the realization that the Period IVb occupation had ended in a widespread sacking and conflagration marked a fundamental change in strategy. Large-scale excavations were started on the High Mound and scores of human victims and thousands of objects were recovered from the well-preserved remains of the monumental structures. Recording the rich and complex contexts of Period IVb in the time available stretched the capacity and abilities of the excavators to the limit. Concomitantly, work on the Low Mound ebbed. Excavations were conducted on the Low Mound in 1959, but the High Mound had by then become the clear focus of the researchers' attention. The excavations conducted between 1959 and 1964 at Hasanlu are the most poorly recorded in the project's history. This had a minimal impact on periods earlier than Period IVb, since the excavation strategy entailed clearing large horizontal exposures of Period IVb on the southern and northwestern High Mound. Publication in 1959 focused on the gold bowl, silver beaker, and other attention-grabbing finds from Hasanlu IVb. The year also saw the publication of the first radiocarbon dates from the site (Ralph 1959; Figs. 2.3–2.4, see color insert).

1960

In *Early Cultures of Solduz* (Dyson 1967c), the publication of the Proceedings of the IVth International Congress of Iranian Art and Archaeology held April 14–May 3, 1960, Dyson explicitly stated the connections between "Period V" and northern Mesopotamia, but this exposition and the late date of publication added to the confusion regarding its definition. The potential existence of Period VI was now recognized. Much of the difficulty encountered in defining "Period V" was connected to attempts at "separating" it from Period VI since, the excavators then believed—correctly—that painted wares overlapped the Early MBW, and these painted wares thus received published coverage wildly disproportionate to their frequency within the assemblages. While painted wares in MBW assemblages are typically sparse, the situation was exaggerated due to the chance find by Stein and the Hasanlu Project of rare graves that included painted wares alongside grey pottery. With regard to the Hasanlu Project specifically, Dyson and Young prioritized painted styles in developing Hasanlu's chronological sequence whenever possible due to the preponderance of painted wares at previously excavated sites in western Iran that they drew on for cross-sequence dating. *Early Cultures of Solduz* reveals another hurdle that confronted the researchers: the distinctive PKW and KW of the High Mound, then known exclusively from scattered chance finds and the small exposure in Operation I, differed from the narrow range of PKW and KW included in the graves of the North Cemetery and the chance finds of painted vessels in 2nd millennium BC occupation deposits from Low Mound soundings. This latter painted ware was a simple form of PKW with annular horizontal painted lines, dubbed "Ring Ware."[4] Dyson provided the following description of the occupation deposits of the High Mound as of the 1960 excavation season:

> A succeeding phase [Period VI], again under western influence, is suggested by sherds of another painted ware with triangular patterns which are similar to Tell Billa IV pottery. *These sherds have been found only on the Citadel* [Operation I], out of reliable stratified context [!], but evidently later than the Painted Orange Ware phase. It is quite possible that they indicate the presence of the missing early second millennium strata somewhere on that mound. Sherds of this type from nearby Dinkha Tepe on the road to Kel-i-shin Pass have been erroneously termed "Chalcolithic" in Stein's report. (1967c: 2957; emphasis my own)

Dyson goes on to define "Period V":

> Sherds of small disc- or button-base vases painted with simple rings belong to the phase overlying the Painted Orange Ware in the Outer Town sequence [only a few such painted vessel were ever found]. In both the Outer Town soundings and on the Citadel this phase underlies the Grey Ware phase of ninth century date. These painted wares reflect the simple forms of the late second millennium B.C. seen at Nuzi, Ashur and elsewhere. At the same time at Hasanlu they are associated with the first appearance of finely made burnished light grey pottery [MBW] in the form of platters, large deep bowls with simple lugs, tall cups or tankards, and rarely jars with free-standing horizontal spouts [only one such spout had been found as a sherd]. (Dyson 1967c: 2957)

It is important to note that extensive excavations in the area of the Low Mound had uncovered no obvious KW occupation despite the presence of 2nd millennium BC deposits. As previously mentioned, in 1956 the excavators had recovered a small, *stratified* deposit of PKW in Operation I, but this assemblage seems never to have been fully analyzed, presumably since it was deemed unreliable. No other operations completed prior to 1960 fit Dyson's description published in *A Survey of Persian Art*, and I assert that the stratigraphy of Operation I appears to be reliable, that is, superimposed, sealed by successive structures and floor levels, and exhibiting few post-depositional disturbances (see below). In dating Period VI and "V," Dyson was influenced by the prevailing view that there were "younger" and "older" varieties of KW (see esp. Hrouda 1957), although he was vague on this point until later. The "younger" variety was dated to the LBA and was associated with the Hurro-Mitanni and Middle Assyrian kingdoms.

Dyson was not the first excavator working in Ušnu-Solduz to note a putative pattern in the spatio-temporal distribution of the painted pottery of the 2nd millennium BC. In 1936, in excavations at nearby Dinkha Tepe, Aurel Stein had found no painted pottery in the uppermost levels, below this a level containing a ware painted only with "simple annular bands" and, below this, a full PKW assemblage, which he misidentified as Chalcolithic (Stein 1940:371, see chapter 4). Stein noted that both assemblages of painted ware also contained unpainted pottery with ribbing, incising, and comb-incising, and that Grey Ware and a Grey-Black Ware were also present (Stein 1940:371–72). Stein also found tombs constructed of large stone slabs that contained jars painted with annular bands (Stein 1940:374–75, XXXI: 1). In the North Cemetery at Hasanlu, graves with painted ceramics of the 2nd millennium BC almost exclusively contained the variety of PKW painted with annular bands or unpainted KW and GW—the latter ware having been initially misidentified as MBW by the Hasanlu excavators, a fact which was usually corrected later (see Chapters 4 and 5).

During the 1960 season, Dyson hired a local well-digger to complete a deep sounding on the High Mound in order to verify his archaeological chronology for Ušnu-Solduz (Dyson 1961b) compiled from his excavations at Hasanlu and small soundings made at neighboring sites (see Chapter 3). The year also marked Dyson's first attempt to attach an ethnonym to the Iron Age "Grey Ware" culture with the publication of *Where the Golden Bowl of Hasanlu Was Found: Excavations near Lake Urmia which Throw New Light on the Little-known Mannaeans* (1960b); this was followed by *Excavating the Mannaean Citadel of Hasanlu* (1961a).

1961–1962

The year 1961 saw no excavation at Hasanlu after a flurry of activity in the late 1950s. In contrast, 1962 was a busy field season with the resumption of large-scale work on the High Mound and renewed excavations in the North Cemetery. T. Cuyler Young, at this point well established as a team member, was charged with setting research objectives, which included conducting an extensive survey in Ušnu-Solduz and visiting other sites farther afield in Iran. Young began a large horizontal exposure on the northwestern High Mound in 1962 that would provide data critical for

understanding the 2nd millennium BC and form a substantial part of his dissertation (Young 1963).

In "The Hasanlu Project," published in *Science*, Dyson explicitly laid out his criteria for the relative and absolute dating of the Button Base Phase, "tentatively called Period V" (1962:639). The example chosen to illustrate the technique of cross-sequence dating was a "Period V" MBW tankard, which was compared to examples recovered from Sialk A, Giyan I, and Geoy Tepe B (Dyson 1962:640–41, fig. 4). Dyson was gradually shifting to an Iranian focus for comparanda, foreshadowing Young's cross-sequence comparisons (Young 1963, 1965):

> Such similarities relate the ceramics of this phase to the general tradition of central and western Iran in the late 2nd millennium B.C. This correlation is supported by the presence of a few button-base vases of buff pottery painted with simple lines. These forms belong to a tradition found in Mesopotamia during the latter part of the second millennium B.C. at the sites of Nuzi, Assur, and elsewhere. The pottery of this phase thus relates the local culture to cultures in the two directions from which influence would be expected, given the geography, and confirms the period of that influence as being 1200–1000 B.C. (Dyson 1962:641)

Here we see early indications of an attempt to trace not just ceramic comparanda but cultural affinities, a short step from concerns with cultural origins/migrations, topics that would be breached in full the following year. Connections to Mesopotamia would eventually fall out of the discussion, as would the Mannaeans.

1963

As previously mentioned, in 1962 T. Cuyler Young began a series of new horizontal exposures on the northwestern High Mound of Hasanlu. One of these trenches, Operation U22–23, was excavated below the Period IVb deposit as a sounding beneath BBVII, and for the first time substantial stratified remains of Period VIb (Strata 11–12) with PKW were reached (see Chapter 3). By 1963, the publications pertaining to Periods V and VI were gradually starting to incorporate these findings, and it was in this year that Young completed his seminal dissertation, *Proto-Historic Western Iran, An Archaeological and Historical Review: Problems and Possible Interpretations*. This work was made widely accessible in two complementary articles in the journal *Iran* in 1965 and 1967, minus the details on the Hasanlu excavations (see below). The greatest lacuna was the omission of a thorough description of the U22 Sounding in publications since it was this sequence more than any other data set that resurrected Ghirshman's punctuated demic diffusion model. Dyson abstractly recounted the results of the U22 sounding with regard to the KW deposit and the seemingly sudden appearance of MBW at the level of general theorizing, it constituted:

> the discovery of *a new stratum,* dating to around 1500 B.C., below the grey pottery "Button-base Phase". It is characterized by a buff ware painted with red bands and triangles—a pottery common in design and form to that of northern Mesopotamia of the same period. This pottery would appear to be the remnant of a "Hurrian" or related occupation of Hasanlu. The new excavations show, furthermore, that *this north Mesopotamian occupation was abruptly terminated by the appearance of a grey-ware culture* characterized by distinctive tankards with button or disc bases, but otherwise sharing all of the main ceramic wares with the following period. We have, therefore, the *sudden appearance of an alien culture* around the end of the thirteenth or beginning of the twelfth century B.C. (Dyson 1963a:33, emphasis my own)

Dyson here assumes a strong migrationist theoretical stance, particularly with the introduction of the idea of a disruption and the abrupt appearance of a new "Grey Ware" culture. This represents the height of the "pots equal people" theorizing of the migrationist paradigm later famously criticized by Carol [Hamlin] Kramer (1977). Dyson's most explicit statement in regard to this period is quite revealing, as he has written "We may be dealing here with an Indo-European intrusion into what is known historically as the Mannaean area" (Dyson 1963a:33). He elaborated with regard to Ušnu-Solduz, "There are historical arguments for placing the Persians in this area upon their entry into Iran but the date suggested has usually been in the ninth–eighth century B.C., at which time they controlled part of the Mannaean area and even had Assyrian governors. *It begins to look as if these three cultural groups are represented at Hasanlu in our Period IV*" (Dyson 1963a:33, emphasis my own).[5]

Two points of clarification ought to be mentioned here. First, in his characterization of the "Button Base Phase," the "distinctive tankards with button or disc bases" were not conclusively found in U22–23; rather, Dyson was alluding to whole MBW tankards found in the Low Mound cemeteries and discussed in earlier publications (Dyson 1963a; see Chapter 5). That is, there was no conclusive evidence in U22–23 that the KW deposit was immediately overlain by an assemblage containing the "classic" forms of MBW associated with "Period V." The occurrence of tankards and other forms considered to be diagnostic of "Period V" are based on a few fragmentary diagnostic, but nonetheless equivocal, sherds (see Chapter 4). Second, the "discovery of a new stratum" in 1962 glosses over the discovery of PKW in Operation I in 1956. This assemblage had apparently been deemed stratigraphically unreliable, not because of depositional or post-depositional processes or errors in excavation or recording, but rather, I suggest, because the deposit also contained MBW. Here we see the crux of the problem with the development of the mid-2nd millennium BC portion of the Hasanlu sequence: Over time, assemblages that contained MBW with a painted ware were deemed unreliable or, in mortuary assemblages, were dismissed as instances of the heirlooming or recycling of Bronze Age painted wares in the early Iron Age periods. In fact, these "Grey Ware" vessels co-occurring with PKW were either: (1) misidentifications of MBA GW, or (2) MBIII graves; the methodological bias is nevertheless evident. The consequences of these biases—the pigeonholing of painted wares in the Bronze Age and "Grey Ware" in the Iron Age—had little impact at Hasanlu largely due to issues of sampling. It seems fairly certain, in fact, that the horizon which bridges Hasanlu VIb and Hasanlu V—designated here as Hasanlu VIa, or the MBIII—simply went unidentified or unexcavated in most soundings completed on the High Mound. The U22 sounding was also lacking the Terminal MBII. The Well Sounding, and possibly Operation I, are notable potential exceptions in this regard. At Dinkha, where a MBIII deposit was encountered above a Terminal MBII level, the dataset was selectively published: the painted and "grey" wares from the same context were separated, with only the painted wares receiving attention.

Dyson further defined the Period "V" and VI assemblages this same year:

> Limited testing of the earlier levels [of U22] produced several building levels and a sample of pottery. The pottery indicates that Period V (Button-Base Phase) is a forerunner of IV, employing the same grouping of ceramic wares (gray, buff, coarse, red-slipped) with simpler shapes. *Rare buff ware vessels with simple lines painted around the shoulder were found.* Below these levels there is *a complete cultural and stratigraphic discontinuity*, with the appearance of a stratum of Painted Buff Ware, Incised Ware and Plain Yellow-buff wares related to northern Mesopotamian pottery of the mid-second millennium. This period, which was previously known only from scattered sherds, now takes its proper stratigraphic position as Period VI. (Dyson 1963b:132, emphasis my own)

Three related points will be examined in greater detail later: (1) Dyson's mention of the presence of a later painted ware in "Period V" of the U22–23 Sounding; (2) his reference to a stratigraphic break recorded in Operation U22, which would be between Strata 10 and 11; and, (3) the fact that it was clear to him that no comparable deposits of KW occurred on the Low Mound. T. Cuyler Young's dissertation (Young 1963) noted the differences between the PKW of the Period VI deposit of U22 and that from the North Cemetery: "These painted wares [recovered from the U22 Sounding] are distinctively different in many respects from the Period V Painted Ware, which appears as a late and simplified survival in that period." (1963:39). Young also includes a cryptic reference to late PKW in Period V in "X37-P37-S38," which, if he was referencing the Hasanlu excavation grid, would be Operations XI, XII, and an unknown area, but which is likely a misidentification of Op. XIII. These three operations were excavated by Young and Dyson in 1958 and were long, narrow trenches laid out radially on the eastern slope of the High Mound, meant to locate what was then thought to be the Period IVb fortification wall (in fact, the Urartian wall of Period IIIc). There is little record of PKW in Operations XI and XII with the exception of a few extrusive painted sherds. The excavators mention the possible presence of a "Ring Ware" phase in the lowest deposit, but nothing more was documented.

Young provided a detailed definition of the EWGW horizon, which was supported by an exhaustive review of the available archaeological evidence and included "Hasanlu V, Giyan I^4–I^3, Sialk V, Geoy Tepe, Khorvin-Chandar, and perhaps Marlik" (Young 1963:133). "All of these sites share three general features: they have essentially a mixed plain grey and buff ware assemblage in which painted ware occurs only very rarely; they display a similar burial tradition in regard to extramural burials and to the positioning of the body within the grave or tomb (flexed on its side); and they only rarely yield objects of iron" (1963:133). Young's essentialist definition originates in Ghirshman's description of Sialk A (1939:103–4). Young identified three vessel shapes common to these sites: simple cups with handles, jars with bridgeless spouts and pedestal-base goblets (Young 1963:133). As Ghirshman before him, Young linked this horizon to Hissar III in northeastern Iran, where "grey ware" was well known. Young cited the presence of *istikhans*, a "slightly divergent" simple cup with handle, bridgeless spouts, and pattern-burnished ware as evidence of the connection between the EWGW and the Hissar III complex (1963:134), concluding that the number and importance of these parallels "suggest that the EWGW Group of sites is definitely related to the earlier Hissar III ceramic complex," and that Geoy and Marlik were outside the main group of EWGW sites (1963:135–36). This became the basis for Young's theory centered on an east-west migration of Iranian populations in the 2nd millennium BC, although chronological (the mid-2nd millennium BC) and spatial (north-central Iran) gaps between Hissar III and the EWGW horizon would prove difficult to reconcile.

1964

Notes on Weapons and Chronology in Northern Iran around 1000 B.C., published in 1964, represented an early attempt by Dyson to summarize how he had defined "Period V" and had attributed absolute dates to it. He states, in a concise and revealing fashion, that

> also present in Period V at Hasanlu, as at Giyan, are objects of North Mesopotamian derivation, button or disc-based vases, footed vases with

painted rings, and buff ware tumblers [*istikhans*]. Parallels to these forms are well documented in northern Mesopotamia and northern Syria in the second half of the second millennium B.C. …the same tumbler shape in pottery occurs at Nuzi in the "Hurrian" strata dated to between 1450–1350 B.C. …The painted button-base and footed vessels at Hasanlu are also related to the "Hurrian" period forms of Tell Billa III. (1964b:36–39)

For the beginning of Period V at Hasanlu a date of about 1200 B.C. was originally estimated on typological grounds. This estimate was based upon the presence of a simple iron ring in one grave [SK29, see Chapter 5], the similarity of the bronze dagger [SK6 HAS57-149, UPM58-4-1, see Chapter 5] to those with inscriptions of the 11th century, and to typological comparisons of the ceramics of Hasanlu V, Sialk V, and Giyan Ib. This evidence seemed to indicate a primary time range of the twelfth and eleventh centuries. The possibility of a somewhat earlier initial date must be kept in mind, however, in view of possibly earlier pottery parallels at Nuzi and less firmly dated at Talish. (1964b:39)

We see a growing concern with "Talish" material (de Morgan 1905:251ff.) and Schaeffer's dating of it—based largely on Mitanni-style cylinder seals (Schaeffer 1948:408–15)—which Dyson would question (1968:32). In 1964, work was confined to small areas of the High Mound and the excavation of large areas in the North Cemetery. Dyson defined the diagnostic ceramic vessel forms of "Period V" drawing on the results from extensions of Operation VI and the previous season's findings from the U22–23 Sounding. Painted vessels are not mentioned. Period V was marked by a narrow range of ceramic types and attributes, including "the presence of a tall, footed goblet [tankard] with vertical loop-handle, and a deep bowl with a vertically pierced horizontal lug. Jars with free-standing horizontal spouts are also indicated by a single sherd from the occupation debris on the Citadel Mound but have not yet been found in graves" (1964b:36). Dyson also noted the presence of a pattern-burnished ware at Hasanlu (1964b). Bridgeless spouts are not characteristic of Hasanlu, and only one was found in a Period V context (Late Bronze Age as defined herein), while three were found in Period IVc contexts. None were ever found in graves at Hasanlu unless in undocumented work conducted prior to the inception of the Hasanlu Project.

1965

The year 1965 represented a critical juncture in the scholarship of the earliest "Iron Age" in western Iran. T. Cuyler Young published *A Comparative Ceramic Chronology of Western Iran, 1500–500 B.C.*, in which he laid out a periodization for northern and western Iran informed by his dissertation research, and Dyson published *Problems of Protohistoric Iran as Seen from Hasanlu*. The two works are closely related and were used in conjunction in building the prevalent chronology of western Iran. Young again defined the EWGW horizon of western Iran as containing three diagnostic vessel forms: (1) simple cups with handles, (2) jars with free standing pouring spouts, and (3) pedestal-base goblets (Young 1965:72). I would argue that these diagnostics are only accurate temporal markers insofar as 1 and 3 identify the second half of the 2nd millennium BC and 2 mainly marks the closing centuries of the 2nd millennium. In 1965, however, this sequence represented an advance in the understanding of Iranian chronology. Young's article recast the question of "Hasanlu V" as one related largely to developments in Iran in the 1st millennium BC, whereas previous treatments had been oriented toward drawing comparisons with LBA Mesopotamia. Painted wares were mentioned as having occurred in Hasanlu "Period V": "In addition to these plain wares, a Painted Buff Ware with a blackish-brown or reddish-brown paint on a tan to buff-white ground is found in very limited quantity in Period V" (Young 1965:55). These vessels were seen as "survivals of the painted ware of Period VI" and the Period VI assemblage was "a markedly different ceramic tradition from that of Period V" (1965:55). While true, I would caution that Young was selectively comparing the MBII to the LBA and Iron I, and the intervening Terminal MBII and MBIII were as yet largely unknown for the Lake Urmia region with the exception of Geoy Tepe late D and C. Dyson defined the diagnostic forms of Hasanlu "Period V" as: (1) burnished bowls, (2) bridgeless spouted vessels, and (3) stemmed goblets with single loop handles [tankards] (1965:195). These assessments did not rest on the frequency of these forms within the assemblage since at this point, for example, only two bridgeless spouts had been found at Hasanlu as sherds on the High Mound, in U22–23 and Q24. The terminology employed for drinking vessels—definitely temporally-sensitive forms of the 2nd millennium BC—introduced much confusion and was employed rather indiscriminately, with "vases," "cups," "goblets," and "tankards" all being cited in combination with the "button-base" and "pedestal-base" attributes. Since the ceramics were seldom if ever shown in illustrations, it is difficult to attain a clear understanding of what is meant with each such use of the various terms. At Hasanlu, early Period V and, probably to a lesser extent, late Period V (the LBA) are characterized by tall, pedestal-base tankards (see Chapters 4 and 5). The trend over time is toward decreasing height and the reduction or loss of the pedestal base. Hasanlu IVc saw increased use of lower pedestal-base carinated cups and flat-base and rounded-base mugs. Lastly, it bears noting that citing the distribution of burnished bowls is of dubious spatio-temporal value.

In both Young and Dyson's works, the inclusion of *istikhan* tumblers (Dyson 1965: fig. 3:11–14; Young 1965: fig. 8:11–14) and painted wares (Dyson 1965: fig. 3:3, 6; Young 1965: fig. 8:3, 6; see also Muscarella 1974:48) in "Period V" subsequently caused confusion (see in particular Medvedskaya 1982 and the response by Muscarella 1994a).[6] There were several efforts subsequently to correct this misconception (Hamlin 1974:148 no. 13; Muscarella 1968:195, and esp. 1994a:141, fig. 12.2). Some published material described as attributable to "Period V" was in fact stratigraphically Period VI; however, (1) initial reports on the U22 Sounding note the presence of ring-painted KW (Dyson 1963b), regardless of how it might be interpreted contextually; and (2) deposits with what appear to be mixes of MBW and painted wares were not fully addressed in subsequent publications. The excavators would later contend there was little to no connection between Periods "V" and VI and that the periods were separated by putative breaks in occupation at both Dinkha and Hasanlu. Publications on Hasanlu are fraught with contradictory statements on this "break" (see Chapter 3), and in fact no major breaks exist at either site.

The date assigned to PKW by other scholars affected Dyson's definitions of both the "Late Bronze Age" and the "Iron I," in particular. Dyson made clear he was drawing on the work of Hrouda (1957):

Period VI has a very close parallel in the "Jüngere Chabur Ware" reported from Assur where it is dated to between 1600 and 1200 B.C. ... In historical terms, this is the period of the first Assyrian expansion during which the kings Adad-nirari I (1307–1275), Shalmaneser I (1274–1245), and Tukulti-Ninurta I (1243–1206) campaigned in the Zagros Mountains ... The intrusion of this western pottery in pure form from Assyria eastward through Solduz to Hasanlu, and its introduction to the local culture of Giyan apparently reflects these activities. (Dyson 1965:195)

Due to this association of Hasanlu VI KW with both its MBA manifestation and its putative later variant of the Mesopotamian LBA, Dyson made Hasanlu VI the "Late Bronze Age" in his influential "Table 2" (1965:211), the equivalent of both the Middle and Late Bronze Ages in Mesopotamia. This dating also reflected the late 2nd millennium BC assignation which prevailed at this time for "Period V," a figure that is now known to be too late for some of the concerned material. Dyson's Table 2 also tacitly introduced the threefold division of the Iranian Iron Age and the designation Hasanlu Period IVc (see below). The rare painted wares and *istikhans* from the North Cemetery were seen as surviving into "Hasanlu V," which was dated to 1350–1000 BC at the earliest. Hasanlu VI was not given a starting date. We see here quite vividly the problems of dealing with "Period V" in the early years of the project—unknown at the time, "Period V" included: (1) objects and iron datable to Period IVc, now the Iron I; and (2) ceramics spanning at least the entire second half of the 2nd millennium BC. The inclusion of Hasanlu IVc (Iron I) within "Period V" (the later LBA) acted to raise the dates, while connections with KW assemblages in turn lowered them. The main, overarching problem was that the definitions of Hasanlu "V"–VI were largely based on grave assemblages from the North Cemetery and limited soundings on the High Mound. Although excavations at neighboring Dinkha Tepe in 1966 and 1968 and the renewal of excavations at Hasanlu (1970–1977) would help to clarify the later 2nd millennium BC sequence to some extent, the designation of a discrete "Middle Bronze Age" would come to be sacrificed to the already established "Late Bronze Age."

1966–1969

Excavations at Dinkha Tepe by the Hasanlu Project conducted in 1966 and 1968 (Muscarella 1968, 1974; Hamlin 1971, 1974) expanded and refined archaeologists' understanding of the "Iron I" and have long provided the best published examples of MBW and KW assemblages from the region. At Dinkha, "Hasanlu V" is known as Dinkha III and is attested by 33 burials and "trash deposits." Dyson initially described the trash deposits and graves in a slightly ambiguous manner, as

> deep deposits of ash and trash into which a number of graves or tombs were sunk. These graves and tombs are characterized by the presence of jars with unbridged horizontal spouts in burnished grey-black ware, polished grey-black goblets [tankards], and bowls with flaring sides and inverted crescent-shaped lugs and two holes ["worm bowls"] … In addition to the grey-black ware, red and buff wares also occurred [these are understood to be early MBW sherds; Dyson shifts to describing the lower "trash deposit" here] along with a polychrome of black and red on cream bands set around the shoulder of jars or bowls [Urmia Ware]. At least one sherd of grey-black pattern-burnished ware was found along with several sherds of white-filled incised ware [Incised and Impressed MBW]. (1967b:137)

This is the earliest mention of Urmia Ware at the site and the first and virtually only mention of the Early MBW and Incised and Impressed MBW found in the "trash deposit." No architecture of "Iron I" date was discovered, but to the excavators the trash deposits indicated a small Dinkha III settlement was probably located in an as-yet unexcavated part of the *tepe*. Below the Dinkha III level were occupation deposits and associated intramural tombs of Dinkha IV/Hasanlu VI (Dyson 1967b:137). Muscarella published a more detailed report in 1968. His definition of Dinkha III/Iron I drew on unpublished material from "Hasanlu V": "The grave goods uniformly consisted of a spouted vessel without a bridge between the mouth and spout, a one-handled goblet on a pedestal base, and a bowl with a small modeled ridge enclosing holes for suspension, *the very same objects that occur at Hasanlu in Period V*" (Muscarella 1968:192, emphasis my own). Such bowls, referred to as "worm bowls," were found in but one "Hasanlu V" grave (SK75, see Chapter 5), although others were known from unpublished sherds from the High Mound (see Chapter 4). The excavators had been aware that bridgeless-spouted vessels did not occur in the extant "Hasanlu V" grave assemblages since 1964. We can thus see here how the excavators' general impressions and recollections of the unpublished occupation deposits recovered between 1956 and 1964 at Hasanlu played a prominent role in their archaeological definition of the period. Muscarella attributed seven graves to Dinkha III based on their stratigraphic position in cases in which the Dinkha III versus II distinction was equivocal using grave goods (1974:36). He also noted that in rare cases the stratigraphic position of some Dinkha III graves allowed them to be dated to the early part of the period concerned (1974:36), which he argued was further supported by the ceramics—in early Dinkha III, the spouts on bridgeless-spouted vessels are seemingly shorter and pedestal-based "goblets" are tall and narrow. The latter observation is borne out by the Period V–IVc assemblages from Hasanlu, which show the same trend of decreasing tankard height (and the loss of pedestal bases) eventually leading to the development of the Period IVb mug (see Chapter 4).

In the fascicle version of *The Archaeological Evidence of the Second Millennium B.C. on the Persian Plateau* (1968, 3rd ed.), revised in 1973, Dyson discussed Hasanlu Period VI on the High Mound in greater detail and included additional information on the recently concluded excavations at Dinkha. The PKW assemblage was again linked to the "older and younger Khabur Ware at Ashur, Tell Billa, Kültepe, Tell Brak, Chagar Bazar, and elsewhere in Mesopotamia and southern Anatolia," which was dated 1900–1200 BC (Dyson 1968:20). This was essentially a rehashing of his earlier position and would soon be modified following Carol Hamlin's (née Kramer; published under both names) study of Dinkha IV KW (1971) and the release of the radiocarbon dates from Dinkha IV. Incised ware was also mentioned, as was MBA Grey Ware: "A certain amount of coarse handmade pottery … with a number of sherds of what appears to be imported burnished light grey ware of a type also found in limited quantities at Chagar Bazar and Brak in similar contexts" (Dyson 1968:20).

Dyson's presentation of the Dinkha stratigraphy is somewhat difficult to follow and contains some inaccuracies and ambiguities with regard to Dinkha IV and the immediately succeeding level of the Control Sounding and other Dinkha IV exposures. He connects some of the polychrome painted Urmia Ware to Dinkha IV by stating, "at Dinkha the best preserved of these sherds have come from the stratum above the early second millennium fortification wall while others, probably not *in situ*, turn up in early Iron Age I trash" (1968:22). Kramer, on the other hand, presents the context differently, "In B10a stratum 7, the collapse immediately overlying the major phase d structures contained half of the total number of burnished polychrome sherds of ware VIII [Urmia Ware], which was also found scattered in different strata in the Iron Age trash excavated in these and adjoining areas" (Hamlin 1971:31). With regard to the earlier sherds, she wrote, "there are two examples of this ware found in pre-Hasanlu V context: one in phase a, and one in phase d, context" (Hamlin 1971:66). In later publications Rubinson is more definitive, stating that "the polychrome sherds are not associated with any architecture, but are stratified above the Hasanlu VI Habur ware period (Dinkha IV) and at the base of a deep stratum of Iron Age (Hasanlu V/Dinkha III) trash" (2004:662). The repeated use of the term "trash" for these strata at Dinkha is unique and was never clarified. Rubinson (2004:662, n. 12), citing Dyson (pers. comm., 2002) indicated that the occupation event connected with "the group associated with this ceramic" was located elsewhere on the mound. The potential association of this hypothetical population with the Early MBW in the same assemblage was not addressed. Rather, Dyson noted the association of polychrome painted Urmia Ware at Geoy late D–C with "Hasanlu V" vessel forms there and the occurrence of polychrome painting on a bridgeless-spouted vessel from Kizilvank (1968:23; see Chapter 4 for further discussion). In the revised 1973 publication, Dyson amended the description of the polychrome sherds to state that "the best preserved of these sherds have come from the stratum above the earlier second millennium *structure* while others, probably *not in situ*, turn up in early Iron Age I trash" (1973a:706, emphasis my own). In both publications Dyson intimates the Urmia Ware sherds are more at home in Dinkha IV based on differential preservation: the familiar "painted ware is Bronze Age" predilection. Doing so enabled him to link the long-necked polychrome painted jars known from Kizilvank to one from a grave at Dinkha and another from Hasanlu (Dyson 1968:23; 1973a:706). He interpreted the occurrence of polychrome-painted high-neck jars in MBW graves as "a terminal stage of the polychrome ware placed in burnished ware graves, a fact which suggests a persistence of the polychrome tradition in western Azarbayjan until the third quarter of the second millennium" (1973a:706). In something of a departure from his previous theories concerning the origins of the EWGW horizon, however, Dyson advanced two potential interpretations: "The whole situation suggests that the *polychrome culture* of north-western Azarbayjan was already in contact with a *Hasanlu V type culture* in the middle second millennium which has yet to be located, or else perhaps implies that *the Hasanlu V burnished grey ware assemblage grew out of the D–C mixed polychrome and plain ware assemblage through the loss of polychrome decoration*. A whole range of new questions is thus raised which cannot be answered at present" (1973a:706, emphasis my own).

This "plain ware" found with Urmia Ware at Dinkha and Geoy Tepe was in fact Early MBW (Dyson and Young's earliest EWGW variant) and Incised and Impressed MBW. As at Geoy Tepe C–B and contemporary sites in the Caucasus, Early MBW at Dinkha occurs in typical "EWGW" forms such as tankards and "worm bowls"—information that was never divulged. The pitfalls involved in equating ceramics with cultures need not be reiterated here with regard to Dyson's first proposition (Kramer 1977). In point of fact, there was as much Early MBW and Incised and Impressed MBW in the early "trash deposit" at Dinkha as there was Urmia Ware—the MBW is labeled "Dinkha III" in UPM sherd collections and the Urmia Ware from the same stratum was labeled "Dinkha IV"! This "trash deposit" assemblage predates the graves cutting it. In sum, there is every reason to believe Dinkha resembled Geoy Late D–C in the mid-2nd millennium BC in terms of ceramics (see Chapter 4). The graves therefore must date to a later phase or period of the MBW horizon than the earliest "trash" strata. Dyson's second idea, that MBW was already present in the ceramic assemblage of the Lake Urmia Basin (herein the MBIII), seems correct. This suggests strong connections with the southern Caucasus, as does the under-reported Incised and Impressed MBW (see Chapter 4). Dyson's "new questions"—especially their implications for the dating of MBW and migration theories—were not pursued and the idea of Hasanlu V representing a punctuated break would prevail in the coming years (see esp. Dyson 1977b). The presence of MBW and Urmia Ware in the lower "trash deposit" at Dinkha was given little interpretive weight, and the assemblage was split to conform with existing views on the chronology despite contradictory evidence from Geoy Late D–C and the southern Caucasus. In this re-analysis, polychrome-painted Urmia Ware is interpreted as a marker of the MBIII (1600–1450 BC) in Ušnu-Solduz; a few apparent imports are still seen to occur in early Period V. Early MBW and Incised and Impressed MBW also typify the MBIII and continue into early Hasanlu Period V (Dinkha III) at Dinkha. Urmia Ware had been found in 1959, in the tiny Well Sounding at Hasanlu, but had gone overlooked at the time (see Chapter 3). Kramer had raised the possibility that the Dinkha Urmia Ware assemblage might be "a very early phase of Hasanlu V" (Hamlin 1971:31) and, with regard to Hasanlu Tepe, that "[t]he [ancient] clearing operation at Hasanlu of Hasanlu V period [the U22 Sounding Stratum 9–11] … could have removed material of this type" (Hamlin 1971:32). It seems as though Kramer was unaware of the Urmia Ware recovered from the Hasanlu Well Sounding—two sherds found in 1959, but impressive given the miniscule excavated exposure—and, more puzzling, did not have access to the Early MBW and Incised and Impressed MBW found at Dinkha with the bulk of the Urmia Ware, as she certainly would have found this co-occurrence noteworthy given her expressed views on the Hasanlu VI–V gap.

During this same period, Dyson published one of his strongest statements to date on his views regarding the origins and meaning of the EWGW horizon in western Iran, revealing the likely influence of Ghirshman's multiple migration wave theory and Young's theory on migration routes:

> Toward the last quarter of the second millennium this complex [belonging to his "Bronze Age" or, herein, Middle Bronze Age] of architecture, burial custom, small objects and ceramics is abruptly replaced at Hasanlu and at Dinkha by *the first wave of grey-pottery using people ushering in the Iron Age* … Their origin appears to have been eastern and they clearly form part of a major cultural movement taking place in central Iran with extensions into Azerbaijan, the Kermanshah Valley, and down into Fars. This pattern of dispersal, beginning with the Gurgan area and carrying with it materials of Tepe Hissar type is currently interpreted as the appearance of the Median and Persian tribes and should be connected therefore, with *the spread of the Indo-Aryan groups* who later emerge in history as the major population of the plateau. (1969:47, emphasis my own)

1970–1977

Following a five-year hiatus work resumed at Hasanlu in 1970. In the next three seasons—1970, 1972, and 1974—important new exposures of the LBA and Iron I were completed on the High Mound and the U22 Sounding was carried down to early 3rd millennium BC deposits. In the 1970s and later, Hasanlu Project publications largely adumbrated and rehashed previous definitions and information with regard to "Period V" ceramics and other diagnostics, with the addition of the columned-hall structure to the roster of supposed culture traits.

Archaeologists had begun to fill in the picture of 2nd millennium BC developments in the northern Lake Urmia Basin with the publication of results from Haftavan Tepe and Kordlar Tepe (Burney 1970, 1972, 1973, 1975; Edwards 1981, 1983, 1986; Kromer and Lippert 1976; Lippert 1976, 1979). There was growing awareness of the connections which existed between the region and the southern Caucasus, reviving theories of EWGW origins and patterns of Iranian migration from north to south (Burney and Lang 1971:117), but a major new development in the prevailing view of 1st millennium BC geography—Levine's assertion that Parsua was not in the northwest Zagros (Levine 1973, 1974a, 1977)—would have a great impact on the old migrationist paradigms regarding the ethnic groups responsible for EWGW, as would the growing realization that the distribution of EWGW was patchy at best outside of Iranian Azerbaijan and did not penetrate the central western Zagros to a significant degree (see Young 1985:364, 366–68; Levine 1987:241, 247). Young's Late Western Buff Ware (LWBW) horizon was also shown to have emerged earlier than he had originally argued in this same area (1985:376).

Young had been definite regarding the association of this ceramic horizon and the Persians (1963:65), and assigning an earlier date to LWBW would qualify this archaeological horizon as a marker for their arrival. Kramer would increasingly drive home the point that pots did not equal people, starting with her dissertation research based on Dinkha Tepe (Hamlin 1971) and continuing in her subsequent writings (Kramer 1977). Accordingly, additional putative culture traits were emphasized in archaeological definitions of the EWGW horizon, such as the columned hall.

1970–1971

In the early 1970s, the results from Dinkha were being incorporated into assessments of the 2nd millennium BC in Iran. This prompted a reappraisal of Hasanlu Period VI, and the onset of the "Late" or "Later" Bronze Age was lowered using the radiocarbon dates from Dinkha. The period would eventually come to include most of the first half of the 2nd millennium BC, and the start of Hasanlu "Period V" was concomitantly lowered, covering much of the second half of the 2nd millennium BC. Again, this was partly based on radiocarbon determinations from Dinkha (Lawn 1970, 1973). The two periods were generally envisioned as having been separated by a 100–150 year hiatus.

Young, who was then working at Godin Tepe, characterized the Dinkha IV/Hasanlu VI assemblage as having PKW like that of Mesopotamia along with "plain, handmade wares [which] tend to have parallels with other areas of the Zagros" (1971:25). In discussing the putative Hasanlu VI–V gap, Young became one of the first scholars, along with Kramer, to mention the Urmia Ware found at the site, although he was clearly unaware of the Early MBW in the same assemblage: "there may be something of a gap between Hasanlu VI and the Early Iron Age of Hasanlu V, into which may fit a polychrome ceramic which appears in the Solduz area [more precisely Ušnu] but is also known in Azerbaijan from Geoy Tepe, Bastam, and Haftavan" (Young 1971:25). Kramer's viewpoints on Urmia Ware have already been discussed with regard to Dinkha (see above). Her dissertation provided some new information on the stratigraphy and architecture of Dinkha IV, but the main thrust of her research was to examine the meaning behind the distribution of KW (Hamlin 1971). Kramer divided Dinkha IV into four phases, A–D, but she was not concerned with changes in the ceramic assemblage over time (see Chapter 4). I have noted Phase D, the latest part of Dinkha IV, exhibits pronounced changes in ceramic production. I refer to Phase D as the Terminal MBII, and it seems highly likely that the MBIII grows directly out of this period, which is in turn the transition to the LBA. Following the suggestion of Kramer, I have introduced the "MBA" designation here into the Hasanlu sequence for the period from 2000 to 1600 BC (Hamlin 1971:256–57).

1972–1973

One stated objective of the 1972 season at Hasanlu was the "excavation of areas of period V date (later 2nd millennium) in an effort to increase the available sherd sample from habitation contexts and to study the question of cultural continuity between V and IV as revealed by architectural remains" (Dyson 1973c:195). This was accomplished in two areas, RS22–23 and YZ27–29 (see Chapter 3). In YZ27–29, below BBIE of Period IVb, the excavators found the "fragmentary remains of a period V building as well as an excellent selection of period V sherds" (Dyson 1973b:304). In fact, they had dug two building levels with multiple phases of construction activity spanning late Period V–early Period IVb, and the bulk of the "Period V" sherds date to Period IVc (see Chapters 3–4). In area RS22–23, the team recovered "a period V building associated with period V ceramics. Its central room, measuring 9x11 meters, contained two columns (stone slabs had been set flush with the floor and surrounded by mud plaster bases), a raised central hearth, a low footing around the walls and a small platform against the center of the rear wall" (Dyson 1973b:304). Dyson was quite specific regarding its significance, stating "its plan, materials, building methods and ceramic wares indicate a direct cultural continuity between periods V and IV at Hasanlu" (1973b:304).

In 1971–1972, Charles Burney and David Lang published *The Peoples of the Hills*, in which they continued in the vein of migrationist theories for EWGW origins, promoting a north-south migratory route along the west side of the Caspian (Burney and Lang 1971:117). Following Young, the authors postulated a close tie between Iranian movements and the distribution of EWGW, and they believed the appearance of this ware in western Iran signaled the beginning of the Iron Age. The archaeological criteria laid out for the Iron I were Grey Ware, pattern burnishing, goblets with button bases, jars with bridgeless spouts, a paucity of iron, an "absence of any large fortified settlements," "extramural cemeteries, at Hasanlu in the lower parts of the mound immediately beneath the citadel," simple inhumations, and in other areas such as Geoy K, Marlik and Talish, stone tombs (Burney and Lang 1971:118). No work was conducted at Hasanlu in 1973.

1974–1976

The 1974 season was the last major campaign of excavation at Hasanlu. Period V was again an objective, and more of the plan of the RS22–23 Building was revealed (Dyson and Pigott 1975:182). The remains of an overlying Period IVc structure were also discovered in a newly opened area (Dyson and Pigott 1975:183) called the "Period IV-V Building." The use of this designation shows Dyson's reluctance to assign late 2nd millennium BC contexts to his Period IVc, which he conceptualized as an initial building phase of the larger monumental structures of Period IVb, such as BBII.

In 1974, Muscarella published the first detailed report on the graves and grave assemblages of Dinkha III. He believed the assemblages, types of burials, and extramural location of the cemetery all served to reinforce the definitional criteria of the Iron I set forward by Young and Dyson for the southern Lake Urmia Basin: "worm bowls," bridgeless spouted jars, and tankards typified the vessel forms. There was a clear separation of KW and MBW in the grave groups. No iron was found in the graves, and the weapons and personal ornaments were similar to those of the unpublished graves of "Hasanlu V."

1977

In the final year of the Hasanlu Project, little fieldwork was completed and efforts were focused on documenting artifact collections stored in the field. Dyson published his most detailed treatment to date of "Hasanlu V," incorporating the important results of 1970–1974 in his *Architecture of the Iron I Period at Hasanlu in Western Iran and Its Implications for Theories of Migration on the Iranian Plateau* (1977b). Here Dyson laid out his expanded criteria for defining the Iron I at Hasanlu accompanied by a cursory overview of the relevant exposures on the High Mound. He included radiocarbon dates and architectural plans of the pertinent "Period V" exposures. In terms of absolute chronology and stratigraphy, I have determined the material presented in this synthesis dates to Period V and Period IVc (see Chapter 3). As the articles title makes plain, punctuated culture change in the mid-2nd millennium BC still dominated Dyson's thinking. He shied away from positing which ethnic group(s) might have introduced EWGW, but he emphasized that the horizon had arrived in western Iran suddenly and fully developed. The putative presence of a columned hall with early "Grey Ware," he believed, greatly strengthened this argument. In this same year, Medvedskaya would challenge the existence of the EWGW horizon and theories linking it to the arrival of Iranians in the Zagros (1977). Her work would gain greater exposure in an expanded English-language publication a few years later.

The Post-Excavation Years

Inna Medvedskaya's *Iran: Iron Age I* (1982) advanced a dissenting view, challenging the migrationist and Iranian-origins stances. In her decidedly partisan work, she deemed Young's EWGW horizon conceptually invalid, and argued the cultures of the "Iron I" of northwestern Iran grew out of the indigenous Bronze Age cultures. Medvedskaya drew a strong rebuke from Muscarella (1994a), who addressed her claims point by point in his *North-Western Iran: Bronze Age to Iron Age*. Muscarella's assessment did not diverge substantially from previous coverage of the period by members of the Hasanlu Project, although it provided some new evidence on the graves of Dinkha III. Muscarella did not advocate a particular ethnonym be associated with the EWGW, but he defended the spatio-temporal definition of the horizon and its punctuated appearance. A more equivocal Young (1985), having amended his own views regarding the EWGW horizon, was somewhat more sympathetic to Medvedskaya's criticisms. By this time, Young had abandoned the purported connection between the EWGW horizon and Iranian origins, shifting his focus to his LWBW horizon while in favor of east-west migratory routes along the southern flanks of the Elburz. The flurry of archaeological activity which was carried out in the 1970s yielded a more complete picture of 2nd millennium BC developments, particularly for central-western Iran. Levine was more conservative than Young (1965) in characterizing the early "Iron Age" in western Iran in terms of ceramic diagnostics, citing only "the button or pedestal based Early Western Grey Ware goblet, and the 'Elamite' or 'Kassite' goblet" (Levine 1987:236). Dyson's later statements on Hasanlu V and VI echoed his earlier work, albeit with less emphasis on population replacements and utilizing a modified chronology:

> The preceding Bronze Age occupation (Hasanlu period VI), characterized by painted buff-colored pottery, appears to have come to an abrupt end. The succeeding occupation of Hasanlu period V represents not only a sudden change in pottery form and manufacturing technology, but also new burial rituals, new types of clothing and ornaments, and new architectural practices and building plans. (1989a:108)

He goes on to make the case for demic diffusion:

> We currently believe that there is a cultural disconformity between Period VI (ending ca. 1450 BCE), which is characterized by Mesopotamian Khabur Ware,[7] and Period V (?1450–?1250 BCE), characterized by completely different burial customs and pottery (burnished red, brown, and gray ware in different shapes) that are of uncertain origin,[8] but are certainly not Mesopotamian … Speculations on ethnicity in the absence of texts … are to be avoided. (Dyson and Voigt 2003:236)

Examined chronologically, we see how views regarding Hasanlu V and Iron I were shaped and modified over a period of roughly 50 years by the members of the Hasanlu Project. The detailed analysis and presentation of the data sets, however, waned in the period following T. Cuyler Young's departure from the project in the mid-1960s, with the notable exceptions of the work of Muscarella (Dinkha III burials), Kramer (KW), and Rubinson (Urmia Ware). Interpretation of the results bearing on 2nd millennium BC chronology was severely hindered by the Balkanization of the research effort: scholars chose or were ceded select, small bodies of material, such as a particular ceramic ware or artifact category, without the benefit of access to the associated finds, the primary field documentation, or detailed stratigraphic and architectural phasing. In many cases, the excavated finds were not analyzed beyond cursory treatment in the field and subsequent partage, especially the ceramics.

The Archaeological Definition of "Hasanlu V"

Ceramics

The archaeological definition of Hasanlu "Period V" has centered on a narrow range of vessel forms and a few other attributes (see Chapter 4). Over the last 40–50 years, scholars have added diagnostics of ware, form, and style to the definition, while other diagnostics have been re-attributed to different periods, predominantly Period VIb. Dyson and other Hasanlu Project members originally identified Hasanlu IV and "V" by the presence of a MBW assemblage. In practice, "Period V" initially comprised MBW deposits below the burned destruction level of Hasanlu Terminal IVb, and so in reality encompassed material that I now attribute to Hasanlu VIa, V, IVc, and early IVb.[9] In High Mound soundings, Dyson and Young eventually separated "Period V" from the Bronze Age (original terminology) in the mid-1960s by the presence of MBW and the absence of a KW assemblage similar to those of MBA northern Mesopotamia (see below). On the Low Mound, 2nd millennium BC deposits overlay an Orange Ware (OW) assemblage diagnostic of the EBA in the southern Lake Urmia Basin.[10] These levels were not attributed to Period V or Period VI at the time, often due to incomplete recording, insufficient artifactual finds, or the failure to systematically collect artifacts. The lack of documentation causes this uncertainty. For the dating of graves, Dyson and Young drew upon comparanda from a fairly far-flung set of MBW and related cemeteries, including Giyan, Sialk, and Khurvin; the criteria used for "Period V" attributions evolved over the course of the project as the excavators gradually accrued data. After having been placed in "Period V," some graves were reattributed to Period VI on the basis of KW, which had been initially viewed as a late—i.e., Mesopotamian LBA—variety of the ware. This view of KW was overturned in Kramer's dissertation (Hamlin 1971). Dyson and Young's analyses of MBW grave groups and other comparanda from sites in Iran led to their identification of type fossils diagnostic of the earliest "Iron Age" in western Iran and, more specifically, of "Hasanlu V" as a regional phenomenon (see especially Dyson 1965; Muscarella 1994a:142; Young 1965). In the years prior to 1962, as the excavators developed the chronological terminology for western Iran, MBA deposits at Hasanlu were not well attested. This period was therefore not clearly defined or properly designated. Simultaneously, "Period V" (initially defined as 1200–1000 BC) and Period VI ("Late Bronze") were steadily pushed back in time with the calibration of radiocarbon dating and the excavation of earlier deposits, until the first half of the 2nd millennium BC in Iran was the "Late" or "Later" Bronze Age and the second half the early "Iron Age."

The MBW assemblage of the later 2nd millennium BC can now be conclusively dated to at least as early as the 16th century BC in Ušnu-Solduz, or the MBIII. The ware gradually emerges in the southern Lake Urmia Basin in some of the forms Dyson and Young previously linked to EWGW, which can in turn be linked to earlier MBA forms. This is followed by the *staggered appearance*, from the MBIII to the Iron I, of other vessel forms and cultural attributes previously cited by scholars as diagnostic of "Hasanlu V" and the EWGW horizon. The Early MBW horizon exhibits *regional variability* with increasingly less regionalization in the Middle MBW and Late MBW horizons. This strongly supports arguments of *local origins* for the horizon rather than the cultural processes espoused by the wave migrationists who allege homogeneity in the early portions of the horizon followed by regionalization. Early MBW is found in association with polychrome painted Urmia Ware at Dinkha, Geoy Tepe, Haftavan, and almost certainly at Hasanlu (Chapters 3 and 4). Early MBW has one stylistic variant, Incised and Impressed Ware, which occurs at Dinkha in the MBIII and early LBA and which appears to be connected to Transcaucasia. This ware is currently unknown in the Solduz valley. Only small exposures of the MBIII and early LBA were achieved at Hasanlu, and site formation processes and sampling issues conspired to create an artificial gap in the mid-2nd millennium BC portion of the Hasanlu sequence (see Chapter 3). I do not believe such a gap exists in the occupation record, and there is a transition from Hasanlu VI to V in the ceramic assemblages of Ušnu-Solduz: MBW emerges from burnished wares of similar appearance present in the MBA—*not MBA Grey Ware, but other burnished and smoothed wares that received little attention in past publications*. The use of PKW steeply declined at Dinkha in the Terminal MBII (Chapter 4), and it is out of this process, and with some influences from northern Mesopotamia, Transcaucasia, and northern Iran which continued into the MBIII, that the ceramic assemblage of Hasanlu V is derived. Dyson suspected as much in the early 1970s (1973a:706), but he quickly abandoned the idea.

Architecture

In the closing years of the Hasanlu Project, Dyson cited the introduction of columned-hall architecture as a diagnostic of "Period V" (1977b:166), adducing a modest "Period V" building with two column bases, a throne seat, benches, and a raised hearth sited on Hasanlu's High Mound in RS22–23 (see Chapter 3). Dyson (1977b) and Young (2002) interpreted the building as a precursor to the monumental columned halls of Period IVb and, far more speculatively, maintained that such structures arrived at Hasanlu as a fully developed form at the start of "Period V." For Dyson, the continuous tradition of columned-hall architecture at Hasanlu disproved an east-west migration of Iranians or other groups for MBW origins since precursors are absent in northeast Iran (Dyson 1977b). Young viewed columned-hall architecture as being derived from the west (1966, 2002), espousing a model of migration in which new populations eclectically drew on the traditions of their neighbors. Young articulated this model most fully following the abandonment of his theory that EWGW represented Iranian demic diffusion (1985).

Other LBA and Iron I architectural exposures on the High Mound revealed structures of monumental character, particularly in Grids YZ27–29, but no other evidence of "Period V" columned halls was forthcoming. The validity of the columned-hall style of architecture as a diagnostic of the earliest "Iron Age" and the arrival of a new population in western Iran is invalid in terms of Dyson, Young, and other's ceramic-centric definition of the EWGW archaeological culture/horizon since *there is no evidence of the architectural form in association with the earliest MBW levels of Hasanlu V*. That is, the earliest known columned-hall architecture dates securely to the *middle* of Period V. Moreover, we lack architecture of the MBIII in the southern Lake Urmia Basin and have an extremely limited dataset of terminal MBII architecture from which to draw valid comparisons. The form might be much earlier than currently attested and represent a native tradition.

Columned halls represent large, central reception areas in elite residences with focal points on the central axis—the raised central hearth and the so-called throne seat. As the primary public space of an elite residence, the form was adopted for temples as well, with a cult target replacing the throne seat. Columned halls are not immediately permeable spaces, and are separated from exterior areas by at least an anteroom and usually a portico as well. The entryway to the hall and the hall itself are designed to impress and serve as a stage for scripted elite activities. The columns provided for wider roof spans, openings for light wells and chimneys for ground floor hearths, and/or possibly supports for balconies. These halls generally have benches along the walls for seating a large audience, and one corner was usually dedicated to fixed storage jars, likely to facilitate drinking and banqueting activities.

I believe columned halls are indicative of a form of sociopolitical organization and a particular conception of political authority and legitimization. At Hasanlu columned halls associated with secular buildings are attested at multiple locations in the Period IVb settlement, suggesting a political organization that emphasized multiple factions, and decision-making processes based at least in part on the crafting of consensus. More generally, columned halls typify polities comprised of geographically dispersed and isolated sociopolitical units characterized by ethnic diversity (i.e., tribal confederations), in mountain and piedmont environments where vertical transhumance and nomadism were crucial parts of the agropastoral economy. The socioeconomics and political exigencies of the region necessitate a fairly high degree of local autonomy, with elites serving as chief negotiators within hierarchically organized networks of segmentary lineages. The tribal confederations of the region historically possessed large tracts of land, which might contain settled, transhumant, and nomadic populations, and often included multiple ethnic groups. The columned-hall form *in toto*, to my mind, denotes a form of sociopolitical organization grounded in socioeconomics. Their increasing monumentality in the late 2nd and early 1st millennium BC connotes a process of secondary state formation that rapidly transformed tribal confederations.

Extramural Cemeteries

An abrupt discontinuity in mortuary practices in the later 2nd millennium BC would lend credence to the notion that the emergence of the MBW horizon embodied demic diffusion. Closer scrutiny shows the intramural/extramural distinction, first postulated by Ghirshman as diagnostic of newcomers heralding the Iron Age, to be invalid. As archaeology progressed in northern and western Iran in the 20th century, the degree of inter-regional and intra-regional variability documented in 2nd millennium BC mortuary practices increased in lock-step, yet scholars clung to the notion that burial practices supported migration theories with little evidence cited.

From the earliest definition of the Iron Age in Iran, Sialk has dominated scholars' thinking regarding the presence of "extramural" cemeteries in the 2nd millennium BC associated with "Grey Ware." Giyan, another influential cemetery, has architecture and graves in the same area of the site and a painted ceramic tradition similar to KW (see especially Overlaet 2003:49–55). This site has been considered iconic of the Bronze Age and Bronze Age-Iron Age transition, but it is noteworthy that the "early Iron Age" graves there were associated with architectural remains. The scholars who posited an intramural/extramural distinction seldom specified the intramural cemeteries to which they were referring prior to the excavation of Dinkha IV in 1966 and 1968.

Given the similarities and close contacts between MBA Mesopotamia and western Iran, and the southern Lake Urmia Basin in particular, one might predict similarities in mortuary practices. Family tombs and burials in close association with residences would represent one such similarity at Dinkha Tepe in Periods IV Phase C and IV Phase D. The intramural, communal stone-built tombs at Dinkha are not typical of the region; however, our picture admittedly remains quite limited (see Chapter 5). The evidence from graves, ceramics, and other material culture suggests that extrapolations from Dinkha IV to the rest of the Lake Urmia Basin, or to northwestern Iran more generally, are likely specious and best viewed as an external influence of Mesopotamian derivation.

Dyson has argued that the shift from intramural cemeteries, with burials within settlements, to extramural cemeteries, where areas were reserved for burials alone, marked the shift from Hasanlu VI to V (1965:196). At Hasanlu, however, there is no evidence of intramural burial in Period VI; the Period VI burials instead lay within an extramural cemetery, and some evidence of early Iron Age occupation exists in the main area of Iron Age graves excavated in the North Cemetery. The Dinkha IV settlement, on the other hand, contained intramural tombs. In short, a number of different mortuary practices are evidenced in the MBA of southern Lake Urmia, including single inhumations, multiple inhumations, intramural communal tombs, extramural tombs, and secondary burial (see Chapter 5). In the MBIII, LBA, and early Iron Age we see a growing preference for single inhumations with significant incidences of secondary burial, multiple interments, cist tombs, and *hypogea* at Hasanlu and Dinkha. Cemeteries were located at the edges of settlements (with shifting boundaries) and, perhaps most significantly, there is an increasing occurrence of "detached cemeteries." "Extramural cemetery" is defined here to mean areas in antiquity designated as cemeteries separate from, but associated with, a settlement. Researchers have not always employed the same definition consistently, and the presence of such cemeteries has been difficult to substantiate since settlements expand and contract in and out of areas used for burials, and archaeological investigations are not always capable of establishing the association of cemeteries with contemporary settlements. In many cases in northern and western Iran in the later 2nd and early 1st millennium BC, we are dealing with detached cemeteries—that is, cemeteries unassociated with permanent settlement. I would argue these are the burial grounds of semi-sedentary and/or non-sedentary populations. Their preponderance in the LBA and early Iron Age seems indicative of the successes of (1) agropastoralism incorporating short-range seasonal vertical transhumance side by side with (2) early nomadism facilitated by and targeted at the production of horses. To my mind, extramural and detached cemeteries do not, perforce, signal demic diffusion, and the use of the intramural-extramural dichotomy was forced onto the data from northwestern Iran to advance wave migrationist theories first promulgated by Ghirshman and Arne and to establish cultural links to the *Eastern Grey Ware* horizon. As with other facets of the wave migrationist position, early conjecture surrounding the "Grey Ware" horizon grew into a series of self-fulfilling prophecies in archaeological practice — *hysteron proteron* reversals of observation and theory validation passing as the hypothetical-deductive method.

Iron Metallurgy

Another potential diagnostic of "Hasanlu V" is the alleged appearance of small amounts of iron, hence the designation "Iron I"; however, consensus has long been that iron rarely occurs in the "Iron I" of western Iran (Burney and Lang 1971:113). Defining archaeological periods with criteria verging on *argumentum e silencio* (scarcity of iron, lack of fortifications) is hardly ideal. The Iron I designation ultimately is linked to comparisons Dyson drew between "Hasanlu V" and other sites in Iran, particularly Tepe Sialk (Ghirshman 1939), where Ghirshman found an iron dagger and punch in Grave 4 of Necropolis A (1939:9). The exact date of these objects is problematic (Moorey 1971:128), and they may just as easily be from the Iron II. We have confirmed the existence of two pieces of iron from Hasanlu IVc (Iron I, 1250–1050 BC) contexts: a fragment of a weapon or tool in grave SK24 and a ring not previously reported from the YZ27–29 Building (HAS72-N188, UPM73-5-82, Grid Y29, Area 4 Stratum 4, on a "Period V" = IVc wall foundation sealed by BBIE). An oft-cited finger ring allegedly recovered from grave SK29 (see Chapter 5, Ring = HAS57-184d, UPM58-4-53; Dyson 1964b:39; 1965:196; 1967a:2957; Muscarella 1974:49; Pigott 1977:223; 1981:125) is almost certainly intrusive from an overlying early Period IVb grave. Suffice it to say, the occurrence of iron in "Hasanlu V" and the "Iron I" of western Iran more generally (Young 1967:24) resembles the pattern seen throughout the LBA and Iron I Near East: iron is extremely rare and was largely confined to personal ornament, only becoming ubiquitous during the Iron II (Pigott 1977:227).

Chronology and Periodization of the "Late Bronze Age" and "Iron I"

Over the last 50 years, dividing the later 2nd millennium BC of the southern Lake Urmia Basin into archaeological periods anchored by absolute dates has proven difficult. Certain ideas have remained fairly fixed since the early years of the Hasanlu Project. Most researchers associate Hasanlu VI with PKW. Dyson and others equate "Period V" with certain diagnostic ceramic attributes in MBW, such as bridgeless spouts, and more generally with archaeological deposits below Hasanlu IVb's destruction level that contained MBW. From 1956 to the present, however, there has been some refinement and modification of Hasanlu's chronology and periodization:

1. the increasingly strong assertion, although not universally accepted, that there is little overlap between "Period V" and Period VI;
2. proposing a potential chronological/cultural gap or break between "Period V" and Period VI;
3. the steady lowering of the dates of "Period V" earlier into the 2nd millennium BC (consensus is generally 1450–1250 BC; the period was originally roughly dated to 1200–1000 BC) and the related re-dating of Period VI to the first half of the 2nd millennium BC; and,
4. the addition, somewhat haphazardly, of Period IVc to the Hasanlu sequence (now 1250–1050 BC).

As previously discussed, in the early seasons of the Hasanlu Project the excavators mixed material from Periods "V" and VI, and conflated them in publication. This was later "corrected," but without adequate presentation and illustration of the relevant evidence. In the late 1960s and early 1970s, reputed evidence for a stratigraphic break between "Hasanlu V"/Dinkha III and Hasanlu VI/Dinkha IV was found at Dinkha Tepe. In the U22 Deep Sounding at Hasanlu, Dyson and Young had already identified a purported break and noted little overlap between the PKW and MBW assemblages (see Chapter 3). As previously mentioned, the excavators have vacillated on this point. Dyson initially asserted that, "[b]elow these levels [U22 Period V Strata 5–10] there is a complete *cultural and stratigraphic discontinuity*, with the appearance of a stratum [Strata 11–12] of Painted Buff Ware, Incised Ware and Plain Yellow-buff wares related to northern Mesopotamian pottery of the mid-second millennium" (1963b:132, emphasis my own). This was contradicted somewhat by Young, who noted that, "no erosion surface was indicated between the upper stratum of VI and the lowest stratum." (1963:43). This point was reaffirmed by Dyson, "There is no visibly eroded surface or erosion deposit between the strata of VI and the overlying *building* of V, a situation which suggests that no period of abandonment intervened" (Dyson 1965:195; emphasis my own). The consistent implication is cultural discontinuity at Hasanlu. There were, however, four intervening strata of Period V predating the "Period V" building to which Dyson was referring (see below).

Dyson's stratigraphic assessment would again change: "At Hasanlu, a clean *stratigraphic break* was provided [between Periods V and VI] by the earliest Iron Age occupants *who leveled off the remains of VI architecture* to make a clean surface for their building operations" (Hamlin 1971:28–29, citing Dyson, pers. comm., emphasis my own). Dyson would eventually settle on a major cultural break linked to the migration of a new population into the southern Lake Urmia Basin and, by extension, western Iran, heralding the start of the Iron Age (Dyson 1977b). I would assert that this theory rests on very little evidence. Comparisons of the Bronze Age and Iron Age in the region should be weighed against the fact that we know little of the Bronze Age at Hasanlu (Periods V–VII) beyond the ceramics. Period VI deposits were seldom excavated, and in the early seasons of the excavations, when deep soundings were dug on the Low Mound (including Operations IV, V, VI, and X), the collection and recording of artifactual assemblages and the delineation of stratigraphy were completely inadequate for the documentation of such a break. Only in the soundings in Operation I, the U22 Sounding, and the Well Sounding on the High Mound were data collected to address the questions of a major stratigraphic break and/or a period of abandonment. As previously mentioned, in Operation I there is overlap in the ceramics of Period VIb, consisting of plain, incised and painted KW and Grey Ware, and a seemingly early type of MBW. The assemblage was too small to allow researchers to completely dismiss a chronological gap, but it does serve as a warning that there are too few adequately documented exposures of the 2nd millennium BC at the site. The stratigraphy of U22 provided Dyson and Young's basis for positing a gap, but the stratigraphic situation is far more complex than has been portrayed (see Chapter 3), and fundamental errors were made during the excavation of these levels. The presence of isolated finds of "Urmia Ware" at Hasanlu in the Well Sounding suggests the presence of a transitional period between Hasanlu VI and "V" at the mound's center, and so I have introduced the designation Hasanlu VIa for this period. Hasanlu VIa is best attested at Dinkha and in the northern Lake Urmia Basin. With regard to absolute chronology, the date range for "Hasanlu V" started out high (Appendix II) and was steadily pushed back by the calibration of radiocarbon dates (Ralph, Michael, and Han 1973) and new samples.

Of the post-excavation reinterpretations of Hasanlu, Dyson's addition of Period IVc to the Hasanlu sequence is particularly relevant and requires some explanation. Dyson first alluded to Period IVc in 1965 (1965:198, 211, table 2), but this subperiod was not adequately defined. The excavators were aware that *several* architectural phases with MBW lay beneath the burned level of Hasanlu IVb, as opposed to a single, widespread level of "Hasanlu V." It was not until the later analysis of the large burned monumental structures of Hasanlu's IVb citadel had revealed traces of an earlier, allegedly widespread construction phase that the IVc designation was explained (Dyson 1989a; Dyson and Muscarella 1989:1; Young 2002:386).[11] Radiocarbon age determinations placed these earlier monumental structures at ca. 1250–1050 BC. The period was defined *only* as the earlier architectural phase present in certain buildings, *but* "Period V" was tacitly shortened to 1500/1450–1250 BC. I would emphasize that it is possible, although not always easy, to differentiate ceramics and other small finds of Hasanlu V from IVc (see Chapters 4–6). Following Dyson's designation of the subperiod IVc, there was no reanalysis of the Hasanlu dataset formerly designated as "Period V" which, according to radiocarbon dates published prior to 1989, ranged from 1450 to 1000 BC—that is, *much of the material Dyson originally had designated as "Period V" now belongs within the Period IVc designation. The major problem with Dyson's IVc designation is that it was de facto an architectural phase, not a defined archaeological subperiod.*

The inability to discern Hasanlu IVc through the assessment of material culture has had important implications. First and foremost, scholars have long grappled with a 400-plus-year span (Hasanlu V–IVc), which offers no internal chronological distinctions.[12] One example serves to illustrate the potential difficulty: In his influential 1965 article on the ceramic horizons of western Iran, T. Cuyler Young noted that the transition from "Period V" to Period IV at Hasanlu was marked by the disappearance of many MBW ceramic forms. This is hardly surprising and not particularly significant given that it is predicated on the comparison of (1) a 600-year agglomeration of Hasanlu grave groups ("Hasanlu V" and VIa) bolstered by comparanda drawn from widely dispersed points in western Iran, to (2) the Hasanlu IVb ceramic assemblage defined almost exclusively using whole forms from grave groups in the North Cemetery that were tacitly proofed against vessels of the Period IVb destruction level on the High Mound which is dated to ca. 800 BC.

The Cultural Character and Cultural Processes of "Period V/Iron I"

Since the discovery of early "Iron Age" deposits in western Iran, scholars have sought to reconstruct the settlement history, ethnic composition, and broader cultural processes at work in the region in the later 2nd millennium BC, often with regard to putative wave migrations and possible links to proto-Iranian populations.[13] The work of archaeologists such as Dyson and Young has had a great impact. In explaining the arrival of Iranian speakers in western Iran, for example, Mallory draws heavily on Dyson and Young's research:

> The period in which we first encounter the Iranians in western Iran is designated Iron Age Period II (1000–800 BC). This in turn is seen as the direct and uninterrupted successor of Iron Age I, which begins about 1400 BC. It is the initiation of Iron Age I that sees a major cultural break in this region. With its earliest appearance we find a shift from painted to plain grey wares, both in settlements and as grave accompaniments. (1989:49)

In an early reconstruction of the cultural processes behind the MBW horizon, Dyson posited:

> The culture of [Hasanlu] Period V plainly represents an intrusion into the area flanking Lake Urmia on the west (from Rezaiyeh south), south, and east (north to Yanik Tepe) of a new group (or groups) of people who used burnished monochrome grey pottery, who buried their dead in

cemeteries, who employed stemmed goblets for drinking purposes, who had virtually no iron, and who settled on scattered mounds throughout the area. (Dyson 1965:197)

Slightly later, in *The Archaeological Evidence of the Second Millennium B.C. on the Persian Plateau* (1968), Dyson came close to linking the Iron I of western Iran with the arrival of Iranian populations: "With the beginning of the Iron Age I in northern Persia, a new stage of development is reached on the plateau which forms the protohistoric background of the Median and Achaemenian dynasties. This change brought to an end all of the second millennium cultures" (1968:29).

As previously mentioned, Dyson (1963a:33) elsewhere joined Young (1963) in directly linking the Iron I to Iranian migrations. The transition from KW to MBW, or the "Bronze Age" to the "Iron Age," is here of particular importance. The difficulties with this terminology aside (see below), many scholars maintain the existence of a pronounced break in the archaeological sequence of Hasanlu and other sites in the southern Lake Urmia Basin and that the MBW horizon signals a new cultural milieu (Dyson 1977b; Levine 1987:233). In the early stages of exploration and interpretation, this was directly linked to the arrival of a new population. Such assertions were later tempered by acknowledging "pots are not people," and it was argued instead that the MBW horizon arrived in a fully developed form from elsewhere and that other aspects of material culture changed simultaneously. In his refinement of the definition of "Iron I" at Hasanlu, Dyson pointed out innovations in construction techniques, building types, and mortuary patterns. For example, Dyson stated with regard to architecture that "the tradition [of "Hasanlu V"] is already one of well-established construction methods which replace those in use during the preceding Bronze Age … this complex was introduced early in the second half of the second millennium BC to the Solduz Valley" (1977b:166). He goes on to emphasize the strong continuities between other aspects of "Hasanlu V" and Hasanlu IV, reinforcing the impression that the advent of the MBW horizon was an exogenously induced, punctuated event.

The publication of *Iran: Iron Age I* (1982) by Inna Medveskaya, in which she interpreted the Iron Age transition of western Iran as an indigenous phenomenon, elicited much stronger declarations regarding "Hasanlu V" from the excavators. Key among the critical responses, Muscarella argued that the introduction of the MBW horizon represented "a major break and a new beginning in the history of the area … recognized by all scholars who have reviewed the evidence," as "a new culture (most probably brought by a new people) entered north-Western Iran," which is but "a basic fact of the archaeological record" (1994a:140).[14] While I concur that the emergence of the MBW horizon is highly significant for archaeological periodization, all the scholars Muscarella cites were principal members of the Hasanlu Project with access to the majority of the evidence, virtually all of it unpublished. Such a rebuttal bordered on a *deus ex machina* explanation.

While the *transition* from Hasanlu VI to "V" is compelling and important, the dataset from "Hasanlu V," heretofore an unpublished archaeological pastiche, seems an inappropriate starting point for the tendentious championing of such cultural constructs and processes as specific ethnicities, dark ages, and punctuated demic diffusion, let alone, for example, gradual stream migration. Furthermore, I question the validity of weighty assertions drawn from comparisons of Hasanlu VIb to its supposed immediate successor. First, scholars have focused on comparing Hasanlu VIb to Hasanlu V and have largely ignored intervening material. Furthermore, little is known about the MBII beyond the Hasanlu ceramic assemblage and the partially published excavations at Dinkha Tepe,[15] weakening any conclusions based on comparisons with later time periods. This highly localized archaeological culture is hardly typical of western Iran as a whole. Hasanlu VIb/Dinkha IV may represent the direct control of the southern Lake Urmia Basin by northern Mesopotamia—an open question in need of further investigation. In many time periods (Hasanlu VII–VI and, in other respects, Hasanlu "V"–IV), the southern Lake Urmia Basin is far from representative of the broader situation in northern and western Iran, or even the entire Lake Urmia Basin for that matter, a fact linked to its important position at a crossroad linking northeastern Mesopotamia, the Zagros, the Iranian Plateau, and the Caucasus.

After a review of the evidence, I contend the prolonged and dogged adherence to EWGW migration theories or the slightly watered-down notion of punctuated demic diffusion stem from two sources. The first is what Karl Popper coined the "Oedipus effect" in the social sciences in his critique of historicism (Popper 1957, 1976), in which he noted that, as is the case here, prediction influences the predicted. I would trace this back to Ghirshman's early grappling with Sialk A in which he popularized a list of putative culture traits and a multiple-wave migrationist model that promised to explicate the arrival of the Iranians onto the plateau: their movements displaced the affiliated "Grey Ware" (Sialk A) culture and their eventual arrival was heralded by Sialk B. Such theories would naturally receive much attention and warm welcome in an emerging, modernizing nation state. As western Iran was further explored, *the model profoundly influenced data collection and interpretation*. Herein lays the reasoning, to my mind, for the origin of and adherence to the unconventional use of the term "Iron Age." "Western Grey Ware" culture, inextricably linked to the definition of the Iron Age (*sensu* Dyson), was in turn linked to Indo-Iranian migrations (*sensu* Young), and for a time it seemed that Persians, Medes, and Scythians might have had a much earlier and easily discernible presence in Iran. These early Iranians were thereby granted a wider geographic distribution (taking in much of the area within the modern borders of Iran and beyond) as connections between "Grey Ware" and "Buff Ware" were strengthened at Hasanlu, Ziwiyeh, and other sites. Pots equaled nation state. The issue of migration became fixed, and Western scholars—although not many of their Soviet counterparts—became preoccupied with migration routes, establishing and reinforcing culture traits and/or archaeological diagnostics, and exploring links between the EWGW, LWGW, and LWBW horizons in lieu of systematic and detailed collection and presentation of data. Biases can be seen to have shaped research and publication efforts nearly from the start. Contradictory findings were glossed over or ignored: the most glaring of these was the mid-2nd millennium BC in Ušnu-Solduz. I would contend that changing the chronological terminology, which was clearly showing strains by the 1970s, might have signified to some the waning of the migrationist–culture change paradigm. Others simply advocated the continued use of the existing terminology for pragmatic reasons: it was already widely used. In many ways, however, maintaining the terminology is a tacit acceptance of the self-fulfilling prophecies entailed in the closely linked theories and acquiescence to the powerful personalities that championed them.

The second source of these models, related to the first, derives from the methodological shortcomings of the Hasanlu Project, by which a gap was artificially created in the archaeological sequence of the Lake Urmia Basin sundering the 2nd millennium BC into two unrelated halves and orphaning the MBIII.

NOTES

2.1. These are Operations IV, V, VI, X, LI, LIII, and LIV.

2.2. It is important to point out that the attribution of these graves to "Hasanlu V" dos not stem from the previous work of the Hasanlu Project and that many are now re-dated to Period IVc or VIa. The graves were excavated in 1957–59 and 1964. The "Period V" designation was predicated on the dating of grave goods and, secondarily, stratigraphy. The majority of said burials were recovered in Operation VI and its various extensions on the northeastern Low Mound. An additional three were recovered in Operation IV on the east Low Mound, and one came from Operation LIII on the northwest slope of the Low Mound. I have added some graves to the time span covered herein that were previously undated or attributed to "Period IV."

2.3. At Hasanlu, KW occupation deposits were excavated on the High Mound in Operation I, the U22 Sounding, the Well Sounding, on the west slope of the citadel mound at the base of Fortification Wall II (Dyson and Pigott 1975:164), in a small sounding in Grid V22, and in a sounding excavated below the Lower Court adjacent to BBV in Grid Y30 (Area 1 Stratum 5, sherds collected but unrecorded). On the Low Mound, architectural remains and occupation strata of undifferentiated 2nd millennium BC occupation deposits were recovered in all operations.

2.4. In unpublished records of the Hasanlu Project, Period VI was often referred to as the "Ring Ware Phase."

2.5. Muscarella has asserted that "neither Dyson nor the author ever stated that the EWGW/Iron I culture represented Iranian speakers" (1994a:145, n9). Muscarella certainly did not state this, but Dyson certainly toyed with the idea in the early 1960s. He later left the question of ethnicity open and simply highlighted the supposed punctuated and wholesale nature of the cultural replacement between Periods VI and "V."

2.6. Dyson (1965) and Young (1965) use an identical figure to illustrate this pottery. The authors do not provide the proveniences of the vessels, but they are as follows: No. 1 (pedestal-base goblet)—HAS59-323, Op. LIII, Burial 2; No. 2 (pedestal-base goblet)—HAS57-126, Op. VI, Burial 15; No. 3 (PKW jar)—HAS59-126, Op. VIa Str. 5; No. 4 (pattern-burnished jar)—HAS59-127 Op. VIa Str. 7; No. 5 (jar with single handle at shoulder)—HAS59-325, Op. LIII, Burial 2; No. 6 (PKW bowl)—HAS59-91, Op. VIa, Burial 12; No. 7 (jar)—HAS57-187, Op.VI, Burial 19; No. 8 (carinated bowl with vertically pierced lug)—HAS59-324, Op. LIII, Burial 2; No. 9 (pedestal-base goblet)—HAS57-188, Op. VI, Burial 19; No. 10 (pedestal-base goblet)—HAS57-159, Op. VI, Burial 19; Nos. 11–14 (*istikhans*)—Op. X, Burial 2. Each *istikhan* shown in this figure was recovered from a single burial (Op. X, Burial 2), which contained 10 such cups, two small, undecorated jars, and a broken fragment of a PKW ring base of less-secure context. Pins found in the burial and its stratigraphic position securely date it to Period VI. The grave contained the articulated burial of a female and the secondary burials of a young male and an infant. With regard to painted wares in Period V, as late as 1974, Muscarella—citing both Dyson (1965:36–37, fig. 3:3, 6) and Young (1965:55, 57, 67, fig. 8, 70ff.)—had stated that "Painted pottery was rare at Hasanlu V but occurs in the form of black or red-brown bands on a buff ground … these seem to be rare examples of continuity from the Bronze Age" (1974:48). The PKW bowl cited here (HAS59-91) comes from burial SK61 and should be dated to Hasanlu VI. The jar was found in fill in Op. VIa Str. 5 and was not associated with skeletal remains.

2.7. I would emphasize here that KW, and especially PKW, does not characterize the period after 1700 BC. The use of the 1450 BC start date by Voigt and Dyson (2003:236) represents the first attempt to incorporate MBIII contexts (1600–1450 BC) within the framework of the Hasanlu sequence.

2.8. Nevertheless, on the same page of this publication we are informed that, "We know that the burial customs and the ceramic assemblage that appear at the beginning of Hasanlu Period V *originate on the Iranian Plateau*" (Dyson and Voigt 2003:236, emphasis my own).

2.9. Monochrome Burnished Ware has been typically called "Grey Ware" or, following Young's terminology (1965), "Early Western Grey Ware" ("Hasanlu V") and "Late Western Grey Ware" ("Hasanlu IV"). These terms are misnomers and do not characterize the ware, which is fired in a range of colors. The use of the term "Grey Ware" has also created a great deal of confusion since it was used to refer to a number of other grey ceramic wares, most notably Middle Bronze Age Grey Ware, which occurs at Hasanlu and Dinkha in conjunction with KW and early MBW.

2.10. In most previous Hasanlu Project publications, Period VII is associated with this "Painted Orange Ware"; the great majority of the pottery from this period, however, is an unpainted ware with grit temper similar to the plain simple ware of the earlier 3rd millennium BC in northern Mesopotamia. The first subperiod of Period VII, Period VIIc (Danti, Voigt, and Dyson 2004), is characterized by the appearance of Orange Ware; the painted varieties of the ware do not appear until the subsequent subperiod, VIIb.

2.11. Dyson has indicated that the period is attested in BBII, BBIVE, and BBV (1989a). A segment of fortification wall on the western High Mound was excavated in 1974 and attributed to Period IVc (Dyson and Pigott 1975:184). In the columned halls, Hasanlu IVc ends in a large fire that destroys the buildings (Dyson and Muscarella 1989:1). Period IVb subsequently begins with the reconstruction and modification of the Burned Buildings atop the Period IVc foundations and wall stubs (Dyson and Muscarella 1989). According to Dyson and Muscarella, all of the IVc buildings were swept clean except for one unpublished *in situ* trash deposit in BBV (1989:1).

2.12. If one considers that MBW appears in the MBIII in Ušnu-Solduz, then this period is even longer.

2.13. See Dyson (1977b) and Muscarella (1994a:140) for reviews of the various theories on this issue.

2.14. Muscarella does not claim that this alleged new population was Iranian, but he strongly supports punctuated demic diffusion. If, in his view, there was such a sudden and large-scale population shift, who might these newcomers have been if not Iranian speakers?

2.15. The recent dissertation by Gabe Pizzorno on Dinkha Tepe has not been released by the author as of this time.

3

The Reanalysis of "Hasanlu V": Stratigraphy, Architecture, and Radiocarbon Dating

The pottery from periods IV and V from Hasanlu has shown that a ceramic assemblage from a cemetery is not necessarily a good sample of the pottery from an entire period.

— T. Cuyler Young 1963:71

Reanalysis of Hasanlu "Period V" has resulted in substantial revisions to the chronological sequence of the later 2nd millennium BC, with the reassignment of a substantial portion of the former "Hasanlu V" to the re-envisioned Period IVc, the designation of Period VIa to cover the MBIII, the discovery of previously unreported and unanalyzed Period VIa–IVc exposures, and the reinterpretation of the later 2nd millennium BC settlements at Hasanlu. Hasanlu V is now considered to be the Late Bronze Age (1450–1250 BC). The designation "Iron I" now refers to Hasanlu IVc (1250–1050 BC), which Dyson previously used to denote an architectural phase of the monumental buildings of the citadel despite his assignment of an absolute date range (effectively making it a subperiod designation). Finally, there is cause to re-evaluate the later MBA (formerly the "Late Bronze Age") if we are to fully understand the origins of the MBW horizon as first conceptualized by Young. I have identified a Terminal MBII, essentially the 17th century BC, as a distinct transitional period, and I have introduced a MBIII to account for the poorly attested 16th and early 15th centuries BC in Ušnu-Solduz. These subperiods are best attested at Dinkha, but are almost certainly present at Hasanlu on the High Mound, where there are hints of MBIII occupation. A MBIII occupation at Hasanlu is also strongly suggested by graves of the period on the Low Mound.

In my reanalysis, I first defined Period V and Period IVc contexts where possible on the basis of recalibrated radiocarbon dates that fell between 1450–1250 cal BC for Period V and 1250–1050 cal BC for Period IVc. Appendix II presents the recalibrated radiocarbon dates from Period V, Period IVc, and from other periods and contexts relevant to the current reappraisal. Having identified a number of excavated contexts, I next turned to the stratigraphic sequences and the available ceramic assemblages from Hasanlu and, to a lesser extent, Dinkha. I was not able to examine archival records from Dinkha Tepe, which would have allowed a fuller incorporation of Dinkha III and IV, together spanning the 2nd millennium BC, into the reappraised sequence. I was able to study the mid-to-late 2nd millennium BC sherds from the Control Sounding area—Operations B9a-b and B10a-b.

Following the mid-2nd millennium BC emergence of MBW in the southern Lake Urmia Basin, the ware came to dominate local ceramic assemblages for roughly 600–700 years with relatively few changes in wares, forms, and styles to provide chronological markers for the archaeologist prior to the onset of the Iron II—the Late MBW horizon. This problem is compounded by a lack of ready comparanda for cross-sequence dating. A full appraisal of the ceramic assemblages of Period IVb is well beyond the scope of the present work. Only a preliminary study of the Period IVb ceramics was completed in order to provide a better understanding of Period IVc.

The MBW horizon is well attested at Hasanlu and Dinkha in mortuary contexts, but the LBA and Iron I graves naturally contain a specific subcomponent of the larger ceramic assemblages. While I have placed these graves into a relative sequence (see Chapter 5, Seriation), the mortuary assemblages appear to be fairly specialized and in developing the ceramic sequence I first turned to occupation deposits. By far the larger part of the MBW assemblage comes from the monumental Burned Buildings of the Period IVb citadel, and only a few excavated exposures went beneath these structures. Fairly extensive excavations were carried out on the eastern Low Mound of Hasanlu, but little of the pottery was drawn or saved. The Hasanlu dataset thus is decidedly biased both functionally and chronologically. The Period IVb and IVc ceramic assemblages are functionally biased since a disproportionate amount of material derives from elite or specialized contexts—elite residences, temples, and buildings of a military nature. The chronological bias is somewhat ironic. We have an amazing view of the MBW assemblage at around 800 BC, with hundreds of whole vessels found *in situ*; because of this remarkable preservation, however, the periods preceding the 9th century are poorly known, with few excavated exposures linking the IVb destruction level to Period V, for example. In the few areas where excavations were taken below the Terminal Period IVb destruction level of the Burned Buildings on the citadel, ancient building activities had often either removed all or substantial portions of the earlier MBW deposits or introduced intentional construction fill containing mixed earlier material. In some small soundings MBII deposits were encountered immediately below the Iron I-II levels of the citadel. Typical household assemblages represent other lacunae, except in a few rare instances on the Low Mound, where stratified MBW deposits were encountered and recorded. Operation V (see below) is the most noteworthy, as it is the best stratified, excavated, and recorded such unit (Danti 2011). The full publication of the artifactual assemblage of the Iron II settlement at Dinkha Tepe would be a welcome addition (Muscarella 1974:56–58), as it would provide insights into smaller, presumably non-citadel settlements that could then be compared to Hasanlu and Zendan (Thomalsky 2006).

We are on firmer footing with the ceramic chronology of our starting point, the earlier 2nd millennium BC. Prior to my study, the 16th century BC had been shown to mark the admittedly rough division between the "Late Bronze Age" KW assemblage (Young 1965; Dyson 1965)—best known for its painted and plain Fine Buff Ware with links to Greater Mesopotamia and the southern Caucasus—and the distinctive "Western Grey Ware" of the "Iron Age" of the southern Lake Urmia Basin. A transitional period had been encountered at Dinkha Tepe, but selective publication of specific wares and contexts had left it difficult to assess. The manner in which the MBA levels were presented, moreover, created the false impression of a rather homogenous MBII when the latter part of the period, the Terminal MBII, in fact witnessed fairly rapid change in keeping with broader trends known from Mesopotamia (see Chapter 4). I have designated the transitional material, roughly datable to the MBIII, as Hasanlu VIa (see below). The earlier portions of the MBA have been divided into Periods VIb (MBII) and VIc (MBI) on the basis of changes in the ceramic assemblages observed at Hasanlu and Dinkha. Monochrome Burnished Ware appears in the southern Lake Urmia Basin no later than Period VIa and so a preliminary overview of the period is included here. This study also assesses ceramics from the Terminal MBII levels of Dinkha (Dinkha IV Phase D, hereafter also Dinkha IVd to create a subperiod designation) since we must first consider this subperiod and the MBIII in order to gain clear insight into the origins of MBW. The Period VIa assemblage at Dinkha was not associated with architectural remains, but I have bracketed it in time using loosely associated radiocarbon dates and a re-interpretation of the stratigraphy as presented in various publications (see below). Monochrome Burnished Ware developed during the late 17th–early 16th centuries BC, steadily replacing the predominant MBA wares. While Dinkha provides our best view of the first half of the 2nd millennium BC, Dinkha Period III (the LBA) is only attested in trash deposits and graves, and Period II is known only from graves and a small excavated exposure of the settlement.

At Hasanlu the U22 Deep Sounding, Operation YZ27–29, and Operation RS22–23 provide the major stratified deposits of the 2nd millennium BC to be compared to Dinkha III–IV. Unlike Dinkha, these sequences contain no transitional material bridging the

Middle and Late Bronze Age, although they do offer a continuous sequence of the LBA and early Iron Age. YZ27–29 dates to the late LBA to Terminal Period IVb; it was not taken down deep enough to investigate the Period VI–V transition. RS22–23 spans the same period, but its primary importance is its exposure of LBA and Iron I–II architecture and it does not contribute substantially to the ceramic chronology due to the poor quality of the excavation and the shallow depth of excavation. The U22 Deep Sounding boasts the most complete sequence from Hasanlu, spanning the early EBA to the Medieval period. The mid-2nd millennium BC sequence, however, is hindered by both a gap—there is no Terminal MBII level equivalent to Dinkha IVd— and what is likely an error in excavation—in antiquity, the earliest LBA level was intentionally cut down into an earlier deposit, possibly of MBIII date, but the two stratigraphic units were collected as one (see below). Regardless of this oversight, this ancient cut removed most of the mid-Second millennium deposit. U22 also represented a poor location for the deep sounding since the area formed the edge/west slope of the mid-2nd millennium mound/settlement. The Well Sounding, which was more centrally located, revealed tantalizing evidence of mid-2nd millennium transitional material in its narrow confines. In sum, we therefore have a weak point in our chronological sequence between the rapid decline of the KW assemblage in the Terminal MBII as seen at Dinkha IVd and the flowering of the LBA documented in early Hasanlu V.

Our view of the LBA is admittedly overly reliant on relatively few excavated exposures at Hasanlu. The Iron I is somewhat better attested. Although Dyson originally defined this period as an architectural phase (Hasanlu IVc; Dyson 1965), I have expanded its definition to include those contexts dated by radiocarbon to the closing centuries of the 2nd millennium BC. The reexamination of this period and its addition to the sequence greatly enhances chronological resolution. A close reexamination of the ceramic assemblage in fact shows that the period can be discerned and distinguished from the LBA and Iron II, a promising development since the later 2nd millennium BC brought sweeping cultural changes to the southern Lake Urmia region, best attested at Hasanlu by the increased monumentality of its citadel, the heightened status differentiation observable in mortuary assemblages from the late LBA and Iron I, growing contacts with northern Mesopotamia, and the eventual spread of iron technology at the end of the period. The primary difficulty in constructing an archaeological chronology stems from the current paucity of individual ceramic type-fossils specific to the LBA MBW assemblage. Several largely unresolvable factors contribute to this situation, and it will continue to hinder our assessment of archaeological survey data, in particular. As previously mentioned, ceramic wares provide few chronological footholds. Ceramic forms in Period V are overall somewhat generic when weighted by frequency, likely owing to the nature of the excavated deposits, which are somewhat mundane when compared to the Period IVc and IVb assemblages recovered from monumental buildings. Many of the utilitarian vessel forms would remain in use for the period during which MBW was a dominant part of the ceramic assemblage.

The following sections provide an overview of the stratigraphic sequences and architecture of the later 2nd millennium BC at Hasanlu and, in outline form, Dinkha Tepe. The later 2nd millennium BC coincides with the Early and Middle MBW horizons in the southern Lake Urmia Basin. These are arranged chronologically, starting with the MBIII (Hasanlu VIa) and ending with the destruction of the Iron I (Hasanlu IVc) settlement at Hasanlu. Within this chronological framework, I have organized the evidence by major excavation areas since preliminary and interim reports were not produced by the Hasanlu Project, and important contextual relationships and patterns would be lost with a higher degree of synthesis.

The Terminal Middle Bronze II, Middle Bronze III, and Late Bronze Age at Dinkha Tepe: Dinkha IVd, IV/III, and III

Dinkha Tepe was first excavated by Sir Aurel Stein in 1936 for six days (Stein 1940:367–76, pls. XXI–XXII, XXX: 1, 3–5; figs. 103–5). He focused on the north slope of the tepe, near the right bank of the Gadar Çay, sinking two trenches and various small units subdivided into horizontal areas dubbed sections i–xi. By the 1960s, the river had washed away this part of the site. Sections iv–vii and ix were located at a higher elevation on the tepe (ibid., 369, Plan 23).

The uppermost 1.60 m of deposit contained a painted ware with "simple annular bands," not the more elaborate painted motifs "typical" of PKW (ibid., 371). In the lower part of these same operations and in sections i–iii and viii, located lower down the slope, Stein found PKW and a grey ware typical of the MBII. This material is the equivalent of Dyson, Muscarella, and Kramer's Dinkha Period IV Phases a–c. Stein describes the painted designs, beyond the annular bands, as, "mainly geometrical, consisting of such simple motifs as zigzags, chequers, circlets, crosses, triangles, hatching and cross-hatching, etc. used single or combined. Figures of stylized birds are found …" (ibid., 372).

Sections i–iii were continued down as a sounding to sterile soil. The original settlement had been situated on a low rise 1.50 m above the level of the river. Both of the main trenches also contained typical MBA incised and plain Simple Ware and presumably plain and incised KW.

Stein seems to have found evidence of a Terminal MBII occupation in the upper deposit—almost certainly equivalent to Dinkha IVd as defined by the Hasanlu excavations of 1966 and 1968. I would include Stein's upper deposit containing a KW assemblage painted with only annular bands, and the graves intrusive to the lower MBII deposit in the Terminal MBII subperiod. Cut into the KW deposit of sections iv and vi, Stein found two burials, here referred to as Burials 1 and 2, respectively. The level from which the burials were cut is not provided and only their depths relative to the river are given. Burial 1, a cist grave containing a child covered over by mudbricks and a large pot sherd, was intrusive to the upper 30–40 cm of the KW deposit of Dinkha IVa–c (Hasanlu VIb). It contained a tripod-footed buff jar with horizontally pierced lugs (Stein 1940: pls. XXI:2, XXX:4), another jar (not described or illustrated), and a coarse simple bowl of undescribed ware (ibid., pl. XXI:3). An identical tripod-footed jar and a similar bowl were found by the Hasanlu Project at Dinkha in a stone-built tomb in Operation B10a Stratum 8 Burial 27 (Figs. 4.12:F, Seriation). This intramural tomb has been dated to Dinkha IVd or my Terminal MBII—the 17th century BC (Rubinson 1991:388–90). Burial 2 was a cist grave, probably of a juvenile male, which contained a small jar with painted annular bands and another plain jar broken during excavation—the ceramics were not illustrated. This grave is most likely Terminal MBII or MBIII in date.

In the lower trenches, two additional graves were found within the KW deposit. Burial 3 of section ii (Stein 1940:373–74) was a jar burial of an adult. Burial 4 of section viii consisted of a stone-lined cist grave covered with stone slabs containing an adult male (Stein 1940:374–75). Grave goods included a dagger (1940: pl. XXI:4), bronze pins—at least one of which had an eyelet in the shaft (1940: pl. XXI:6)—a stone burnisher or whetstone (1940: pl. XXI:12), a large bronze ring (1940: pl. XXI:7), two small jars with ring bases (not illustrated), a jar painted with annular bands (1940: pl. XXI:1), four ovoid jars (1940: pl. XXIX:7, 16), an incised ovoid jar (1940: pl. XXIX:18), and four small jars (1940:XXX:1). The latter are of interest since one contained a flake of glass, which, given the ceramics, would support a date no earlier than the 17th century BC considering the history of glass manufacture in the Near East (McGovern, Fleming, and Swann 1991; Moorey 1999:192–93) and the disappearance of the annular painted ware in the region in the 16th century. Given the depth of the tomb and the massive amount of stone sealing it, the glass was almost certainly found in a primary context. This tomb is similar in terms of construction technique and objects to grave SK49 from Hasanlu, excavated in 1958 in Operation X and attributed to "Period VI," as well as the intramural tombs of Dinkha IV Phases C and D (see Chapter 5). The ceramics support a later MBII date.

The KW deposit recovered in the lower parts of Stein's trenches clearly belongs to the MBII (Dinkha IVa–c, Hasanlu VIb). The dating and nature of the upper deposit of sections iv–vii and ix, characterized by painted ceramics with simple annular bands, is more open to debate. Stein is quite definite on the character of the painted assemblage and mentions no MBW or Urmia Ware, with which he was quite familiar at the time of writing. In fact, I would argue Stein misidentified the KW assemblage as Chalcolithic because of the absence of these more familiar wares. Some scholars have proposed a period of Late KW to account for this depleted stylistic repertoire in Mesopotamia (see esp. Hrouda 1957:22, 35, 45; see also discussion in Hamlin 1971:298), and buff ware with simple annular bands continues, albeit rarely, into the MBIII in Ušnu-Solduz, as it does in the LBA of Mesopotamia. This simple painted ware from the upper levels of Stein's excavations at Dinkha and the material from the aforementioned graves closely resemble certain assemblages from Hasanlu that were previously designated "Period VI." Relatively little elaborately painted KW was found in occupation deposits at Hasanlu, with the exception of some painted sherds from the U22 Sounding and stray sherds from the Low Mound and surface. Painted Khabur Ware examples recovered from Hasanlu VI graves bore only annular band motifs. This in fact made a strong impression on the excavators, as Dyson's initial, informal designation for the period at Hasanlu was the "Ring Ware Phase." The reports published on the 1966 and 1968 seasons at Dinkha provided no evidence for such a distinction in the ceramic sequence of the mid-2nd millennium BC in nearby areas of the northern mound. Kramer had concluded, moreover, that there was little evidence for dividing the KW period (Hamlin 1971:136). A closer examination of Dinkha IVd nevertheless shows that PKW (Kramer Ware Ie) becomes markedly less common in the mid-2nd millennium BC, constituting only 8% of the assemblage in the Terminal MBII (Fig. 4.6, see Chapter 4). Annular bands are, moreover, the most frequently occurring motif applied to PKW, and this design element is the last to disappear. I would submit that Stein's later occupation deposits and graves date to Dinkha IVd—the Terminal MBII.

The Hasanlu Project conducted excavations at Dinkha Tepe in 1966 and 1968. Three horizontal clearances were undertaken (B9/10a–b, G10, and H1), as were well soundings, long test trenches, and small test pits (I–XI). Unlike Stein's trenches, LBA and early Iron Age graves and occupations had disturbed the lower levels in the Hasanlu Project operations. Operations B9a–b and B10a–b, four 10 m x 10 m units separated by 1 m baulks located on the northern mound, provide the best stratified sequence. In 1966, only B9a and B10a penetrated below Iron Age "trash levels." In 1968, the intervening baulk was removed and the excavation area truncated. This new operation, referred to as the Control Sounding, or Operation B9/10a, measured 5 m x 11 m and was carried down to sterile soil. This is the most complete stratigraphic sequence from Dinkha, spanning the late 3rd/early 2nd millennium BC to the LBA, although the MBIII and early LBA levels survived only as poorly preserved "trash deposits" which were cut by LBA and Iron I graves. The MBII ceramics from this sounding formed the core of Carol Hamlin's dissertation research (1971, 1974), and the Control Sounding and immediately adjacent operations constitute the most complete sequence of the Terminal MBII and MBIII for the southern Lake Urmia Basin.[1]

Dinkha Period IV: The Middle Bronze Age II

There are few published details regarding the earlier MBII or Dinkha IV Phases A–B. In the area of the Control Sounding, the 1968 excavations were carried down to sterile soil. Dinkha IVa consisted of "massive walling found in B9a stratum 11 and B9/10a stratum 4" (Hamlin 1971:33). Phase B, above this, consisted of "a series of superimposed walls" in B9/10a Stratum 3 (Hamlin 1971:33). Elsewhere at the central area of the site in Operation G/H, the excavators found a fortification (Muscarella 1968:194) or alternatively a massive mudbrick structure (Dyson 1973a:704) with a later occupation stratum abutting it (Dyson note in Lawn 1970:579; Appendix II, P-1429/1431). Three radiocarbon dates are available from the architectural level sealing the earlier use phase of the fortification/structure (Appendix II, P-1233, P-1430, P-1431),[2] and suggest the use-phase dates to the late 3rd–early 2nd millennium BC, or MBI, and a MBII date (Dinkha IVa–c) for the overlying level(s). The ceramic assemblage from this area contained a typical KW component—that is, not Terminal MBII—but was not published by Kramer due to the heavy disturbance noted in the area and the "massive and heavily reconstructed nature of the architecture there" (Hamlin 1971:35). Most of the ceramics presented here are from the uppermost levels.

In the B9/10a Control Sounding of the northern mound, Phases C and D consisted of the remains of three burned structures (Hamlin 1971:31),[3] along with three intramural tombs, two of which were stone-built (Dyson 1973a:704). Phase C architecture in B9/10a Stratum 9 included mudbrick walls on stone footings associated with stone-built tomb B10a B28, which contained plain KW (Muscarella 1968:195); the tomb was "surrounded by the joints of animals" (Hamlin 1971:33). As with the preceding periods, we know little of this settlement save that it was destroyed by fire and rebuilt on a similar plan, constituting Phase D. This latest Period IV occupation provides a rare dataset on the 17th–16th centuries BC. The Phase D plan—which consists of B9a and B10a Stratum 8 and B9/10a Strata 1 and 1a—has been published, as has a detailed report of stone-built intramural tomb B10a B27 (McGovern, Fleming, and Swann 1991; Rubinson 1991). Three radiocarbon samples (Appendix II) are available for the phase. Sample P-1450, "Charcoal from burned structural beams in fill near floor of final major structure of Bronze age in Area B10a(8)" (Lawn 1970:578), falls within the 18th–early 17th century and, given the material, provides the bottom date for the construction and use of the building. P-1232, "Charcoal from main floor of final Bronze age structure in Area B10a(8)" (Lawn 1970:578), is slightly later than the previous date, at 1750–1625 cal BC. P-1231 was described as "Charcoal from terminal Bronze age deposit (8) directly underlying Iron age fill (7)," and falls between 1620–1500 cal BC (Lawn 1970:578). I would assign the structure to the Terminal MBII and possibly the earlier MBIII. The ceramic assemblage of Phase D shows a dramatic decline in typical PKW and provides early attestations of wares and forms that occur in Hasanlu VIa/early Dinkha III (see Chapter 4). Tomb B10a B27 was constructed of stone slabs and contained between five and nine interments and almost certainly served as a family tomb, used over an unknown period of time. The tomb contained a large number of objects and 42 ceramic vessels. No painted ceramics were found in the tomb, although it did contain plain KW in standard forms along with other wares. Rubinson convincingly dates the tomb to the 17th–16th centuries BC on the basis of the artifact assemblage and the aforementioned radiocarbon dates associated with the adjacent architecture, arguing for a date in the 17th century specifically (Rubinson 1991:388–90).

Dinkha III/IV or Hasanlu VIa

Following the destruction of the final Period IVd occupation phase, layers of trash accumulated which

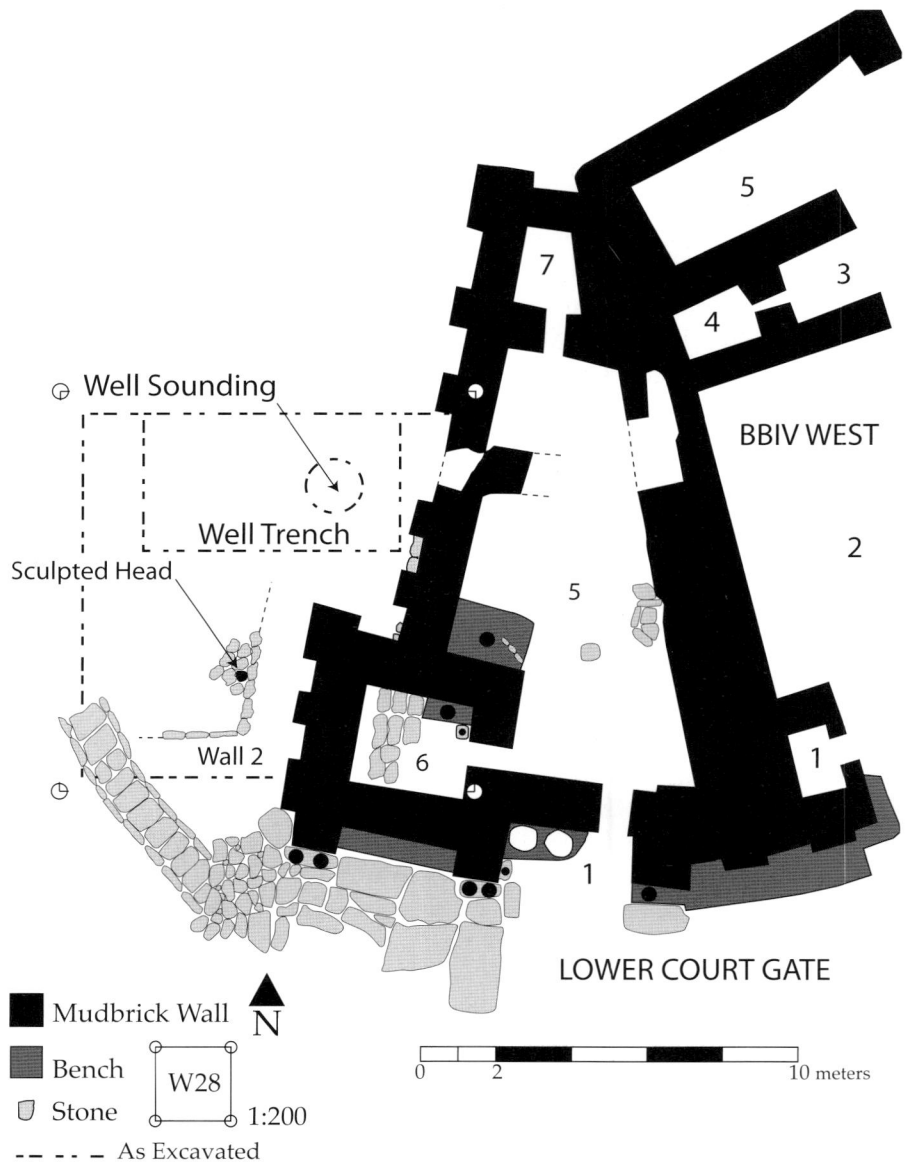

Fig. 3.1 Hasanlu Tepe: Operation W28/LXXX in 1960 showing the Well Trench and Well Sounding.

contained sherds of a polychrome painted ware commonly referred to as Urmia Ware (Edwards 1981, 1983, 1986; Muscarella 1994a; Rubinson 2004), along with Early MBW, often decorated with incised and impressed designs. Similar Dinkha IV/III transitional material was found in Operations B9a Strata 7–8, B10a Strata 5–7, and B10b Strata 3–5 (these collection units comprise a stratigraphically coherent chronological phase). The majority of the polychrome painted ware was found in B9/10a Stratum 7 and B10b Stratum 5. In the strata immediately above this phase, Urmia Ware was rare, but Early MBW was still present and the forms and decorative styles exhibited continuity with the earlier assemblage. The ceramic sequence of this lower "trash deposit" evinces close ties with those of the northern Lake Urmia Basin and the southern Caucasus.

The so-called trash deposits were cut by graves as they accumulated. It was challenging for the excavators to arrange the graves in a sequence, since the burial cuts were difficult to trace stratigraphically (Muscarella 1974:37). The graves can be placed in a general sequence by comparing the ceramics within them to stratified sequences of Late Bronze and Early Iron Age ceramics from Hasanlu occupation deposits independently dated by radiocarbon determinations, or when other object categories provide dates (see Chapter 5, Seriation). I attribute the "Dinkha III" graves to Hasanlu V (LBA or early Dinkha III) and Hasanlu IVc (Iron I or late Dinkha III) or, in sum, the period from approximately 1450–1050 BC. I date the majority to the latter part of this time range. "Trash pits" were also cut down from unspecified levels into the trash deposits, and three radiocarbon dates (Appendix II, P-1474, P-1475, P-1449) confirm the long period of time during which the trash deposits accumulated and, concomitantly, during which the cemetery was in use. These dates range from the late 16th–12th centuries BC. Only Burial 25, found in the lower post-Dinkha IV trash deposit, might be assigned to Period VIa (see Chapter 5; Muscarella 1974:39, 48, figs. 3, 5; 1994a:fig. 12.4.1). The grave reportedly contained an Early MBW tankard and an Urmia Ware jar. As discussed in Chapter 2, this grave resembles another from Hasanlu excavated by Stein (1940:401, fig. 110, pls. XXIV, 3, XXXI, 8). The fact that Dinkha Burial 25 cuts the lower "trash deposit" of Period VIa, which contains Urmia Ware and Early MBW sherds, sug-

gests this period of co-occurrence between these wares was significant and that the grave likely dates to early Hasanlu V and not VIa. The ceramic assemblage from the lower Dinkha trash deposit sealing Stratum 7 of the Control Sounding has virtually no painted ware and consists almost entirely of Early MBW and Incised and Impressed MBW, occasionally with white infilling (see Chapter 4). This suggests the continuation of close ties with the southern Caucasus. Such influences are not well attested in the Hasanlu dataset.

Hasanlu V and IVc: The High Mound of Hasanlu Tepe

The Central High Mound

The Well Sounding/Operation LXXX/Grid W28 (Periods IVc–IX)

In 1960, Dyson hired a local well digger to complete a sounding on Hasanlu's High Mound in Grid W28, with the goal of obtaining a more complete ceramic sequence (Fig. 1.3; Dyson 1967a). This sounding represents one of the few operations near the center of the High Mound which investigated the pre-MBW occupation, the other being Operation I in Grid T28 (see below). Both the Well Sounding and Operation I were located in the area of the site's central depression. These soundings verify that, as is the case with Dinkha Tepe, Hasanlu has Terminal MBII, MBIII, and early LBA levels at its center.

In the late 1950s, survey and excavations at other sites in the Ušnu-Solduz area (Dyson 1958; Dyson and Young 1960; Young 1959) had provided enough chronological information for the researchers to begin developing an archaeological sequence which stretched back to the pottery Neolithic, but there remained a need to verify the ordering of the chronological segments and to address possible gaps. Up to this time only isolated, extrusive sherds found in Iron Age contexts had hinted at pre-Period VI occupation on the High Mound. Soundings and graves excavated on the Low Mound had provided some evidence for earlier periods of occupation, dating back to Hasanlu VIIc—now known to be the early 3rd millennium BC (Danti, Voigt, and Dyson 2004; Dyson 1958:27).

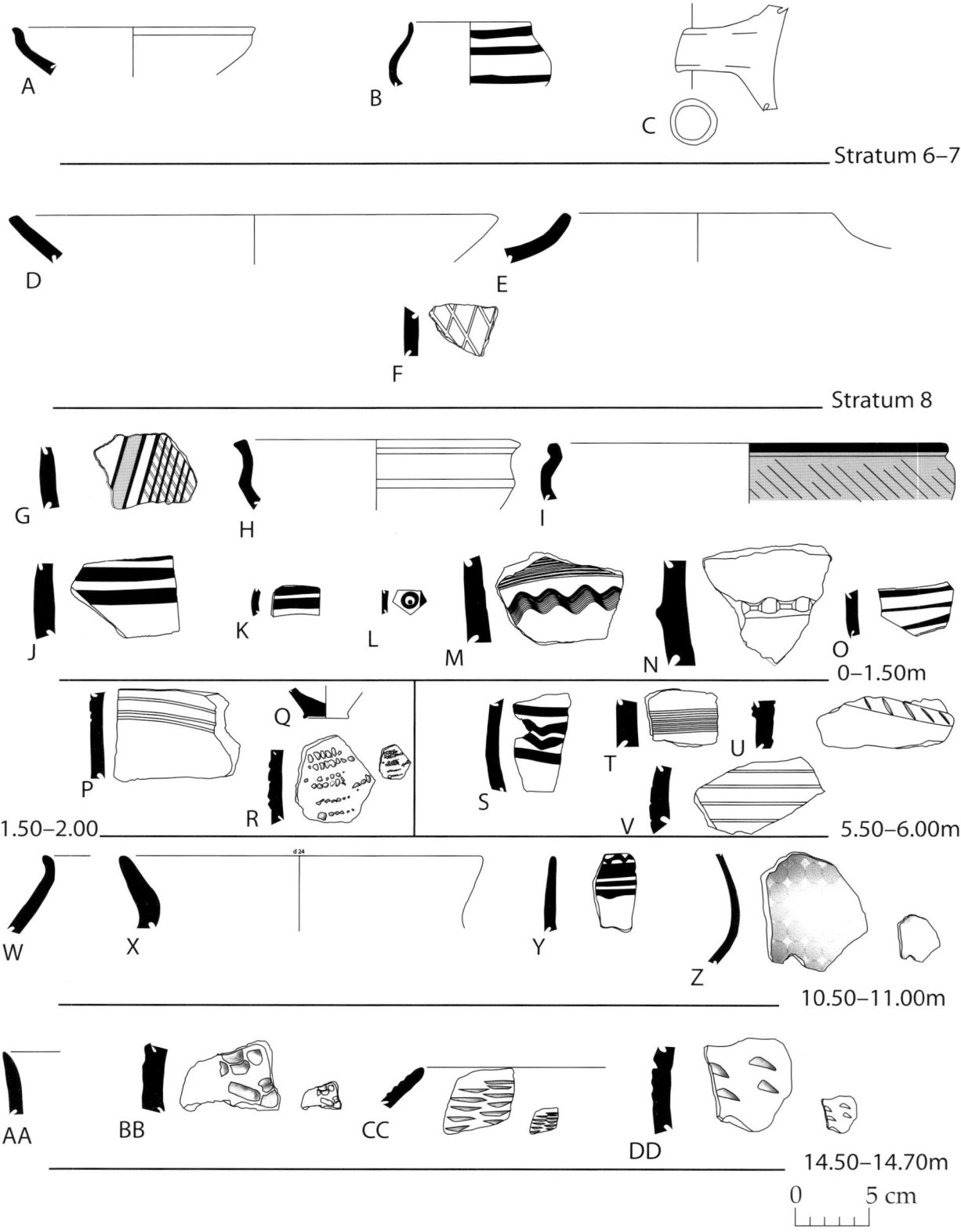

Fig. 3.2 Hasanlu Tepe: sherds from the Well Trench and Well Sounding (Op. LXXX/Grid W28).

Operation LXXX/Grid W28 was located on the east side of the 3- to 4-m deep depression near the center of the High Mound (Figs. 1.3, 3.1). The main focus of work in this area in 1960 was the well-preserved Upper Court Gate of Period IVb. At the level of Stratum 3b, while excavating an architectural phase likely attributable to early Period IVb, the operation was truncated. An area measuring 3.80 m x 6.80 m, the Well Trench, was then continued down an additional 0.85–1.30 m to Stratum 8 at the north end of the original operation. A few objects were collected from the sounding and cursory notes were taken on the pottery, but few sherds were drawn (Fig. 3.2:A–F). The circular Well Sounding measured 1.5 m in diameter and ended at a depth of 17.80 m below the base of "Period V" (Stratum 8), just below the water table but not yet at sterile soil (Pl. 3.1). Sherds were collected in arbitrary 50 cm units. According to the excavators, the Well Sounding produced 2.00 m of Period VI deposits, 6.50 m assigned to Period VII, 6.00 m of Period VIII (Pisdeli) material, 3.00 m of Period IX (Dalma), and *ex situ* sherds of early Period IX and Period X (Hajji Firuz) (Fig. 3.2:G–DD).

Notes on the pottery from Strata 6–7, collected as a single unit, and Stratum 8 provide few details beyond confirming that the assemblage contained an Early MBW component. The few sherds that have been illustrated show at least one annular band–painted KW shouldered beaker from Strata 6–7 (Fig. 3.2:B). Stratum 8 yielded a MBW bowl of Type 1a (see Chapter 4), dated to the mid-2nd millennium BC or Period VIa or early Period V (Fig. 3.2:D), as well as a sherd of pattern-burnished MBW (Fig. 3.2:F). The units immediately below Stratum 8 yielded a sherd of polychrome Urmia Ware, almost certainly a Type 6a jar in light of the sherd profile and painted motif (Fig. 3.2:G; see Chapter 4), a weathered sherd of a distinctive Urmia Ware bowl (Fig. 3.2:I)—a type well known at Dinkha in the MBIII (Rubinson 2004)—along with PKW (Fig. 3.2:J–L, O) and other MBA material (Fig. 3.2:M, N). The W28 sequence, from Stratum 6 of the Well Trench to the 1.50 m depth marker of the Well Sounding, strongly suggests chronological continuity during the mid-2nd millennium BC at the central Hasanlu High Mound which is undocumented elsewhere at the site, with the possible exception of Hasanlu Operation I. Bearing in mind the arbitrary collection units used in the Well Sounding, this deposit seems to cover the MBIII–early LBA and is similar to Dinkha Tepe's Control Sounding except for the absence of Incised and Impressed MBW.

Operation I (Periods VIc–I)

Operation I (Grid T28) was excavated in 1956 in the central depression of the High Mound near a small trench excavated by Stein in 1936 (Pls. 3.2a, 3.2b). The central depression was initially believed to be an ancient well, although this was later disproved by excavation. Operation I measured 9 m x 7 m but was truncated to 3 m x 7 m in its lower levels (Stratum 5c and below) and reached a maximum depth of 4.6 m below the surface (Fig. 1.3). The lowest two strata, Strata 6a and 6c, consisted of ashy matrices. I have found no evidence these lowest levels were disturbed. In particular, Strata 6a and 6c were sealed by two strata of ashy fill (Stratum 5d) which were in turn overlain by two intact floor levels associated with a wall and a stone paving of "Period IV" date (Strata 5a–5c). Strata 5d–5e yielded MBW ceramics and a radiocarbon sample (Stratum 5e, P-0185) ranging from 1400–1100 cal BC, or Periods V–IVc (Figs. 3.3, 3.4). I date Stratum 6a to Period VIb based on its ceramic assemblage (see Chapter 4, Fig. 4.14), and Stratum 6c to Period VIc. Stratum 6c contained SW and incised SW. The assemblage recovered from Stratum 6a was comprised of PKW, incised SW, MBA Grey Ware (GW), and small amounts of MBW. The excavators recorded the Period 6a deposit as "Ring Ware" and "Grey Ware" in excavation records. The Stratum 6a assemblage is another tantalizing hint that there are deposits at Hasanlu of the mid-2nd millennium BC that would fill in the Period VI–V transition. The PKW recovered in Stratum 6a is not "Ring Ware," but rather "Classic" KW—typical of Dinkha A–C. Operation I along with the Well Sounding and Well Trench demonstrate that Early MBW and painted wares were found in association with one another, despite numerous claims to the contrary in the subsequent publication record.

The Northwestern High Mound

In 1962, T. Cuyler Young began the excavation of a new series of trenches on the northwestern High

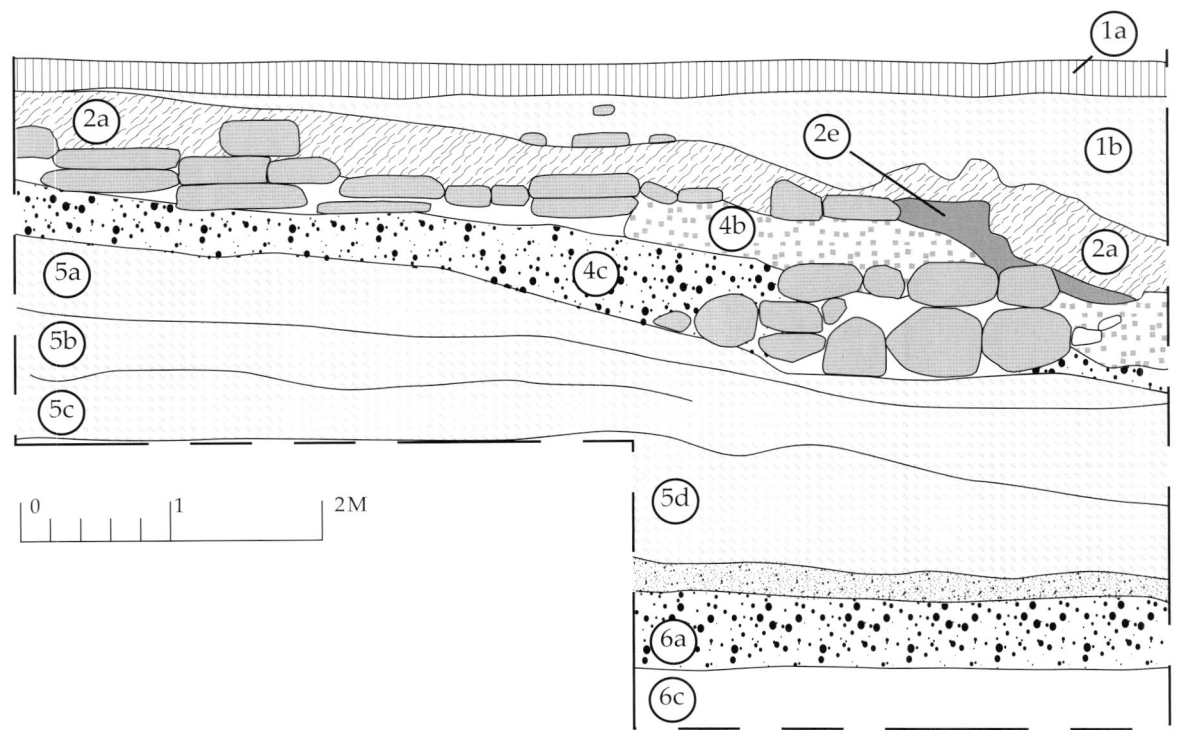

Fig. 3.3 Hasanlu Tepe: north section of Operation I (T28).

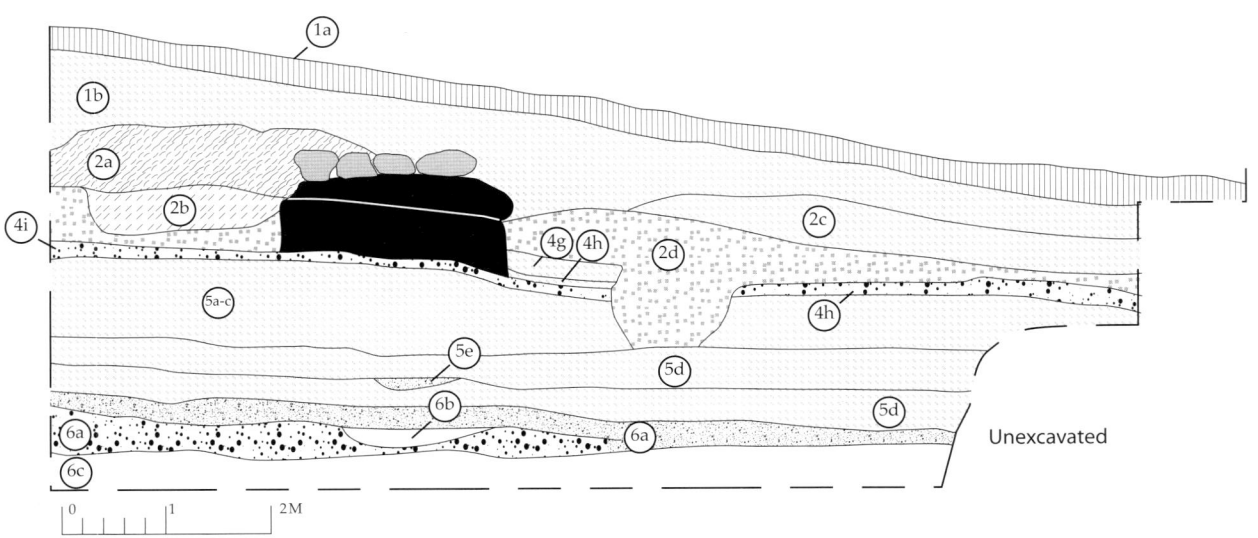

Fig. 3.4 Hasanlu Tepe: east section of Operation I (T28).

Mound. Work started with narrow test trenches strategically located along the sloping surface of the mound, most of which ran east to west. This was followed by the excavation of two large horizontal exposures that would reveal Period IVb BBIII and the west end of BBVIII in the north and BBVI, BBVII and BBVIIE in the south (Fig. 3.5). Work continued in this area until the close of large-scale excavations in 1974. Soundings were possible in this quadrant of the High Mound since it often contained poorly preserved Period IVb remains, as well as what were large open spaces in the Iron II.

A review of the entire northwestern High Mound sequence is well outside the scope of the current work, but a review of the stratigraphy and some of the basic premises that informed the excavators would be useful in guiding the current discussion. The shape of the northwest citadel exposure reflects the topography of the mound and the extent of well-preserved Iron II architecture in that area of Hasanlu. In the northwest, the excavators were essentially tracing an arc of monumental structures aligned to the contours of the mound's edges, the central depression, and by default, the Iron II fortifications and large, unexplored open space which separated the two major areas of Iron II monumental architecture of the northwest and southern citadels, respectively. The Iron II fortification wall was difficult to trace in all areas of the High Mound since it had been obscured and damaged by the overlying Period IIIc (Urartian) wall, but small exposures were achieved in Grids QR20 (Fig. 3.6) and at the northwest end of BBIII (see below). On the northern High Mound, a possible Iron II fortification wall was also found in Operation II, in Grids MN28 (Fig. 3.7); on the southern mound, certain architectural features in Operation DD30–31 suggest the presence of such a wall, as well (see below).

Burned Building III and the Dating of the Hasanlu IVb Destruction

The northern end of the northwestern mound exposure was dominated by the large columned-hall structure dubbed BBIII, most likely an elite residential compound, as well as the southwest corner of BBVIII. Southwest of BBIII was the BBVIIE gateway, occasionally referred to as the "Double Gate." As with other structures originally assigned a Hasanlu IVb date, these buildings were burned and contained victims of an attack on the settlement and a large number of *in situ* finds. The attribution of BBIII to the Terminal Period IVb citadel as originally defined by Dyson forms a crucial part of our understanding of Hasanlu, since contexts within this structure provided the short-lived radiocarbon samples (carbonized grain and grapes) that were used in establishing the dating of this destruction (Dyson and Muscarella 1989: fig. 13). Magee has recently challenged the association of the terminal phase of BBIII with the rest of the terminal Iron II citadel, the short-lived characterization of the BBIII radiocarbon samples, the absolute dating of Period IVb using samples from the northwest citadel and, concomitantly, the dating of the destruction of the entire Iron II citadel (Magee 2008). Medvedskaya had similarly questioned the prevailing dating of the destruction (Medvedskaya 1988), arguing for a later date in the 8th century BC on the basis of styles of horse harness and ivory carving, which triggered a detailed response from Dyson and Muscarella (1989) and another article by Medvedskaya (1991). The rebuttal Dyson and Muscarella put forth has gained strength from the recent re-dating of the destruction of Gordion (DeVries et al. 2003). While it behooves us to challenge the assumptions embedded in the original interpretations of Hasanlu, particularly in the case of the dating of various excavated exposures from the northwest citadel, Magee's assertions cannot be maintained (see also Danti 2011). In large part, his arguments are flawed because they lack a firm foundation—they are based on the early publication record, which is widely known to be error-ridden, contradictory, incomplete, and lacking in detail (cf. Muscarella 2006).

Magee's arguments are founded on four propositions. First, Magee rightly points out that all short-lived radiocarbon samples bearing on the Terminal Period IVb destruction—assuming there is only one such destruction event—were collected from within BBIII and proceeds to question the association of BBIII with the rest of the citadel: "Only Building III has provided samples that might be relevant to the destruction: this building is located at some distance from the main group of buildings and there is *no published evidence* of it being stratigraphically linked to the other citadel buildings that have provided the bulk of the Hasanlu IVb material" (Magee 2008:102, my emphasis). Magee also cites the alleged paucity of objects from BBIII as evidence of its stratigraphic "isolation"

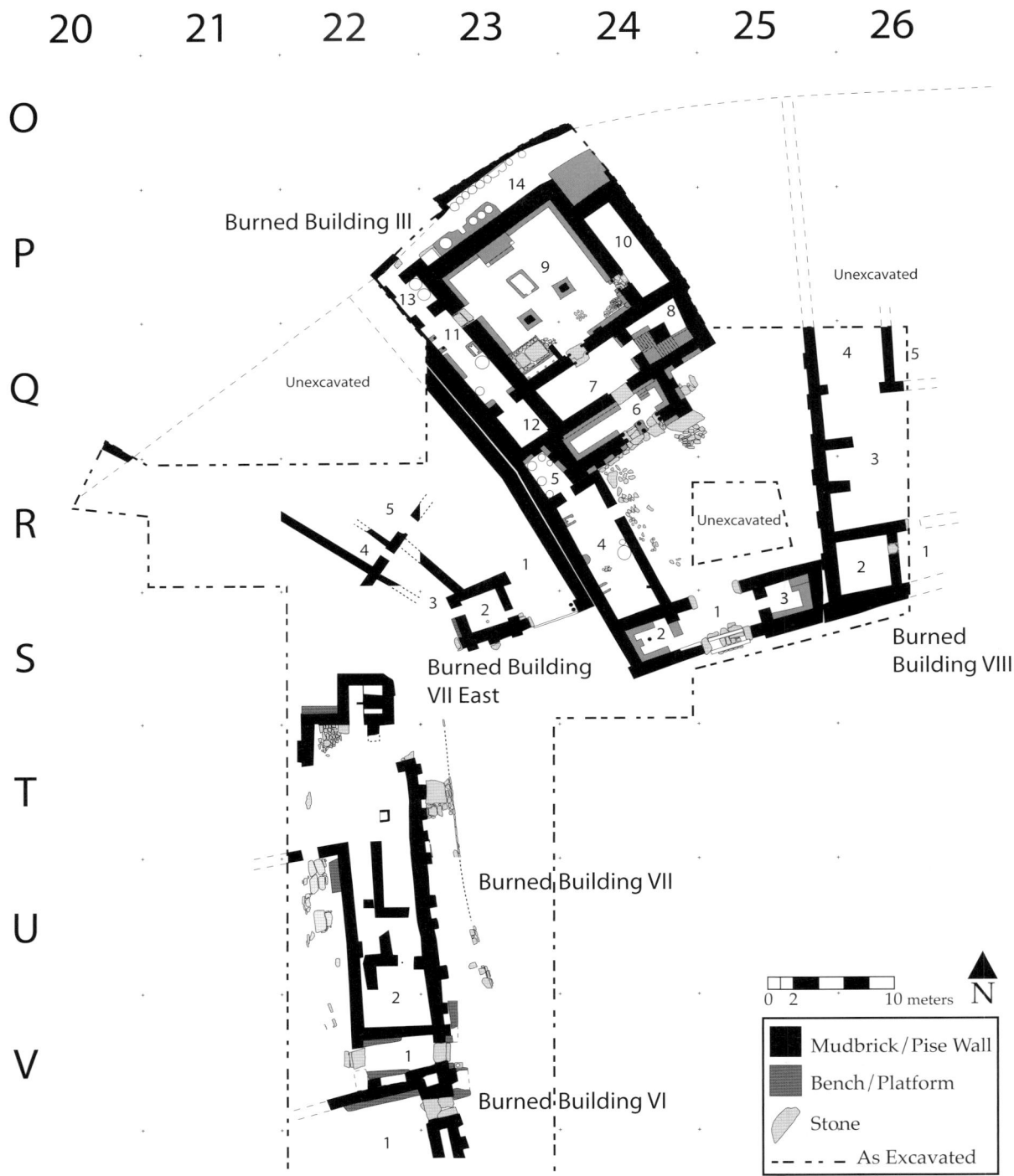

Fig. 3.5 Hasanlu Tepe: the northwest citadel in Period IVb.

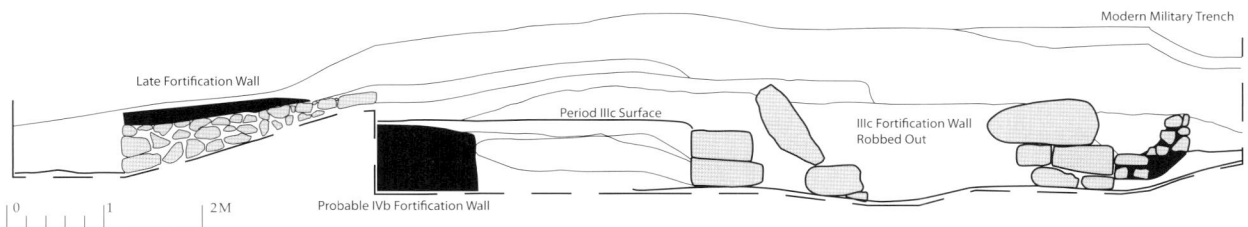

Fig. 3.6 Hasanlu Tepe: north section of Operation QR20 showing IIIb fortification wall and the probable IVb fortification wall.

and independent destruction date (2008:91–92). While it is not the objective of the current volume to present Period IVb in detail, by default this project involved the careful examination of Period IVb stratigraphy, especially in the area of BBIII. In short, BBIII is stratigraphically connected to other Period IVb contexts such as BBVIII, BBVIIE, BBVII, and BBVI. The building contained at least 26 victims from a Terminal Period IVb attack (Pl. 3.3a) and approximately 1,370 objects (Pl. 3.3b). Were we to re-date the Terminal IVb destruction level of BBIII it would set off a chain reaction following stratigraphic and architectural connections that would result in the re-dating of the entire northwest citadel and all the victims found there in the burned level. This does not falsify Magee's theory but obviously renders specious his main premise—that the northern and western citadel and the southern citadel were destroyed in separate major conflagrations with scores of victims and thousands of objects left by each separate event. Each putative event would represent the end of Iron II occupation in that respective area—Kroll has recently asserted the so-called Squatter Occupation of Hasanlu IVa is nonexistent (Kroll 2010:22).

Second, Magee has also questioned the relationship between the samples from BBIII and the building's function, arguing "the function of Building III casts doubt on the relationship between the charred grain samples and the destruction of the building" (2008:102). This implies that the association of the samples with the destruction event is questionable (the samples are earlier in terms of context), the short-lived characterizations of the samples are invalid (they are, for example, the remains of carbonized dung fuel,

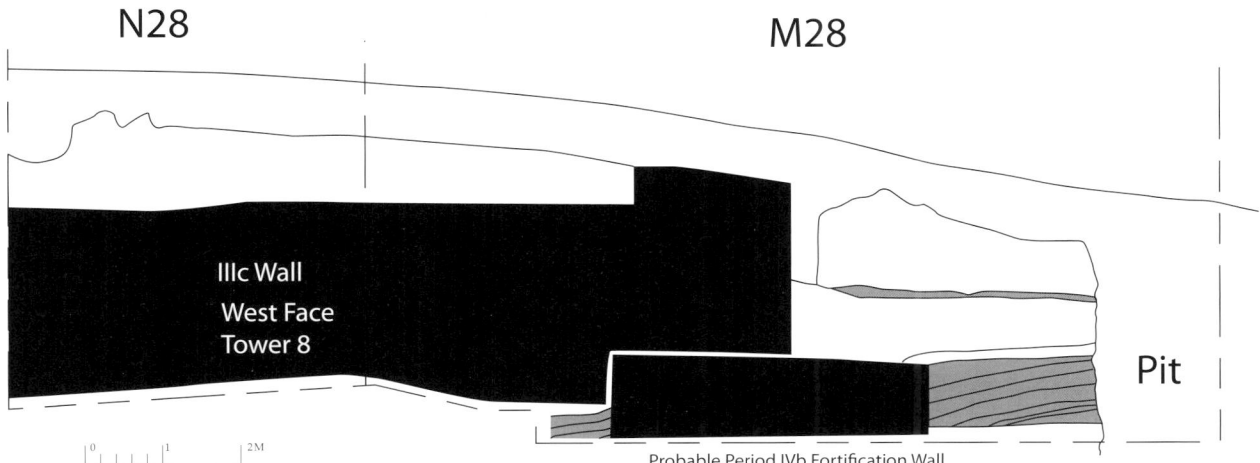

Fig. 3.7 Hasanlu Tepe: Operation II west section showing IIIb fortification wall and the probable IVb fortification wall.

ergo the behaviors they represent are substantially earlier than the destruction), and the sample materials disagree with the imputed uses of the building (plant remains are out of place given the uses of the building and are therefore contextually suspect). This is simply not the case. Stratigraphically, the grain samples were found on the final floor surface of the ground-floor level of the building, covered in a thick layer of burned destruction debris that was in turned sealed by a massive layer of mudbrick collapse. The major wall collapses occurred during or immediately after the fire—the state of preservation of fragile carbonized remains proves this. The samples collected from BBIII are foodstuffs stored in the building in jars and bins—such foodstuffs would date to just before the destruction event. Finally, BBIII naturally did not have a single function, and there was abundant evidence of food preparation on a large scale. BBIII was a building complex with 14 rooms on its ground floor, a second floor, and a multitude of activity areas, including a columned hall, anteroom, portico room, large kitchens (Rooms 11 and 14), storerooms containing fixed storage jars, as well as a large enclosed courtyard entered through a fortified gatehouse (Rooms 1–3) flanked by a *kitchen complex* (Room 4) *and a storage facility containing foodstuffs* (Room 5). One group of radiocarbon samples consisting of clean barley (Appendix II, P-860, 861, and 863) was collected from the floor of a kitchen/grain processing area (Room 4, North Kitchen, Pl. 3.4) in association with *in situ* storage jars, bins, grinding stones, ash deposits, and an oven built against the west wall (Fig. 3.5). All of the grain recovered was *Hordeum polystichum* (Botanical Notes, Hasanlu Publication Archive). The evidence was so overwhelming that T. Cuyler Young concluded his assessment of the area with the statement, "The evidence, taken together, clearly indicates that the room was a kitchen—cooking area—probably the main kitchen area which supported all of Burned Building No. III" (Hasanlu Excavation Notebook 23:4, Hasanlu Publication Archive). While this kitchen was not mentioned in later reports, Young did mention the kitchen in Room 11 (1966:53). The grain samples were collected from lenses of grain associated with the bins; they are not flotation samples from fuel deposits (i.e., carbonized in the bread oven). Another radiocarbon sample—P-577, consisting of carbonized grapes and a fig—was recovered from inside a small buff jar (HAS62-209) in the upper part of the destruction deposit in Room 5. This storeroom adjoined the kitchen/grain processing area and had five large storage jars set into mudbrick benches (Pl. 3.5).[4] The small jar containing the grapes and fig lay against the west wall in a heavy ash deposit sealed by wall collapse. The exterior of the jar containing the fig and grapes—not a cooking vessel—was fire-blackened almost certainly during the conflagration (Table 3.1). The excavator believed the jar and many other artifacts had fallen from the upper story or the roof during the fire that destroyed the building.

Another group of grain samples was recovered from the south end of the BBIII complex, in the area generically described as the "gate building" (Stuckenrath, Coe, and Ralph 1966:349–50). These samples were collected in 1962. Examination of the excavation notebooks has revealed these grain samples to have come from the south end of Room 4, which was

TABLE 3.1. Radiocarbon Samples from Burned Building III North Kitchen (Room 4 North) and Storeroom (Room 5)

P-0860	Room 4 North Kitchen	Carbonized grain (*Hordeum polystichum*): pile of grain on floor, south of oven (Sample 62-26)
P-0861	Room 4 North Kitchen	Carbonized grain (*Hordeum polystichum*): pile of grain on floor (Sample 62-24 or -25)
P-0863	Room 4 North Kitchen	Carbonized grain (*Hordeum polystichum*): pile of grain east of grinding stone (Sample 62-24 or -25)
P-0577	Room 5 from possible upper story	Carbonized grapes (*Vitus vinifera*, Sample 62-22): in jar HAS62-209 with fig (*Ficus carica*, Sample 62-23)

TABLE 3.2. Radiocarbon Samples from Burned Building III Room 4 South

| P-0905 | Room 4 South Kitchen | Carbonized grain (*Hordeum polystichum*): grain in smashed storage jar near hearth (Sample 62-149) |
| P-0906 | Room 4 South Kitchen | Mixed carbonized grain (*Triticum vulgare, Triticum dicoccum, Hordeum polystichum*): grain scattered on floor (Sample 62-12) |

excavated within the operation that also cleared BBII Room 2 and the west end of Room 1 (the gate). The samples are from two smashed storage jars beside an oven built against the building's west wall and from a lens of mixed grain on the floor just to the north (Pls. 3.3b, 3.6). The area contained a large amount of pottery and quern stones, and represents a second kitchen.

Two short-lived samples from the area of BBIII are difficult to account for due to irregular research methods and publication errors. Magee notes that sample P-0907, "dried grapes from vase on floor of BBIII," is not listed as "charred" in the attendant publication (Magee 2008:100; Stuckenrath 1963:350). Carbonized-grape radiocarbon sample P-0577, consisting of "dried grapes from Operation R-24, Stratum 3, Area 2, inside Container 8," is similarly not listed as carbonized (Stuckenrath 1963:88), although this fact is not noted by Magee. Magee reasons that P-0907, and by extension P-0577, cannot be from the destruction level of BBIII since they were not carbonized/burned (2008:100). These nevertheless represent two samples taken from among the same grapes found within Buff Ware jar HAS62-209, which was not found on the floor and was incorrectly and inadequately described in the attendant publication. The object card for this jar records, "Has C14 sample of *burned* grapes inside" [emphasis my own]. With this established, there is no reason to discount the samples. With regard to preservation, in the Room 4 North Kitchen the excavators also found a string of "dried" figs on a copper/bronze tray, such was the preservation (Pl. 3.7). The excavators doubtless meant the figs were in a dried state *prior to the fire*—that is, they had been dried and strung as a form of food preparation and preservation. In other parts of the building, preservation was so good due to carbonization (the Terminal IVb fire) and rapid deposition (the building's collapse) that samples of textiles, rope, and even hair were collected. Such samples were not listed as "burned," "carbonized," or "charred," however—the excavators working in the Terminal Period IVb destruction level were immersed in the ruins of a burned city and often the evidence of burning simply was deemed self-evident and thus was not recorded. The "charred" or "dried" grapes and other organic material attributed to Period IVb are from the Terminal IVb destruction level of BBIII based on *basic principles of stratigraphy*—as Magee states, "if it stratigraphically belongs to IVb, then it belongs to IVb" (2008:102), issues of semantics in earlier publications aside. The high degree of preservation in the Burned Buildings of Hasanlu IVb was caused by direct burning, high temperatures, and the rapid deposition of thick layers of building collapse.

P-0865 constitutes another problematic sample of "charred wheat from Floor 3 of citadel" (Stuckenrath et al. 1966:350). Magee writes that, "a sample initially published as coming from Hasanlu IVb almost excludes the possibility of this level coming to an end at 800 BC. The stratigraphic position of this sample has not been convincingly reassigned in any publication" (2008:102). First, it is in fact a level, or a stratum, and re-dating a stratum does not necessitate changing the dating of an entire occupation. This is an oversimplification in which Magee slips into the same interpretative mindset as the early excavators, who misrepresented the stratigraphy of the site in preliminary publications such that it seemed to have a "IVb level," a "IVc level," etc. Magee rightly notes that subsequent publication (e.g., Dyson and Muscarella 1989:5) changed the attribution to "IV grain" and dated the sample to Period IIIb without further explanation. Magee declares that, "It is difficult to understand what this means. If it stratigraphically belongs to IVb, then it belongs to IVb—it cannot be placed into a later period on the basis of its age." (2008:102). While this is certainly sound in principle, it represents a severe contradiction of his own logic with regard to the seven samples sealed within the ruins of BBIII—five on the destruction-level floor and two sealed in a jar—which he throws out on vague notions of association, sample characterization, and building function. Most important is the case of P-0865: Stuckenrath lists this sample as "undersized" (Stuckenrath et al. 1966:350) and, on this basis alone, it should not have been used for dating! Excavation records show this sample came from R23 Stratum 3 Floor 3. This sample was the remainder of the wheat used in sample P-0576—too little was left for an accurate date, but oddly the radiocarbon determination was published with little explanation and, as with so many other aspects of Hasanlu, *literally* took on a life of its own. R23 Floor 3 is the Terminal Period IVb surface in the area of gateway BBVIIE, located just to the southwest of BBIII. The excavation supervisor did not record the exact location from which this sample was collected in 1962: a large pithos was found in this area sitting on the Terminal IVb floor surface, and it is likely but not certain that the wheat came from there. The area inside this former gateway was the focus of heavy building activity and pitting following the Terminal IVb destruction. Many of these pits and wall trenches, which constitute what can best be described as a complex stratigraphic situation, were not noted during excavation. In the end, samples P-0576 and P-0865 should be thrown out due to a lack of information on their exact contexts, the minor problems with the R23 excavation, and the insufficient size of sample P-0865.

Magee concludes that "the carbon-14 dates do not…reinforce an 800 BC date for a radiocarbon event in this building or anywhere in the citadel" (2008:102); closer examination of the contexts of the BBIII carbonized grain samples, however, has revealed no reason to question their association with the Terminal Period IVb phase of the kitchens of BBIII, and the carbonized grapes were found in the same jar in a sealed deposit within the building. The pooled mean of the short-lived dates for the Terminal Period IVb phase of BBIII is 836–808 cal BC at the one-sigma level and 895–802 cal BC at the two-sigma level (Fig. 3.8). We see that the current radiocarbon evidence supports a dating of around 800 BC *or slightly earlier* for the close of Terminal Hasanlu IVb.

While there is little support for Magee's reinterpretation, his points that we need more radiocarbon dates from Hasanlu IVb and that we must challenge long-held assumptions regarding Hasanlu are valid and constructive. To achieve the latter goal, however, we must work from the excavation records and collections rather than the early publication record, or we risk substituting modern textual exegesis for archaeological interpretation—that is, substituting researching the Hasanlu Project for researching Hasanlu. Admittedly, in the past conducting primary research on Hasanlu was difficult, to say the least, and redressing the project's shortcomings will require diligence, time, and patience. While the radiocarbon dates support a late 9th century BC destruction of Period IVb, some scholars have argued for an 8th century BC destruction, citing object styles. It is beyond the scope of the present work to address this complex topic here, but suffice it to say that, as I have shown with the radiocarbon samples, the archaeological contexts provided in previous publications are equally an issue for many of the small finds. From the standpoint of stylistic arguments, I would counter that the lack of 8th century BC MBW at Hasanlu similar to that of Zendan-e Suleiman I carries more interpretive weight (Thomalsky 2006). Ultimately, I believe the door remains open for a slightly later *or earlier* dating of the citadel's Terminal Period IVb destruction.

The Northwest Citadel in the MBA, LBA, and Iron I

Excavations were carried below the Period IVb destruction in several places in the northwestern High Mound, providing exposures of the MBA, LBA, and Iron I settlements. Evidence for an earlier destruction or destructions associated with MBW was found in all such exposures. The dating of this destruction is difficult to ascertain since it is not pinned to radiocarbon determinations in the area of the northwest High Mound, but a similar sequence was encountered in most areas of the High Mound and on the Low Mound in Operation V (Danti 2011). This earlier burned level is associated with wall stubs and cut-down architectural remains that generally determined the alignment and plans of the superimposed Period IVb structures; the Iron II buildings occasionally incorporated these earlier remains. The earlier destruction is not associated with human victims or large numbers of artifacts; in fact, these earlier deposits were often associated with few artifacts at all. When ceramics were collected and separated from overlying terminal Period IVb con-

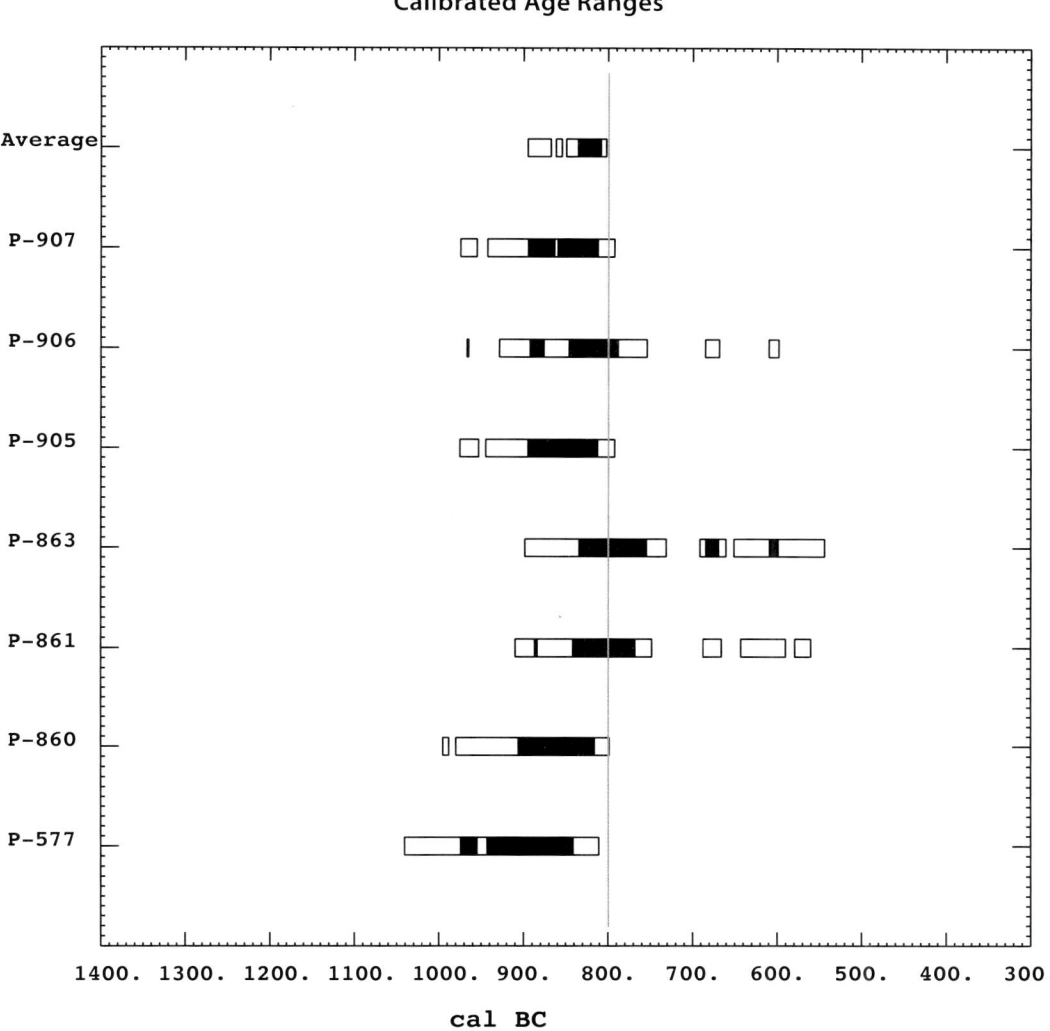

Fig. 3.8 Hasanlu Tepe: calibrated one-sigma radiocarbon date ranges and pooled mean from carbonized grain and grape samples found in the Terminal IVb phase of Burned Building III.

texts, it consistently appears the earlier destruction is associated with material of a Period IVc–early Period IVb date (see Chapter 4). This has previously been interpreted as a widespread, single destruction of the site at the end of Period IVc—that is, sometime during the 11th century BC—based on radiocarbon dates from the southern High Mound (Dyson and Muscarella 1989:1). These samples are mostly carbonized wooden structural elements from the Terminal Period IVb destruction phase of the southern High Mound, which provide a date for the early Period IVb rebuilding of the destroyed IVc structures. The settlement was rebuilt after a widespread Period IVc destruction in Dyson's conceptualization of the occupational sequence. Given the current scarcity of radiocarbon dates for the period, particularly from short-lived samples, it is difficult to further investigate these issues.

The architectural remains of Hasanlu V and IVc reveal the long history of development of the famous Iron II citadel of Terminal Hasanlu IVb (Figs. 3.5, 3.9). The Iron II citadel is an adaptation of the Iron I. Most Iron II building plans were based on Period IVc and early Period IVb precursors. Below Period IVc levels, the similarities begin to erode away (Fig. 3.10),

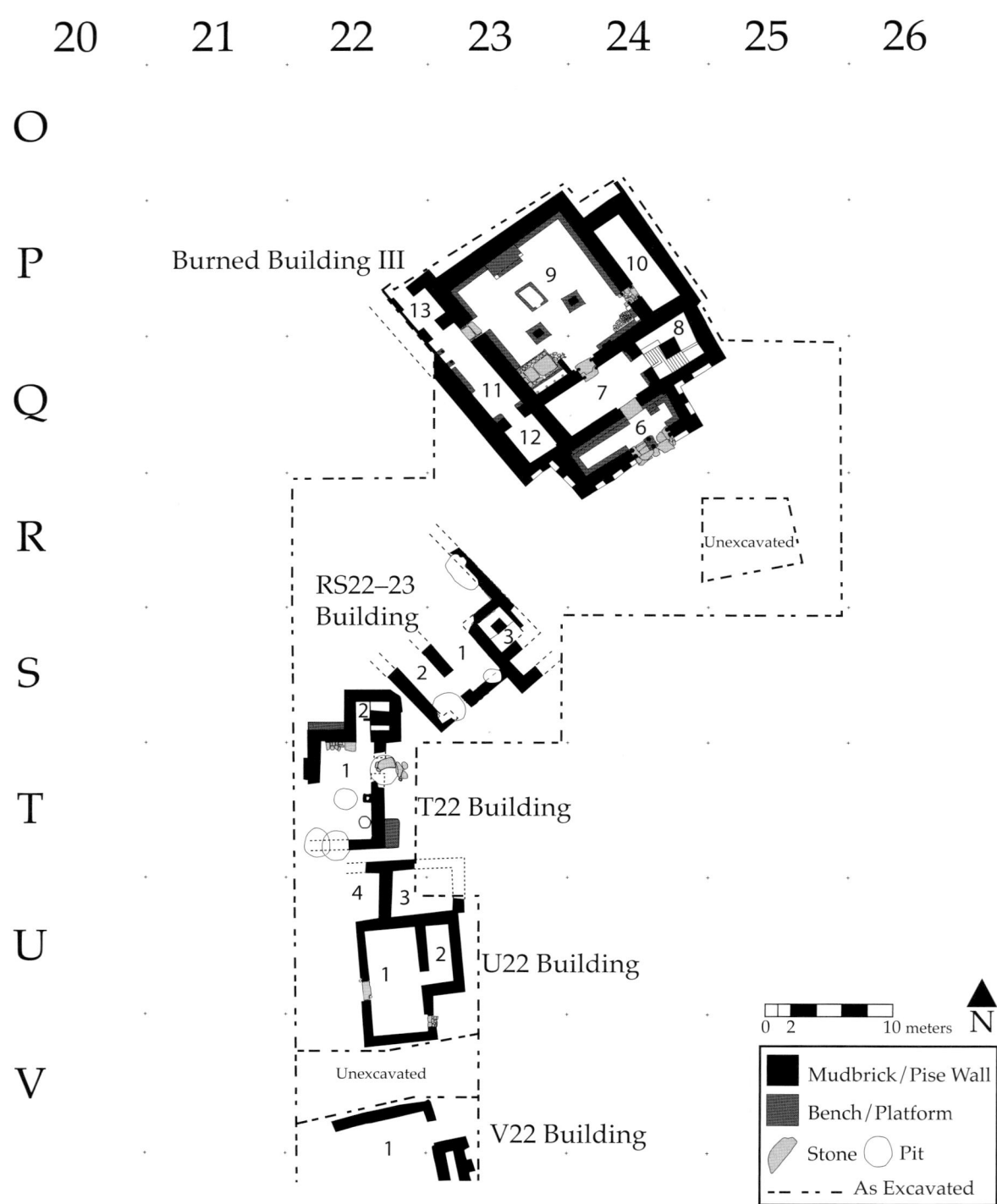

Fig. 3.9 Hasanlu Tepe: the northwest citadel in Period IVc.

although the layout of High Mound architecture in the LBA is familiar, as are building plans and general patterns in the use of space. It is currently impossible to comment on the transition from the MBA to the LBA at Hasanlu with regard to architecture and stratigraphic relationships. There are simply too few excavated exposures of the mid-2nd millennium BC, and in the one major sounding to have reached these levels, located in Operation U22, early LBA construction activities appear to have removed earlier remains.

The LBA and Iron I Northwest Citadel

The U22 Sounding

The U22 deep sounding is the most complete archaeological sequence from Hasanlu, in part due to the fact that its lower levels—Periods VIc–VIIc—were excavated in the 1970s using more systematic archaeological recording and collection strategies. The upper levels (Periods I–VIb), largely excavated in the 1962 campaign, were not as well recorded, but the excavators did recognize the importance of the pre-Period IVb artifactual assemblage and retained the majority of the ceramic diagnostics for Periods IVc–VIb. This assemblage formed a significant portion of T. Cuyler Young's dissertation (1963), although the ceramic assemblage was not and never has been presented despite its critical role in the later interpretation of the EWGW horizon. The alleged presence of a gap was of major significance, the gap having been variously interpreted as either cultural—fitting into migrationist interpretations—or stratigraphic. In later publications this gap became synonymous with the disjuncture between the Bronze Age and the earliest Iron Age. Portions of surrounding excavation grids, including U23, T22, and V22–23, were also excavated to varying depths below the Iron II occupation, but the maximum depths in these areas did not typically penetrate below the Iron I levels with the exception of T22 (see below). Much has rested on the interpretation of the small U22 Sounding and, as will be seen, it should not have been used to argue for a sudden arrival of a fully developed EWGW horizon at Hasanlu.

The Excavation of the U22 Sounding

The U22 Sounding is perhaps the most important excavation currently available from Ušnu-Solduz for understanding the 3rd and 2nd millennia BC. With this in mind, it seems necessary to review its history of excavation rather than to proceed in a traditional bottom-up chronological approach. The phasing of the various strata and the periodization are presented in Table 3.3, while Table 3.4 provides the stratigraphic links to contiguous excavation areas. The first EBA subperiod, Hasanlu VIIc, has been published (Danti, Voigt, and Dyson 2004) as has the last period of occupation, the Ilkhanid Period (Danti 2004).

Work in the area of the U22 Sounding began in 1962 with the excavation of test trenches measuring 1.40 m wide and running east-west across Grids U20–22. These trenches were carried down to the Period IVb destruction surfaces. Grids U22–23 and T22–23 were chosen for a horizontal clearance, as was a larger area to the northeast that would provide the exposure of BBIII (see below). Preservation was generally good in the eastern part of this area (up slope), with Hasanlu I, II/III, and IVb occupations present. To the north and west, approaching the steep slopes of the High Mound, erosion and later disturbances had taken a toll on materials associated with the later periods of occupation.

Periods I–IVb. In U22, beneath a well-preserved Ilkhanid Period house (Danti 2004) near and at the surface of the mound, fairly poorly preserved Period II/III levels were found, which sealed a large rectangular Iron II structure, or the eastern portion of a larger structure, called BBVII. The artifactual assemblage and a radiocarbon sample P-2384, 1038–813 cal BC (Appendix II), date the building to Period IVb. BBVII contained at least 12 skeletons lying on its Terminal Period IVb floor. The structure resembles BBVIII and possibly served as a military installation in light of its architectural form and artifactual assemblage. The architectural plan represents an adaptation of two earlier, separate buildings (Fig. 3.9) of the Iron I–early Iron II found in UV22–23 (hereafter the U22 Period IVc Building) and UTS 22 (hereafter the Period IVc T22 Building). The northeast corner of BBVII incorporated parts of the earlier T22 Building. The construction surface of BBVII in some areas lay immediately on the tops of the stone footings of portions of the earlier T22 Period IVc Building that were not incorporated into BBVII (Pl. 3.8). The excavators at first dated some of these earlier stone footings to Period IVb BBVII before later realizing that victims of the Period IVb destruction lay atop the footings.[5]

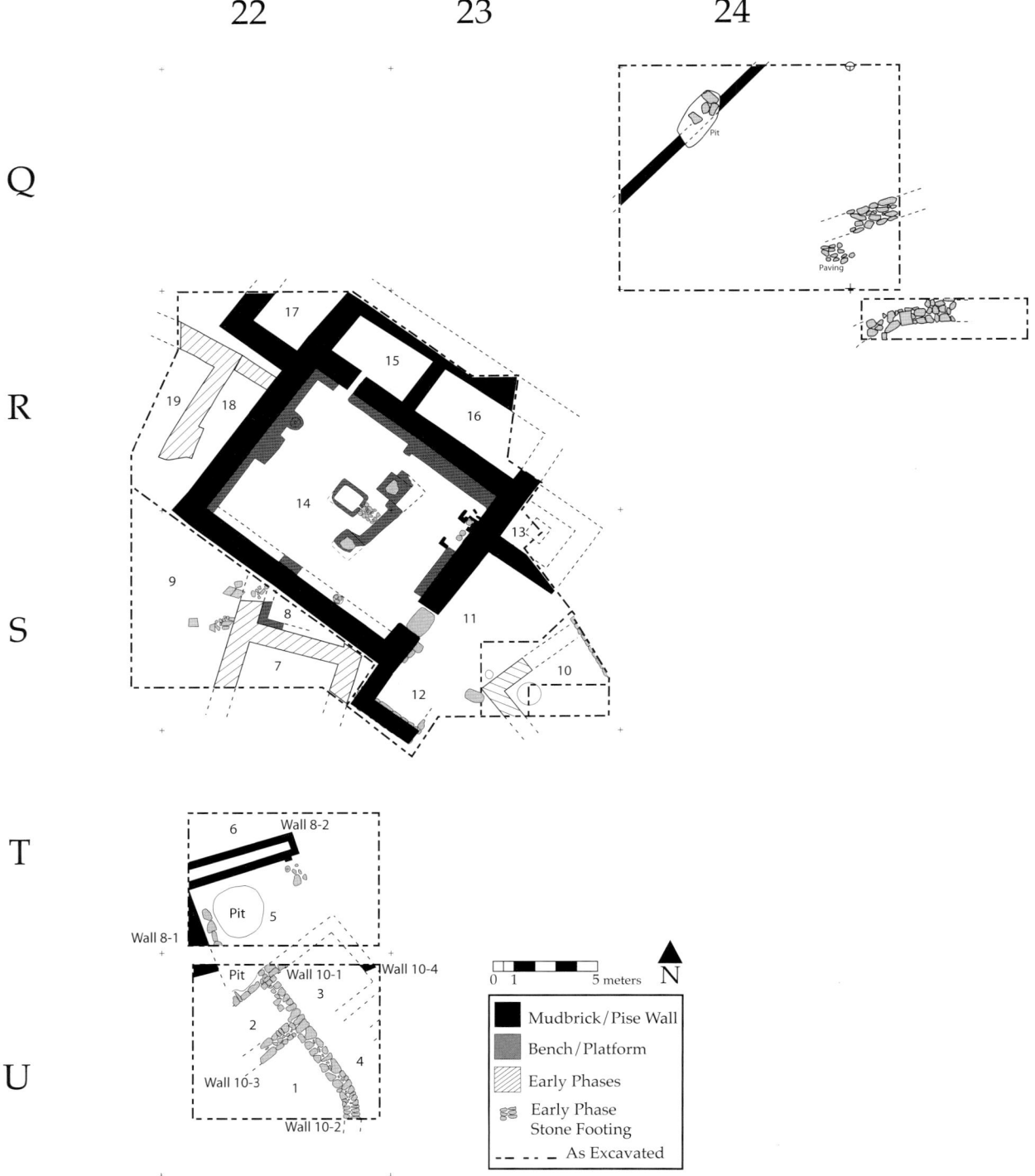

Fig. 3.10 Hasanlu Tepe: the northwest citadel in Period V.

TABLE 3.3. The Periods, Subperiods, Phases, and Strata Designations of the U22 Sounding

Period/Subperiod	Phases/Subphases	Strata	Comments
I (Ilkhanid)	I: 1	1–2	Architectural Level Lajvardina Ware, Monochrome Green-Glazed Ware, Red Earthenware
II/IIIa–IIIb (Iron III–IV)	Undetermined	3	Unanalyzed LWBW, Triangle Ware
IVb (Iron II)	IVb:1	4	Burned Building VII Late MBW
IVc (Iron I)	IVc:1	5–6	Period IVc Structure Middle and Late MBW
V (Early and Late LBA)	V: 1–2	7–10	Period V Structure Early MBW
VIa (MBIII)	–	–	Problematic—partly removed in antiquity and also collected by the excavators with the overlying LBA
VIb (MBII)	VIb:1	11–13	No Architecture MBII KW similar to Dinkha IV Phases A–C
VIc (MBI)	VIc:1–2	14–18	One Architectural Phase SW as at Dinkha V
VIIa (EB)	VIIa:1	19–20	One Architectural Phase POW, OW
VIIb (EB)	VIIb:1	21–29	No Architecture OW, POW
VIIc (EB)	VIIc:1–5	31–42	Multiple Architectural Phases ETC Ware, OW, Streaky Ware, Soapy Ware, Gritty Ware, Gird-i Hassan Ali Ware

To the south, in Grids U22–23 and V22–23, the Period IVb U22 Building was founded on fill deposits, which separated it from the underlying U22 Period IVc Building. In Period IVc much of the area of Grid V22 appears to have been an open space, which separated the U22 Period IVc Building from BBVI of the same period (Fig. 1.4). Grid U22 was chosen for a deep sounding in 1962, and excavation was continued in the area in a truncated trench to Stratum 12 of the MBII in 1962 and to lower deposits in the 1970 and 1972 seasons (Pl. 3.9).

The U22 and T22 Buildings of Period IVc–Early Period IVb. Directly below the clay floors of the terminal phase of BBVII (Strata 4h, 4l, 4s; Figs. 3.11–3.12) lay an ashy deposit containing sherds and stones (Stratum 5) and bricky collapse (Stratum 6) resting on another floor level (also Stratum 6) associated with mudbrick walls and stone footings of the U22 Period IVc Building. This architectural level and the contemporary T22 Period IVc Building to the north represent the Iron I–early Iron II precursors of BBVII (Fig.

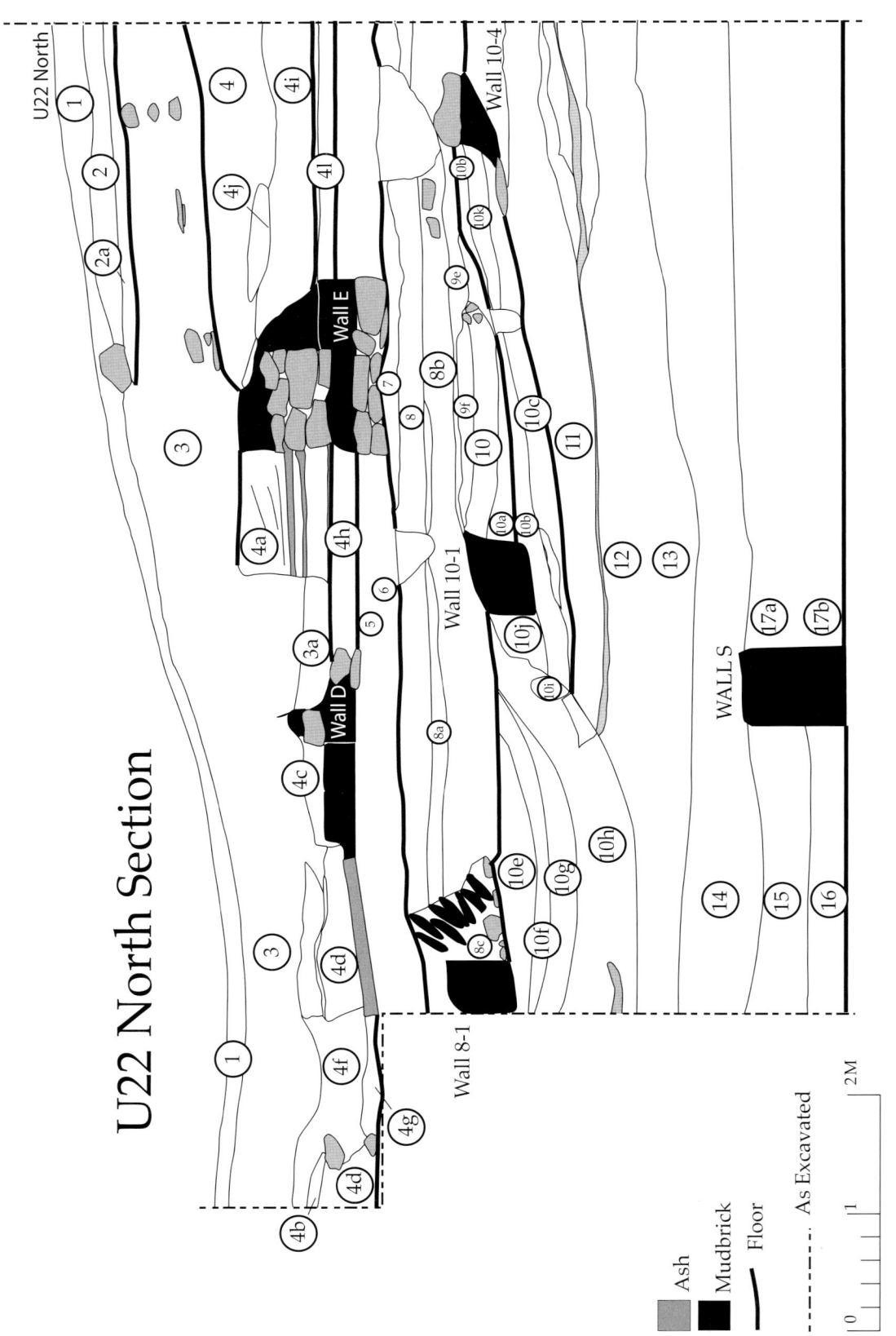

Fig. 3.11 Hasanlu Tepe: north section of the U22 Sounding.

TABLE 3.4. Stratigraphic Concordance of Northwest Mound Excavations.

Phase	R22	R23	S22	S23	T22	U22
IVb: 1	Str. 4 (1962)	–	Str. 3b (1962), 6–8a (1972)	4–5 Area 5 Str. 5	Str. 4 (1962)	Str. 4 (1962)
IVc: 1	Eroded and cut away by the excavators	Largely eroded and cut away by the excavators	Str. 8–9 (1972)	Area 7 Str. 6 S23E Area 1 Str. 1	Str. 5 (1962)	Str. 5–6 (1962)
V: 1	Area 7 Str. 11 Area 8 Str. 11	?	Str. 10–11 (1972)	–	Str. 6–8 (1962, 1972)	Str. 7–8 (1962)
V: 2	–	–	Area 12 Str. 9 (1972)	S23E Str. 2–3	–	Str. 9–10 (1962)

3.9). Dyson previously attributed the U22 Period IVc Building to "Period V" (1977b:160, fig. 5); the T22 Period IVc Building, never presented in detail, was dated to an early phase of Period IVb (see below). The east sections of U22 and T22 show how U22 Walls E and F of the Period IVc U22 and T22 Buildings were incorporated into the earliest phases of the later Period IVb rebuilding (Figs. 3.11–3.12). The excavators did not note this architectural continuity. I have reattributed the U22 Building to Period IVc–early IVb in light of the Strata 5–6 ceramic assemblage and the radiocarbon dating of the overlying Period IVb building. According to Dyson (1977b:160), his "Period V" U22 building—by which he was actually referring to the T22 Period IVc Building—lay beneath the north end of BBVII. He dates the construction of BBVII and the underlying architectural level using the radiocarbon date (P-2160) of 931–832 cal BC at the one-sigma level (Appendix II). Dyson has stated that, "The northern end of B.B. VII cut into two secondary walls and an associated surface which produced a radiocarbon date 940–990 B.C. (P-2160). This fact indicates an even later date for the construction of B.B. VII and the sealing over of the ruins of U22–23 [my Period IVc T22 Building] which lie below" (1977b:160). The context of this radiocarbon sample, however, is insecure and has been wrongly associated with this area. In a publication of the radiocarbon dates (Fishman and Lawn 1978:221), this sample's context is provided as S22 Stratum 10 Area 13, from a posthole intrusive to the "Period V" deposit (see below, RS22–23). First, this sample was not associated with the T22 Period IVc Building (Dyson's U22–23). This error aside, such a posthole at a lower level associated with surfaces and walls would imply an earlier architectural phase of Period IVb: naturally this would have major implications for the dating of the entire northwest citadel. However Dyson's interpretation is not correct: inspection of the S22 excavation notes shows this to be Sample 4, collected August 2, 1972. The sample is listed as "charcoal of floor [Area] 13 base of [Stratum] 10 at west W[all]-D1, Pit 12 in the north." (Hasanlu Excavation Notebook 56:17, Hasanlu Publication Archive). Pit 12 was located in the southwest quadrant of Operation S22 and cut the early Period V deposit. No posthole was ever recorded by the excavators, the pit was extensive, and the sample must come from the pit fill. The pit measures at least 130 cm in diameter, and the north end of BBVII did not cut or seal this area—there was in fact an intervening Period IVc occupation cut by the pit as well. This sample is irrelevant to the dating of the U22 sequence—the pit was cut down from the Terminal Period IVb surface level, there was no posthole, and the walls mentioned by Dyson are confused.

The U22 Building of Period V. In 1962, directly below the U22 Period IVc Building of Strata 5–6, Young excavated a deposit containing Early and Middle MBW—there was some mixing of earlier and later material in these collection units (see below). The ceramic assemblage of U22 Strata 7–8 (Phase V:1)

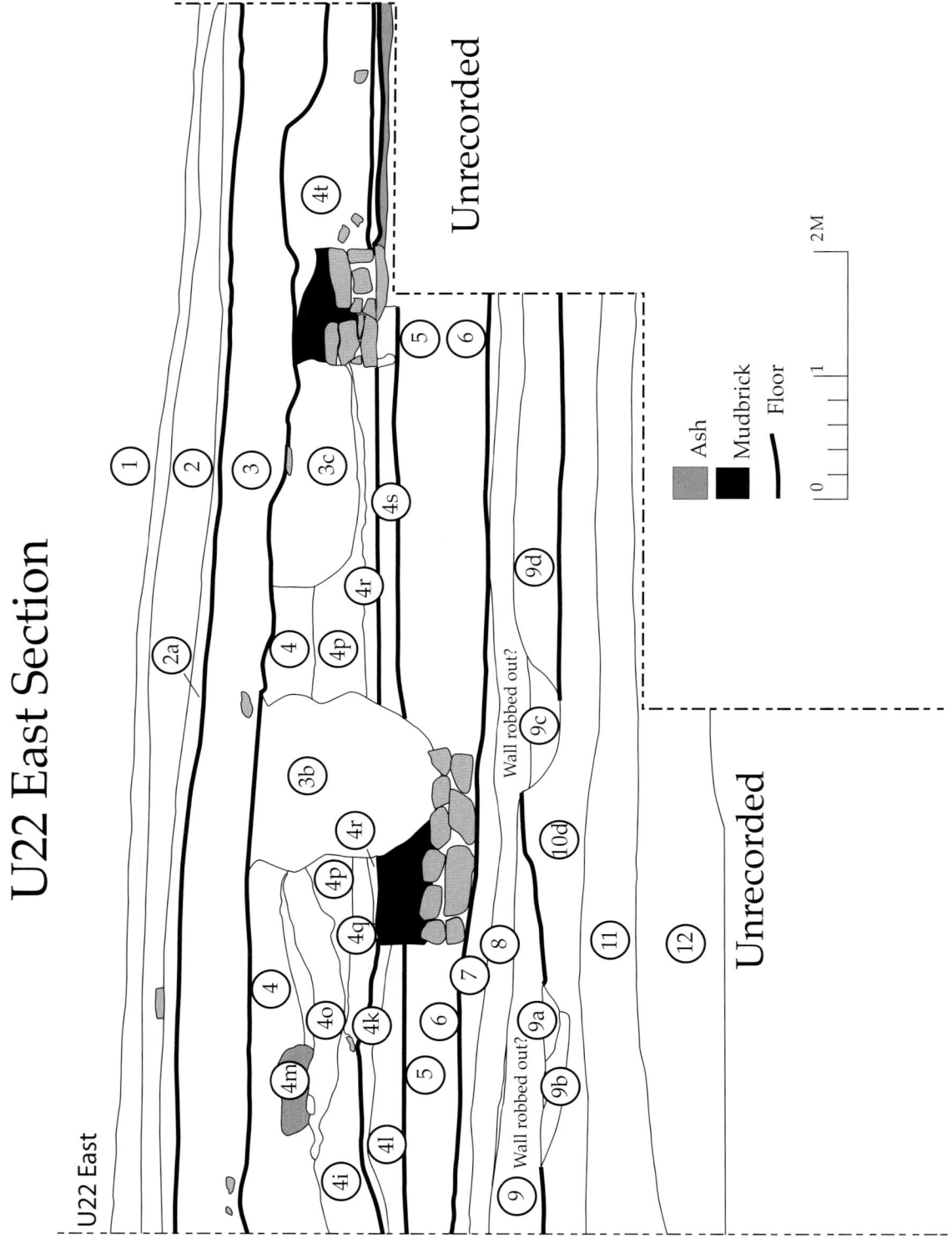

Fig. 3.12 Hasanlu Tepe: east section of the U22 Sounding.

dates to late Period V–Period IVc (see Chapter 4). The pottery of U22 Strata 9–10 dates to early Period V and constitutes Phase V:2, but the exact dating remains somewhat open since we lack comparable ceramic assemblages from Ušnu-Solduz, and the only radiocarbon dates bearing on the deposit come from neighboring Operations RS22–23. The U22 Strata 7–10 sequence can be stratigraphically linked to that of T22 and RS22–23, although there are some difficulties. T22 was not excavated to as great a depth as the adjacent U22 and RS22–23, and Phase V:2 levels were not reached there. This operation did provide a substantial assemblage of Phase V:1 ceramics of the later LBA (see Chapter 4). Operations RS22–23 produced a stratigraphic sequence similar to that of U22 and T22, along with the aforementioned radiocarbon dates (see below). Unfortunately, few ceramics were collected from RS22–23 in a reliable, stratigraphically controlled manner.

In U22, Young uncovered a fragmentary structure consisting of stone footings (Walls 10-1, 10-2, and 10-3) in Stratum 10 (Fig. 3.10), which has never been reported in detail (Young 1963).[6] The western end of this U22 Period V Building had been cut away in antiquity, and the excavators missed an eastern wall of the structure (Wall 10-4) visible in the section and in a 1972 excavation photo (Fig. 3.11, Pl. 3.9a). The associated ceramics are largely early Period V, which corresponds with radiocarbon dates from stratigraphically linked deposits in RS22–23.[7] However, I must emphasize that the associated U22 ceramic assemblage potentially contains some earlier and later material due to errors in excavation.

The north section (Fig. 3.11) shows a large pit in its west end (Strata 10e–h). The pit is cut down from the level of late Period V/IVc—it was not noted during excavation and was only recorded in 1972, when excavations were re-opened to dig below Strata 12–13. This same section also shows what are almost certainly two architectural phases of the northeastern wall of the U22 Period V Building (Wall 10-4); these, too, were not recorded or noted in 1962. *Wall 10-4 is cut into an earlier deposit* (also designated Stratum 10 in 1962, here Stratum 10d). Strata 9e, 10b, 10k, and 10c run against the western face of Wall 10-4 in the 1972 section, and do not appear in the eastern section recorded in 1962 (the east side of Wall 10-4), also suggesting an intervening wall (Fig. 3.12). In most periods in an-

tiquity, this area constituted the tepe's northwestern edge, and was partially leveled for the construction of the western end of the Period V U22 Building, removing parts of the earlier Stratum 10d. This implies that a small portion of the northeastern part of the sounding pre-dated the Stratum 10 structure, and that some earlier artifacts were inadvertently included in the Stratum 10 collection (see Chapter 4). In terms of its spatial extent, this earlier deposit designated as Stratum 10d corresponds to the reconstructed area of Room 4 of the U22 Period V Building (Fig. 3.10). This Stratum 10d deposit was collected with the strata associated with the later U22 Period V Building—the material from within Rooms 1–3 and the late Period V–IVc pit of Strata 10e–h. This in part accounts for the seeming superposition of a "fully developed" Early MBW assemblage overlying a MBII deposit containing KW (Strata 11–13). There is no evidence of a Terminal MBII occupation in this area. Moreover, deposits potentially dating to early Period V or the MBIII (Stratum 10d) were partly removed by ancient building activity *and* were mixed by the excavators within the Stratum 10 collection unit. This is the sum total of the physical evidence of the famous "cultural" gap between the "Bronze Age" and "Iron Age" of Ušnu-Solduz—everywhere else at Hasanlu and Dinkha Tepe, intervening material separated these ceramic horizons or, at the least, is strongly suggested.

This contradictory evidence was largely ignored, and the unpublished and problematic U22 sequence was used to support the cultural break. To be sure, much contradictory information has been published on the relationship of Stratum 10 to Stratum 11, as previously mentioned, including assertions of stratigraphic discontinuity (Dyson 1963b:132), stratigraphic continuity (Dyson 1965:195; Young 1963:43), intentional leveling (Hamlin 1971:28–9, citing Dyson, pers. comm.), and a clear cultural break (Dyson 1977b; Muscarella 1994a:140, n7)! The stratigraphic details of this critical juncture were difficult to ascertain since the excavators in 1962 sketched only one small section showing the relationship of Wall 10-1 to other major stratigraphic markers (Fig. 3.14) and drew only the east section (Fig. 3.12, Strata 7–12)—a section lacking intact early Period V architecture. A more detailed north section was drawn in the U22 Sounding in 1972, from the base of the Strata 5–6 building, but naturally the stratigraphic details had changed some-

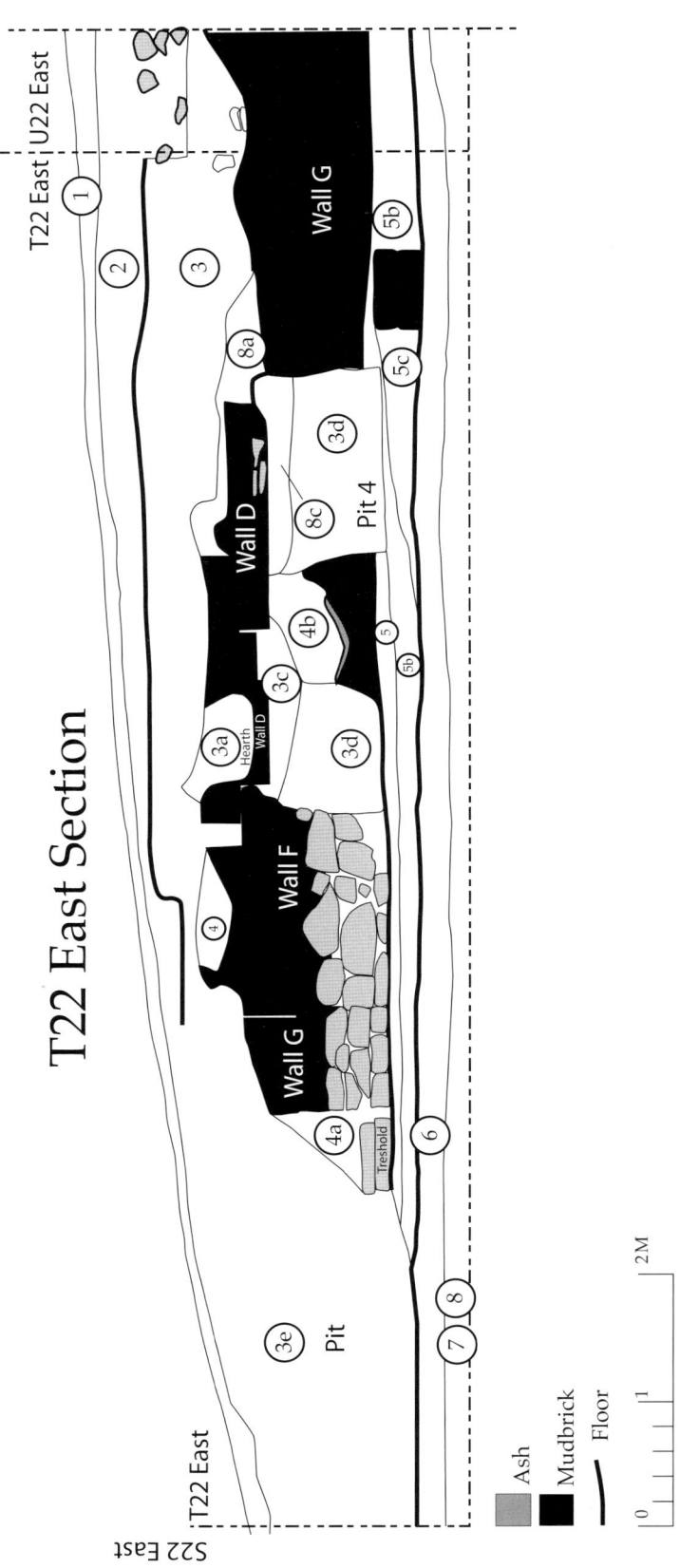

Fig. 3.13 Hasanlu Tepe: east section of T22.

what due to erosion and the cleaning of the baulks, and the 1972 excavators assigned arbitrary stratum numbers to the strata previously excavated in 1962.

In 1962, excavations in U22 were carried down to Stratum 12; however, the excavator did not take notes on Strata 7–12 and only one architectural plan of "Stratum 10" was recorded along with the aforementioned sections. The sherds from this sounding were saved and are currently (as of 2012) in the University of Pennsylvania Museum. Only small amounts of KW were found in Strata 9–10, a fact easily accounted for by its position immediately atop a MBII deposit with large amounts of this ware. The Strata 11–12 deposit, not surprisingly, contained virtually no MBW and is characterized by a KW assemblage similar to that of Dinkha IVa–c (Figs. 4.1, 4.2).

In 1970, work was resumed in the U22 area to expand the excavated area in order to complete the architectural plan of the "Period V" building—that is, the U22 Period IVc Building. Excavations were conducted in the south ends of U22 and U23 and the northern parts of V22 and V23. The eastern doorway and southern end of Room 1 were added to the plan (Fig. 3.9).

In 1972, the U22 Sounding was re-opened to recover earlier levels. This excavation was relatively well recorded and systematic. The excavations of 1962 had ended on the base of Stratum 12, which coincidentally represented the bottom of the PKW deposit (Pls. 3.9a, b). Renewed excavations showed the MBII level lay above a Period VIc deposit (Strata 13–18) characterized by plain and incised SW with vessel forms and styles of incising and appliqué which show it to be the precursor of Period VIb (Pl. 3.10a).

Finally, in 1974 the sounding was taken down in a progressively truncated area to the base of the EBA deposit (Pl. 3.11). This sounding provides our best view of Hasanlu VIIa, b—the later EBA or mid-to-late 3rd millennium BC—and Hasanlu VIIc—the late Chalcolithic/early EBA transitional period or the early 3rd millennium BC (Danti, Voigt, and Dyson 2004).[8]

The Excavation of T22 and S22 (Periods IVc–V)

Similar to U22, excavations in the area of S22 and T22 were begun in 1962. These excavations were re-opened in 1972 and some limited work was conducted to clarify architectural details in 1974. Many mistakes were made in this area that can be attributed to the mainte-

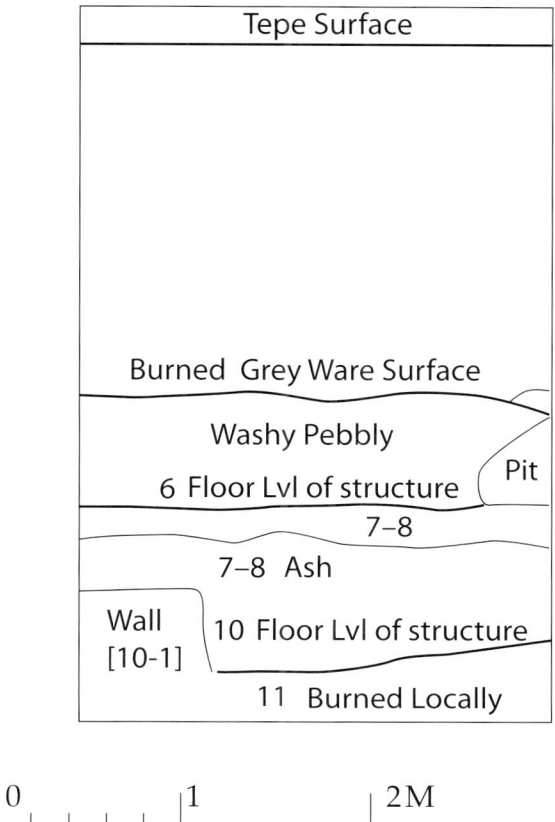

Fig. 3.14 Dyson's sketch of the U22 north section of 1962.

nance of wide east-west balks separating S22 and T22 (they were eventually removed) and the ten-year break in excavations.

In T22, the Period IVc T22 Building (Fig. 3.9) lay immediately below the earliest floor level of Period IVb BBVII (Fig. 3.13). The extant structure consisted of a large rectangular room (Room 1) oriented on long axis north to south (Fig. 3.9). A square stairwell stood at the north end of the building and had a central mudbrick pillar on a stone footing abutting the east wall (Room 2). A doorway in the northeast corner of Room 1 led to what was likely a large open space to the east. The only intact internal features were partial stone pavings and a mudbrick platform abutting the east wall of Room 1. Mudbrick benches abutted the exterior faces of the southeast corner and north end of the building. Room 1 was excavated in 1962 and Room 2 was found in 1972 and 1974 as balks were removed. The

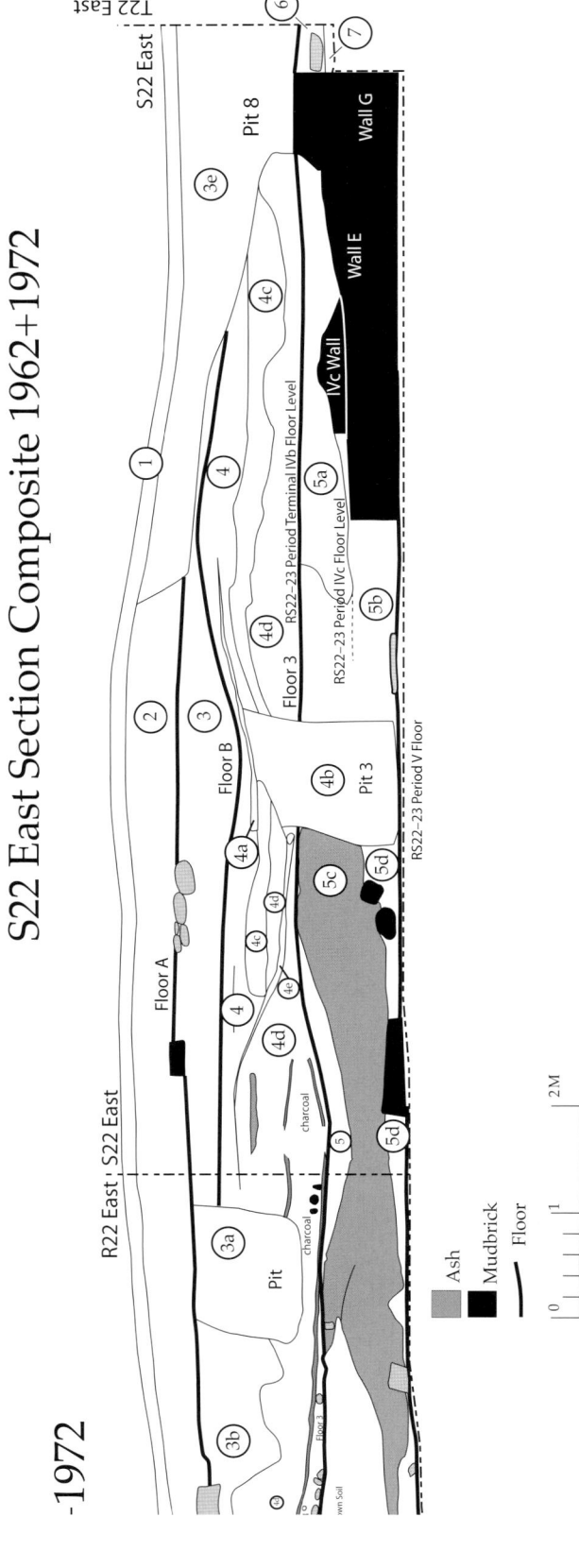

Fig. 3.15 Hasanlu Tepe: east section of S22.

Period IVc T22 Building, collected as T22 Stratum 5 and substrata, is the equivalent of U22 Strata 5 and 6. The structure was not preserved in the southwest and a large pit had cut down to its floor level in the area of the eastern doorway of Room 1 (Figs. 3.9, 3.13). While much of Room 1 of the Period IVc T22 Building was recovered, little was recorded. This was in part due to substantial cuts into and erosion of the western slopes of the mound and the incorporation of parts of the structure into BBVII by its builders (see above). The floors of Period IVc (Stratum 5) were seldom noted during (or separated from) the excavation of BBVII with the exception of areas with stone paving.

Below the Period IVc Building were Strata 6–7, which consisted of "bricky fill with sherds—not distinctively different from typical Grey Ware but somewhat."[9] Only the east section of T22 was recorded, which shows these strata precede the U22 Period IVc Building (Fig. 3.13) and are the equivalent of U22 Strata 7–8. A "T22 Stratum 8" was recorded in the labeling of sherd drawings from 1962 but is not mentioned in the excavator's notes, although we can be reasonably certain it represents the continuation of Stratum 8 in the adjacent U22 based on relative elevations and the stratigraphic sequence. Work ceased in T22 at this point in the 1962 excavations. When work was resumed in 1972, five days were spent cleaning and excavating Operation T22, continuing the strata numbering where the 1962 excavators had left off (Pl. 3.9a, Background). After the initial cleaning the operation was taken down to an unknown but shallow depth (Strata 8–10). Stratum 10 was only excavated as a small, shallow sounding. No sections were drawn and no sherd collections were saved or recorded. Architecture was uncovered in the western part of the operation (Fig. 3.10). Section drawings from U22 help to date this architectural level: the level of T22 Wall 8-1 was recorded in a newly drawn 1972 north section of U22 (Figs. 3.10, 3.11), although this wall was not recognized as the continuation of T22 Wall 8-1.[10] The southern continuation of the wall was evidently cut away in U22 in 1962. The U22 north section (Fig. 3.11) shows T22 Wall 8-1 and Strata 7–8 equate with the late Period V deposit in U22 (Strata 7–8). The wall seals a large pit cut into the early Period V deposit in U22 (Fig. 3.11, Stratum 10). Wall 8-1 and the associated architecture in T22 (Fig. 3.10, Rooms 5 and 6) appear to be a rebuilding of the north and west end of the structure found in U22. Wall 8-2 was unusual in terms of its construction. The wall consisted of thin, parallel mudbrick walls with rubble packed between them. A small buttress-like projection on the south face of Wall 8-2 may mark the position of a doorway into Room 5.

In 1962, Grid S22 was excavated to a depth of 1.75 m below surface, but a wide east-west baulk was left standing between T22 and S22 creating a temporary stratigraphic discontinuity with serious consequences. Stratigraphic continuities between the adjacent R22 and T22 were documented for Period IVb, but the southeastern end of S22 contained a large pit (Pit 8), which had removed the upper strata (Fig. 3.15).[11] This combined with the baulk complicated the interpretation of the stratigraphy during the fieldwork. The stratigraphy of S22 is especially important since it provides a vital link between three large excavated exposures on the northwest High Mound: the east baulk of S22 represents a kind of stratigraphic bottleneck tying together BBVIIE, BBVII, and a large area to the west allegedly devoid of pre-Period III remains.

The southern and eastern portions of S22 and the S22–T22 baulk contained the larger part of a stairwell used in both the T22 Period IVc Building (Room 2) and BBVII of Period IVb (Figs. 3.5, 3.9, Pl. 3.12) and a small part of the RS22–23 Period IVc Building (Fig. 3.17). The lower levels of S22 of Period V date were better preserved and contained the RS22–23 Period V Building (Fig. 3.16), as well as rare early Period V architecture (Fig. 3.19).

Previous interpretations of the stratigraphy of S22 have been plagued by assumptions regarding the Hasanlu stratigraphic sequence that entered the excavation records in 1962. The uppermost strata comprised at least two architectural phases (Strata 2 and 3, Floors A and B). The latest consisted of ephemeral architectural remains in the northeast quadrant of S22 (Stratum 2 Floor A, Fig. 3.15) and a ceramic assemblage with at least one sherd of painted "Triangle Ware," dated to Hasanlu IIIa (Dyson 1999a, 1999b; Kroll 2000, In press b). Below these late levels lay a thick deposit of burned material (Stratum 4). Excavations conducted in S22 in 1962 ended at the base of Stratum 4d (Fig. 3.15), a hard surface level designated as Floor 3, which was easily defined across the entire operation. In the west, Floor 3 seemed associated with stone footings (not shown here). The excavators correctly attributed these to "Period III," but failed to note

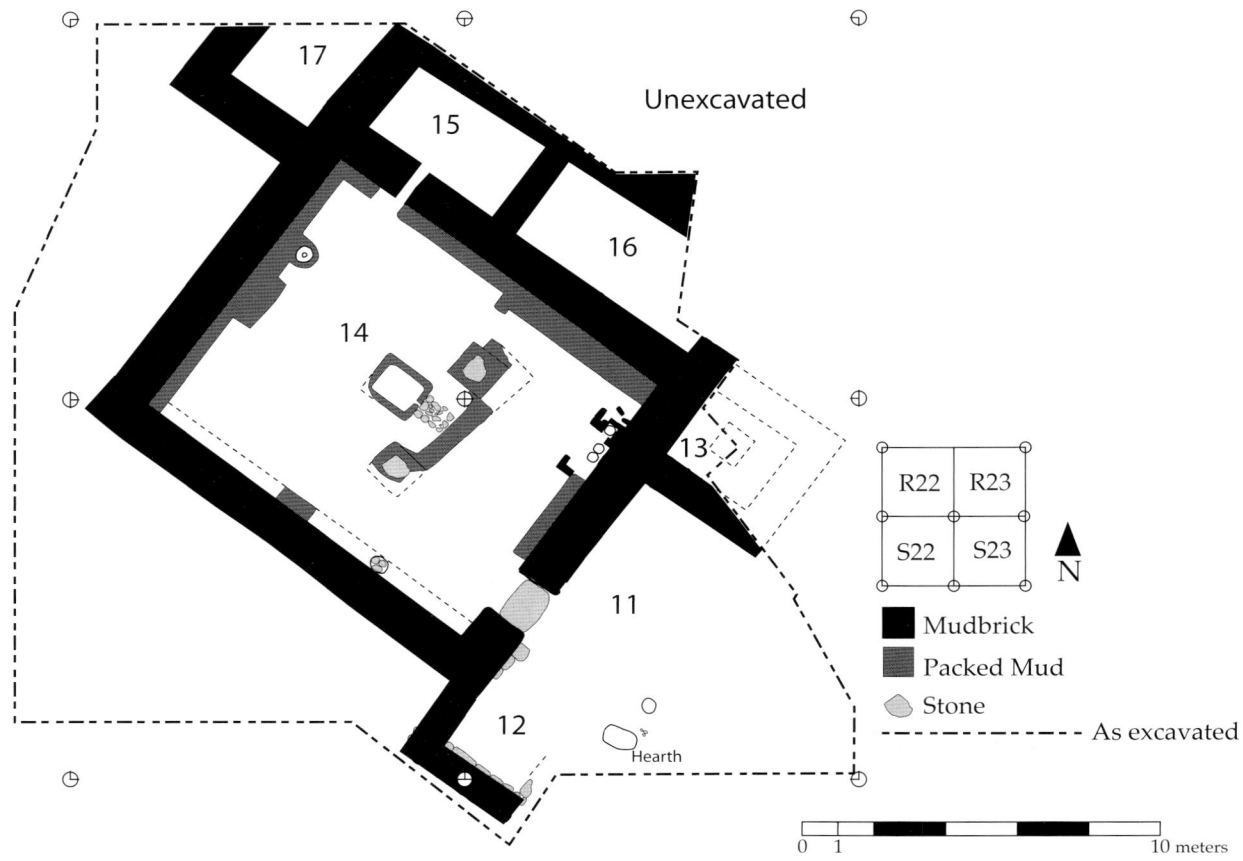

Fig. 3.16 Hasanlu Tepe: RS22–23 Period V columned hall.

these footings lay in the foundation trench cutting the Stratum 4 burned deposit. In short, there was a stratigraphic conflation of Period III and Period IVb. Seen another way, since Stratum 4, a thick layer of burned debris, lacked some of the "obvious" signs of a Period IVb destruction, such as large numbers of *in situ* finds and skeletons, the entire level was attributed to Period III—that is, what Stephan Kroll now designates Period IIIc or the Urartian "fortress" and IIIb, the later Iron III occupation. Superficially this seemed correct since the position and alignment of the stone footings could not be reconciled with the Period IVb citadel plan and in other operations excavated to the west other stone footings of "Period III" could be linked up with them architecturally. The date assigned by the excavators to S22 Stratum 4 affected their subsequent interpretation of the lower levels of S22.[12] Such errors were compounded over time and became deeply embedded in the archival record, greatly hindering later efforts to publish "Period V" and ultimately resulted in the publication of idealized plans of buildings in isolation (compare Fig. 3.10 to Dyson 1977a: fig. 6). Moreover, the lack of a stratigraphic concordance within and between excavation units prevented the publication of the artifactual assemblages.

Excavations were reopened in S22 in 1972, and a 1.50 m baulk was maintained in the southern portion of the excavation; part of the 1962 south baulk was removed. Work started with a layer of soft grey ash, which represents the slumped remains of 1962 Stratum 4 and Stratum 5a (Fig. 3.15). In the southern end of the unit where the earlier baulk was removed, the stone footings of the northern end of the aforementioned stairwell of Period IVb and IVc were found (Figs. 3.5, 3.9, 3.17). Its interior contained a layer of ash and a large number of finds (originally designated

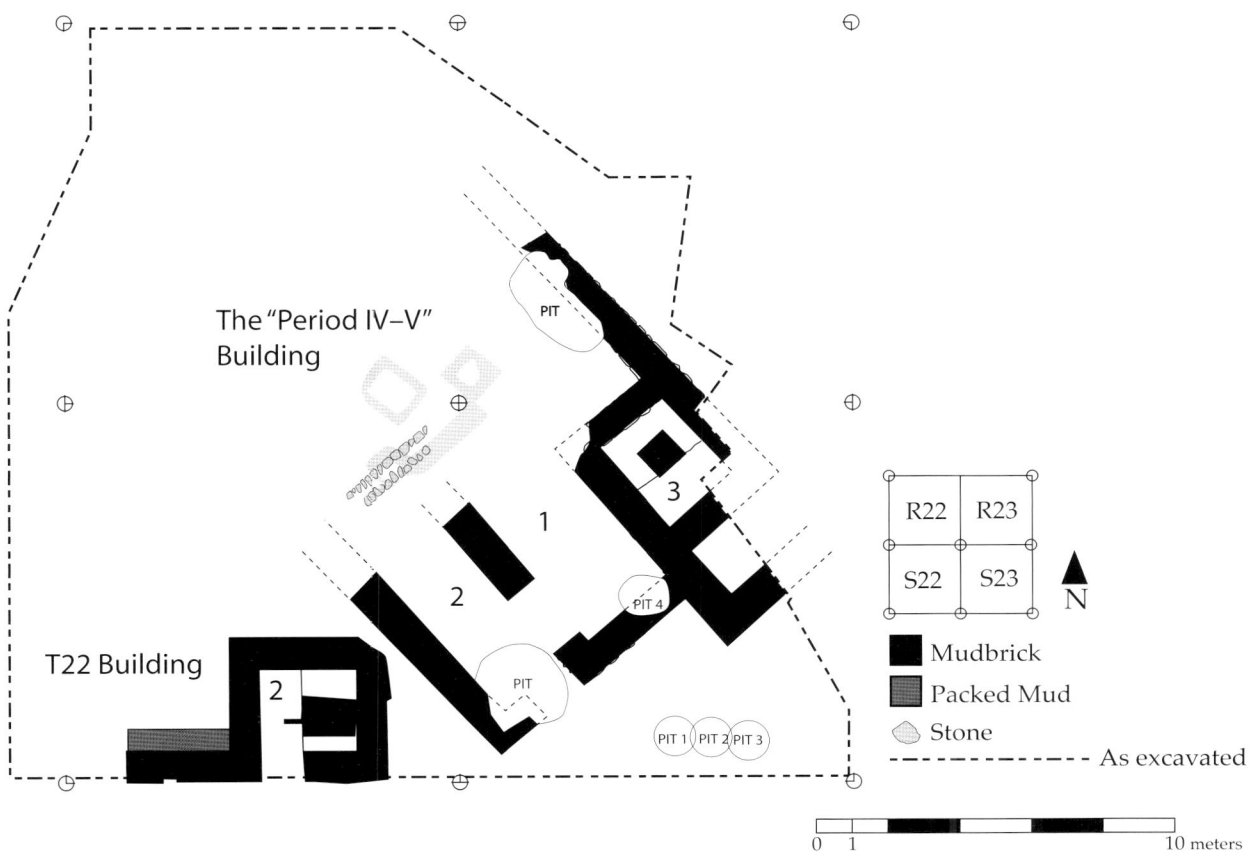

Fig. 3.17 Hasanlu Tepe: RS22–23 Period IVc columned hall.

Area 10 Stratum 6–7, Pl. 3.13). The stone foundations rested on the top of Strata 5b and 7, the Period IVc construction surface in this area (Fig. 3.15). *Outside* of the stairwell, S22 Stratum 5a (Fig. 3.15) ran against the base of the stone footings of the stairwell and *under* the stone foundation of the Stratum 4 building to the northwest, which had been originally excavated in 1962 (see above). The excavators interpreted this to mean that the stairwell dated to Period IVb since the Stratum 4 structure had been previously attributed to Period III, a conclusion bolstered by the assumption that the abundant finds from inside the stairwell linked it to Terminal Period IVb as did its position and alignments. This interpretation is partly incorrect. First, the Stratum 4 structure was cut into Stratum 5a from a higher elevation. Furthermore, the stratigraphic position, elevation, and alignment of the stairwell show it originally formed the north end of the Period IVc T22 Building and was later re-used in the Period IVb BBVII along with other architecture to the south. This stairwell was founded at the base of Stratum 5a, and later excavation in RS22–23 showed that another structure of Period IVc (the RS22–23 Period IVc Building) *was founded on this same level and was sealed by BBVIIE of late Period IVc–Terminal Period IVb* (see below). The north stairwell of the Period IVc T22 Building had the exact same dimensions as the contemporary stairwell of the RS22–23 Period IVc building and its eastern corner was constructed *so as to neatly align to the adjacent Period IVc structure* (Figs. 3.9, 3.17, Pl. 3.12a). Stratigraphy and architectural attributes demonstrate the stairwell originated in Hasanlu IVc–early Period IVb and was re-used along with other walls of the north end of the Period IVc T22 Building in the construction of Period IVb BBVII. The other stratigraphic and architectural de-

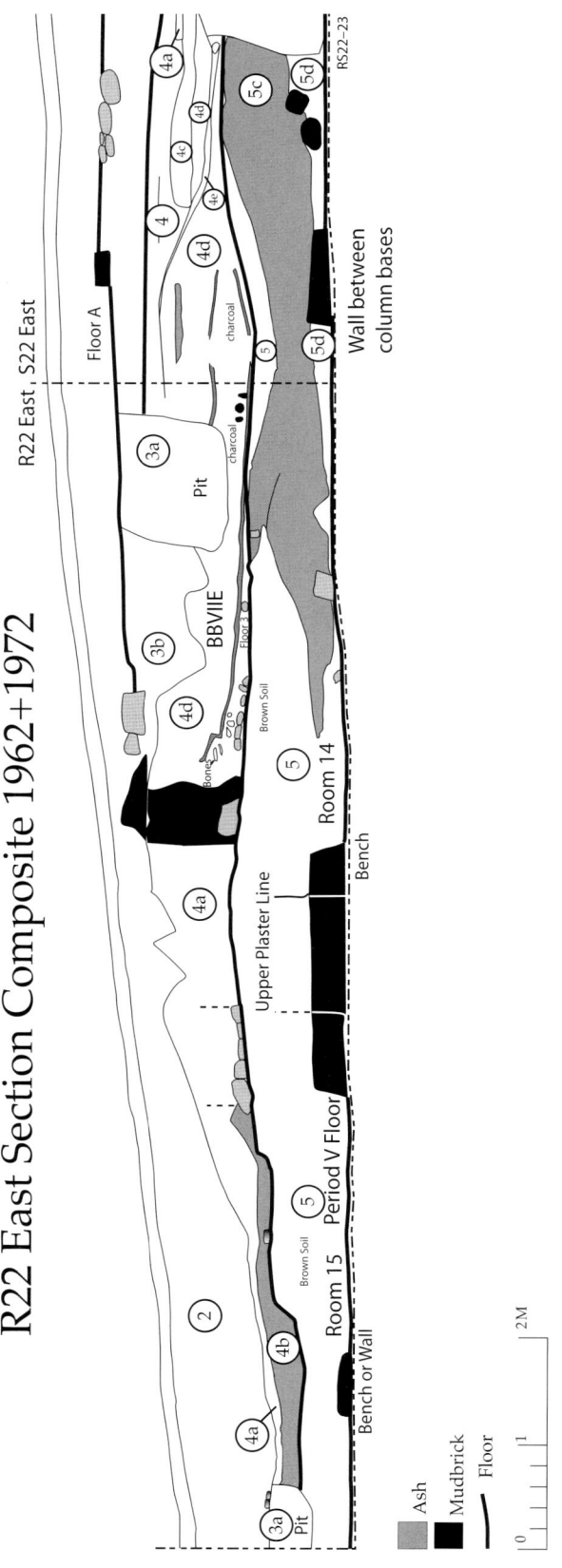

Fig. 3.18 Hasanlu Tepe: east section of R22.

tails of S22 are discussed in the following section on RS22–23.

The Excavation of RS22-23 (Periods IVc–V)

A sequence of architectural levels and MBW deposits on the northwest High Mound was recovered from 1962–1974, spanning Period V to Terminal Period IVb in an important horizontal exposure in RS22–23. Dyson published one architectural phase of this area, referred to here as the RS22–23 Building, which he dated to Period V and which was critical to his assertion that "Early Iron Age" culture arrived in the southern Lake Urmia Basin suddenly and in a fully developed form (Dyson 1977b:160–64, fig. 6). Young also cites this structure as the earliest attestation of columned-hall architecture:

> Our sequence of columned halls in Iran begins shortly after 1500 BC with the modest structure of Hasanlu V. The hall itself (11 x 9 m) has all the later standard features: columns, central hearth, benches and "throne seat". The hall is fronted asymmetrically by an anteroom whose door is off-centre with that leading to the hall. To your left as you enter the anteroom is a small square room with the footings for a stairway to the second storey [the stairwell, stair footing, and anteroom were never actually found; see below]. Clearly, hall and anteroom were built as one unit. (2002:386)

While Dyson, Young, and others believed that the RS22–23 Building represented the earliest attestation of this form that typifies the monumental buildings of the MBW horizon, the current reassessment forces us to significantly alter this view and a revised plan of the building is presented here (Fig. 3.16).

Late Period V–Period IVc

In Terminal Period IVb, the RS22–23 area was occupied by BBVIIE,[13] a buttressed tower and associated walls that formed a gateway, possibly a double gateway, linking the inner citadel to the system of fortifications located along the western High Mound, where the citadel's main gate was almost certainly located (Fig. 3.5). The northern part of this entrance was formed by the heavily reinforced south wall of BBIII and the southern portion by the north end of BBVII. The earlier Iron I architecture shows the area probably served a similar function (Fig. 3.9). The Period IVb and later levels were excavated in 1962. As previously mentioned, the excavators believed that they had only excavated down to "Period III" in Operations S22 and R22, but they had in fact already reached Period IVb or slightly earlier deposits.

In 1972, work was resumed in RS22–23. This ten-year hiatus contributed to a disjuncture in the understanding of the stratigraphic sequence among the excavation supervisors. The cleaning of Operations S22 and R22 almost certainly removed the ephemeral remains of Period IVc—most tellingly, the preserved remains of the Period IVc building of RS22–23 largely end at the western baulk line of RS23 (Fig. 3.17). As previously mentioned, at the critical stratigraphic juncture in S22, the excavators thought they were at the "level" of Period III due to assumptions made in 1962 and anticipated the thick, burned destruction level of Terminal Period IVb to appear after cleaning out the operation. The built environment of the Iron II citadel was different in the area of BBVIIE, however, as it was there characterized by large open spaces. Site formation processes had therefore not resulted in a readily identifiable thick, burned level in all places. Across much of the area there were relatively few signs of the violent sacking of the citadel such as the familiar *in situ* objects and skeletons. Finally, post-depositional processes had heavily altered the Iron II remains—this area was particularly exposed to pitting and the cutting of wall trenches and terraces in later periods. These factors combined to confound interpretations of the subsequent results in the northwest citadel in the areas outside of BBIII and BBVII.

Below BBVIIE in S23 and R23 lay the poorly preserved remains of a building of Period IVc, dated by two radiocarbon samples (Appendix II, P-2161, P-2370). P-2161 falls between 1320–1190 cal BC and P-2378 to 1316–1126 cal BC. The contexts of these charcoal samples are not especially informative. The structure was excavated as a series of extensions of RS23 in 1972 and 1974. The ceramic assemblage was unsystematically collected and the area was heavily disturbed, but the excavators noted that there were few diagnostics of the Iron II.[14] This building was almost certainly a columned-hall structure and represents the rebuilding of a similar structure of Period V located almost directly beneath it (see below). The Period IVc stone footings lay on or immediately above the wall stubs of the Period V columned hall, and there was likely no intervening period of abandonment in this part of the settlement. The extant Period IVc walls at the northwest end of the building sealed rubble-filled trenches where the stone footings of the Period V structure had been robbed out.

While only the southeastern portion of the building was preserved—including a stairwell and entry—the overall layout and alignment of the Period IVc building follows that of the preceding Period V columned-hall building (Fig. 3.17). This suggests it, too, centered on a columned hall, and the Period IVc plan presented here shows the location of a reconstructed hearth in the area of ash and debris found directly above the Period V hearth along with the column bases dated to Period V (Fig. 3.17). No column bases were previously attributed to the IVc structure, but the column bases and low mudbrick wall between them of Period V date curiously align to the Period IVc structure rather than the Period V building. Since the bases were raised above the level of the Period V floor by at least 15 cm based on the height of the stone bases, the columns they supported could easily have been incorporated into the Period IVc structure. Architectural details are presented in Appendix V. A Period IVc wall preserved as a low stone footing was built over the southern column base at a later date (Fig. 3.17). This wall was oriented along the same line as an earlier underlying wall built between the column bases and directly over its southern end, which was founded on the earlier Period V surface. The Period IVc columned hall was located just south of the Period IVc phase of BBIII (see below), and the open space between the two buildings may have served as an entrance into the citadel as it did in the succeeding Period IVb when this area contained the BBVIIE gateway (Dyson 1989a:112).

Period V

Dyson has previously published the columned-hall building that lay beneath the Period IVc level (Dyson 1977b), albeit in a cursory fashion (Pls. 3.13–3.17). The ceramic assemblage (see Chapter 4) and the radiocarbon dates from the overlying level indicate it dates to the LBA. The structure had at least two architectural phases—an initial construction and later modifications. In Room 14, a raised mudbrick and stone hearth and two column bases made of plaster and stone indicate a columned hall (Fig. 3.16). The several stratigraphic sections recorded that run through the center of this room failed to record the column bases and in most places do not show the Period IVc floor level (Fig. 3.18). Excavation photos show that the column bases were founded on the initial floor of the building (Pls. 3.14–3.17). The sections record that the low wall built between the column bases was founded on the building's initial construction floor (Fig. 3.18, Stratum 5d). Room 17 was a later addition, as was the wall dividing the northern storeroom (Rooms 15–16). These later additions were not shown on the original plan published in 1977.

Dyson reported that the front (southeast) portion of the building was not preserved (1977b:161–62, fig. 6), and he reconstructed a stairwell and antechamber there, locating the stairwell south of the main entrance (Fig. 3.16, the area of Room 12). For Dyson, the existence of this reconstructed stairwell rested on two pieces of evidence: (1) a stone that possibly formed the southwest corner of the stairwell, and (2) the plan of the overlying Period IVc building, which contained a stairwell. The Period IVc structure was only mentioned in passing in Dyson's 1977 publication (1977b). Dyson cited the ubiquity of antechambers and stairwells in Period IVb as additional support for his reconstruction of the stairwell and antechamber of the Period V building, introducing circular logic into discussions of the origins of the columned-hall structure in Iran since RS22–23 represents the earliest example but was partly reconstructed using analogies drawn from the Iron II. Later publications neglected to mention that parts of the building were reconstructed (Young 2002). Regarding the stone purported to have formed the corner of the southwest wall of Room/Area 2 (Fig. 3.16), naturally, one stone does not prove the existence of a wall, especially in buildings with buttresses, pilasters, and benches. The question thus becomes: Was there evidence that the eastern end of the building had been disturbed and the reconstructed antechamber and stairwell had been cut away?

Closer examination of the excavation records shows that there is no evidence the eastern end of the building had been extensively disturbed (see be-

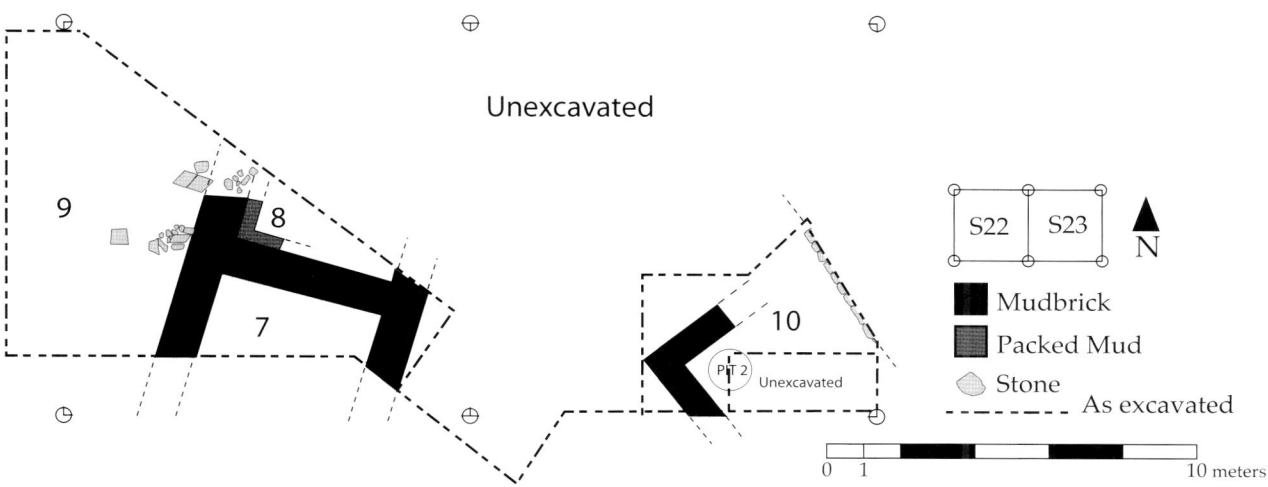

Fig. 3.19 Hasanlu Tepe: RS22–23 early Period V architecture.

low) and that there is little basis for the antechamber and stairwell reconstructed to the left of the main entrance; in fact, there were intact features (Fig. 3.16) to the east of the building that virtually preclude the existence of the southeastern wall on Dyson's plan (1977b: fig. 6). In the eastern end of the excavated area of Grid S23, the excavators were able to easily trace the hard-packed construction surface associated with the columned hall, which was covered by approximately 30 cm of Period V occupational debris prior to the construction of the Period IVc Building. Some small pits dated to Periods III and IVb had disturbed the area; however, intact features—including a small hearth located 10 cm above the Period V building surface and an area of postholes—were found in the southern and eastern portions of S23, indicating it was an exterior space in Period V rather than an antechamber or stairwell. This same use of space is evidenced in the Period IVc architectural plan (compare Fig. 3.16 with 3.17). Dyson argued that the reconstructed stairwell of Period V would have had dimensions that were nearly identical to the stairway of the Period IVc building. In point of fact, such a reconstructed stairway (Fig. 3.16, Area 13) could have been located directly below this later IVc stairway located in the northern end of Grid S23 (Fig. 3.17), where the thick northeast wall of Room 11 of the Period V columned-hall structure seems to indicate the presence of such a feature. This area was not excavated to the level of the Period V building. As previously mentioned, there are no signs of major disturbance to the southeast of the building that would account for a missing stairwell. Moreover, there is a great deal of architectural continuity between the Period V columned hall and the putative columned hall of Period IVc in terms of their alignment and position, thus making the likely location of the stairwell in Period V to the right of the entrance, if one existed.

Our overall picture of the RS22–23 area in Periods V and IVc is one of successive domestic spaces with modest columned halls in the Late Bronze and early Iron Age. Sometime in late Period IVc or early Period IVb, this pattern was modified: RS22–23 became a fortified internal gateway in the northwestern citadel. The structures of RS22–23 Period V and IVc probably served as the southern end of a more modest entryway or gateway, the north end of which was formed by BBIII of Period IVc and its Period V precursor (see below, Q24). The changes of Period IVb here as elsewhere were on an order of scale, they bolstered citadel security at access points, and did not represent a qualitative departure from earlier patterns in the built environment save the sacrifice of one residential structure. Residential space was simultaneously added in the same area with the enclosure of BBIII's forecourt, which perhaps represents the reorganization/consolidation of elite households as citadel space reached a new premium in the Iron II.

Early Period V?

The RS22–23 stratigraphic sequence begins with three unreported exposures of architecture represented by poorly preserved mudbrick walls, stone footings, and associated surfaces that predate the construction of the Period V building (Figs. 3.10, 3.19, Rooms 7, 8, 10, 18, 19). No radiocarbon dates were directly associated with these contexts and only a few ceramic diagnostics were recorded, which offer few additional clues to assist in dating other than the observation that MBW dominates the assemblage (see Chapter 4). This earlier architectural phase or phases *lay at or below* the absolute elevation of the nearby U22 Stratum 10 structure, but cannot be directly linked stratigraphically to Grids T22 and U22 (Figs. 3.11, 3.12).[15]

A partially preserved wall corner was found in Operation S23, and the edge of a similarly aligned wall was protruding from the eastern section. The interior of the reconstructed Room 10 (Fig. 3.19) has the same east-west dimensions as the roughly contemporary Rooms 7 and 8 of S22. The S23 walls were sealed by the hard, pebbly surface on which the Period V columned-hall building was founded (Fig. 3.10). The walls consisted of packed clay (*tauf*) atop a single course of white limestone river cobbles and measured 80 cm wide.

The mudbrick walls on stone footings in Grid S22 rested on the same level as the columned-hall structure, but its north end was almost certainly demolished as part of the construction of the Period V columned hall (Pl. 3.18). The earlier building likely had a bench which abutted its fragmentary northwestern interior corner in Room 8 (Fig. 3.19), although little was recorded of this feature—if it is a bench it is an interesting link to later styles of Late Bronze and Iron Age architecture and provides strong evidence that Room 8 was in fact a usable room and not an architectural "filler" contemporary with the Period V building to the north and meant to close the gap between Room 8 and Room 7. When this building was removed during excavation, a layer of white powder was found beneath its stone foundations, which the excavators identified as the remains of reeds or reed matting (Pl. 3.19).

To the north of the Period V columned hall, Rooms 18–19 likely represent the remains of another early Period V structure (Fig. 3.10, Pl. 3.16). Little information was recorded pertaining to these mudbrick walls. Dyson's notes mention, "To west of rear wall of main room of V house another structure visible in floor—half-full-half brick walls." (Observations 1974).

The presence of these earlier building phases associated with a MBW assemblage proves the overlying RS22–23 columned hall postdates the earliest phase of the MBW horizon. In the early LBA, we instead see an unusual, repeated architectural form on the northwest High Mound consisting of square stalls or closed cells in rows following the mound's major contours (Fig. 3.10). While the architectural exposure is woefully limited, it bears little in common with the architecture of the later LBA and Iron I in the same area. To be sure, we must exercise caution when citing columned halls as a hallmark of the arrival of the MBW horizon and as evidence for the stark contrast between Hasanlu V and VI. *We currently have no evidence of columned halls from the earliest MBW levels at Hasanlu and the earliest attested architectural phase(s) indicate a radically different architectural form.* We must also remember that we lack architecture dating to the MBIII in Ušnu-Solduz from which to draw comparisons, and little from the Terminal MBII aside from Dinkha.

The excavations in RS22–23 were not continued to the base of the MBW deposit, and no indications of Period VI material were recorded. The earliest possible date for MBW in this area thus remains an open question. I would tentatively place the earliest MBW levels excavated in RS22–23 in the 15th–late 14th centuries BC. The later columned-hall structure of Period V predates the 13th century BC by radiocarbon (P-2161). The Period V deposit was in turn sealed by what is likely another columned hall of late Period V–Period IVc dated to the 13th–12th centuries BC (P-2378). This chronology is confirmed by the ceramic sequence (see Chapter 4).

Q24–25 and R24/Burned Building III (Period V–IVc)

Burned Building III dominated the northwestern High Mound in Hasanlu IVb and presumably also Period IVc (Figs. 3.5, 3.9). Ephemeral remains of earlier MBW occupation were also found in this area predating the construction of BBIII (Stratum 11). As is the case with the RS22–23 buildings of Periods V and IVc, BBIII was a columned-hall structure and provides important information on the development of the built environment in the LBA and early Iron Age of western Iran.

The destruction of the Terminal Period IVb phase of the BBIII complex has been dated on the basis of radiocarbon to the late 9th century (see above). This date is naturally open to some revision pending additional radiocarbon determinations, but stratigraphically the destruction of BBIII can be linked to the same Terminal IVb destruction in all adjacent excavated areas. Work conducted by T. Cuyler Young in 1964 revealed the initial construction of the building dated to Period IVc and yielded evidence on the evolution of columned-hall architecture, especially the supposed later addition of porticos to many of these structures in the Iron II (Dyson 1965:198; Young 1966:66; 2002:387). The central point with regard to BBIII concerned the question of the addition of the portico room (Room 6) to the original building in Period IVb (Fig. 3.5, Pl. 3.20). The columned hall (Room 9) and anteroom (Room 7) were interpreted as the core area of the initial construction. A similar developmental sequence was posited for BBII on the basis of the limited evidence available at the time (see below). By extension, Dyson and Young's hypothetical evolution of the architectural form was used to date other structures with porticos in their original plans to the later part of the Iron II sequence—most notably, the BBI complex (see, for example, Dyson and Muscarella 1989:1; Young 2002:388). With regard to the BBI complex, Young has declared: "Clearly the architects of Hasanlu IV had now reached the conclusion that a well planned monumental building with a columned hall, such as BBIW, should have both a portico and anteroom. The concept of the portico on the facade of a building has arrived in Iron Age Iran" (2002:388). Closer inspection shows the portico rooms of BBs II and III were original features, however, and undermines the notion they were Iron II innovations. It is important to differentiate here between the portico—a wide entry with columns—and the portico room itself. *For the excavations at Hasanlu, the floor levels on which the actual column bases of the portico entries rested were not recorded; rather, the stratigraphic relationships of the portico rooms were investigated.* We do not know whether the early phases of the columned halls all had porticos, but they did have portico rooms. With regard to the dating of the initial phase of BBIII, we have only one ceramic assemblage collected from Grid Q24, circumstantial evidence, and similarities in its use-life to other Burned Buildings on the citadel with which to attribute it to Period IVc. Radiocarbon samples were not collected for the early phases of the building. The overall body of evidence from Hasanlu, however, suggests that porticos were introduced in Period IVc.

The majority of BBIII was excavated to the Terminal Period IVb destruction level in 1962. In 1964, the area of BBIII Rooms 6–8 and areas outside of the structure to the south (Fig. 3.5) were excavated below the level of the Terminal Period IVb destruction in Grids Q24–25 and R25 (Figs. 3.20–3.23). Operation Q24 was excavated 70 cm below the Terminal Period IVb floor. To the south, three trenches were excavated in Grid R25 along the walls of BBIII and BBVIII and perpendicular to both, leaving an unexcavated block in the middle of the grid (Fig. 3.5). These trenches were roughly 2 m wide, and the northern trench was carried down below the earliest phase of the BBIII courtyard (Figs. 3.5, 3.20). Few notes were taken for the 1964 excavations in Q24–25 and R25, although Dyson did record the overall excavation strategy and results in an unpublished Hasanlu Newsletter, reporting that:

> Cuyler [Young] demolished Burned Building III in order to clear a reasonable area to go deeper hoping to find more evidence concerning the overlap of periods IV and V. We gambled that somewhere in the area would be a structure of some sort but lost as there was only a deep accumulation of ash and animal bones mixed with broken pottery [Grid Q24 Strata 10–11] and one enclosure wall [Grid Q24 Stratum 11]. *We did learn, however, that Burned Building III had not been built all at once, the portico having been added sometime after the main building was built. We also found that the main building had two earlier floor levels accumulated during its long history and two pavement levels in the open courtyard out in front.* (Hasanlu Newsletter, July 26, 1964, emphasis my own)

The excavators first removed the walls and destruction-level floors of BBIII, leaving some stone footings *in situ* as reference points. Below the Terminal Period IVb destruction surfaces of Rooms 6–9, Young found evidence of earlier floor levels and fill layers—amounting

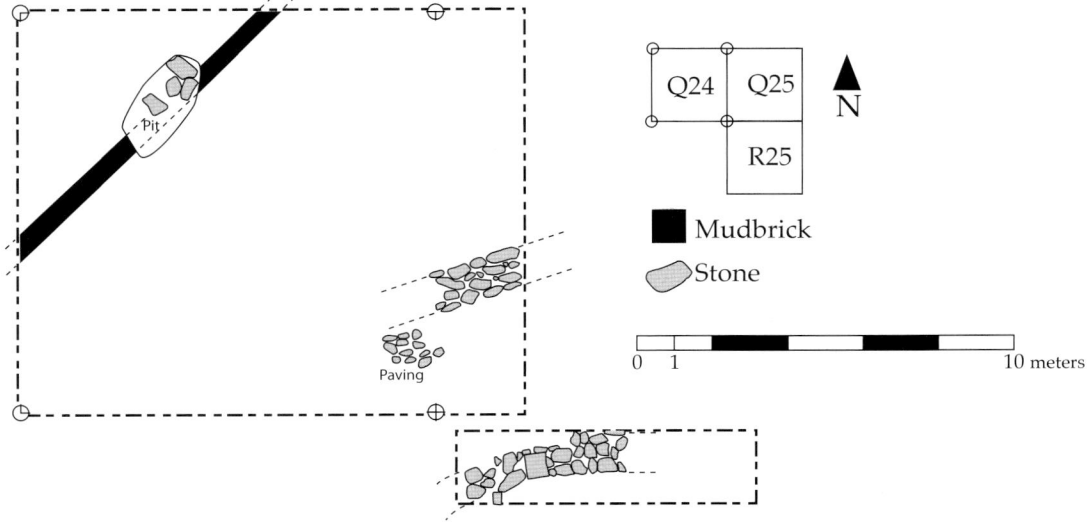

Fig. 3.20 Hasanlu Tepe: the Q24 Area Pre-Burned Building III.

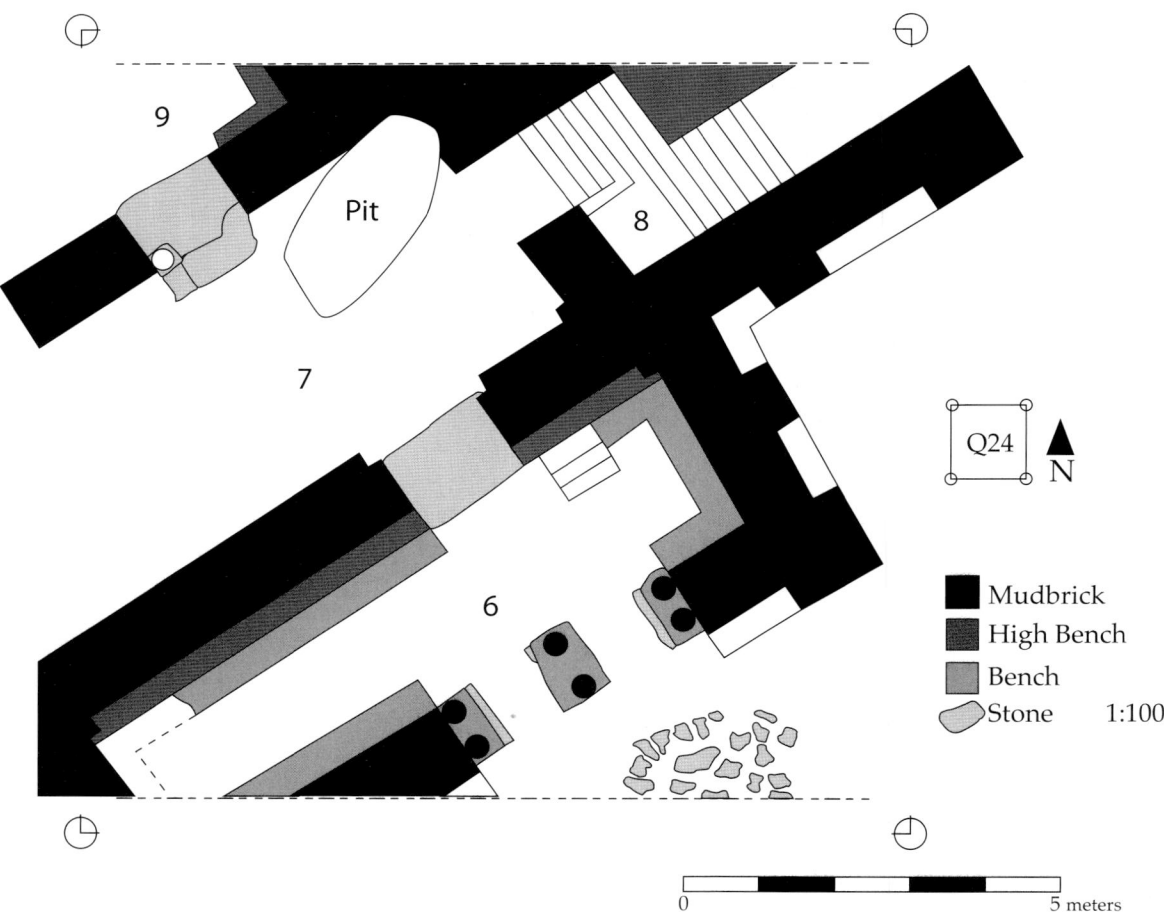

Fig. 3.21 Hasanlu Tepe: the entry to Burned Building III of probable Period IVc as excavated in 1962–64.

to approximately 30 cm of deposit—which ran against the lower stone footings of the structure along with evidence for widespread burning.[16] This material was designated Stratum 10. The manner in which material was collected and recorded in Q24 hinders us somewhat since many strata, divisible into three architectural phases, were recorded under the single Stratum 10 designation. Not all these strata, however, were associated with BBIII (see below). The "lumped" ceramic assemblage recovered from these phases nevertheless represents one of the few of early Period IVb–IVc from the site (see Chapter 4).

The majority of the architecture and stratigraphy recorded in 1964 relates to the building's southeast corner, where Young drew two important sections (Fig. 3.21).[17] In an L-shaped north-south and east-west section (Section A–A′), deposits running against the exterior south faces of Rooms 6 and 8 and predating the building were drawn and described (Fig. 3.22). Young did not describe all strata in the section, which include: loose, bricky flooring (Stratum 10a); ashy, striated layers (Stratum 10b); and brick wash with striated layers of burned material (Strata 10c–d).[18] In this section, this same deposit seems to run against the exterior face of the eastern wall of Room 6 (the portico), but at the 90° turn in the section Young recorded stratigraphic disjunctions.[19] Curiously, in another north-south section running from this same face of the portico room (the matrices were not recorded), he noted that the stone foundations of the portico *continued down, as had the other walls of the building, and were associated with a lower stone pavement to the south*, in the BBIII courtyard (Fig. 3.23). *No cut line of a foundation trench for the portico was recorded.* Conversely, the south wall of the stairwell (Room 8) of BBIII *appears on the recorded section to have been constructed in a foundation trench that cuts through two earlier architectural phases* (Fig. 3.22). This probable foundation trench is not labeled on the original section. It might alternatively be interpreted as a layer of plaster, but plasters were seldom recorded by the excavators in sections and, to my knowledge, were never recorded in such a manner by Young. It therefore seems certain that these footings were set in a foundation trench, which cut through Strata 10c3 and 10d (Fig. 3.22).[20] Stratum 10h, the only stratum *potentially* separating the anteroom and stairwell from the portico, might in fact represent intentional fill brought in to level the area under the portico at the time of the construction of the rest of the building.

The buttressed façade of BBIII also provides supporting evidence that the portico room was original to the structure. These buttresses span the entire southern façade, comprising the south walls of Room 6, 8, and 12 (Fig. 3.5). The buttresses were original to the building and so date to the Iron I. Later, the buttresses on the south end of the building were incorporated into Room 5 in Period IVb, when Rooms 1–5 were added to the BBIII complex. These buttresses (Pls. 3.21, 3.22) were not mentioned in the publication record associated with BBIII (cf. Dyson 1965: fig. 5; 1989a:112, figs 6a, 6b; Young 1966: fig. 3; 2002: fig. 2). The niching and buttressing start at the top level of the stone footings of the building—thus the footings form a shelf inside the niche. The top level of the footings was the same across the southern façade. If the portico room was also a Period IVb addition we have a rather strange developmental history for the building, with buttresses added to a façade, which were then quickly covered over by the addition of a storeroom (Room 5) and kitchen (Room 4).

Finally, the Section B–B′ recorded by Young in 1964 for deposits against the southern wall of Room 6 shows it to be associated with the earliest known surface of the BBIII courtyard, which in all other cases had been interpreted as belonging to the earliest phases of construction of the BBIII complex (Fig. 3.23). The strata of this section (here called Strata 10x1–10x6) were not labeled or described, but they are clearly the same strata as 10a–10c1 of Section A–A′. The positions of these two sections would indicate that both recorded the strata in the courtyard just southeast of the building. Therefore, the strata should be expected largely to match; however, they do not match in terms of their details, although both show two floor levels in the courtyard associated with the portico room and Room 8. The fact that the lower stone paving/plaster surface is obviously associated with the portico room wall was never accounted for in interpretations of the phasing of the portico room. With regard to the earlier paved surface, Young wrote in his excavation notes that it

> represents the earliest front courtyard pavement of B.B. III at ca. 30 cm below last floor level of Period IV excavated in 1962 [Terminal Period IVb]. [The] Section against southeast corner [of] portico room, B.B. III indicates Pavement

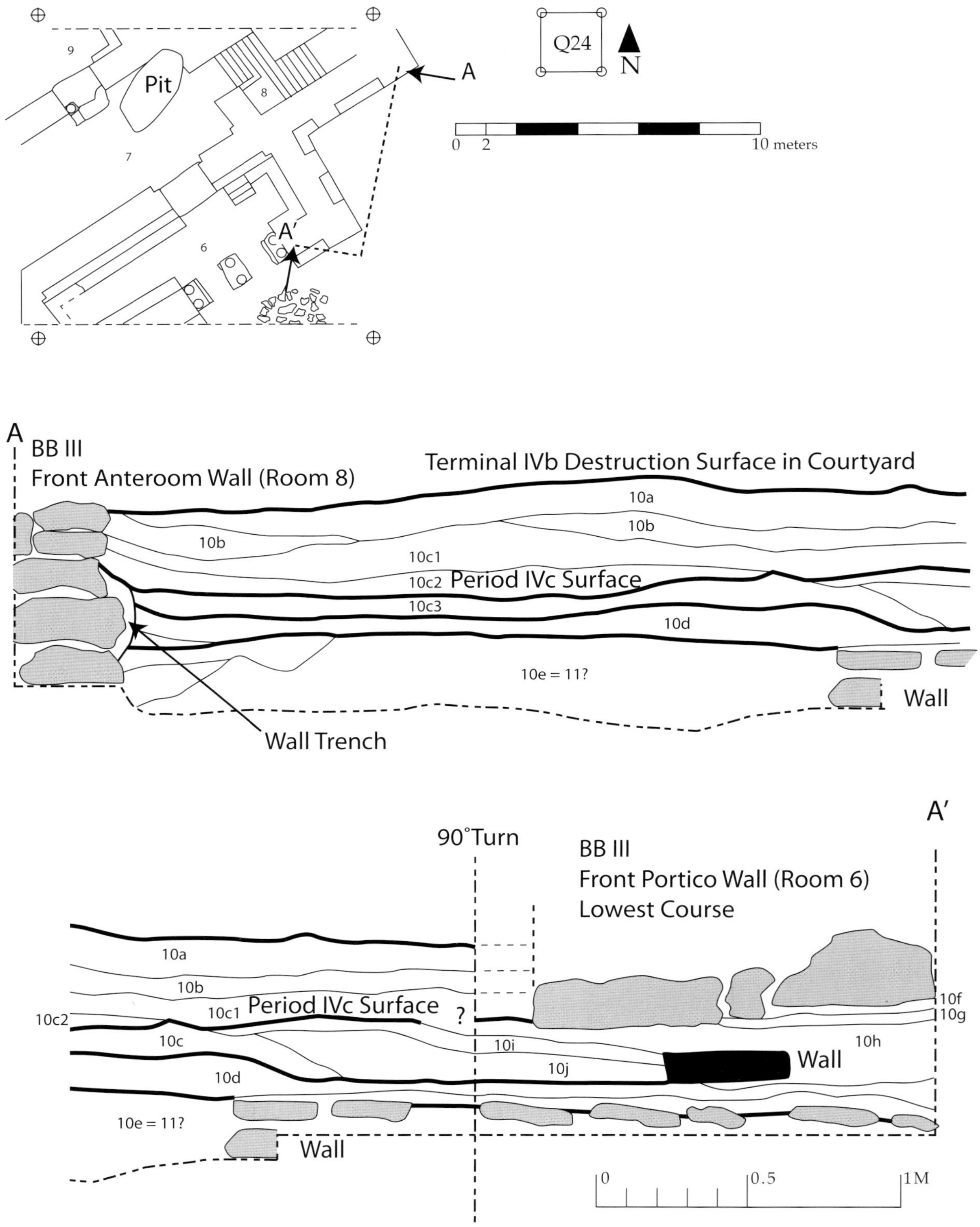

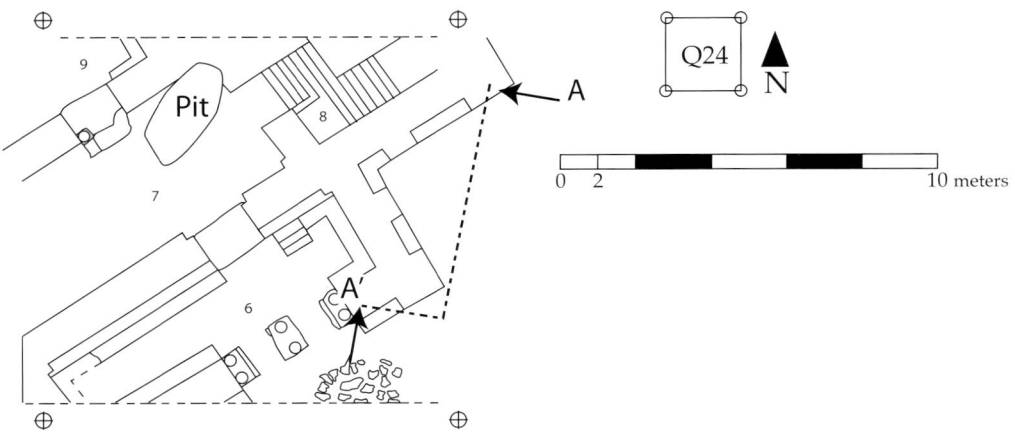

Fig. 3.22 Hasanlu Tepe: section A–A' of the entry area of BBIII.

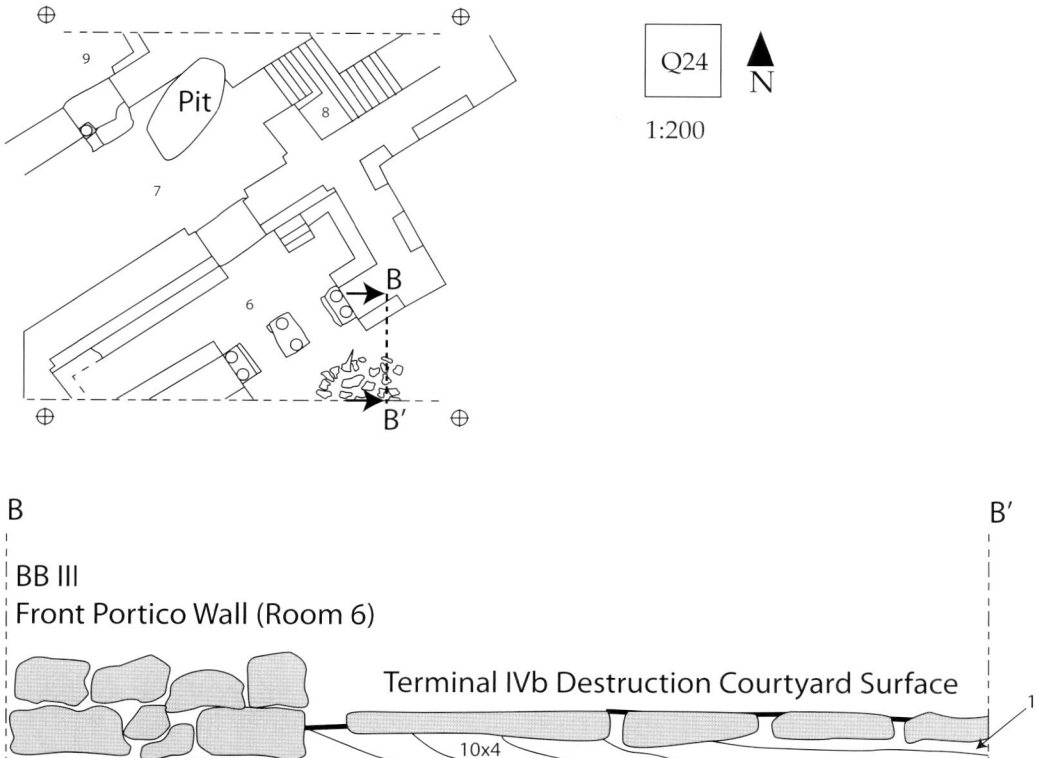

Fig. 3.23 Hasanlu Tepe: section B-B' of the entry area of BBIII.

Z gradually covered over during course of building's occupation. Steep accumulation of debris against wall face and eventually over pavement. Area then artificially leveled, without adjustment in wall, and upper pavement and floor as excavated in 1962 laid. (Hasanlu Excavation Notebook 18, Hasanlu Project Archives)

I am uncertain why these multiple lines of evidence were not taken into account in the phasing of the building: the clear conclusion is the portico room dates to the building's earliest phase.

Below the level of BBIII in the northwest corner of Q24 lay a narrow mudbrick wall cut by a pit (Fig. 3.20). The pit postdates Period IVb, cutting that level as well. This was the lowest level reached, and was designated Stratum 11. While this stratum/building phase was not linked to the sections recorded for the southeastern part of Q24, these remains likely correspond to the lower walls shown in Young's Section A–A´, designated Strata 10c3–10e (Fig. 3.22). For the sake of argument, were we to discredit the existence of the previously mentioned foundation trench associated with the stone footings of Room 8 (Fig. 3.22), its south wall would be potentially contemporary to this earlier architectural level, and thereby the Room 8 stairwell would predate BBIII—an architectural argument *reductio ad absurdum*!

In summary, BBIII was constructed sometime in Period IVc. The portico room formed part of the original building plan, and the southern façade of the building was buttressed. Evidence was found of burning associated with the earlier phase(s) of use designated as Stratum 10. The ceramics from Q24 Stratum 10, while drawn from mixed contexts, do not contain substantial amounts of Late MBW and can be placed within the timeframe of Middle MBW or the Iron I period (see Chapter 4). The building's stratigraphic position and orientation indicate it was contemporary to the Period IVc RS22–23 Building and its successor BBVIIE, as well as the T22 and U22 Period IVc buildings (Fig. 3.9). For Period IVc there are no continuous sections that link the structure to surrounding areas. The narrow open space between BBIII and the RS22–23 IVc Building served as an entrance to the large open space located on the northwestern citadel, as in Period IVb. The Period IVb northwest citadel resembles that of Period IVc in terms of its plan with the exceptions that a large enclosed forecourt was added to BBIII in Period IVB and in late Period IVc the RS22–23 IVc Building was demolished and a tower was constructed over its staircase. This tower—BBVIIE—flanked a gateway previously called the Double Gate, but little evidence of the southern half of this supposed double gate was recorded.[21]

The Southern High Mound

Excavations commenced on the southern High Mound in 1957 as part of a trans-citadel trench running north-south across the entire mound in Operations II, VII, IX, and XIV. A large horizontal clearance to the Terminal Period IVb destruction level was begun in 1958 and would continue until the close of work by the Hasanlu Project, moving from southwest

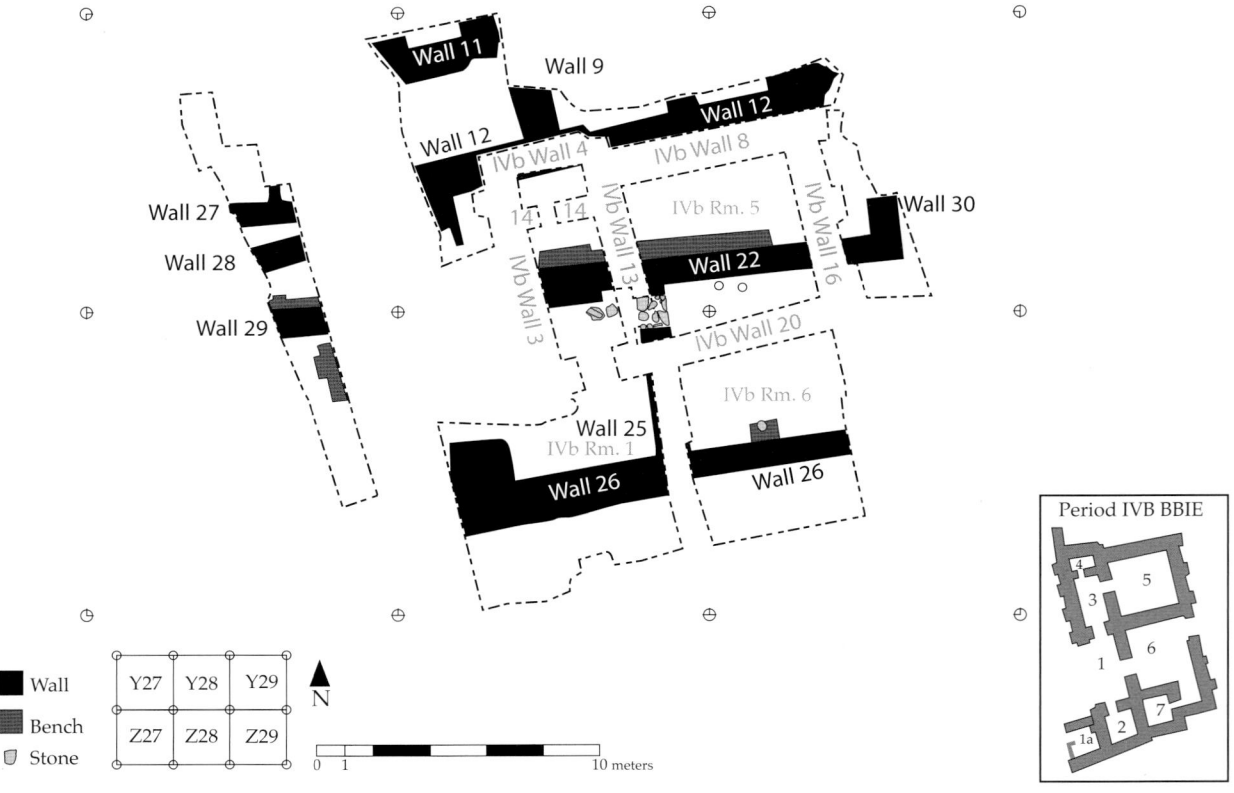

Fig. 3.24 Hasanlu Tepe: the YZ27–29 area as excavated showing remains of Periods V–IVc below Period IVb Burned Building I East.

TABLE 3.5. The Phasing of the YZ27–29 Building and BBIE

Phase	Period	Comments
IVb: 1	Terminal Period IVb	Widespread destruction level with victims on final floor levels of BBIE and BBIW
IVb: 2	Period IVb	BBIE Portico (Room 1) and Rooms 1a, 2, and 7 added.
IVc: 1	Late IVc–early IVb	YZ27–29 demolished. Core of BBIE constructed in major building project. Radiocarbon date of late 12th–11th century BC from BBIE (P-0423). BBIW constructed.
IVc: 2	Late IVc–early IVb	YZ27–29 substantially altered to a form resembling later BBIE.
IVc: 3a	Period IVc	East-west passage completely blocked and north-south passage blocked as the gateway's position was relocated, probably to the west. Radiocarbon date (P-2391A) of later 13th–12th centuries cal BC. Building activities suggest major modifications in the area of the Lower Court/southern citadel.
IVc: 3b	Late Period V–IVc	Gateway modified to limit east-west access. Mudbrick floor of Rooms 2, 4, and 5.
V: 1a	Late Period V	Known from soundings and collected as "Stratum 11."
V: 1b	Late Period V	Initial gateway built. Known from soundings and collected as "Stratum 11." Precursor to BBII built to the southeast.

to northeast. Since the excavation of the southwestern High Mound was conducted in the early seasons of the project, it is often difficult to interpret the dataset due to poor recordkeeping—sometimes notes are wholly absent—and excavations tended to be fast paced and rather unsystematic. Work conducted from 1970–1977 was of far better quality, and many of the earlier areas dug in the 1950s and 1960s were revisited in follow-up studies to clarify architectural and stratigraphic details.

As in the area of the northwestern High Mound, the first major period encountered in most excavated areas dated to the late 13th–14th centuries AD, or the Ilkhanid Period (Danti 2004). Below this were confusing levels of fragmentary and ephemeral Period II/IIIa remains. In Hasanlu IIIc, the peripheries of the High Mound were heavily disturbed by the construction of a massive Urartian fortification wall (Kroll 2011). This wall sat in a deep, wide construction trench, which often obliterated Period IVb remains. Dyson associated this wall with "garrison rooms"; a recent reanalysis by Kroll, however, has suggested that this is less directly related to the Urartian presence at Hasanlu (2011), and this occupation is now distinguished as subperiod Hasanlu IIIb. As in most other areas of the High Mound, the excavators found a massive layer of ash and burned debris beneath the Period III deposits representing the destruction of the Period IVb citadel. Period IVb remains were particularly well preserved in the south and include the buildings of the Upper Court and Lower Court—BBIW, BBIE, BBII, BBIV, and BBV—and two small structures at the southwestern corner of the citadel referred to as BBIX (the "Square House") and BBX (the "Bead House"). Given the remarkable preservation, few soundings were excavated beneath Terminal Period IVb. The most important exposure of pre-Period IVb remains is the YZ27–29 Building, part of a late Period V–IVc internal gateway on the citadel. Small soundings were also completed below BBII and in the area of BBIX and BBX.

YZ27–29 (Early Period IVc)

Reanalysis of the YZ27–29 Building, first published as Period "V" (Dyson 1977b:156–58, fig. 2), has resulted in substantial revision of its dating, phas-

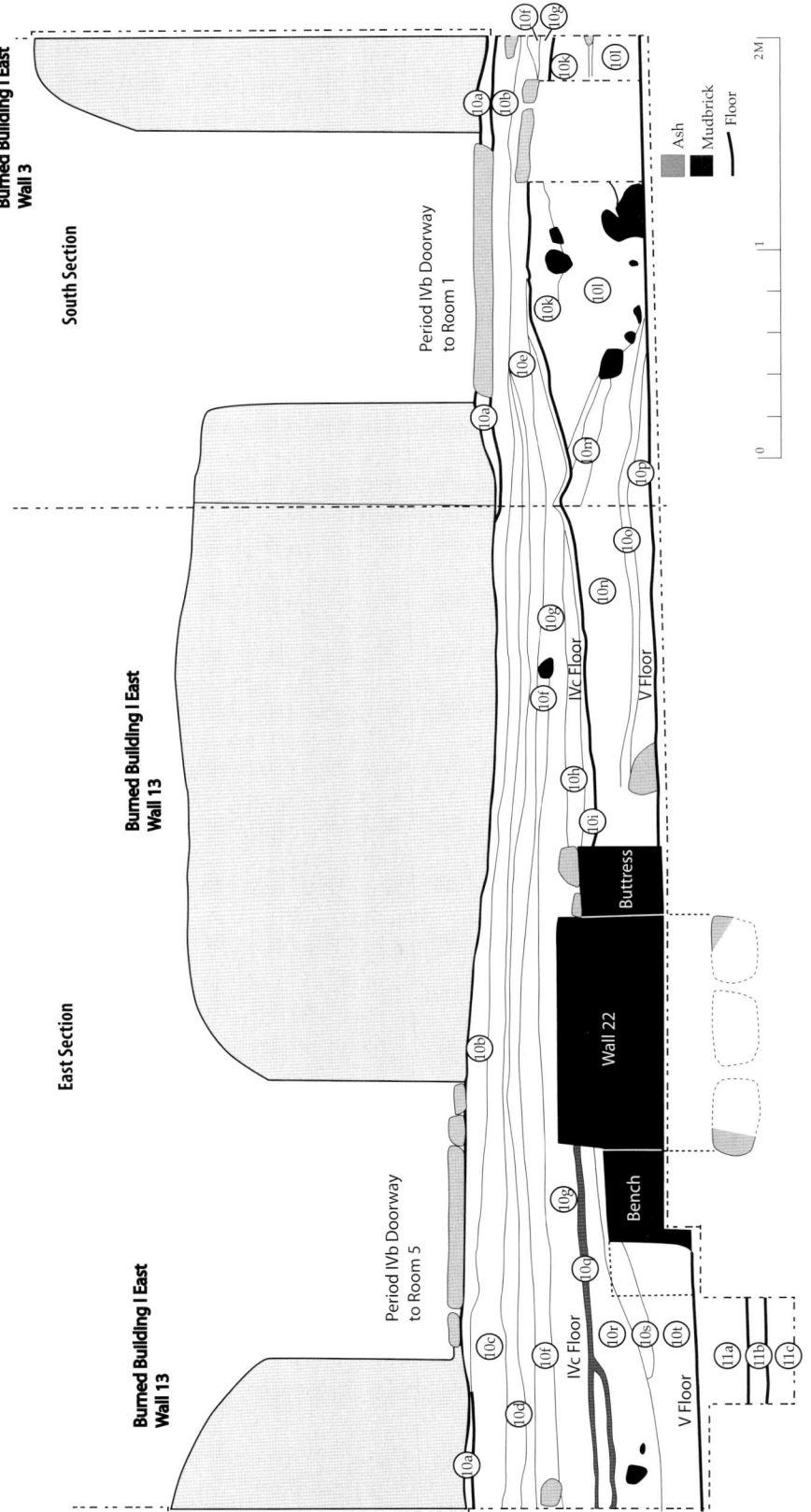

Fig. 3.25 Hasanlu Tepe: east and south sections below BBIE Room 3 of Period IVb.

ing, and architectural plans. Dyson called this structure the "largest and most impressive of the Iron I buildings" and referred to it as a "monumental public building" (1977b:155). He identified only two architectural phases beneath Terminal Period IVb: "The YZ28–29 structure lies stratigraphically below a fragmentary foundation which in turn directly underlies the standing B.B. IE structure of Iron II. The latter structure is dated by radiocarbon dates from its adjoining part (B.B. IW) to a construction date in the 11th century" (1977b:155). In fact, the YZ27–29 Building formed part of an internal gateway during late Period V and Period IVc (Table 3.5), and these structures were thus the precursors of BBIE, which served as the eastern side of the monumental gateway/passageway to the Upper Court. The Upper Court, oriented north-south, linked BBIW and the Lower Court area to the open area to the north (Fig. 1.5).

The YZ27–29 "structure" consists of at least three major architectural phases—IVc:2, IVc:3, and V:1—and was used and modified over a long period of time (Table 3.5). Dyson lumped Phases IVc:3 and V:1 into a single building (1977b: fig. 2). The "fragmentary foundation" above the structure forms part of the IVc:2 building, and the overlying BBIE of late Period IVc–Terminal Period IVb is preliminarily divisible into at least three architectural phases or subphases (Phases IVb:1–2 and IVc:1). A single radiocarbon sample (Appendix II, P-2391) places Phase IVc:3a between the later 13th–12th centuries BC, or squarely within Period IVc/Iron I.[22]

The Excavation of YZ27–29

Excavations in the area of Grids YZ27–29 began in 1958 with the opening of Y27 and Z27 as part of the clearing of the eastern end of Period IVb BBIW.[23] Work was not carried out below the Terminal Period IVb destruction level. The area of YZ28–29 was excavated in 1959.[24] As in YZ27, Period III deposits lay just below the surface. The area contained some post-Period IV burials above, and occasionally cutting into, the Terminal Period IVb destruction level. YZ28–29 took in the larger part of BBIE and the southern end of the Upper Court Gate. Burned Buildings IE and IW formed the boundaries of the V-shaped Upper Court, a paved area fronted to the north by stone steps. In a few areas the excavators revealed the tops of underlying early Period IVb and Period IVc features. In 1960, the north end of Grid Y28, having not been completely cleared in 1959, was excavated as part of Grid X28 to the north.[25] The area between the Upper Court Gate's southern tower (Room 4) and the area between it and BBIE were explored (Fig. 1.5). Pre-Period IVb features were uncovered in some areas and were subsequently included on architectural plans of Period IVb (see below).

In 1972, the areas beneath BBIE and the eastern façade of BBIW were carefully excavated and relatively well recorded by Greg Gorton and Eric Pasternak. Excavations were largely conducted within the bounds of the rooms of BBIE to preserve the Iron II standing remains (Fig. 3.24). Walls and architectural features of the late Period V–IVc building were also traced in short tunnels. In most areas excavations were carried down through an earlier floor level of Period IVb to the floor level of late Period V–Period IVc (Phase IVc:3, see below). The Phase IVc:3b building found in YZ28–29 had contemporary mudbrick paved floors in Rooms 2, 4, and 5, providing a certain degree of stratigraphic control. Collections from this "level" were given the single stratum designation "Stratum 10," which is mainly Period IVc with a potential mix of some early Period IVb from above and late Period V material from below. A few deeper test trenches were also excavated, but these were not clearly delineated on any plans. Collections from these strata were grouped under "Stratum 11" (Phases V:1a and V:1b). The ceramic assemblage of YZ27–29 is the largest and best available for Hasanlu IVc.

Phase V:1

The earliest phase, divided into subphases 1a and 1b, was reached only in a few limited soundings located along the east baulk of Grid Z28 within the confines of the overlying BBIE Room 3 (Figs. 3.25, 3.26), the east end of the baulk of Z28 within BBIE Room 6 (Fig. 3.30), and the east end of BBIE Room 1. The plan of the building is largely reconstructed (Figs. 3.35, 3.36). The initial construction date of the tower (Room 1, Walls 9, 11) and the northern façade of the trapezoidal room (Room 2, Wall 12 west) are not known, but they date before Phase IVc:3a (see below). Wall 22 was constructed and plastered before the buttresses on its southern face and the bench to its north, marking Phase V:1a (Pl. 3.23). It was not determined whether Wall 22 and its buttress and bench rested on

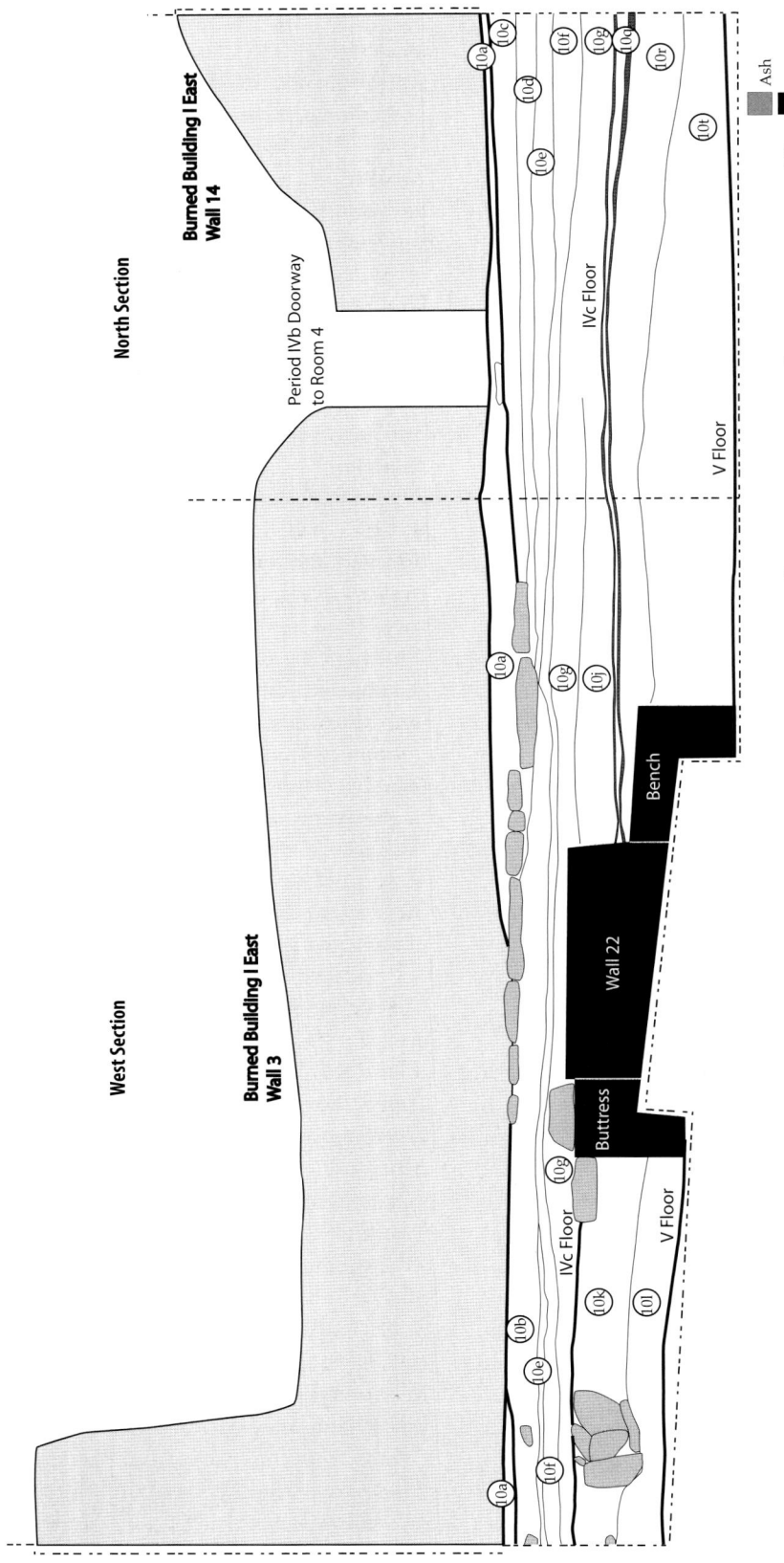

Fig. 3.26 Hasanlu Tepe: west and north sections below BBIE Room 3 of Period IVb.

the same floor level. A doorway was located at the east end of Room 2, but its dimensions are not known since its northern doorjamb lay in an unexcavated area covered by the massive stone paving of the Period IVb Lower Court. The southernmost wall of the building (Wall 26) was almost certainly constructed in this period; however, in Phase IVc:3a (Fig. 3.38), the eastern end of this wall was almost completely cut away and rebuilt slightly off it original alignment following the addition of Wall 24 (Pl. 3.24, see below). The Phase V:1–IVc:3b northern face of Wall 26 and its east buttress were preserved as low wall stubs in Phase IVc:3a, in a reused Phase IVc:3b bench on the south side of Room 4, and as a low wall stub between the abutment of Wall 24 and the rebuilt Wall 26E (Figs. 3.27, 3.36–3.38; Pl. 3.24). In Phase V:1, Room 4 likely formed a dog-leg passageway linking the open space to the north with one to the east (just north of the BBII area, see below), as in Period IVb. Gravelly occupation debris was found in the soundings that reached this level. Opposing buttresses—one is reconstructed—possibly formed part of a gate (Fig. 3.36).

Phase IVc:3b

In this phase, Rooms 2, 4, and 5 were paved with mudbricks (Fig. 3.37, Pls. 3.25–3.26). The plan of Phase IVc:3b shows the substantial modifications made to the internal gates, passageways, and porticos following a plan familiar from later periods at Hasanlu, as a partitioning wall with a doorway (Rooms 4/5 Wall 25) was added across what had been a wide opening (Figs. 3.28, 3.30, 3.37). Based on analogy with contemporary and later architecture, the western entrance to Room 5, if any north-south wall existed there, would have been offset from the eastern doorway—that is, it would have been situated in the southwest. The Room 4/5 doorway had a stone threshold and a door pivot was found inside Room 4 flush with the northern doorjamb (Figs. 3.32, 3.37; Pl. 3.26b). Postholes located on the northern and southern edges of the room (Fig. 3.37) likely mark the roofline (Pl. 3.24), and the eastern end of the room was probably open to the sky; a fire pit or hearth was found in this area. A sunken area for a jar, with fragments of a jar base, was found at the southern edge of the roofline, probably meant to catch runoff from the roof. The southern posthole was set in a mudbrick bench and was stone lined.

Phase IVc:3a

At this point, the building was substantially altered with the blocking and narrowing of passageways (Fig. 3.38). The first modification involved the construction of Wall 24 between the eastern buttresses of Walls 22 and 26, probably to erect a more permanent roof over the western end of Room 4. This modification indicates that access to the probable court to the east was relocated, likely to the southwest in light of the changes to the west end of the building and concordant with points of access in later periods. In places, Wall 24 sat atop a thin layer of occupation debris which had accumulated on the IVc:3b mudbrick floor (Fig. 3.34, Stratum 10g1). Sometime later but before Phase IVc:2, the eastern end of the southern wall of Room 4 (Wall 26) was torn down and rebuilt slightly off its original position and alignment. Portions of the northern face of the wall were preserved in a reused bench and as wall stubs in the abutments of Wall 21, Wall 24, and Wall 26. Room 2 was shortened on its east end to align with the modifications in the east end of Room 4: Wall 21N was added as a new southeast corner and presumable doorjamb. This may be ultimately linked to modifications in the Lower Court and its associated monumental structures such as BBII and BBIV. As with Wall 24, Wall 21N sat atop a thin layer of occupational debris on the IVc:3b mudbrick floor. The northern façade of the structure was also modified with the construction of a new span of buttressed wall (Wall 12E). The excavators dug a tunnel from the northern baulk of Grid Y28 Room 2 (Fig. 3.33) to examine the wall's southern face and the associated IVc:3a floor level. They had missed this floor in Room 2 and/or it was not well preserved there. The ancient builders reinforced the join between the western (older) end of Wall 12W and the new, narrower eastern portion with a buttress, and a similar buttress on the same east-west alignment marks the older and newer portions of Wall 26/26E.

Excavations in Grids YZ27 uncovered evidence of IVc:3 walls blocking the putative gateway (Figs. 3.38, 3.40). These remains lay beneath the eastern façade of BBIW. Radiocarbon dates place this building's construction in the 11th century BC (Appendix II). The floor levels and elevations of these additions correspond to the IVc:3a floors of the western end of the main part of the YZ27–29 Building.

Based on comparisons to later gate structures of the Iron II, Walls 28 and 29 may have formed a trian-

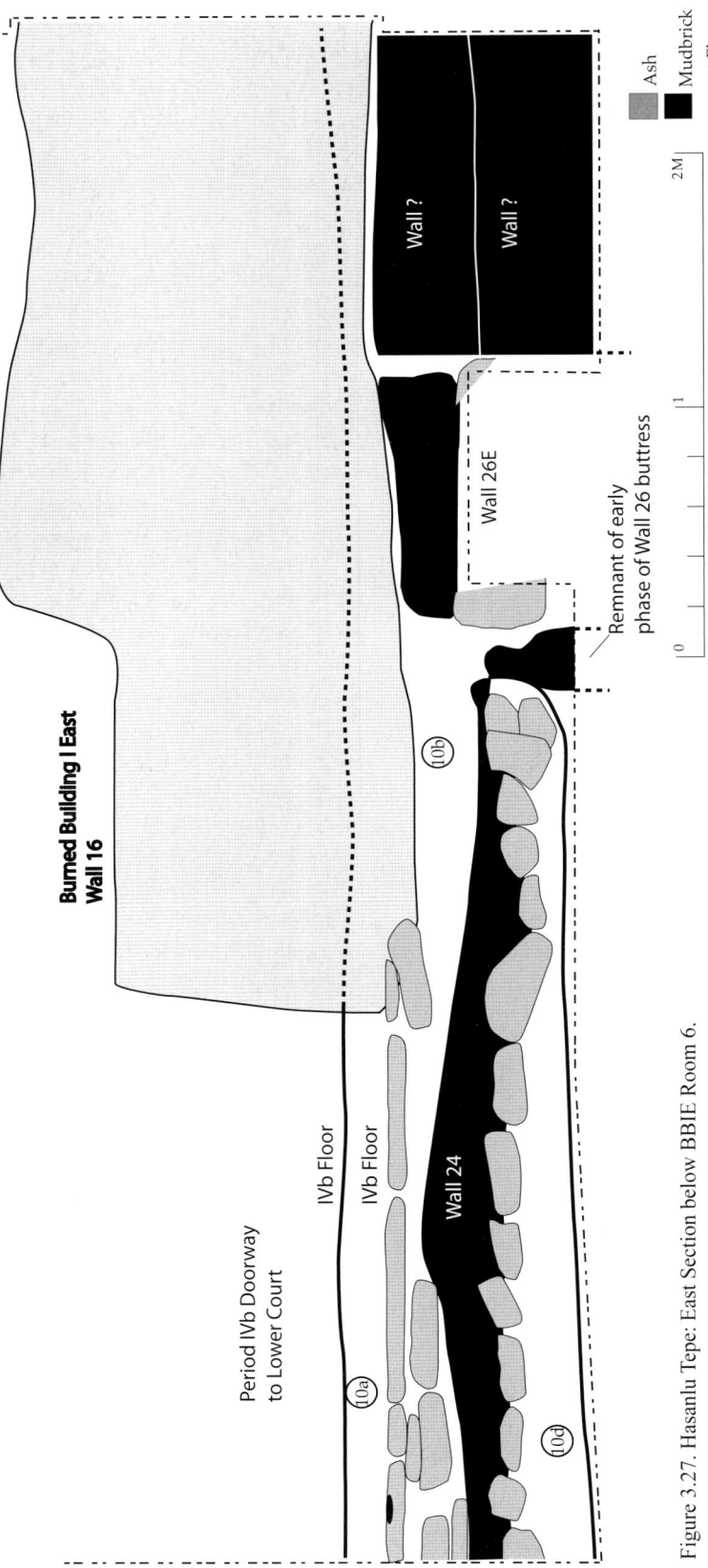

Figure 3.27. Hasanlu Tepe: East Section below BBIE Room 6.

Fig. 3.27 Hasanlu Tepe: east section below BBIE Room 6.

gular room, Room 3, similar to Room 7 of the Iron II internal gateway BBIVW (Fig. 3.41). The reconstructed line of Wall 29 is aligned with the projected southern buttress line of Wall 22, and Walls 28 and 27 would converge at the reconstructed western face of Tower 1 at the position of a reconstructed corner buttress (Fig. 3.38). A mudbrick bench with a projection was located on the north face of Wall 29. A similar bench was found just south of the wall and on the same alignment as Building Y27–29. This feature may mark the location of the west wall of Room 5.

Phase IVc:2
This phase is not well preserved and went largely unrecorded by the excavators. It is best attested in the northeast of Room 4/5 (Figs. 3.33, 3.39), where the excavators missed a wall that was shown in the sections but not otherwise identified. A large matte orange storage jar with vertical ribs was found at the level of the probable floor of this new building (Fig. 4.50:HH, Pl. 3.26a). The strata running against this wall sealed most of the interior walls of the former IVc:3 building, which had been almost completely leveled. The eastern wall of the building was cut down and a new wall, Wall 21, was built atop the wall stub (Fig. 3.39). Fragmentary stone footings were found at the northwest end of this wall that likely represent its continuation—they lay at the same level as the wall shown in the north section of Room 4/5 (Figs. 3.31, 3.33).[26] Earlier versions of the building would suggest a doorway was located in this northeast corner of Room 4/5—it had been relocated westward in Phase IVc:3a, presumably as the probable courtyard which preceded the Lower Court of Period IVb to the east took shape. The southern end of the building lay immediately below the initial floor level of Period IVb (Figs. 3.27–3.30). While little more can be said of the plan of this phase, overall the building foreshadows the general layout and alignment of BBIE. The end of Phase IVc:2 is marked by the leveling of the area and the construction of BBIE Phase IVc:1. This building was modified at least once, in Phase IVb:2, before it was destroyed by fire in Phase IVb:1.

Summary
Similar to the RS22–23 area, the reassessment of the construction history of the YZ27–29 Building and its functions provide additional support for the interpretation that the High Mound served as a fortified citadel in late Period V–IVc. This structure, with its buttressed façade, thickened exterior walls, trapezoidal room (Room 2), small buttressed tower (Room 1), and narrow triangular room (Room 3), resembles the Lower Court Gate of Period IVb (Fig. 3.41) which was located directly to the north slightly later in time. In the Hasanlu IVb citadel such buttressed façades faced large open courts and gave the impression, although not necessarily the reality, of architectural strength. The YZ27–29 Building therefore likely represents the remains of an internal gate. This interpretation is further supported by the fact that the passageway through the gate, reconstructed to the west of the tower, lies immediately below a passageway leading to the Upper Court of the IVb citadel—that is, there is a monumental entry below a later monumental entry. This continuity in the function of space attested over several centuries accords well with other late Period V and Period IVc exposures such as the late Period V and IVc buildings of U22 and RS22–23, as well as DD30–31 and BB28–29 (see below), the rooms of a Period IVc temple (and possibly one of late Period V) predating the overlying temple of BBII of Period IVb (Dyson and Voigt 2003). Many of the artifacts of the Terminal IVb (Iron II) level have long been thought to represent heirlooms of an earlier period of the citadel given their LBA and Iron I dates. We can now argue that a fortified citadel with elite spaces was present at Hasanlu during these periods.

Burned Building II (Periods IVc–IVb) and BB28–29 (Late Period V–Early Period IVc)

The delineation and dating of the various phases of BBII, a large temple dominating the southern citadel of Hasanlu, form the linchpin for understanding broader developments in the southern citadel. Early excavations in BBII were grossly under-recorded, but later efforts focused specifically on studying its development through time.

In 1974, soundings were dug in BBII to investigate its portico room and flanking storerooms. The most important work for understanding Period V and IVc are soundings through the Terminal IVb destruction-level floors of Room 13 (Test Trenches A–C) and Room 14 (a noncontiguous extension of Test Trench

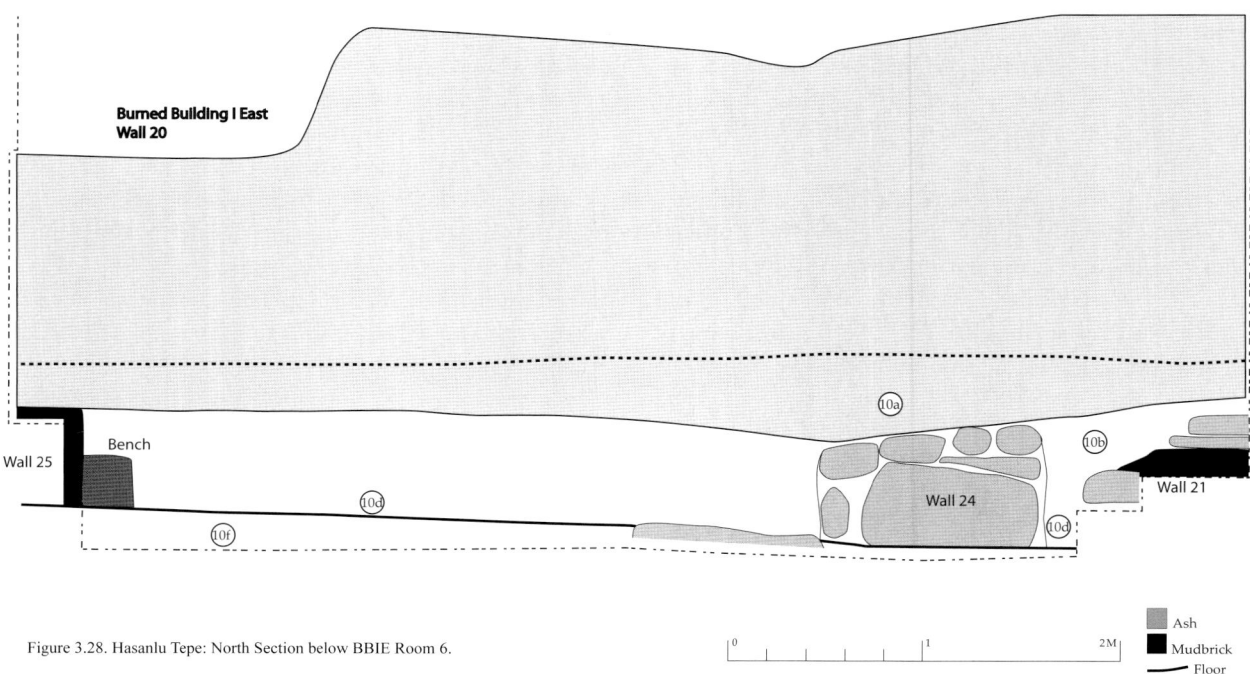

Fig. 3.28 Hasanlu Tepe: north section below BBIE Room 6.

C and Test Trench D) (Fig. 3.42, Dyson 1977b:158). There is no record of the results from Test Trench D. According to Dyson and Voigt, the western storerooms of BBII were added sometime after a widespread fire on the citadel that marked the *terminus ante quem* of the final use-phase of the Period IVc monumental buildings of the citadel (2003:222)—that is, the end of Period IVc. They wrote:

> Rereading of the original field notes and examination of computer-enhanced photographs indicate that the end of Period IVC is marked by a major fire (dated around 1100 BCE by radiocarbon), after which Burned Building II was reconstructed. The fire and rebuilding are visible archaeologically as a layer of pebbles and small pieces of charcoal enclosed in a double layer of mortar that runs between the first and second courses of brickwork above the free-standing stone foundation of the first construction phase. The storerooms on the east (room 12) and west (rooms 13–15) lack this feature and were therefore added after the IVC fire and date to Period IVB. The walls of room 16 are too poorly preserved to determine its date of construction, but since the foundations abut the west wall of the IVC building in a manner similar to that found in rooms 13–15 there is a good possibility that room 16 is also a VIB [SIC IVb] addition. (Dyson and Voigt 2003:222)

The authors assumed that the earliest phase of BBII dated to Period IVc (1250–1050 BC), following Dyson's use of this terminology as an architectural phase representing a chronological period, and not early Period IVb, which is essentially squeezed out of existence. The conflagration which ended Period IVc is not dated by radiocarbon; rather, samples from carbonized wooden beams (Appendix II, P-0421, P-0437, P-0440) found in the Terminal Period IVb destruction level provided radiocarbon dates for the rebuilding after the fire as did a date from carbonized debris found sandwiched in the rebuild line of the mudbrick walls of BBII (Appendix II, P-1230, see below). The assumption is that this building and other buildings of the IVb citadel were rapidly reconstructed after the IVc fire. The pooled mean for the three timbers is 1114–1005 cal BC at the one-sigma level and 1191–929 cal BC at the two-sigma level. The sample from within the walls of

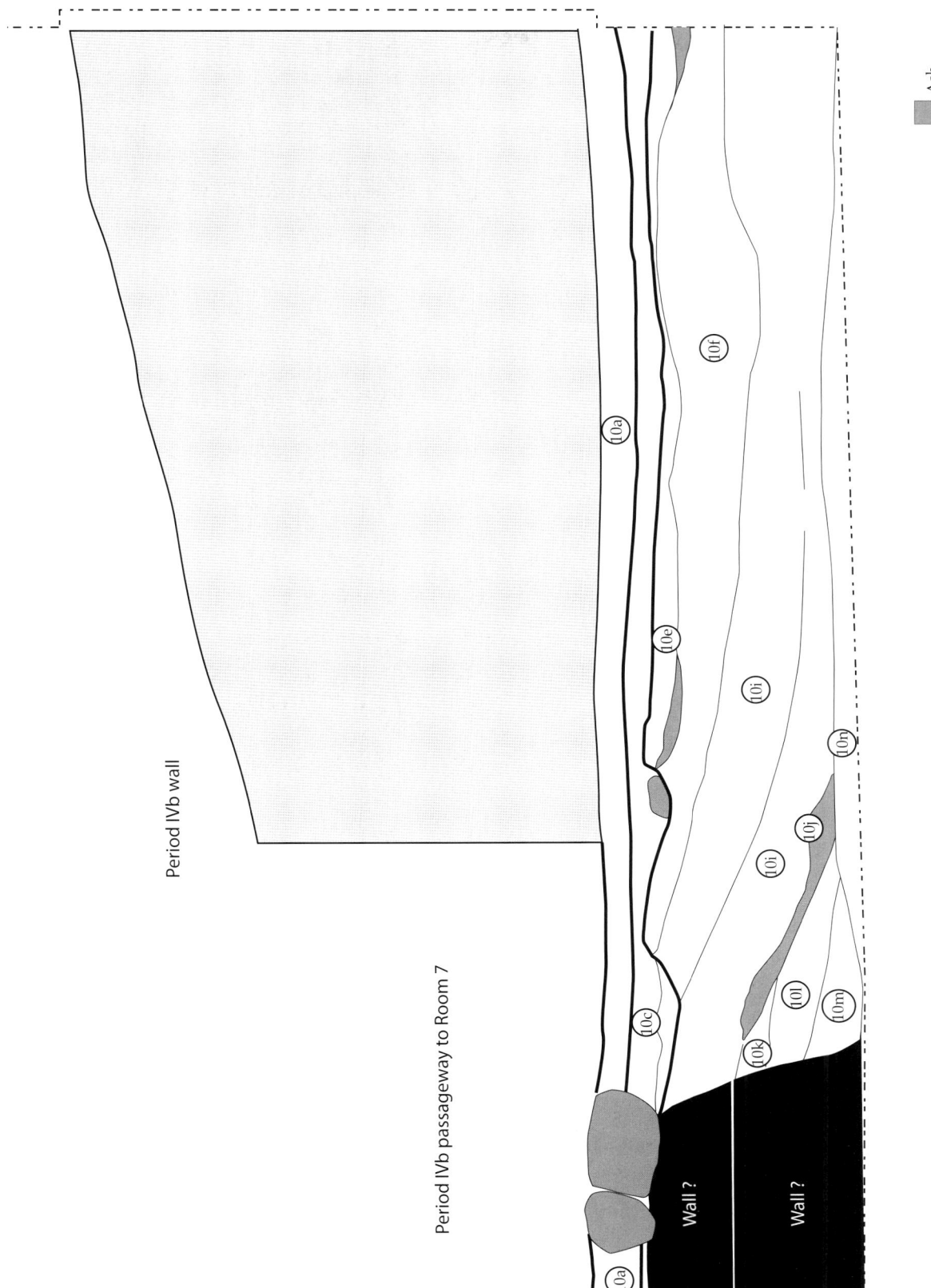

Fig. 3.29 Hasanlu Tepe: south section below BBIE Room 6.

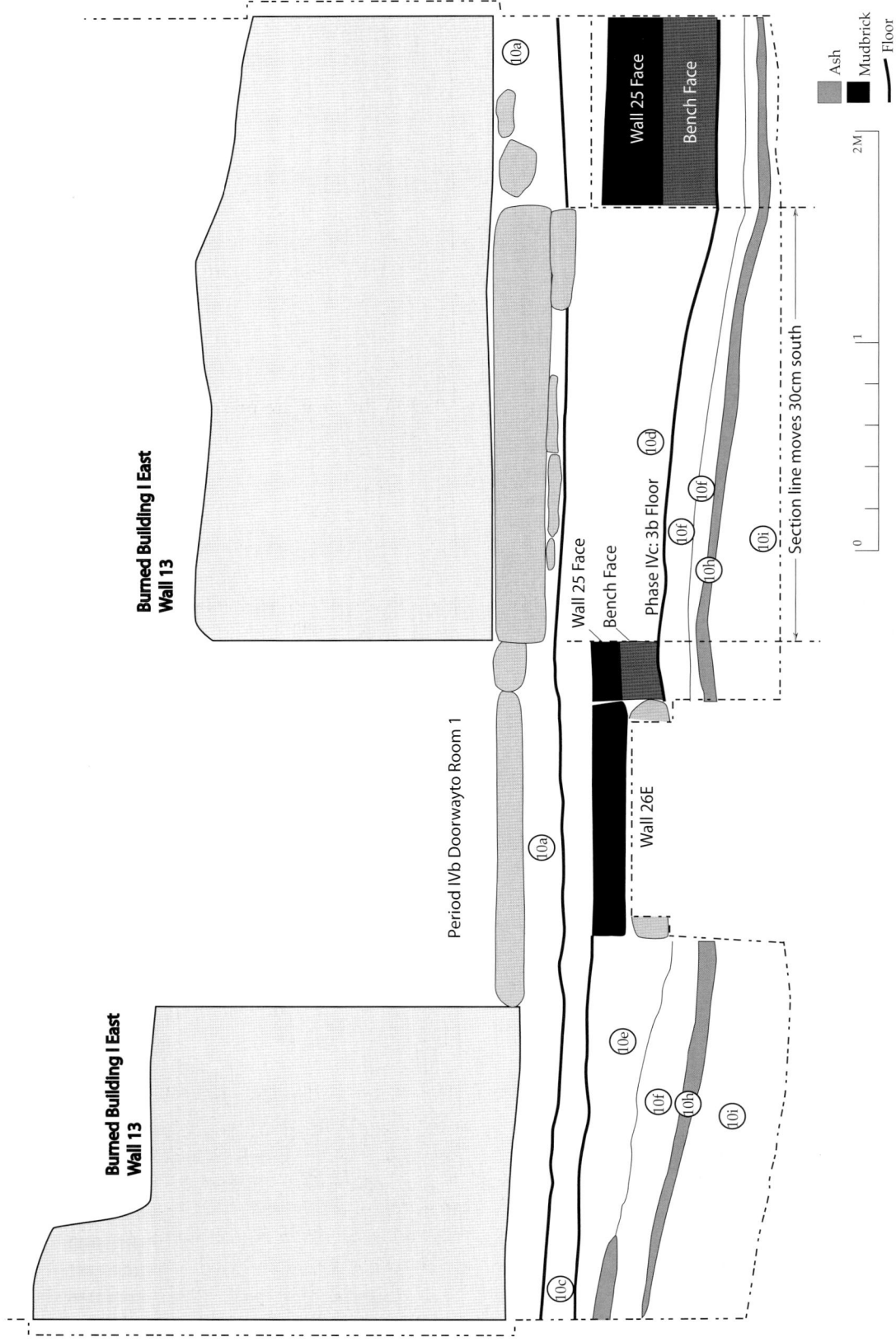

Fig. 3.30 Hasanlu Tepe: west section below BBIE Room 6.

BBII dates between 1110–906 cal BC at the one-sigma level and 1192–836 cal BC at the two-sigma level. A construction date for the final major version of BBII would thus seem to fall within the 11th–10th centuries BC, or late Period IVc–early Period IVb. Similar date ranges are available from other burned buildings on the citadel; hence the current estimated start date of 1050 BC for Period IVb at Hasanlu.

In its lowest level, Test Trench C in Grid BB28 exposed the foundations of the northeast corner of a building which ran diagonal to the axes of the overlying BBII (Figs. 3.43, 3.44, North Section Test Trench C; Dyson 1977b:158, fig. 3). The north wall was quite wide, measuring 1.50 m thick, and it was constructed on a leveled surface. The fragmentary remains of two southwest-northeast running walls ran south from this wall to form a room 3.25 m east-west with a stone-paved floor. To the north of the structure the excavators found an associated clay floor that lay 35 cm above the interior floor of the building. To the east, the building was separated from the eastern wall of an adjacent structure by a mudbrick blocking. Dyson notes that the construction technique of the BB28–29 foundations is similar to that of the Period IVb buildings (1977b:158), and that only one other room constructed in a similar manner has been found at Hasanlu—Room 3 in the northwest corner of BBII (Fig. 1.5), which he interprets as the lustral chamber of a temple given the presence of a hearth, a subterranean drain, and its stone-paved floor (1977b; Dyson and Voigt 2003). Dyson hints that the "Period V" structure might have had a similar function (1977b:158) and thus would provide evidence for continuity in the use of space in this area. He also notes that only the YZ27–29 Building (see above) has walls as thick as the north wall of the structure (but see CC27, below), implying that the BB28–29 structure might have been monumental in character. Dyson attributes the BB28–29 Building to "Period V" on the basis of:

1. the building's stratigraphic position immediately below the earliest phases of BBII, radiocarbon dated to Period IVc (12th century);[27]
2. the fact that BB28–29 "lies in the same relative horizon as the YZ28–29 Building [YZ27–29];
3. the associated ceramics, which were not illustrated and are unavailable for analysis (Dyson 1977b:158).

All three of these dating criteria are open to debate. In particular, since Dyson's 1977 interpretation of the BB28–29 structure the internal phasing of BBII has been revised, and so the date of the BB28–29 structure must be reconsidered. This re-dating is also important since a rare assemblage of late Period IVc–early Period IVb ceramics was recovered from the sounding (see below and Chapter 4).

As previously mentioned, Dyson and Voigt now argue the western storerooms of BBII which sealed the BB28–29 Building were not original to the building and were added in Period IVb to the plan of the original IVc structure shortly after the Terminal IVc fire: here, Dyson's use of "IVc" as an architectural phase must be kept in mind (Dyson and Muscarella 1989:1). In what are presumed to be the older parts of the building, the original mudbrick wall stubs of Period IVc were often separated from the overlying IVb brickwork by a layer of burned debris (Dyson and Voigt 2003:222). The aforementioned radiocarbon sample (P-1230) was collected from this layer in the north wall of the anteroom of BBII (Room 2) and dates to 1050–900 BC (Fig. 1.5, Appendix II). The authors do not elaborate on the depositional processes and/or the construction techniques which might have been responsible for these unusual intervening layers of mortar and debris, although other sources more explicitly attribute this intervening layer of charcoal, ash, and pebbles to construction work (Fishman and Lawn 1978:221, P-1230). Other evidence for the internal phasing of BBII is currently unavailable since plasters were not regularly removed from mudbrick walls to record masonry joins and abutments. The primary question is how putative destruction debris became lodged neatly atop existing mortar and then was covered by a new layer of mortar within the masonry of walls that were heavily plastered in Period IVc. The only tenable conclusion would be that this occurred during the rebuilding, when the Period IVc walls were cut down to the first course of brick above the existing surface in cases where Period IVc use-debris and destruction-debris had accumulated, and it is this destruction-debris that presumably came to be introduced into the mortar joints during the construction of the new walls. In terms of deposition, the debris layers present in the mortar must be the result of proximity to ground level rather than wind action given the introduction of pebbles and large pieces of charcoal and the fact that the debris formed a distinc-

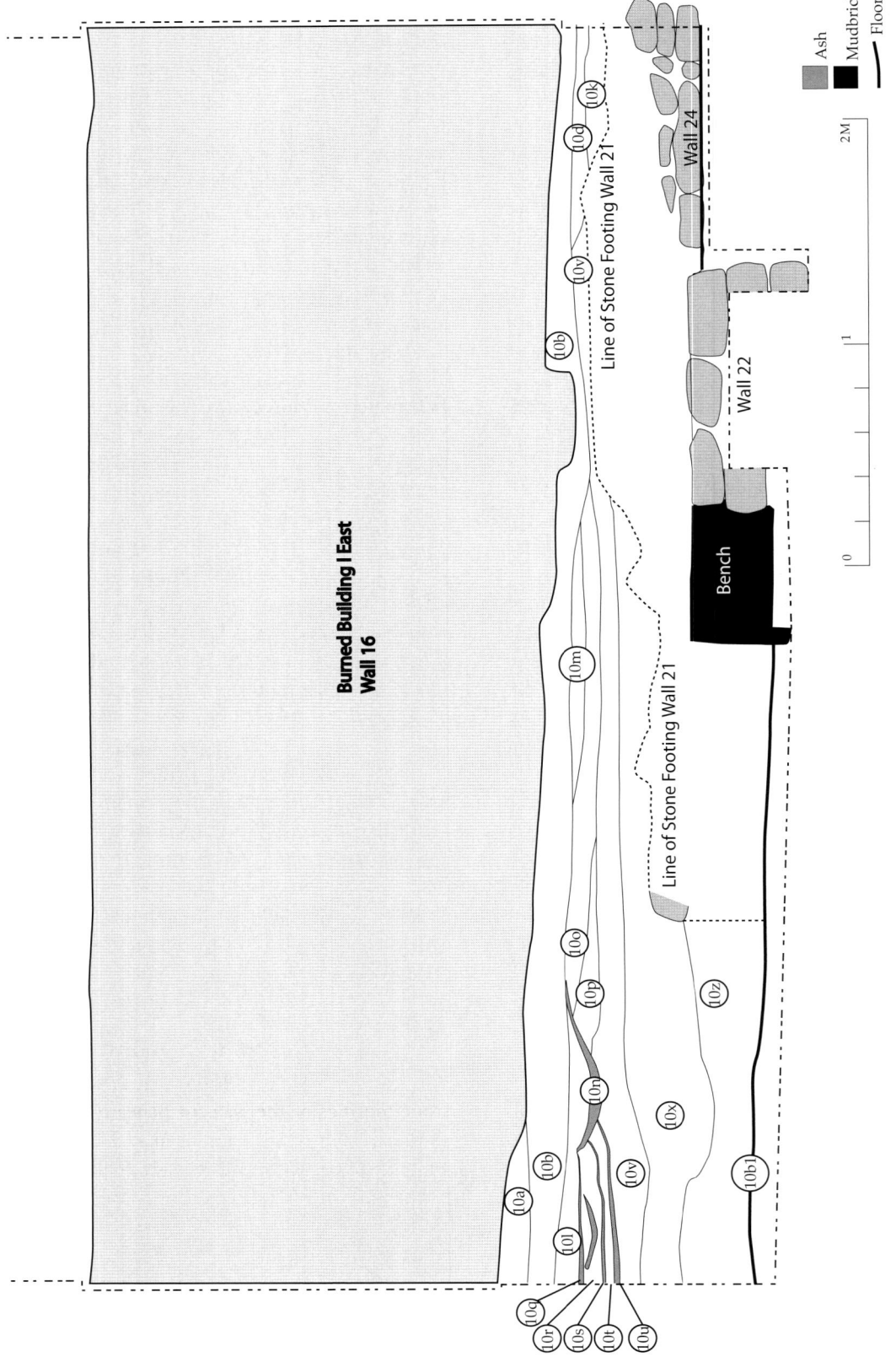

Fig. 3.31 Hasanlu Tepe: east section below BBIE Room 5.

tive layer. This mortar-debris-mortar line would thus likely mark the surface level after the IVc destruction or be close to it. Sections recorded in the soundings made in the western storerooms (Fig. 3.44) and in Grids CC27 (Fig. 3.45, Operation XVI, see below) and BB28 (Fig. 3.46, Operation XXXIX) help to clarify this situation to some extent, but also undermine Dyson and Voigt's interpretation of the architectural development of BBII: the western storerooms of BBII must be dated to BBII's earliest phase.

Returning to the BB28–29 sounding, the level of the tops of the aforementioned stone footings of the BB28–29 Building lie at the lowest level of the north section of Test Trench C (Fig. 3.44). These footings were covered by a layer of fill above which the excavators encountered a burnt plaster surface that marked the floor level at the time of the putative Period IVc fire. Curiously, this is the only lower floor level associated with BBII to have been recorded in this area by the excavators: this is not typical of other areas of the citadel. In Test Trench A, the east section indicates that the excavators encountered earlier deposits underlying the burnt floor (Fig. 3.44). The stone footing of Room 13's eastern wall (the western exterior wall of Period IVc BBII in Dyson and Voigt's interpretation/the western wall of BBII Rooms 4 and 5) was founded at the level of this burned floor and this wall shows evidence of the layer of pebbles, ash, and carbonized debris sandwiched between mortars (Fig. 3.44, Line of Period IVb Rebuild). If the floor was burned and the debris was introduced in the same event, as seems to have been the case, then the accumulated destruction debris in this area from the IVc fire was presumably around 1.30 m deep (the distance from the burned floor to the rebuild line)! The potential problems introduced by such a scenario are manifold in light of past interpretations of Hasanlu. First, the rebuild line containing the burned debris might lie above the level of later Period IVb floors; the number of these floors and their levels were never recorded. Possible scenarios include: (1) part of the debris layer from the Period IVc destruction was dug out *after* the construction of the new IVb walls, (2) the sandwiched layer of debris incorporated into the walls was introduced in some other manner than simple proximity to the upper surface of the burned debris, or (3) the burning of the floor and the sandwiched wall debris derive from separate events and we are missing later IVc floor levels. A second implication has even greater ramifications: *BBII and other buildings of the Hasanlu citadel contained substantial deposits below the Terminal Period IVb floor*. According to Dyson and Muscarella, the Period IVc structures had been "swept clean" prior to the Period IVb rebuild event and hence contained virtually no artifactual finds (1989:1). On the contrary, review of the available evidence indicates that all Period IVb buildings of the citadel contained earlier use-related deposits and multiple floor levels ranging in date from late Period IVc–early Period IVb. We have already seen such evidence from BBIII and BBIE. In practice, Dyson's use of Period IVc as an architectural phase virtually excluded the possibility of early Period IVb material. Moreover, rather than only a few pre-IVb deposits having been encountered and having been "swept clean," *the excavators in fact began digging stratified deposits below the burned Terminal Period IVb surfaces in the area of BBII as early as 1959 in Operation XXXIX (BB28), but did not record the results of this work except in section drawings,* where three major earlier surface levels are shown predating the Terminal IVb destruction surface and labeled "Grey Ware I" (Fig. 3.46). Work in Operation S22, discussed above, shows how the excavators anticipated finding a major burned debris level associated with Terminal Period IVb and used this as a kind of universal guiding principle for stratigraphic control, occasionally incorrectly. The existence of two major, superimposed burn strata of Terminal IVb date added to the confusion in the early excavation seasons. The upper burned deposit had resulted from the collapse of the roofs and upper stories of the monumental buildings; the lower material derived from the burned ground-floor levels of the citadel. Initially these deposits were dug as one massive layer. The excavators only later began to anticipate two separate contexts.

In western BBII, the excavators did not record whether the Period IVc burned surface ran against the stone footings of the walls or beneath them, and it is assumed herein that it ran against the footing of this wall. The floor level, not its stratigraphic relationship to the walls of BBII, is recorded in the excavators' sections and is shown in the sections included here. The north wall of Room 13 (Fig. 3.44: north sections of Test Trench A and B) was clearly *founded atop a layer of fill overlying the burned surface and did not have the intervening layer of burned material in its masonry* (Pl.

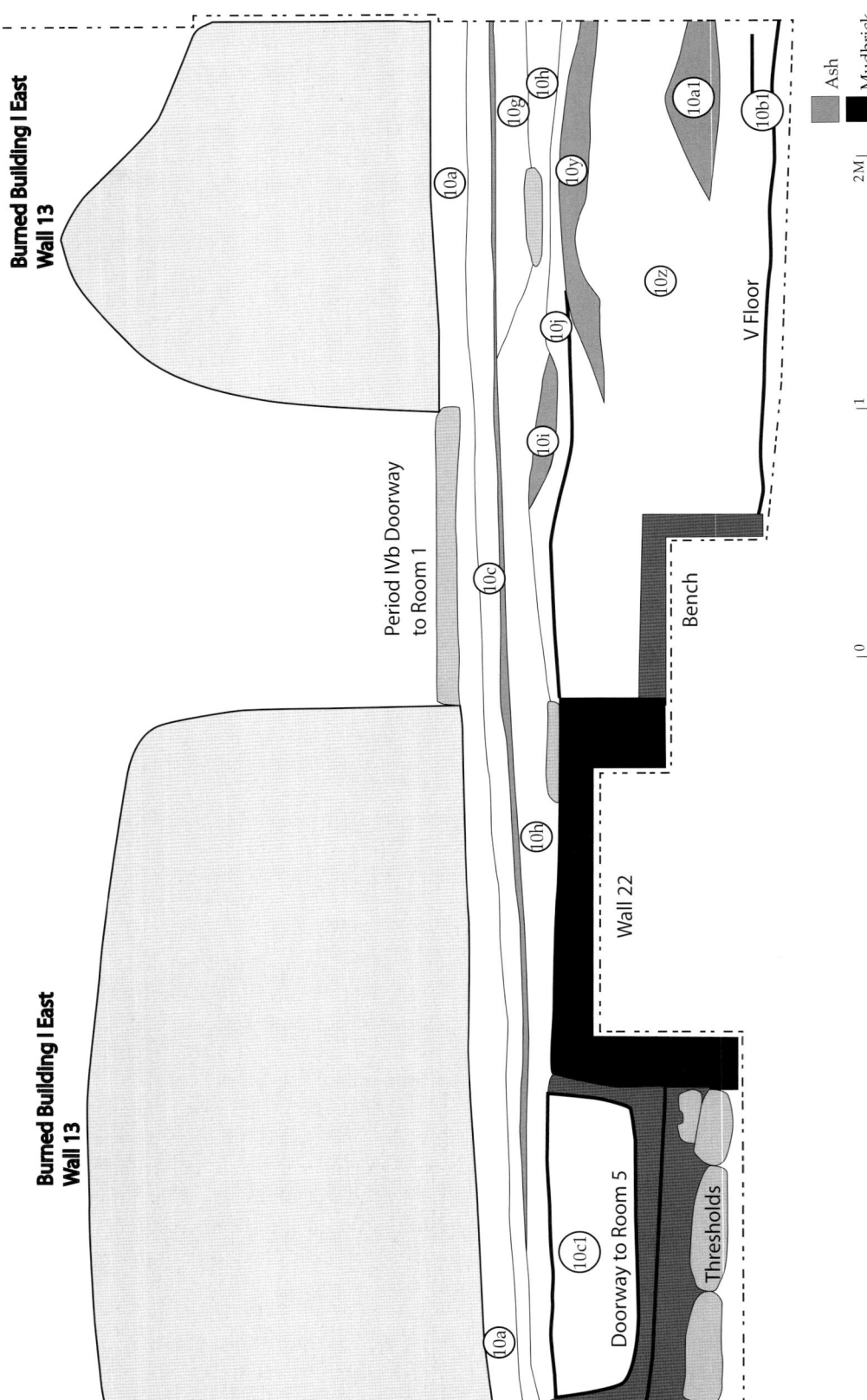

Fig. 3.32 Hasanlu Tepe: west section below BBIE Room 5.

3.27a). These architectural and stratigraphic features all accord with Dyson and Voigt's general phasing of the building; however, other stratigraphic details do not. The west walls of Rooms 13 and 14 were founded *at the same level* as the burned surface of Period IVc (Fig. 3.44: Test Trench C North Section; Fig. 3.46: BBII Wall B and Floor 12a). These sections show no evidence of foundation trenches from a higher level nor any traces of the intervening layer of mortar and debris in the masonry but, based on stratigraphy and overall construction techniques, there is no reason to date this wall to the post-IVc fire reconstruction of the building. Moreover, the south wall of Room 13/north wall of Room 14 was also founded on or at the level of the burned surface (Fig. 3.44: Test Trench A East Section; Pl. 3.27b). The destruction-level floor associated with Terminal Period IVb in the northwest storeroom appears to lie below the Terminal IVb destruction surface outside (to the southwest), where BBIX and BBX were sited (Fig. 3.44, Pl. 3.28). In summary, the only wall of the western storerooms dating exclusively to the Period IVb BBII is the north wall of Room 13. This calls into question previous definitions of Period IVc—often confused with early Period IVb—and the efficacy of delineating the "IVc" phases of the Burned Buildings based on the presence or absence of sandwiched debris.

A radiocarbon sample from a charred beam from the Terminal Period IVb destruction-level floor of Room 13 falls within Period IVc at 1200–1000 BC (Appendix II, P-0421). This is consistent with other beams from the Terminal IVb citadel, which generally date to late Period IVc–early Period IVb. Such dates provide a *terminus post quem* for the rebuild of the Period IVb structures, and the possibility that older beams were re-used in new construction must be kept in mind. Sections recorded by the project in 1959 show that a structure to the southwest of BBII, in Grid CC27, previously interpreted as belonging to Period "V," was founded on the same construction surface as the western wall of the BBII storerooms (Figs. 3.45–3.47). Two radiocarbon samples taken from charcoal on the floor of the CC27 structure (Appendix II, P-0418, P-0419), not seemingly from carbonized beams but unspecified as to potential sources, fall within the same late Period IVc–early Period IVb range *and* match those from the burned beams in BBII (Appendix II, P-0421, P-0440). Critical for dating, the CC27 structure was demolished in Period IVb and replaced by BBIX and X (Fig. 3.44: north section Test Trench C; Fig. 3.45)—both structures were destroyed in the Terminal Period IVb fire, along with BBII (see also CC27, below).

It seems highly likely that the Hasanlu IVc citadel was burned late in Period IVc or early in Period IVb. Radiocarbon dates place this event in the 11th century BC. These buildings were then rebuilt according to similar architectural plans. Previous plans of the architecture of Hasanlu IVc and IVb are incorrect, and it seems that the general plans of the columned halls were established in late Period V to early Period IVc and that many modifications of the buildings attributed to Period IVb are in fact original to them. The dating of the western end of BBII to Period IVc–early IVb does not securely date the underlying BB28–29 "Period V" structure to Period V (1450–1250 BC), since it might date to early Period IVc. BB28–29 is similar in alignment and dimensions to the CC27 structure (see below) and indicates that this area of the southern citadel had a very different built environment prior to BBII. One is reminded of the developmental history of the northwest citadel where we see in early Period V small square rooms laid out radially with the contours of the High Mound that were replaced in late Period V and early Period IVc by monumental structures foreshadowing the IVb citadel.

In Test Trench A, a deposit containing MBW was found beneath the Terminal Period IVb floor level of Room 13 (see Chapter 4, Fig. 4.57a). These sherds are noted as coming from "below the floor of IVb and above the foundation base [of the east wall of Room 13]" (Hasanlu Excavation Notebook 69, Hasanlu Publication Archive). This dates this material to Period IVc–early IVb. The excavators did not record the level of the terminal Period IVb destruction-level floor relative to the lower burned surface, but it can be reconstructed (Fig. 3.44). The accumulated deposit in the room was likely 1.00–1.30 m. The southern end of the east section of Test Trench A shows that other strata were excavated from below the earlier burned construction surface of the stone footings of BBII, but no sherds are recorded from these strata (Fig. 3.44, section Test Trench A). Moreover, no sherds are recorded from Test Trench C, which exposed the BB28–29 Building. Both such contexts most likely date to Period IVc or possibly late Period V. Again, the dating of the BB28–

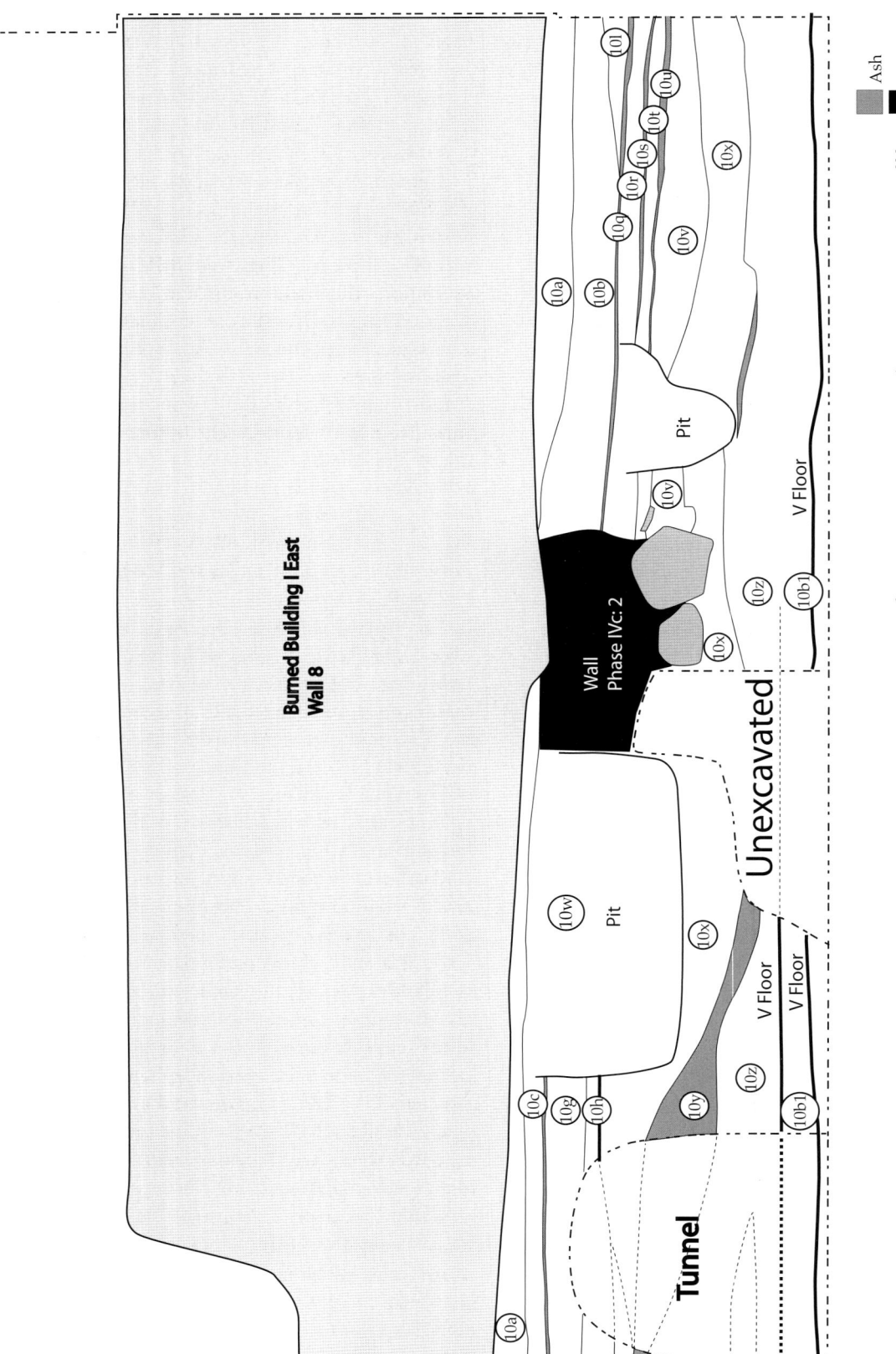

Fig. 3.33 Hasanlu Tepe: north section below BBIE Room 5.

29 Building, previously attributed to "Period V," must be called into question since the radiocarbon dates from BBII carbonized beams are largely irrelevant to its dating, there are no sherds recorded from the concerned "Period V" contexts, and the building cannot be easily linked to YZ27–29, which in fact has a long history of development.

CC27 (Period IVc–IVb)

In 1959, the Hasanlu Project excavated Operation XVI in Grid CC27 on the southern High Mound as part of the exploration of the triangular area defined by the southern end of BBIW, the western end of BBII, and the Period IIIc fortification wall (Fig. 1.5). In Period IVb this was the area of "South Street," a paved passageway along the southern end of BBIW. In CC27, below walls associated with "Period III," the excavators found the southern extremity of BBX at the level of the nearby paved walkway dubbed "South Street" (Figs. 1.4–1.6, 3.45). The entire operation, largely devoid of Period IVb architectural remains, was cleared to the succeeding architectural level, which was designated as the "Button Base Phase," the equivalent of "Period V" in the early years of the Hasanlu Project. Although architectural remains were found, the exposure was little reported in later publications (Fig. 3.47), except with regard to two radiocarbon samples (Appendix II, P-0418, P-0419) from the "Period V" building level which were used to support the absolute dating of the YZ27–29 Building and, by extension, the BB28–29 Building, to "Period V": "P-418 and P-419 are from a building level immediately beneath the South Street of period IV on the Citadel mound, and yield dates of 1036±45 B.C. and 1016 ±45 B.C. respectively. The overlap of these dates with the average starting date for Period IV indicates that there is probably no chronological gap between Periods V [now Period IVc] and IV. This conclusion is supported stratigraphically by the absence of erosion products between the deposits of the two periods" (Dyson 1965:39). The sections recorded in CC27 and BB28 (Figs. 3.45, 3.46) show this building to be contemporary with Period IVc BBII; this lower building is likely the precursor to late Period IVb BBX. The Period IVc–early Period IVb structure exhibits an alignment and plan similar to BBX. The recalibrated dates from Period IVc Stratum 5 place the structure securely in the late Iron I–early Iron II, or the late 12th–11th centuries BC (Appendix II). Few notes were recorded for this MBW deposit, although a north section and plan were drawn, a few objects were recorded from the relevant strata, and blurry field photos were taken (Pl. 3.29). The north section of CC27 and the south section of BB28 (Figs. 3.45, 3.46) show the structure founded on the same construction surface as Period IV BBII—thus, through association, the radiocarbon dates from the CC27 structure help to date the earlier phases of BBII and, as previously mentioned, are strong evidence that the western storerooms of BBII were original to it (see above). The CC27 structure was modified multiple times prior to its replacement by the overlying BBX of late Period IVb.

DD30–31/Burned Building II (Late V/IVc–IVb)

In 1972, Room 7a at the south end of BBII was investigated, with excavation continuing below the Terminal Period IVb floor level. This structure, which abuts the south end of BBII (Fig. 3.48), was originally attributed to "Period V"–Period IVb; as with the rest of BBII, however, it is almost certainly Period IVc–IVb in date (Figs. 1.4, 1.5). The ground floor of this area was used for storage and as a kitchen, in a manner similar to that of Room 14 of BBIII (Fig. 3.5) and, as in BBIII, BBII Room 7a likely abutted the Period IVb citadel wall (see above). Evidence in support of a Period IVb date includes: (1) the stratigraphic position of this building; (2) the available data on the levels of its foundations; (3) its alignment with and abutment to BBII; (4) the presence of a Terminal IVb destruction level above at least one earlier floor; (5) the continuity in function; (6) the presence of glazed ceramics, iron, and Period IVc–IVb ceramics; and (7) the lack of Period V ceramics. DD30–31 formed part of the original BBII structure and continued in use up to the Period IVb destruction. DD30–31 appears to have been grouped into Period V (Dyson 1977b) on the basis of radiocarbon dates alone. Recalibration of these dates, which were taken from carbonized wooden beams used in construction, places them in Period V–Period IVb, ranging from 1409–1125 cal BC (P-2156) and 1379–999 cal BC (P-2392) at the two-sigma level.

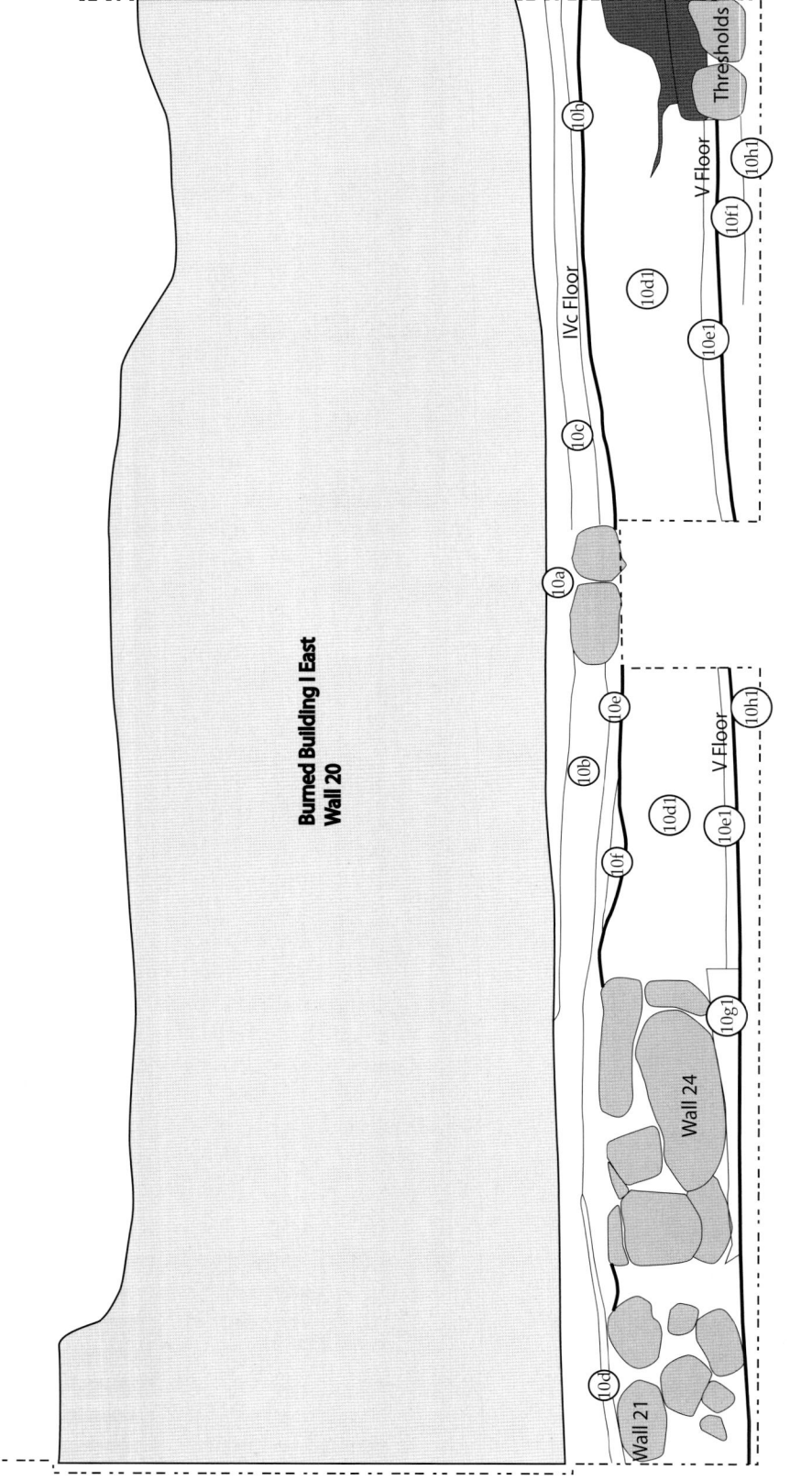

Fig. 3.34 Hasanlu Tepe: south section below BBIE Room 5.

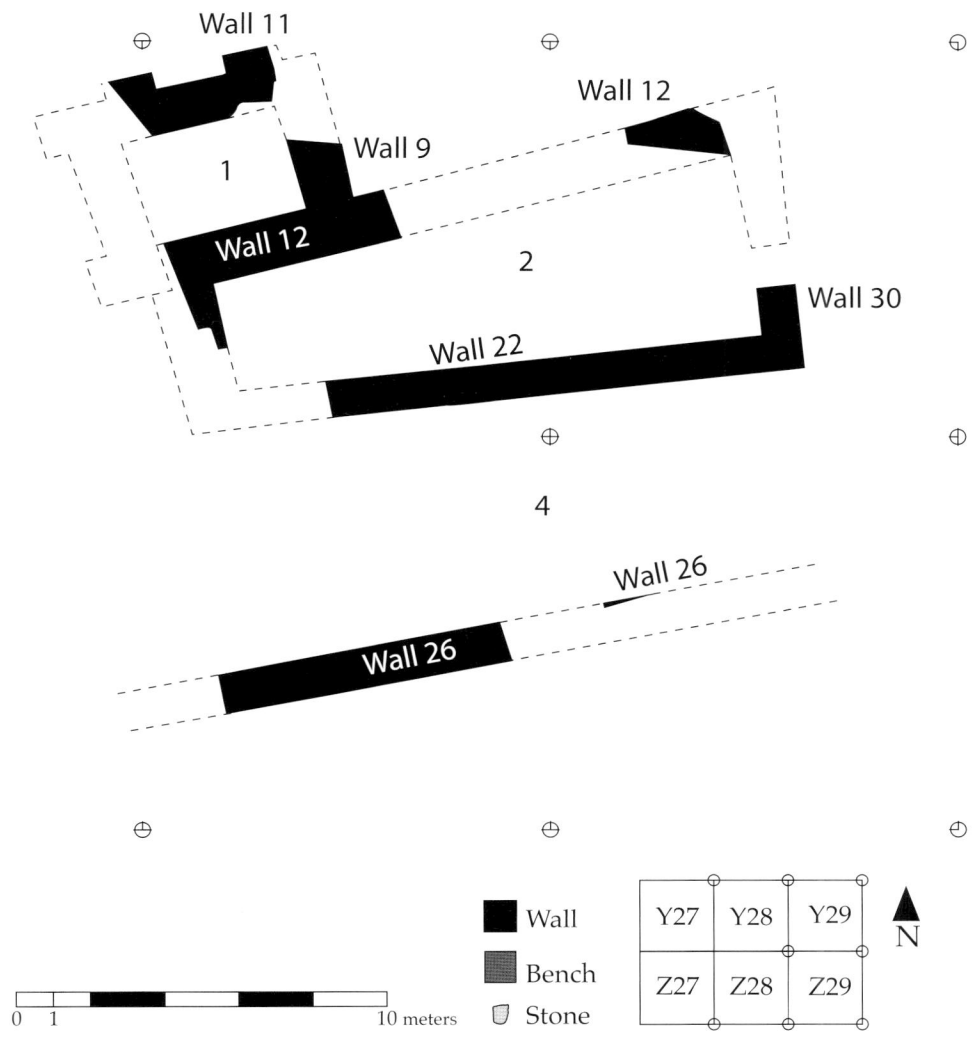

Fig. 3.35 Hasanlu Tepe: YZ27-29 Phase V:1b.

For much of the excavation, the supervisor of DD30–31 was largely unaware that the Iron I–II deposit was cut by the substantial foundation trench of the Period IIIc Urartian fortification wall, and consequently mixed material from this foundation trench with stratified material in primary contexts from the DD30–31 structure. Later in the excavation this cut was identified and the separate floor levels of the building were delineated so that the location of the earlier IVc deposit was clarified. Pithoi were found on both of these floor levels. Overall, the stratigraphic situation is reminiscent of that found in the western storeroom of BBII and the storerooms of BBV, but the material collected in this area is too unreliable to use in defining Period IVc material culture (see below).

V31 (Early Period IVc–Late Period V)

In 1974, test trenches were excavated through the Terminal Hasanlu IVb destruction level floor of BBIVE (Fig. 1.6) in the northern area of its columned hall and anteroom to clarify the building sequence of the IVb Building and its relationship to earlier architectural levels first noted in 1972 (Dyson 1977b:158–

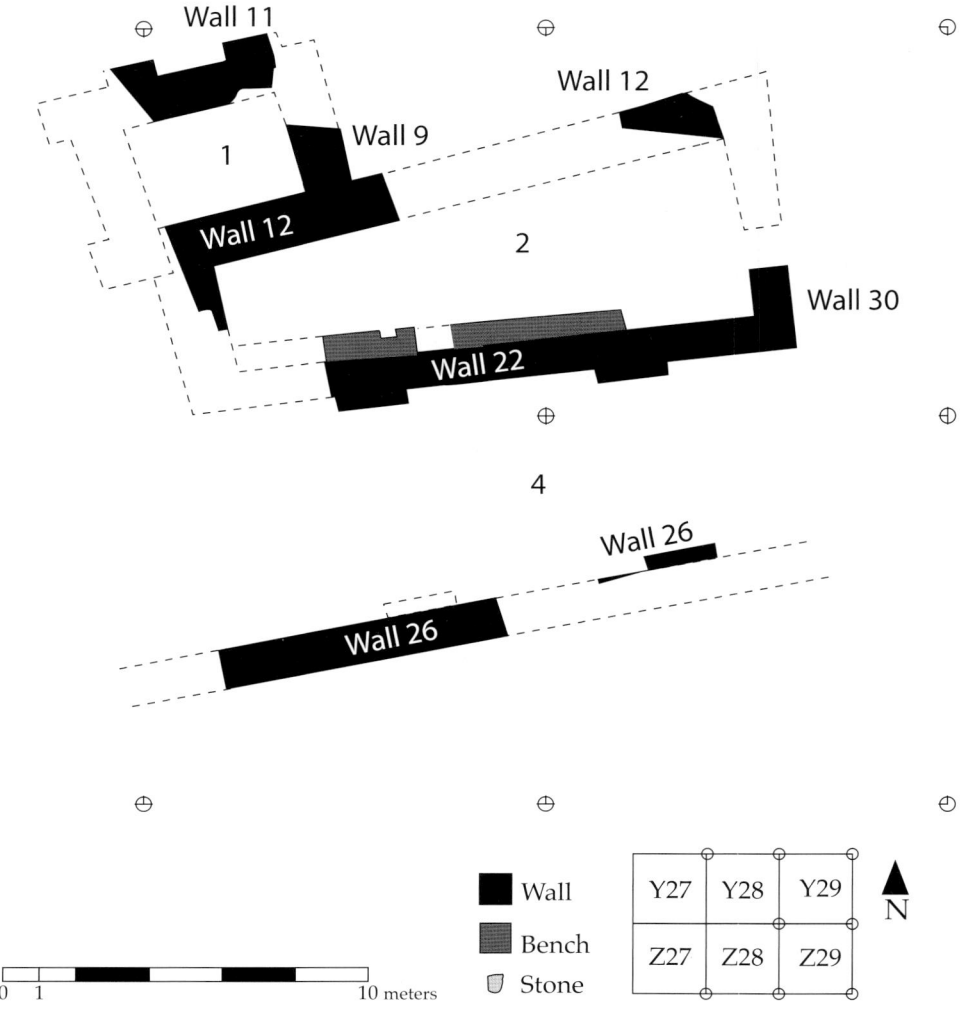

Fig. 3.36 Hasanlu Tepe: YZ27–29 Phase V:1a.

60). The tops of earlier walls were visible at the same level as the Terminal Period IVb floor in some places. A Period IVc–early Period IVb building phase of BBIVE was documented (Fig. 1.5), as well as the remains of two pre-BBIVE structures, which were separated by a trash-filled alley (Fig. 3.49). Three floor levels were found inside each of the buildings, all of which showed evidence of burning. In the south, the excavators found robber's trenches where the stone footings had been removed, probably in preparation for the construction of BBIVE. A radiocarbon sample from between the second and third floors (P-2393) provided a date in the 13th century BC, or late Period V–early Period IVc (Appendix II). A sample (P-2390) collected from between the last floor of the structure and the floor of BBIVE dates to the mid-15th–early 14th century BC, or Period V (Appendix II). The structure therefore likely dates to Periods V and early IVc. Burned Building IVE contained two floor levels—the earlier likely dating to Period IVc–early IVb and showing evidence of burning and the later representing the Period IVb destruction of the settlement. Ceramics from this area were collected but the uppermost lots show evidence of intrusive Period IVb material, which is not surprising given the shallow depth of the deposit. The Period V–early Period IVc architecture suggests large rectan-

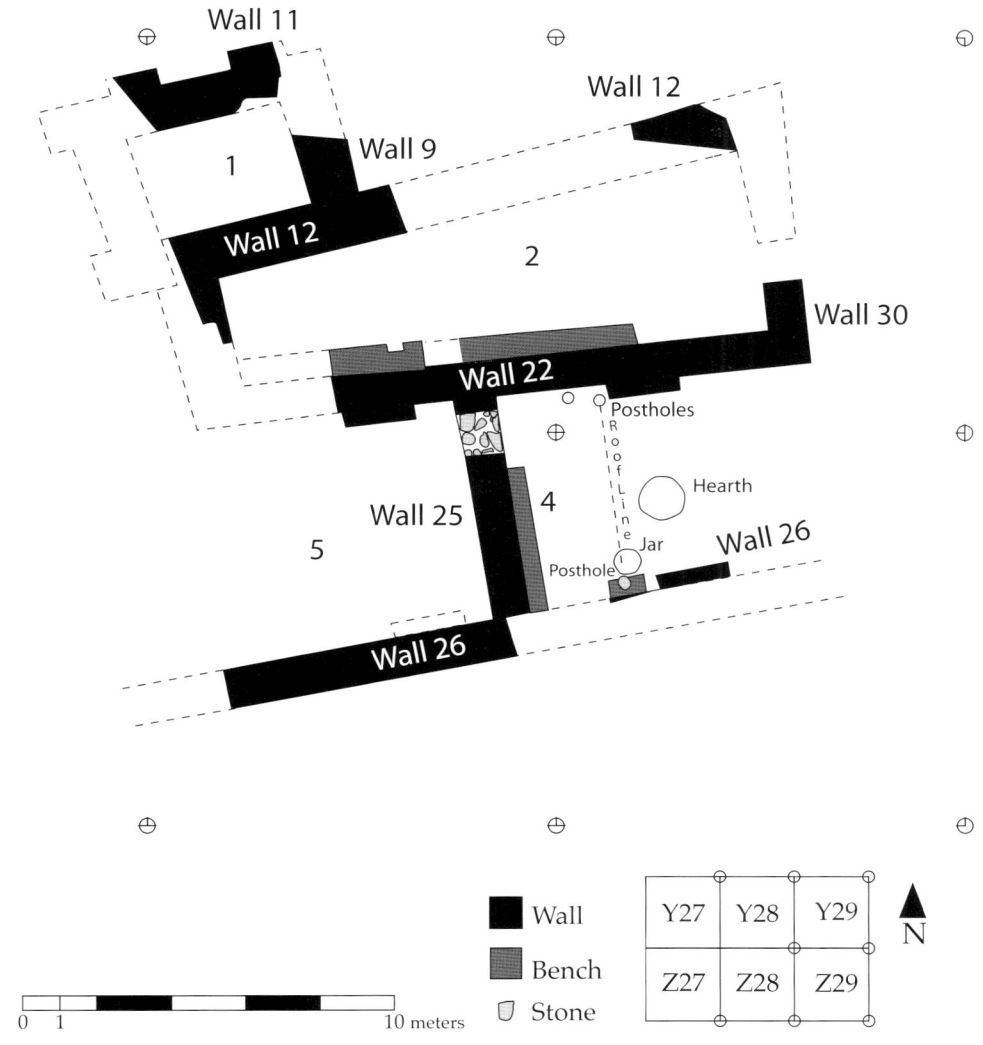

Fig. 3.37 Hasanlu Tepe: YZ27–29 Phase IVc:3b.

gular rooms oriented southeast to northwest, which is similar to the overlying BBIVE. As with YZ27–29, we see additional evidence that the southern citadel had a long developmental history rooted in the late LBA.

Additional Period IVc Contexts

Many contexts formerly attributed to "Period V" have been shown to date to Period IVc–early IVb. Other Period IVc–early Period IVb deposits were never reported in detail, such as CC27 and Operation XXXIX (B28), both excavated in 1959, or were mentioned only in passing—such as lower floor levels in BBV (see below). Separating Period IVc from early IVb will require additional excavation. The following contexts fall within this span, and we see the development of attributes in the ceramics which are typical of the Iron II but which maintain other elements typical of the Iron I (see Chapter 4).

AA32/Z32 and Y31, Burned Building V (Pre-IVb Destruction)

In 1972, the Hasanlu Project dug below the level of the Terminal Period IVb destruction in two areas of BBV, providing rare MBW collections from pre-

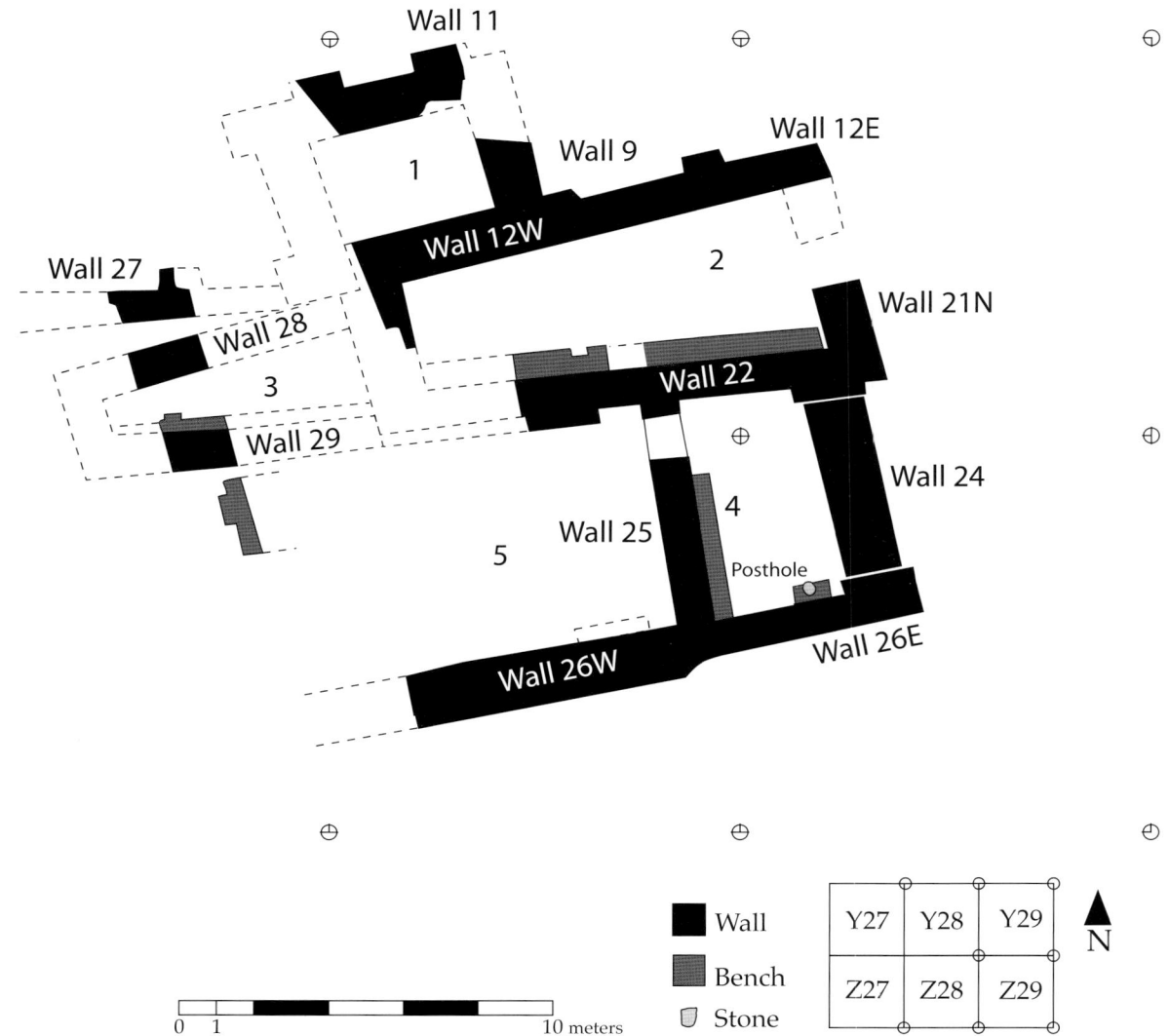

Fig. 3.38 Hasanlu Tepe: YZ27–29 Phase IVc:3a.

Terminal IVb destruction-level contexts. The ceramics indicate these contexts date from late Period IVc–early Period IVb (see Chapter 4). Burned Building V, a columned-hall structure already quite old in the Iron II, lies on the western side of the Lower Court and might originally have functioned as a temple—Dyson believed the building contained a fire altar (1989a:115, fig. 9). At the time of the Period IVb destruction, part of its ground floor served as a stable. Soundings were made in the southern storeroom (Room 6) and the western storeroom (Room 4) (Fig. 1.5). Parts of these storerooms had been previously cleared to the Period IVb destruction level in 1970. In both storerooms, the excavators found large amounts of Period IVb pottery dating to the late 9th century BC destruction of the citadel and, below this, thin trash deposits sealed by the Terminal IVb floor that contained MBW (Dyson and Muscarella 1989:1). Burned Building V was founded prior to the Terminal Period IVc burning of the citadel—traces of the Period IVc fire and a subsequent rebuilding were found throughout it. Thus we would expect the pre-Terminal IVb deposits in the storeroom to fall somewhere within the range of Period IVc–early Period IVb.

In Room 6 (southern storeroom) in Grids AA32–Z32, the excavators found *in situ* pithoi and other ves-

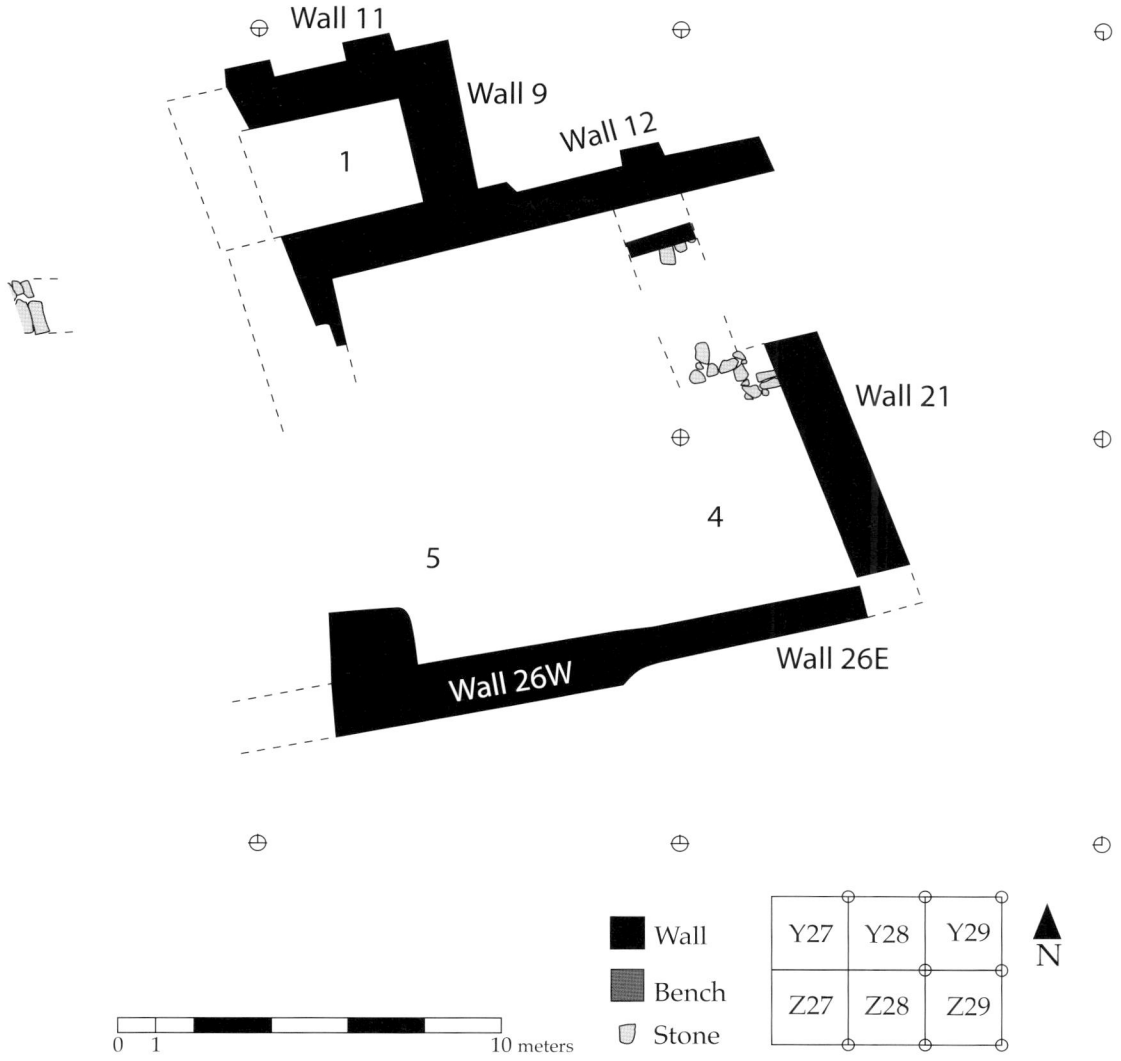

Fig. 3.39 Hasanlu Tepe: YZ27–29 Phase IVc:2.

sels on the Terminal IVb floor level. Below this floor was a layer of occupational debris lying on the earliest floor of the building. Sherds were saved and recorded; however, this material, designated as Stratum 5a, was not initially separated from the overlying Stratum 5, which the excavator indicates dated to Period IVb and had likely been contaminated by slump from the upper levels that had been excavated in 1970. Some whole vessels were collected separately as Stratum 5a (Figs. 4.51, 4.52). The floor consisted of laminated clay surfaces and had numerous indentations for pithoi, showing that in the earlier phase Room 6 was likely a storeroom as in Terminal Period IVb.

In Room 4 (western storeroom) in Grid Y31, the excavators found a similar stratigraphic situation to that in Room 6. In this instance, the excavator separated material from the overlying Period IVb deposit (see Chapter 4, Fig. 4.60). The early floor in this area also showed that the room had been used for storage.

Summary of the High Mound

The High Mound of Hasanlu served as a fortified citadel in Period IVb and similarities in architectural plans and broader patterns in the use of space in the

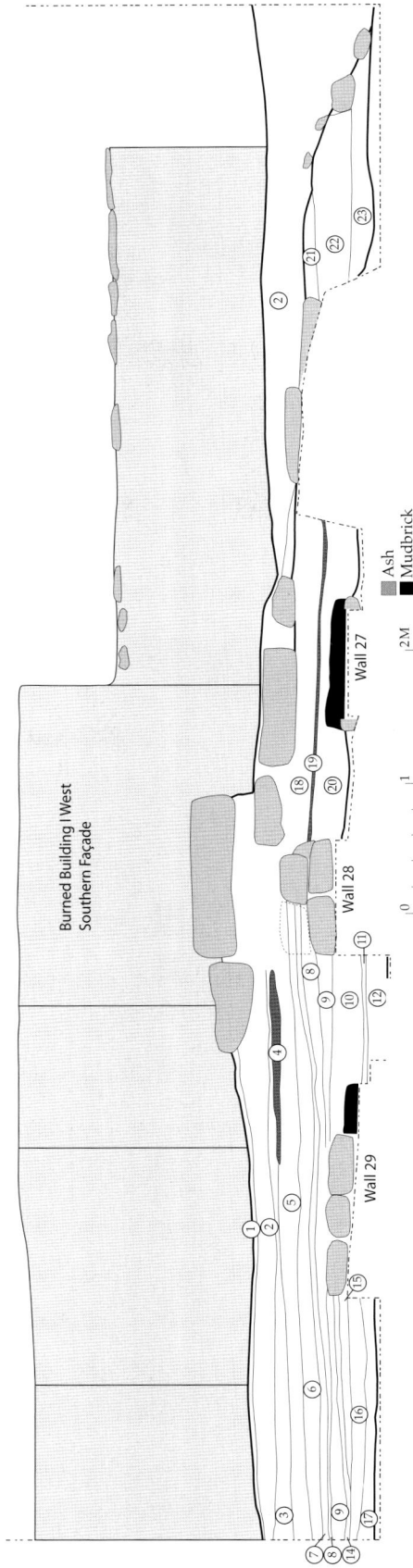

Fig. 3.40 Hasanlu Tepe: YZ27 west section below the façade of BBIW.

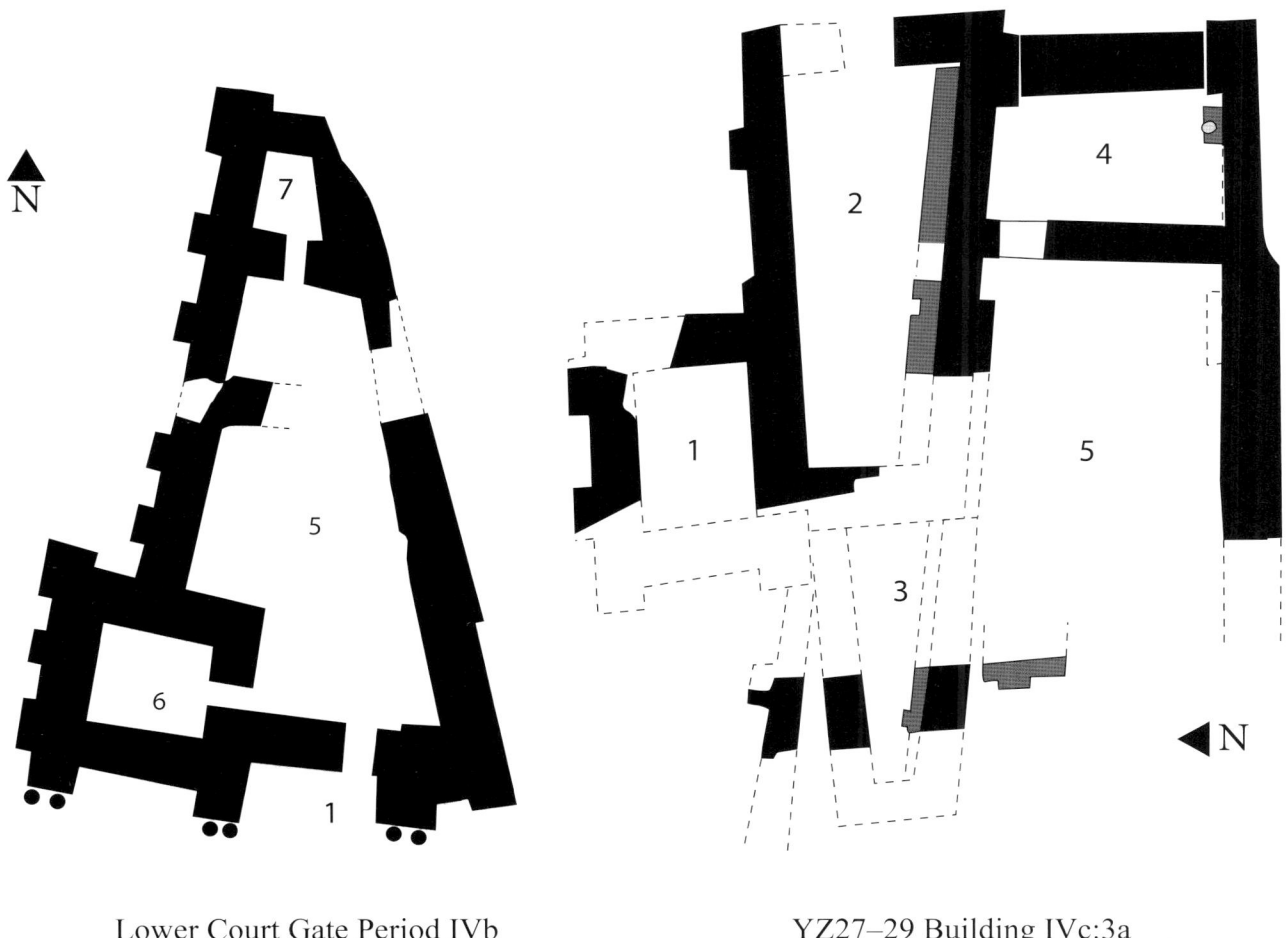

Lower Court Gate Period IVb

YZ27–29 Building IVc:3a

Fig. 3.41 Comparison of the YZ27–29 Building and the Lower Court Gate.

northwest and southern High Mound show conclusively this citadel first took shape in late Period V–Period IVc. There is strong circumstantial evidence that the site was fortified in the late LBA–Iron I, given the presence of an internal gateway (YZ27–29) and broader similarities in the settlement plan. Temples such as BBII and other elite monumental structures (BBIVE and BBV, in particular) are attested in the southern citadel by late Period V–Period IVc, although the layout of this area appears to have been different from that of the Iron II citadel—the Iron I southern citadel may have had a larger rectangular open space compared to the Lower Court of the Iron II (Figs. 1.5, 1.6). In the Iron I and Iron II, the main entrance to BBII formed the main focus of this part of the citadel. Columned-hall structures are first attested in late Period V at Hasanlu, and larger columned halls with portico rooms occupied the citadel no later than Period IVc. Evidence from early Period V is too limited to make inferences regarding the site's built environment save that it was very different from later LBA and early Iron Age. There is no evidence of monumental architecture in early Period V.

The Low Mound

The majority of "Period V" contexts on the Low Mound previously reported by the Hasanlu Project are burials in the North Cemetery (Fig. 1.4, Pl. 3.30), although occupation deposits of the 2nd millennium BC were encountered in most areas. The Low Mound was excavated in the early seasons of the project, and

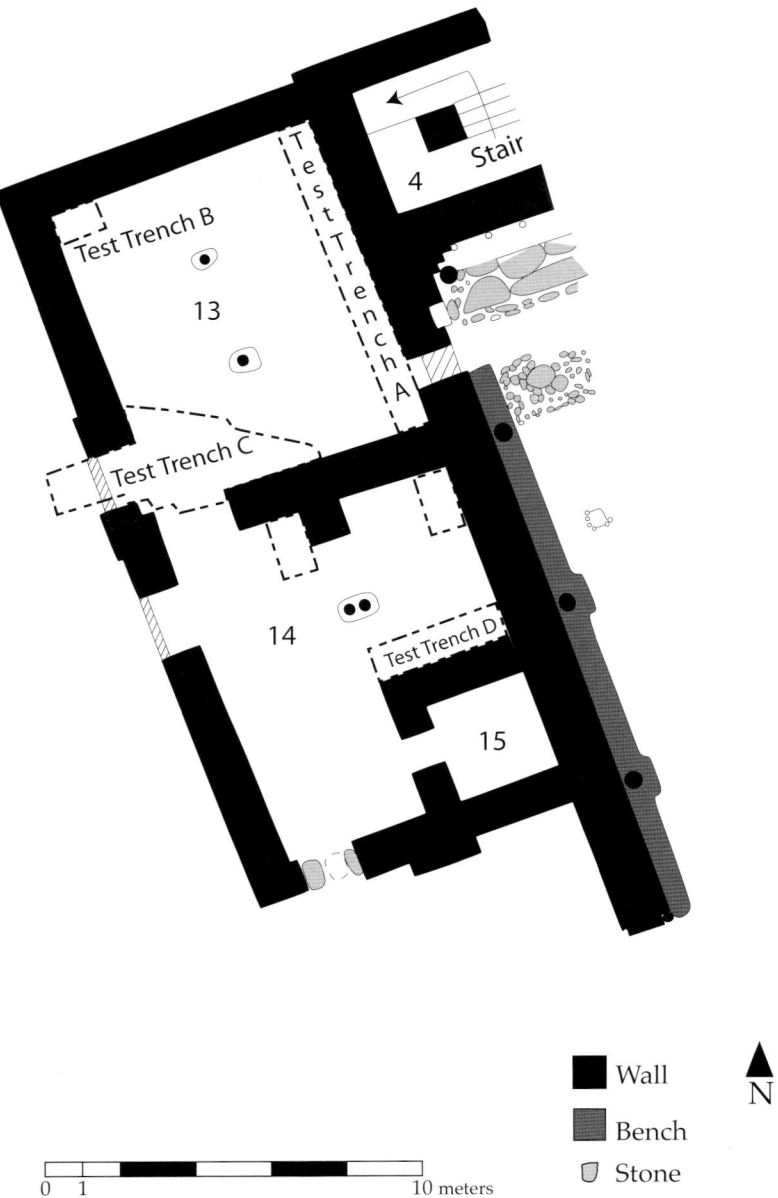

Fig. 3.42 Hasanlu Tepe: the location of the soundings in the Burned Building II western storerooms.

work was not well recorded. Few sherds were saved or drawn from these seasons, and architectural and stratigraphic information is often sketchy or wholly lacking (Danti 2011). Relative to the High Mound, the often-complex stratigraphy cut by numerous burials and pits frustrated the excavator's attempts to reconstruct even a general stratigraphic sequence for some operations.

The earliest occupation attested in the deep soundings (Operations IV, V, and X) dates to Period VIIc (Danti, Voigt, and Dyson 2000). The Period VII deposit, spanning the 3rd millennium BC, was quite substantial (usually 2 m or more) and shows that Hasanlu was an important EBA center. Evidence for Period VI occupation is scant. While there were areas with 2nd millennium BC occupation deposits, the paucity of artifact assemblages makes their dates difficult to determine. Periods VIb–VIa are largely represented by burials found in the same areas as the later MBW graves of Period V–IVb (see Chapter 5). Occupation strata of Period V are attested on the eastern and northern Low Mound, but were often poorly preserved and incompletely recorded. On the eastern Low Mound, Period V–IVb occupation in Operation V appears fairly continuous and this area was densely settled (Danti 2011). The same may be said of Operation IV. In the north, Operations LI, LIV, and X indicate this area was occupied in early Period V to Period IVc and was later abandoned and used as an Iron II cemetery. The lack of sampling on the western and southern Low Mound and the low quality of excavations prevents all but the most general interpretations there. A small sounding on the western Low Mound (Operation LIII) revealed MBW graves, as did earlier work in the same area by Ali Hakemi (Hakemi and Rad 1950). Extensive modern cemeteries cover the southern Low Mound making it virtually inaccessible to archaeologists.

Operation IV (Period VIIc–II/IIIa)

Operation IV was located in Grids S48–49 and measured 8.50 m x 10.0 m. The Operation was carried out in 1957 with the specific objective of investigating the occupation sequence of the eastern Low Mound in

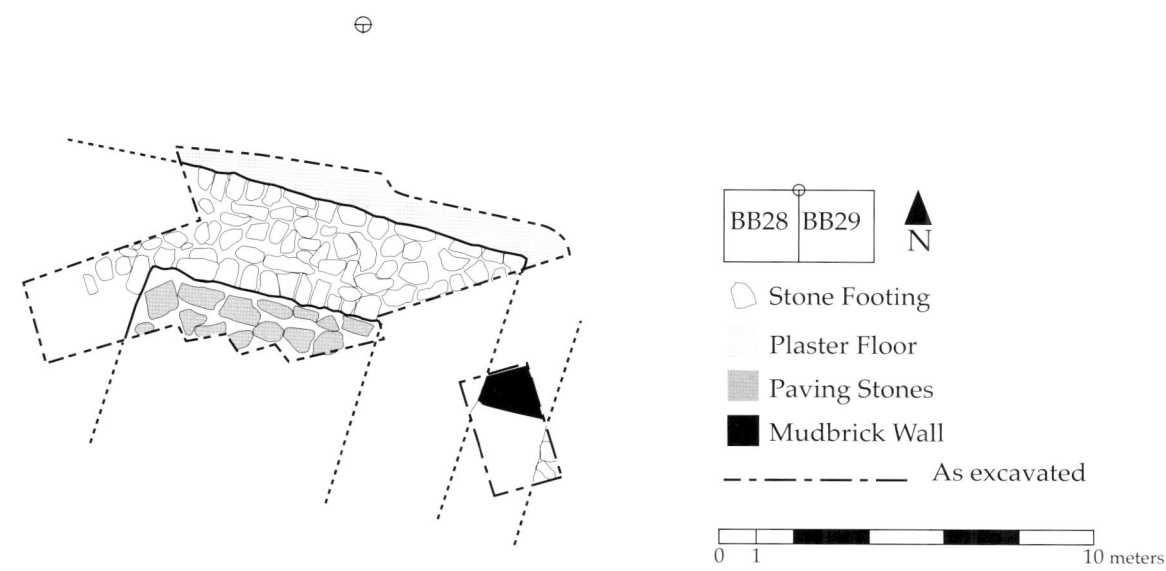

Fig. 3.43 Hasanlu Tepe: pre-Burned Building II remains in BB28–29.

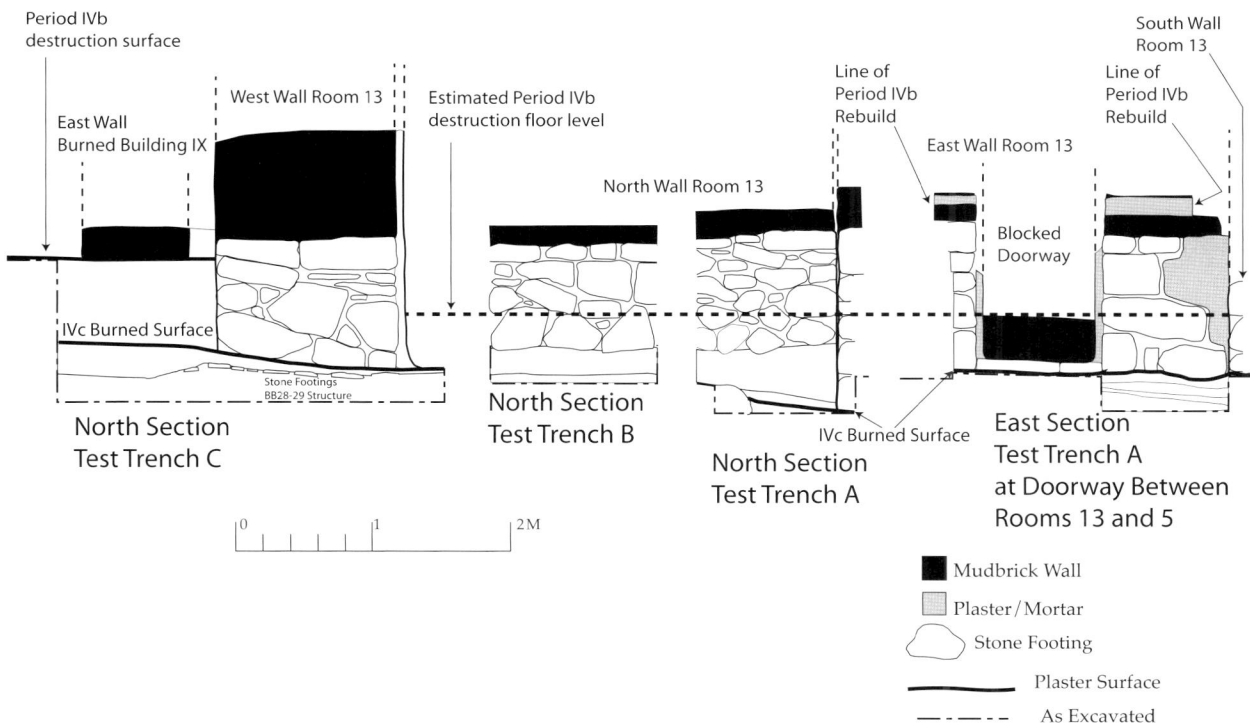

Fig. 3.44 Hasanlu Tepe: sections from the soundings in the western storerooms of Burned Building II.

122

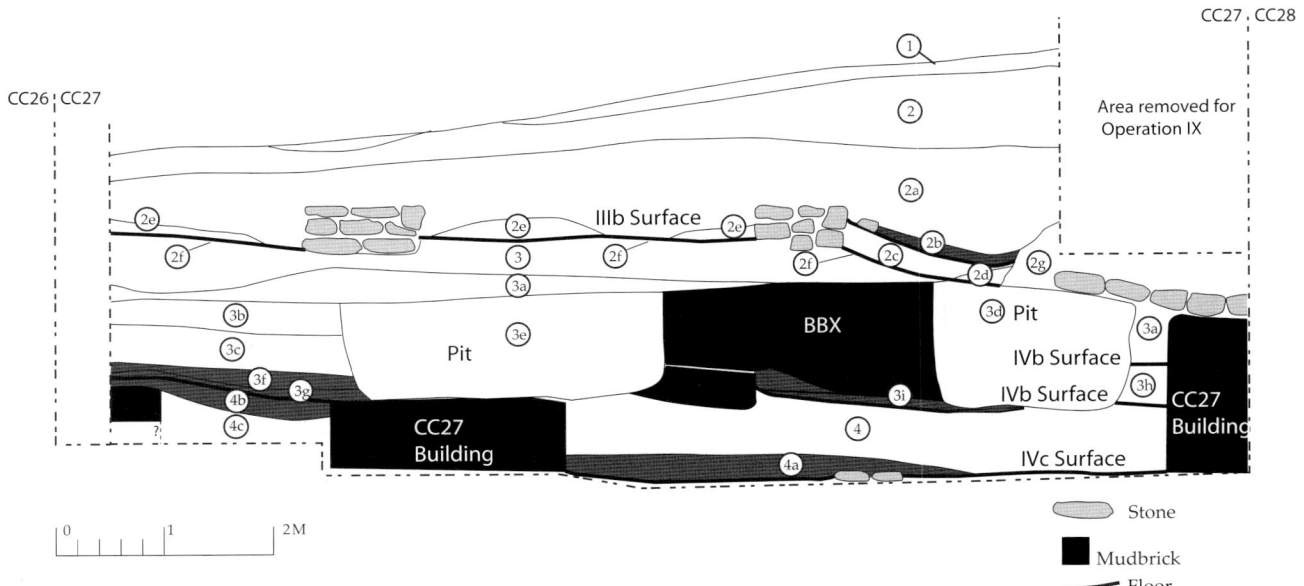

Fig. 3.45 Hasanlu Tepe: north section of CC27.

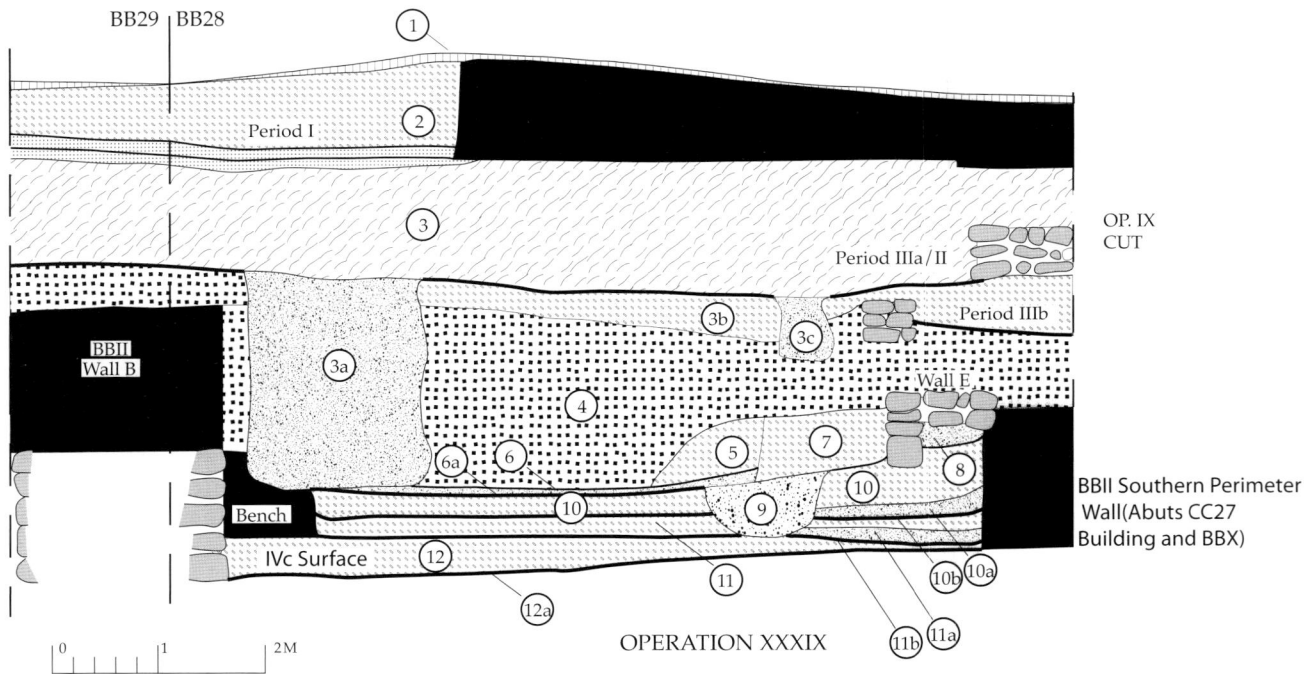

Fig. 3.46 Hasanlu Tepe: south section of BB28–29.

the area just south of the village schoolhouse (the expedition's headquarters), near an area of the East Cemetery excavated by Hakemi and Rad (Fig. 1.4, Hakemi and Rad 1950). The digging of a well nearby revealed a total of 8.50 m of occupation deposit in this area above sterile sand (Dyson 1958). In total, 34 strata and six burials were documented (SK1–6) in a progressively truncated sounding. The major periods of occupation were the early EBA (Hasanlu VIIc) and the Late Bronze and Early Iron Age (Hasanlu V–IVb).

Above sterile sand lay a thick deposit of Period VIIc (Strata 15–34)—the earliest occupation of the Low Mound to be archaeologically attested (Figs. 3.50–3.52). Stratified deposits of Period V were recovered in Strata 9–14, but sherds were not saved or drawn. The deposit was recorded as a "Button Base" assemblage in the notes on the ceramics and largely consisted of MBW. Only two sherds of PKW were documented in the entire sequence—one of "Ring Ware" in Stratum 8 and another of standard PKW in Stratum 10. Given the practice of carefully collecting painted wares, if there had been more PKW we may presume it would have been saved and documented. The remainder of the upper Operation IV deposit dated to Period IVc/IVb and later, and contained multiple architectural phases of Period IVb dated on the basis of ceramics and a radiocarbon sample from Stratum 3 (Appendix II, P-0187). Post-Period IVb graves cut these levels. While it is not within the scope of this study to review the evidence for Period IVb and later occupation, it is important to note the alternating use of space on the Low Mound between cemetery and occupation in Periods IVb–VII and especially between

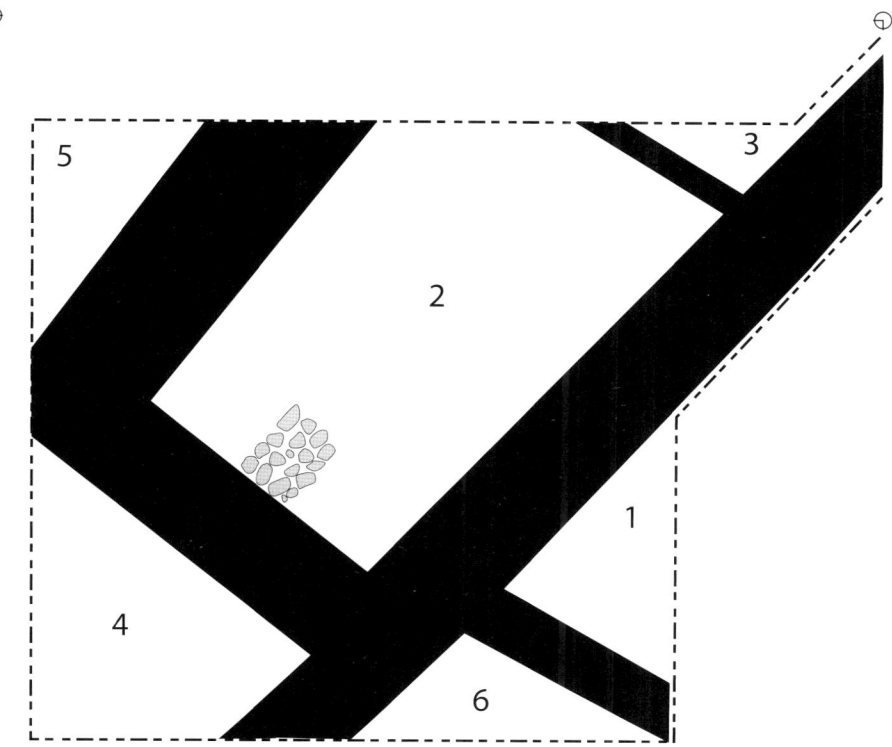

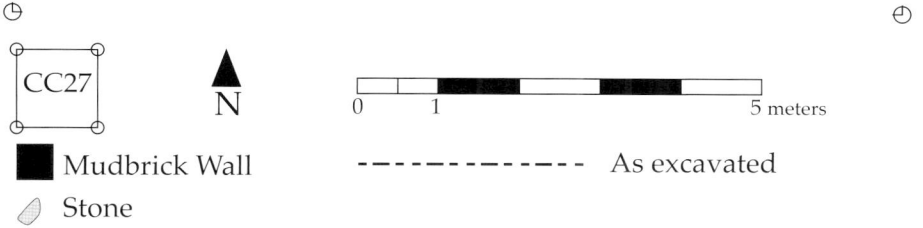

Fig. 3.47 Hasanlu Tepe: Operation CC27 Period IVc.

different periods of the MBW horizon.

Multiple grave SK4–5 of the MBII was cut into the Period VII deposit (Stratum 15, Figs. 3.50–3.52) from its uppermost extant surface. The excavators noted that the grave lay below the level of Floor 7, the surface associated with Wall G, and did not mention the floor as having been cut by the grave. The stratigraphic relationship between the top of the grave cut and the overlying occupation phases of Strata 9–13 is difficult to assess. Wall G (actually two walls, one atop the other) was cut into Stratum 15 (Fig. 3.51). Stratum 15 represents an erosional sealing of the underlying Period VII depos-

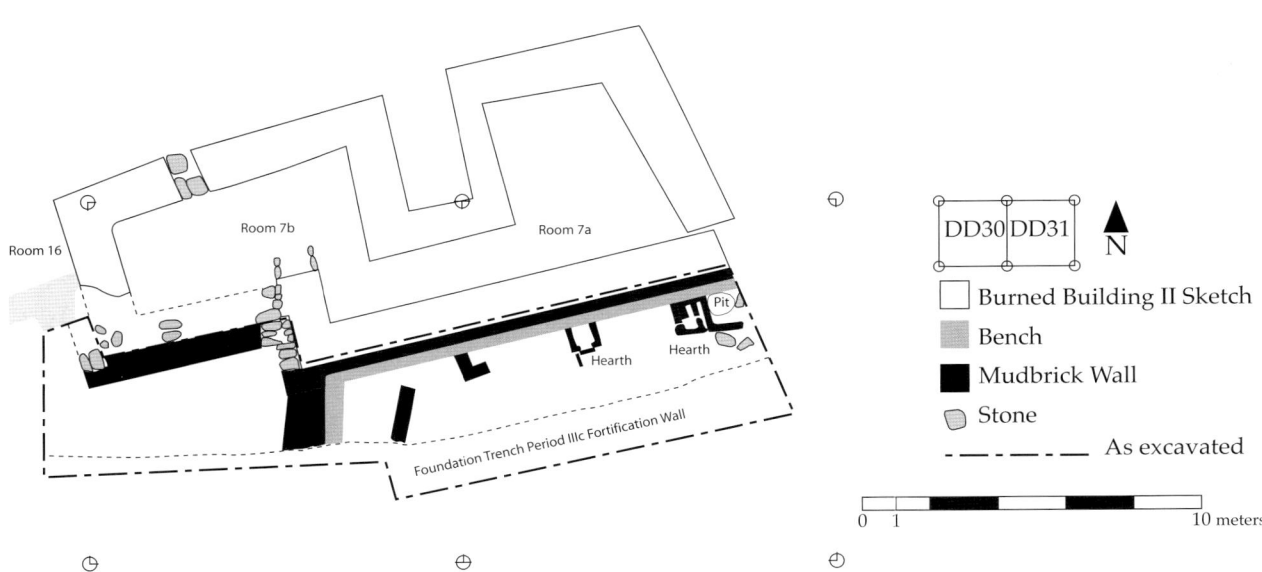

Fig. 3.48 Hasanlu Tepe: DD30–DD31 Periods IVb and IVc.

it. While I date this multiple grave to the MBII/Hasanlu VIb (see Chapter 5), Dyson originally considered it two separate graves of Hasanlu IV since they contained "Grey Ware" (Dyson 1958:31). He later reattributed SK4–5 to "Period V" and associated both graves with SK6 (1964b:34–36, 39) on the basis of the small ceramic assemblage in SK4, a dagger from the supposedly associated SK6 (1964b:34–36, 39), and similar beads allegedly found in all three graves (SK4–6) that linked them. SK4–6 were found at the same absolute elevation, but Dyson's interpretation of them cannot be maintained. SK4–5 clearly represents a multiple inhumation, and SK6 is an unrelated grave of the early Iron Age (Fig. 3.52). I have dated SK6 to Hasanlu IVc on the basis of stratigraphy and the grave goods (see below and Chapter 5). SK4–5 was situated immediately east of the west baulk. The west section (Fig. 3.51) shows the large mudbrick Wall G in the level immediately above this grave and not cut by it. The actual position of this wall is not shown on the architectural plan of the operation completed by the excavator, so it is unclear whether this wall was missed during excavation, was cut by the burial, or terminated before the excavated area. The most likely scenario was that the wall was cut away during excavation, as were nearly all other mudbrick walls of the Low Mound, and that Wall G and Floor 7 sealed SK4–5. Wall G and Floor 7 represent the reoccupation of this area of the Low Mound following the Early Bronze Age, and as in other areas of the Low Mound it contains Period VI graves that are likely associated with the contemporary occupation of the High Mound.

The grave cut for SK6 was visible in the south baulk of the operation (the pit shown as Stratum 9 and Strata 15b–15e), but the excavators did not recognize it as such, believing that this grave was cut from a lower level (Fig. 3.50), which strongly influenced Dyson's "Period V" dating. At the line of the south section, however, the grave is clearly cut from the level of Floor 6. The excavator noted the burial cut had penetrated as deep as Floor 8, which corresponds exactly with the pit visible in the south section. Greatly strengthening my argument that the grave was cut from Floor 6, the feature "Wall E" at the level of Floor 6, a line of flat stones, is almost certainly the stone covering for grave SK6 (Fig. 3.52). The skeleton of SK6 was positioned directly below these stones. Thus we see that the pit for SK6 cuts down through the "Period V" deposit but is sealed by the Period IVb architecture of Stratum 5 and higher—a Period IVc date for the grave seems most probable (See Chapter 5).

Operation V/Burned Building XIII (Period VIIc–IIIa/II)

Operation V was situated west of the Hasanlu village schoolhouse in Grids QR42–44 near a former

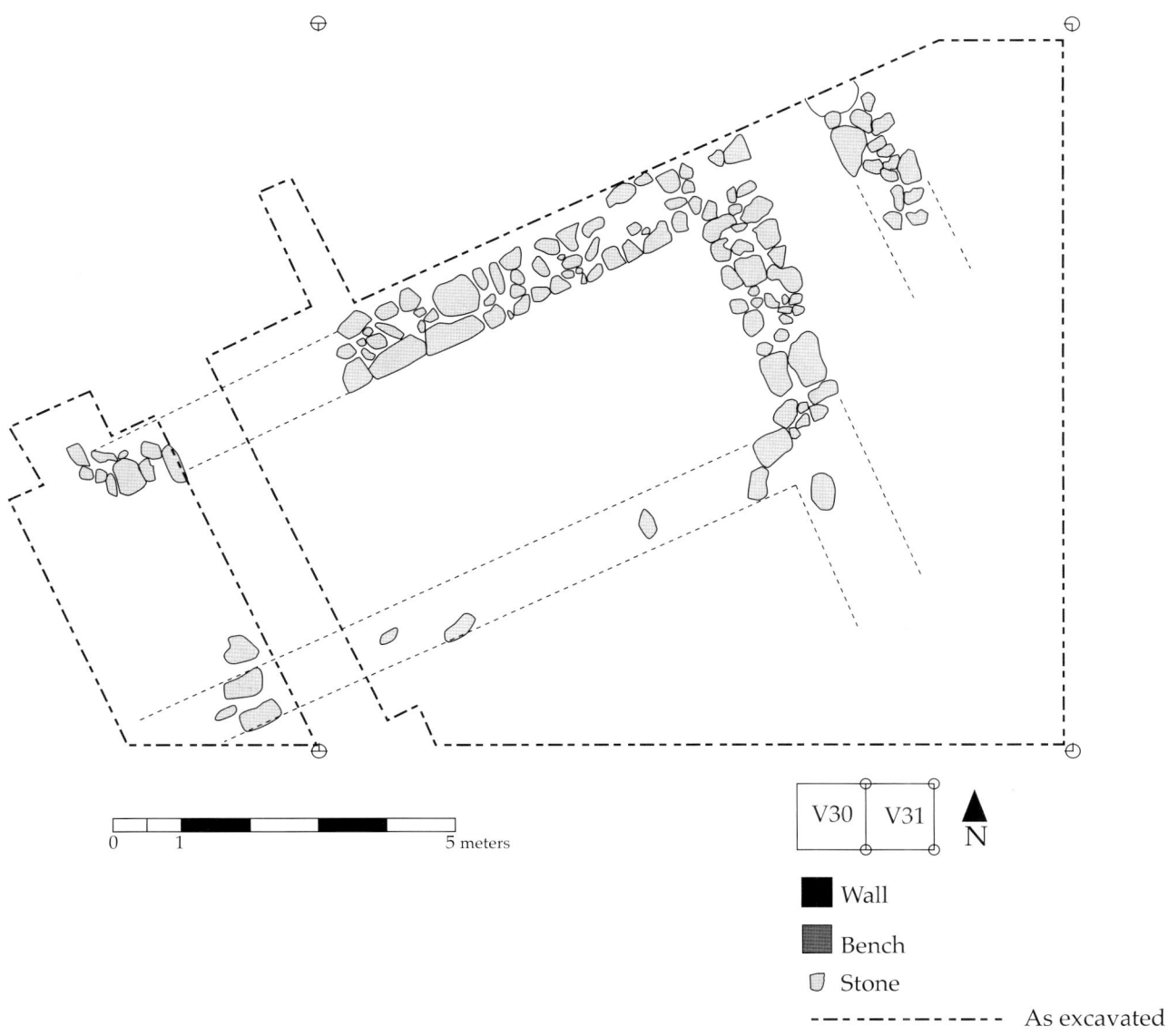

Fig. 3.49 Hasanlu Tepe: V30–V31 Period V.

excavation of Hakemi and Rad (Danti 2011; Dyson 1960a:121; 1962:645; Hakemi and Rad 1950). The unit measured 8.0 m x 8.0 m in 1957 and was expanded in 1959 with three additional 8.0 m x 8.0 m squares to recover the plan of a burned building of Period IVc–b dubbed the "Artisan's House"—now BBXIII. The 1957 operation was renamed Vb and the new squares were Vc, Vf, and Vg. In 1957, Operation V/Vb was repeatedly truncated to complete a sounding, which was excavated to sterile soil at a depth of 8.75 m (Stratum 37), exposing an area 2.60 m east-west by 2.40 m north-south. The results were similar to those from Operations IV and VI (see below) in terms of the occupation sequence.

The "Artisan's House" of Period IVb consisted of an entry area, an antechamber (Room 1), a main room (Room 2), a likely storeroom (Room 3), and possibly a courtyard (Room 4). This structure seems to have been a center for metallurgical production in Period IVc–IVb: metal-casting molds, planishing hammers, slag, and ingots were found in and around the building (Danti 2011). The Period IVc/Early Period IVb building was destroyed by fire and rebuilt on a similar plan (Fig. 3.53). The Terminal Period IVb structure had been burned and razed; one human victim was found inside the building with a substantial number of *in situ* artifacts. Outside the structure were two equids and four canids that seem to have died in the destruction. The excavators attributed the earlier architectural phase (Preliminary Phase C) to the "Button Base Phase" in notes. Below this, the excavators found three strata or 1.2 m of total deposit (Strata 8–10) of Period IVc–Period VI date in the Operation Vb sounding, but almost no pottery was drawn (Danti 2011). Period VII was reached by at least Stratum 12, and the earliest occupation encountered was Period VIIc.

Operation VI

Operation VI is a large area containing a number of subunits located near a canal that flowed along the northern and eastern perimeters of the *tepe* (Fig. 1.4). In various periods in antiquity the settlement surely extended beyond this area, but the modern village of Hasanlu and associated agricultural activities have obscured the surface and prevented most excavation beyond this point. The various trenches of Operation VI were situated in an area known to be a cemetery as demonstrated by the previous excavations of commercial antiquities dealers, Sir Aurel Stein, and Hakemi and Rad. Operation VI was excavated in 1957 (Figs.

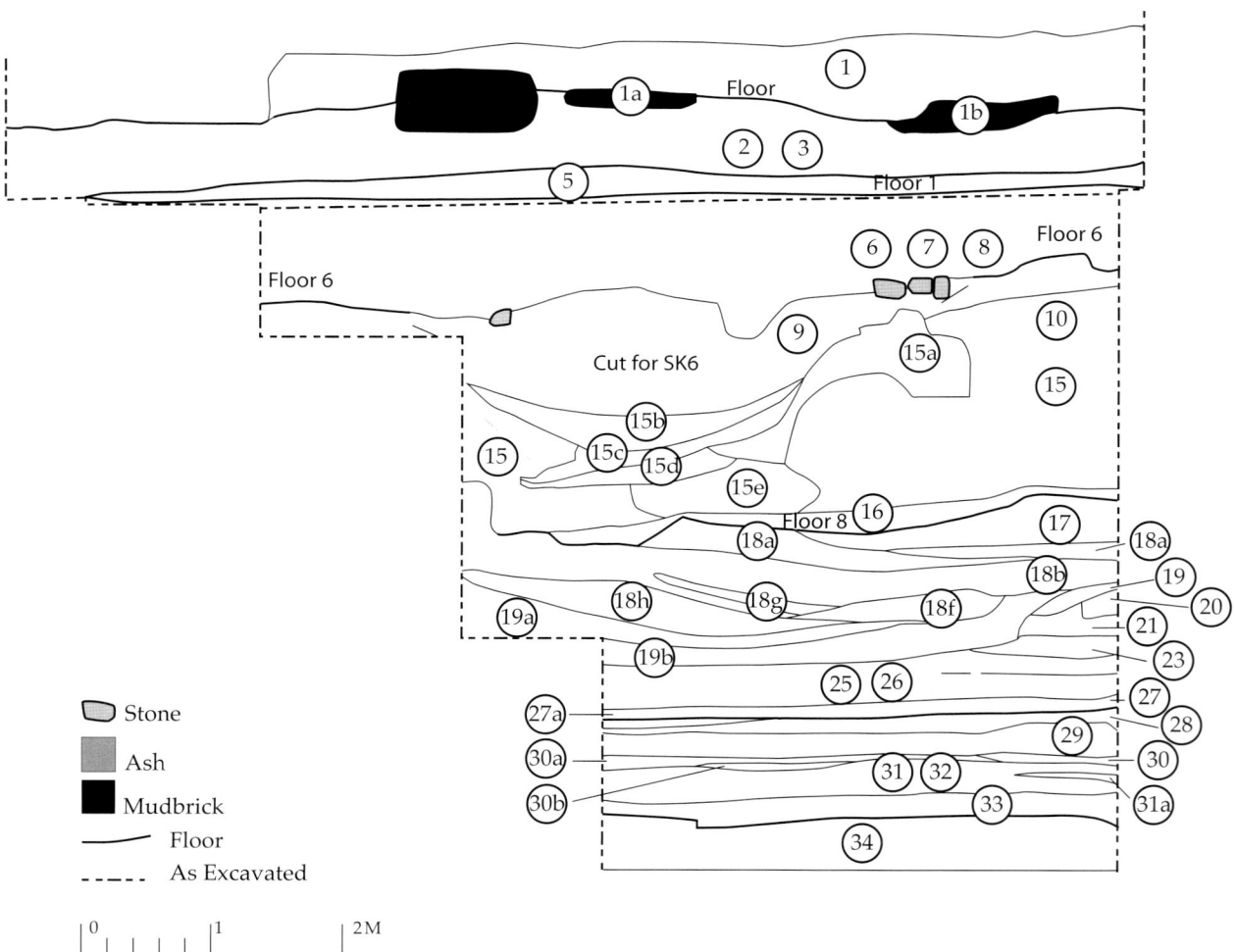

Fig. 3.50 Hasanlu Tepe: south section of Operation IV.

1.4, 3.54). Operations VIa and VIb were dug in 1959. In 1964, Operations VIc–h and j, all noncontiguous extensions of the original operations, were excavated by Ted Rathbun and William Bass to collect additional skeletal material (Rathbun 1972). There are no sections or detailed notes on the stratigraphy and architecture from the 1964 excavations. Most troubling, architectural remains and evidence of burning were found in Operation VIf, and skeletons there interpreted in the excavation notes as Iron II "burials" likely represent victims of an attack.

Operations VI, VIa, and VIb were inhabited in Period VII with some Period VII burials found in the same area but not associated with contemporary use-phases of architecture. The area was then abandoned and was used as a MBA cemetery and continued as such in the LBA, Iron I, and Iron II with some traces of contemporary architecture. In the Iron II/III, the northern mound was reoccupied.

Operation VI (Period VIIb–IIIa/II)

Operation VI measured 4.0 m north-south by 8.0 m east-west and lay just north of an Iron II *hypogeum* excavated by Hakemi and Rad (see Operation VIb below). The project excavated 23 graves in this area (SK11–34) from July 7–15, 1957 (Fig. 3.55). The lowest stratum reached in 1957 was Stratum 6, a level with architecture that had been burned (Wall E/Floor 3). This phase was not included in the sections recorded in 1957 (Figs. 3.56, 3.57). A radiocarbon sample from the Stratum 6 floor provided a date ranging from 2900–2550 BC or Hasanlu VII (Appendix II, P-0194). The excavation was taken down further

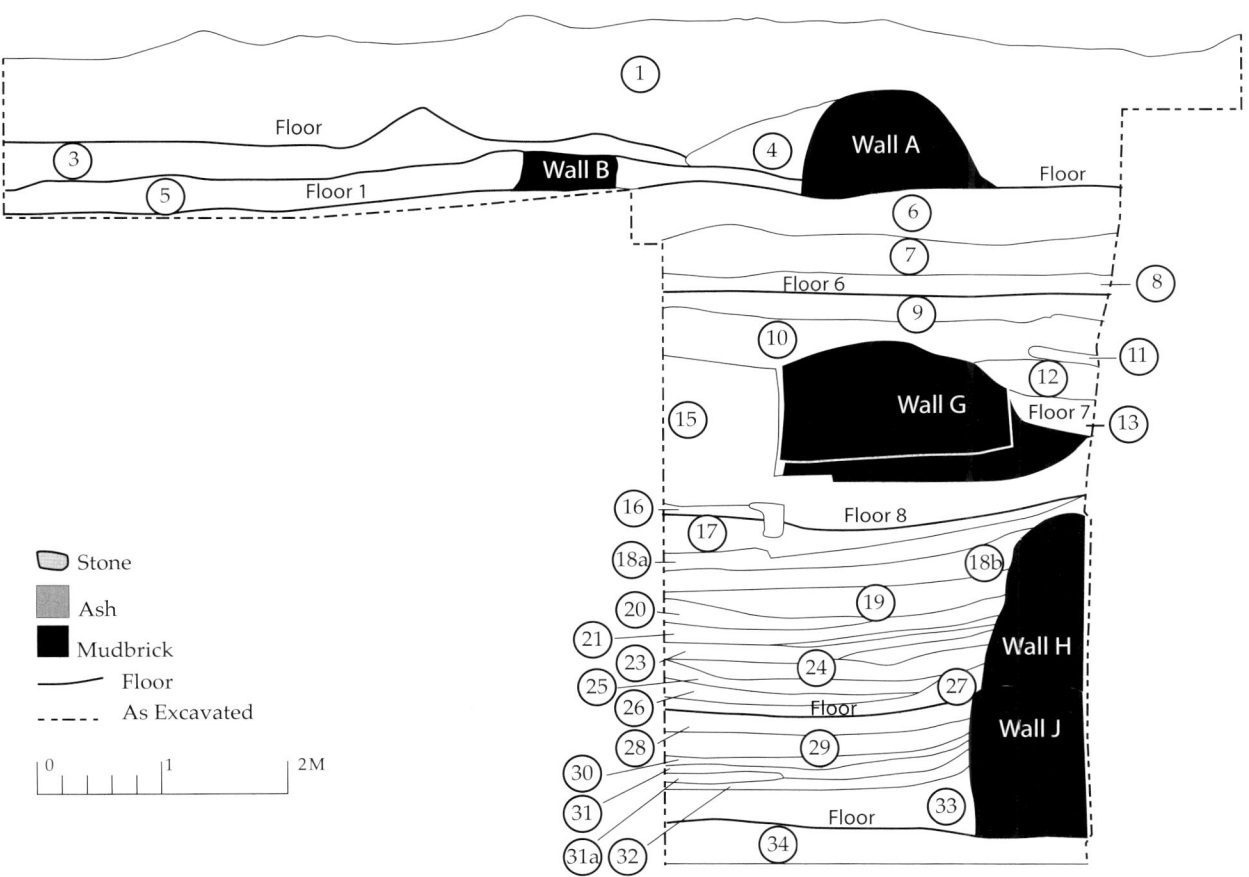

Fig. 3.51 Hasanlu Tepe: west section of Operation IV.

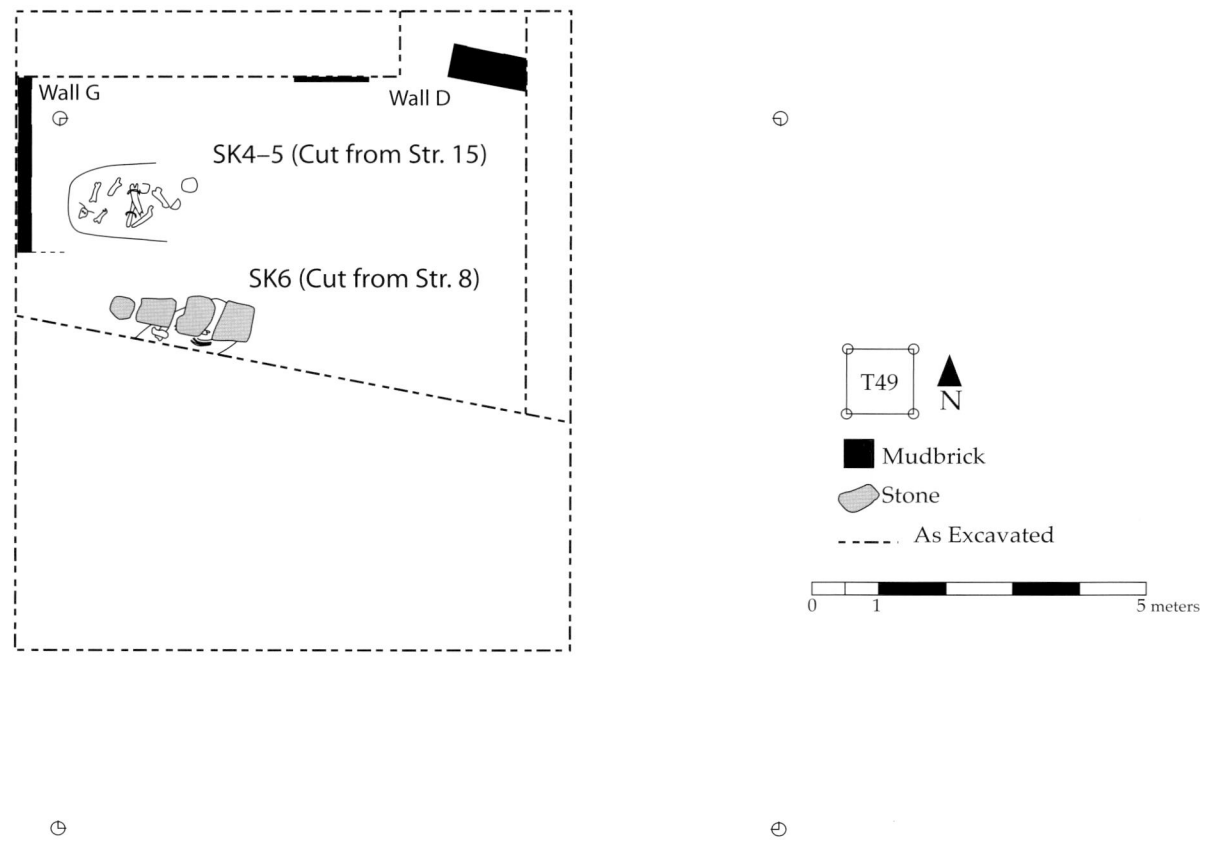

Fig. 3.52 Hasanlu Tepe: graves in Operation IV.

in 1958. Another architectural phase was documented in Stratum 7 similar to that of Stratum 6 in terms of layout. The unit was truncated an unspecified amount, and a sounding was carried down 50 cm in the northwest corner. A posthole digger was then used to document the depth and nature of the deposit (1.10 m, Strata 7–10).

Above these early levels lay two more occupation deposits with architecture of Period VII designated Strata 4–5 (Figs. 3.56, 3.57). A radiocarbon sample from Stratum 4/Floor 2 dated to the mid-3rd millennium BC (Appendix II, P-0191), but no sherds were collected from this architectural phase, which was cut into the Stratum 5 deposit. Stratum 5 was cut by or sealed (the excavators could not tell) Burial SK31 of Period VIIa-b (Figs. 3.55, 3.56). This grave had been disturbed by the digging of at least one other grave of Period VIa (SK29), which in turn lay beneath Burial SK15 of Period IVb (Figs. 3.55, 3.56). Floor 2 was cut by grave SK25 of Period VIa, also in the northeast corner of the operation (Fig. 3.55). Overall, the northeast corner of Operation VI was heavily disturbed with tightly packed burials. There were clearly also numbering problems and difficulties in attributing finds to the graves in this area as reflected in the recordkeeping. SK29 (Fig. 5.9), an "old male represented by a skull" (Rathbun 1972:53, UPM58-4-109), contained the oft-cited example of iron from "Period V" (Dyson 1964b:39; 1965:196; 1967a:2957; Muscarella 1974:49; Pigott 1977:223; 1981:125); however, this attribution seems highly unlikely given the mid-2nd millennium BC date of the grave and evidence that mixing occurred with Period IVc–IVb contexts (see Chapter 5).

Above the occupation strata of the EBA was a severely cut-through deposit (Stratum 3) with burials attributed to the "Grey Ware Phase" and "Button Base" or "Ring Ware Phase" (Figs. 3.56, 3.57). Grave SK24

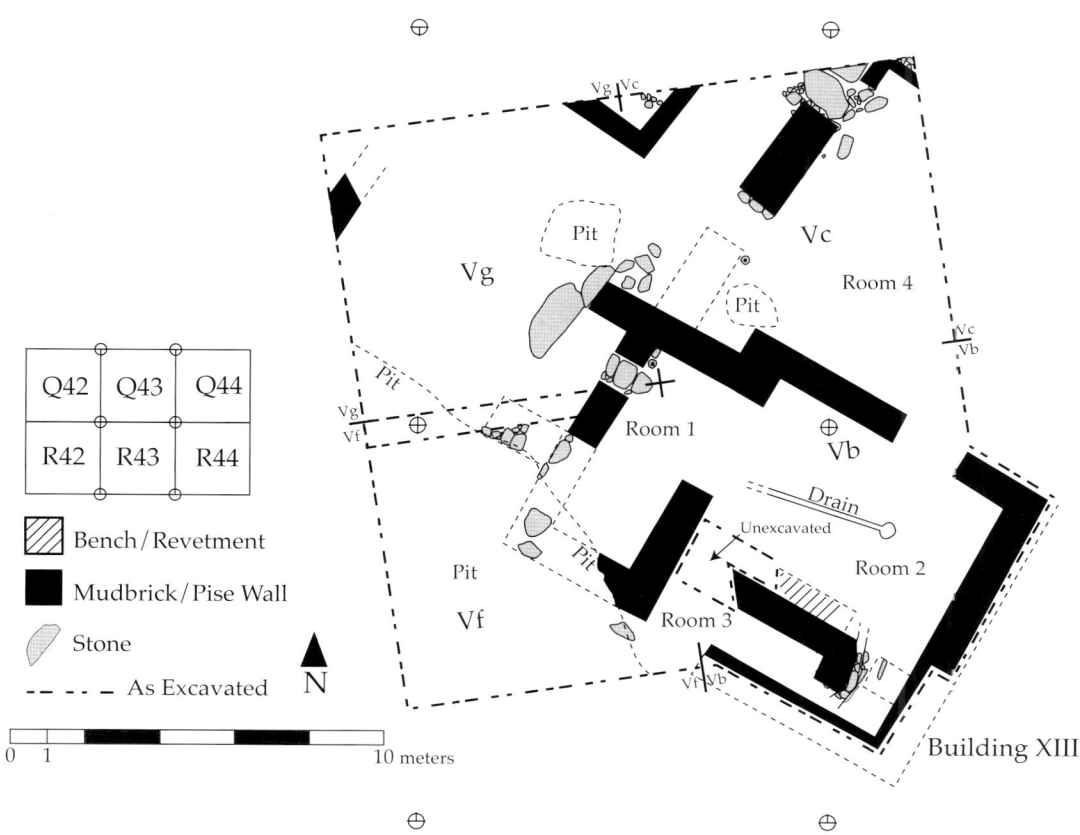

Fig. 3.53 Hasanlu Tepe: Operation V BBXIII Artisan's House Phase C.

cut this layer and contained a pattern-burnished jar (HAS57-121) and an unplaced piece of poorly preserved iron (HAS57-120, UPM58-4-46) that resembles the socket of the iron spears typical of Period IVb (Figs. 3.55, 5.18; HAS57-120, UPM58-4-46). This grave is dated to Period IVc on the basis of a pattern-burnished holemouth jar and a copper/bronze pin with incised head of likely early Iron Age type.

One radiocarbon date (Appendix II, P-0198) from Stratum 3 of ca. 1450–1200 BC (the old uncalibrated range) was important for Dyson in establishing the lower date of "Period V" at Hasanlu and, along with the dates from late Dinkha IV and Dinkha III, formed the basis for the absolute dating of the division or purported hiatus between Period VI and Period V. This sample is described as "small lumps of charcoal mixed with ash from Outer Town area, Op. VI stratum 3, above burial 13 [SK23], East baulk. Comment: this is one of the earlier burials ..." (Ralph 1959:50). In addition, Dyson provided that: "from the lower Iron I fill in the Outer Town cemetery area (Op. VI)" (1977b:164). Dyson and Muscarella (1989:15, fig. 17) include this date in "Period V." However, the ceramics in grave SK23 securely date it to Period IVb, and the relationship between the radiocarbon sample and the grave has never been clarified.[28] Moreover, the elevation of SK23, an intrusive grave, is largely irrelevant to the dating of the deposit. In summary, this radiocarbon sample should not be used to date Period V or the Period VI/V division and only provides a general date, and not an especially reliable one, for the Operation VI Stratum 3 occupation (see Operation VIa, below). This leaves no secure radiocarbon samples from the early part of Period V at Hasanlu and no evidence with which to assign an absolute date to the Period VI/V transition at the site.

Above Stratum 3 and just below the surface the excavators encountered a fairly well preserved occupation with architecture of "Period III" (probably Period IIIa–II; Stratum 2, Floor 1, Walls A1–2).

Operations VIa and VIb (Period VIIb–IIIa/II)

Operations VIa and VIb were contiguous, irregular-shaped trenches measuring 6.0 m east-west by 11 m north-south situated west of and adjacent to Operation VI and separated from it by a 1 m baulk, which was partly removed during the excavation (Figs. 3.54, 3.55). Below a layer of substantial Period IIIa/II architecture linked to that in Operation VI Stratum 2 were 26 burials (SK51–76), most of which are datable to Periods VIb–IVb (Fig. 3.55; see Chapter 5). These burials were cut into occupation levels of Period VII.

In Operation VIa, the lowest levels were occupation strata consisting of tightly packed surfaces and floor levels separated by striated layers of ash and mudbrick wash (Fig. 3.58, Strata 12–21). All but one of the mudbrick walls shown in the north and east sections were cut away during excavation (Wall D). In light of the excavation results from Operation VI, these lower levels can be dated to Period VII. No sherds, artifacts, or radiocarbon samples were collected from these phases. The lower Period VII occupation was probably followed by another major phase of the EBA (Fig. 3.58, Strata 4–11). The excavators identified no walls, but characteristics in the sections such as a pronounced vertical break in the stratigraphy of Strata 4–13 in the north section in the area cut by Stratum 7/Burial SK57 may mark a missed wall(s) (Fig. 3.58). This wall was likely cut down into Strata 8c, 9, and 13. This occupation level was not well recorded to the east in Operation VI where it would equate with the lower part of Stratum 3—this "stratum" was drawn rather schematically in the sections. The EBA occupation was followed by a period of abandonment equivalent to the base of Stratum 3a. Graves SK70 and SK72 date to Terminal Hasanlu VIb and cut the terminal Period VII occupation (Fig. 3.58). The Operation VIa west section and the west end of the north section show the ancient mound's surface was subsequently cut away following the MBII: the line of this cut is marked by the base of

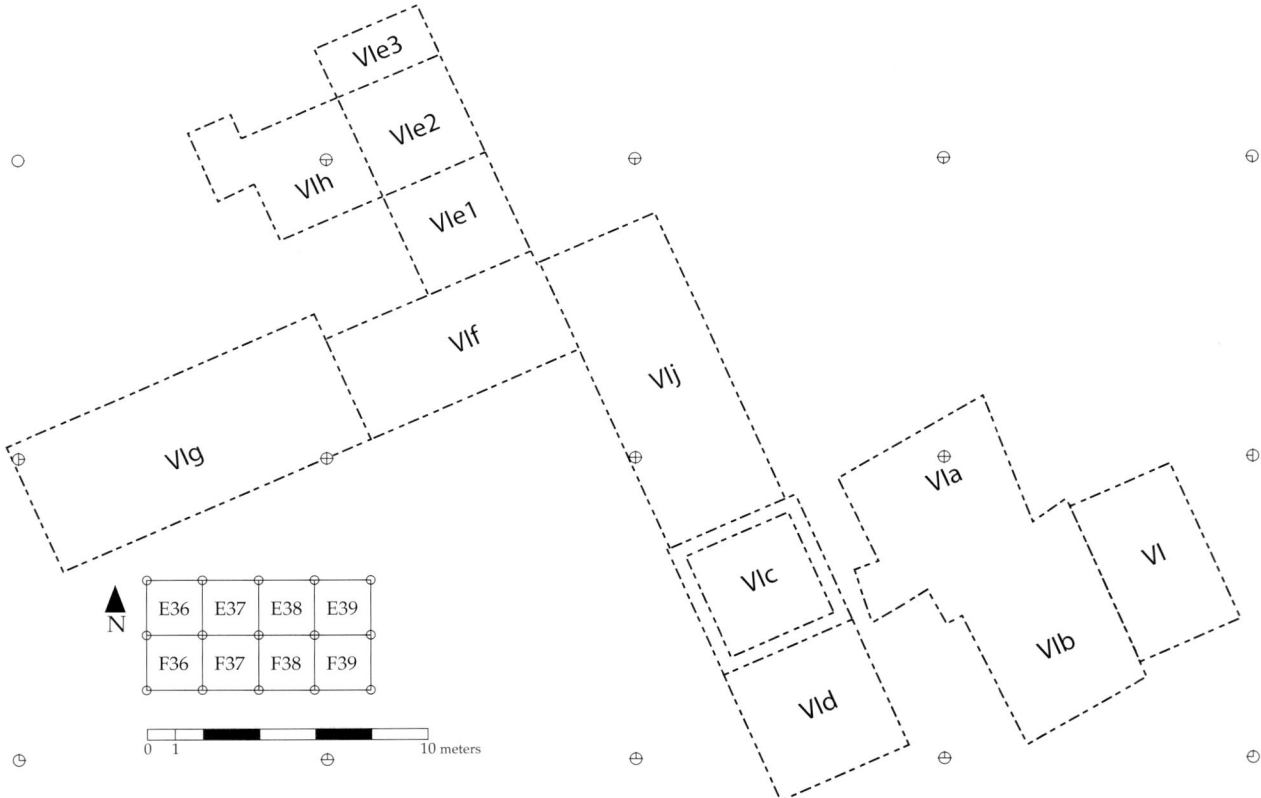

Fig. 3.54 Hasanlu Tepe: Operation VI and extensions.

Stratum 3 and removed the upper part of the burial cut for SK70 and SK72. In Operation VIa, a few whole vessels, not recorded as having come from grave cuts, were found in the Strata 3–3b deposit; a few were also found in Operation VI Stratum 3. These vessels date this level to between Periods V–VIa (Fig. 3.59), but some might derive from the lower Period VII deposit as well (Fig. 3.59:D). The 2nd millennium date of the ceramic assemblage agrees with the single radiocarbon date from Operation VI Stratum 3 of 1610–1003 cal BC at the two-sigma level (Appendix II, P-0198). Grave SK57 contained ceramics dating to Hasanlu IVc or early IVb, and a cylinder seal was found clenched in the individual's teeth (see Chapter 5). The excavators did not discern the level from which this grave was cut, but it seems to be at least the base of Stratum 3a (Fig. 3.58). Other graves of Period IV, either of Period IVb or an unidentifiable subperiod, were also cut from this general level. The early Iron Age cemetery was sealed by a Period IIIa/II architectural phase(s) encountered previously in Operation VI and also present in Operation VIb (Fig. 3.58, Walls A–B, Strata 2a–2c).

Records on the excavations in Operation VIb are even more cursory. The overall stratigraphic sequence seems similar to that of VIa. The excavators found a feature of large stone slabs they believed was too irregular in terms of placement and elevation to be a stone footing or pavement (Fig. 3.55). It appears to be a tomb of Period VIb designated SK61, SK66, and SK76. This feature sat within an unspecified level of Stratum 11 (Fig. 3.60): the sections from Operation VIb were highly schematized. Moreover, the strata designations

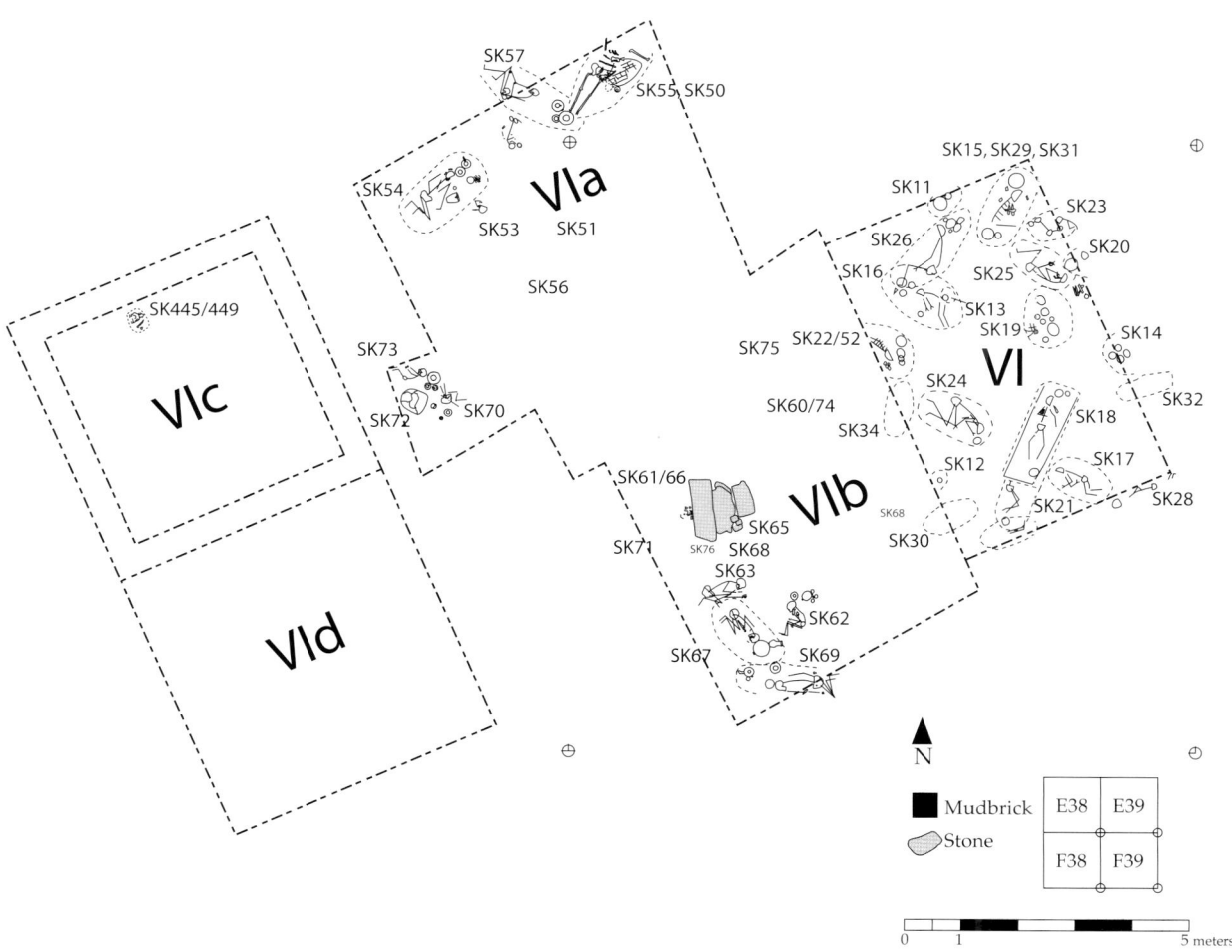

Fig. 3.55 Hasanlu Tepe: burials in Operations VI, VIa, VIb, and VIc.

132

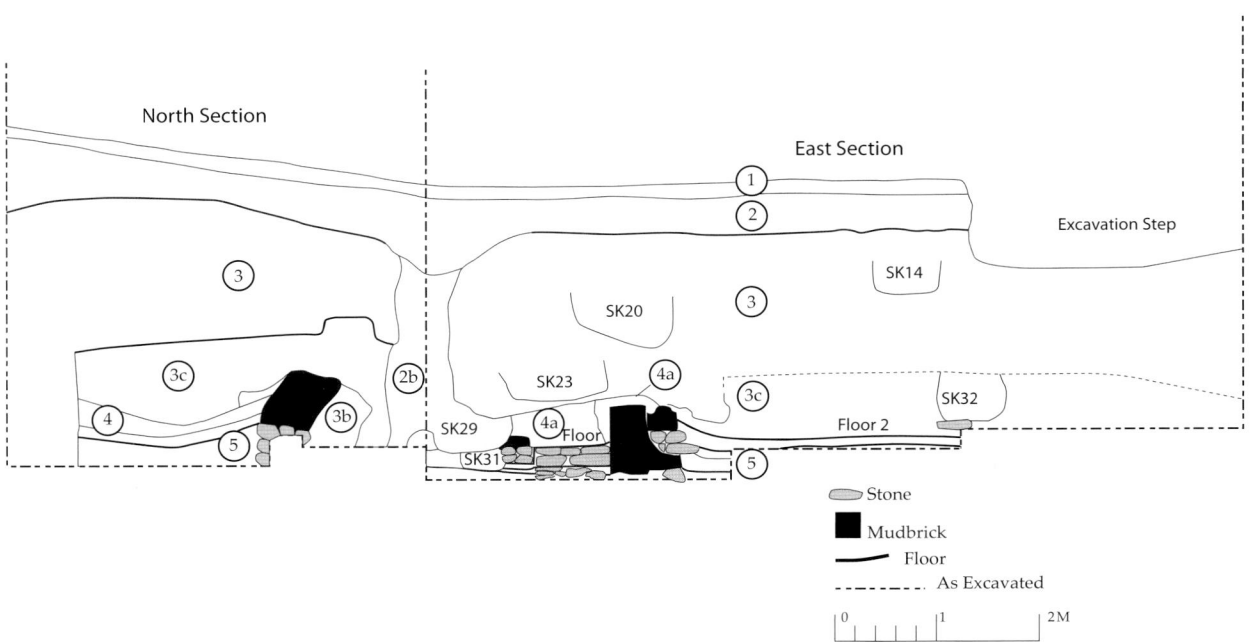

Fig. 3.56 Hasanlu Tepe: east and north sections Operation VI.

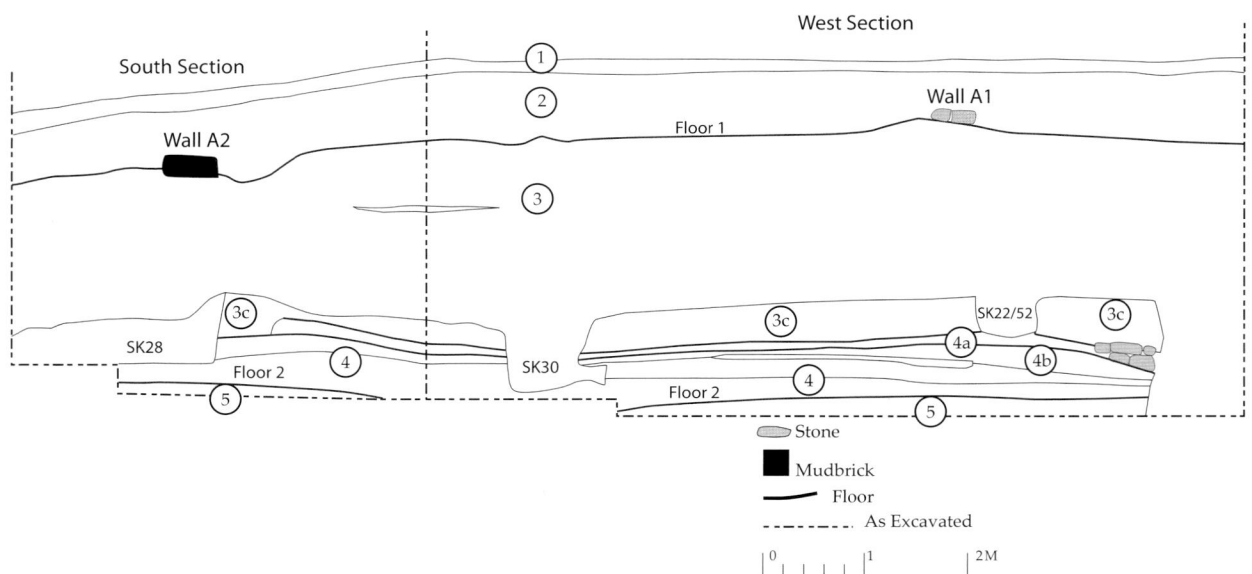

Fig. 3.57 Hasanlu Tepe: south and west sections Operation VI.

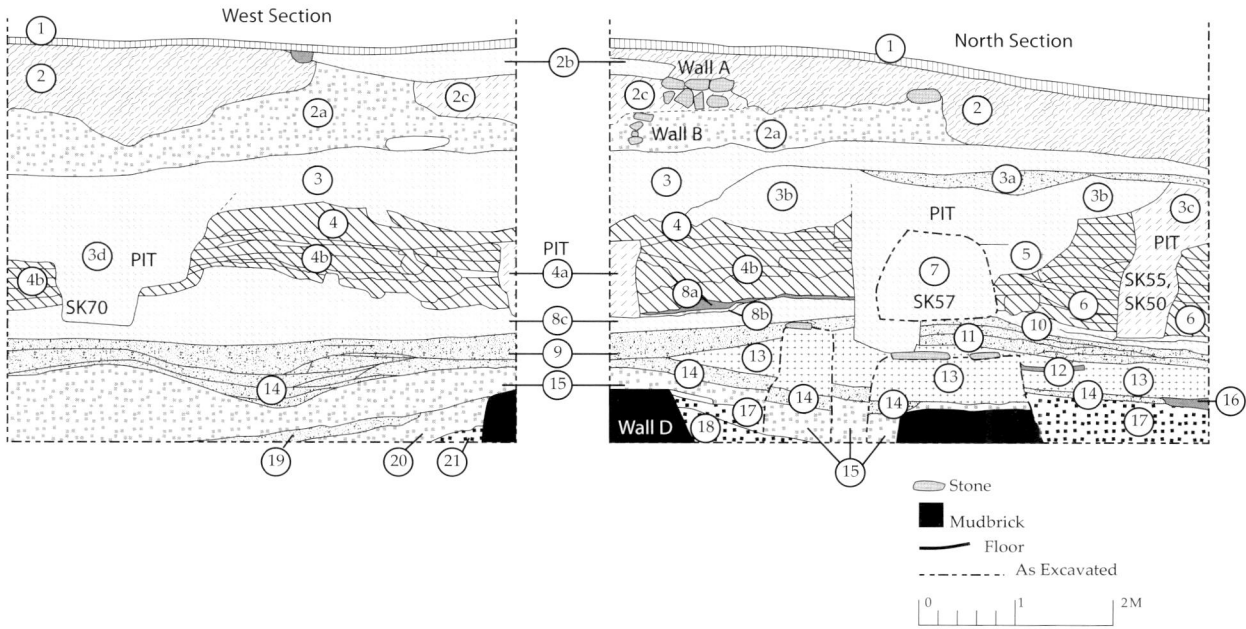

Fig. 3.58 Hasanlu Tepe: north and west sections Operation VIa.

of Operation VIb cannot be precisely correlated with those of Operation VIa. The stones covered two graves of Period VIb, and vessels of this same period as well as animal bones were situated atop the stones. One of the graves below the slabs, SK66, contained three *istikhans*, while the other, SK76, had only a copper/bronze finger ring (see Chapter 5). The vessels on top of the stones, considered an incomplete burial by the excavators (SK61), included a PKW bowl and jar of the annular band-painted variety and a small incised GW jar. Other burials dated to the 2nd millennium BC were SK62, the simple inhumation grave of a child of unspecified age and gender of Period IVc cut into Stratum 5 (just 90 cm below the surface), and SK67 of Period V, another simple inhumation of a woman of over 40 years of age, in the thick fill deposit of Stratum 11. Operation VIb was located near a *hypogeum* excavated by Hakemi and dated to the Iron II (Hakemi and Rad 1950). The reconstructed location of this tomb relative to Operations VI and VIb reveals that it extended into Operation VIb, and the south section of the operation shows a large pit matching the dimensions of the *hypogeum* and even containing a stone slab of the size reported for the stone structure (Fig. 3.60). No early Iron Age graves were found in the southeast corner of Operation VIb where the *hypogeum* would have been situated (Fig. 3.55), and it seems fairly certain that the Hasanlu Project re-excavated this collapsed and in-filled *hypogeum*.

Operations VIc–h, j (Periods V–IIIA/II)

In 1964, seven noncontiguous extensions of varying sizes were excavated north and west of Operation VI and VIa, b (Figs. 1.4, 3.54, 3.61), extending the excavated area to the edges of the modern irrigation canal skirting the unoccupied portions of the northern and eastern Low Mound. The objective was to rapidly recover skeletal material for study by William Bass and Ted Rathbun. In all, 64 graves of Periods III–"V" and VII were recorded; most of these graves date to Period IV with at least 22 definitely assignable to Period IVb in light of the associated grave goods. The excavations in Operation VIc–h and j were not fully recorded—no detailed architectural plans or notes exist and no sections were drawn. Some burials were not drawn or plotted on the plans of the operations. Operation VIc measured 4.0 m x 4.0 m and produced 5 burials (SK445–449). Operation VId measured 5.0 m x 5.0 m and there is no record of burials having been found in this area. Operation VIe, divided into three

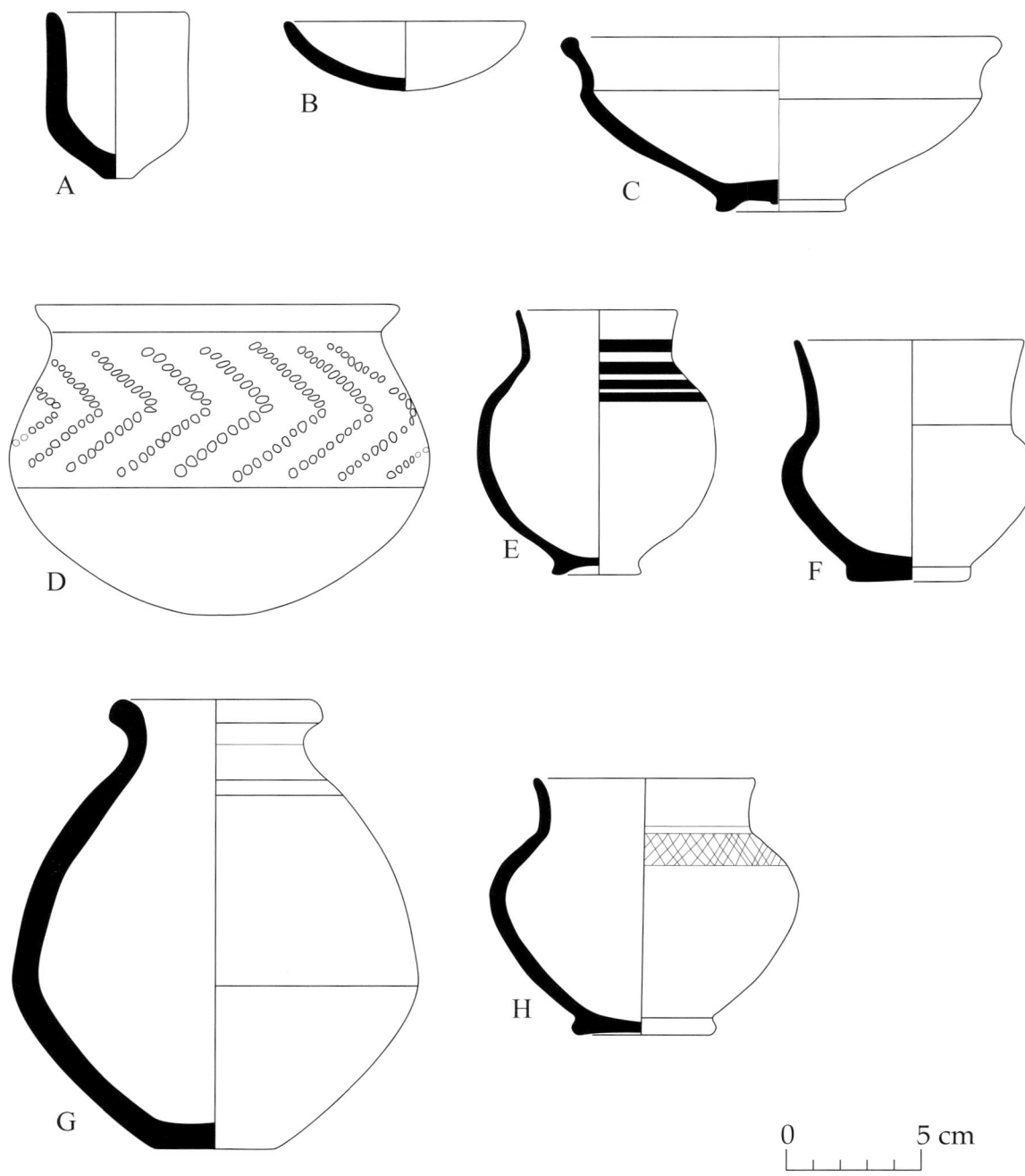

Fig. 3.59 Hasanlu Tepe: vessels from Operations VI and VIa.

subunits, measured 4.0 m x 10.0 m and contained 22 burials (SK450–471). Operation VIf covered an area of 4.0 m x 8.0 m and contained 14 burials (SK472–485). Architectural remains of the early Iron Age were also found in this operation. Operation VIg measured 5.0 m x 12.0 m and contained 5 graves (SK486–490). Operation VIh measured 4.0 m x 4.0 m and 9 graves were recovered in the area (SK491–499). Operation VIj covered 4.50 m x 11.50 m and included 10 burials (SK500–509). Only a few of the burials from this

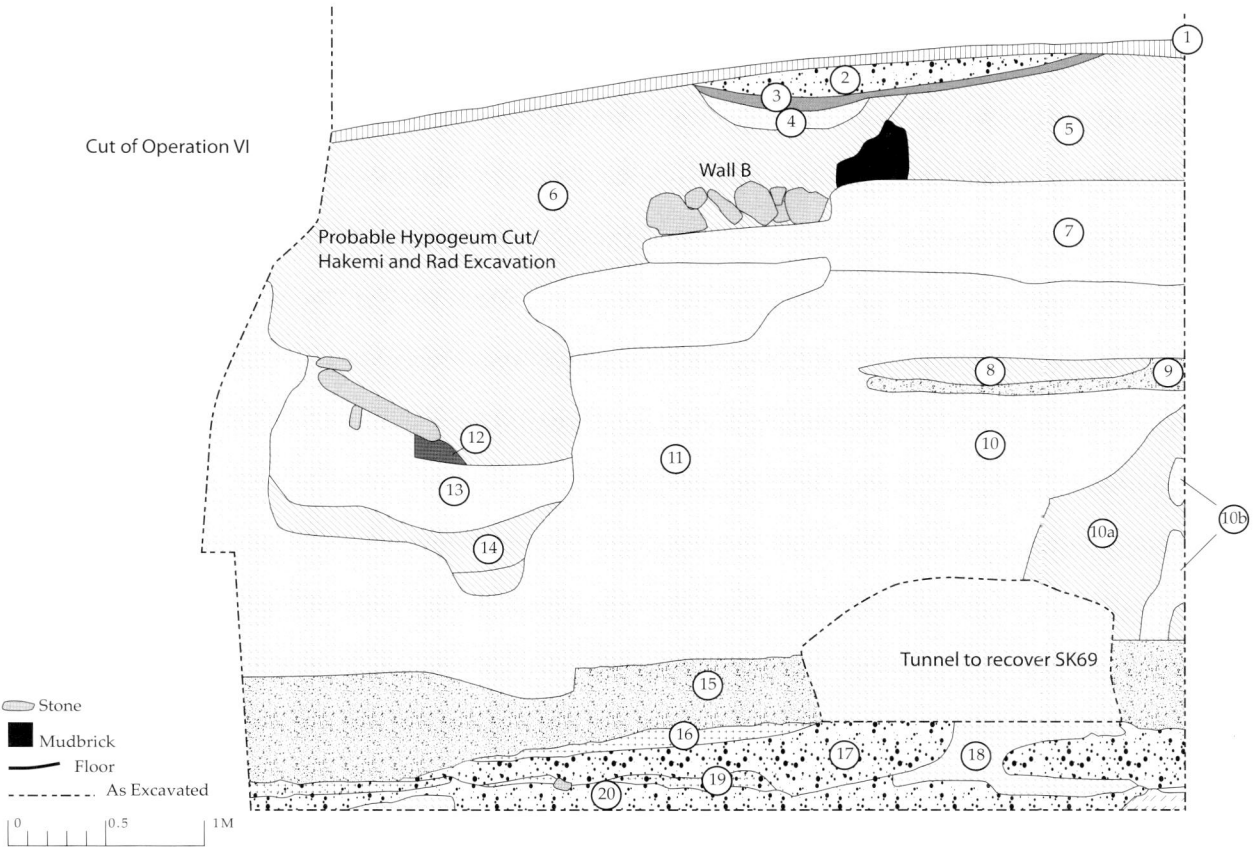

Fig. 3.60 Hasanlu Tepe: south section Operation VIb.

group of trenches can be assigned to Periods IVc–V and most date to Period IVb (Fig. 3.61). Details on the earlier graves are provided in Chapter 5, and Period IVb graves have not been plotted due to the difficulty of accurately placing them on plans. The paucity of 2nd millennium BC graves in this area and their presence to the southeast suggests the growth of the Low Mound cemetery outward over time. Moreover, Operations VI, VIa, and VIb contained 2nd millennium BC burials that had been disturbed by later graves, especially intrusive graves of the Iron II, indicating the reuse of the area as the memory of earlier graves faded or prohibitions on disturbing them were relaxed.

Operation X (Periods VII–IIIa/II)

One of the more revealing stratigraphic sequences recorded for the Low Mound as well as some of the more interesting Bronze Age burials in the Northern Cemetery came from Operation X (Fig. 1.4). Operations X and Xa, located in Grids B27 and B28, respectively, were excavated on the northern Low Mound in 1958. Operation X measured 9.0 m north-south x 4.0 m east-west. It was located 10 m south of the irrigation canal near a large back-filled hole, probably dug by commercial antiquities dealers, and was laid out adjacent and west of one of Hakemi's trenches of 1949 and trenches excavated by Stein. The main objective of the operation was to recover burials, but the trench was roughly in line with the Trans-Citadel Trench (Operations II and VII)—part of an attempt to construct a section of the entire site (Danti 2004:9, 43–45). In all, seven phases comprising 25 major strata were recorded in Operation X, spanning Periods VII to IIIa/II (Figs. 3.62, 3.63). The earliest attested occupation was Period VIIc, as in other northern areas of the eastern Low Mound. Phase VIIc:1 consisted of Strata 21–25. No architectural remains were found in these strata. At the

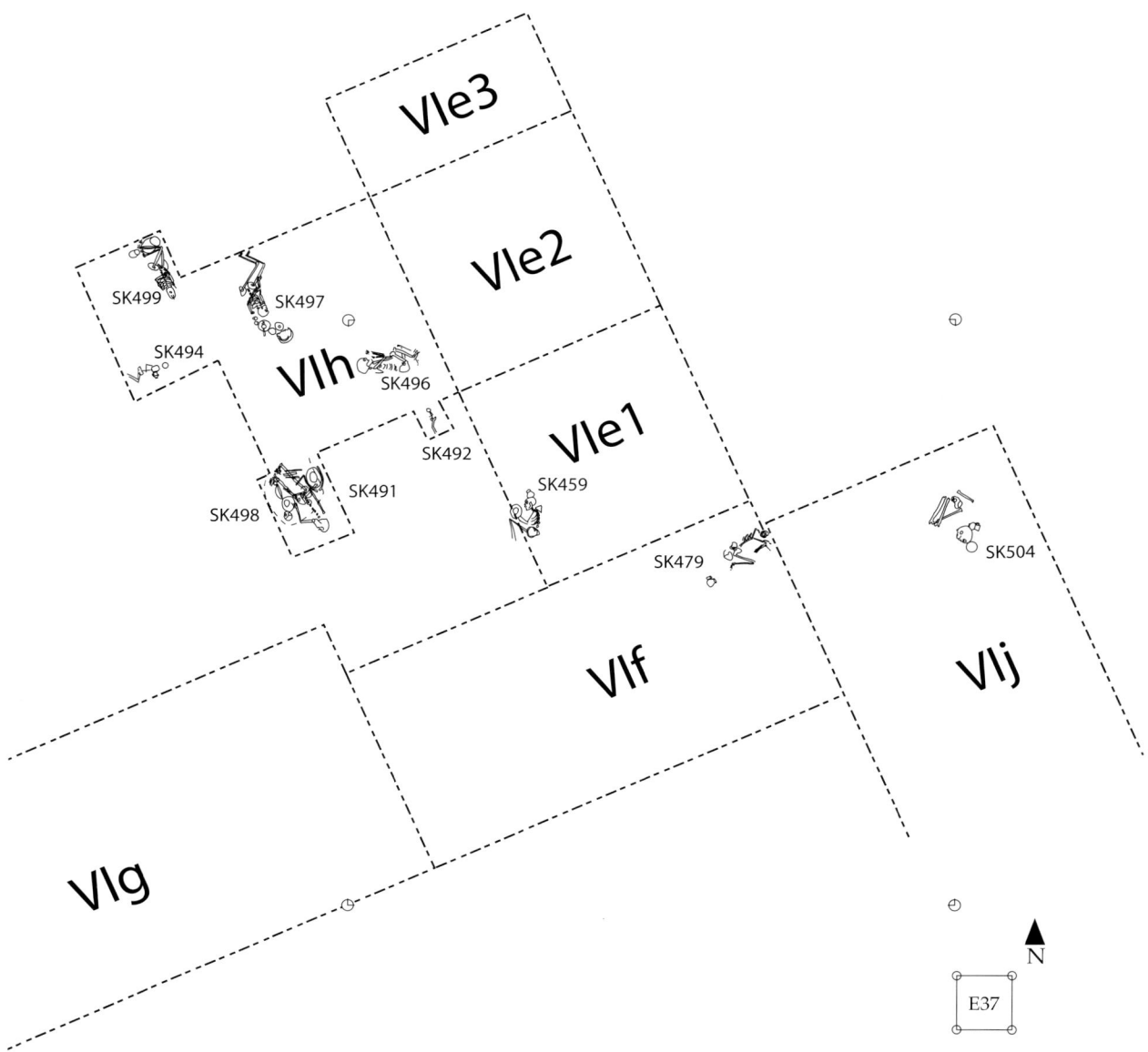

Fig. 3.61 Hasanlu Tepe: select burials in Operations VIe, VIf, VIh, and VIj.

level of Stratum 23, the excavation effectively stopped and only a narrow hole was dug down to probe for sterile soil. The earliest stratum, Stratum 25, consisted of sterile sand and lay at the level of groundwater, reached at 8.45 m below the surface. Phase VIIb:4 (Strata 18–20) is the first construction level found in the operation. Mudbrick Wall G and pisé Wall H, located in the southwest corner of the operation, were cut into Stratum 21, a layer of striated ash. The associated fill, contemporary with both Walls G and H, consisted of brick collapse (Stratum 20). Wall H was then sealed by ash (Stratum 19), which ran against Wall G. The phase ends with Stratum 18, the bricky collapse of Wall G. Sherds found in these levels date the phase to Period VIIa, b, the EBA. Phase VIIb:3 comprises Strata 12–17. The operation was truncated following Stratum 11. No architecture was associated with this phase, which was made up of three successive episodes of striated ash layers capped by brick collapse. Ceramic diagnostics date the phase to Period VIIa, b.

Phase VIIb:2 consisted of Strata 8–11 and may be divided intro three subphases on the basis of architecture (Phases 2a–c). No plans exist for the alignment of the three mudbrick walls associated with this phase, but it appears as though they represent an initial construction phase followed by superimposed rebuilds. Phase 2c is marked by the initial construction of mudbrick Wall E, which was subsequently rebuilt twice (Phases VIIb:2b–2a) directly over existing wall stubs. Wall E is associated with Strata 11/11a (ash) and 10 (brick collapse) and floors of unspecified construction technique abutted it in the north and south (Stratum 11a and an un-numbered stratum). Wall D was built directly atop Wall E. Stratum 10a (brick collapse) ran against it. Wall D is also contemporary with ash accumulations to its north (Stratum 9), and a floor of unspecified construction technique ran up against it in the north (Stratum 9c). The final rebuild episode, Wall C, is associated with layers of ash (Stratum 9a) and brick collapse (Strata 8 and 8a) that probably derive from its destruction. A floor (Stratum 9b) ran against it in the south. Sherds from Phase D date it to Hasanlu Period VIIa, b.

The construction of mudbrick Wall B marks the beginning of Phase VIIb:1 (Strata 6–7) since it seems much larger than the preceding Walls C–E of Phase VIIb:2. No plans exist which inform on the alignment and extent of this wall. Stratum 7 was composed of debris layers of ash and green clay on the floor of the structure (Stratum 7a). The composition of this floor was not recorded. Thick layers of brick collapse were cleared on either side of the wall (Strata 6a–6b). An erosional surface developed over these ruins and a layer of powdery brown soil containing sherds (Stratum 6) accumulated to the north, marking the end of the phase. A single burial, SK48, was found in this level, which the excavator believed to have been associated with the occupation debris of a Stratum 6 structure or to have been located just outside this structure. This burial contained no grave goods and the level from which the grave was cut was not recorded. Sherds from this phase date it to Period VIIa, b.

Phase VIb:1 (Strata 5–5a) followed the abandonment and erosion of the Phase VIIb:1 structure. A shaft (Stratum 5a) was dug through Stratum 6a to Stratum 10a for the construction of a stone-built tomb (Figs. 3.62, 3.63). Only a small portion of this cut lay within the excavated area—it was located in the southwest corner of the operation—and to reach the entrance to the tomb the excavators undercut the southwest corner of the operation (Pl. 5.4). At the bottom of this shaft cut the

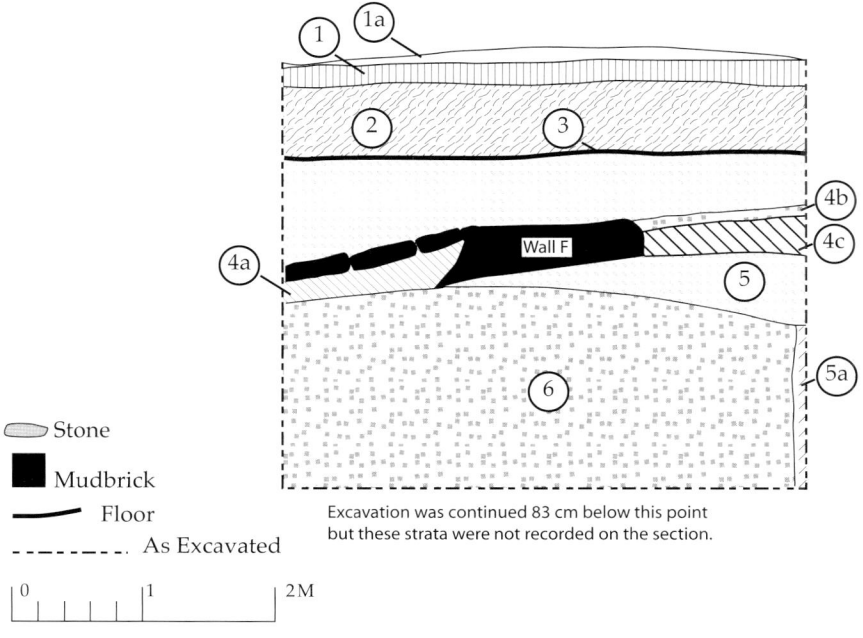

Fig. 3.62 Hasanlu Tepe: south section Operation X.

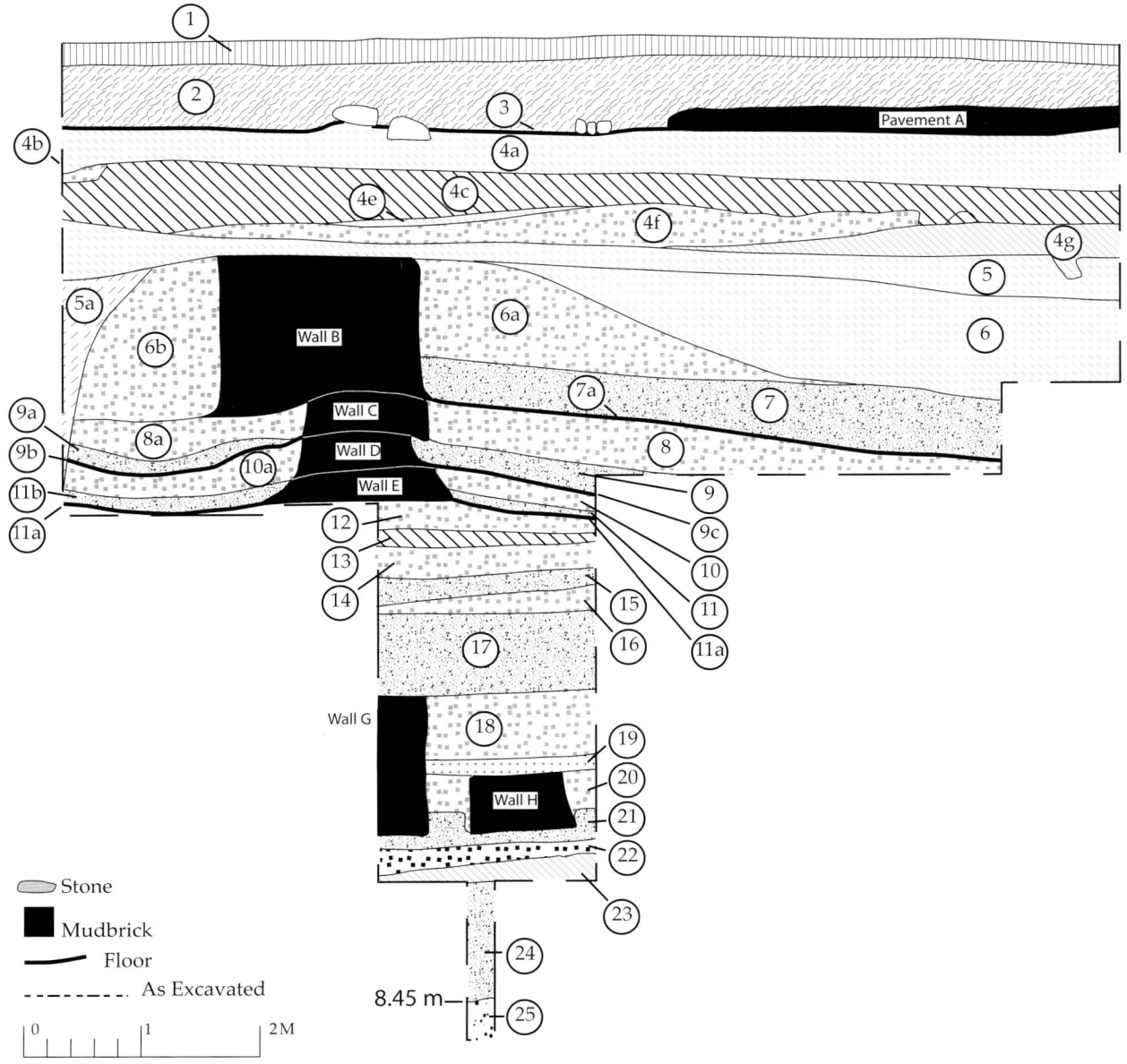

Fig. 3.63 Hasanlu Tepe: west section Operation X.

excavators found a tomb containing a single interment, SK49 (see Chapter 5). They assigned this grave to Period VI—more specifically, it likely dates to Period VIb.

Phase VIb:1 may be dated on the basis of stratigraphy and associated graves to Period VIb. In the same stratigraphic position—that is cutting Phase VIIb:1–2 strata and sealed by those of Phase IV:1 (cut down from the base of Stratum 5 and cutting Strata 6 and 7)—was the multiple interment SK45–47 of Period VIb (see Chapter 5). Stratum 5, a layer of clean brown soil, sealed these grave cuts and an erosional surface formed atop it.

Phase V:1 (Strata 4a–g) contained the approximately 1-m-thick Wall F, which was associated with mudbrick paving to the east (Fig. 3.62). No plans of this architecture exist. The excavator's notes recorded a "probable wall" in Stratum 4, presumably in reference to Wall F. A layer of soft brown soil accumulated

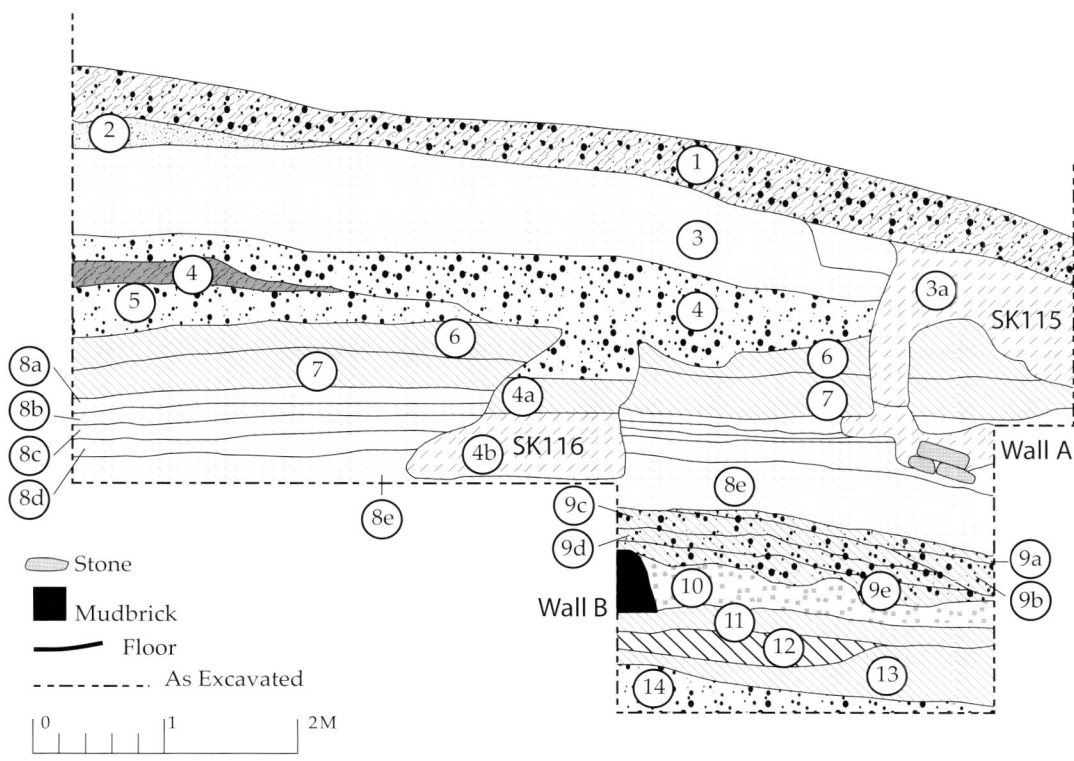

Fig. 3.64 Hasanlu Tepe: south section Operation LIII.

on the east side of this wall prior to the construction of the mudbrick paving (Stratum 4a). Ceramics were of buff, red, and grey fabrics—they were not drawn or collected—and date to Period IV–V. At this same general elevation a poorly preserved Period IVc–V occupation was discovered in neighboring Operations LI and LIV (see below). No early Iron Age graves were found in Operation X, which is in marked contrast to nearby Operations LI and LIV where the LBA–Iron I occupation was superseded by an Iron II cemetery. Phase III:1 (Strata 1–3) began with the construction of a stone and brick pavement 2.00 m wide and 8.90 m long with poorly preserved remains of stone wall footings to the east and west. The excavators believed this formed part of a walled courtyard. The pavement ended in the south in a straight edge and was not found in Operation Xa (Fig. 1.4). Three walls were recognized, Walls A, B, and C. Mudbricks measured 12 cm x 12 cm x 28 cm. In the west baulk, the excavator reports having found flat stones that likely formed a threshold for a doorway. Stratum 2 represented a continuation of top-soil and was composed of a soft greyish-brown powdery soil with some large rocks. One diagnostic sherd of a Hasanlu IIIa "Triangle Ware" bowl was recovered from the stratum. Stratum 1 consisted of sod and soft grey-brown topsoil. A Period IIIa/II occupation was also documented in Operations LI and LIV.

Operations LI and LIV (Periods VI–IIIa/II)

These long trenches were excavated in the northern Low Mound in 1959 (Fig. 1.4). They were originally opened by the site's landlord, Mr. Djanahmad-lou, for the commercial collection of antiquities prior to the inception of the Hasanlu Project. In 1959, the old trenches were cleaned out and subdivided into a series of adjacent subunits, each measuring 4.0 m east-west x 6.0 m north-south. Operation LI had six subunits (LIa–f) and Operation LIV had seven (LIVa–g), labeled from southeast to northwest. Few sections were recorded due to the extensive disturbance in the area. These operations lay just to the south of Operations X and Xa, and LIf adjoined Operation Xa.

After cleaning out the trench, subunits LIc–f were excavated to a depth 1.00–1.35 m below the level of the landlord's excavation, to a total depth of approximately 2.35 m. Eleven burials were found in the operation (SK98–107, 114), including an Iron II *hypogeum* similar to that found by Hakemi in 1949 (Danti and Cifarelli n.d.). Nine graves can be attributed to Period IVb and two are not assignable to a particular period at this time.

In Operation LIV, subunits LIVe–f were excavated below the bottom elevation of the landlord's excavations, and an additional 1.40–1.75 m of deposit was cleared. Five graves, SK108–112, were excavated; of these, three were datable to Period IVb, one to "Period VI," and one cannot be assigned to a period. The grave attributed to Period VI, SK112, was the disturbed and disarticulated burial of an adult of unspecified gender (see Chapter 5). The grave contained an *istikhan* (HAS59-223), an annular band-painted PKW beaker (HAS59-224), and a large storage vessel (HAS59-225), as well as a large number of sheep/goat bones mixed with the human skeletal remains. The small, shouldered beaker is similar to others of Old Babylonian type (cf. Postgate, Oates, and Oates 1997: pl. 79 nos. 879–98, particularly 897).

Strata 4–5 in Operations LI and LIV provided evidence of a Late Bronze and Iron I occupation in this area. Sherds from Operation LI Strata 4–5 and Operation LIV Stratum 4 date to late Period V to Period IVc. Stratum 5 of Operation LI seems to extend into early Period V. These strata were associated with poorly preserved architecture and features. The associated ceramics were not used in the reassessment of the chronology

of "Hasanlu V" because of the heavy disturbance of this area and the incomplete recording of the Hasanlu Project excavations (Danti and Cifarelli n.d.).

Operation LIII (Period VIIc–IIIa/II)

Operation LIII was located in Grid L11 and was the only excavation conducted by the Hasanlu Project in the area of the western Low Mound (Fig. 1.3). The trench was situated on the slope of a dry seasonal streambed or derelict canal near a trench excavated by Hakemi in 1949. Little documentation exists for this unit, which was excavated in 1959.[29] The trench measured 7.20 m east-west; the north-south dimensions were not recorded. Fourteen major strata and two burials were encountered (Fig. 3.64). SK115 of Period IVb was cut down from near the existing surface of the Low Mound (the top of Stratum 3) into the lowest portion of Stratum 3. The burial was sealed by Stratum 1 (topsoil) and had been disturbed by a later cut. SK116 of "Period V" (early Period V, see Chapter 5) was cut down from Stratum 4 through Strata 5–8e and the burial cut was sealed by the upper part of Stratum 4 (Fig. 3.64). Stratum 4, a deposit measuring 20–40 cm in depth and without architectural features, was recorded as "Painted Ring Ware"—an informal name for Period VI. I have found no sherds or sherd drawings from this level. Stratum 5 and lower strata belong to Period VIIa–c based on the labeling of the south section and sherds in the collections of the UPM. Two architectural levels of Period VII are shown in the sections, labeled Walls A and B, but no plans exist of these walls. The operation reached a

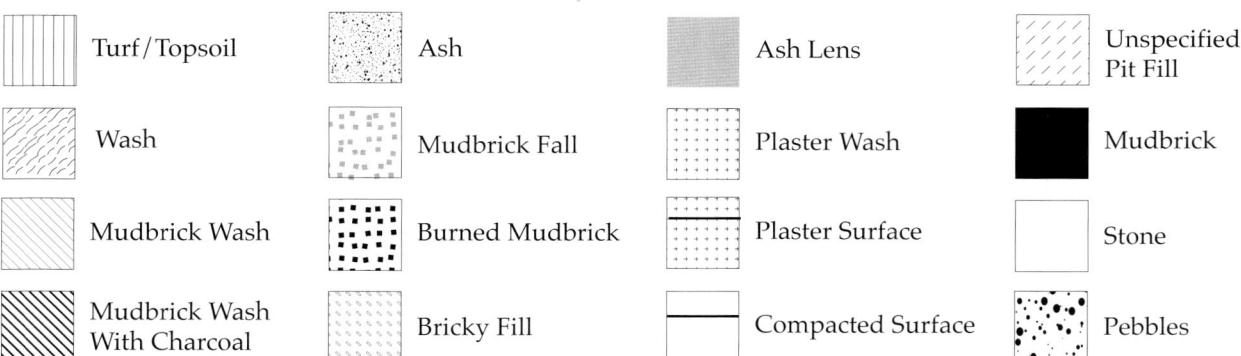

Fig. 3.65 Key to sections.

depth of 4.60 m at which point there was a clean layer of sterile sand.

Low Mound Summary

The Low Mound of Hasanlu was settled in the late 4th–early 3rd millennium BC or Hasanlu VIIc. The area was occupied extensively and fairly continuously through the 3rd millennium BC as evidenced by the deposits of POW of Hasanlu VIIa–b. Graves of Hasanlu VIIa–b were cut into the occupation deposits following their abandonment—this does not constitute intramural burial. I have found no indication that the Low Mound was occupied or used as a cemetery in Hasanlu VIc—the MBI of the late 3rd to early 2nd millennium—although this horizon, typified by buff and greenish-buff SW, might have easily been overlooked during the early years of the Hasanlu Project. Such an occupation is attested in the U22 Sounding on the High Mound and in the lower levels at Dinkha Tepe. No definitive evidence of occupation of Hasanlu VIb or VIa was found on the Low Mound. Stray sherds and whole vessels of annular-band painted KW were found in deposits immediately above the Period VII strata, always in association with MBW. Too little information is currently available to allow for further interpretation. Graves of Period VIb and VIa were cut into the Period VII deposit, as were graves of early Period V (see Chapter 5). These graves were not associated with architecture; rather, they appear to have been part of an extramural cemetery. Occupation deposits yielding Early and Middle MBW were found on the northern and eastern Low Mound, but documentation is lacking. The best evidence for occupation comes from Operation V, the so-called Artisan's House or BBXIII (Danti 2011). Here, coherent architectural remains date as early as early Period IVb and almost certainly Period IVc (Danti 2011). These levels rested above a deposit of MBW of likely LBA date (Danti 2011). The MBW occupation continued in Hasanlu IVb on the eastern Low Mound as seen in Operations IV and V. The evidence from Operation V suggests a number of closely spaced buildings with streets/alleys occupied at least parts of the Low Mound. The topography of the Low Mound seems to suggest areas of likely early Iron Age occupation where low rises exist, but the larger part of these areas was not investigated, especially on the southern Low Mound, where a modern Islamic cemetery prevented excavation.

NOTES

3.1. For an assessment of the period from the standpoint of archaeological survey, see Kroll 1994a, 1994b.

3.2. These samples come from different areas of the central mound. P-1233 is from Stratum 2 of Operation G10g (see Muscarella 1968: fig. 1 for the layout of the operations). This context was sealed by Floor 1A and the associated Walls F and G. P-1430 was charcoal from a floor associated with Wall D of Operation H1g. The context of P-1429/31 seems unreliable, as the sample comes from a floor and pit cutting Wall G in Operation H1h. The pit was cut from Stratum 3 and Walls F and G abutted the top of the earlier massive Wall H1h-E.

3.3. Dyson refers to "several levels of houses" (1973a:704).

3.4. Harris (1988:23) has stated that, "a jar full of figs and grape pips (Ficus carica, Vitis vinifera) was found in burned building III, in a room that may have been a kitchen. In the same room, what seems to have been a string of figs was found in a copper/bronze basin with iron handles." In fact, the jar (HAS62-209) contained only one fig and was found in a storeroom (Room 5). The string of figs on the tray (HAS62-256) was found in Room 4.

3.5. This is one of many examples that revealed the excavators' use of the burned deposit of Period IVb—with its *in situ* finds, skeletons, thick ash deposit, and intense burning—as an assumed universal stratigraphic benchmark. The floors of BB-VII were cut through in many places during excavation in areas without stone pavings or such "obvious" evidence of the Period IVb destruction. When such conditions were not present, errors in excavation were fairly common.

3.6. Young mentions this deposit and briefly discusses the ceramics (1963); the important material from the lowest MBW level (Stratum 10), however, curiously goes unmentioned. Citing ware frequencies, Young believed there was a clear distinction between the upper and lower parts of the deposit. This is supported by closer examination, but rather the distinction is one between Period V (Strata 7–10) and Period IVc (Strata 5–6).

3.7. The U22 Strata 9–10 deposit dates prior to Strata 8 and 8a of S22, which date fairly securely to the late 14th–12th centuries BC, or late Period V–early Period IV according to radiocarbon determinations from samples P-2161 and P-2378.

3.8. Muscarella (2006) is confused as to the periodization.

3.9. Hasanlu Notebook 30, Hasanlu Publication Archive, University of Pennsylvania Museum.

3.10. Dyson correctly noted in 1972 that Wall 8-1 could not be the continuation of the wall of the U22 Stratum 10 structure.

3.11. Figure 3.15 is entitled "S22 East Section Composite 1962+1972" because it represents two different but complementary section drawings that I have combined. The 1962 and 1972 sections differed in some details with regard to Strata 1–4, which they both depicted. I chose to show the more detailed stratigraphic features in the composite drawing—by far the more reliable section was that of 1962. The lower levels were only shown on the 1972 section and were aligned to the upper strata of 1962 by overlaying the two sections and aligning their major features (mainly pits and walls)—the balk lines had naturally shifted over the intervening years and no instrumental mapping was completed in this area—this often poses a major challenge when working on Hasanlu. I followed a similar procedure to produce Figure 3.18.

3.12. The Hasanlu Project excavators frequently interpreted the periods they were excavating while working and this influenced their recordkeeping when notes were taken in the field. At times this can complicate the analysis of the dataset.

3.13. Archival records show that at one point Dyson had designated BBVIIE as BBXIII and he later revised this to BBVIIE. BBXIII now refers to the so-called Artisan's House of the Period IVb eastern Low Mound (Danti 2011).

3.14. Dyson recorded in his notes, "This is either early IV or late V in date. Sherds not adequately segregated but little of IV type below that surface" (West Slope Observations 1972, Hasanlu Publication Archive, University of Pennsylvania Museum).

3.15. In 1972, Dyson believed the early walls of S22 were in fact contemporary with the Period V columned hall. He wrote that the "level to south of V house [Grid S22] held brick walls set on reed layer. Contemporary with V house, which does not open on this side. This building runs under baulk to south and lies below D Structure [the north stairwell of the T22 Building of Period IVc and BB VII of Period IVb] of Period IV" (West Slope Observations 1972, Hasanlu Publication Archive, University of Pennsylvania Museum). Dyson linked the structure to the late Period V architecture of Grid T22, noting the T22 building was "on level of reed wall in S22" (West Slope Observations 1972, Hasanlu Publication Archive, University of Pennsylvania Museum).

3.16. Young noted that there were, "fragments of burned brick in section, and patches of burned fill over most of the square in Stratum 10 which indicate some kind of burning prior to final destruction, Period IV" (Hasanlu Notebook 18). This burned deposit was sealed by the Terminal Period IVb floor of the building.

3.17. I have reconstructed the general lines of these sections, which were not recorded by the excavator. The sections do not match the architectural plans of Periods IVb and earlier architecture exactly, and I have not attempted to correct these spatial discrepancies.

3.18. While all material was collected from the Q24 sounding as Stratum 10, I have introduced substrata to clarify the construction sequence.

3.19. Young labels this turn as such, and it cannot be interpreted as a cut line.

3.20. The excavators almost never recorded the presence of foundation trenches in the 1956–64 seasons of work at Hasanlu.

3.21. Definitive evidence of the northern wooden gate was found. Dyson reconstructed the southern gate.

3.22. This sample was collected July 26, 1972, from Area 1/4 Stratum 10a. The excavator notes that this sample consisted of "reeds, wheat grains, etc." and was collected just south of Wall 26, "in the layer of trash even with the top of the foundation stones of Wall [26]." This is Stratum 10a7 of Phase IVc:3a (Hasanlu Excavation Notebook 65: 10).

3.23. Y27 was Operation XXVII and Z27 was XXIV. Work in this area was supervised by T. Cuyler Young.

3.24. The Operations were XLV (Z28), XLIV (Z29), XLVIII (Y28), and XLVII (Y29). This area was supervised by Vaughn Crawford and T. Cuyler Young.

3.25. X28 was excavated as Operation LXXVIII and supervised by Young and Dyson.

3.26. Stratum 10x of Figure 3.31 does not seal Wall 21—the section shows the projected elevation of this wall, which was located south of the actual drawn baulk/section showing Stratum 10x. Stratum 10x runs under the stone footings of the upper wall in Figure 3.33.

3.27. When Dyson initially interpreted this structure (1977b:158), Period IVc was poorly defined and these radiocarbon dates were attributed to the "Iron II" period. The relevant samples are P-0421, P-0437, P-0440, and P-1230 (see Appendix II).

3.28. In the notebook for Operation VI (1957), of the five ceramic vessels listed for this grave (HAS57-90–94), numbers 91–93 have been crossed out for no discernable reason.

3.29. Operation LIII was supervised by Dyson, who became extremely ill in the latter part of the 1959 season. Work continued for a short period in the area, but he was unable to record the results in detail (Robert H. Dyson, pers. comm. 1999). The trench was completed at a time when excavation notes were compiled after the excavation from various sources and no daily running records of the excavations were usually kept. It is possible the digging continued during the supervisor's absence.

4

Overview of the Ceramic Assemblages of Hasanlu VIa–IVc

We know that the burial customs and the ceramic assemblage that appear at the beginning of Hasanlu Period V originate on the Iranian Plateau.

— Dyson and Voigt 2003:236

Introduction

The archaeological cultures of the LBA and Iron I of the southern Lake Urmia Basin have traditionally been viewed as a radical departure from those of the first half of the 2nd millennium BC (Dyson 1965:195; Muscarella 1994a)—albeit with a few notable exceptions (Medvedskaya 1982). As previously discussed, the punctuated nature and magnitude of this change—best attested by the ceramic assemblages—has been exaggerated by gaps in our sequence, conflations of chronological periods, and biased sampling and data presentation, leading to invalid comparisons and artificial lacunae. The most distinctive material from the graves of Hasanlu "Period V," a pastiche covering roughly 600 years or more, was informally and selectively compared to the occupation assemblages of Dinkha IV Phases A–B and Hasanlu VIb, the MBII period which spanned some 300 years. The datasets on which all such comparisons rested have never been adequately published or fully analyzed.

Dinkha IV ends around 1600 BC and "Hasanlu V" as previously described begins in the mid-15th century BC. A smattering of earlier material of the MBA was mistakenly included in it. The intervening "gap" between the original Hasanlu VI and V, now covered by Hasanlu Period VIa, has seldom been considered, nor has the terminal MBII (Dinkha IV Phase D) been singled out to search for potential change—the MBII was essentially presented as a 300-year homogeneity. Moreover, there have been few explicit statements pertaining to the exact lines of comparison between the relevant ceramic assemblages. The presence/absence of painted ware with "early Iron Age Grey Ware" has loomed large in the distinction between the early "Iron Age" and Hasanlu VI. Tracing the publication record through time we read of "Hasanlu V" having some annular band-painted wares (Dyson 1965:195; Young 1963, 1965) followed by steadily strengthening assertions that there is virtually no painted ware in "Hasanlu V," and subsequently no PKW in Hasanlu V (Muscarella 1994a:141). Yet the co-occurrence of painted Urmia Ware with Early MBW at Dinkha was little considered and went virtually unreported (see Chapter 2). MBA "Grey Ware" received similar treatment. Early statements by Young and Kramer suggested potential connections between Bronze Age and early Iron Age "Grey Wares" (Hamlin 1971; Young 1963). Any relation between the two was later viewed as spurious at best, with Muscarella stating, "No one who has closely worked with the pottery in Iran would confuse the two [citing Dyson, pers. comm., and Young 1985]… There is no evidence for any *in situ* evolution" (Muscarella 1994a:141). Naturally, such an assertion rests solely on how the noted authorities defined or subsequently re-defined MBA "Grey Ware." The ware's definition and distinction were apt in terms of a consistently light grey, dense, burnished fabric (Kramer's Ware Va), but other types of monochrome smoothed or burnished ceramics occurring in Dinkha IV/Hasanlu VI—particularly in the period's terminal Phase D—went virtually ignored with regard to connections to the early "Iron Age."

While the LBA (Hasanlu V) represents a period of change, as with any time period one should not immediately assume it is the result of a wholesale, punctuated cultural replacement dating to the 16th century BC. First of all, when such theories were first advanced, inaccuracies in the absolute dating of this cultural transformation placed it at the end of the 13th century BC (Dyson 1965:195). Clearly we need to reframe our research questions and build our arguments from the ground up. From the standpoint of the ceramic assemblage, two key questions are: Can we discern changes during Dinkha IV Phase D (the Terminal MBII or Hasanlu VIb) that provide links to the succeeding Hasanlu VIa/MBIII? Similarly, are there connections between Period VIa and the LBA? In both cases, the answers are in the affirmative but rest on limited data, and I must be forgiven for seeking egress in the *via media* and in the threadbare adage "more research is needed."

Hasanlu Project Ceramic Analysis: Field Methodology and Analytical Procedures

There was no consistent strategy for the collection, recording, and saving of sherds from 1956–1964 at Hasanlu. During this period sherds and other finds were sporadically collected according to Strata-Area designations, although in practice Area was far less likely to guide collection or be recorded. Area designations most often encompassed rooms or pits. Strata often represented architectural levels rather than discrete distinctions in excavated matrices. In the later seasons of the project (1970–1977), a Locus-Lot system was introduced which allowed the excavators to designate smaller collection units that were not necessarily tied to the higher order interpretive level embodied by Strata and Area designations.

Painted, glazed, and other decorated sherds were far more likely to be collected, recorded, and saved. A type-series method was initially being developed to classify the ceramics and thus sherds were saved if they best represented a diagnostic of form, ware, or style. Many decorated sherds and most whole vessels were thus given a Hasanlu Number in the field. Hasanlu Numbers were field numbers designated by the site prefix "HAS" followed by a two-digit year designation followed by a sequential number assigned to objects entered into the registry for a given season (e.g., "HAS59-232"). Some sherds and whole vessels were saved and various collections are currently in the Tehran Museum, the Metropolitan Museum of Art, the University of Pennsylvania Museum, and the Royal Ontario Museum (ROM); small collections of material were subsequently distributed to many other institutions. Where museum accession numbers are known, they have been provided herein with the standard TM, MMA, and UPM prefixes, respectively. No material analyzed in this study appears to be housed at the ROM.

In certain trenches, sherds were saved in large number—mainly in operations that were excavated with the intention of clarifying the chronological sequence, such as the U22 Deep Sounding and Operation I, both located on the High Mound. On the Low Mound nearly all ceramics were discarded during the digging or shortly thereafter. For some operations, general notes on ceramic wares and forms were kept. The excavators of other operations occasionally provided information on the ware and in one case representative forms of each attested formal type were illustrated. Project records dating to ca. 1964 lay out the prescribed procedure by which site supervisors were to analyze the ceramics from their operation(s): "Sort into reduced or oxidized groups. Sort each group into shapes—see major types: bowls, jars, pots, etc. Sort these into types of surface finish or decoration: glazed, painted, burnished, etc. Check for significant association between type, shape and finish" (Pottery Analysis and Drawing in the Field, Hasanlu Project Archives Document). Wares were then recorded using the following system. First, sherds and vessels were assigned to a Series comprising five general categories reflecting the initial sorting based on surface color:
GREY—pottery of dark brown, grey, or black surface color—reduced firing atmosphere;

BUFF—pottery of light brown, buff, orange, reddish, yellowish, whitish, or greenish surface color—oxidizing firing atmosphere;
SLIPPED—pottery with a surface coating of a color distinctly different from that of the interior of the core;
PAINTED;
and
GLAZED.

"Paste," and concomitantly the "coarseness" or "fineness" of wares, was categorized based on temper and coded with a Roman numeral. Eight categories were designated, but only six are described in project documentation:

I. Medium-sized grit or sand (medium paste of unwashed clay);
II. None visible or very small (fine paste–washed clay best for burnishing);
III. Small pebbles (coarse paste);
IV. Large grit and lime (coarse paste);
VII. Lime pops;
VIII. Fiber or straw.

Surface finish was coded into four categories that were designated by letters:

a. Matte (or plain);
b. Smoothed or scraped (but not shiny);
c. Burnished (stroke marks visible);
d. Polished (no stroke marks visible).

Finally, paste color or surface treatment was often recorded, rather informally, as a gloss, since the actual Ware Series designations could be highly deceptive, for example, "light greyish-buff Grey IIc" or "reddish Buff Ia."[1]

This sorting system resulted in ware categories based primarily on *surface color*, which were then secondarily sorted by vessel form. A great deal of significance was placed on visual observation of an oxidizing versus reducing atmosphere. The influence of Ghirshman's findings at Sialk shows through here: "Grey" pottery precedes Buff pottery. This system worked well for ceramics produced under fairly standardized manufacturing conditions, such as the KW of the MBII or the fully developed Late MBW of the Iron II. This system proved wholly inadequate for assemblages with a high degree of variability within and between wares—that is, ceramics that were the product of more localized, non-standardized manufacture such as was the case in the late MBII, MBIII, and early LBA. Compounding problems, the ware designations developed by the Hasanlu Project were not consistently employed from 1956–1977 at Hasanlu. Munsell charts were rarely employed. The Ware Series designations were heavily reliant on unsystematic assessments of firing color but, as already alluded to, within each Series—and even on a single vessel—color often varied markedly and graded into other Series, causing typological overlap. The end result was not the intended differentiation of different firing atmospheres and, by extension, alternative methods of production, but rather the splitting of ceramics into types based on perceived coarseness, degree of burnish, presence or absence of painting, and vessel forms. The best-known product of this system is so-called Grey Ware, now MBW, which occurs in buff, red, grey, and black. As originally defined, the Series generally meant simply "not buff in color," but the definition of "buff" varied widely. Sherds and vessels of darker variants of buff or that had been smoothed or burnished were more likely to be classified as "Grey Ware." Matte or smoothed black, grey, or greyish-buff ceramics were almost always classified as "Grey Ware."

Another difficulty with this system is the Slipped series, since the Buff and especially the Grey Series are often slipped in colors close to the underlying body. Red-slipped Buff Ware was accounted for in the typology, while slips and self-slips in "Grey Ware" were seldom recorded unless they markedly contrasted with the underlying color of the core or the line between a slipped and unslipped portion was preserved on a vessel or sherd. Finally, vessel forms in the Buff and Grey Series generally overlap: surface finish (burnishing and polishing) and coarseness-fineness, irrespective of firing color, correspond more frequently to vessel forms. An exception is coarse Buff Ware, which appears to have been the standard ware for cooking vessels. A reassessment of the ceramic ware typology employed by the Hasanlu Project is well beyond the scope of the present work and is in any case extremely complicated, since the majority of the ceramics were discarded and ware designations were inconsistently recorded. I would suggest that coarse Buff Ware be maintained since it represents a utilitarian cooking and food processing ware. Few storage jars were ever recorded by the project, and they were generally discarded and thus the typical ware(s) of these vessels is difficult to ascertain. In smaller vessels, the Series distinctions between Buff and Grey have little value and appear to have been imposed upon the LBA and early Iron Age assemblage.

Seen another way, the typologies developed by the Hasanlu Project were designed to facilitate cross-sequence comparisons between the highly diagnostic ceramics of Ušnu-Solduz with other known (published) assemblages—this was of course how chronologies were initially developed. During the cultural-historical phase of Iranian archaeology, such methods naturally led to explanations for such connections—conquest, migration, and trait diffusion being the great causal triumvirate. The biases inherent in the methodology and theoretical stance of the Hasanlu Project were amplified to a certain extent by the research foci of the scholars developing the ceramic chronology. For the 2nd and early 1st millennia BC, two typologies were developed: Young produced one for the Iron II that was extended to the Iron I and LBA, and Kramer developed a related system for the MBII. Both works are classics of Near Eastern archaeology. Young's work was focused on facilitating study of his Early and Late Western Grey Ware horizons as attested in Ušnu-Solduz as a conceptual springboard for approaching a larger phenomenon—these same horizons throughout northern and western Iran. Kramer's study was similar but oriented to the west: she sought to compare the KW phenomenon of Dinkha Tepe to northern Mesopotamia, western Syria, and Syro-Cilicia.

Two studies with very specific, preconceived goals produced equally specific ceramic typologies. One was designed with the typical MBII ceramic assemblage of Mesopotamia in mind and the other was aimed at articulating the Iron I–II assemblage of Hasanlu with similar ceramics from northern and western Iran known largely from grave assemblages. Conceptually these two systems "met," but were never tied together, in the mid-2nd millennium BC or the MBIII and early LBA. Neither was tooled to deal with this period of high ware variation and reduced diagnosticity in vessel forms, resulting in typological lumping, lacunae, and ultimately highly idealized notions of the Bronze Age and the Iron Age.[2] Moreover, connections to the southern Caucasus and eastern Anatolia, regions often closely linked to the Lake Urmia Basin, took a backseat to Assyria and Persia. In the end, the putative chronological and cultural void dividing the Bronze and Iron Ages was inadvertently widened by research agendas rather than migrations or punctuated culture change, per se.

Ceramics of Late Dinkha IV/ Hasanlu VIb—The Terminal Middle Bronze Age (1700–1600 BC)

To enable research to proceed on a firmer footing, Hasanlu VI/Dinkha IV must first be more closely examined. Kramer has provided an in-depth study of the ceramics of the period (Hamlin 1971, 1974), but detailed stratigraphic and architectural information have yet to be published. One potential bias in our understanding of Hasanlu VI/Dinkha IV stands out—since Kramer focused specifically on the KW phenomenon of the MBII, her interpretations and data presentation were heavily weighted toward the earlier Phases A–C of Dinkha IV, that is, the highpoint in the ware's production and by default not the terminal phase of the MBII, Dinkha IV Phase D. Moreover, the overlying material of early Dinkha III was not systematically analyzed. While this assemblage is small, its existence alone is significant, as we shall see.

Overview of Dinkha IV Ceramic Wares and Types

The Bronze Age–Iron Age transition as previously envisioned was often typified as the rapid, wholesale abandonment of painted pottery and the equally sudden emergence of MBW. As previously mentioned, other lines of evidence bearing on this putative cultural break—stratigraphic continuity, architectural forms, styles of burial, and types of cemeteries—do not support arguments of rapid change or wholesale cultural replacement. The evidence from ceramic production is by far the most difficult to address owing to weak points in our sequence and the quality of the available dataset. The first half of the 2nd millennium BC in the southern Lake Urmia Basin, moreover, presents certain unique problems for archaeologists.

The MBI–II can be characterized as a period of close contacts with Mesopotamia if not the actual colonization of the region, best attested by the so-called KW ceramic assemblage found at Dinkha and Hasanlu and known to occur at other sites such as the large, unexcavated mound of Naqadeh (see Chapter 1 regarding Naqadeh; see also Kroll 1994b:164–65 for other sites in the valley which have produced KW). Dinkha and Hasanlu might have been *karum*, or trading posts, as such colonies attached to indigenous settlements are known textually and archaeologically in southern Anatolia. This line of fortified sites suggests direct control of the main east-west line of communication that linked Ušnu, Solduz, and Mahabad. Unless texts are discovered, however, we cannot be certain regarding the presence of *karum*. If this represents colonization, can we discern potential autochthonous traditions in the region? Given the current biased dataset—the product of excavating two high mounds representing the remains of strategically located and almost certainly fortified MBI–II centers—the answer is unfortunately no. Future meticulous excavation of Hasanlu's Low Mound might hold the key, but the quality of the work conducted there in the late 1950s and early 1960s was not adequate to address such questions. It is therefore difficult to deal with this potential source of bias in our current view of the Middle Bronze–Late Bronze transition. The emergence—or, perhaps more accurately, increased visibility—of the MBW horizon in the MBIII and early LBA might be the result of the sudden removal or replacement of a "foreign" presence or influence—the KW horizon, representing only one intrusive part of the larger cultural milieu of the 2nd millennium BC northwestern Zagros.

A major question confronting us is whether there is a gap in the Dinkha sequence between the destruction of Dinkha IV Phase D and the MBIII "trash deposit." While no evidence of post-Dinkha IV occupation other than "trash deposits" was forthcoming in the Dinkha Control Sounding, Sir Aurel Stein alludes to a fairly substantial deposit sealing the "classic" KW levels in his uppermost trenches (1940:376; see Chapter 3). What is the date of this material? The Hasanlu Project Control Sounding was located near Stein's uppermost trenches. Stein's upper levels must either postdate Dinkha IV Phase D or be roughly contemporary. Stein was an avid reporter of painted wares. He mentions only vessels with annular painted bands in the uppermost levels and does not refer to the Urmia Ware typical of MBIII/Hasanlu VIa and known to occur in Operation B9/10a-b, only a "sherd's throw" away from Stein's trenches. Did Stein simply fail to notice Urmia Ware here? This is extremely doubtful. We know Stein was fully aware of the presence of Urmia Ware prior to his 1940 publication, having found two graves with Urmia Ware jars at Dinkha and Hasanlu (see below). Did the area of the mound investigated by Stein, washed away by the Gadar River shortly after his work, touch upon the remains of an occupation dating to Dinkha IVd or that even extends this period? If so, it would appear that, based on the scant evidence at hand, the ceramic assemblage retained some Mesopotamian affinities. Was there evidence for such an occupation at Hasanlu that was overlooked? In short, some graves and occupation deposits might belong to this period. Bear in mind, we are trying to identify an archaeological *rara avis*—a late 17th to early 16th century archaeological culture, the MBA-LBA transition using the terminology of Mesopotamia, or the MBII-MBIII transition if one prefers the chronology of the southern Caucasus. A key point here is that we should not assume that Dinkha IV Phase D marks the end of external influence on the local ceramic assemblage; that for a short time after the terminal MBII Ušnu-Solduz might have maintained such traditions within what was surely a disrupted sociopolitical and economic environment in Mesopotamia. One would predict, using later LBA Mesopotamia as a hypothetical point on the interpretive horizon, that we would be searching for a ceramic assemblage like Stein's: one largely devoid of "classic" PKW elements. Indeed, we already see a trend at Dinkha in the Terminal MBII that explains Stein's uppermost ceramic assemblage. I have demonstrated that Classic PKW was already in steep decline in the Terminal MBII (see below), as was PKW more generally, but undecorated KW continues in typical forms and some simple painting is attested. I believe this explains Stein's upper ceramic assemblage—it is transitional, like the Control Sounding assemblage from Dinkha, and helps to fill the gap between Hasanlu VI and V. Insufficient sampling and selective publication are likely the key culprits in the "cultural break" of the mid 2nd millennium BC in the southern Lake Urmia Basin.

Kramer's Ceramic Analysis

In her pioneering ceramic study, Kramer approached the Dinkha IV assemblage with the goal of understanding the cultural forces behind the distribution of KW—Ušnu-Solduz marks the northeastern extent of its large distribution zone and thus occupies a position of special economic and sociopolitical import for any attempt to explain this phenomenon. Kram-

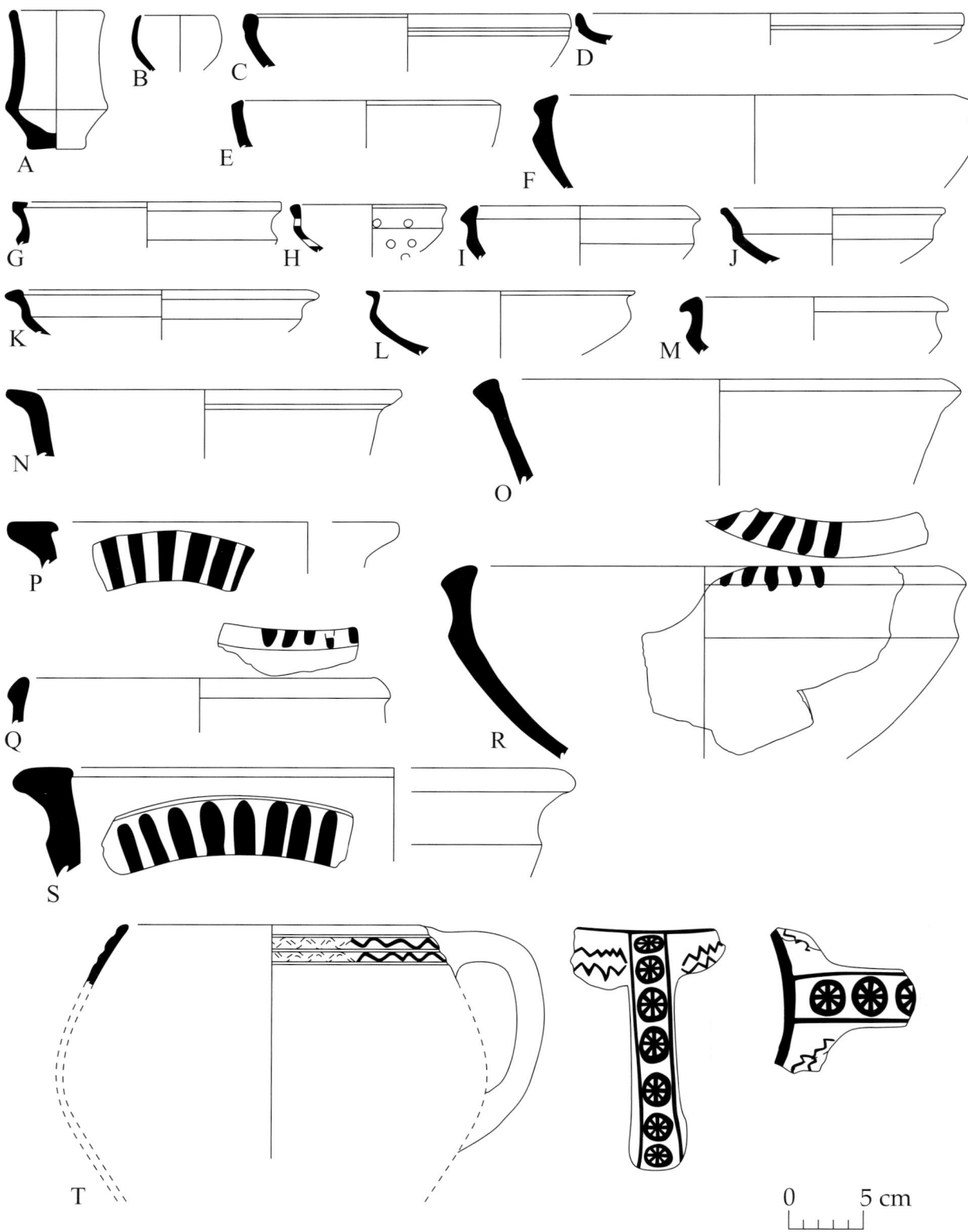

Fig. 4.1

Fig. 4.1 Hasanlu Tepe: U22 ceramics of Period VIb (opposite).

Fig.	Op.	Context	Description	Dia.	Disposition
A	U22	Area 7 Str. 13	Buff Ia (Cream)	6.5	UPM 73-5-159, HAS72-N234
B	U22	11	Buff IIb	6	UPM Sherd
C	U22	11	Buff Ib (Ext. Grey)	22	UPM Sherd
D	U22	11	Buff IIb (Cream), Incised	26	UPM Sherd
E	U22	11	Buff IIb (Grey)	18	UPM Sherd
F	U22	11	Buff Ib (Orange)	30	UPM Sherd
G	U22	11	Buff IIa (Cream)	18	UPM Sherd
H	U22	11	Buff Ia (Cream)	11	UPM Sherd
I	U22	11–12	NR	16	UPM 73-5-799.22
J	U22	11	Buff IIb (Cream)	15	UPM Sherd
K	U22	11	Buff Ib (Orange)	21	UPM Sherd
L	U22	11	NR	18	UPM 73-5-797.19
M	U22	11	NR	18	UPM 73-5-797.43
N	U22	11	Buff IIc (Orange)	27	UPM Sherd
O	U22	12	NR	30	UPM 73-5-798.1
P	U22	11	PKW Buff I	25	UPM Sherd
Q	U22	11	Buff II	16	UPM Sherd
R	U22	11	PKW Buff I	22	UPM 73-5-797.33
S	U22	11	PKW Buff I	32	UPM Sherd
T	U22	11	PKW Buff I (Cream), Black Pt., Incised	13	UPM Sherd

er was largely concerned with making cross-sequence comparisons between Dinkha and other KW sites, and less emphasis was placed on eliciting and communicating intra-assemblage variations at Dinkha. While Kramer presented detailed descriptions of the wares attested at Dinkha and breakdowns of form types by wares, for example, the frequencies of wares within and between phases were not summarized for the sample, making trends in ceramic production difficult to track.[3] To be sure, the Dinkha IV Phase D assemblage reveals changes in the patterns of ceramic production and links to the MBIII/Hasanlu VIa. Kramer made similar observations, as well, but such lines of inquiry were not followed up on and a planned final publication was regrettably never produced.

The Dinkha IV assemblage analyzed and presented by Kramer (Hamlin 1971, 1974) was composed of 965 diagnostics of formal types (Hamlin 1971: figs. 7–9, 11). A small number of other sherds diagnostic of rare forms and ware types were also presented to illustrate the full range of variability, particularly the painted motifs of KW.[4] Types were defined primarily by vessel rim forms and were divided into three general form categories—jars, bowls, and pots (holemouth vessels). Kramer defined nine major ware groups (I–IX) based on the surface color of the fabric, groups which were then divided into subcategories to account for differences in ware based mainly on the presence of painting, temper, and coarseness and, secondarily, slipping and burnishing. Fine Buff Ware (Ware I), also commonly called Khabur Ware, was the primary focus of her study, with special attention paid to Ware Ie, Painted Khabur Ware. Coarse Buff Ware (Ware II) was something quite different from Ware I, as discussed below. Wares III–IV were orange fabrics—Coarse Orange Micaceous Ware and Fine Orange Micaceous Ware, respectively. Wares V and VI, Fine Grey Ware and Coarse Grey Ware, have received some attention subsequently in the literature on the MBA of the southern Lake Urmia Basin in debates regarding the potential connections of these wares to the MBW assemblages of the Late Bronze and early Iron Ages (Hamlin 1971:137; Medvedskaya 1982:38, 98; Muscarella 1994a:131; Young 1985:373, n11). The terms

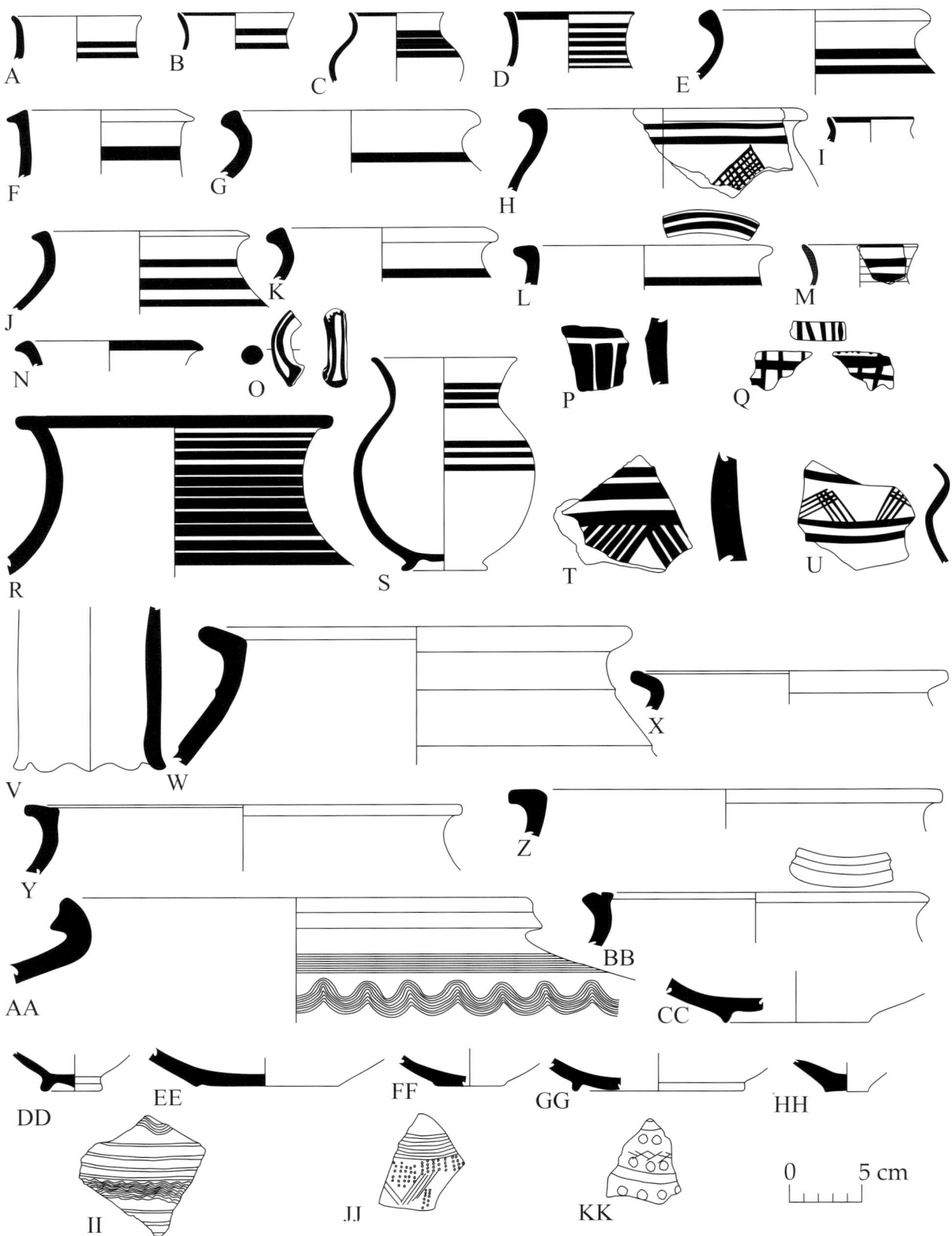

Fig. 4.2

Fig. 4.2 Hasanlu Tepe: U22 ceramics of Period VIb (opposite).

Fig.	Op.	Context	Description	Dia.	Disposition
A	U22	11–12	PKW	9	UPM 73-5-797.56
B	U22	11	PKW Buff II	8	UPM Sherd
C	U22	11	PKW Buff II	7	UPM Sherd
D	U22	11	PKW Buff II	9	UPM Sherd
E	U22	11	PKW Buff I	16	UPM Sherd
F	U22	11	PKW	13	UPM 73-5-797.58
G	U22	11	PKW	18	UPM 73-5-797.57
H	U22	11	PKW	20	UPM 73-5-797.74
I	U22	11–12	PKW	6	UPM 73-5-799.6
J	U22	11	PKW Buff II	15	UPM Sherd
K	U22	11	PKW Buff	16	UPM 73-5-797.56
L	U22	11	PKW Buff I	18	UPM Sherd
M	U22	11	PKW Buff	8	UPM 73-5-797.62
N	U22	11–12	PKW Buff	13	UPM 73-5-797.64
O	U22	11–12	PKW Buff	–	UPM 73-5-797.69
P	U22	11	PKW Buff	–	UPM Sherd
Q	U22	11	Grey, Brown Pt.	–	UPM Sherd
R	U22	11	PKW Buff I	22	UPM Sherd
S	U22	11	PKW Buff II	10	UPM Sherd
T	U22	11–12	PKW Buff	–	UPM 73-5-799.15
U	U22	11–12	PKW Buff II	–	UPM Sherd
V	U22	11	Buff IIa (Cream)	11	UPM Sherd
W	U22	11	Buff IIb	30	UPM Sherd
X	U22	11	Buff Ib (Cream)	22	UPM Sherd
Y	U22	12	NR	32	UPM 73-5-798.4
Z	U22	11	Buff IIb (Cream)	30	UPM Sherd
AA	U22	11	Buff Ib (Orange) Incised Deco.	34	UPM Sherd
BB	U22	11–12	NR	24	73-5-799.2
CC	U22	11–12	NR	10	UPM Sherd
DD	U22	11	Buff IIb (Cream)	5	UPM Sherd
EE	U22	11–12	NR	10	UPM Sherd
FF	U22	11	NR	5	UPM 73-5-797.77
GG	U22	11–12	NR	12	UPM Sherd
HH	U22	11	NR	3	UPM 73-5-797.17
II	U22	11	Buff IIb Incised and Impressed Deco.	–	UPM Sherd
JJ	U22	11	Buff IIb Incised and Impressed Deco.	–	UPM Sherd
KK	U22	11–12	NR Incised and Impressed Deco.	–	UPM 73-5-799.17

have also caused some confusion given Young's earlier use of "Grey Ware" to describe the MBW assemblages of Late Bronze and early Iron Age Iran.

It is debatable whether Kramer's typological categories for the non-KW assemblage are wholly valid given the primacy accorded to ware color, particularly grey, in defining and recording ware types. This often obscures more important patterns in ceramic production, specifically the burnishing of buff and other "non-grey" wares. Moreover, preoccupation with the color grey in defining MBA ware types reveals the influence of already existing "Iron Age" ceramic taxonomy on Kramer, particularly the misconception that "early Iron Age" pottery tended to be grey.[5]

Kramer's remaining ware categories were designated to account for certain rarities in the assemblage. Ware VII, Pattern Burnish Ware, made up a very small part of the assemblage, but is also of interest since such surface treatment is fairly common in the LBA and early Iron Age. Kramer based this ware designation on a specific type of surface decoration, unlike the previous wares mentioned which had been defined by fabric, suggesting her tacit recognition of its importance for dating, establishing continuities with the LBA, and in facilitating cross-sequence comparisons. The same may be said of the remaining ware categories Polychrome Ware (Ware VIII) and Bichrome Ware (Ware IX). Kramer mentions these painted wares only in passing, as they were quite rare in the Dinkha IV assemblage and occurred primarily in the strata that immediately sealed the terminal MBA occupation. Rubinson later published a detailed assessment of the polychrome painted Urmia Ware (1991).

The Ware Types of Dinkha IV Phase D

To discern trends within the Dinkha IV assemblage, I first quantified the occurrences of the 965 type-ware diagnostics (Hamlin 1971: figs. 7–9, 11) according to wares and the three main form groups, since Kramer mainly approached the dataset through form types. Viewing the assemblage by form types masks a great deal of chronological variability; such data were revealed by examining the relative ware frequencies by phases in the Dinkha Control Sounding. In this light it is hardly surprising that painted wares drop out of the ceramic assemblage of Ušnu-Solduz shortly after 1600 BC. Rather than being seen as a cultural break, this development can *in part* be seen as the continuation of an ongoing process of the late 18th–17th century BC (the terminal MBII).

I focused on the Phase A–D sequence of Operation B9a-b, B10a-b, and the B9/10a Control Sounding, since this area provides the most complete and relatively secure MBA sequence from Dinkha. Kramer designated some of this material as "Phase C-D," but this designation was not fully explained (Hamlin 1971). Since comparisons between Phase C and Phase D are especially important to this study, sherds from the combined Phase C-D designation are not included here. Additionally, statistics on Phase A are not always included in the examination of chronological trends owing to the small size of the sample—the bottom of the sounding was quite small and the sample is not statistically significant.

Figure 4.3 (see color insert) presents the ware percentages within the jar category for Dinkha IV (n=112). Subtypes of Ware I, unpainted and painted KW, dominate the subassemblage at 95.7%. Painted Khabur Ware (Ware Ie) makes up 44.0% of this number. While PKW jars make up a high percentage of the overall Period IV subassemblage, there is a noticeable decrease in their frequency over time. In Phase B, there are 23 examples, comprising 63.9% of all jars. In Phase C we see a similar pattern with 21 examples or 53.8%. In Phase D, however, there are only 11 examples or 35.5% of jars. Plain KW makes up the majority of the difference. Grey wares were almost never used for jars.

Within the bowl category, we see a great deal of ware diversity (Fig. 4.4, see color insert). Fine Buff Ware makes up 58.85% of the total subassemblage with 11.88% having been described as PKW. Fine Grey Ware constitutes 17.39% of the subassemblage and Coarse Grey Ware another 8.99%. The remaining bowls are divided between Coarse Buff Ware (8.99%) and Fine Micaceous Orange Ware (5.80%). Again, there is a decrease in PKW toward the end of the period. A total of 16 examples were found in B9/10a, with 5 in Phase B (18.52%), 9 in Phase C (24.10%), and only 2 (3.64%) in Phase D. Fine Grey Ware holds steady throughout Phases B–D at 25.93%, 20.48%, and 21.8% of this vessel class.

The final category, "pots," more often referred to as holemouth vessels, exhibits the highest degree of ware diversity (Fig. 4.5, see color insert). Fine Buff Ware makes up 35.49% of the subassemblage, while Coarse Buff Ware also weighs in at 35.49%. The Fine Buff Ware variant was almost never painted (n=1, 0.26%). The remainder of the subassemblage consists of Coarse Orange Micaceous Ware (20.98%), Fine Orange Micaceous Ware (4.92%), Coarse Grey Ware (2.59%), and Fine Grey Ware (0.52%). I discerned no trends in ware frequencies over time, as might be expected from such utilitarian vessels.

The breakdown of wares by phase reveals patterns masked as a result of Kramer having considered the Phase A–D assemblage as a whole (Fig. 4.6, see color insert).

We see a steady decline in the production of PKW, from 24.1% of the Phase B assemblage to only 8.0% in Phase D. One would predict virtually no PKW in the subsequent MBIII, and by extension a move away from painted wares more generally, and such is in fact the case. At the same time, the unpainted Fine Buff Ware (Ware Ia) of the KW assemblage holds steady from Phase B (19.0%) to Phase D (16.7%), and there is an increase in medium KW (Ware Ib) from 9.5% to 17.3%. This pattern matches that seen in the ceramic wares of Phase D Tomb B10 B27 (see below). There is a similarly steep decline in the production of both the Coarse and Fine Orange Micaceous Wares from Phase B to Phase D.

The decline in PKW is paralleled by a proportionate increase in wares produced by an alternative method of ceramic production. Coarse Buff Ware (Ware IIa), not to be confused with the Buff Ware designation used for KW, increases from 12.1% in Phase B to 25.3% in Phase D. Kramer describes this ware as having,

> [s]mall, medium, and occasional large grit inclusions…The inclusions are generally poorly sorted, which could reflect different clay sources and/or different treatment of the raw clay than that used for Ware I. *The largest white grit inclusions break the surface in some sherds…pitting and lime pops are also common, as is surface crackling and crazing. The center of the core is not fully oxidized, having a grey or black central stripe. The core itself often shows signs of lamination paralleling the surface, suggesting manufacture by hand…exteriors are sometimes matt and sometimes lightly and irregularly burnished. Slips appear to have been applied in some instances; and in a few cases slip and burnish are distinguishable…*Surface color is light brownish-grey (Munsell 1954: 10YR 6-7/2-4; 2.5 Y 7/2), *often mottled from pale buff to dark brown, with local patches of red, brown, and/or grey… Fracture is often jagged and uneven…the fabric is often friable…surfaces often look lumpy, suggesting manufacture without the use of the wheel.* (Hamlin 1971:62–63, emphasis my own)

Other mentions of the ware by Kramer (Hamlin 1971) demonstrate that slipping and/or burnishing are common to Phase D. This ware is similar to much of the Early MBW of the MBIII and early LBA. As with Early MBW, Coarse Buff Ware has both a red-slipped variant (Ware IIb), which makes up 5.6% of the Phase D sample, and a matte cream-slipped variant (Ware IIc), which often has a smoothed surface. Kramer's Coarse Grey Ware is incredibly similar to this ware, *and was separated from it presumably based on its darker color alone.*[6] This ware:

> is characterized by small and medium white grit inclusions, occasionally breaking through the surfaces. Surfaces are often crackled, color is commonly mottled from medium grey to black, sometimes having spots of tan or brown (Munsell 1954: 2.5YR 5/0–2.5/0)…Fracture is usually uneven; fabric appears to be friable but is actually fairly dense. The surfaces of this ware are sometimes crazed as though they had been slipped and then either burnished or dried too quickly. The cores are always dark grey or black. (Hamlin 1971:65, emphasis my own)

This ware has a highly burnished variety (Ware VIa) and a matte variety (Ware VIb), and Kramer notes "a few sherds of this group are grooved" (Hamlin 1971). The ware constitutes 5.7% of the Phase D assemblage.

Considering Ware II and Ware VI as a whole, we see material remarkably similar to the Early MBW of the MBIII and early LBA (see below). Ware II/VI represents a starkly different method of ceramic production compared to that employed in the production of KW. Ware II/VI is grit tempered, often with white inclusions, and is friable, or seemingly so, and breaks unevenly. Vessels were handmade. Surfaces were often smoothed or burnished, and the technique often resulted in surface crackling, crazing, and pitting. The ware is irregularly fired under seemingly poorly controlled conditions resulting in mottled surfaces and dark inner cores, indicating the ware was not fully oxidized during firing. Vessels range in color from buff to tan, grey to black, and pinkish buff to red.

This ware group of the Terminal MBII should be our focus with regard to further investigations of the origins of the MBW horizon. Moreover, the point of comparison should be with Hasanlu VIa and early V rather than "Hasanlu V" as originally defined by Dyson (1965) and Young (1965). Previous arguments denying connections between the ceramics of the MBA and LBA were too narrowly focused on comparisons of Kramer's Ware V—Fine Grey Ware—to the grey MBW of the chronologically mixed "Hasanlu V," which was on the whole representative of the late 2nd millennium BC. Kramer was clearly considering whether the "Grey Ware" of Dinkha IV Phase D could be connected to the Early MBW of Hasanlu when she wrote: "it seems safe to conclude that a variety of grey wares were indigenous to Dinkha in what is more familiarly known as the Hasanlu VI period. This finding may have important cultural historical (as well as technological) implications for the interpretation of the early Iron Age (Hasanlu V) in western Iran" (Hamlin 1971:137). While there is support for this in regards to Ware VI, as has been previously pointed out by both Young (1971) and Muscarella (1974), *Ware V* is not connected to Early MBW. Its method of manufacture is akin to that of KW—it is made from a well-levigated clay with small grit temper or no visible temper. The fabric is hard and dense and evenly fired. Ware color is remarkably consistent with only occasional mottling. Vessels are wheelmade. Fine Grey Ware makes up 6% of the Dinkha IV assemblage (Hamlin 1971:136) and occurs in 16 of the 104 types defined by Kramer (see below). Production of Ware VIa peaks in Phase C, at which point it constituted 10% of the assemblage, and declines to 6.8% in Phase D. Its popularity parallels that of PKW. As is the case with PKW, it does not occur in significant amounts in the MBIII.

The Formal Types of Dinkha IV Phase D

Turning to vessel forms, we must consider two questions: Can we detect changes in the attested Phase D types defined by Kramer? and, What are the links, if any, between late MBA types and the MBIII and early LBA? Figures 4.7–4.12 show the formal types defined by Kramer that are attested in Phase D. She provided illustrations only to explicate her types (Hamlin 1971, 1974), so in some cases the sherds shown herein are from Dinkha IV Phases A–C.

Bowls of Dinkha IV Phase D
We see a great deal of variability in the open forms of Dinkha IV Phase D and a decline in the number and variation in PKW types.[7] This discussion is organized on the basis of Kramer's Type Numbers. Bowl 1 (Fig. 4.7a:A, n=3 or 5.88% of Dinkha IVd bowls) is a typical PKW type in Dinkha IV, usually with its rim painted in stripes or triangles, and is the only bowl type found in Ware Ie in Phase D. The form and style of decoration are ubiquitous to the broader KW distribution area, and the type was found in all phases of Dinkha IV and at Hasanlu VI. A similar form is attested in Early MBW in the MBIII at Dinkha (Fig. 4.16:D). An especially common type in Phases C–D is Bowl 8 (Fig. 4.7a:B, n=6 or 11.76% of Dinkha IVd bowls), which often occurs in either Fine Grey Ware or burnished Buff Ware. A bowl of this type is also attested in the MBIII deposit at Dinkha in Early MBW (Fig. 4.16:C), and carinated bowls are common in the early LBA, as are vertically pierced tabular lugs. A double version of the bowl (Type 8b) with a vertically pierced tabular lug was found in Dinkha IV Phase D Tomb B10a B27 (Fig. 4.12:F).

Incurving Bowl 35 (Fig. 4.7a:C, n=6 or 11.76% of Dinkha IVd bowls) is typical of Dinkha Phases C–D and the ware in which it occurs alternates between Ware Va in Phase C and Ware Id (Micaceous Khabur Ware) in Phase D. Similar incurving bowls, albeit with thickened rims, are attested in the early LBA at Hasanlu (see Bowl Type 4, below), and Stein found one in a Hasanlu VIa grave at Hasanlu alongside an Urmia Ware jar (Seriation: Section XV).

Kramer's Bowl 36 (Fig. 4.7a:D, n=5 or 9.8% of Dinkha IVd bowls) of Phases C–D is a generic form present throughout the later Bronze Age at Hasanlu; a similar bowl is attested in polychrome painted Urmia Ware in MBIII Dinkha (Fig. 4.17a:B). The form is attested at Haftavan—Edwards Type 6a—in Early and Late Period VIB (e.g., Edwards 1983: figs. 92:16, 94:13, 95:8–9) and is similar to bowls in both Sagzabad Ware (Piller 2003–2004: pl. 12:1) and Central Grey Ware at Sialk A (Ghirshman 1939: pl. XXXVII:443).

Kramer's Bowl Type 38a–b (Figs. 4.7a:E, 4.8:A, n=3 or 5.88% of Dinkha IVd bowls) appears to be a catch-all category. Kramer grouped the two rims of her Ware VIII (Urmia Ware) in this type (Hamlin 1971:95) and other examples of Urmia Ware confirm the presence of Bowl 38a in the MBIII assemblages of both Dinkha (Figs. 4.17a:A, C, H, 4.17b:A–E) and Geoy Tepe C (Burton-Brown 1951: fig. 31 no. 60). The form is well known at Haftavan in Early and Late

Period VIB, where it occurs in Urmia Ware—thus the Urmia Ware examples in Dinkha IV hardly need be considered out of place here—and in Early MBW (Edwards Type 6b, e.g., Edwards 1983: figs. 98:13, 14; 99:3). Kramer's Bowl 38a is also attested in Tomb B10a B27 (Fig. 4.12:H) of the Terminal MBII. This bowl occurs in Sialk A in Central Grey Ware (Ghirshman 1939: pl. XXXVII:443) and a slightly taller version is known in Sagzabad Ware (Piller 2003–2004: pl. 12:1). This is truly a transitional form of the Terminal MBII–MBIII.

Bowl Type 32 represents another form common to Phases C–D that is also attested in the Phase D tomb (Figs. 4.7a:F, 4.12:A, n=4 or 7.84% of Dinkha IVd bowls). Kramer's Bowl 42 (n=3 or 5.88% of Dinkha IVd bowls), an incurving type with a simple rim similar to Type 40 (Fig. 4.8:D), was represented by sherds in occupation deposits and two smaller whole examples from Tomb B10a B27 (Figs. 4.7a:G, 4.12:E, G). All were made either in smoothed Ware IIa or were burnished (Hamlin 1971:96). While such bowls are not attested in Hasanlu VIa at Dinkha, a similar bowl occurs in early Hasanlu V in Early MBW (see Bowl Type 5, below, Fig. 4.21:C, O, Q). A bowl similar to Kramer's Type 40 is known from Hassanabad Marafi (Piller 2003–2004: pl. 5:5) and another from Xurabad (Piller 2003–2004: pl. 2:1–3) in north-central Iran, both in Central Grey Ware. Kramer's Type 42 bowls from Tomb B10a B27 find their strongest parallels with a bowl of Sialk A (Ghirshman 1939: pl. XLVII:674d).

Kramer's Bowl Types 24, 33, and 34 represent a class of large shallow bowls (Fig. 4.7a:H–J). Kramer's Bowl Type 33, attested by a single occurrence in Phase D (Terminal MBII) in Fine Grey Ware, as well as Type 34 (also a late MBII type in Ware Ib), have strong parallels with a bowl in Piller's Central Grey Ware from Xurabad (Piller 2003–2004:Pl. 3:3). Two of Piller's 'Knickwandschüsseln' forms (2003–2004: pl. 3:2–3) bear strong similarities to bowls of the early "worm bowl" class of the MBIII and LBA, particularly Type 1b (see below), in the Lake Urmia region. This class of bowls represents one of several linkages between the Terminal MBII and MBIII of the Lake Urmia region and the period of overlap between painted Sagzabad Ware and Central Grey Ware in north-central Iran and at Sialk A—I would date this period of overlap to the 17th–16th centuries (cf. Piller 2003–2004: table I). Bowl 34 (Fig. 4.7a:J, n=2 or 3.92% of Dinkha IVd bowls) may be tentatively linked to MBIII–LBA Bowl Type 1 (see below) attested at Dinkha, Hasanlu, and Geoy Tepe (Burton-Brown 1951: fig. 30 no. 949). Kramer lists the occurrences of Bowl 24 (Fig. 4.7a:I, n=2 or 3.92% of Dinkha IVd bowls) as being attributable to Phase C, but they are recorded as Phase D in her figure 9 (Hamlin 1971:90). Bowl Type 33 (n=1 or 1.96% of Dinkha IVd bowls) is a rare example of a decorated bowl in Ware Vb (Kramer's Burnished Grey Ware) with an impressed wavy line (Fig. 4.7a:H); it is unique to Phase D and resembles Early MBW.

A number of bowl types are attested in the Phase D assemblage in low numbers, including Bowls 13, 18, 21, 28, 29, 31, 34, 39, 40, 44, 47, and 51–53 (Figs. 4.7b:A–M, 4.8:B–E). Many are typical of the earlier MBA and likely represent late holdouts of these types or possibly extrusive material from the lower levels. Small-to-medium carinated bowls with thickened rims and rills certainly represent the latest occurrence of this type, particularly the use of multiple rills at the rim (Fig. 4.7b:C–H). The same may be said for overhanging ledge rims and rilling on barrel-forms and incurving bowls (Fig. 4.8:C–E).[8] Kramer classified Figure 4.8:C as a "pot" (Type 17), but it is most likely a bowl form. She also attributes it to Phase C, but it has been shown to come from Phase D (Hamlin 1971:108) and it is similar to Bowl Type 14b, which occurs in Phases C and C–D (Fig. 4.7:E). Both examples are in Ware Va (Kramer's Fine Grey Ware). Pot Type 6 is also likely a bowl and was used as a cooking vessel (Fig. 4.8:B). The sharp decline in these formal types and stylistic attributes parallels the decline in PKW, which is in keeping with the late MBII as it is known more generally in the Near East.

Other types rarely attested in the Control Sounding may be linked to the emergence of the MBIII assemblage or intrusive material. Bowl 39 (Fig. 4.7b:A, n=1) was typically shaved, creating a lustrous finish, or burnished. The type was fairly common at Dinkha, but its lone occurrence in the Control Sounding did not reflect that fact and it is likely a late Dinkha IV type. Such bowls seem to be related to Kramer's Type 36 (Fig. 4.7a:D) which, as previously mentioned, occurs in succeeding periods. Bowl Type 29 (Fig. 4.7b:I) is quite similar to Kramer's Pot Type 9 (Fig. 4.7b:J), which she notes (Hamlin 1971:106), and both types are similar to her Type 8 (Fig. 4.7a:E), which again

156

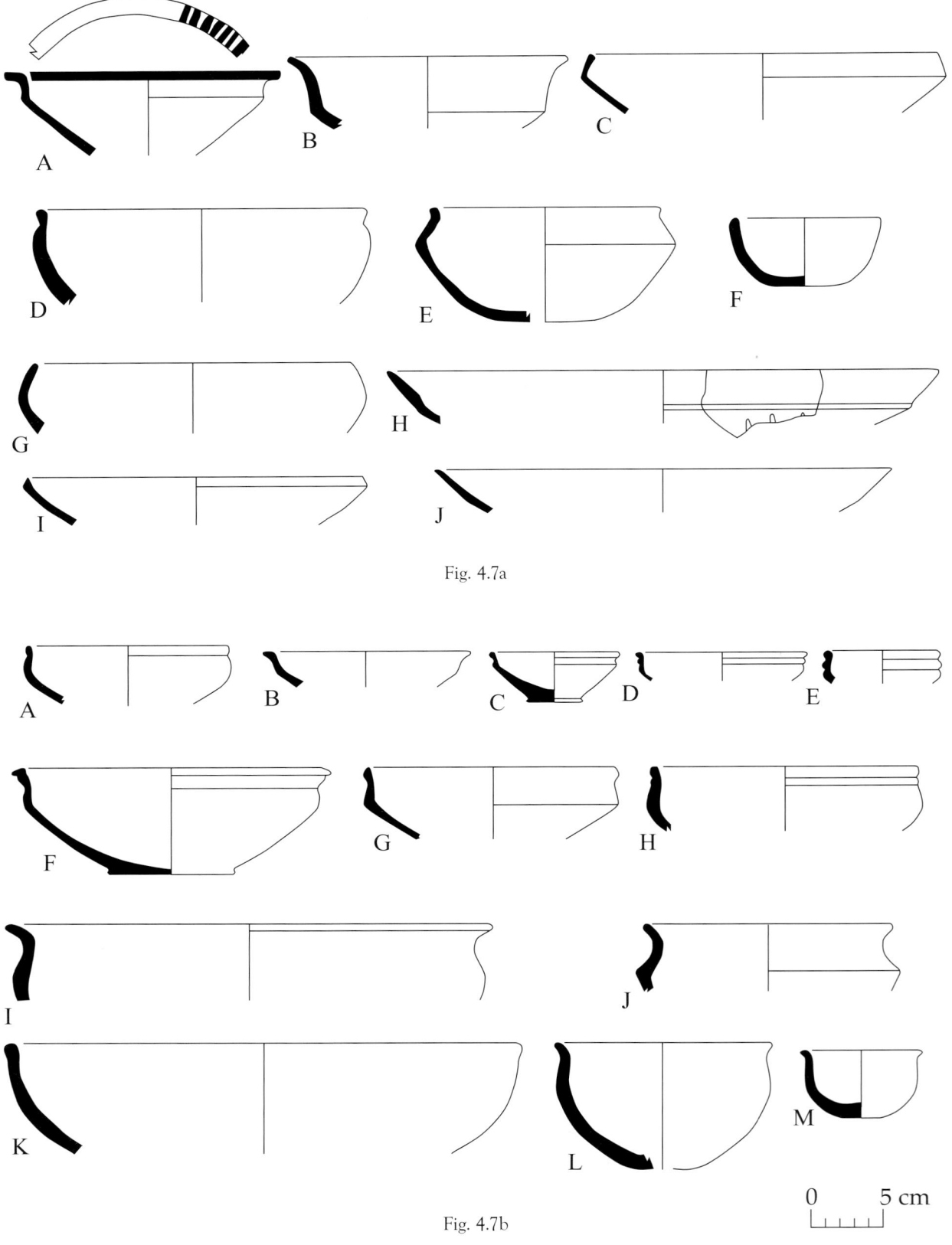

Fig. 4.7a

Fig. 4.7b

Fig. 4.7a Typical Terminal MBII (Dinkha Period IV Phase D) bowls (opposite, top).

Fig.	Op.	Context	Type	Description	Dia.	Disposition
A	B9a	8	Kramer Bowl 1a	Ware Ie	19	UPM Sherd
B	B9a	10	Kramer Bowl 8a	Ware VIa	19	UPM Sherd
C	B9/10a	1a	Kramer Bowl 35	Ware Va	24	UPM Sherd
D	B10a	9	Kramer Bowl 36	Ware IIa	23	UPM Sherd
E	B9a	10	Kramer Bowl 38a	Ware IIa	16	UPM 66-23-232
F	B10a	8	Kramer Bowl 32	Ware Ib	10	NR
G	B9a	8	Kramer Bowl 42	Ware IIa	22	UPM Sherd
H	B9/10a	1	Kramer Bowl 33	Ware Vb	38	UPM Sherd
I	B9/10a	1	Kramer Bowl 24	Ware Va	24	UPM Sherd
J	B9a	8	Kramer Bowl 34	Ware Ib	32	UPM Sherd

Fig. 4.7b Rare Terminal MBII (Dinkha Period IV Phase D) bowls (opposite, bottom).

Fig.	Op.	Context	Type	Description	Dia.	Disposition
A	B9/10a	2b	Kramer Bowl 39b	Ware Ic	14	UPM Sherd
B	B10a	8	Kramer Bowl 21	Ware Ia	14	UPM Sherd
C	B9/10a	1a	Kramer Bowl 18	Ware Va	9	UPM Sherd
D	B9a	8	Kramer Bowl 53	Ware Id	12	UPM Sherd
E	B9a	8	Kramer Bowl 44	Ware Ia	8	UPM Sherd
F	B9/10a	1	Kramer Bowl 51	Ware Va	22	UPM Sherd
G	B10a	9	Kramer Bowl 47	Ware IIc	18	UPM Sherd
H	B9/10a	8	Kramer Bowl 8	Ware Va	19	UPM Sherd
I	B10a	8	Kramer Bowl 29	Ware IIc	34	UPM Sherd
J	B10a	9	Kramer "Pot" 9	Ware VIa	17	UPM Sherd
K	B9a	8	Kramer Bowl 31	Ware IIb	36	UPM Sherd
L	B9/10a	2a	Kramer Bowl 28	Ware IV	15	UPM Sherd
M	B9/10a	1a	Kramer Bowl 13	Ware Ib	8	UPM Sherd

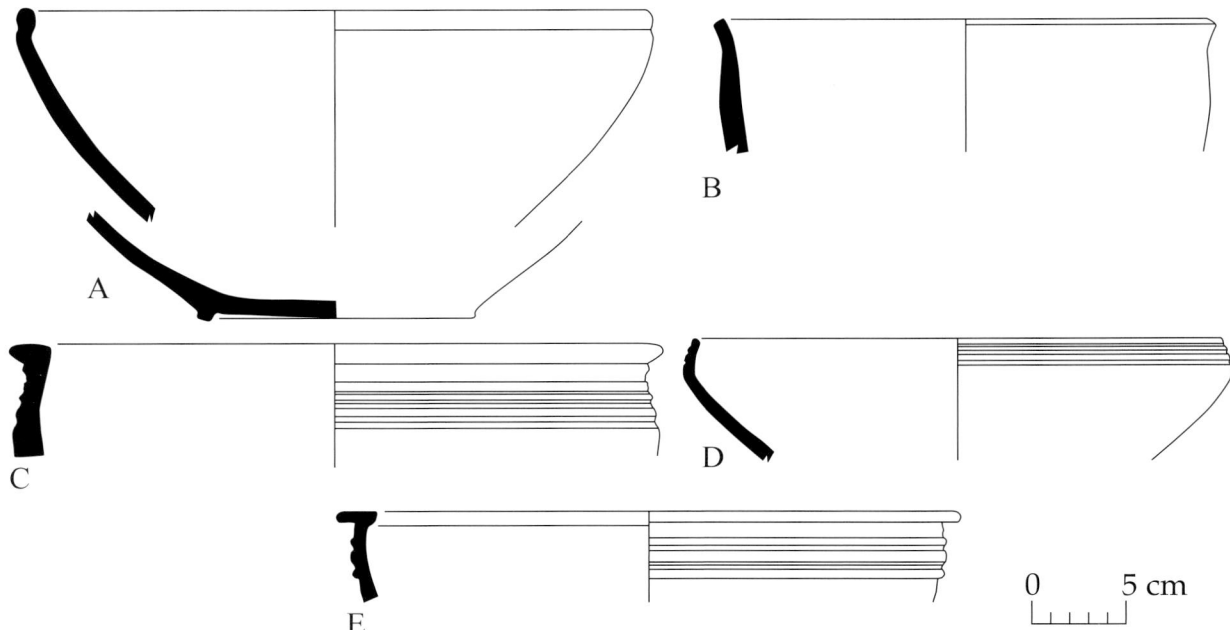

Fig. 4.8 Rare Terminal MBII (Dinkha Period IV Phase D) bowls.

Fig.	Op.	Context	Type	Description	Dia.	Disposition
A			Kramer Bowl			UPM Sherd
B	B9/10a	3	Kramer Pot 6	Ware IV	26	UPM Sherd
C	B9a	8	Kramer Pot 17	Ware Ib	34	UPM Sherd
D	B10a	9	Kramer Bowl 40	Ware Ia	28	UPM Sherd
E	B9a	8–9	Kramer Bowl 14b	Ware Ia	33	UPM Sherd

can be linked to succeeding periods. The majority of examples of this class of vessel are handmade in Ware VIa. Bowl Type 31 (Fig. 4.7b:K) is unique to Phase D. This vessel was handmade in Ware IIb and covered in heavy red slip (Hamlin 1971:92). It resembles Bowl Type 8 of the early LBA (see below). Bowl Type 28 occurs in Ware IV and Ware VI, was handmade, and all examples were burnished (Fig. 4.7b:L). This type is similar to Type 13, a likely late form that was also handmade (Fig. 4.7b:M).

Pots of Dinkha IV Phase D

We see the appearance of new holemouth forms in Phase D (n=80) and an increase in the use of burnishing. Smaller pots of Kramer's Type 1, many of which are likely cups, are highly diagnostic of the terminal MBII (Fig. 4.9:A–B, n=28 or 35% of Dinkha IVd pots). Nearly all attestations belong to Phase D, excepting two from C–D and one from a Period C context. At Hasanlu, however, one such pot was found in grave SK45 of the MBII along with 10 *istikhan* cups (Fig. 5.2:C). These small beakers or tumblers are rare at Dinkha and are absent from Tomb B10a B27. The Hasanlu example possibly represents an early occurrence of the type. Kramer states that Tomb B10a B27 contained 14 of these pots, but it is not clear to which vessels she is referring (Hamlin 1971:99, 103). A number of vessels of this basic form are present in the tomb assemblage (Fig. 4.12:I–S, Y, AA, BB). Many such pots, particularly the smaller examples and those with loop handles at the rim, should instead be labeled as "cups" (Figs. 4.9:B, 4.12:Y, AA, BB). Decoration is present in the form of incision or appliqué. In occupation deposits, one occurrence in Ware Ia from Phase

C–D was decorated with an appliquéd "worm" and others have appliquéd crescents—stylistic motifs typical of MBIII, LBA, and Iron I bowls and holemouth vessels (Hamlin 1971). Other examples have a vertical lug, and one is incised (Fig. 4.9:A). Kramer compared this incised design to examples from Nuzi and Tell Shamlu (Hamlin 1971; Starr 1937: pl. 115:E; al-Janabi 1961). The smaller beakers and cups with handles from Dinkha (esp. Fig. 4.12:O, AA) are closely related to the MBIII button-base tankards of Dinkha and Hasanlu (Seriation, see below). Similar small beakers and cups with handles are known from Sialk A in Sagzabad Ware and Early MBW (Ghirshman 1939: pls. XXXVII:444, XLVII:677c), and they occur in primary association with button-base tankards (Ghirshman 1939: pls. I:5, XXXVII:436). A low tankard from Dinkha Tomb B10a B27 provides the best link to the later button-base tankards of the MBIII (Fig. 4.12:Z) and has a form remarkably similar to a button-base tankard in Early MBW from Sialk A (Ghirshman 1939: pl. XXXVIII:450).

Kramer's Pot 11 (I would classify this as a bowl) occurs in Ware IIb and both examples were burnished (Fig. 4.9:C, n=2 or 2.5% of Dinkha IVd pots). This "pot" is similar to Kramer's Bowl Type 38a (see above) and is attested at Geoy C in burnished ware and bichrome-painted ware (Burton-Brown 1951: fig. 31 nos. 60, 708, fig. 32 no. 698). Kramer writes of Pot 4 (Fig. 4.9:F, n=2 or 2.5% of Dinkha IVd pots) that, "there is one very highly burnished example, with small rim diameter, which has a vertical strap handle" (Hamlin 1971:104). This interesting vessel was not illustrated. She compares this *burnished, cream-slipped vessel* to the "tankards" found at Godin Tepe, which were made in a burnished black ware similar in appearance to Dinkha Ware VIa (Young 1969: fig. 23:14, 15). A similar vessel of identical size with a "polished cream slip" and polychrome painting occurs in Geoy C (Burton-Brown 1951:137, fig. 31 no. 692). Kramer was certainly aware of connections between the "pots" of Phase D and the holemouth jars and cups/tankards of "Hasanlu V." She suggests that Pot 31 (Fig. 4.10:B) "may represent an early version of a slightly different form found at Dinkha in Hasanlu V context. The phase d sherd is made of ware VIa and is highly burnished" (Hamlin 1971:113).

Painted Khabur Ware is all but absent in the pot category. Kramer's Pot 15 (I would classify this as a bowl) is a fairly common type that occurs at other KW sites and which has a PKW variant (Fig. 4.9:E; Hamlin 1971: pl. VII:15b, n=3 or 3.75% of Dinkha IVd pots). Burnishing and slips appear to be fairly typical surface treatments.

We see that closer inspection of Kramer's ware descriptions reveals a fairly high incidence of slipped-and-burnished surface treatments in the pot category. Without a complete phase-by-phase re-analysis of the Dinkha IV assemblage, we cannot gauge to what degree burnishing was employed, but it appears that the forms which characterize Phases C–D were frequently burnished and that the ware categories, formulated to facilitate analysis of the KW assemblage, obscure this important change. On the other hand, among Kramer's pots we see a large number of storage vessels exhibiting little change since the beginning of the MBA (Hasanlu VIC), such as Pot Types 10, 18, 20, 22a–b, 24, 27, 29, 31, 33, and 36 (Fig. 4.10). Modeled and ledge rims, comb incising, and horizontal ribs are typical of the holemouth jars of the Terminal MBII at Dinkha. These attributes are present in the smaller holemouth jars of MBIII Dinkha, but drop out of the assemblage prior to the early LBA (Fig. 4.16:E–G). Large storage jars are especially well attested in Dinkha IV Phase D since the phase represents the destruction level of a residential area. It is perhaps unremarkable that these large utilitarian vessels of long use-life were not as susceptible to stylistic change as compared to other vessel classes such as serving bowls and drinking vessels.

Jars of Dinkha IV Phase D
There is a limited range of jar types in Phase D or, put another way, a high degree of standardization. Kramer recorded 31 jars from Phase D (Hamlin 1971: fig. 7). In the MBA, jars are the form most likely to have been painted or incised in KW assemblages. Jar Type 1 (Fig. 4.11:A, n=17 or 54.84% of Dinkha IVd jars) occurs primarily in Buff Ware, with five in PKW. Three Fine Grey Ware examples are reported (Hamlin 1971:71), but elsewhere Kramer notes only two (Hamlin 1971: fig. 7). Three of these jars were found in Tomb B10a B27 (Fig. 4.13:A–C; Rubinson 1991). These S-profile beakers have parallels with S-profile tankards and beakers in Sialk A (Ghirshman 1939: pls. XL:473b; XLI:494b, 495; XLVII:671a).

Jar Type 2 (Fig. 4.11:B, n=2) was made exclusively in PKW and constitutes 6.45% of jars—almost

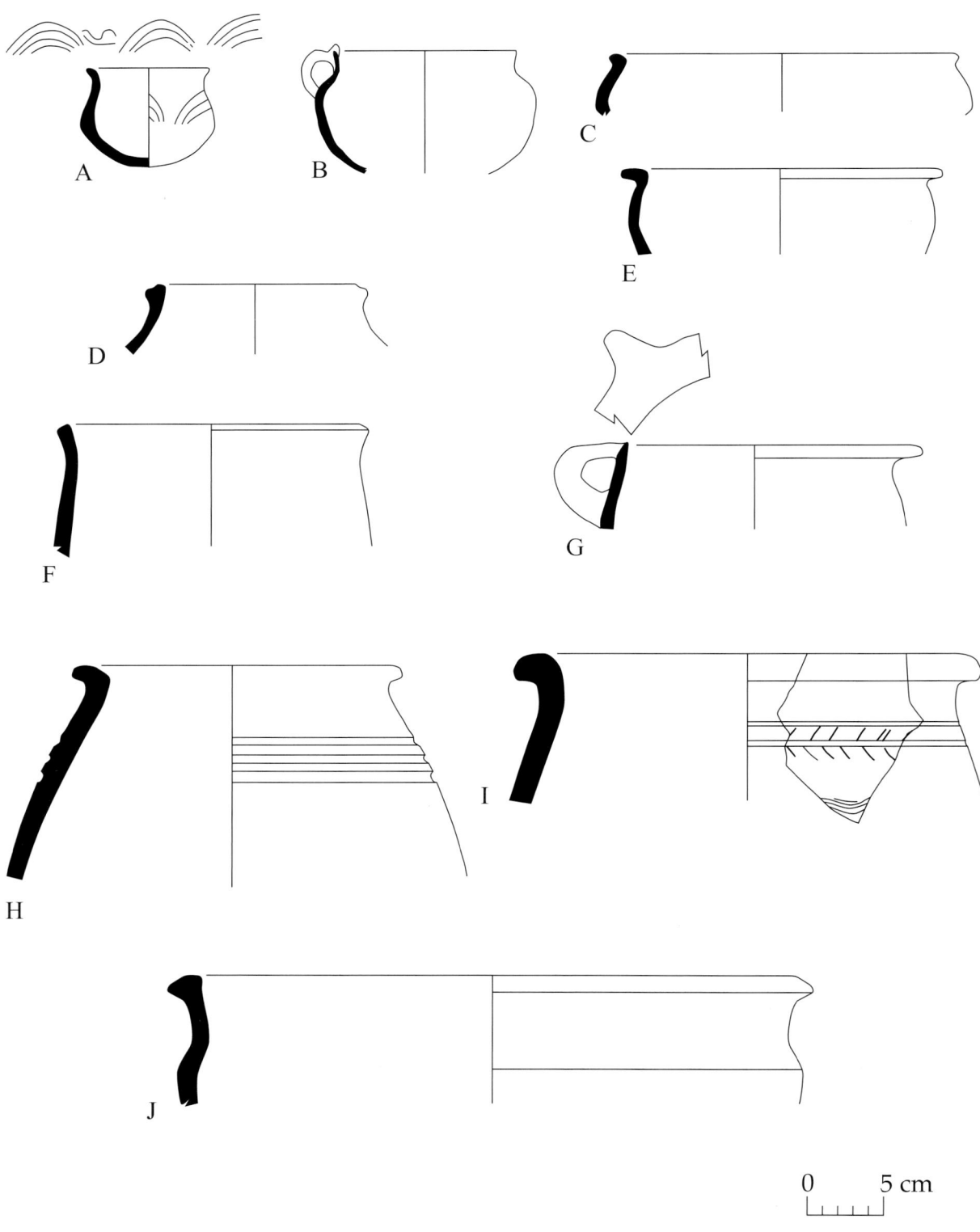

Fig. 4.9

Fig. 4.9 Terminal MBII (Dinkha Period IV Phase D) pots (opposite).

Fig.	Op.	Context	Type	Description	Dia.	Disposition
A	B10a	8	Kramer Pot 1	Ware IIb	8	UPM Sherd
B	B9a	8	Kramer Pot 1	Ware Ib	12	UPM 66-23-512
C	B9/10a	2	Kramer Pot 11	Ware IIc	22	UPM Sherd
D	B9a	8	Kramer Pot 25	Ware Ib	14	UPM Sherd
E	B10a	8	Kramer Pot 15c	Ware Ia	22	UPM Sherd
F	B9/10a	2a	Kramer Pot 4	Ware Ib	20	UPM Sherd
G	B10a	8	Kramer Pot 21	Ware Ia	20	UPM Sherd
H	B9a	8	Kramer Pot 22a	Ware Ib	21	UPM Sherd
I	B9a	8	Kramer Pot 22b	Ware Ib	30	UPM Sherd
J	B9/10a	2c	Kramer Pot 16	Ware Ib	42	UPM Sherd

all occurrences are limited to annular band painting (Hamlin 1971:71–72). One jar of this type was associated with a Hasanlu Tomb of Period VIb (SK61/66, Figs. 5.4:B, 5.5). Jar Type 3 (Fig. 4.11:C, n=4) mainly occurs in Phases C–D. One of these jars in Fine Grey Ware with an incised and impressed design was found in the Phase D Tomb (Fig. 4.12:V; Hamlin 1971: pl. I:3b). It appears to imitate painted geometric motifs found on KW (cf. Fig. 4.11:H). There are examples of similar incised and impressed designs in Early MBW at Dinkha in the MBIII (see below). In Phase D, this type usually occurs in Fine Buff Ware with a matte surface (Ware 1a, n=3). Kramer informs us that, "Several examples of this jar type are decorated with narrow ridges and grooves on the shoulder" (Hamlin 1971:72, pl. I:3a) (Fig. 4.10:C). A jar of this type was found at Hasanlu in Tomb SK61/66 (Figs. 5.4:A, 5.5).

Jar Type 4 occurs only in Phase D (n=3 or 9.67% of Phase IVd jars). One example made in Ware VIa has a tripod base with two vertically pierced lugs and was found in Tomb B10a BB27 (Fig. 4.13:F). The other two examples have a single vertically pierced lug; both are Ware Ia, as well. Such lugs are typical of Hasanlu V (see below). As previously mentioned, Stein found a jar of this type with a tripod base and vertically pierced lugs in a grave (1940: pl. XXI:2). Similar jars have been found at Sialk A (Ghirshman 1939: pl. XLI no. 492) and Godin III$_1$ (Henrickson 1987a: fig. 32:21). Piller has previously highlighted the potential overlap in this jar form in north-central Iran in Sagzabad Ware and Central Grey Ware (2003–2004:163–64; see also Dittmann 1990:133–34, pl. 11:7–9). Type 11 (n=5 or 12.9% of Phase D jars) is a large jar typical of Dinkha IV Phases B–C, which is usually found in PKW (n=4; Fig. 4.11:G).

MBA Grey Ware Vessel Forms

Given the attention previous scholars have paid to potential connections between MBA Grey Ware and LBA and early Iron Age grey MBW, it is useful to review the vessel forms from Dinkha that occur *only* in Grey Ware (Kramer's Wares V and VI and associated subtypes). Kramer states that Pot Types 8, 9, 19, 31, and 35 and Bowl Types 4, 17–19, 24, 26, 33, 35, 41, 46, and 52 were made exclusively in Grey Ware (Hamlin 1971:136). In fact, Kramer lists one occurrence of Bowl 17 in Ware Ia and five examples of Bowl 35 in Ware Id (Fig. 4.15:C, K; Hamlin 1971: fig. 9). As we have seen, there are substantial differences in "Grey Ware" in Dinkha IV, as recognized by Kramer; however, her exclusive Grey Ware types include both Wares V and VI. Bowls 4, 17–19, 24, 26, 33, 46, and 52 are Fine Grey Ware/Ware V (Fig. 4.15:A–I). Bowl 41 and Pots 8, 9, 19, 31, and 35 were produced in Coarse Grey Ware/Ware VI (Fig. 4.15:J, L–P). Significantly, only Bowl 35 is attested in both Ware V and Ware VI (Fig. 4.15:K). In chronological terms, most occurrences of these types date to Phases C and D. Of the bowls, 1 is Phase A (14.0% of Phase A bowls), 2 are Phase B (7.4% of Phase B bowls), 10 are Phase C (12.0% of Phase C bowls), and 6 are Phase D (10.9% of Phase D bowls). Seven of the pots belong to Phase C (7.2% of pots) and 2 to Phase D (4.7% of pots).

Of the Ware V vessels, only Bowl 52 is possibly attested in later periods, and it is admittedly a fairly generic form (Fig. 4.15:I). Among the Ware VI vessels, Bowl 41 is also attested in Geoy B Tomb K (Burton-

162

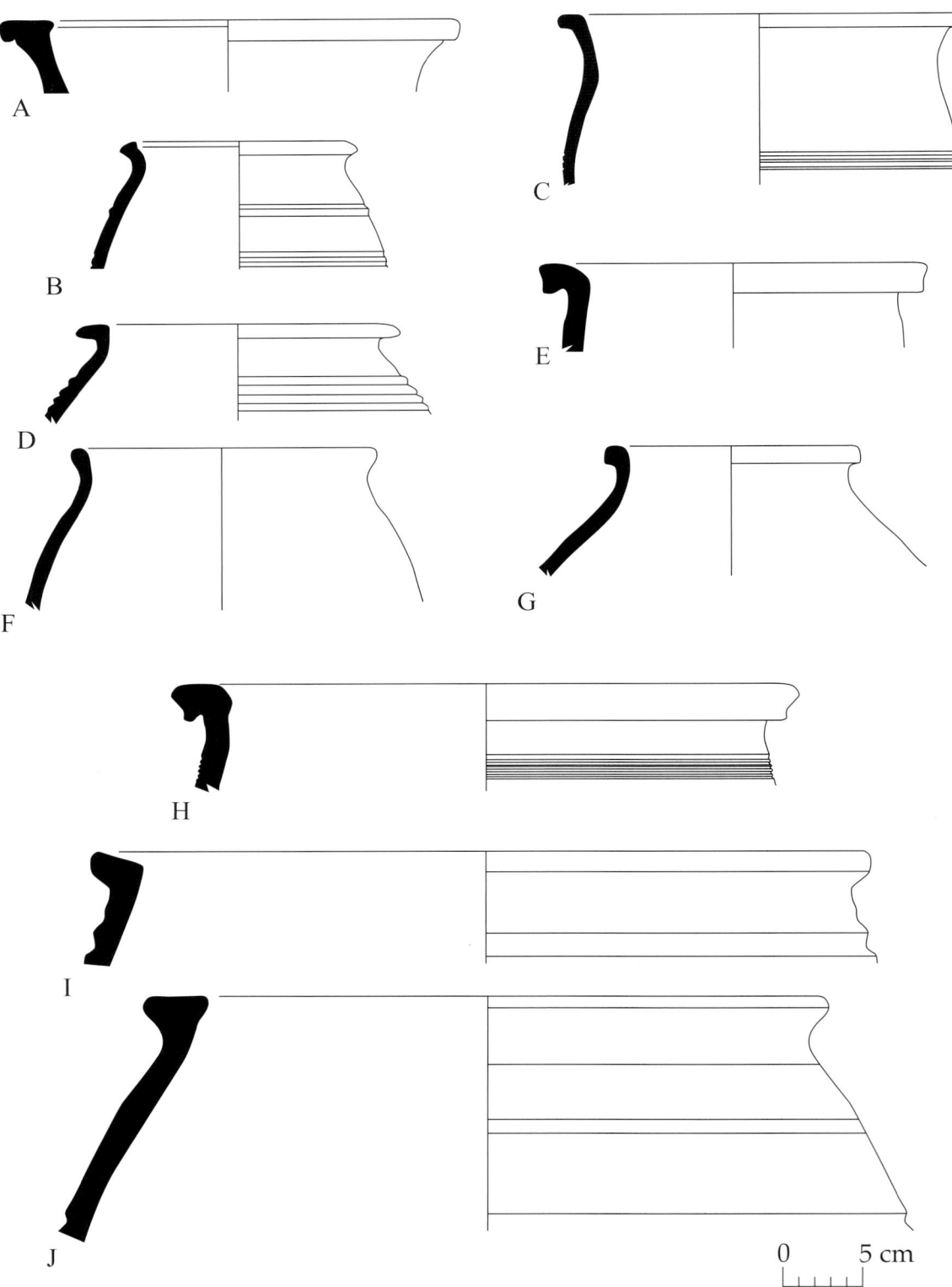

Fig. 4.10

Fig. 4.10 Terminal MBII (Dinkha Period IV Phase D) pots (opposite).

Fig.	Op.	Context	Type	Description	Dia.	Disposition
A	B10a	8	Kramer Pot 33	Ware Ib	29	UPM Sherd
B	B10a	8	Kramer Pot 31	Ware VIa	15	UPM Sherd
C	B9a	11	Kramer Pot 18	Ware IIc	25	UPM Sherd
D	B9a	10	Kramer Pot 20	Ware IV	20	UPM Sherd
E	B9a	10	Kramer Pot 27	Ware Ib	24	UPM Sherd
F	B9a	11	Kramer Pot 2	Ware IV	19	UPM Sherd
G	B10a	9	Kramer Pot 24	Ware Ia	16	UPM Sherd
H	B10a	9	Kramer Pot 36b	Ware III	40	UPM Sherd
I	B10a	8	Kramer Pot 29d	Ware Ib	49	UPM Sherd
J	B10a	8	Kramer Pot 29c	Ware Ib	43	UPM Sherd

Brown 1951: fig. 32 no. 402) and Pot 9 (Fig. 4.15:O) resembles vessels of Geoy Tepe C (Burton-Brown 1951: fig. 31 no. 705).

Ceramics of Dinkha Tomb B10a B27

The ceramic assemblage of Tomb B10a B27 underscores both the importance and biases inherent to the use of mortuary assemblages to build chronological sequences. If this assemblage were the only one from Dinkha IV Phase D, we would doubtless have a markedly different view of the ceramics of the period. Fortunately, in the case of Dinkha Tomb B27 we have the benefit of stratigraphic links with Phase D architectural levels and an occupation deposit with radiocarbon age determinations with which to date and balance our view of the terminal MBA. While there are connections between the Phase D occupation assemblage and that found in the tomb, the differences are also quite striking—particularly in the number of drinking vessels and the absence of PKW. The pottery finds its best parallels with Sialk A.

Most vessels are of plain Buff Ware and have matte surfaces. While KW jars (often actually beakers) are present (Fig. 4.13:A–C, E), there is no painted ware. Burnishing, incising, and appliqué are present. The majority of vessels are "pots," small bowls, and cups. The latter provide a crucial link to the cups and tankards of the MBIII and LBA (Seriation) and demonstrate that important Hasanlu "V" diagnostics— button-base and pedestal-base beakers and tankards— in fact have their origin in the terminal MBII. The cup form most typical of the earlier MBA, the so-called *istikhan*, is not found among the Dinkha IV Phase D Control Sounding assemblage. Only one was found in Dinkha Phase C of the Control Sounding and six more were recovered from other contexts. Two small beakers or jars were found in Tomb B10a B27 (Figs. 4.12:DD, 4.13:D), but these lack the distinctive profiles characteristic of true *istikhans*. At Hasanlu, *istikhans* are one of the most common cup types in graves of Period VIb (Figs. 5.2, 5.4–5.6; see below, SK45–47 n=10, SK61/66 n=3, SK112 n=1) and were also found in Strata 11–12 (Period VIb) of the U22 Deep Sounding (Fig. 4.1:A, 4.2:HH). In Hasanlu graves, they are only associated with annular band–painted KW as opposed to "classic" PKW. The Hasanlu and Dinkha sequences show that *istikhans* were likely developing into (or being replaced by) S-profile cups, and this type bridges the gap between the earlier MBII and the Terminal MBII and MBIII. The small beaker from Dinkha Tomb B10a B27 is attested at Sialk A (Ghirshman 1939: pl. XLI:488), with the addition of a handle. The various comparanda for a small jar with vertically pierced lugs and a probable tripod base (Fig. 4.13: F) have already been discussed (see above), but Sialk A provides the strongest comparison (Ghirshman 1939: pl. XLI no. 492). Tomb B27 also contains some vessels that are unique within the Hasanlu sequence, including a theriomorphic vessel (Fig. 4.13:H) and two small pots with pointed bases and decorated with incising and appliquéd bosses (Fig. 4.12:W, X).

The Terminal MB II at Hasanlu

No stratified occupation deposits of Terminal Period VIb were excavated at Hasanlu due to limited sampling, but at least one grave of the period was found

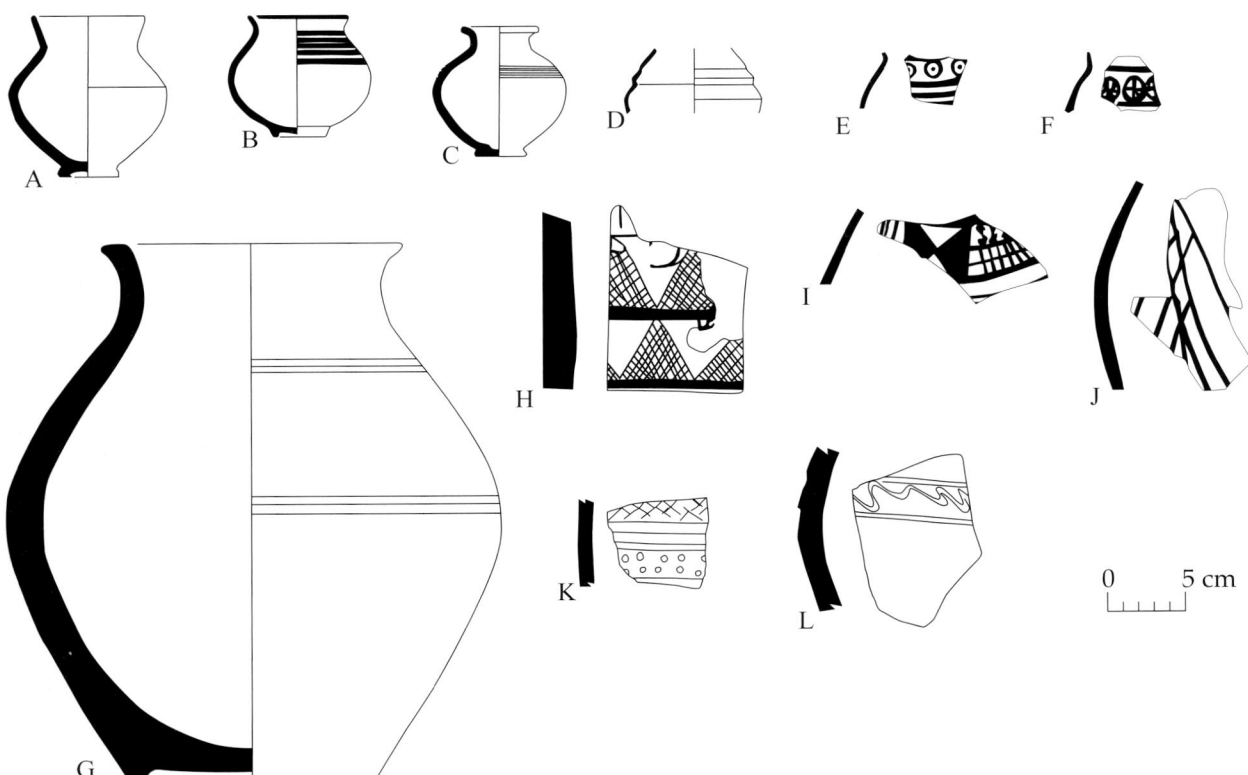

Fig. 4.11 Terminal MBII (Dinkha Period IV Phase D) ceramics.

Fig.	Op.	Context	Type	Description	Dia.	Disposition
A	B9/10a	3	Kramer Jar 1	Ware Ia	7	UPM Sherd
B	H1h	3	Kramer Jar 2	Ware Ie	7	UPM Sherd
C	B9/10a	3	Kramer Jar 3a	Ware VIa	5	UPM Sherd
D	B9/10a	1a	—	Ware Vb	—	UPM Sherd
E	B9/10a	1a	—	Ware Ie	—	UPM Sherd
F	B9/10a	1a	—	Ware Ie	—	UPM Sherd
G	B9/10a	3	Kramer Jar 11	Ware VIa	19	UPM Sherd
H	B9/10a	1	—	Ware Ie	—	UPM Sherd
I	B9/10a	1	—	Ware Ie	—	UPM Sherd
J	B9a	8	—	Ware IXb	—	UPM Sherd
K	B10a	8	—	Ware III	—	UPM Sherd
L	B10a	8	—	Ware Ib	—	UPM Sherd

in the North Cemetery (SK70, Fig. 5.7). In the U22 Deep Sounding the earliest MBW deposit, Strata 9–10, was mixed during excavation. There are some indications that this assemblage spans Hasanlu VIa–early V (see below). Below this level, in Strata 11–12, the excavators found a KW assemblage of MBII date. No evidence of a terminal MBII deposit equivalent to Dinkha IV Phase D was forthcoming. In Operation I Stratum VIa, an assemblage falling somewhere between MBII–early LBA was recovered (Fig. 4.14).

Dinkha IV Phase D Summary

Dinkha IV Phase D, the Terminal MBII, represents a period of marked change. Recognition of the shifting trends in ceramic production already present in the late 18th–17th century BC blunts the supposed punctuated change between the ceramics of Hasanlu VI and V. As we shall see, adding the succeeding Period VIa to the Hasanlu Sequence and careful separation and examination of the earliest Period V from later material goes even further in filling the largely artificial gap between the periods.

The terminal MBII slipped and burnished wares that occurred in a range of colors continued into the MBIII/Hasanlu VIa (early Dinkha III) — at this point I designate the ware early MBW (see below). The burnished sherds of early Dinkha III (Hasanlu VIa) were not previously published and were referred to in archival documentation as "Dinkha III," while the painted material of the same strata tellingly received the label "Dinkha IV." Unfortunately, when an INAA study of Dinkha and Hasanlu material was conducted in the late 1990s, the "Grey Wares"/Early MBW of Dinkha IV and Hasanlu VIa were not sampled for comparison to the MBW of the "Iron Age."

In Phase D, we see the emergence and increasing importance of new forms, some of which can be linked to Hasanlu VIa–V, as well as the continuation of a limited repertoire of typical KW forms and a precipitous decline in the use of painted decoration and an attendant increase in the use of slips and burnishing. Drinking vessels represent a highly diagnostic category for relative dating throughout the 2nd and early 1st millennium BC. *Istikhans*, the typical MBII cup, were already falling out of production in Dinkha IV Phase C, likely evolving into cups with S-profiles and loop handles located at the rim, as seen in Tomb B10a B27 and in grave SK70 at Hasanlu.

There is little KW with elaborate designs in Phase D. The possible mixing of contexts between the 1966 and 1968 seasons and the inevitability of extrusive sherds from the lower deposit appearing in the assemblage may account for much of what was found in the Control Sounding. This possible mixing of material occurred when excavations were renewed in the Control Sounding in 1968 following the 1966 season. The north-south baulk running between B9/10a was removed and Operation B9/10a was truncated, at which point a new series of stratigraphic designations was used starting with Stratum 1 (Hamlin 1971:30–31). The hiatus between excavations, the baulk removal, the truncation of the excavated area, and disjunction in the numbering of strata occurred at or near the base level of the Phase D deposit. Where provenience information is available, some of the "classic" KW of Phase D is found to have come from the 1968 designations Strata 1 and 1a, which raises the question of the mixing of Phases C-D (Hamlin 1971:31). Kramer's use of the "Phase C-D" designation, never fully explained, also indicates there was difficulty in reconciling the strata designations of 1966 with those of 1968. Perhaps the assemblage found in Dinkha Phase D, which contained little painted ware, is in fact the equivalent of Stein's upper deposit with annular band–painted ware.

Some parallels for the unpainted portion of the Terminal MBII assemblage are found in north-central Iran, in the core area of the Sagzabad (painted) and Central Grey Ware horizons summarized by Piller (2003–2004). The presence of polychrome painted ware in Sagzabad I, exhibiting generic similarities to polychrome painted Urmia Ware, provides links to the MBII of the northern Lake Urmia Basin and the MBIII of the northern, western, and southern parts of the same region, highlighting the transitional nature of the Terminal MBII and MBIII across a broad swathe of northern and western Iran.

Ceramics of Hasanlu VIA/Middle Bronze III (1600–1450 BC)

Hasanlu Period VIa is something of a misnomer, since the period is best attested at Dinkha Tepe. During the Terminal MBII (late Hasanlu VIb), as seen at Dinkha in Period IV Phase D, there were likely shifts in the patterns of ceramic production. In this regard, Dinkha Tepe and presumably Hasanlu are no different from northern Mesopotamia, Transcaucasia, and north-central Iran in the timing or nature of these shifts. The end of Dinkha IV can be dated to no later than the early 16th century BC. In the succeeding Period VIa or MBIII, there are some pronounced changes in the ceramic assemblage, which again fits rather neatly within the sequence established for Transcaucasia. The Dinkha ceramic assemblage from this period

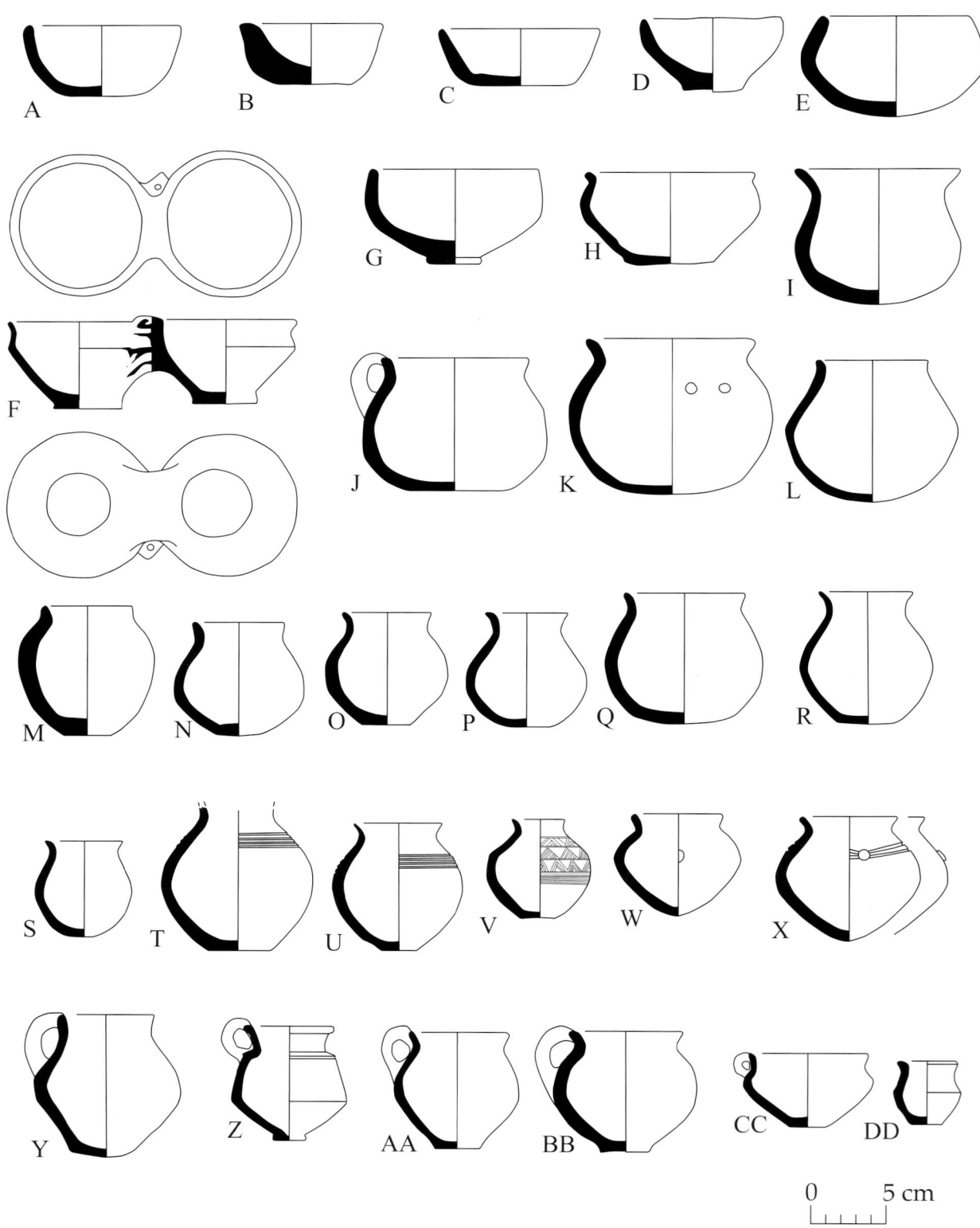

Fig. 4.12

Fig. 4.12 Terminal MBII Dinkha (Period IV Phase D) ceramics from Tomb B10a B27 (opposite).

Fig.	*Op.*	*Context*	*Description*	*Dia.*	*Disposition*
A	B10a	Burial 27	Buff Ia	11	Di66-674, Tehran
B	B10a	Burial 27	Buff IVa	10	Di66-775, Disc.
C	B10a	Burial 27	Buff IVa	11	Di66-671, UPM 66-23-9
D	B10a	Burial 27	Buff IIa	10	Di66-670, Tehran
E	B10a	Burial 27	Buff IIa	10	Di66-672
F	B10a	Burial 27	Kramer Ware II (Reddish Brown, Burnished)	10	Di66-651, UPM 66-23-1
G	B10a	Burial 27	Buff VIIa	12	Di66-673, Disc.
H	B10a	Burial 27	Buff IIa	12	Di66-677, UPM 66-23-10
I	B10a	Burial 27	Buff IVa	12	Di66-671, UPM 66-23-9
J	B10a	Burial 27	Buff IVa	10	Di66-690, Disc.
K	B10a	Burial 27	Buff (Grey) IIa	11	Di66-689, Disc.
L	B10a	Burial 27	Buff IIa	8	Di66-691, Disc.
M	B10a	Burial 27	Buff IIa	6	Di66-679, Disc.
N	B10a	Burial 27	Buff IIa	6	Di66-678, Tehran
O	B10a	Burial 27	Buff IIa	6	Di66-665, Tehran
P	B10a	Burial 27	Buff (Reddish) Ia	6	Di66-653, UPM66-23-3
Q	B10a	Burial 27	Buff Ia, Red Slip	8	Di66-680, UPM 66-23-11
R	B10a	Burial 27	Buff Ib, Red Slip	6	Di66-664, UPM 66-23-7
S	B10a	Burial 27	Buff VIIc, Red Slip	5	Di66-657, UPM 66-23-4
T	B10a	Burial 27	Buff IIa	—	Di66-686, Disc.
U	B10a	Burial 27	Grey Ia	6	Di66-66, Tehran
V	B10a	Burial 27	Grey IIc, Incised and Impressed Deco.	4	Di66-658, UPM 66-23-5
W	B10a	Burial 27	Buff IIb Red Slip	6	Di66-667, UPM 66-23-8
X	B10a	Burial 27	Buff	6	Di66-662, UPM 66-23-6
Y	B10a	Burial 27	Buff	7	Di66-663, Tehran
Z	B10a	Burial 27	Buff	6	Di66-656, Tehran
AA	B10a	Burial 27	Buff IIa	7	Di66-655, Disc.
BB	B10a	Burial 27	Buff VIIa	7	Di66-655, Disc.
CC	B10a	Burial 27	Grey Ia	8	Di66-660, Tehran
DD	B10a	Burial 27	Grey IIc	4	Di66-654, Tehran

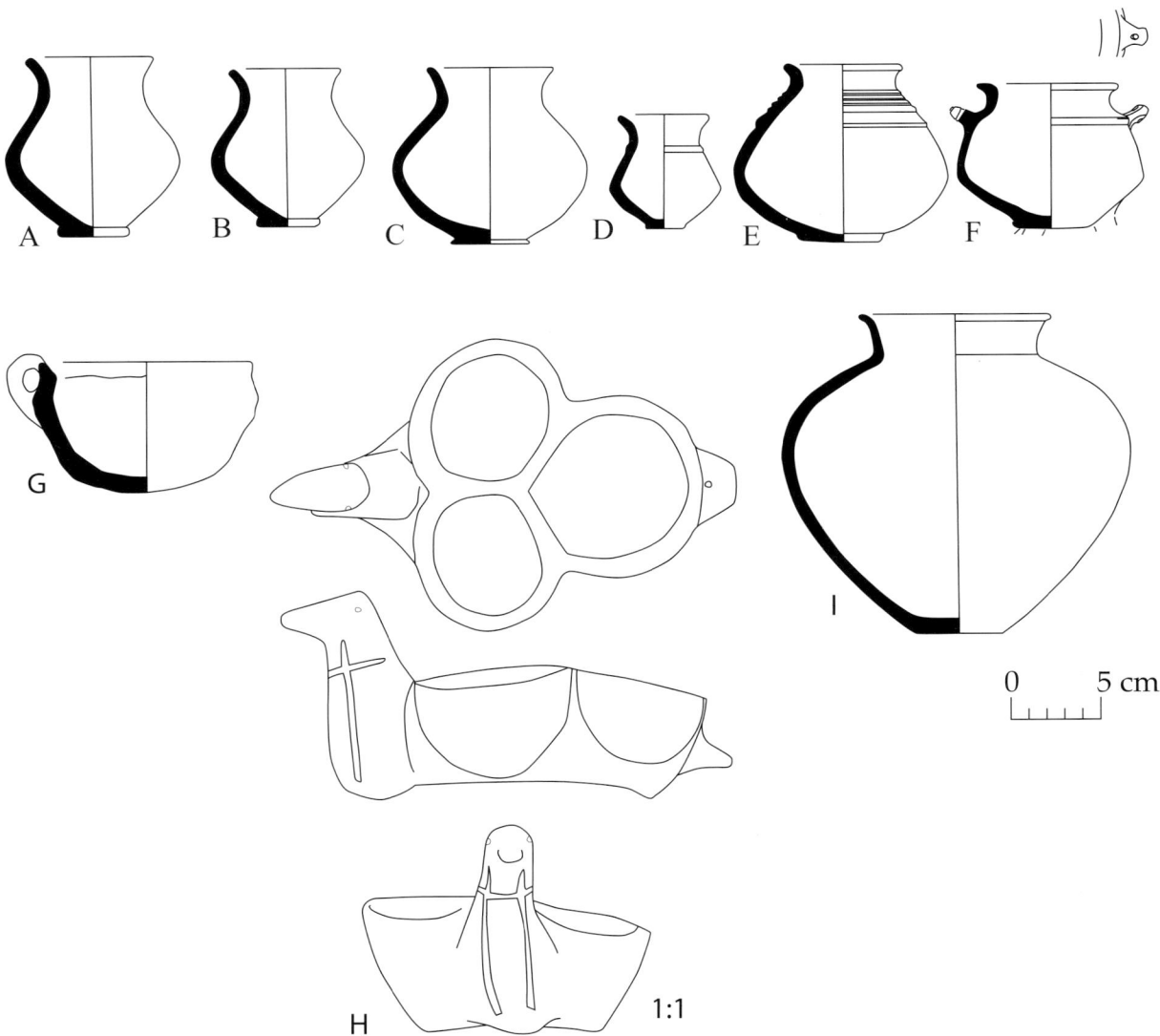

Fig. 4.13 Terminal MBII Dinkha (Period IV Phase D) ceramics from Tomb B10a B27.

Fig.	Op.	Context	Description	Dia.	Disposition
A	B10a	B27	Buff IIa	7	Di66-652, UPM 66-23-2
B	B10a	B27	Buff VIIa	6	Di66-659, Tehran
C	B10a	B27	Buff IIa	7	Di66-683, UPM 66-23-13
D	B10a	B27	Buff IIa	5	Di66-665, Tehran
E	B10a	B27	Buff IIa	6.5	Di66-676, Disc.
F	B10a	B27	Di66-682	8	Di66-682, UPM 66-23-12
G	B10a	B27	Buff IIa	12	Di66-675, Disc.
H	B10a	B27	—	—	Di66-584, Tehran
I	B10a	B27	Buff IIa	10.5	Di66-669, Disc.

is quite small, and I have mainly used the sequence from the Control Sounding (Operation B9/10a) and immediately adjacent trenches to inform this overview. Ceramics from graves at Hasanlu and Dinkha are discussed here and covered in more detail in Chapter 5.

Following the final destruction of the Dinkha IV Phase D structures, a layer of mudbrick collapse and wash accumulated in which were found painted sherds with clear connections to the western and northern Lake Urmia Basin and the southern Caucasus. This painted ware was associated with Early MBW. The most obvious link with assemblages to the north is the polychrome painted Urmia Ware (Dyson 1967b:137; 1973a:705–6; Muscarella 1968:195; Rubinson 2004). Urmia Ware has been identified in Geoy Tepe Late D–C, Haftavan Late VIB (Edwards 1981, 1983, 1986), and at sites of the Karmirvank archaeological complex of the MBIII period of the Caucasus. While the bulk of these painted sherds were found in B9a and B10a Stratum 7 and B10b Stratum 5, a few such sherds were found in Dinkha IV Phase D contexts and in all strata up to the surface. Incised and Impressed (Punctate) MBW, a variety of Early MBW, was also found associated with the Urmia Ware. In terms of fabric, the undecorated Early MBW in the early post-Dinkha IV deposit is identical to the Incised and Impressed MBW, but morphologically the plain ware belongs to the ceramic traditions of northern and western Iran. At Hasanlu, only a few sherds of polychrome Urmia Ware were found and no Incised and Impressed Ware is known from the miniscule number of High Mound soundings. Early MBW occurs in the lower levels of the U22 Sounding, and certain diagnostic forms indicative of the mid-2nd millennium BC there indicate the possible presence of material of Period VIa in these strata, which were mixed during excavation (see Chapter 3).

Early Monochrome Burnished Ware

Early MBW is a grit-tempered ware ranging in color from light grey to black, pinkish-buff to red, and buff to brown. The ware is typically slipped or wet smoothed, creating a self-slip, and burnished. On Early MBW burnishing is frequently inconsistent, giving the vessel a streaky appearance. The ware differs from the Fine Grey Ware of Dinkha IV in terms of its density, the consistency of its surface color, and the range of attested forms with which it is associated. Dinkha MBII Grey Ware exhibits a fairly consistent light grey color indicative of controlled firing and a preconceived standard for ware color. This accords well with the high-quality level of ceramic production evinced by the contemporary KW assemblage. Early MBW exhibits more variety in color, often on the same vessel, and has a more friable and less dense fabric. I believe the ware developed from Kramer's Wares II and VI.

Forms

I have established type numbers for all vessel forms of Periods VIa–IVc presented in this study. There are four Type Series, which correspond to the four major vessel classes: cups, bowls, holemouth jars (pots), and jars. These Types are independent of the type series established for the Dinkha MBII material by Kramer. Open forms in Early MBW include bowls of the "worm bowl" class, holemouth jars, button-base goblets and tankards, carinated bowls, and a bowl with an outturned simple rim. Closed forms are poorly attested.

Bowl Type 1a
This bowl with flaring sides and a flat base is typical of the early "worm bowl" class of the MBIII and early LBA, and one sherd has the distinctive appliquéd crescent and a drilled hole on its interior, sometimes referred to as a lug (Fig. 4.16:A, B). Bowls of this type occur at Geoy Tepe in Period C in both Early MBW and Urmia Ware (Burton-Brown 1951: fig. 30 nos. 949, 950, 961). The "plates" of Haftavan VIb, especially Edwards' Type 7 (1981: figs. 9, 15), appear to be related to this class of vessel, particularly Bowl Type 2a of early Hasanlu Period V (see below). Type 1 bowls continue into early Hasanlu V (see below). A rim sherd from the Hasanlu Well Sounding is the earliest attestation of a Type 1a bowl there (Fig. 3.2:D).

Bowl Type 3d
This tall, carinated bowl produced in Early MBW, while fairly rare in Hasanlu VIa and early V, occurs throughout the later 2nd and early 1st millennium BC (Fig. 4.16:D). The form is also typical of the MBII.

Bowl Type 18
This hemispherical bowl (Fig. 4.16:C) with a simple everted rim is unique in the Hasanlu Period VIa assemblage, but is a well-attested type in Dinkha IV

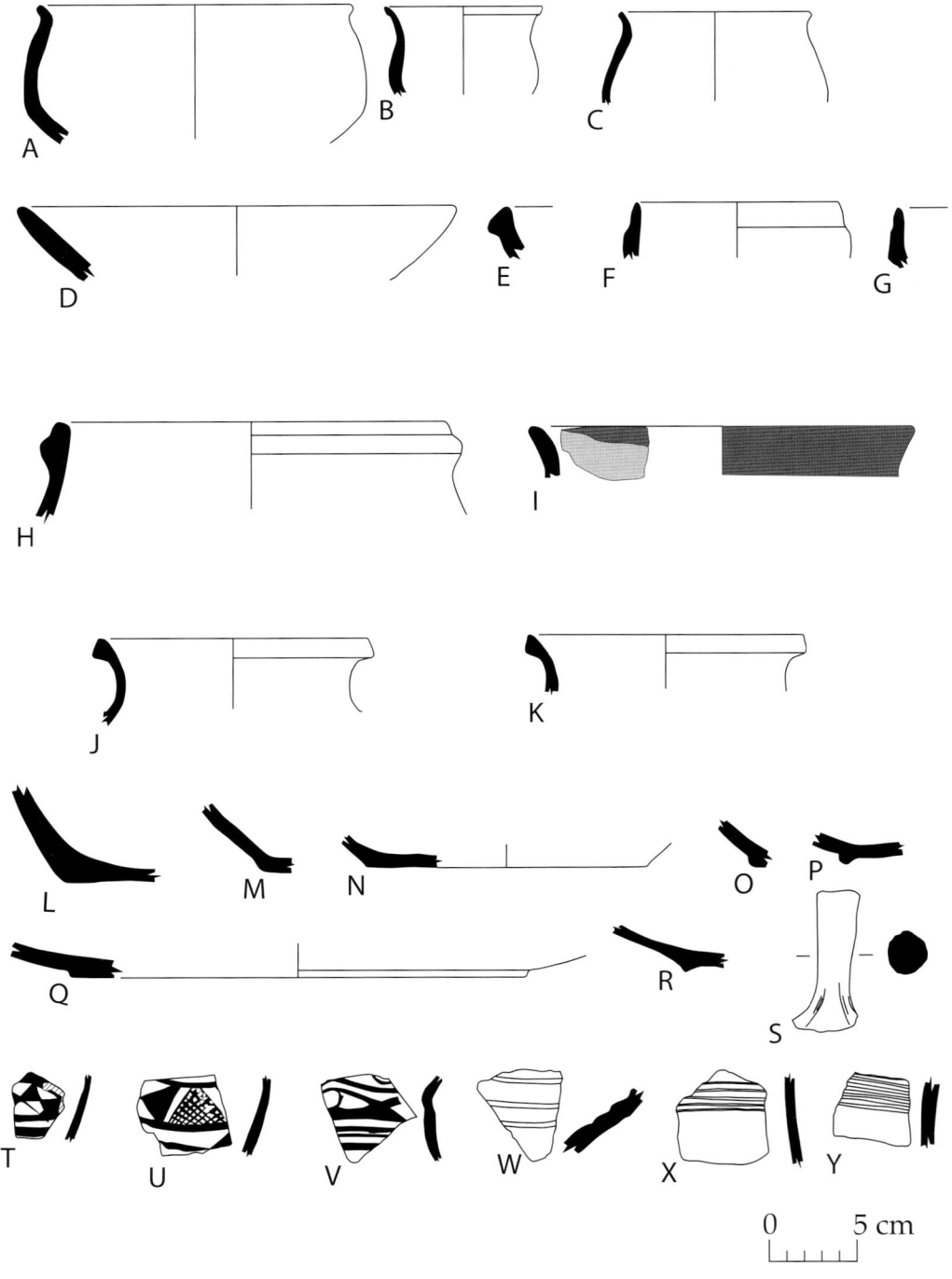

Fig. 4.14

Fig. 4.14 Hasanlu Tepe: sherds from Operation I Stratum 6a (opposite).

Fig.	Op.	Context	Ware	Type	Description	Dia.	Disposition
A	I	6a	MBW IIc	Bowl 19	Ext. Black Burnished Int. Greenish Buff	18	UPM Sherd
B	I	6a	Grey Ia	Cup 1a		9	UPM Sherd
C	I	6a	Buff Ia	Cup 8a/b	Buff Grit Temper	11	UPM Sherd
D	I	6a	MBW IIc	Bowl 1a	Black, Burnished and Slip	25	UPM Sherd
E	I	6a	MBW Ic	Bowl 13	Grey, Burnished and Heavy Slip	–	UPM Sherd
F	I	6a	MBW Ia	Bowl 21	Grey	13	UPM Sherd
G	I	6a	MBW IIc	Bowl 21	Black, Slipped and Burnished	–	UPM Sherd
H	I	6a	Buff Ia	HM 5	Int. and Ext. Pinkish Buff	24	UPM Sherd
I	I	6a	Polychrome Slip IIIb	HM 1	Ext. Black Wash Int. Red Slip	22	UPM Sherd
J	I	6a	Buff Ia	Jar 2	Int. and Ext. Pinkish Buff, Grit Temper	16	UPM Sherd
K	I	6a	Buff Ia	Jar 2	Int. and Ext. Pinkish Buff	16	UPM Sherd
L	I	6a	Buff Ia	–	Int. and Ext. Pinkish Buff, Grit Temper	–	UPM Sherd
M	I	6a	MBW IIc	–	Ext. Black, Slipped, Burnished, Int. Green Buff	–	UPM Sherd
N	I	6a	Buff Ia	–	Int. and Ext. Pinkish Buff, Grit Temper	–	UPM Sherd
O	I	6a	Buff Ia	–	Int. and Ext. Pinkish Buff	–	UPM Sherd
P	I	6a	Buff Ia	–	Int. and Ext. Pinkish Buff	–	UPM Sherd
Q	I	6a	MBW Ic	–		–	UPM Sherd
R	I	6a	MBW IIc	–	Buff, Slipped Tan	–	UPM Sherd
S	I	6a	Grey Ia	–		–	UPM Sherd
T	I	6a	PKW	–	Ext. Buff, Slip, Black Pt. Int. Buff Matte	–	UPM Sherd
U	I	6a	PKW	–	Ext. Buff, Slip, Black Pt. Int. Buff Matte	–	UPM Sherd
V	I	6a	PKW	–	Ext. Buff, Slip, Black Pt. Int. Buff Matte	–	UPM Sherd
W	I	6a	MBW Ib	–	Ext. Incised, Dark Red Slip Int. Buff	–	UPM Sherd
X	I	6a	Buff I/VIIIa	–	Ext. Buff, Incised Int. Buff	–	UPM Sherd
Y	I	6a	Buff Ia	–	Ext. Incised	–	UPM Sherd

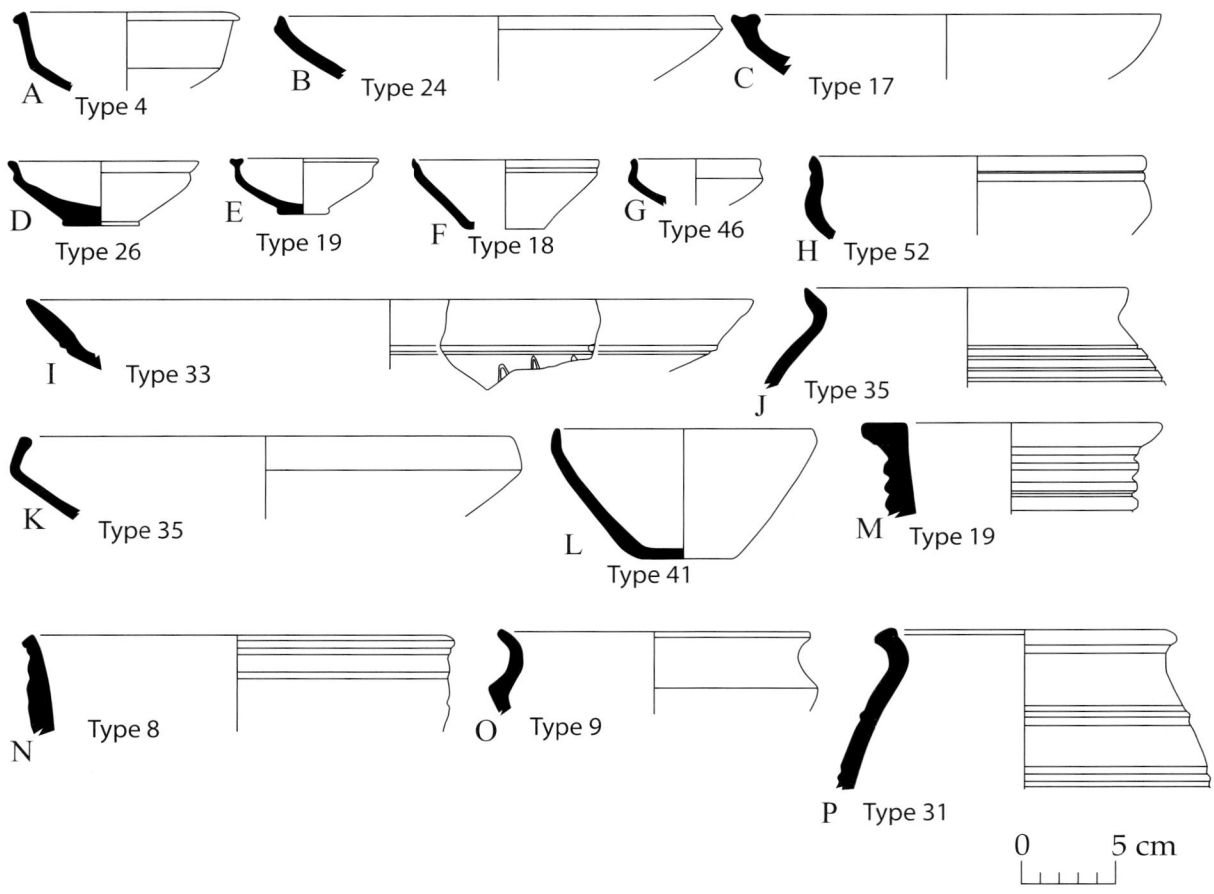

Fig. 4.15 Dinkha Tepe: Kramer's ceramic types exclusively in Grey Ware.

Phases B–D (Kramer's Type 28, Hamlin 1971:91, pl. III:28). These earlier examples are of Kramer's Ware IV and VI and all have burnished exteriors (Hamlin 1971:91). The type also occurs in Haftavan early VIb in Urmia Ware (Edwards 1981: figs. 16, 18). An identical bowl in Coarse Grey Ware was found at Hasanlu in Period VIb Burial SK4–5 (Fig. 5.1:A). Considering this chronological distribution, this bowl either represents an *ex situ* occurrence or, seemingly just as likely, a late MBIII holdover of a typical MB II type which is unattested in the LBA.

Holemouth Jar Type 1

Ovoid holemouth jars with everted to out-turned simple rims of this type are well attested at Dinkha in Early MBW (Fig. 4.16:E–G), Incised and Impressed MBW, and Urmia Ware (see below). Such jars are reminiscent of MBII forms with ledge rims. One jar with a distinctive strap handle (Fig. 4.16:E) is also attested at Geoy Tepe C (Burton-Brown 1951: fig. 30 no. 934).

Holemouth Jar Type 13

This hemispherical holemouth jar with thickened rim is rare throughout the chronological range covered here (Fig. 4.16:H). This Early MBW example seems to be related to the range of holemouth and/or deep incurving bowls in Urmia Ware from the same context (Fig. 4.17a:A–C, G, H).

Holemouth Jar Type 9

Small holemouth jars of this type in the LBA are often provided with cylindrical spouts (teapots) or bridgeless spouts (Fig. 4.16:I). Bridgeless-spouted jars are not present in the MBIII at Dinkha and Hasanlu. This jar is somewhat taller than those of later periods, and other jars of this type occur in Urmia Ware in the MBIII (Fig. 4.17a:D).

Holemouth Jar Type 5
This medium-to-large jar was likely a storage vessel and is better attested in the late LBA and Iron I at Hasanlu (Fig. 4.16:J).

Holemouth Jar Type 15
This small "teapot" likely represents a feeding jar for infants (Fig. 4.16:K). Later examples have basket handles.

Cup Type 1a Button-Base Tankards
Although no complete examples of this type were found at Dinkha, such drinking vessels are attested by the rim of what appears to be a tall tankard with twisted handle (Fig. 4.16:L). Two examples of this type were found in graves SK25 and SK29 at Hasanlu; I date both to Period VIa (Figs. 4.26:C–D, 5.8, 5.9, Seriation). The tankard from grave SK25 was found with an annular band–painted KW shouldered beaker (Figs. 4.26:B, 5.8:A, B). The tankard from grave SK29 was found associated with an Early MBW Type 6 jar (Figs. 4.25:E, 5.9:A, B). As with terminal MBII cups, these tankards have an S-profile and the handles are attached near the rim.

Cup Type 1b Pedestal-base Tankards
Although fragmentary, the form of this vessel remains distinctive (Fig. 4.16:O). This tall pedestal-based tankard is the earliest stratified example from Dinkha; the form is much better attested in the LBA in graves at Dinkha and Hasanlu (Fig. 4.26:E–I) as well as in occupation deposits, and examples have been identified from Geoy Tepe Tomb K (Fig. 4.22:C) and Hajji Firuz (Fig. 4.32:H). To securely date this form to the MBIII will require additional data, but the reconstructed height of the vessel is consistent with the earlier range of the form, whereas it decreases in height markedly by the Iron I.

Cup Type 8a Shouldered Beakers
This vessel form is well known in northern Mesopotamia from Tell Brak (Oates, Oates, and McDonald 1997:63–64, fig. 195:381, 382) and Tell al-Rimah (Postgate, Oates, and Oates 1997: pls. 72–76). The best parallels are with the shorter shouldered beakers of the Late Old Babylonian and early Mitanni periods. Button bases are common on such vessels in Mesopotamia and the southern Lake Urmia region. At Hasanlu, the type is attested in the MBII/Period VIb (Fig. 4.2:A–C), Period VIa, and possibly early Period V (see below). A shouldered beaker with annular band painting was found in the Hasanlu Well Sounding in association with Early MBW (Fig. 3.2:B). Shouldered beakers are contemporary with the closely related button-based tankard (Cup Type 1a) of the MBIII and early LBA. At Dinkha, this beaker is represented by one base in Early MBW (Fig. 4.16:N) and a PKW rim with black annular band painting (Fig. 4.16:M). In the MBIII and the early LBA the type is difficult to distinguish from the button-base tankard (Cup Type 1a), which is particularly evident in the lowest MBW level of the U22 Sounding (Fig. 4.27).

Miscellaneous MBW
One sherd of Pattern-Burnished MBW (Fig. 4.16:Y) and a modeled MBW face-lug at the rim of a vessel (Fig. 4.16:Z) provide links to Dinkha IV Phase D (cf. Dyson 1973a:704; Hamlin 1974:127, 129, fig. XIV, i). Pattern-Burnished MBW was also found in the Early MBW deposits at Hasanlu (see below). One tray with circular indentations and a lug or perhaps a leg is unique in the assemblage (Fig. 4.16:AA).

In summary, we see already in this early period some of the key markers used by scholars to define the early "Iron Age" of western Iran, including "worm bowls," button-base shouldered beakers, and pedestal and button-base tankards. The close relationship between shouldered beakers and tankards, their contemporaneity, and the fact that the beaker occurs in MBW and late KW strongly contradicts previous assessments of the ceramic assemblages which asserted no such relationship between the two existed. While the assemblage from Dinkha is quite limited, occupation assemblages and grave groups at Hasanlu corroborate this picture (see below). We also see some overlaps between Urmia Ware vessel forms and those in Early MBW. If one must seek an origin for Early MBW, the burnished wares of later Dinkha IV that are present in a similar range of colors—which have thus far received little attention—seem better able to provide likely precursors than does the Fine Grey Ware (Kramer's Ware 5) characteristic of the MBII. The shifts in ceramic

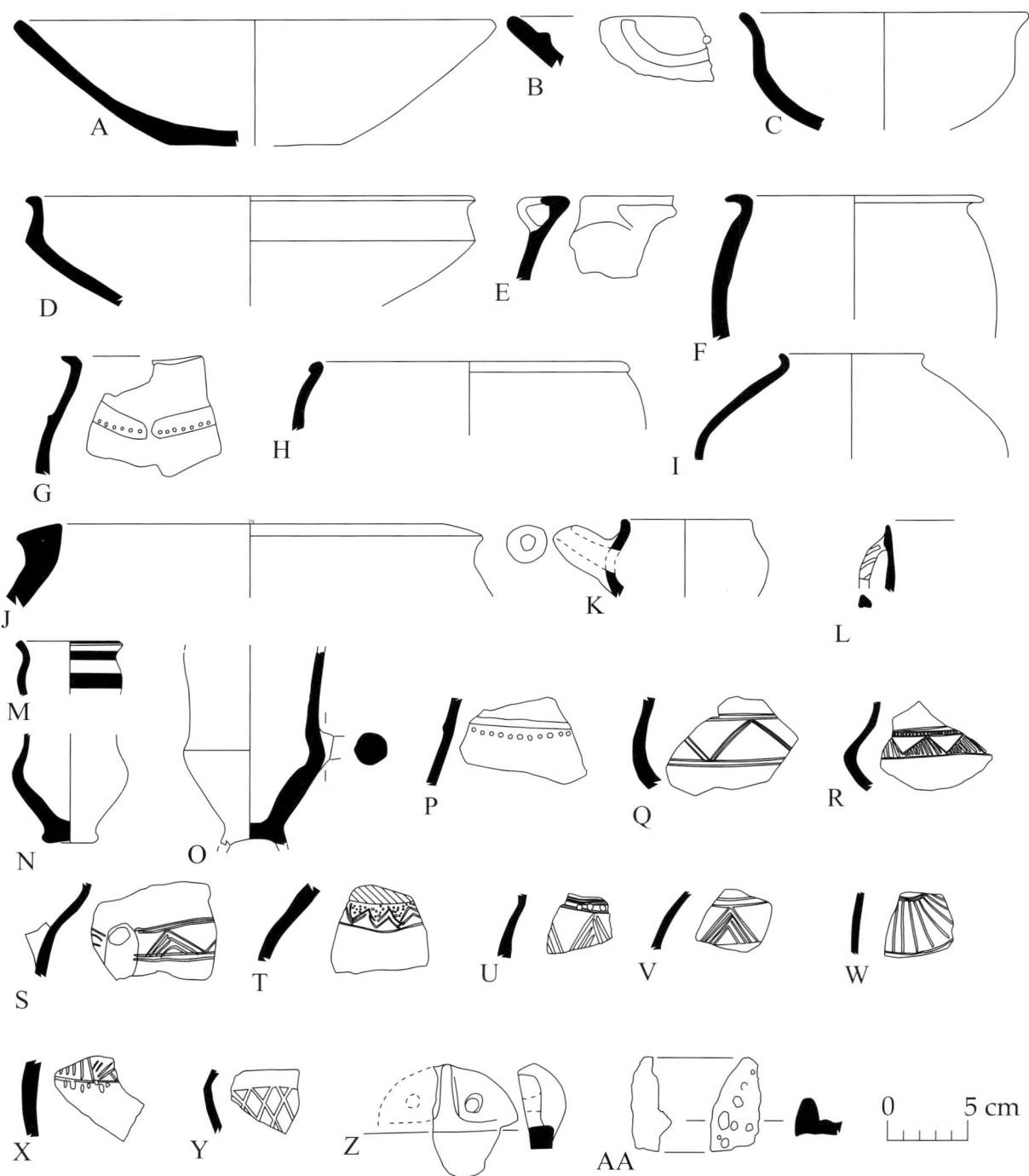

Fig. 4.16

Fig. 4.16 Dinkha Tepe: Hasanlu VIa ceramics.(opposite)

Fig.	Op.	Context	Ware	Type	Description	Dia.	Disposition
A	B9a	7	MBW IIc	Bowl 1a	Tan, Burnished	30	UPM 66-23-535
B	B9a	7	MBW IIb	Bowl 1a	Pale Brown, Appliqué Crescent and Drilled Hole	—	UPM Sherd
C	B9a	7	MBW IIc	Bowl 18	D. Brown	20	UPM 66-23-538
D	B9a	7	MBW IIc	Bowl 3d	Grey	32	UPM 66-23-571
E	B9a	7	MBW IIc, Red Slip	HM 1	Buff, Red Slip, Loop Handle	—	UPM 66-23-598
F	B9a	7	MBW IIc, Red Slip	HM 1	Buff, Red Slip	18	UPM 66-23-570
G	B9a	7	MBW IIc	HM 1	Grey, Raised Band, Impressed Deco.	—	UPM 66-23-604
H	B9a	7	MBW IIb	HM 13	Reddish-Yellow	2	UPM Sherd
I	B9a	7	MBW IIc	HM 9	Ext. Burnished, D.Grey, Int. Matte, Reddish Brown	10	UPM Sherd
J	B9a	7	MBW IIb	HM 5	Reddish-Brown	33	UPM Sherd
K	B9a	7	MBW IIc	HM 15	Pinkish Buff, Tube Spout	22	UPM Sherd
L	B9a	7	MBW IIc	Cup 1a	Grey, Twisted Loop Handle	—	UPM 66-23-537
M	B9a	7	PKW	Cup 8a	Ext. Orange, Black Pt. (Grey Core) Int. Matte, Buff	8	UPM Sherd Collection
N	B9a	7	MBW IIc	Cup 8a	Grey		UPM 66-23-536
O	B9a	7	MBW IIc	Cup 1b	Light Red, Loop Handle	Min. 9	UPM Sherd Collection
P	B9a	7	MBW IIc	—	Grey, Raised Band, Impressed Deco.	—	UPM 66-23-663
Q	B9a	7	MBW IIc	—	Grey-Brown, Incised Deco.	—	UPM 66-23-600
R	B9a	7	MBW IIc	—	Grey, Incised and Impressed Deco.	—	UPM 66-23-594
S	B9a	7	MBW IIc	—	Grey, Incised Deco., Loop Handle	—	UPM 66-23-599
T	B9a	7	MBW IIc	—	Orangish Buff, Incised and Impressed Deco.	—	UPM 66-23-614
U	B9a	7	MBW IIc	—	Orangish Buff, Incised and Impressed Deco.	—	UPM 66-23-597
V	B9a	7	MBW IIc	—	Grey-Brown, Incised Deco.	—	UPM 66-23-601
W	B9a	7	MBW IIc	—	D. Grey, Incised Deco.	—	UPM 66-23-596
X	B9a	7	MBW IIc	—	Grey, Incised Deco.	—	UPM 66-23-595
Y	B9a	7	MBW IIc	—	Black, Pattern Burnish	—	UPM 66-23-605
Z	B9a	7	Buff IIb	—	Possible Red-Brown Pt., Double Pierced "Face" Lug	—	UPM Sherd Collection
AA	B9a	7	MBW IIb	—	Ext. Reddish-Grey Int. Reddish Brown, Impressed, Tray Fragments		UPM Sherd Collection

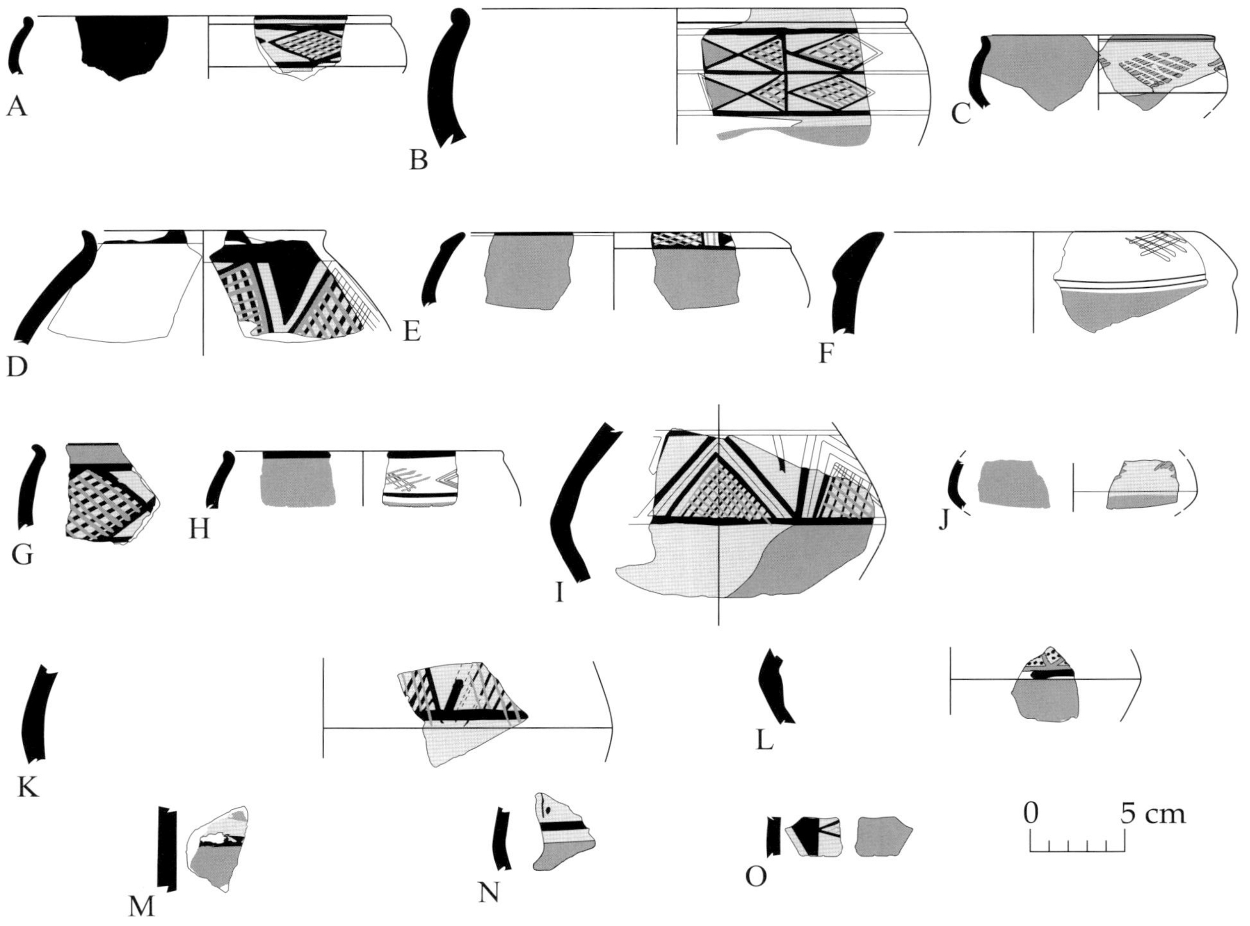

176

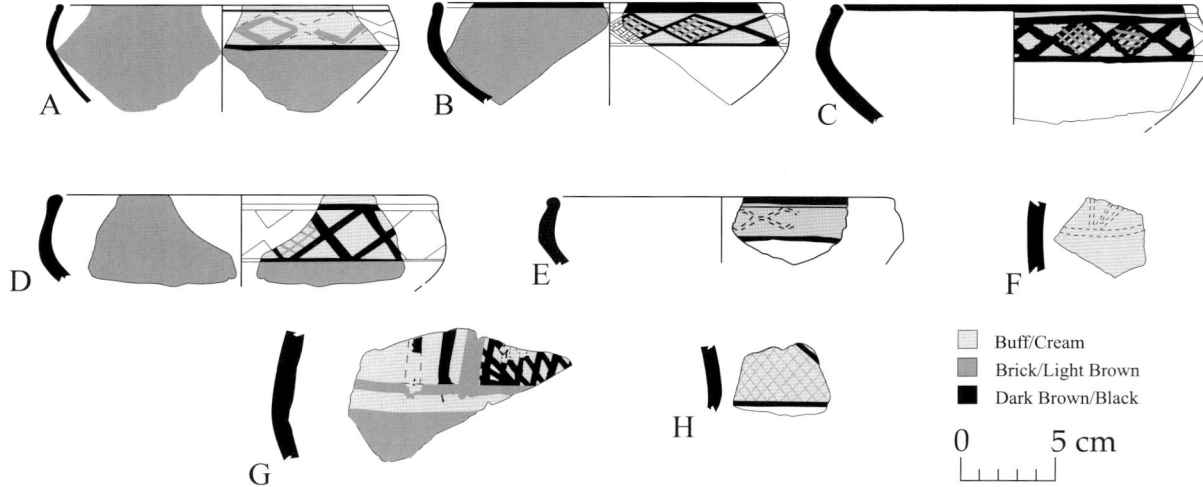

Fig. 4.17a

Fig. 4.17b

Fig. 4.17a Dinkha Tepe: Hasanlu VIa Urmia Ware (opposite, top).

Fig.	Op.	Context	Ware	Type	Description	Dia.	Disposition
A	B10a	7b	UW	—	—	21	UPM 66-23-412
B	B10b	5	UW	—	—	26	UPM 66-23-672
C	B9a	7	UW	—	—	12	UPM 66-23-584
D	B9a	7	UW	—	—	12	UPM 66-23-586
E	B9a	7	UW	—	—	16	UPM 66-23-585
F	B10b	5	UW	—	—	20	UPM 66-23-674
G	B10b	5	UW	—	—	—	UPM 66-23-411
H	B10b	5	UW	—	—	16	UPM 66-23-675
I	B10b	5	UW	—	—	—	UPM 66-23-410
J	B9a	7	UW	—	—	—	UPM 66-23-588
K	B9a	7	UW	—	—	—	UPM 66-23-581
L	B9a	7	UW	—	—	—	UPM 66-23-582
M	B9a	7	UW	—	—	—	UPM 66-23-583
N	B10b	5	UW	—	—	—	UPM 66-23-671
O	B10a	7	UW	—	—	—	UPM 66-23-673

Fig. 4.17b Dinkha Tepe: Urmia Ware from various contexts (opposite, bottom).

Fig.	Op.	Context	Ware	Type	Description	Dia.	Disposition
A	B10b	1	UW	—	—	17	UPM 66-23-670
B	B9b	4	UW	—	—	18	UPM 66-23-625
C	G10g	1	UW	—	—	18.5	UPM 66-23-590
D	G10g	1	UW	—	—	20	UPM 66-23-591
E	B10b	4	UW	—	—	18	UPM 66-23-623
F	H1h	2	UW	—	—	—	UPM 66-23-645
G	XI	2	UW	—	—	—	UPM 66-23-646
H	G10g	1	UW	—	—	—	UPM 66-23-674

production seen at Dinkha—most notably the gradual reduction in painted wares and the proliferation of burnished wares—can be linked to broader geographic patterns in which the ceramic traditions of northern and western Iran and the southern Caucasus developed gradually and in tandem in the mid- to late-2nd millennium BC from MBII precursors.

Incised and Impressed MBW

Incised and Impressed MBW was produced using the same technique as other Early MBW. Such decoration is generally confined to the shoulders of jars, while decorated bowls were polychrome painted (see below). Typical decoration consists of a frieze of pendant triangles or stacked chevrons framed by double incised lines (Fig. 4.16:Q–V, X). Triangles are sometimes hatched (Fig. 4.16:R, X). Rows of impressed circles occasionally occur at the top border of the frieze (Fig. 4.16:R, U). One sherd has a row of stacked chevrons with a field of impressed dots above (Fig. 4.16:T). Holemouth jars were also decorated with raised bands on the shoulder, with a horizontal row of impressed circles on or below the band (Fig. 4.16:G, P). With the exception of the holemouth jars, the incised decorative style echoes that of the contemporary polychrome painted ware.

Forms

Little can be said of the attested forms of Incised and Impressed MBW in Hasanlu VIa save that they are almost exclusively jars or cups too fragmentary to assign to types or they are Type 1 holemouth jars (Fig. 4.16:G). Jars with low shoulders (Fig. 4.16:G) and carinated vessels (Fig. 4.16:R, S) are present. One small jar or tankard has the vestige of a handle (Fig. 4.16:S). Only one sherd may be from a bowl (Fig. 4.16:Q).

Remarks

If the southern Caucasus is used as a guide to inform on developmental trends within entire ceramic assemblages, plain "polished" wares are certainly present in the MBIII and early LBA assemblages alongside monochrome and polychrome painted ware and Incised and Impressed (punctate) ware. It is nevertheless currently efficacious to treat the Incised and Impressed Ware of the southern Lake Urmia Basin as separate from the MBW of the same region since the two wares might potentially be the product of separate traditions that converged in the region in the mid-2nd millennium BC. Incised and Impressed Ware at Dinkha shows strong connections to the southern Caucasus in terms of styles of decoration and possibly in terms of attested vessels forms, although few morphological types are attested. These vessel forms only slightly overlap the range of forms attested in Early MBW and this overlap is quite generic—e.g., Type 1 holemouth jars and possibly tankards. Incised and Impressed decoration does not currently seem to adorn the contemporary Early MBW forms that have traditionally been used by scholars to define the "Early Western Grey Ware horizon," such as "worm bowls," bridgeless-spouted jars, or closely affiliated forms, and these vessel forms in Early MBW are not found in significant numbers in the MBIII and earliest LBA in the Caucasus. The styles of decoration associated with Incised and Impressed Ware are related to the contemporary painted styles of the north rather than earlier styles of incised and impressed decoration known from Hasanlu VIb/Dinkha IV, such as comb-incised bands and wavy lines and incised and impressed designs meant to imitate cordage (Fig. 4.2:II–KK). Finally, this ware has not been found at Hasanlu or sites documented by archaeological survey in Ušnu-Solduz. There are too few excavated exposures at Hasanlu to categorically state that the Incised and Impressed Ware is absent—especially since there are a few examples of the related polychrome Urmia Ware. Future research may show that the ware was typical of all Hasanlu VIa assemblages in the region, as opposed to our current view, in which Dinkha appears to represent a highly localized anomaly.

Urmia Ware

Urmia Ware is a highly distinctive grit-tempered red ware with slip and polychrome painting attested at Dinkha Tepe and Hasanlu in a narrow range of forms. Fifteen sherds of the ware were found in the MBIII deposit of the Dinkha Control Sounding and contiguous units (Fig. 4.17a). Rubinson identifies another 8 sherds of the ware from other operations (Fig. 4.17b) and 11 fragments (Rubinson 2004:662, n10).

With the exception of Hajji Firuz (Hamlin 1971:32), no sites with this ware were discovered by archaeological survey in the southern Lake Urmia region (Edwards 1986). Vessels are usually slipped red and burnished. Painted designs in combinations of red and brown–black are applied over a lighter field typically of tan, off-white, or "apricot" paint or slip on the upper portions of vessels. Vessels are handmade. There is some variation within this ware category in terms of paint color and the amount of painted design; such variation is not always present in the Dinkha corpus. The slip/paint colors and vessel forms provide ample evidence that these sherds belong to the broader Urmia Ware tradition.

Forms

Rubinson identified four forms among the Urmia Ware sherds from Dinkha: a low open bowl with rolled rim; a bowl with incurving, folded, and flattened rim; a high form with incurving rim that might be a deep bowl or pot; and a jar type (Type 6a, see below) with narrow neck and rounded body (Rubinson 2004:664). As mentioned previously, some of these same forms were manufactured in Early MBW in the same assemblage at Dinkha and other Early MBW forms are attested at other sites in Urmia Ware. One Urmia Ware bowl with "incurving, folded and flattened rim" was found on the High Mound at Hasanlu in the Well Sounding, as was a body sherd from a Type 6a jar (see Chapter 3, Fig. 3.2:G, I). Surface sherds of Urmia Ware were also found at Hasanlu, and one grave found by Stein contained a Type 6a jar. In Nakhichevan, at sites such as Sortepe, Qızılburun, and Kizilvank, similar painted designs in monochrome and polychrome are found on forms typical of the MBIII and LBA of northwestern Iran, such as tankards and jars with bridgeless spouts (Seyidov 2003: figs. 43:6, 8; 44:3, 10). The chronological and cultural significance of such vessels in Azerbaijan is currently difficult to assess since we cannot gauge the spatio-temporal spread of the painted style and these vessel forms. Such Urmia Ware–EWGW "combinations" are not attested at Dinkha or Hasanlu and may reflect a general trend of 2nd millennium BC painted pottery traditions persisting longer in the north (from the Urmia region northward) than in the south. The "worm bowls," tankards, and carinated bowls typical of Hasanlu VIa–early V occur in Urmia Ware in Geoy Tepe C and in the southern Caucasus. Moreover, small amounts of Urmia Ware were found in LBA contexts at both Dinkha and Hasanlu, and should not be dismissed out of hand as *ex-situ* based on the continuation of painted decoration in the southern Caucasus into the early LBA.

Hasanlu VIa: Dating/Conclusions

Using the Dinkha Tepe assemblage and that from Geoy Tepe late Period D and Period C, we can trace the following developments in Hasanlu VIa in the southern Lake Urmia Basin:

1. The proliferation of polychrome painted ware at Dinkha—so-called Urmia Ware—in open forms and the development of new styles of geometric decoration, especially pendant triangles and lozenges which are frequently crosshatched. Concomitantly, PKW continues its rapid decline. Only a small amount of Urmia Ware is attested in Dinkha IV, and the polychrome painted ware of early Geoy D (contemporary to Dinkha IV Phase D) differs from that of Late D and C.

2. The development of Type 1a bowls. These are the earliest examples of so-called worm bowls (Fig. 4.16:A, B). At Geoy Tepe one such bowl was decorated with polychrome painting (Burton-Brown 1951:131, fig. 30 no. 950) and others are MBW (Burton-Brown 1951: fig. 30 nos. 949, 961).

3. The use of shouldered beakers and carinated tankards with flaring sides, button-bases, pedestal bases, and simple rims (Fig. 4.16:M–O) in Early MBW and late KW. Rim sherds from what Burton-Brown believed to be cups in painted wares from Geoy Tepe C appear to be unusually large for drinking vessels—with rim diameters of 17.5 and 19.3 cm, respectively—especially as compared to the beakers and tankards typical of the mid-2nd millennium BC (Burton-Brown 1951: fig. 30 no. 51; fig. 31 no. 692). For comparison, an obvious pedestal-base tankard from Geoy Tepe Period B has a reconstructed rim diameter of only 9.5 cm (Burton-Brown 1951: fig. 34 no. 38), typical of similar vessels from the MBIII and early LBA at Hasanlu. I would tentatively link the development of drinking vessel forms to influences from Mesopotamia; one would thus predict they would appear in Ušnu-Solduz somewhat earlier than they appear at sites further north in the Lake Urmia Basin.

4. The appearance of Incised and Impressed MBW at Dinkha.

The date of Hasanlu VIa in the southern Lake Urmia Basin is closely connected to interpretations of Dinkha IV Phase D. Stratigraphic details are currently lacking from the Dinkha Control Sounding. This final architectural phase belonged to Stratum 8 in Operation B9/10a. The excavators report that a radiocarbon sample (Appendix II, P-1232, 1754–1626 cal BC) was collected from the floor of the main Phase D structure (Appendix II, P-1232; Dyson 1973a:705) and that, "following this disaster there was a short re-occupation of the area [also designated Stratum 8] with some additional wall construction and then final abandonment before the accumulation of Iron Age I trash [actually MBIII, LBA, and Iron I] over the area and its use as a cemetery" (Dyson 1973a:705). Artifacts from this late phase rebuild were apparently not separated from the earlier phase(s) of Stratum 8 during excavation. One radiocarbon sample, P-1231, was collected from the reoccupation and it yielded a 16th century date (Appendix II). Hasanlu VIa thus likely dates from at least the later 16th century to the early 15th century BC.

Similarities between MBIII Dinkha and the mid-2nd millennium BC ceramic traditions of the southern Caucasus, namely the 'Kizilvank' or 'Karmirvank' archaeological culture, provide some bases for cross-sequence dating. Recent comprehensive assessments date this archaeological culture to 1700–1500 BC (Smith, Badalyan, and Avetisyan 2009). The radiocarbon dates from late Dinkha IV (Appendix II) suggest the MBIII assemblage dates to the latter part of this period and slightly later—the later 16th–early 15th

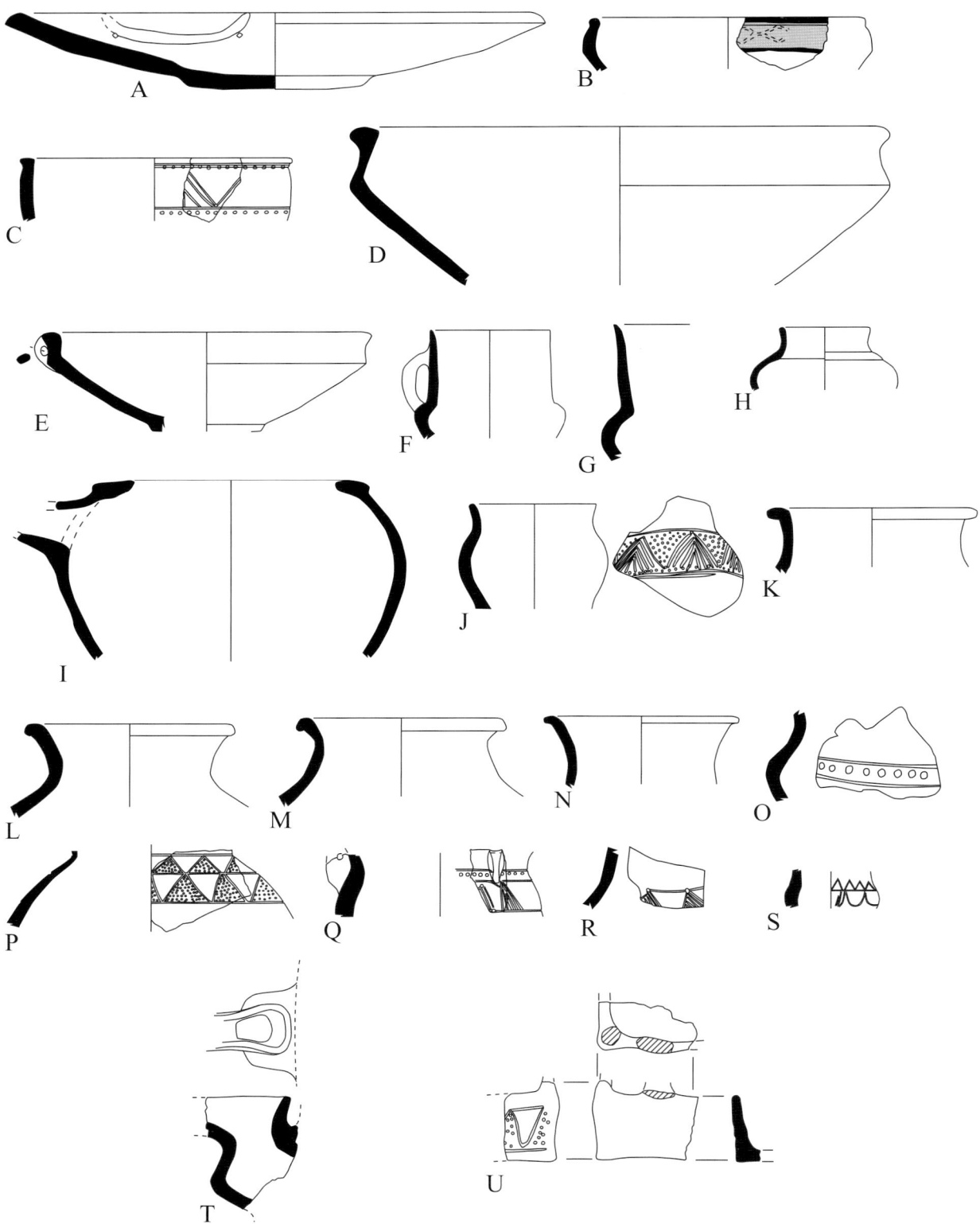

Fig. 4.18

Fig. 4.18 Dinkha Tepe: early Hasanlu V "Trash Deposit" (opposite).

Fig.	Op.	Context	Ware	Type	Description	Dia.	Disposition
A	B9a	6	MBW IIc	Bowl 2a	Grey	34	UPM 66-23-517
B	B10b	4	UW	—	—	18	UPM 66-23-623
C	B10a	1	MBW IIb	Bowl 10	Dark Brown, Incised and Impressed with White Infilling	18	UPM Sherd
D	B10b	4	MBW	Bowl 6		36	UPM 66-23-503
E	B10a	5	MBW	Bowl 3a		22	UPM 66-23-566
F	B9a	6	MBW	Cup 1a		8	UPM 66-23-533
G	B10a	5	MBW	Cup 1a		—	UPM 66-23-565
H	B10a	5	MBW IIc	Cup 8a	Orangish Buff	6	UPM Sherd
I	B10b	4		HM 3		18	UPM 66-23-504
J	B10b	4	MBW IIc	Jar 4	D. Grey-Brown, Incised and Impressed, White Infilling	9	UPM 66-23-621
K	B9a	6	MBW IIc	Jar 2	Tan	14	UPM 66-23-530
L	B9a	6	MBW IIc	Jar 2	Tan	14	UPM 66-23-532
M	B9a	6	Buff IIa	Jar 2	Pinkish Buff	14	UPM 66-23-516
N	B9a	6	MBW IIb	Jar 2	Grey	13	UPM 66-23-534
O	B10a	5	MBW Ic	—	Grey, Incised and Impressed	—	UPM 66-23-512
P	B9a	6	MBW IIc	—	Grey, Incised and Impressed, White Infilling	—	UPM Sherd
Q	B7e		MBW	—	Incised and Impressed, Pierced Lobe Lug	—	UPM Sherd
R	B9a	6		—	Incised and Impressed Deco.	—	UPM 66-23-622
S	B9a	5	MBW IIc	—	D. Grey, Incised Deco.	—	UPM 66-23-592
T	B9a	5	MBW IIc	—	Grey-Brown, Bridgeless Spout	—	UPM Sherd
U	B8d	2	MBW	—	Incised and Impressed, Fenestrated, "Box Basin"	—	UPM Sherd

century. An earlier starting date would not be surprising given the presence of small amounts of Urmia Ware and Incised and Impressed Ware in Dinkha IV Phase D—this material might belong to the aforementioned later rebuild phase. The ceramic assemblage from the layers sealing the Dinkha Stratum 7 (MBIII) deposit suggests an end date. This assemblage belongs to early Hasanlu V or the early LBA and contains virtually no painted ware, instead being characterized by Early MBW and Incised and Impressed Ware, paralleling developmental trends the Lchashen-Metsamor archaeological complex (see below). This supports a date in the late 15th–13th centuries BC for Hasanlu V (Smith, Badalyan, and Avetisyan 2009), and concomitantly a date range for Hasanlu VIa which spans the 16th–early 15th centuries. Dinkha and Geoy Tepe appear to run in tandem with the ceramic sequences of the northern Lake Urmia Basin (Haftavan) and southern Caucasus sequences. This was noted by Dyson in his preliminary and only assessment of the Hasanlu VIa assemblage from Dinkha: "Some contact between Dinkha Tepe and Geoy Tepe D–C is indicated through the occurrence at Geoy Tepe of several incised sherds of Dinkha type[9] and the occurrence at Dinkha of sherds of Geoy late D–C polychrome type [Urmia Ware]…This polychrome ware at Geoy Tepe is associated with vessel types of the local Iron Age I (Hasanlu V) culture, for bowls of plain burnished red or grey of Iron Age shape and fabric occur along with the polychrome" (Dyson 1973a:705–6). Curiously, the same applies to the Dinkha Hasanlu VIa assemblage as a whole, and at both sites there is even overlap between forms occurring in MBW and Urmia Ware, but it would appear that the heavy focus on the painted wares from Hasanlu and Dinkha in preliminary analyses resulted in this point being overlooked. Dyson concluded that an archaeological culture characterized by polychrome painted ware must have been in contact with the Hasanlu V culture from the mid–2nd millennium BC, or that this, "perhaps implies that the Hasanlu V burnished grey ware assemblage grew out of the D–C mixed polychrome and plain ware assemblage through the loss of polychrome decoration" (1973a:706). This latter interpretation seems the most plausible, even in light of the intervening 40 years of exploration in the southern Caucasus. I would merely emphasize that the MBIII in turn develops from the MBII. Burney and Lang also championed the possible Transcaucasian origins of the Early MBW horizon (1971:117), and Dyson's later work continued to attack connections between Early MBW origins and Tepe Hissar and southern Turkmenistan (1977b:167), while advocating punctuated culture change and demic diffusion.

Ceramics of Hasanlu V/ Late Bronze Age (1450–1250 BC)

Our understanding of the early LBA ceramic assemblage of Ušnu-Solduz is largely informed by the lower levels of the U22 Sounding at Hasanlu, which comprise Operations T22–23, U22–23, and V22–23, and the Dinkha B9/10a Control Sounding and operations immediately adjacent to it. A few sherds of obvious early LBA date from other operations are also included to illustrate the range of variation in the assemblage, and other Period V assemblages at Hasanlu from less secure contexts are briefly discussed at the end of this section. Gradual changes in the predominant Early MBW types and the seriation of Period V graves (see Chapter 5) provide some means for dividing the LBA into earlier and later subperiods. Future research may justify the subdivision of the LBA into an LBI and LBII. Overall, the early LBA assemblage exhibits a significant degree of linkage to northeastern Mesopotamia.

T. Cuyler Young was the first scholar to analyze the Period IV–VI ceramic assemblage from Hasanlu (1963), and his work had a profound influence on later scholarship. The Hasanlu ceramics formed the core of Young's definition of the Early and Late Western Grey Ware horizons of northwestern Iran, with Hasanlu and Ziwiyeh essentially providing the chronological and typological spine of a larger study of northern and western Iran. Hasanlu offered a rare stratified ceramic sequence from occupation deposits with radiocarbon dates and grave groups with which to structure a larger, chronologically floating dataset composed of grave groups from previously excavated sites in Iran. In developing his ware typology, Young clearly started with Hasanlu IVb, the better-attested and more familiar part of the sequence at the time of his writing in the early 1960s and then applied this typology to "Period V." In Young's dissertation, "Period V" included whole vessels from Hasanlu graves dating mostly to my early Hasanlu V—mixed with a few of Periods VIb, VIa, and IVc—and occupation deposits mainly of Hasanlu V and IVc date. While the majority of Young's analyses of the wares and types characteristic of "Hasanlu V" focused on assemblages from the U22 Sounding and graves, the small group of ceramics he chose to illustrate the period were, as we have seen, from a wide range of largely insecure or non-Period V contexts.

Young defined three ware types for Period V, broken down into varieties (Table 4.1). Coarse Ware was defined as a fabric of poorly levigated clay with large grit temper (approaching small pebbles) that was fairly well fired. Vessels in this fabric were handmade. Young distinguished three varieties using widely differing attributes. Plain Buff Coarse Ware was distinguished by surface color, ranging from tan-buff to a dark brown or reddish brown. Typical shapes were coarse, flat trays, large storage jars, and pithoi. Smudged Coarse Ware was based on the premise that smoke-blackened surfaces marked certain vessels as cooking ware. The ware was not appreciably different from Plain Buff Coarse Ware in terms of fabric. Forms attested in the ware include large and small "cooking pots" (holemouth jars) with small strap handles or upturned tabular lugs, small jars, bottles, trays, and low, plain holemouth vessels. In practice, Young seems to have distinguished this ware

Table 4.1. Young's "Period V" Ware Types

Ware	Color Range	Surface Treatment	Paste Levigation	Temper	Firing	Manufacture	Density/ Hardness	Porosity	Break Fracture
Coarse ware	buff, tan, reddish brown	matte, smoothed, rare burnishing of red-slipped variant	poor	large grit	fairly well	wheelmade, some hand-made	soft	porous	uneven
Common ware	buff, tan, dark brown	matte, smoothed, light burnishing, burnishing of red-slipped variant	well	medium	well	wheelmade	dense	non-porous	even
Fine ware	90% grey	burnished, rarely smoothed	well	medium to fine	well	wheelmade	highly compact, brittle [?], hard	non-porous	even

from other Coarse Ware using vessel forms rather than the presence or absence of smoke-blackened surfaces. This attribute can occur on any ceramic intentionally or accidentally subjected to fire and such accretions are often washed off of sherds during processing. Re-examination of the assemblage has shown, moreover, that not all of the cited forms in Smudged Coarse Ware show evidence for such "smudging." Red-Slipped Coarse Ware was "very rare" in the Hasanlu IVb–V assemblage. Young does not describe the fabric, but it tends to be buff to pinkish buff and is finished with a reddish-brown slip on the exterior, often inconsistently applied, and then burnished. Fire smudging is not unusual. Attested forms include holemouth jars, small-to-medium bowls, carinated holemouth jars with opposing strap handles, large holemouth jars with pairs of triangular lugs, and large storage jars and pithoi. The forms described by Young for Coarse Ware overall typify Period IVc–IVb and are less well attested in Periods V and VIa. Given the dubious value of "smudging" as an attribute in a ceramic typology, I would argue that Plain Buff and Smudged Coarse Ware should be collapsed into a single Coarse Ware category. Red-Slipped (and burnished) Coarse Ware should be redesignated a variant of MBW.

Common Ware fabric consists of a well-levigated clay with small-to-medium grit inclusions—although Young defined it as having only medium grit temper. It tends to be well fired and its surfaces are matte, wet-smoothed or, more rarely, burnished. Vessels were wheelmade and occurred in a broad range of forms—essentially the same as Medium Fine Ware (see below). The same three varieties defined for Coarse Ware were used to subdivide Common Ware—Plain Buff, Smudged, and Red-Slipped.

Although Young never explicitly states it, he primarily based his ware types on ware color, temper, and vessel thickness. While this typology appears valid for the Iron II ceramics of Hasanlu IVb—and it is almost certain that Young developed his ware typology using this assemblage and his knowledge of the succeeding Iron III in western Iran—major inconsistencies emerge when it is applied to the earlier Period IVc and, especially, Periods V and VIa assemblages that are demonstrably the precursors of the late MBW horizon. These inconsistencies likely stem from underlying assumptions regarding the origins and evolution of the Iron II–III assemblages, particularly the importance and putative cultural significance of the buff and grey-black wares. Key inconsistencies for Periods V and IVc include:

Young always assigned the grey- and black-colored ceramics of Period V and IVc to Fine Ware, regardless of vessel wall thickness, temper or any other attributes of the ware. This bias was reflected in the coding system employed for the ceramics, in which the two main signifiers of ware categories are "Grey" and "Buff". Medium-to-fine burnished buff, tan and red ceramics were assigned to Common Ware and rarely Fine Ware, in a seemingly arbitrary fashion. Nevertheless, as Young makes clear, the vessel forms attested for Fine and Common Ware overlap. Moreover, this re-examination of the Hasanlu assemblage and archaeological research conducted since the 1960s at Hasanlu and related sites have revealed a great deal more variation in the color of "Fine Ware" than was originally defined by Young.

1. Burnishing is a key attribute in the definition of Fine (black and grey) Ware, but is of tertiary importance in classifying other (buff and red) wares. In point of fact, in Periods VIa, V and, to a lesser extent, IVc, Young's Fine (grey and black) Ware includes matt-surface ceramics. At the same time, Young tacitly used the degree of burnishing to distinguish between Common Ware and buff-colored Fine Ware, the former being only occasionally lightly burnished and the latter being "almost always burnished and…only very rarely simply smoothed" (Young 1963:36). This conclusion is something of a tautology since heavily burnished wares should have been, by definition, Fine Ware and thus not Common Ware, regardless of color, albeit with the exception of Red-Slipped Common Ware.

2. Young only recognized slips when the slip color contrasts with that of the paste—that is, only in the case of red-slipped varieties of Coarse and Common—i.e., buff spectrum—wares. An important attribute of so-called Fine Ware is the frequent application of a slip or the development of a self-slip, achieved through wet smoothing, usually in the same color as the paste, facilitating and enhancing the effect of any subsequent burnishing of the surface. Red-slipped and burnished vessels, which replicate the vessel forms of Medium Fine (grey and black) Ware, were included in the typology as a variety of Common (buff) Ware, presumably due to their paste color. There is, moreover, a red-slipped variety of red fabric Fine Ware. As with burnished buff ware, these red-slipped wares likely represent an unintentional difference in the firing atmosphere in what is otherwise MBW in terms of production techniques—that is, in terms of paste, temper, throwing method and surface finish.

3. Fire-blackened or "smudged" surfaces were used to define varieties of Coarse and Common (buff) Wares. Blackened surfaces are naturally readily apparent on light-colored ceramics and are harder to detect on grey and black ware. Grey and black ceramics occur in "cooking" forms in Periods VIa, V and IVc and, although more difficult to detect, are fire blackened from use.

In sum, Young always categorized highly burnished and grey-to-black ceramics as Fine Ware. Ceramics in colors other than grey and black were only Fine Ware if they were heavily burnished. Slips and fire blackening were only taken into account if they occurred on buff spectrum fabrics. We see that ware color and surface treatment—matte, smoothed, or burnished—were especially important in defining ware types, but these and other attributes were used inconsistently throughout the typology *and were only made explicit* at the lower level of ware variety in Young's definitions, despite their importance at the highest level of ware definition in practice.

Young's Coarse Ware appears to be a valid category given the correspondence between the ware attributes, attested vessel forms, and imputed vessel functions. The ware served utilitarian purposes such as storage, food processing, and cooking and therefore is designed to withstand breakage. Accordingly, temper is coarse and vessel walls tend to be thick. The ware is found in occupation contexts, and especially in midden deposits. It is not found in graves. Coarse Ware was frequently handmade and its color, which varies considerably within the type and even on the same vessel, probably indicates open firing—many of the vessels were likely too large to be effectively and economically fired in a kiln. These factors suggest a household-level of non-specialized production.

So-called Common Ware and Fine Ware, on the other hand, seem to be the product of specialized craft production in terms of achieved standards and the required degree of expertise to produce. Other than the degree to which burnishing co-occurs with certain colors at Hasanlu, these wares were produced using similar techniques in the MBIII, LBA, and Iron I. The archaeological findspots, the range of attested forms, and the frequency of stylistic elaboration demonstrate the use of these "wares" in social and ritual settings—the serving of food and drink, cult practices, and mortuary rituals. Although it is beyond the bounds of the current work, there is a need to reconsider Young's distinction between Common Ware and Fine Ware for the LBA and early Iron Age. These ware definitions appear arbitrary and stem from implicit assumptions regarding emic, diachronic preferences in ware color and, secondarily, in burnishing. The Hasanlu researchers were certainly aware of the predominance of buff-colored wares in the Iron III–IV of western Iran, and apparently they developed a ceramic typology for the earlier Iron Age that was designed to measure assumed diachronic changes in proportions of grey versus buff ceramics. In the LBA and early Iron Age, ware color varies significantly in northern and western Iran and the southern Caucasus. The methods used to produce ceramics, especially the table and serving ware, seem to have been driven by a desire for consistently monochrome, burnished/smooth-surfaced ceramics in a range of colors, especially grey, black, red, and buff in the late 2nd–early 1st millennium BC. These ceramics are often imitations of metal vessels, which are far more rarely attested in the archaeological record.

With regard to diachronic patterns in ware frequency, Young noted that Period V at Hasanlu was divisible into an earlier and later subperiod: "In the Deep Sounding [U22] it is perhaps possible to distinguish an upper and lower phase in Period V. Grey Fine Ware appears to be slightly more common in Stratum 6 (late) than in Stratum 9 (early)…the red-slipped variety of Common Ware is more characteristic of the early strata" (1963:40). The higher incidence of grey in Stratum 6 (Period IVc or the Iron I) fits with the general trend of firing color varying to a higher degree in the earlier MBW horizon.

In U22, the LBA and Iron I MBW assemblage was contained within Strata 6–10. Young oddly made no reference to the Stratum 10 pottery in his dissertation. Young also noted the presence of PKW in the MBW deposit when comparing it to Hasanlu VIb, saying, "These painted wares [from Hasanlu VIb] are distinctively different in many respects from the Period V Painted Ware, which appears as a late and simplified survival in that period" (1963:43).

Early Hasanlu V: Dinkha

At Dinkha Tepe, the lower strata of the so-called early Iron Age trash deposit date to the early LBA. This makes the transition to the LBA somewhat clearer at Dinkha Tepe than at Hasanlu. While the corpus of material from Dinkha is quite small, what it lacks in numbers it surely makes up for with diagnosticity.

As in Period VIa, the LBA ceramic assemblage contains wares and forms that link it to the southern Caucasus. Curiously, such material is absent at Hasanlu V or, for that matter, at Geoy Tepe B,[10] and thus Dinkha presents us with a highly localized phenomenon. In both cases, this absence is likely an effect of sampling and in particular we should not assume chronological continuity between Geoy C and B. Fortunately, certain Early MBW types facilitate cross-sequence comparisons between Dinkha and other sites of the southern and western Lake Urmia Basin and beyond. The general trend at Dinkha from Period VIa to Period V is quite similar to that documented at Shirakavan: the MBIII assemblage containing Karmirvank painted ware and Sevan-Uzerlik black ware is replaced by: "a more homogeneous assemblage containing only ceramics with the distinctive punctate ornamentation of the Sevan-Uzerlik tradition. However, except for this continued tradition of punctate decoration, the pottery from Shirakavan's upper layer is quite distinct morphologically from the shapes of the Middle Bronze III phase" (Smith, Badalyan, and Avetisyan 2009:68). This difference in morphology is not as pronounced at Dinkha, where the assemblage exhibits at least a modicum of continuity in the Early MBW forms of the MBIII and LBA. Given the close parallels between the Early MBW assemblages of Dinkha and Hasanlu in the LBA, it would not be surprising if future excavations at Hasanlu were to reveal more definitive evidence of a MBIII-LBA transition like that of Dinkha.

Hasanlu

At Hasanlu we have few secure early LBA contexts relative to the number of areas excavated, and none are associated with radiocarbon dates. Unlike Dinkha, the Hasanlu assemblage is largely composed of undecorat-

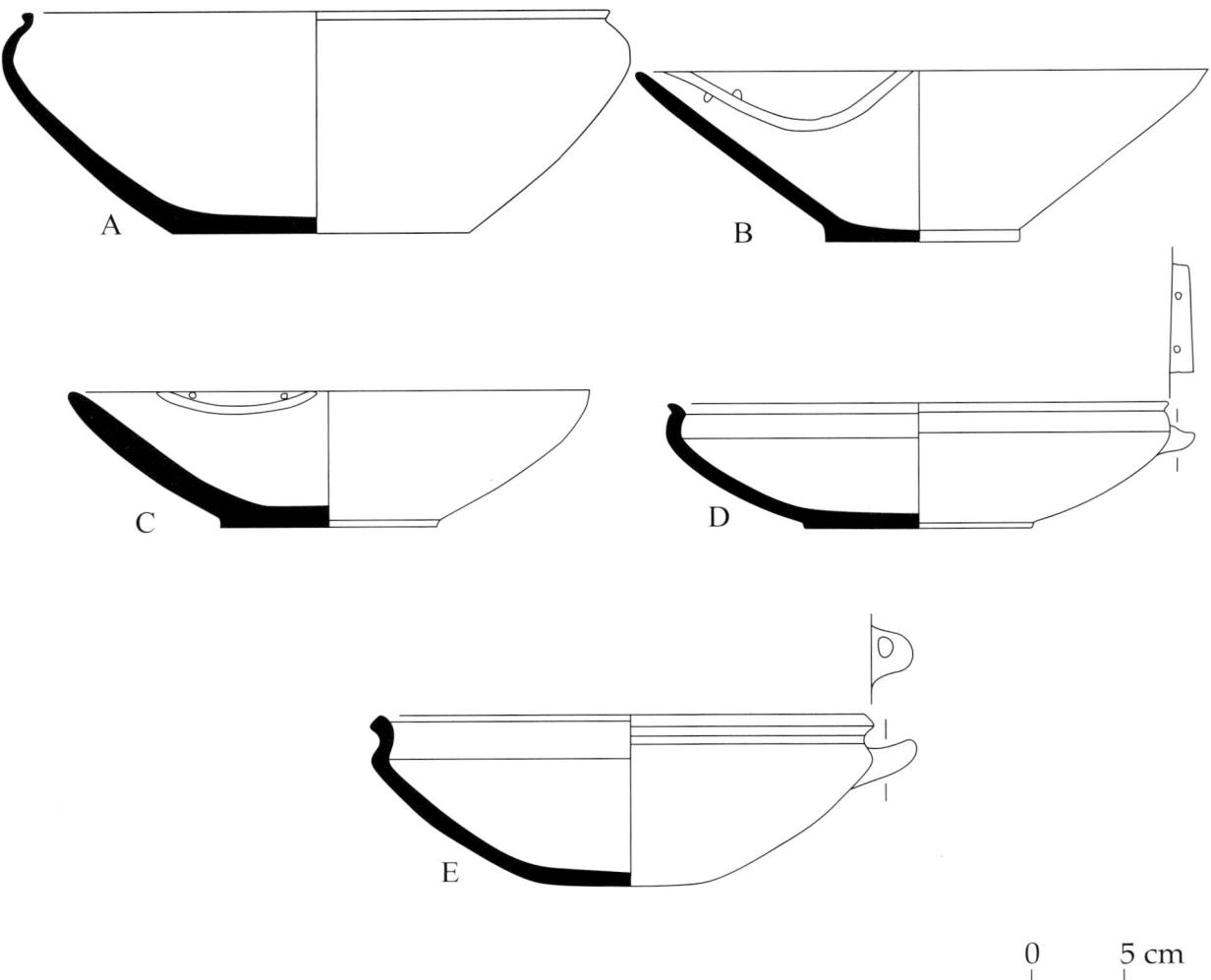

Fig. 4.19 Hasanlu and Dinkha Tepe: bowls from Periods VIa and early V graves.

Fig.	Op.	Context	Ware	Type	Description	Dia.	Disposition
A	Stein Section XV	Grave		Bowl 4		32	—
B	B10b	Burial 15		Bowl 1a	Appliqué Crescent, Drilled Holes	20	—
C	B8a	Burial 17		Bowl 1a	Appliqué Crescent, Drilled Holes	28	—
D	VIa	Grave SK67	MBW IIIc	Bowl 3c	Grey, Double-Pierced Bar Lug	27	TM, HAS59-146
E	LIII	SK116/ Burial 2 LIII	MBW Ic	Bowl 3b	Grey, Pierced Lob Lug	27	UPM60-20-76, HAS59-324

ed MBW. Moreover, Hasanlu provides no "clean" Period VIa/MBIII occupation deposits. By interpreting Hasanlu V–VI in isolation, one could easily exaggerate the degree and rate of change in material culture. Only the lowest mixed deposit of the U22 Sounding (Strata 9–10) and the miniscule samples from Operation I and the Well Sounding yield signs of dating to the earliest part of Period V and VIa. One is immediately struck by the prevalence of Early MBW in types that are largely unattested in the MBA. We must exercise caution in interpreting this "break," however, since the mid-2nd millennium BC sequence from Dinkha provides strong evidence for continuity from the MBIII to the LBA.

The Hasanlu Period V ceramic assemblage of Ušnu-Solduz can no longer be equated with the "Early Western Grey Ware horizon" as previously defined—the ceramic sequence is far more complex and, as we have seen, the old "Hasanlu V" was defined using a mix of periods. In comparison to the succeeding Period IVc/Iron I, the assemblage exhibits a narrow range of simple forms and the rare use of decoration or elaboration of form.

Early Monochrome Burnished Ware and "Buff Ware"

The MBW of early Hasanlu V (early Dinkha III) is not appreciably different from that of the preceding period in terms of the ware itself. Period V is defined by the prevalence of MBW, the paucity of painted ware, and the presence of certain diagnostic formal types. We see some of these types appear for the first time in the lower Dinkha trash deposit and Hasanlu Stratum 10. I have included vessels of "Buff Ware" in MBW, as defined by Young (1965), since such vessels are not appreciably different from MBW in terms of the attested range of forms and often are simply burnished or smoothed buff vessels, with or without slip, and grit temper—that is, only the color might set these vessels apart.

Early Hasanlu V Bowls
One of the more obvious changes in early LBA ceramic assemblages is the decline in Urmia Ware bowls at Dinkha, which are replaced by new forms that occur instead in MBW. At Hasanlu, incurving, carinated, and "worm bowls" are in the majority.

Bowl Types 1–2 "Worm Bowls." One of the more obvious and important markers of the LBA is the so-called worm bowl, which often has an appliquéd crescent ("worm") and/or a pair of drilled holes near the rim. Such large open bowls with simple rims first appear in the MBIII at Dinkha and Geoy Tepe late D–C, but are far better attested in the LBA, and this class of bowls lasts until the early Iron II at Hasanlu. This class exhibits important developmental trends that I believe provide us with one effective means for dividing the LBA and Iron I. Type 1a bowls are high, with straight, flaring sides with angles of 35°–45°. Type 1b bowls also have straight, flaring sides but are a good deal higher, with sides angled as steeply as 60°–70°. Type 1 bowls have flat bases. Type 2 bowls, which approach plates or chargers, are lower and more open. Type 2a examples tend to be finer bowls with straight sides with angles of 15°–30°. Type 2b bowls are also lower, open bowls with the same angling sides as Type 2a; the subtype is differentiated by the appearance of curving sides. A similar range of large bowl types is well attested in northern Mesopotamia in the LBA, albeit in different wares and without appliquéd crescents and drilled holes: such sites include Tell Brak (Oates, Oates, and McDonald 1997: figs. 184:63–73, 185:81–88, 186:110, 187:140–45), Nuzi (see esp. Starr 1937: pl. 85), Tell al-Rimah (Postgate, Oates, and Oates 1997: pls. 34:105–12; 35; 36:138–46; 37), and even in the Syrian Middle Euphrates more broadly (Dornemann 1979: figs. 20:12–13; 24:1), to name but a few locales. The developmental sequences from the MBA to the LBA in Ušnu-Solduz and northern Mesopotamia follow very similar patterns in terms of the prevailing bowl types.

One crude bowl of Type 2a appears in the lower Dinkha trash deposit (Fig. 4.18:A) and two of Type 1a come from Dinkha graves cut into the trash deposit (Fig. 4.19:B–C). At Hasanlu, there are two types of large bowls attested within this class in early Period V (Fig. 4.20:N–R, T). None of the fragmentary bowls from the occupation deposits have extant double drilling or appliquéd crescents. Higher-angled Type 1 bowls are typical of the MBIII and early LBA (Figs. 3.2:D, 4.14:D, 4.20:O, Q, T, 4.19:B–C). As previously mentioned, the type first occurs in Geoy late D–C in Early MBW and Urmia Ware and in Dinkha MBIII in Early MBW (Fig. 4.16:A–B; Burton-Brown 1951: fig. 30 nos. 51, 949, 950, 961; fig. 31 no. 692). Type 2a is attested in early Period V in occupation deposits (Fig. 4.20:R), as is Type 2b (Fig. 4.20:N, P). In the MBIII, a similar type but with a thickened rim oc-

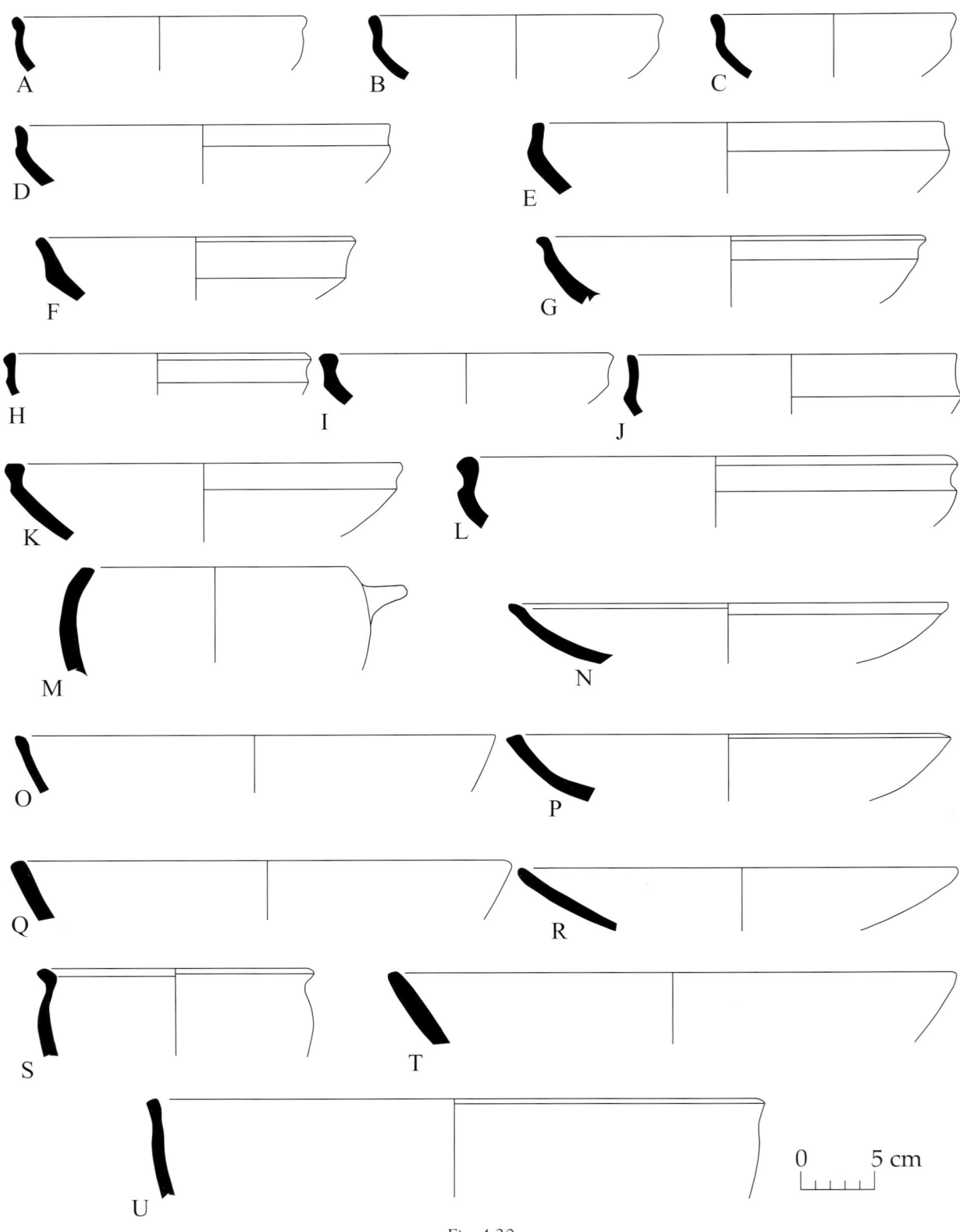

Fig. 4.20

Fig. 4.20 Hasanlu Tepe: early Period V ceramics from the U22 Sounding.

Fig.	Op.	Context	Ware	Type	Description	Dia.	Disposition
A	U22 Str. 10	10	MBW	Bowl 3c	Int. Grey, Matte; Ext. Black, Slipped, Burnished Med.	20	UPM Sherd 81
B	U22 Str. 10	10	MBW	Bowl 3c	Black	20	UPM Sherd 47 UPM63-5-1059
C	U22	10	Grey IIc	Bowl 3c	Greyish Brown, Burnished	17	UPM Sherd 15b
D	U22 Str. 10	10	Buff Ib	Bowl 3c	L. Pinkish-Grey, Smoothed, Coarse	26	UPM Sherd 46
E	U22 Str. 10	10	MBW Grey IIc	Bowl 3a	Grey, Burnished, Medium	28	UPM Sherd 53
F	U22 Str. 10	10	MBW Grey Ib	Bowl 3	Int. L. Grey, Matte Ext. L. Grey, Smoothed, Medium	22	UPM Sherd 45
G	U22 Str. 9	9	MBW Ic	Bowl 3c	Red	28	UPM Sherd 04
H	U22 Str. 10	10	MBW Grey IIb	Bowl 3b	Int. L. Grey Matte Ext. L. Grey, Smoothed, Medium	21	UPM Sherd 59
I	U22 Str. 10	10	MBW	Bowl 3a	Int. Grey, Matte Ext. Black	20	UPM Sherd 80
J	U22 Str. 10	10	MBW Buff Ic	Bowl 3d	Int. L. Grey, Matte Ext. L. Grey	23	UPM Sherd 25
K	U22 Str. 10	10	MBW Grey Ic	Bowl 3a	Black	27	UPM Sherd 65
L	U22 Str. 10	10	MBW Grey IIc	Bowl 3a	Grey	34	UPM Sherd 48
M	U22 Str. 9	9	MBW Ib	Bowl 5	Int. Pink Slip, Burnished Ext. Pink Slip, Red Slip at Lip, Black Slip or Fire-blackened Body	18	UPM Sherd 08
N	U22 Str. 10	10	MBW IIc	Bowl 2b	L. Grey	30	UPM Sherd 21
O	U22	10	MBW IIc	Bowl 1b	Greyish Brown	32	UPM Sherd 14b
P	U22 Str. 10	10	MBW IIc	Bowl 2b	L. Grey. Probably same vessel as No. 21	30	UPM Sherd 22 –
Q	U22 Str. 10	10	MBW IIc	Bowl 1b	Grey	34	UPM Sherd 49
R	U22 Str. 10	10	MBW IIc	Bowl 2a	Grey	30	UPM Sherd 67 UPM63-5-1062
S	U22 Str. 9	9	Grey Ib	Bowl 19	Ext. Black, Burnished Int. Grey, Matte	19	UPM Sherd 01 UPM 63-5-1008
T	U22 Str. 10	10	MBW Ic	Bowl 1b	Int. Grey, Smoothed Ext. Black, Slipped, Burnished, Coarse	39	UPM Sherd 50
U	U22 Str. 9	9	MBW Ic	Bowl 17	Int. Orangish-Buff, Matte Ext. Orangish-Buff, Red Slip, Burnish, Coarse	42	UPM Sherd 06

190

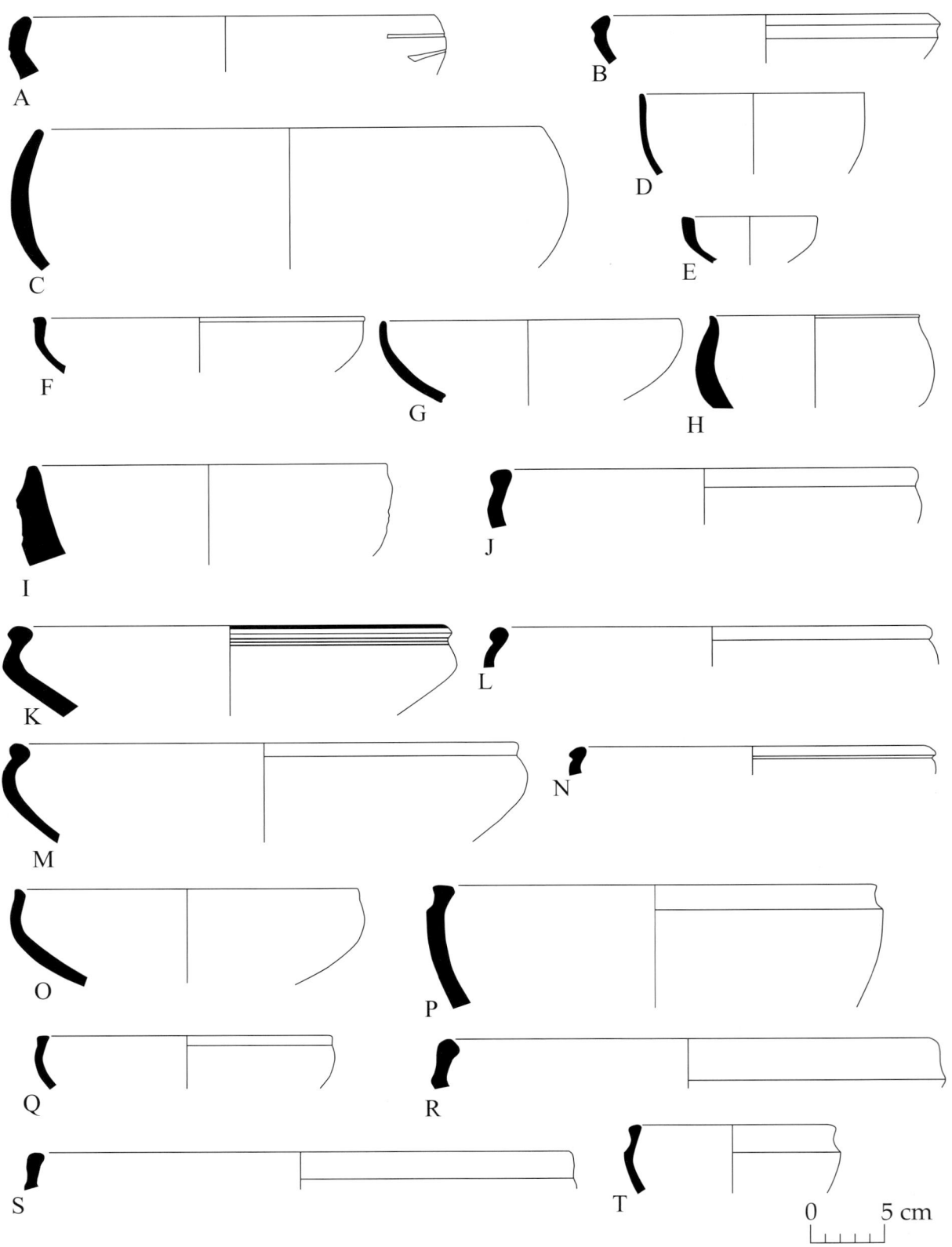

Fig. 4.21

Fig. 4.21 Hasanlu Tepe: early Period V ceramics from the U22 Sounding.

Fig.	Op.	Context	Ware	Type	Description	Dia.	Disposition
A	U22	10	"Red Ware"	Bowl 7	Red, Matte, Incised	28	UPM Sherd 15
B	U22	10	MBW IIc	Bowl 7	Grey, Burnished	23	UPM Sherd 26
C	U22	10	MBW	Bowl 5	Int. Orange, Matte Ext. D. Grey, Burnished	35	UPM Sherd 02
D	U22	10	MBW IIc	Bowl 8	Int. L. Grey, Matte Ext. Black, Slipped, H. Burnished	15	UPM Sherd 64
E	U22	9	MBW IIc	Bowl 8	Ext. Grey, Burnished Int. Grey, Matte	9	UPM Sherd 02
F	U22	10	MBW IIc	Bowl 8	D. Grey, Burnished, Medium	22	UPM Sherd 58
G	U22	10	MBW IIb	Bowl 8	Red-Orange	20	UPM Sherd 06
H	U22	10	MBW IIb	Bowl 8	Red, Tan Slip, Smoked	14	UPM Sherd 08
I	U22	10	CPW	Bowl 12	Buff, Coarse, Mold-Made	24	UPM Sherd 05
J	U22	10	MBW Ic	Bowl 4	Int. Grey, Matte Ext. Grey, Burnished, Medium	29	UPM Sherd 52
K	U22	10	MBW Ic	Bowl 4	Reddish-Buff, Burnished, Red Painted Horizontal Bands, Lower Body Black-Slipped or Fire Blackened, Coarse	30	UPM Sherd 88
L	U22	10	MBW IIc	Bowl 4	Black	30	UPM Sherd 62
M	U22	10	MBW IIc	Bowl 4	Grey	30	UPM Sherd 51
N	U22	10	MBW IIc	Bowl 4	Int. L. Grey, Matte Ext. D. Grey, Slipped, Burnished	25	UPM Sherd 61
O	U22	10	MBW IIc	Bowl 5	Grey	23	UPM Sherd 24
P	U22	10		Bowl 6	Grey	30	UPM Sherd 77
Q	U22	10	MBW IIc	Bowl 5	Black	20	UPM Sherd 66
R	U22	10	MBW IIb	Bowl 6	Ext. D. Grey, Smoothed Int. Pinkish-Buff, Matte, Medium	34	UPM Sherd 11
S	U22	10	MBW IIc	Bowl 6	D. Grey	37	UPM Sherd 60
T	U22	10	MBW Ic	Bowl 6	Grey	14	UPM Sherd No #

curs in Geoy C in Urmia Ware (Burton-Brown 1951: fig. 32 no. 959). Type 2 continues into later Period V and, in a modified hemispherical form, occurs in Period IVc, as well. Type 1 probably represents the forerunner of Type 2. The co-occurrence of the two types in U22 Stratum 10 is inconclusive with regard to establishing the degree of overlap between the two types since the assemblage derives from a mix of strata, possibly Period VIa and early V, which was cut by a later (late Hasanlu V/early Hasanlu IVc) pit that was not detected during excavation (see Chapter 3). A certain amount of contamination of the context thus seems inevitable. Turning to grave groups to resolve the issue, we see that this class of bowl is one of the more common vessels included in LBA and Iron I burials (Seriation), but only one bowl was included per grave and thus we cannot document the co-occurrence of the two types in these critical short-term contexvts. Neither type occurs in grave groups with button-base or early pedestal-base tankards at either Hasanlu or Dinkha.[11] Type 2 tends to co-occur with later varieties of bridgeless-spouted jars, and one example of Type 1 occurs with the early variety of such jars, lending support to a developmental sequence, which pro-

192

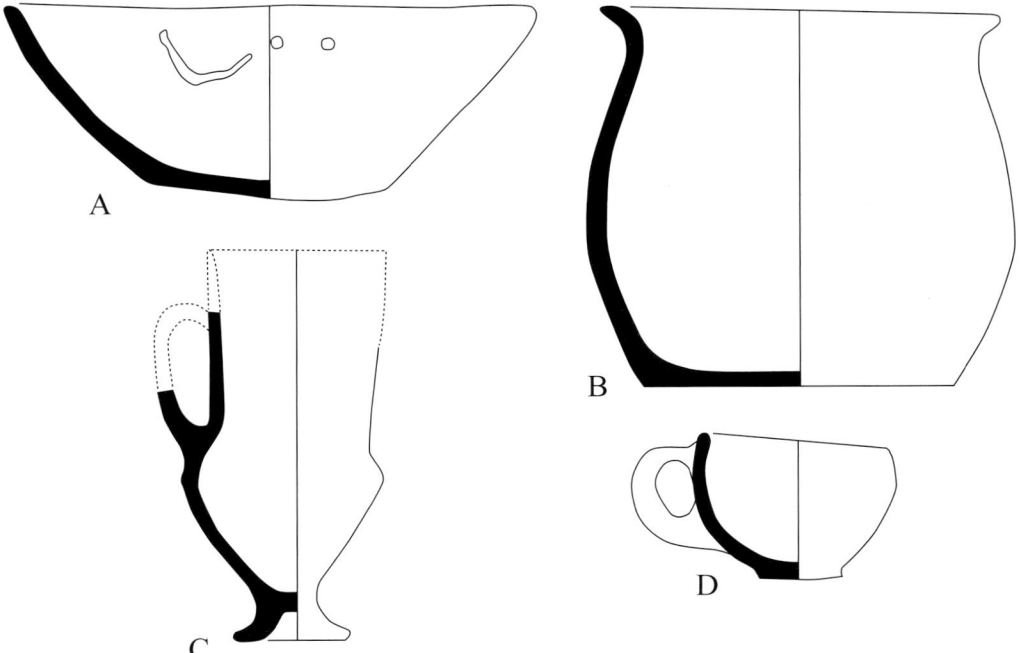

Fig. 4.22a Geoy Tepe: lower Tomb K.

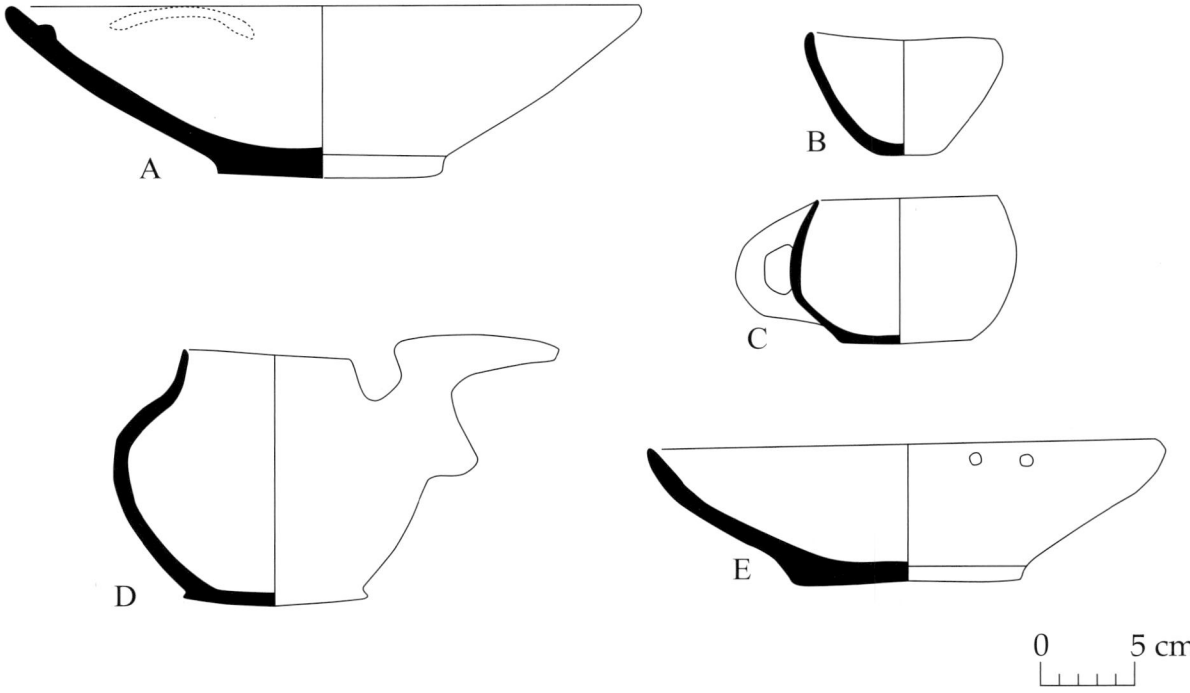

Fig. 4.22b Geoy Tepe: upper Tomb K.

gressed from Type 1 to Type 2 (Seriation). At Geoy Tepe B, a bowl of Type 1 and two of Type 2 were found in Tomb K, but rather than refuting the argument for a developmental sequence this assemblage appears to lend support. This tomb was used over an extended period of time and contained multiple interments (Burton-Brown 1951:142–45). Twelve bodies had been placed in the stone tomb and then covered with earth, seemingly in a gradual succession, creating an internal stratigraphic sequence. In the lowest part of the tomb, a Type 1b bowl with crescent and double drilling was found alongside a pedestal-base tankard, vat, and mug (Fig. 4.22a). In the upper/later part of the tomb (Fig. 4.22b), two Type 2 bowls, one with a crescent that Burton-Brown described as a "crescent-shaped handle in relief" (1951:149 no. 2, fig. 16 no. 2)—the crescent is not illustrated—and another with double drilling (drilling not illustrated, Burton-Brown 1951:149 no. 478, fig. 32 no. 478), were found with a bridgeless-spouted jar, beaker, and mug. At Dinkha and Hasanlu, over time the "worm bowl" class seldom bore the appliquéd crescent and instead was double-drilled or, in occupation deposits at Hasanlu, received a double crescent (see late Period V and IVc, below).

Bowl Type 3 Carinated Bowls. Carinated bowls which grade into semi-hemispherical bowls, with straight or slightly everted rims, are typical of Period V; examples occasionally have single loop handles (Figs. 4.18:E, 4.20:A–L). Five subtypes occur in Period V that are defined by rim type and body height above the point of carination, both of which appear broadly indicative of time period. Type 3a bowls are carinated by pinching the sides of the vessel to form the carination and, usually, a slightly thickened rim. Type 3b is similar to 3a, although the indentation left by forming the carination is more pronounced. Type 3c is characterized by a more rounded body form and a slightly everted simple or thickened rim. Type 3d occurs in Period VIa and early V but is typical of later Period V and represents a trend toward bowls with lower carination points and concomitantly the presence of vessel walls above the point of carination. These bowls generally have everted simple rims. The type is likely the predecessor of bowl Type 9 (see Late Period V and IVc, below).

There is a great deal of variation within Type 3. A single occurrence of Type 3a has a slightly inverted rim (Fig. 4.20:E). Bowls with markedly inverted rims are grouped under Type 6 (see below). Some Type 3c bowls lack obvious points of carination (Fig. 4.20:A, C) and, with a larger sample, might be found to constitute a new type. Rims are occasionally thickened (Fig. 4.20:H, I, K, L). Such bowls, admittedly a fairly generic form, are present throughout Period VIb, but most of the bowls in Period VIa were made in Urmia Ware and were ellipsoid. The sheer number of these bowls at Hasanlu in early Period V is noteworthy. Two were found in graves at Hasanlu (Fig. 4.19:D–E). Both have vertically pierced lugs and were found with tall tankards of Type 1 (Seriation: SK116, SK67).

Bowl Types 4–7 Incurving Bowls. The incurving bowl with various rim treatments typifies early Period V. Type 4, medium-to-large bowls with thickened rims, is one of the more diagnostic types of this class (Fig. 4.21:J–N). Stein found one red-slipped and burnished bowl of this type at Hasanlu in a grave with an Urmia Ware jar of Type 6 (Figs. 4.19:A, Seriation; see Chapter 5). Type 4 continues into late Period V but is quite rare in Period IVc. With the exception of the grave excavated by Stein, Type 4 is absent in the graves of Hasanlu or Dinkha. Type 5 incurving bowls have simple rims (Fig. 4.21:C, O, Q). Type 6, inverted carinated bowls with thickened rims (Figs. 4.18:D, 4.21:P, R–T), resemble bowls from Geoy Tepe B (Burton-Brown 1951: fig. 33 nos. 1003, 336), and the form is typical of Lchashen-Metsamor 1 (Smith, Badalyan, and Avetisyan 2009: fig. 24: g–h). Similar but smaller bowls are also known from LBA Mitanni contexts in northern Mesopotamia (Oates, Oates, and McDonald 1997: fig. 186 nos. 96–98). Type 7 bowls are sharply incurving, thick-bodied bowls that probably developed from Urmia Ware bowls of Period VIa; one example is incised (Fig. 4.21:A, B).

Bowl Type 8 Simple Bowls. Small bowls of this type may be drinking vessels (Fig. 4.21:D–H), and larger examples do not differ appreciably. Such bowls/cups occur in many time periods and taken alone are of little value in dating assemblages.

Bowl Type 19. This deep bowl with simple everted rim is rare within the assemblage and verges on classification as a holemouth jar (Fig. 4.20:S). A similar vessel was found in the lower MBW deposit of Hasanlu Operation 1 (Fig. 4.14:A).

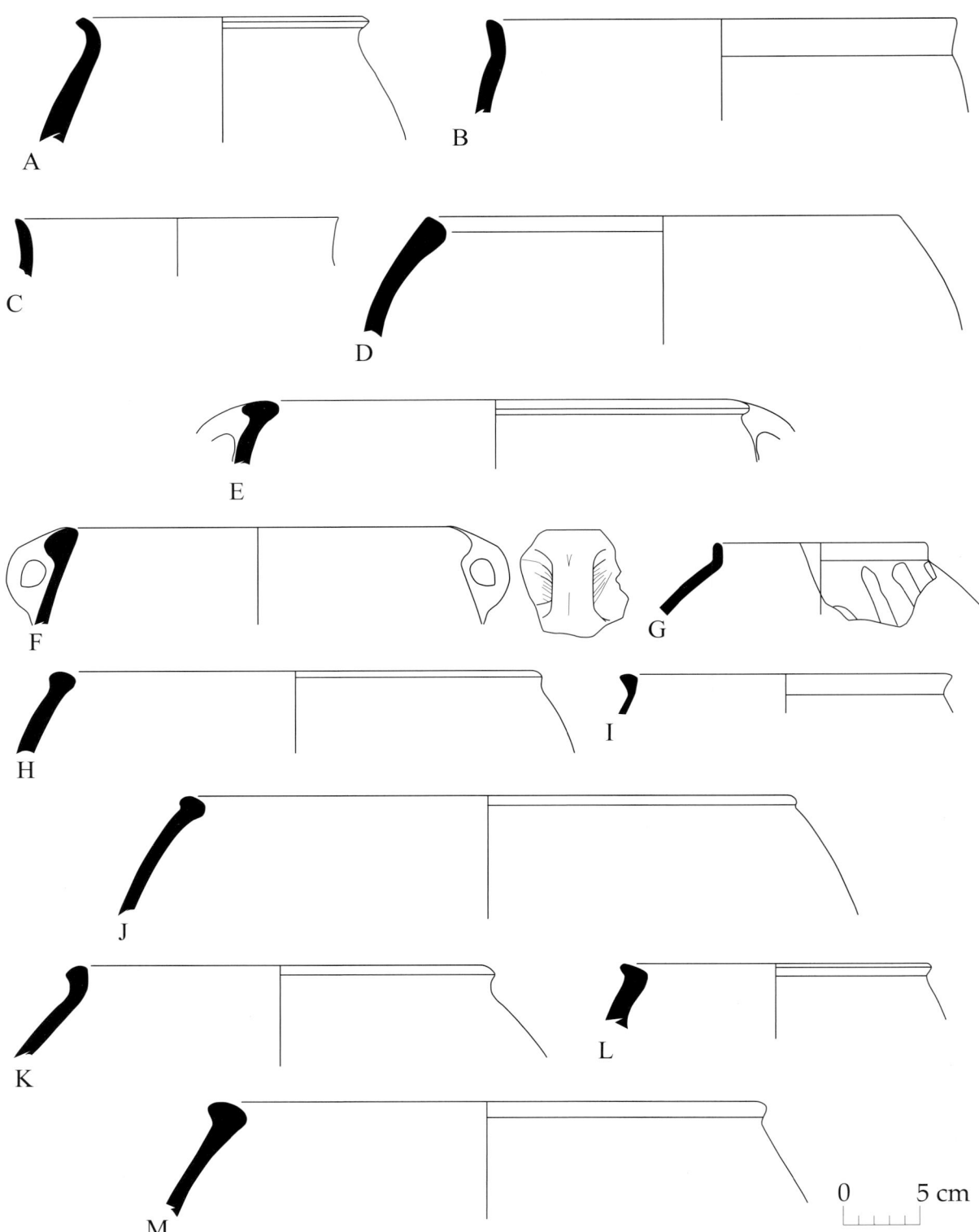

Fig. 4.23

Fig. 4.23 Hasanlu Tepe: early Period V ceramics from the U22 Sounding (opposite).

Fig.	Op.	Context	Ware	Type	Description	Dia.	Disposition
A	U22	10	MBW IIb	HM 1	Int. Red, Matte Ext. Red, Smoothed	19	UPM Sherd 18
B	U22	10	MBW IVc	HM 1	Int. Reddish Buff Matte Ext. Red-Black Mottled	31	UPM Sherd 14
C	U22	10	MBW IIIc	HM 1	NR	21	No#
D	U22	10	MBW IIb	HM 2	Orangish-Buff	32	UPM Sherd 13
E	U22	10	MBW IVb	HM 3	Int. Red, Matte Ext. Red Slip, Blackened	33	UPM Sherd 12 UPM63-5-1015
F	U22	10	Buff Ia	HM 3	Red, Matte, Loop Handle(s)	28	UPM Sherd 17 UPM63-5-1017
G	U22	10	MBW	HM 9	Int. Grey, Matte Ext. Black, Burnished Appliqué	14	UPM Sherd 79
H	U22	10	MBW IVa	HM 4	Grey	32	UPM Sherd 04 Coll.
I	U22	10	Misfired MBW IIb	HM 5	Mottled Black, Greyish-Buff, Purplish Buff	21	UPM Sherd 27
J	U22	10	MBW IIb	HM 4	Red	40	UPM Sherd 03
K	U22	10	MBW Ic	HM 1	Int. L. Grey, Matte Ext. D. Mottled Grey, Slipped, Burnished	28	UPM Sherd 01
L	U22	9	MBW Ic	HM 6	Ext. Orangish Buff Slipped and Burnished Int. Reddish Buff Matte	21	UPM Sherd 05 63-5-1058
M	U22	10	Buff IIa	HM 4	Pinkish Buff, Matte	36	UPM Sherd 16

Early Hasanlu V Holemouth Vessels

Holemouth vessels are abundant in the early LBA deposit at Hasanlu, but few were found at early LBA Dinkha or Geoy Tepe B. In MBIII Dinkha, such vessels are attested in MBW and Incised and Impressed Ware (see above). Their scarcity in early LBA Dinkha is an effect of sampling and possibly the nature of the excavated context, which might be functionally specialized even though a "trash deposit."

Holemouth Jar Type 1. This ovoid jar/pot is defined by its low, sloping shoulder and simple out-turned rim (Figs. 4.23:A–C, K, 4.24:B, H). Type 1 jars endure from the MBIII to the Iron II.

Holemouth Jar Types 2–5. This class of holemouth jar dominates this vessel series at Hasanlu. Type 2, a large ovoid jar with slightly thickened rim, is unique within the assemblage (Fig. 4.23:D). Type 3 consists of medium-to-large ovoid jars with slightly everted, thickened rims or ledge rims (Figs. 4.23:E, F, 4.24:F). Handles are common, and one jar was decorated with a band of pattern-burnish decoration at the shoulder (Fig. 4.24:F). Type 4 represents large storage vessels with round rim profiles (Figs. 4.23:H, J, M, 4.24:D, G). Type 5 is a finer version of Type 4 (Fig. 4.23:I) and is unique. One Type 3 jar from Dinkha Tepe has a spout (Fig. 4.18:I).

Holemouth Jar Type 6. This small jar has a flattened rim (Fig. 4.23:L) and is virtually unique. The type is typical of EBA cooking pots and may be extrusive from the lower U22 Sounding deposit—one other example occurs in Period IVc–early IVb (see below).

Holemouth Jar Type 7. This large holemouth jar has a vertical rim that is round in profile (Fig. 4.24:E). It is unique in the U22 assemblage.

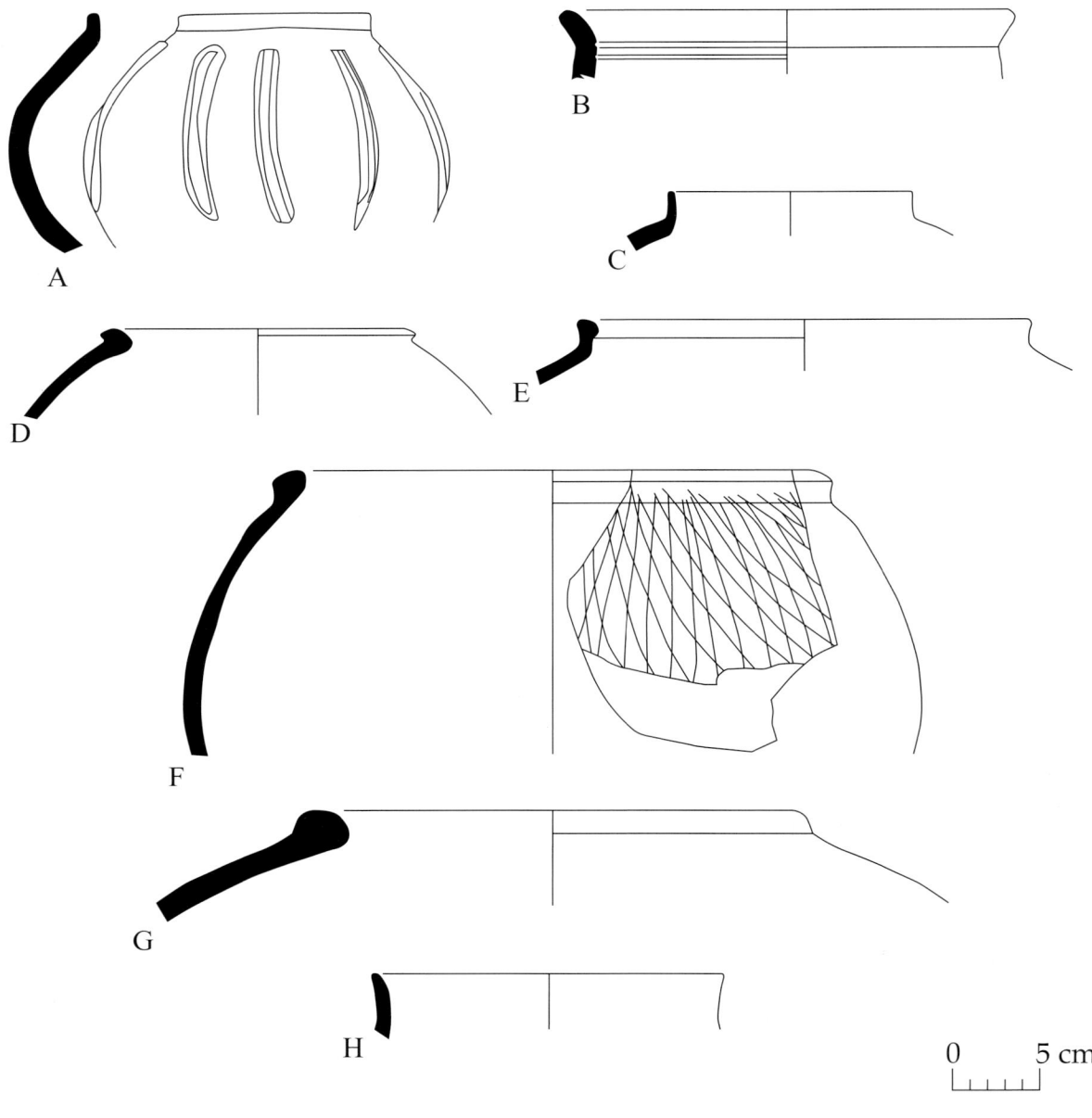

Fig. 4.24

Holemouth Jar Types 8–10. When found whole in graves at Dinkha Tepe, small holemouth jars of this class—comprised of three types—always have bridgeless spouts (see Chapter 5); these same jar types, however, are found without extant spouts at Hasanlu in occupation deposits. This assertion is based on whole or nearly whole vessels since, in sherd collections from occupation deposits, spouts and rims are virtually never preserved on the same sherd, confounding classification. Bridgeless spouts are arguably the most recognizable and ubiquitous single ceramic attribute associated with the later 2nd millennium BC of northern and western Iran—at least insofar as material has been chosen for publication. They date to the LBA and the Iron I in the southern Lake Urmia Basin, but are far more common in the later LBA and Iron I, and this class of

Fig. 4.24 Hasanlu Tepe: early Period V ceramics from the U22 Sounding (opposite).

Fig.	Op.	Context	Ware	Type	Description	Dia.	Disposition
A	U22	10	MBW IIa	HM 9	Int. Matt Grey-Black Ext. Grey-Black Smoothed Mottled	12	UPM Sherd 72, 78 UPM 63-5-1021
B	U22	10	Buff Ia	HM 1	Buff, Matte	26	UPM Sherd 15
C	U22	10	MBW IIc	HM 9	Int. D. Grey, Matte Ext. D. Grey, Slipped	14	UPM Sherd 70
D	U22	10	MBW IIc	HM 4	Int. Black, Matte Ext. Black, Burnished	18	UPM Sherd 69
E	U22	10	MBW IIc	HM 7	Grey	26	UPM Sherd 82
F	U22	10	MBW IIC	HM 3	Int. Purplish-Grey, Matte Ext. Purplish Grey, Pattern Burnish Deco.	32	UPM Sherd 84
G	U22	10	MBW IIc	HM 4	Black	29	UPM Sherd 85
H	U22	10	MBW IIc	HM 1	Int. Pinkish-Buff, Matte Ext. Pinkish Buff, Slipped, Burnished	20	UPM Sherd 09

vessel evolves over time. Such spouts were added to holemouth jars and "true" jars.

Holemouth Jar Type 8. This ovoid jar has no neck—making it a true holemouth vessel—a small rim diameter and a bridgeless spout (Fig. 4.25:F). The spout is partly missing, but appears to be angling upward, a feature unique to this vessel. The vessel has a "tail," defined as an appliqué element opposite the jar's spout end, and only the slightest indication of a "beard"—a thin protuberance aligned to the transverse midline of the spout aperture but in this case uniquely attached to the vessel body. Bridgeless-spouted and bridge-spouted jars seem to be highly stylized theriomorphic bird vessels (depicting pelicans and possibly other aquatic birds common to Lake Urmia and neighboring lakes?) popular from the LBA to the Iron II. A similar type of bird vessel occurs in the MBA Tomb B10a B27 (Seriation). In Hasanlu IVb, one bridge-spouted jar was provided with clearly defined anatomical features (HAS64-863), and it is possible such vessels grew out of MBA traditions of theriomorphic vessels and spouted bowls and jars (e.g., at Dinkha, Salmas, Geoy). The bridgeless spout is the one morphological feature in the LBA ceramics of Ušnu-Solduz that might have originated in the Iranian Plateau and southwestern Central Asia. Unlike the southern Caucasus, in Ušnu-Solduz jars with bridgeless spouts do not occur with painted wares and are never painted. This vessel, from a Dinkha grave, is unique and is possibly the earliest attested bridgeless-spouted jar from Hasanlu and Dinkha. Significantly, it is the only vessel of this class to be found with a high tankard (Fig. 4.26:F), a marker of the early LBA (Seriation: Dinkha VII Burial 2). The early date of this vessel is additionally supported by the grave's stratigraphic position (Muscarella 1974:38–40). While no bridgeless-spouted jars occur in the LBA graves of Hasanlu, one bridgeless spout was found in Stratum 10 of the U22 sounding. *It is the only securely attested LBA spout of this kind from the site* (Fig. 4.27:FF). Two bridgeless spouts were found in Period IVc contexts (Fig. 4.47:J, K) and another was found in a mixed Period V–IVc deposit (Fig. 4.40:P). One bridgeless spout was found in the lower trash deposit of Dinkha (Fig. 4.18:T). None of these spouts were found with preserved vessel rims. The marked contrast in the presence of bridgeless-spouted jars in Dinkha graves versus those of Hasanlu is possibly due to differences in the dates of the cemetery exposures (in other words, issues of sampling). The graves from Hasanlu largely date to early Period V, while the Dinkha graves date mostly to late Period V and Period IVc. Alternatively, regional differences in

198

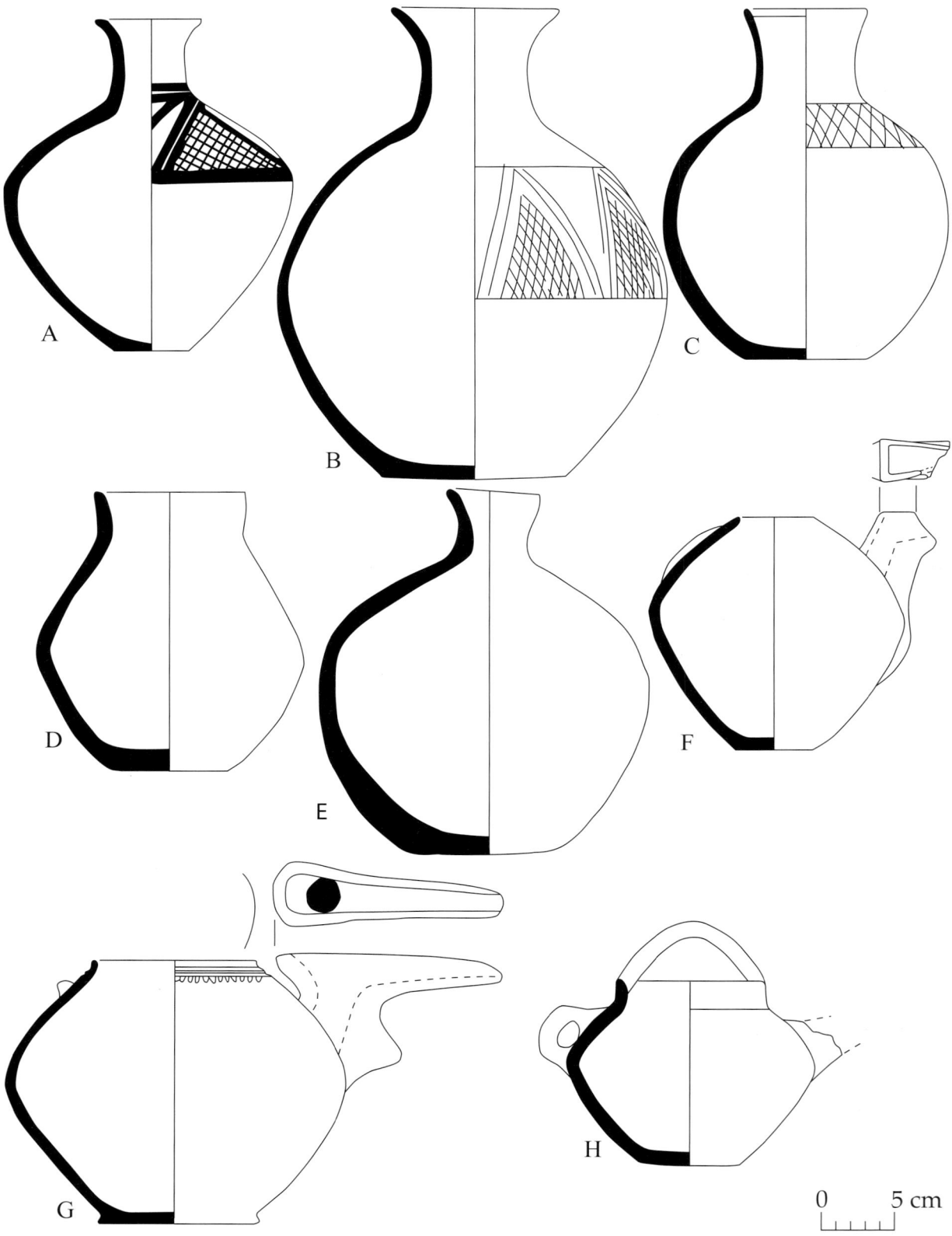

Fig. 4.25

Fig. 4.25 Hasanlu and Dinkha Tepe: jars from Periods VIa and early V graves.

Fig.	Op.	Context	Ware	Type	Description	Dia.	Disposition
A	Dinkha B9a	Burial 25	UW	Jar 6a	NR	7.5	—
B	Stein Section 15	Burial	UW	Jar 6a	NR	11	—
C	VIj	Str. 5 Burial SK504	MBW	Jar 6a	Pattern Burnish	8.5	HAS64-580
D	Dinkha B10b	Burial 13	—	Jar 1a	NR	10.5	—
E	VI	Burial SK29	—	Jar 6b	NR	6	HAS57-187
F	Dinkha VII	Burial 2	—	HM 8	NR	5	—
G	Dinkha B10b	Burial 13	—	HM 10	NR	11	—
H	Dinkha B8e	Burial 7	—	HM 15	NR=	10	—

the early LBA ceramic assemblages of Ušnu and Solduz—seemingly present in the MBIII and early LBA assemblages in the presence/absence of Incised and Impressed MBW, for example—might also have contributed to this situation.

Holemouth Jar Type 9. Type 9 jars only occur in occupation deposits at Hasanlu (Figs. 4.23:G, 4.24:A, C), but the type represents the most common holemouth form in the graves of Dinkha in late Period V (Seriation). The type has a slightly out-turned simple rim and later whole examples exhibit a more pronounced carination at mid-body, as do other contemporary jar types of later Period V and IVc, often giving the vessel a slightly elliptical shape. One globular jar from U22 has raised vertical ribs on the upper body (Fig. 4.24:A) and another has oblique excised bands (Fig. 4.23:G). Such decoration is not typical of the jars of Dinkha and stylistic elaborations in the attested spouted varieties are generally more common in the late 2nd millennium BC.

Holemouth Jar Type 10. This jar is also unique and was found in a LBA grave at Dinkha with an early (Type 1) "worm bowl" (Figs. 4.25:G, 4.19:B) and a bag-shaped jar of Type 1a (Fig. 4.25:D). The bridgeless-spouted holemouth jar has a slightly out-turned rim but otherwise is of the true holemouth variety similar to Holemouth Type 8. The form is globular and the rim diameter is larger than that seen in Type 8. The vessel has a more pronounced "beard" than Type 8, a lug-like tail, a disc base, and a band of incised decoration just beneath the rim.

Holemouth Jar Type 15 Teapots. One so-called teapot of early Period V was found at Dinkha Tepe (Fig. 4.25:H). The whole example, found in a grave with a Type 1 "worm bowl" (Figs. 4.19:C, Seriation: Dinkha B8e Burial 7), has a basket handle and loop handle at the back. The jar is hemispherical with a short, vertical simple rim. An example from Geoy Tepe has two spouts (Burton-Brown 1951: fig. 33 no. 19). Other than this teapot, there is a noticeable lack of holemouth vessels at Geoy Tepe.

Early Hasanlu V Cups and Jars

Jars and cups make up a small proportion of the MBW assemblage from Hasanlu and Dinkha Tepe. The absence of jars/closed forms in Period VIa Dinkha is difficult to explain, but the published assemblage from Geoy C lacks true jars as well and instead has semi-open forms such as vats, tall "casserole" forms (to borrow a term from Late Chalcolithic ceramic terminology), and holemouth jars—often referred to as "pots" or, for smaller vessels, *pyxides*.

Cup Type 1 Tankards. The mid-to-late 2nd–early 1st millennia BC drinking vessels of northwestern Iran are especially diagnostic for dating purposes. Tall, carinated tankards of Type 1 are a hallmark of Period V, although they first appear in Period VIa. Shorter button-base tankards and shouldered beakers also date to Period VIa and early Period V. I have subdivided the tankards according to the style of base. As previously discussed, Type 1a are button-base tankards and appear to be an early type occurring in Period VIa and early V. The early examples are shorter than the later

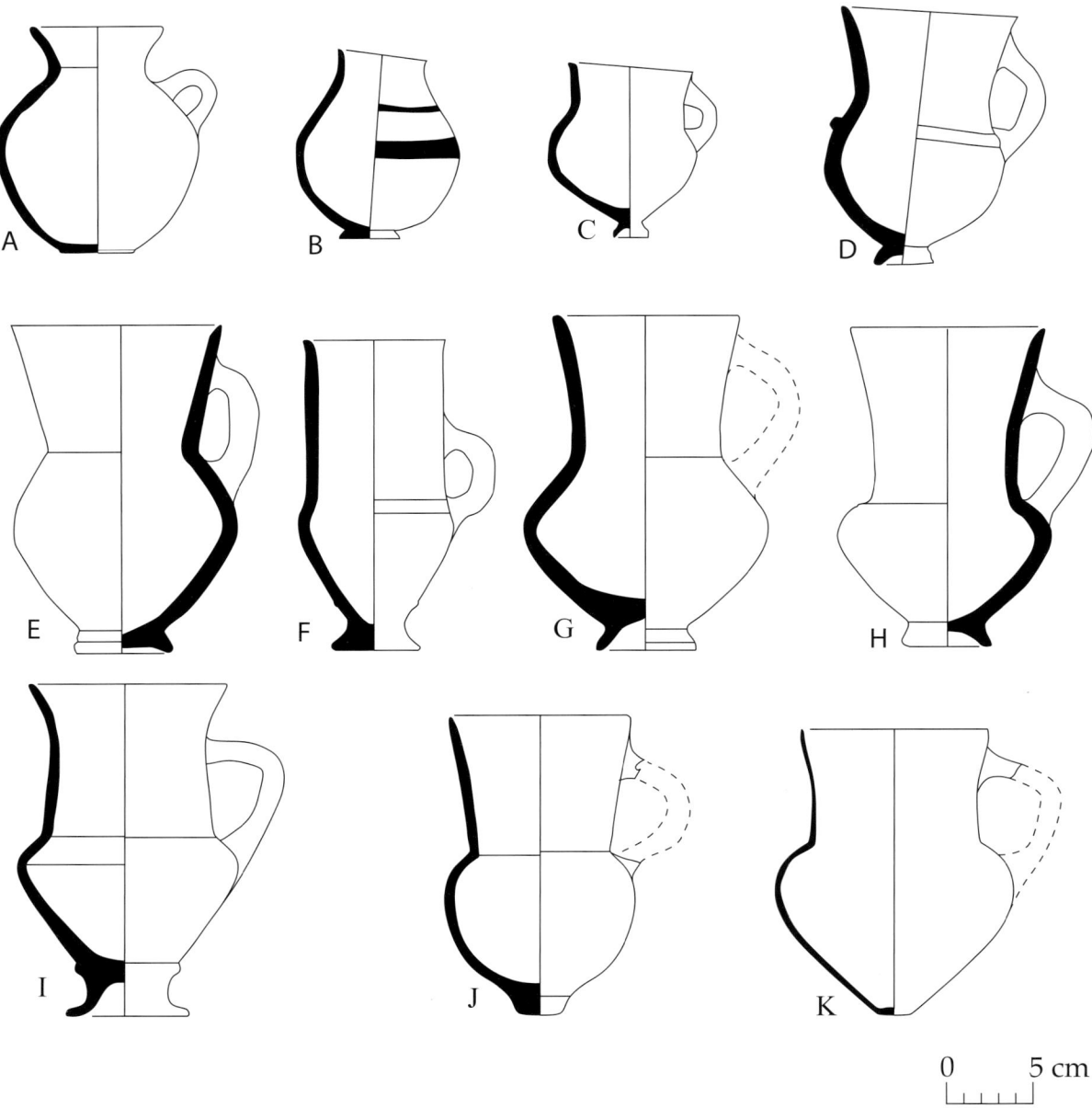

Fig. 4.26

Type 1a–b tankards. Type 1b is a broader category encompassing pedestal bases, including solid-footed and ring bases (Fig. 4.26:E–I). Type 1c is attested by only two vessels from early LBA graves at Hasanlu (Fig. 4.26:J–K). Fragments of tankards were also found in early LBA occupation deposits at Dinkha and what are likely mixed MBIII/early LBA occupation deposits at Hasanlu. These tankards appear to be earlier if their low height is in fact chronologically diagnostic (Figs. 4.18:F, G, 4.27:H). They are usually made from grey-to-black MBW and tend to be heavily burnished.

Type 1 tankards often have a sharp carination or shoulder at the join between the upper and lower half of the vessel. Several bases, handle fragments, and rim sherds from Hasanlu represent portions of this ubiquitous form (Fig. 4.27:A, C, D, I, N–T, V, W) or derive

Fig. 4.26 Hasanlu and Dinkha Tepe: cups and small jars from Periods VIa and early V graves (opposite).

Fig.	Op.	Context	Ware	Type	Description	Dia.	Disposition
A	LIII	Burial SK116	MBW Ic	Jar 1a	Grey	8	HAS59-325
B	VI	Burial SK25	PKW	Cup 8a	NR	3.5	HAS57-127, TM10534
C	VI	Burial SK25	MBW - -	Cup 1a	Grey	6	HAS57-126, TM10538
D	VI	SK29	MBW - -	Cup 1a	Grey	10	HAS57-159, UPM 58-4-52
E	Dinkha B9a	Burial 25	MBW	Cup 1b	NR	12	—
F	Dinkha VII	Burial 2	MBW	Cup 1b	NR	8	—
G	VIJ	Str. 5 Burial SK504	NR	Cup 1b	NR	11	HAS64-579, MMA 65-163-75
H	Dinkha B10a	Burial 23		Cup 1b	NR	11	—
I	LIII	Burial SK116	MBW Ib	Cup 1b	Grey	12	HAS59-323, UPM 60-20-58
J	VIa	Str. 11 Area 2 Burial SK67	MBW Ia	Cup 1c	Grey	11	HAS59-147, TM 10915
K	VIc	Str. 5 Burial SK445/449	MBW	Cup 1c	NR	11	HAS64-335, UPM 65-31-88

from shouldered beakers. The upper portion of such vessels consists of a straight or flaring neck with simple rim. The lower body tends to be globular, conic, or ovoid depending on the form of the base. Handles tend to be round in profile and are usually attached below the rim and at the widest point of the carination. Terminal MBII cups with handles have the same rudimentary form as the LBA tankards, but almost always lack bases and have handles attached at the rim. I would argue for continuity between the MBA and LBA for this important diagnostic in Ušnu-Solduz and, more generally, such is likely the case for the footed goblets/beakers and tankards of northwestern Iran, as well—perhaps best seen in the developmental sequence of Giyan (Henrickson 1983–1984:211–14, fig. C). As is the case with the button-base beakers and tankards of the MBIII and early LBA, the tall tankards of the early LBA seem to follow developments in contemporary drinking vessels in Mesopotamia. Henrickson has indicated parallels with Kassite drinking vessels and one example from Nuzi (1983–1984:n38), the key difference being the addition of handles in northwestern Iran and the obvious differences in wares. I would add to this list other Mitanni shouldered beakers as strong parallels to tall tankards (Postgate, Oates, and Oates 1997:fig. 72:750, 751).

The terminology employed by various authors to describe the bases of 2nd millennium BC drinking vessels has tended to gloss over the high degree of variation manifest in the beakers, goblets, and tankards of the MBIII and LBA, with most bases described as belonging to the "button" or "pedestal" types. True button bases, defined as having a constricted joining point with the lower body and a short concavo-convex profile, seem to date quite early in the ceramic sequence of Ušnu-Solduz, to Period VIa–early V (Figs. 4.16:N, 4.26:C–D). At Hasanlu, whole tankards with such bases were found only in MBIII and early LBA graves (see Chapter 5, SK25 and SK29) and have profiles reminiscent of the drinking vessels of MBII–III rather than the sharply carinated body form typical of other tall LBA tankards. Button bases appear to develop into increasingly higher and wider ring and pedestal bases in Period V (Seriation) with the notable exception of two vessels with nipple bases, likely a Mesopotamian influence (Fig. 4.26:J–K).

The two fragmentary tankards from the lower Dinkha trash deposit lack bases (Fig. 4.18:F–G), but we know from other examples from Hasanlu and Geoy Tepe that pedestal bases are the norm in Period V. At least one tankard with a low pedestal base was found

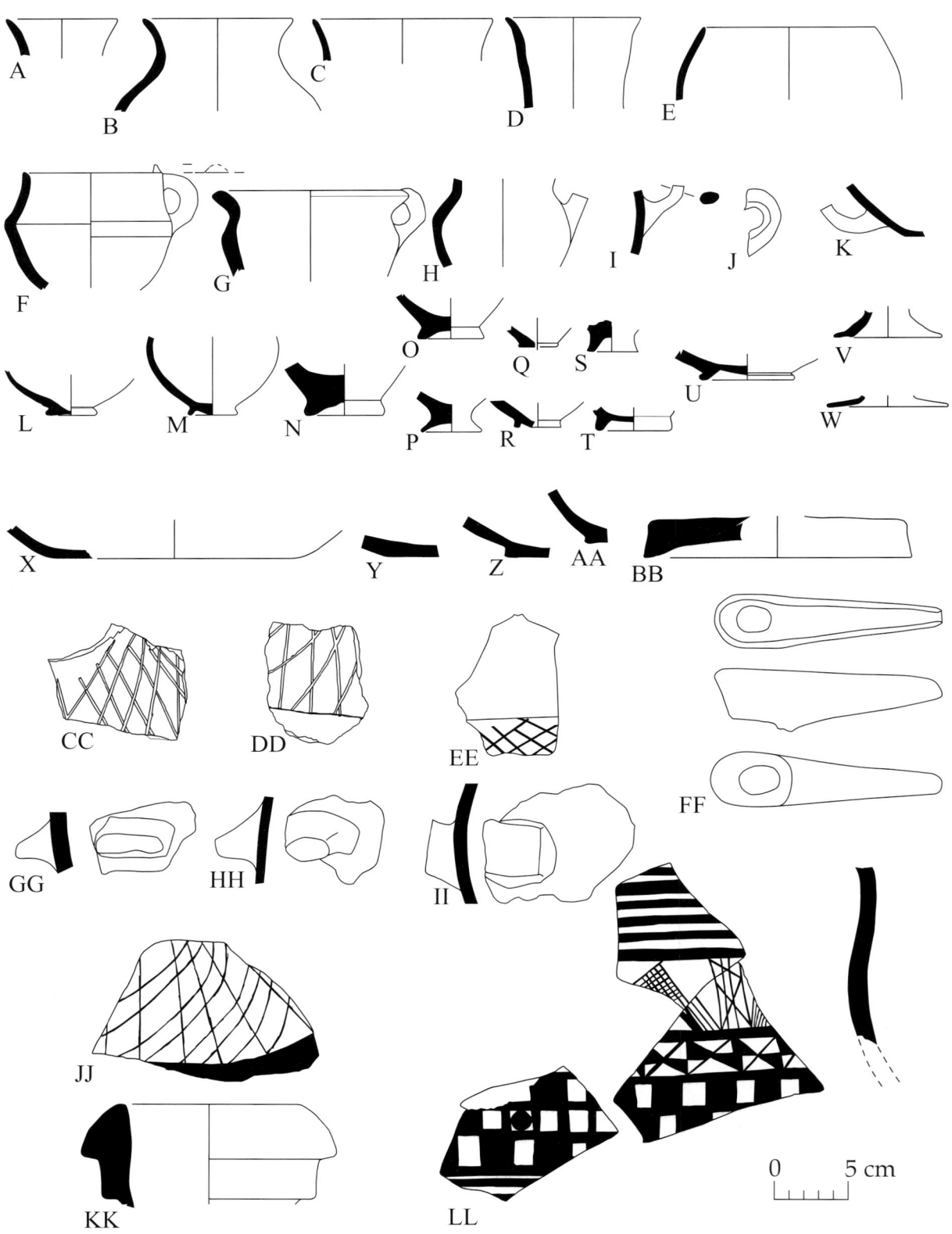

Fig. 4.27

Fig. 4.27 Hasanlu Tepe: early Period V ceramics from the U22 Sounding (opposite).

Fig.	Op.	Context	Ware	Type	Description	Dia.	Disposition
A	U22	10	MBW Ic	Jar 1	Int. Grey, Matte Ext. D. Grey, Burnished	8	UPM Sherd 55
B	U22	10	MBW IIc	Jar 1	Int. D. Grey Matte Ext. D. Grey Burnished	10	UPM Sherd 56
C	U22	10	MBW IIc	Jar 1	Grey	12	UPM Sherd 54
D	U22	10	MBW IIc	Cup 1	Int. Black, Matte; Ext. Black, Burnished	9	UPM Sherd 63
E	U22		MBW	Cup 5	Int. Black, Matte Ext. Black, Slipped, Burnished	12	UPM Sherd 73
F	U22	10	MBW Ib	Cup 2	Grey, Matt, Med.	11	UPM Sherd 40
G	U22	9	MBW Ic	Cup 6	Ext. Grey, Smoked or Black Slip, 2.5YR3/0 Int. Brownish Grey, 5YR5/3	13	UPM Sherd 07
H	U22	10	MBW IIc	Cup 1	Int. Grey, Matte Ext. Grey, Burnished	–	UPM Sherd 43 UPM63-5-1012
I	U22		MBW – –	Body Sherd with Handle	Int. Grey, Matte Ext. Black, H. Burnished	–	UPM Sherd 68
J	U22	10	MBW IIc	Handle	Grey	–	UPM Sherd 44
K	U22	10	MBW IIc	Flat Base and Handle	Int. Grey, Matte Ext. Black, Burnished	–	UPM Sherd 175
L	U22	10	KW	Disc Base	Buff, Matte	3.5	UPM Sherd 19
M	U22	10	KW	Ring Base	Buff, Slipped	3.5	UPM Sherd 87
N	U22	10	MBW IIc	Ring Base	Int. Grey, Matte, Ext. Grey	5.5	UPM Sherd 42
O	U22	10	MBW IIc	Button Base	D. Grey, Burnished	4	UPM Sherd 39
P	U22	10	MBW Ic	Button Base	Int. Grey Matte Ext. Black Burnished	4	UPM Sherd 29
Q	U22	10	"Tan"	Disc Base	Buff, Matte	2.5	UPM Sherd 23
R	U22	10	MBW IIb	Ring Base	Grey	3	UPM Sherd 28 UPM63-5-1060
S	U22	10	MBW IIc	Button Base	Grey	3	UPM Sherd 41
T	U22	10	MBW Ic	Ring Base	Grey	5	UPM Sherd 33
U	U22	10	MBW IIc	Ring Base	L. Grey	6	UPM Sherd 38
V	U22		KW	Pedestal Base	Buff, Matte	7	UPM Sherd 20
W	U22	9	MBW IIc	Pedestal Base	Ext. Grey, Burnished; Int. Grey, Matte	8	UPM Sherd 03
X	U22	10	MBW IIb	Flat Base	Int. L. Grey Matte; Ext. D. Grey, Burnished	16	UPM Sherd 31
Y	U22	10	MBW IIb	Flat Base	L. Grey, Burnished	–	UPM Sherd 32
Z	U22	10	MBW	Flat Base	Black	–	UPM Sherd 83
AA	U22		NR	Disc Base	NR	–	No #
BB	U22	10	CPW IVa	Lid/Tray	Buff, Matte	18	UPM Sherd 07
CC	U22	10	MBW Ic	Pattern Burnished Body Sherd	Int. Grey, Matte Ext. Grey, Burnished	–	UPM Sherd 34 UPM 63-5-1014
DD	U22	10	MBW Ic	Pattern Burnished Body Sherd	Int. Grey, Matte Ext. Grey, Burnished	–	UPM Sherd 35
EE	U22	10	MBW IIc	Flat Base	Grey, Burnished, Incised Crosshatching on Base	–	UPM Sherd 36
FF	U22		MBW Ic	Bridgeless Spout	Grey	–	UPM Sherd A
GG	U22		CPW IVa	Lug Handle	Int. Orangish-Red, Matte; Ext. Fire Blackened	–	UPM Sherd 89
HH	U22	10	CPW IVa	Lug Handle	Reddish Orange, Matte	–	UPM Sherd 91
II	U22	10	CPW IVa	Lug Handle	Reddish Orange	–	UPM Sherd 90
JJ	U22	9	MBW Ic	Painted Grey MBW Body Sherd	Ext. Grey, Burnished, Black Paint Int. Matte, Grey	–	UPM Sherd 09 UPM 63-5-1009
KK	U22	10	MBW IIa	Jar	Grey, Matte	13	UPM Sherd 10
LL	U22		PKW	PKW Body Sherds	Int. Buff, Matte Ext. Buff, Slipped, Black Pt.	–	UPM Sherd I

at Geoy Tepe B in lower Tomb K, where it was associated with the early type of "worm bowl" (Seriation, Fig. 4.22:C; Burton-Brown 1951: fig. 34 nos. 22, 38).

Cup Types 2–3 "Mugs". I have dubbed Cup Types 2 and 3 "mugs" given their height to width ratio and single loop handle. This class is common throughout the LBA and early Iron Ages. Mugs are attested in the early LBA at Geoy Tepe (Fig. 4.22:F). The lone attestation of Type 2 is a carinated mug with a handle attached at the rim and indications of a thumbstop (Fig. 4.27:F). The form is reminiscent of MBA mugs. Cup Type 3 represents a thick-bodied mug unique for both its ware type and form (Fig. 4.27:G). The carinated body with everted rim resembles Terminal MBII cups and small jars, and this vessel may be extrusive or a late holdover (Seriation).

Cup Type 6. This unique example of a hemispherical cup or small holemouth vessel is unique to the early Hasanlu V assemblage (Fig. 4.27:E).

Cup Type 8a. This shouldered beaker in Early MBW has a small ovoid form with short neck and simple everted rim (Fig. 4.18:H). This beaker provides an important link between the MBII, where the type is common, and the Early MBW Horizon.

Jar Type 1a. These small jars with flaring necks and simple rims are rather indistinct (Fig. 4.27:B). Several similarly fine rims with small diameters may be from Type 1 jars, but are just as likely to represent tall tankards (see Cup Type 1, above). Whole examples are known from graves at Hasanlu and, as previously noted, at Dinkha (Figs. 4.25:D, 4.26:A).

Jar Type 2 Ovoid Jars. Jars with a medium-to-high flaring neck and simple out-turned rim in Early MBW and matte buff ware are present in early Period V and are also typical of later Period V and IVc (Fig. 4.18:K–N). Later occurrences of Type 2 jars have a low sloping shoulder and ovoid to bag-shaped body form.

Jar Type 6 High-necked Jars. Small globular to ellipsoid jars with high necks, simple everted rims, and flat bases (Fig. 4.25:A–C, E) are of particular importance to understanding the MBA–LBA transition. These jars were found only in the graves of adult males at Dinkha (B9a Burial 25) and Hasanlu (SK29, SK504, and the Stein Section XV grave; see Chapter 5, Seriation). This distinctive jar occurs in Early MBW, pattern-burnished Early MBW, and polychrome Urmia Ware. The type co-occurs with Bowl Type 4 and Cup Types 1a and 1b. Type 6 jars are attested in contemporary Sialk A in grey-black MBW with pattern-burnish decoration (Ghirshman 1939: pl. XLII 503d).[12] Jars of this type are also known from Haftavan in polychrome Urmia Ware, as well as the southern Caucasus and eastern Anatolia, but are not attested at either Geoy Tepe or Kordlar. At Haftavan, these vessels constitute Jar Type 1a, "raised neck jars with everted rims" (Edwards 1981:112–13, fig. 11 nos. 1–4, 6–8). They occur in both early and late Period VIb, the MBII, and MBIII, with some changes in the style of painting in the MBIII. The painting on the Urmia Ware Type 6 jars of Ušnu-Solduz, with a frieze of pendant triangles filled with crosshatching, differs from that of Haftavan. As pointed out by Rubinson with regard to these jars: "The polychrome jar shape is not characteristic of the most distinctive 'Urmia Ware' forms [at Dinkha]. In Nakhichevan, Azerbaijan, similar polychrome painting is found on many examples of shapes considered Iron Age I ('Early Hasanlu V') in Iran, especially the unbridged spouted vessels, primarily from Kizil-Vank, but also from Sortepe" (2004:663).

At Hasanlu, these jars also occur in Early MBW and co-occur with Early MBW diagnostics such as Type 1 Tankards and Type 4 Incurving Bowls of at least early Hasanlu V and possibly Hasanlu VIa as well. At Dinkha, grave B29a Burial 25, which contained a Type 6 jar, *cut* Stratum 7 (Muscarella 1974:38–40) and so must postdate the MBIII Urmia Ware deposit. In light of the painted style of the Urmia Ware jars, the stratigraphic evidence from Dinkha and the co-occurrence of types at Hasanlu, I assign this jar type and these graves tentatively to Hasanlu VIa and definitely to early Hasanlu V. High-necked jars are a key diagnostic of the LBA Lchashen-Metsamor 2, but these jar forms differ from Type 6 and probably represent the continuation of a tradition of such jars first seen in early Haftavan VIb.

Miscellaneous Early Period V MBW

Among the sherds from early Hasanlu V are a few occurrences of pattern-burnished MBW (Fig. 4.27:CC–EE). One unusual sherd of black-painted grey MBW and a small number of PKW sherds (Fig. 4.27:JJ, LL) make up the entirety of painted ware at Hasanlu in early Period V. The PKW found in Operation U22 Stratum 9 likely all derives from a single jar, which in turn is likely extrusive from Strata 11–12. Tabular lugs in Coarse Buff Ware, a Coarse Buff jar rim and a lid or tray round out the miscellaneous material from the deposit (Fig. 4.27:BB, GG–II, KK).

Incised and Impressed Ware of Early Period V

This ware was found only at Dinkha. As with the Incised and Impressed Ware of the MBIII, the fabric is identical to the plain Early MBW in the same assemblage. Design motifs are similar to those of the MBIII. An important variant of this ware has incised and impressed decoration in-filled with a white grit (Fig. 4.18:C, J, P). No whole forms are attested in this ware, but it is highly important given its links to the early LBA of the southern Caucasus. White-filled decoration occurs in Lchashen-Metsamor 1 (Smith, Badalyan, and Avetisyan 2009:73). Similar impressed burnished grey ware with white in-filled designs is also known in Mitanni occupations in northern Mesopotamia at Tell el-Rimah (Postgate, Oates, and Oates 1997:56–57, pl. 23d–f), Tell Brak (Oates, Oates, and McDonald 1997: fig. 108 lower, fig. 208 nos. 588, 589), and Nuzi (Starr 1939:401–2, pls. 91:N–R, T–W; 92:A–S). At Nuzi the ware is quite similar to MBW, but impressed decoration occurs almost exclusively on bowls, unlike at Dinkha; the design elements and arrangement, however, are comparable.

Bowl Type 10
This unique example of white in-filled Incised and Impressed MBW has a simple square rim, a slight indentation beneath the rim and fairly straight sides (Fig. 4.18:C). Decoration consists of a frieze of incised, stacked chevrons bordered above and below by incised horizontal lines and rows of impressed circles. All design elements were in-filled in white. This sherd was found near the surface and is included here owing to its distinctive decorative style.

Jar Type 4
This small jar or cup with simple out-turned rim (Fig. 4.18:J) resembles other vessels found in Terminal MBII and MBIII levels at Dinkha Tepe (Figs. 4.9:A, 4.12:N–P, S, V, 4.16:K). Its white-filled decoration consists of a frieze of stacked chevrons interspersed amid a band of impressed dots bordered by horizontal incised lines. Other likely incomplete examples of this type include an incised and impressed burnished grey sherd with horizontal incised lines bounding a row of impressed dots and a vessel with a pierced suspension-lug and a frieze of stacked chevrons bounded by incised lines and surmounted by a band of impressed circles (Fig. 4.18:O, Q).

Miscellaneous Incised and Impressed Ware
Among the remaining sherds of incised and impressed ware are a few fragments of what are likely beakers or jars (Fig. 4.18:R, S). A fragmentary prism-shaped "box-basin" with incised and impressed decoration and fenestrations (Fig. 4.18:U) resembles those of Lchashen-Metsamor 1 (Smith, Badalyan, and Avetisyan 2009: fig. 24:M). One fragmentary jar with white-filled incised and impressed decoration likely belongs to Holemouth Jar Type 9 (Fig. 4.18:P).

Urmia Ware

Only one Urmia Ware sherd was found in the lower trash deposit at Dinkha (Fig. 4.18:B). As we have seen, two Urmia Ware Type 6 jars were found in graves at Dinkha and Hasanlu and, at least in the case of Dinkha, the grave can be dated to the early LBA. Such jars seem to represent imports and polychrome painting is only common in the MBIII.

Late Hasanlu V

Analysis of the ceramic assemblages from Hasanlu and Dinkha indicate that we might be able to distinguish between the early and late LBA in the future, but more data will be needed from controlled excavations to verify this and enhance chronological precision. Late Hasanlu V is best attested in stratified occupation deposits at Hasanlu in the U22 Sounding and, to a lesser extent, in RS22–23—the Period V columned-hall building. The material from RS22–23 is divisible into a late Period V assemblage found on the floors of the RS22–23 Building (Fig. 4.30) and a separate assemblage that spans late Period V and early Period IVc (Fig. 4.31). There are also graves of this period, mainly at Dinkha. The Dinkha and Hasanlu assemblages are comparable in terms of developmental trends, but the

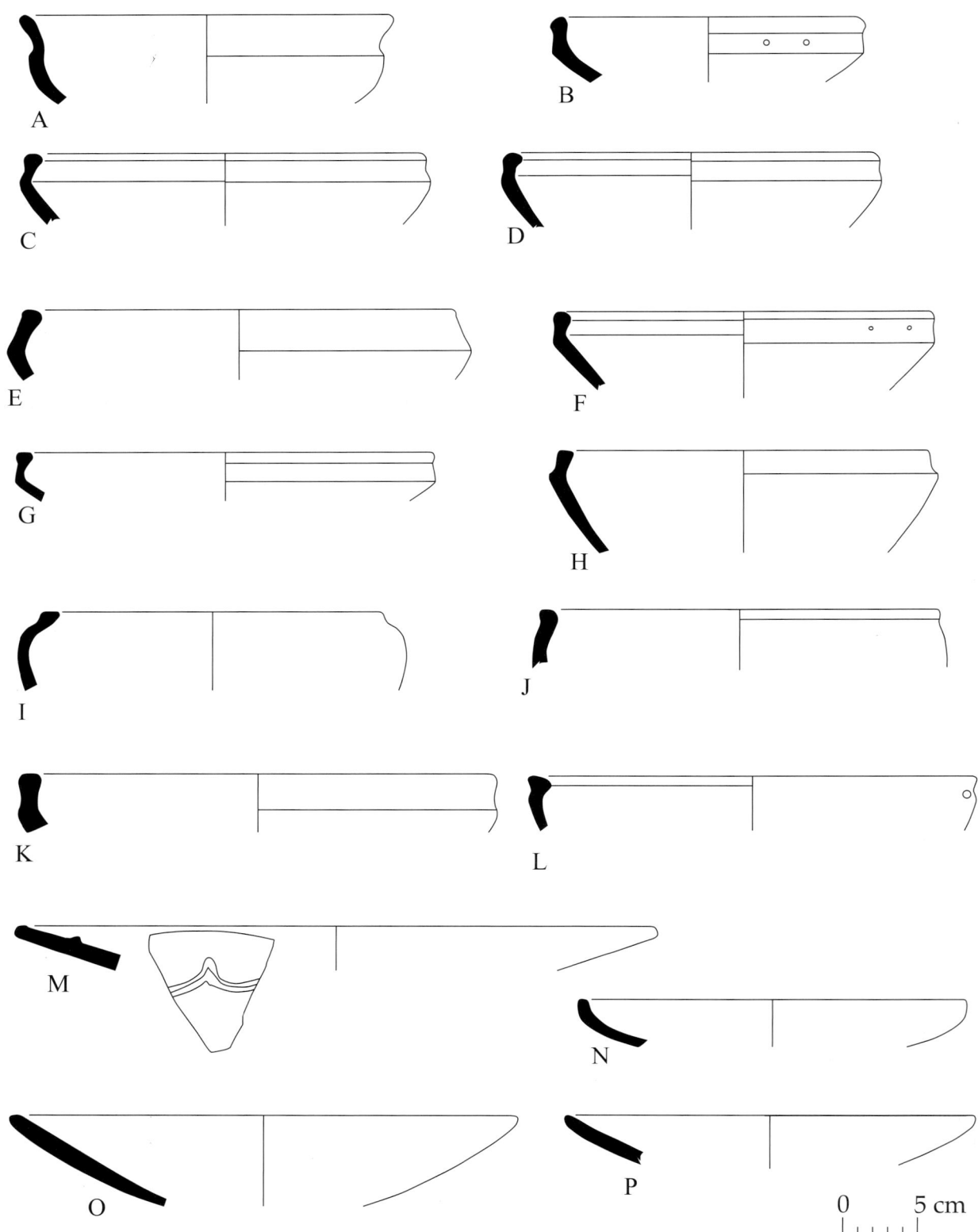

Fig. 4.28

Fig. 4.28 Hasanlu Tepe: late Period V ceramics from the U22 Sounding (opposite).

Fig.	Op.	Context	Ware	Type	Description	Dia.	Disposition
A	T22	7	MBW IIc	Bowl 9	Brown	25	UPM Sherd 24
B	T22	7	MBW Ic	Bowl 3a	Orange, Double-Pierced	21	UPM Sherd 21
C	U22	8	MBW IIc	Bowl 4	Ext. Black, 2.5Y3/0 Int. 2.5Y6/2	26	UPM Sherd 02
D	U22	8	MBW IIc	Bowl 4	Ext. Black, Burnished, 2.5YR4/0 Int. Matte, 7.5YR4/0	24	UPM Sherd 06
E	T22	7	MBW Ic	Bowl 6	Red-Orange	29	UPM Sherd 19
F	U22	8	MBW IIc	Bowl 6	Ext. Black, 7.5YR4/0 Int. 10YR5/1	25	UPM Sherd 04
G	T22	8	MBW IIc	Bowl 4	Black	28	UPM Sherd 23
H	T22	7	MBW Ic	Bowl 6	Grey	25	UPM Sherd 26
I	T22	8	MBW IIc	HM 16	Ext. Red	23	UPM Sherd 16
J	U22	7	MBW Ib	Bowl 4	Ext. Reddish-Orange Slip, Streaky Burnish 7.5YR6/4 Int. Matte 7.5YR6/4	27	UPM Sherd 02
K	T22	8	MBW IIc	Bowl 3a	Red	32	UPM Sherd 27
L	T22	8	MBW Ic	Bowl 4	Black	30	No #
M	T22	7	MBW IIc	Bowl 2a	Grey, Double Crescent Appliqué	43	UPM Sherd 15
N	T22	7	MBW Ib	Bowl 2b	Grey	26	UPM Sherd 25
O	T22	7	MBW IIc	Bowl 2a	Grey	34	UPM Sherd 22
P	U22	7	MBW Ic	Bowl 2a	Red Slip	28	UPM Sherd 10 UPM 63-5-1053

scarcity of late Period V graves at Hasanlu and occupation deposits at Dinkha somewhat complicates efforts to develop a ceramic chronology. The main diagnostics in graves are "worm bowls" with low flaring sides and double drilling, bridgeless-spouted jars with low necks and mid-body carination, and mid-body carinated jars with flaring necks (Seriation). These developments anticipate the more obvious changes seen in the Iron I/Hasanlu IVc ceramic assemblage.

Too few sherds were found and/or recorded from the Control Sounding at Dinkha from the upper levels of the "trash deposit" to draw any significant conclusions regarding developments in the ceramics. The assemblage from the Hasanlu U22 Sounding is dominated by MBW with a small component of matte Coarse Buff Ware. This latter ware represents the standard "cooking pot ware" of the Late Bronze and early Iron Age, serving a variety of utilitarian functions as indicated by the range of forms. The late Period V assemblage is noteworthy for the predominance of MBW—this includes the burnished and smoothed "Buff Ware" and Red-slipped Buff Ware identified and described by previous researchers, which should simply be seen as color variations within MBW.

Bowls

We see a continuation of most of the major classes of bowls that were common to early Period V. The double drilling of small carinated and incurving bowls parallels developments in the "worm bowls" in the contemporary graves at Dinkha (see Chapter 5). Carinated bowls significantly outnumber the other classes.

Bowl Type 2a–b "Worm Bowls"

"Worm Bowls" of Type 1 are not found in occupation deposits of late Period V. Two Type 1a bowls were found at Dinkha in graves—both have double drilling, which is more common in the later LBA (Fig. 4.32:D, E). Type 2a bowls in MBW and what was previously designated Young's Ware Ic, or burnished Buff Ware, are attested in the Hasanlu U22 Deep Sounding (Fig. 4.28:M, O, P). One example has a double crescent motif (Fig. 4.28:M), which is also found on two bowls

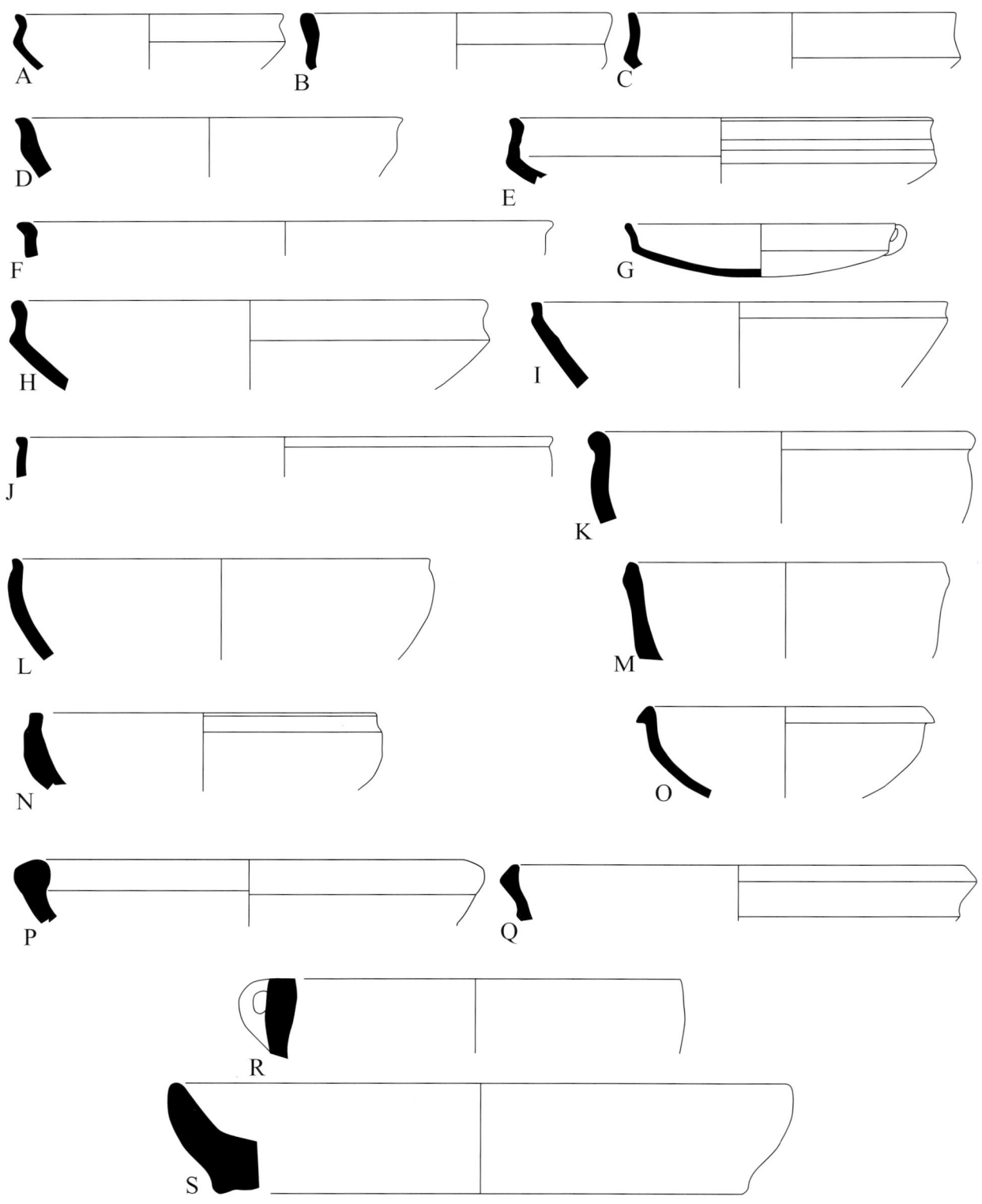

Fig. 4.29

Fig. 4.29 Hasanlu Tepe: late Period V ceramics from the U22 Sounding.

Fig.	Op.	Context	Ware	Type	Description	Dia.	Disposition
A	T22	7	MBW IIc	Bowl 3d	Grey	18	UPM Sherd 18
B	T22	8	MBW IIc	Bowl 3d	Grey	21	UPM Sherd 40
C	T22	7	MBW IIb	Bowl 3d	Grey	22	UPM Sherd 17
D	T22	8	MBW	Bowl 3c	Grey	26	UPM Sherd 31
E	U22	8	MBW Ic	Bowl 3d	Grey	28	UPM Sherd D
F	T22	8	MBW IIc	Bowl 3c	Grey	36	UPM Sherd 37
G	T22	7	MBW IIc	Bowl 3d	Loop Handle	18	UPM Sherd 25
H	T22	7	MBW Ic	Bowl 3d	Grey	32	UPM Sherd 16
I	T22	8	MBW	Bowl 3a	Black	28	UPM Sherd 11
J	T22	8	MBW	Bowl 8	Grey	36	UPM Sherd 36
K	T22	8	MBW	Bowl 8	Grey	38	UPM Sherd 26
L	T22	8	MBW	Bowl 8	Black	28	UPM Sherd 09
M	T22	8	Buff IVa	Bowl 12	Grey	22	No #
N	U22	8	MBW	Bowl 12	Ext. Black, 7.5YR3/0 Int. Red, 5YR6/4	24	UPM Sherd 07
O	T22	8	MBW	Bowl 13	L. Red	20	UPM Sherd 03
P	U22	7	MBW Ic	Bowl 14	Int. Brown, Matte, 5YR6/2 Ext. Brown, Slipped, Burnished, 5YR6/3	32	UPM Sherd 09
Q	T22	8	MBW IIc	Bowl 16	Grey	32	UPM Sherd 18
R	T22	8	Buff Ia	Bowl 11	Buff	28	No #
S	T22	8	Buff IVa	Bowl 15	Buff	42	UPM Sherd 14

from Period IVc at the site (see below). Type 2a bowls with this motif are usually larger and lower than other bowls in this class. The smaller Type 2a bowls associated with this same stratum (Fig. 4.28:O, P) are typical of later Period V with double drilling, an attribute common to the graves at Dinkha. Bowl Type 2b is a lower variety of these bowls (Figs. 4.28:N, 4.32:C).

Bowl Type 3 Carinated Bowls
As in early Period V, carinated bowls with everted or vertical rims are a common type (Figs. 4.28:A–B, K, 4.29:A–I, 4.31:A, D–I, K). One example has double drilling (Fig. 4.28:B). Another bowl from RS22–23 exhibits attributes, such as its greater height and horizontal rib, which are far more at home in Period IVc (Fig. 4.30:F).

Bowl Type 4 Incurving Bowls
This class of bowl continues in use from previous periods, although later Period V examples tend to lack the smoothly curving sides seen in Period VIa and early V (Figs. 4.28:C, D, G, I, J, L, 4.30:C) and are approaching the carinated Type 6. One has a drilled hole (Fig. 4.28:L).

Bowl Type 6
Incurving/inverted carinated bowls are fairly common (Figs. 4.28:E, F, H, 4.30:D, E, 4.31:J, M). One has double drilling (Fig. 4.28:F).

Bowl Type 8
Hemispherical bowls with slightly thickened rims (Figs. 4.29:J–L, 4.30:A–B, 4.31:B–C, L) make up a small part of the assemblage.

Bowl Type 11
This slightly incurving coarse bowl or vat in matte Buff Ware (Buff Ia) has a thickened square rim and a loop handle. It is unique in the Period V assemblage (Fig. 4.29:R).

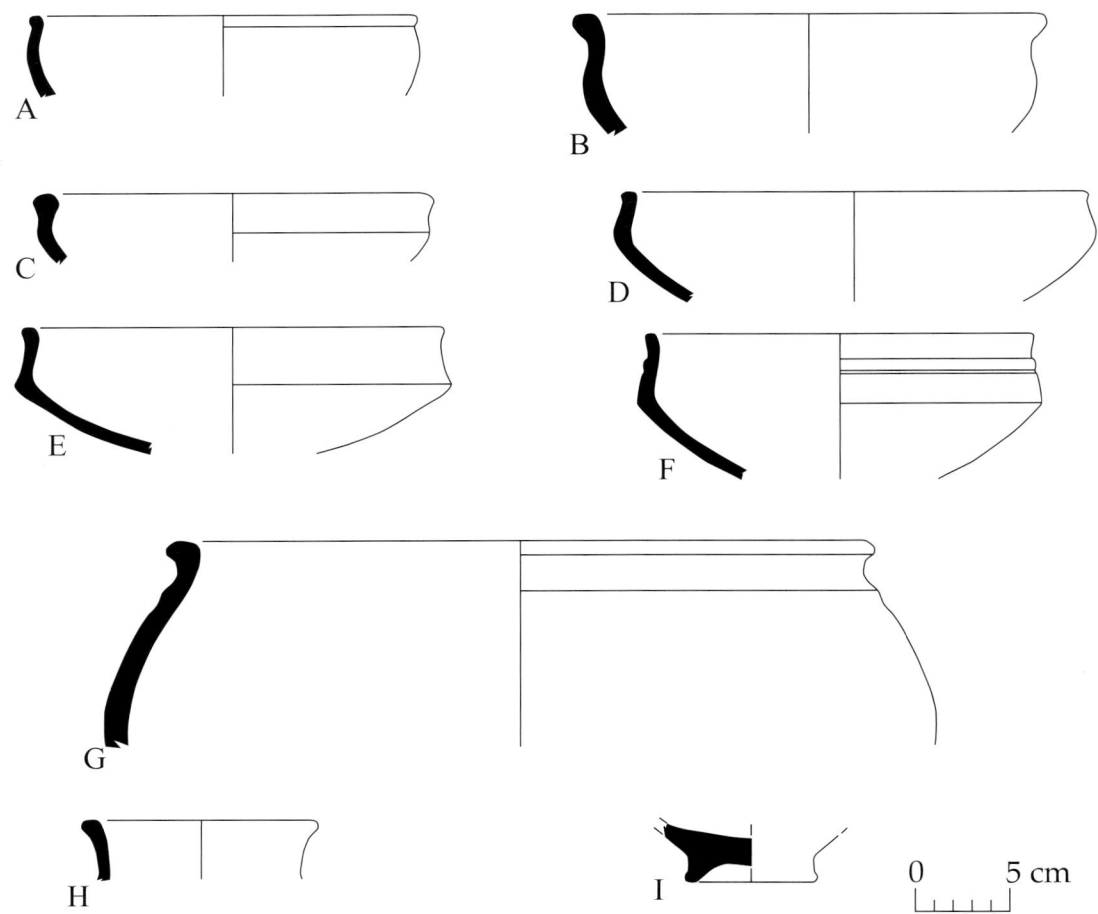

Fig. 4.30 Hasanlu Tepe: late Period V ceramics from RS22-23.

Fig.	Op.	Context	Ware	Type	Description	Dia.	Disposition
A	S22	Area 11 Str. 12	NR	Bowl 8	NR	20	Sherd Drawing 400
B	S22	Area 11 Str. 12	NR	Bowl 8	NR	25	Sherd Drawing 401
C	S22	Area 13 Str. 11	NR	Bowl 4	NR	21	Sherd Drawing 410
D	S22	Area 13 Str. 11	NR	Bowl 6	NR	25	Sherd Drawing 411
E	S22	Area 11 Str. 11	NR	Bowl 6	NR	22	Sherd Drawing 422
F	S22	Area 11 Str. 12	NR	Bowl 3d	NR	20	Sherd Drawing 402
G	S22	Area 11 Str. 12	NR	HM5	NR	37	Sherd Drawing 404
H	S22	Area 11 Str.12	NR	Jar 3a	NR	13	Sherd Drawing 400a
I	S22	Area 11 Str. 12	NR	Ring Base	NR	7	Sherd Drawing 403

Bowl Type 12

This coarse, hemispherical bowl with simple rim in Buff IVa ware is among the more utilitarian forms attested in the assemblage (Fig. 4.29:M). I have provisionally included a similar bowl in MBW (Fig. 4.29:N).

Bowl Type 13

This hemispherical bowl with triangular rim profile is unique in the assemblage (Fig. 4.29:O).

Bowl Type 14

This medium Buff Ware bowl with round rim profile is burnished on the exterior (Fig. 4.29:P).

Bowl Type 15 Coarse Basins

Large coarse basins in Buff Ware form a small part of most midden and domestic deposits of the LBA and early Iron Age at Hasanlu (Fig. 4.29:S).

Bowl Type 16

This unique straight-sided bowl with simple incurving rim (Fig. 4.29:Q) resembles examples from Geoy Tepe B (see esp. Burton-Brown 1951: fig. 33 no. 1008).

Holemouth Jars

True closed forms remain quite rare in late Period V, with the majority of jars falling within the holemouth series. Small-to-medium holemouth jars are better attested than in early Period V, probably owing to the larger excavated area in the U22 Sounding having taken in a wider range of contexts.

As in early Period V, the generic holemouth jar Type 1 is well represented in the latter part of the period (Figs. 4.31:T, 4.33:J, 4.34:E–F). One has pattern-burnished decoration (Fig. 4.34:J). The ovoid class of jars comprised of Types 3–5 is also present in late Period V (Figs. 4.30:G, 4.31:Q, S, 4.33:C, F, I, K–M, 4.34:A–D, G), as is Type 9 (Figs. 4.31:N, R, U, 4.33:B). One Type 5 jar has a pattern-burnish design (Fig. 4.33:M) and another was painted in black (Fig. 4.34:A). A Type 9 strainer jar with tripod legs and two handles is unique in the holemouth series (Fig. 4.31:N).

Holemouth Type 8

Only one true holemouth jar has been attributed to this period (Fig. 4.36:F). It comes from a rare late Period V burial at Hasanlu (see Chapter 5, SK459).

Holemouth Type 11

This jar type, generally referred to as a pyxis, is newly introduced in late Period V and has a simple or slightly thickened vertical or everted rim and carination at mid-body, giving the vessel a biconic form (Fig. 4.33:A, G). Pyxides continue at Hasanlu in Period IVc and IVb and are known from Geoy Tepe A (Burton-Brown 1951: fig. 35 nos. 101, 108, 188).

Holemouth Types 12–14, 16

Type 12 jars, small ovoid jars with thickened rim (Fig. 4.33:D–E, H), first appear in late Period V. One jar has an appliquéd "horn" motif and the remains of a simple spout (Fig. 4.33:H). A similar raised design is found on vessels at Giyan in Graves 9, 10, 24, 25, 31, and 57 (Contenau and Ghirshman 1935; Overlaet 2003:51, fig. 35). Henrickson dates Giyan Grave 57 to his Carinated Pedestal-Base Goblet Group, which he places between 1450–1200 BC or essentially Hasanlu V (Henrickson 1983–1984). A bridgeless-spouted vessel from a late Period IVc grave at Dinkha Tepe (Seriation: B9a Burial 24) also bears this motif. These two attestations are the earliest examples of a common stylistic attribute of the Iron II. Unique or virtually unique holemouth jars include Type 13, a jar with what is probably an ellipsoid form and a simple vertical rim (Fig. 4.34:H); Type 14, a coarse ovoid jar with thick, flaring simple rim (Fig. 4.34:I); and Type 16 (Fig. 4.28:I), a deep vat or bowl with a collar rim. One Type 15 "teapot" with basket handle was found in grave B9a B26 at Dinkha (Fig. 4.36:C).

Jars/Cups

Mid-body carinated jars begin to emerge as a dominant form in late Period V. We are overly reliant on grave assemblages to document this pattern since no whole vessels were found in occupation deposits and undecorated body sherds, which would provide an estimation of the frequency of carination, were seldom collected. Tankards and beakers are still found in occupation deposits, but fall out of mortuary assemblages. This cannot be established as a broader pattern since we are largely reliant on the graves of Dinkha Tepe for our view of mortuary practices in the late LBA.

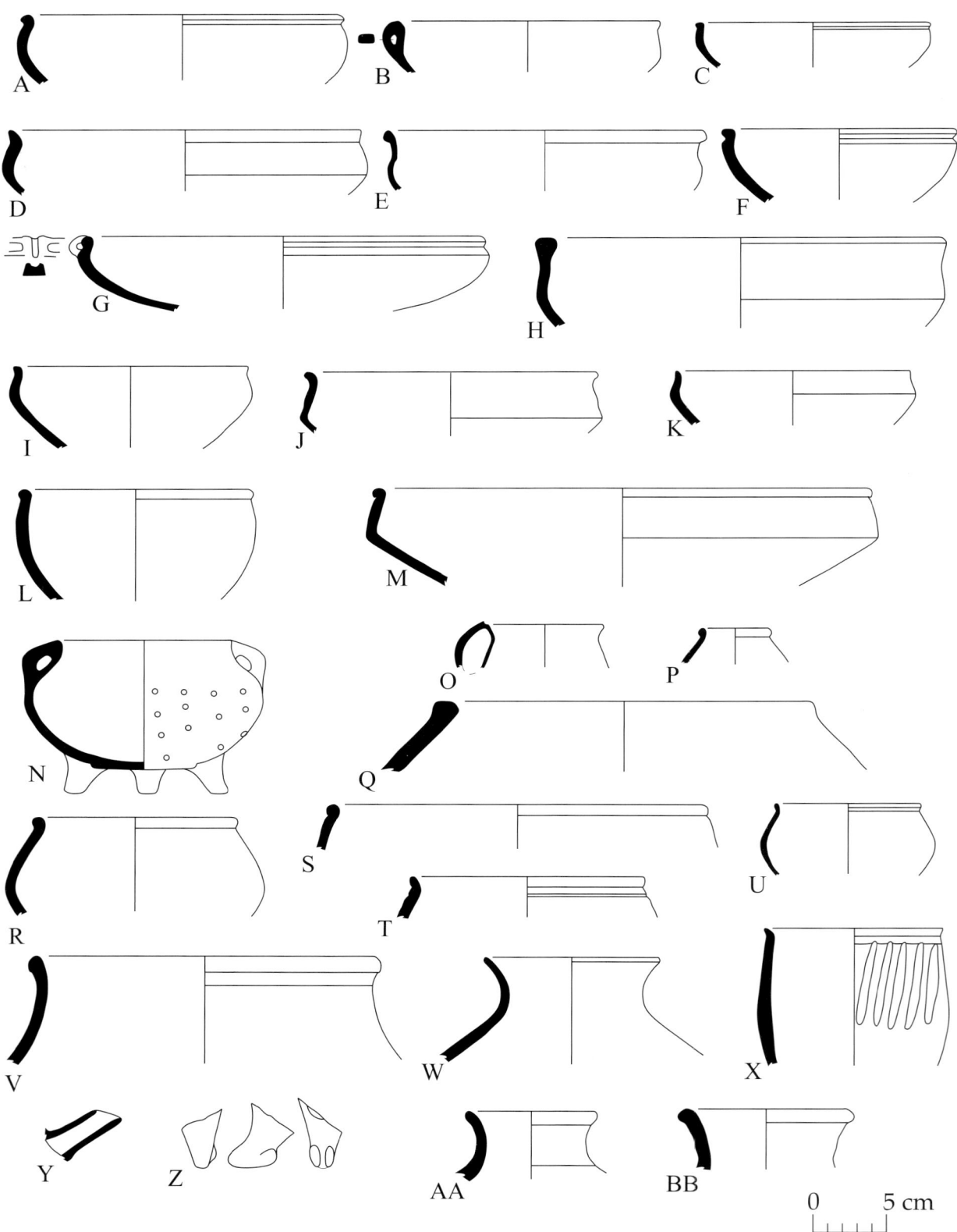

Fig. 4.31 Hasanlu Tepe: Late Period V–IVc ceramics from RS22–23.

Fig. 4.31 Hasanlu Tepe: late Period V–IVc ceramics from RS22–23 (opposite).

Fig.	Op.	Context	Ware	Type	Description	Dia.	Disposition
A	R22	10-11	MBW IIIc	Bowl 3c	Tan-Buff	22	Sherd Drawing
B	R22	10-11	MBW Ic	Bowl 8	Grey	18	Sherd Drawing
C	R22	10-11	MBW IIIc	Bowl 8	Tan-Buff	16	Sherd Drawing
D	R22	Area 8 Str. 11	MBW IIIc	Bowl 3c	Grey	24	Sherd Drawing
E	R22	10-11	MBW IIIb	Bowl 3c	Orangish-Buff	22	Sherd Drawing
F	R22	10-11	MBW IIIc	Bowl 3a	Grey, Int. Pattern Burnish	16	Sherd Drawing
G	R22	10-11	MBW IIIc	Bowl 3c	Grey-Black	27.5	Sherd Drawing
H	R22	10-11	MBW IIIc	Bowl 3d	L. Grey	28	Sherd Drawing
I	R22	10-11	MBW IIIc	Bowl 3c	Ext. Grey, Int. Brown	16	Sherd Drawing
J	R22	10-11	MBW IIIc	Bowl 6	Grey-Black	20	Sherd Drawing
K	R22	10-11	MBW IIIc	Bowl 3c	Grey	16	Sherd Drawing
L	R22	10-11	CPW Ia	Bowl 8	D. Brown, Smudged	16	Sherd Drawing
M	R22	10-11	MBW IIIc	Bowl 6	Grey	34	Sherd Drawing
N	R22	10-11	MBW IIIb	HM9	Buff, Pierced Holes	12	Sherd Drawing
O	R22	Area 8 Str. 11	MBW IIIc	Cup 7	Grey	8	Sherd Drawing
P	R22	10-11	MBW IIIb	HM2a	Buff	5	Sherd Drawing
Q	R22	Area 8 Str. 11	Buff IIa	HM5	Scraped	26	Sherd Drawing
R	R22	10-11	MBW Ib	HM9	Orangish Buff	14	Sherd Drawing
S	R22	10-11	MBW IIIc	HM4	Grey	26	Sherd Drawing
T	R22	10-11	MBW IIIc	HM1	Grey	16	Sherd Drawing
U	R22	10-11	MBW IIIc	HM9	Tan-Grey-Black	10	Sherd Drawing
V	R22	10-11	NR	Jar 5	NR	24	Sherd Drawing
W	R22	10-11	MBW IIIc	Jar 2	Grey	12	Sherd Drawing
X	R22	10-11	MBW IIIc	Pot Stand 1	Grey, Gadrooning	12	Sherd Drawing
Y	R22	10-11	MBW IIIc	Tube Spout	Black	–	Sherd Drawing
Z	R22	10-11	MBW IIIc	Foot	Black	–	Sherd Drawing
AA	R22	10-11	NR	Jar 1a	NR	9	Sherd Drawing
BB	R22	10-11	MBW IIIc	Jar 1b	Black	12	Sherd Drawing

Jar Type 1a

These small simple jars are more abundant in the area of the Hasanlu U22 Sounding in late Period V than earlier in the period (Figs. 4.31:AA, 4.35:A–B, D–E, G, L–M). One whole example comes from a grave at Dinkha (Fig. 4.36:G).

Jar Type 1b

These jars are similar to Type 1a but are larger and have a short neck (Figs. 4.31:BB, 4.35:C, I–K). These jars likely evolve into the *hydriai* of the early Iron II with three handles.

Jar Type 2

Only one of these jars is attested in late Period V–early IVc (Fig. 4.31:W).

Jar Type 3

Type 3a jars are rare in occupation deposits in late Period V (Fig. 4.30:H). In the graves of Dinkha and Hasanlu we see a range of mid-body carinated jars in this period (Fig. 4.36:A–B, D–E, H–J). The type becomes far more prevalent in Periods IVc and IVb. Type 3a jars have medium-to-high necks and simple everted rims (Fig. 4.36:D, H–J). Type 3b jars tend to have bridgeless spouts, short

214

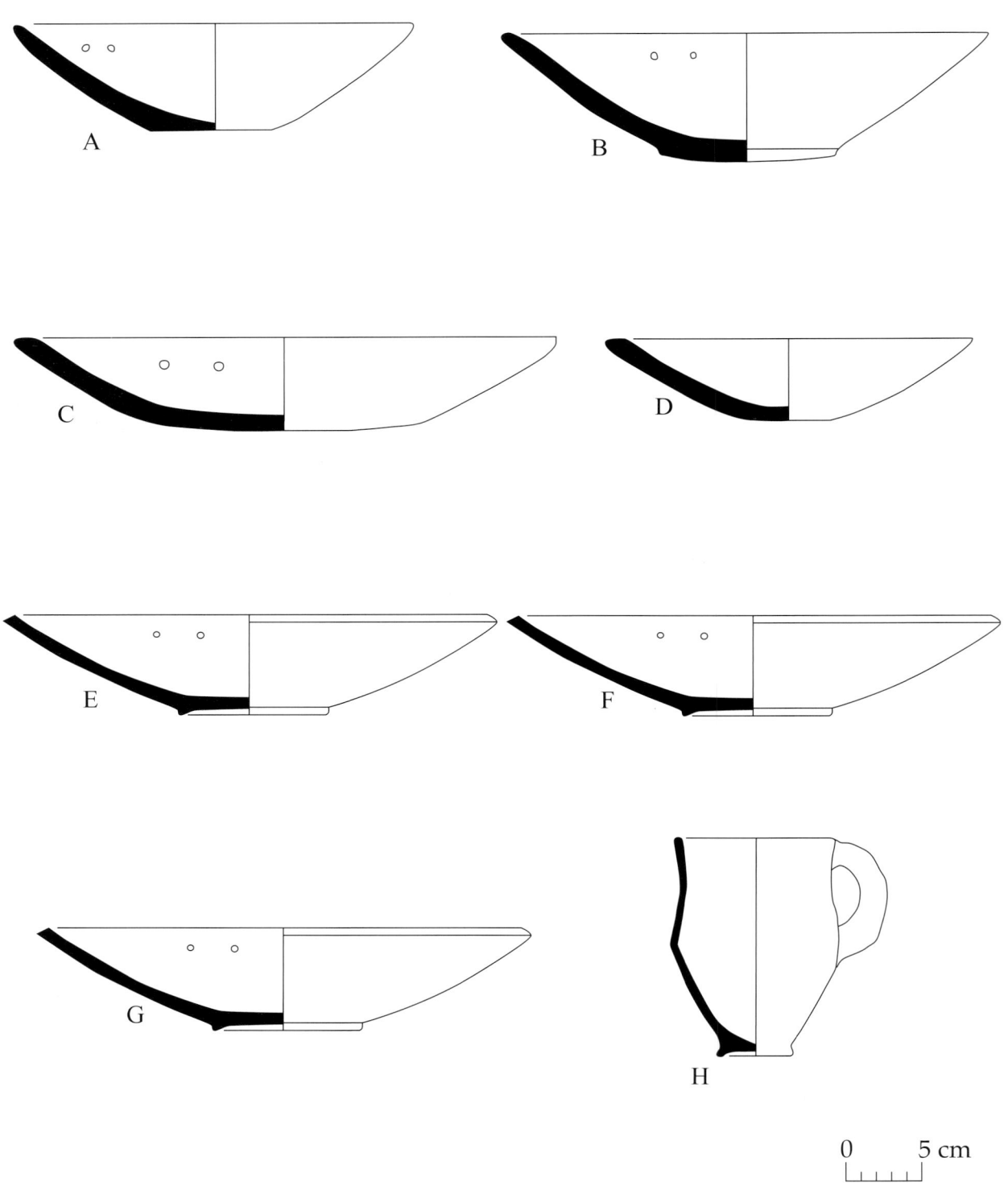

Fig. 4.32

Fig. 4.32 Hajji Firuz and Dinkha Tepe: bowls and cups from late Period V graves (opposite).

Fig.	Op.	Context	Ware	Type	Description	Dia.	Disposition
A	Hajji Firuz K10	Burial 1	MBW	Bowl 1a	NR	26.5	HF68-36
B	Dinkha B9a	Burial 17	MBW	Bowl 1a	NR	32	—
C	Dinkha B9a	Burial 27	MBW	Bowl 2b	NR	36	—
D	Dinkha B9a	Burial 26	MBW	Bowl 2a	NR	24	—
E	Dinkha B10b	Burial 10	MBW	Bowl 2a	NR	32	—
F	Dinkha VII	Burial 1	MBW	Bowl 2a	NR	32	—
G	Dinkha B9a	Burial 23	MBW	Bowl 2a	NR	32	—
H	Hajji Firuz K10	Burial 1	MBW	Cup 1b	NR	10	HF68-47

necks, and simple straight or slightly everted rims (Fig. 4.36:A–B, E). Most Type 3 jars have flat bases, although one ring base is present (Fig. 4.36:B). Mid-body carinated jars are not well attested at Hasanlu until Period IVc.

Jar Type 5
This small-to-medium jar with shoulder, constricted neck, and simple rim (Figs. 4.31:V, 4.35:H) is unique to late Period V–early IVc.

Cup Type 1 Tall Tankards
This LBA diagnostic occurs in the assemblage of the U22 Deep Sounding in late Period V as rim, carination, handle, and, possibly, base sherds (Fig. 4.35:F, P, U, W, AA). Only one tankard, of unusual form, was found in graves of the period at the nearby mound of Hajji Firuz (Seriation: Hajji Firuz K10 Burial 1, Fig. 4.32:H). By no means does the lack of tankards in the late Period V graves at Dinkha indicate such vessels were declining in popularity given their presence in occupation deposits of the period and the ubiquity of the successor to the tall tankards, short carinated cups with pedestal bases, in Period IVc (see below). Rather, the absence of these cups in grave groups may indicate changing ideas surrounding mortuary ritual and appropriate grave goods. In Period VIa and early Period V, tall tankards were almost exclusively placed in the graves of adult males. In the late Period V graves at Dinkha, nearly all the deceased were provided with a large bowl, spouted jar, and a medium-size jar. Cups re-appear in the Period IVc graves of Hasanlu and Dinkha in the form of short carinated cups with pedestal bases, but only in the graves of children (see Chapter 5, Graves Hasanlu SK494 and Dinkha B9a Burial 10 and B9b Burial 12). Despite their meager attestation as a grave good, these cups (Cup Type 7) are well attested in the occupation deposits of Period IVc at Hasanlu and surely represent a popular Iron I drinking vessel.

Cup Type 2
One fragmentary example of this type was found in late Period V (Fig. 4.35:V).

Cup Type 4 'S'-Profile Mug
This cup (Fig. 4.35:T) seems out of place within the assemblage along with sherds of obvious MBII–III date in Fine and Coarse Buff Ware (plain KW; Fig. 4.35:N–O, Q), which are likely extrusive or miscollected material from the lower MBA deposit. Coarse mugs occur in LBA and early Iron Age deposits in the Lake Urmia region. To the north, this class—which exhibits a great deal of variation—is attested in the later LBA–Iron I at Geoy Tepe (Burton-Brown 1951: fig. 33 nos. 1004, 1013; fig. 32 nos. 33, 18) and at Kordlar (Lippert 1979: fig. 7, no.13). Yet in the southern Lake Urmia Basin, styles of drinking vessels were more closely linked to northern Mesopotamia in the LBA and such mugs are thus relatively rare.

Cup Type 5 Short Carinated Cups/Beakers
These two short, sharply carinated cups or beakers likely represent the early appearance of a class of vessel common to Hasanlu IVc with pedestal base and handle (Fig. 4.35:R–S). Neither has a preserved base or handle, but the form is quite distinctive. Alterna-

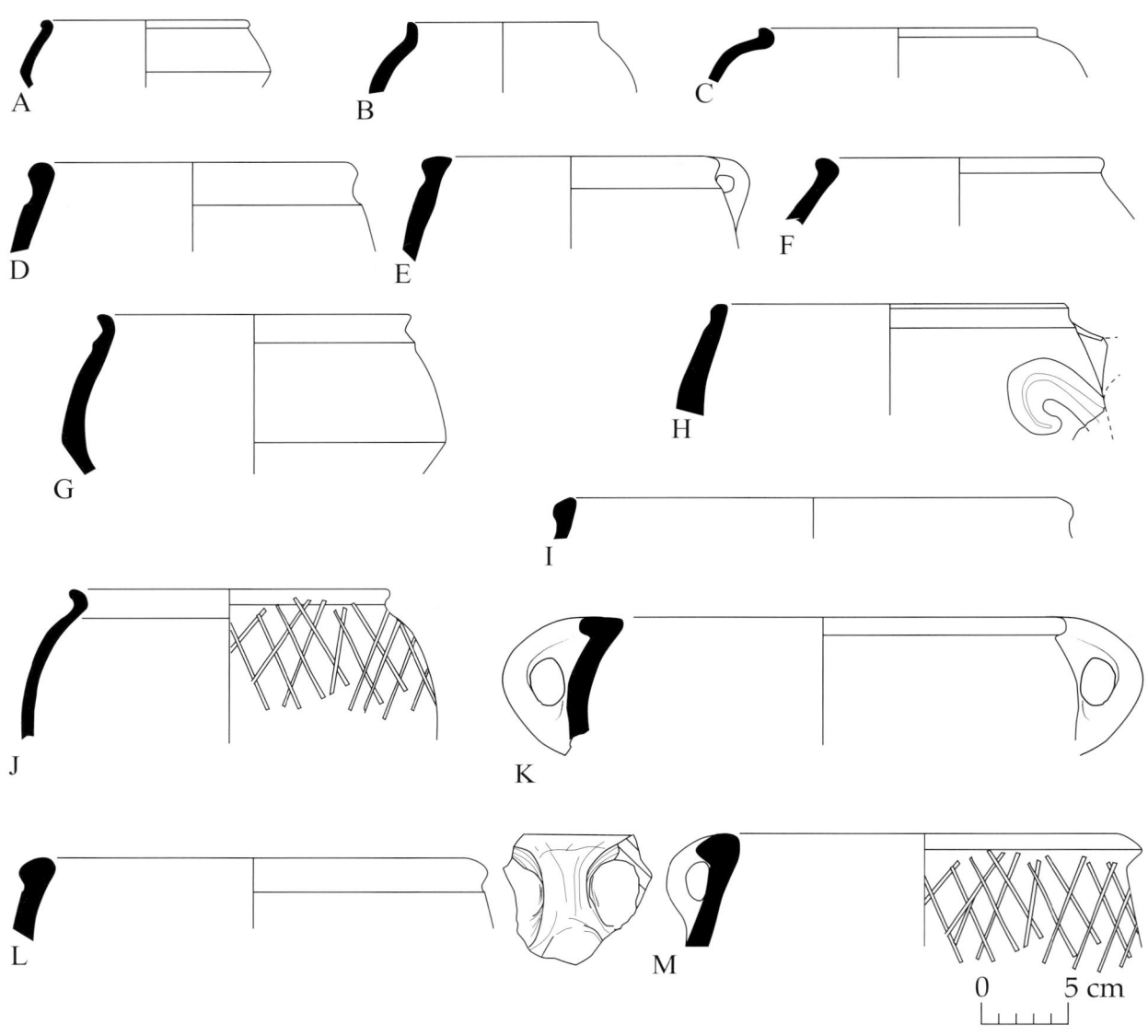

Fig. 4.33

tively, these vessels may be intrusive from the overlying IVc deposit. A similar cup was found in a LBA–Iron I grave at Haftavan alongside a bridgeless-spouted jar (Burney 1970: fig. 8, no. 7).

Cup Type 7 Short Carinated Pedestal-base Cups
As with the Type 5 cups, this tentatively identified Type 7 cup (Fig. 4.31:O) is more common in Period IVc (see below). It differs from other examples in that the handle is attached at the rim and there are vestiges of a thumbstop on the upper handle.

Potstand Type 1

This potstand in grey MBW with fluting on its upper portion (Fig. 4.31:X) represents the earliest attestation of a type known in the graves of Hasanlu IVb, where they are usually paired with bridge-spouted vessels. The stands of the Iron II frequently have ibex-head handles and are slightly larger, with rim di-

Fig. 4.33 Hasanlu Tepe: late Period V ceramics from the U22 Sounding (opposite).

Fig.	Op.	Context	Ware	Type	Description	Dia.	Disposition
A	T22	8	MBW	HM 11a	Black	12	UPM Sherd 08
B	T22	8	MBW Ib	HM 9	Black	11	No #
C	T22	8	MBW IIb	HM 4	Buff	16	UPM Sherd 17
D	T22	8	MBW IIa	HM 12	Greyish-Buff	19	UPM Sherd 04
E	T22	7	Buff Ia	HM 12	Buff	17	UPM Sherd 24
F	U22	8	MBW Ib	HM 4	Ext. Grey, Smoothed; Int. Grey, Matte	17	UPM Sherd 12
G	T22	7	MBW Ib	HM 11	Orange	18	UPM Sherd 22
H	T22	7	Buff Ia	HM 12	Buff	20	UPM Sherd 22
I	T22	8	MBW	HM 3	Red	30	UPM Sherd 38
J	U22	8	MBW IIc	HM 1	Ext. Black, Pattern Burnish, 2.5YR3/0 Int. Black, Matte 5YR6/3	19	UPM Sherd 01
K	U22 Str. 8	8	MBW IIa	HM 3	Ext. 7.5YR6/4, 2.5Y3/0 Int. 2.5Y6/4	28	UPM Sherd 09
L	T22	8	Buff Ia	HM 3	Buff	27	UPM Sherd 34
M	T22	8	MBW IIa	HM 5	Red, Pattern-Burnish	25	UPM Sherd 21

ameters averaging 16 cm. As opposed to the potstands of LBA and early Iron Age Mesopotamia, which are open at the base, those from Hasanlu have flat bases.

Theriomorphic Vessel

Among the ceramics from the columned hall (Room 14) of the RS22–23 Period V building is a unique oblong, almost boat-shaped theriomorphic vessel in black MBW (Pl. 4.1a–b; HAS72-173). The extant portions of the vessel measured a maximum of 39.2 cm long, 15.6 cm wide and 15.6 cm high. Pierced flanges extended from the rim of the vessel at 90° and it originally stood on four feet, with the opposing pairs of feet facing in opposite directions. The vessel was found with only three feet; the other was found in Stratum 10/11 of RS22–23, although the exact findspot was not recorded and it was likely discarded after illustration (Fig. 4.31:Z). The opposing feet suggest the vessel had heads at either end; both were missing, but two "sheep's head figurines" and one "dog's head" figurine were found but not saved or recorded.[13] The crudely fashioned feet possibly represent the cloven hooves of an artiodactyl. A dewlap hanging along the midline of the neck below the jaw is suggestive of a bovine or waterfowl. Both bovids and waterfowl were favored subjects of zoomorphic vessels in northern and western Iran. A similar vessel was discovered at Kordlar Tepe II/III (Lippert 1976: fig. 7, no. 1a).

Miscellaneous Late Period V MBW

Among the Late Period V sherds recovered from the Hasanlu U22 Sounding are typical pattern-burnished MBW (Fig. 4.35: BB–DD, FF–GG) and appliquéd dots (Fig. 4.35:EE). A bi-lobed lug represents an early attestation of a type more common to Hasanlu Period IVc–IVb, which often has double piercing (Fig. 4.35:Y). Tube spouts are increasingly more common (Fig. 4.31:Y).

Other Potential Period V Assemblages at Hasanlu

A small sample of sherds was collected from the earliest Period V deposit in Operation RS22–23 (see Chapter 3). Unfortunately, the ceramics collected from the Period V columned-hall building and the overlying Period IVc level are somewhat unreliable in terms of stratigraphic separation and the collection units employed by the excavators, and thus are detailed here rather than in the previous discussion. The earlier assemblage does not add significantly to our understanding of the period (Fig. 4.37), with Type 3 bowls well represented.

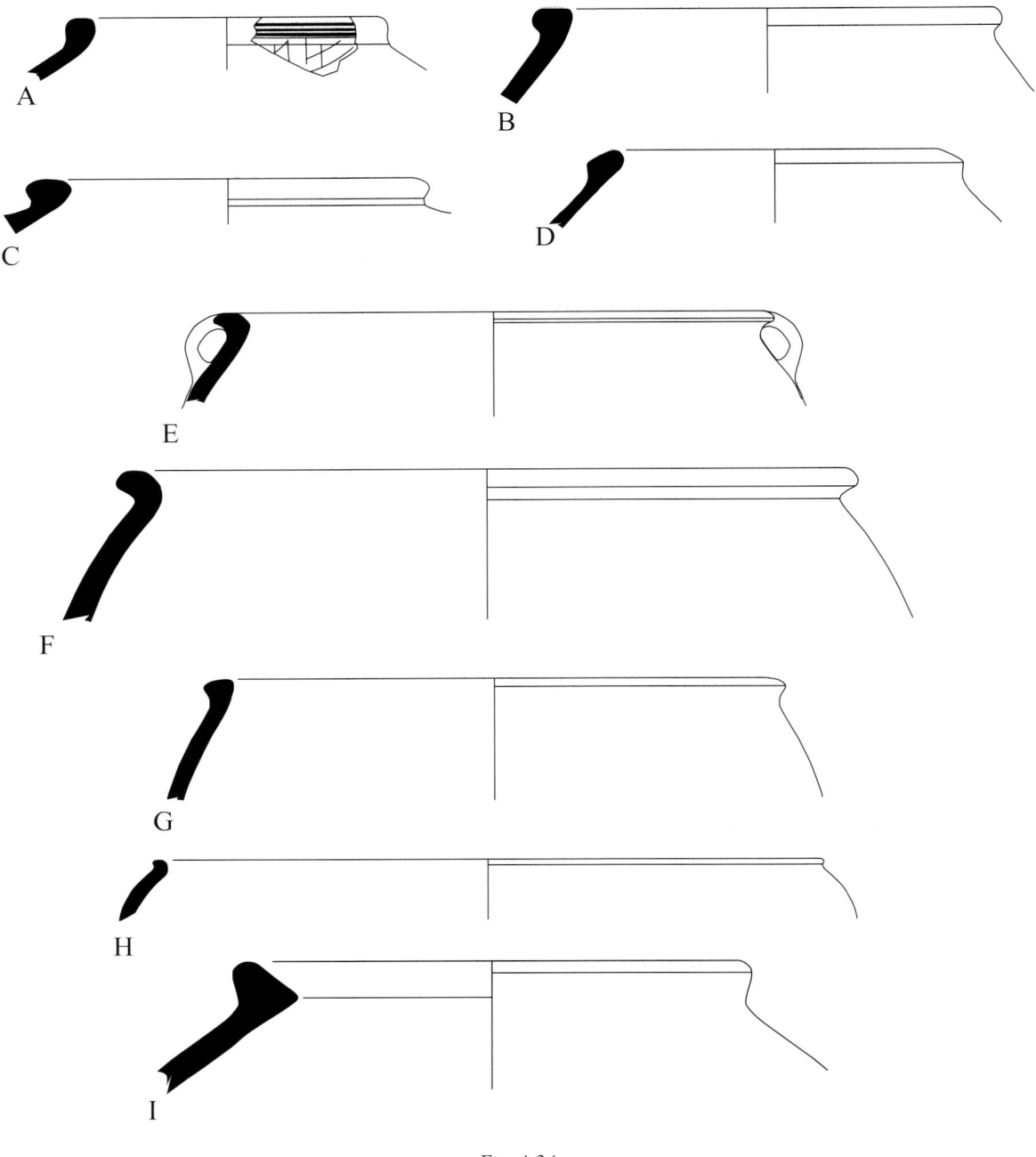

Fig. 4.34

Soundings excavated beneath BBIII of Period IVc–IVb recovered deposits dating at least in part to late Period V and early Period IVc (see Chapter 3). The Q24 Stratum 10 assemblage recovered in 1964 is fairly sizable, but the recordkeeping from this area was poor during the excavation and there is evidence for the mixing of strata, which was noted by the excavators at the time. For the most part, the attested forms fit within Period V, although to avoid circular logic it is best to use this material only to supplement our view constructed from the U22 Sounding, Dinkha, and the Dinkha/Hasanlu grave groups. A small amount

Fig. 4.34 Hasanlu Tepe: late Period V ceramics from the U22 Sounding (opposite).

Fig.	Op.	Context	Ware	Type	Description	Dia.	Disposition
A	U22	8	MBW	HM 5	Black with Black Paint/Slip	20	UPM Sherd 14a
B	T22	8	MBW	HM 5	Red	28	UPM Sherd 13
C	T22	8	MBW	HM 4	Black	24	UPM Sherd 12
D	U22	8	CPW Ia	HM 5	Ext. Orange, Smoked, 5YR5/3 Int. 5YR6/6	22	UPM Sherd 11
E	U22	7	CPW Ia	HM 1	Ext. Orangish-Red, Smoked, 7.5YR7/4, 7.5YR3/0 Int. 7.5YR7/4	34	UPM Sherd 03
F	U22	7	MBW Ic	HM 1	Ext. Grey, Burnished, 2.5Y6/2 Int. D. Grey, Matte, 7.5YR4/0	44	UPM Sherd 04
G	U22	7	MBW Ic	HM 5	Ext. Grey, Burnished, 10YR4/1 Int. L. Grey Matte, 10YR6/2	34	UPM Sherd 07
H	T22	8	MBW	HM 13	Black	40	UPM Sherd 30
I	U22	8	MBW	HM 14	Ext. Black, 10YR6/ Int. 10YR6/2	31	UPM Sherd 03 2

of MBA material is present, including a barrel-form jar with overhanging-ledge rim (Fig. 4.39:C) and one probable *istikhan* base (Fig. 4.40:K). The MBW assemblage includes Types 3 and 9 carinated bowls (Fig. 4.38:E–G, I–J, L–O, Q, T–W, Z), Type 6 incurving bowls (Fig. 4.38:H, R), and Type 8 hemispherical bowls (Fig. 4.38:K, S, Y). As in the U22 Deep Sounding, holemouth jars are prevalent, with Types 1–5 being typical (Fig. 4.39). Jars are relatively rare and are largely confined to Type 2 (Fig. 4.40:B–H). There is some incising (Fig. 4.40:N, O), a bowl with impressed design (Fig. 4.38:P), a rare example of a bridgeless spout (Fig. 4.40:P), and a tab lug (Fig. 4.40:Q).

Period V Conclusions

The most obvious change in Period V is the preponderance of Early MBW in the available assemblages, making up the majority of material available for this study. Surface treatment on the exterior of vessels normally consists of a slip or self-slip, generally of the same color as the vessel's fabric, and varying degrees of smoothing or burnishing. Burnishing is sometimes inconsistent and appears streaky. Other vessels, especially thin, fine ones, are highly burnished and have a glossy appearance. Temper tends to be grit and/or sand of medium grain size with both fine and coarse temper being fairly rare. Surface color ranges from light grey to black, buff to dark brown, and pinkish buff to dark red. Surface decoration is rare, with appliqué, incising, and pattern burnishing used conservatively. The Incised and Impressed MBW present at Dinkha is absent at Hasanlu. Cooking Pot Ware (Coarse Buff Ware) makes up a small percentage of the assemblage. The fabric is fairly porous and contains coarse grit temper. Surfaces are wet smoothed. The color range is limited to pinkish buff to reddish orange, and surfaces are often fire blackened from use. Small amounts of painted and plain KW are found in Period V deposits at Hasanlu, but until larger samples of material are available it would be mere speculation to say whether it is extrusive or was still produced in small amounts.

A wide variety of bowls were used during the period. The predominant types are "worm bowls" (Types 1 and 2), carinated bowls (Types 3, 6, 9), incurving bowls with thickened and simple rims (Type 4–5), and hemispherical bowls with simple or thickened rims (Type 8). There is a change during the period in "worm bowls," with Type 1 tending to be earlier than Type 2.

Carinated tankards are the typical drinking vessel in use during the period. These vessels are short and have button-bases in Period VIa and early Period V. In early Period V, tall tankards gain in popularity and exhibit a wide range of bases.

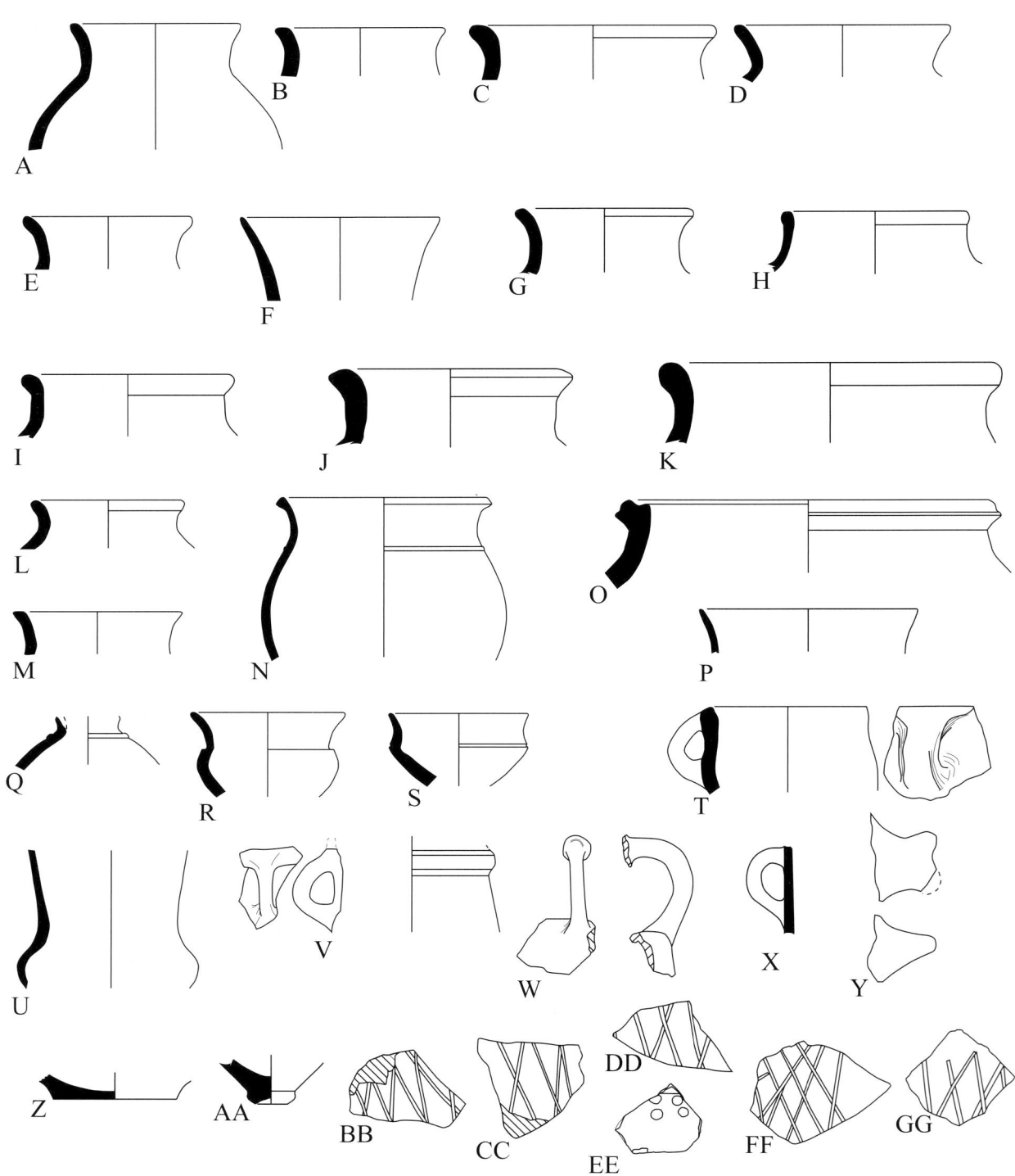

Fig. 4.35

Fig. 4.35 Hasanlu Tepe: late Period V ceramics from the U22 Sounding (opposite).

Fig.	Op.	Context	Ware	Type	Description	Dia.	Disposition
A	T22	8	MBW	Jar 1a	Black	11	UPM Sherd 02
B	T22	8	MBW	Jar 1a	Grey	11	UPM Sherd 29
C	T22	8	MBW	Jar 1b	Red	16	UPM Sherd 32
D	T22	8	MBW IIc	Jar 1a	Grey	14	UPM Sherd 33
E	T22	8	MBW	Jar 1a	Black	11	UPM Sherd 24
F	T22	8	MBW IIc	Cup 1	Grey	13	UPM Sherd 28
G	U22	7	MBW Ib	Jar 1a	Orange, Red Slip	12	UPM Sherd 06 UPM63-5-1055
H	U22	8	MBW	Jar 5	Ext. Tan, 10YR6/2 Int. Grey, 2.5Y4/0	12	UPM Sherd 05
I	U22	7	Buff Ia	Jar Ib	Ext. Matte 7.5YR6/4 Int. Matte 7.5YR6/4	14	UPM Sherd 01
J	U22	7	MBW Ic	Jar Ib	Ext. Red Slip Int. Matte	16	UPM Sherd 05 UPM63-5-1054
K	U22	7	MBW Ib	Jar Ib	Ext./Int. Reddish-Orange, Smoothed, 5YR6/6	22	UPM Sherd 08
L	T22	8	MBW Ib	Jar Ia	Buff	10	UPM Sherd 25
M	T22	8	MBE Ib	Jar Ia	MBW I	11	UPM Sherd 35
N	T22	8	KW Ib	—	Buff	14	UPM Sherd 01
O	T22	7	KW Ib	—	Buff	25	UPM Sherd 23
P	U22	7	MBW IIc	Cup 1	Ext. Red Slip	14	UPM Sherd 13
Q	T22	8	Buff	—	NR	—	UPM Sherd 06
R	T22	8	Buff	Cup 5	NR	10	UPM Sherd 07
S	T22	7	MBW Ic	Cup 5	Red Slipped	10	UPM Sherd 20
T	T22	8	Buff	Cup 4	NR	10	UPM Sherd 39
U	T22	8	MBW	Cup 1	Black	ca. 10	UPM Sherd 10
V	T22	8	MBW	Cup 2	Black	ca. 10	UPM Sherd 19
W	T22	8	MBW	Cup 1	Grey	—	UPM Sherd 20
X	U22	8	MBW Ib	Handle	Ext. 2.5Y4/0 Int. 2.5Y6/2	—	UPM Sherd 15
Y	T22	8	MBW	Bi-Lobed Lug	Red	—	UPM Sherd 15
Z	U22	8	MBW Ib	Flat Base	Grey	—	UPM Sherd E
AA	U22	8	MBW Ib	Button Base	Grey	—	UPM Sherd C UPM63-5-1018
BB	T22	8	MBW	Pattern-Burnished Body Sherd	Buff Pattern Burnished	—	UPM Sherd 5c
CC	T22	8	MBW	Pattern-Burnished	Buff Pattern Burnished	—	UPM Sherd 5a
DD	T22	8	MBW	Pattern-Burnished Body Sherd	Buff Pattern Burnished	—	UPM Sherd 5b
EE	U22	7	MBW IIc	Body Sherd with Appliqué	Ext. Grey–Brown, Burnished, Appliqué Dots, 5Y5/1. 2.5Y3/0 Int. Grey Matte, 2.5Y6/2	—	UPM Sherd 14
FF	T22	8	MBW	Pattern-Burnished Body Sherd	Buff Pattern Burnished	—	UPM Sherd 5d
GG	T22	8	MBW	Pattern-Burnished Body Sherd	Buff Pattern Burnished	—	UPM Sherd No #

222

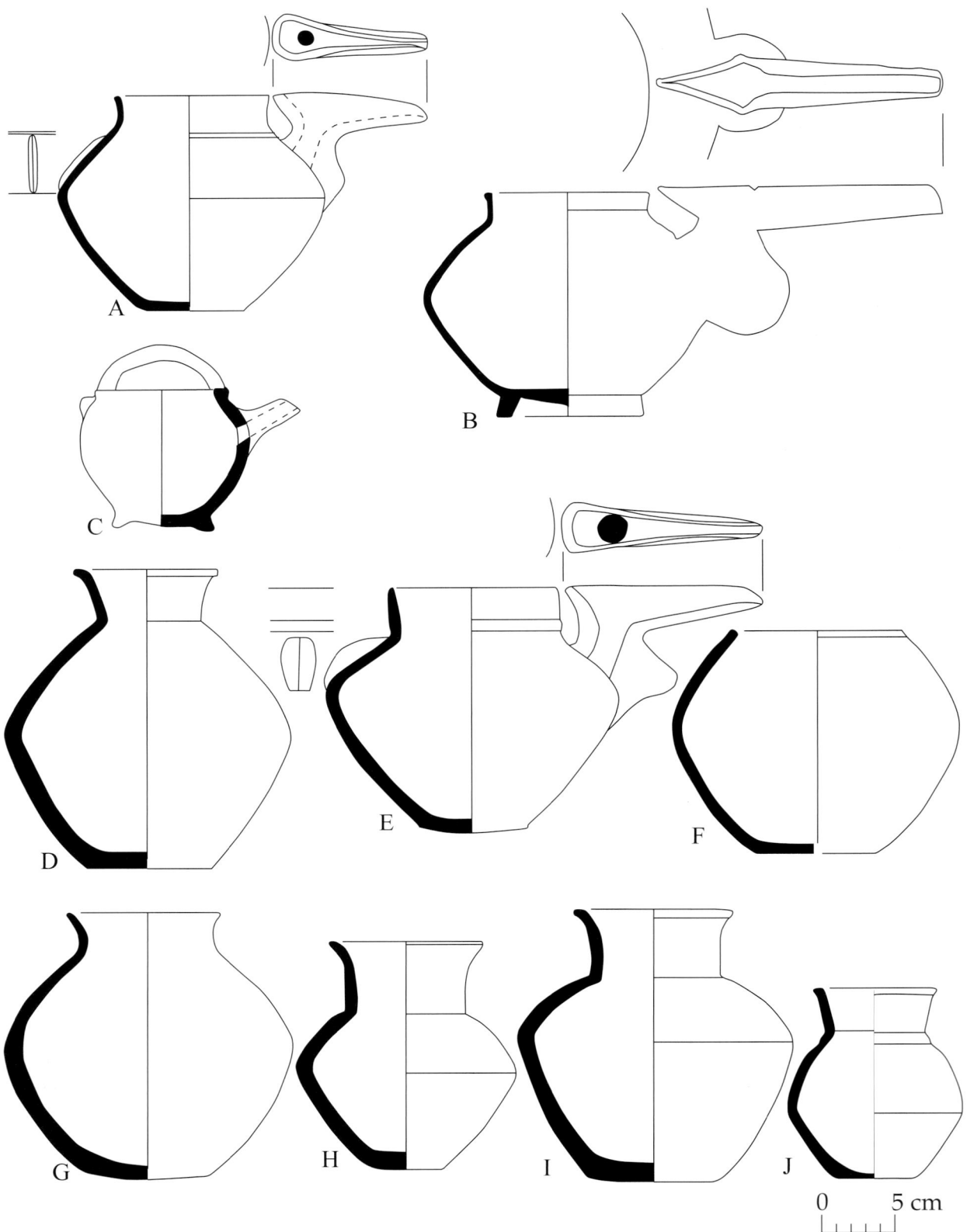

Fig. 4.36

Fig. 4.36 Hajji Firuz, Hasanlu, and Dinkha Tepe: bowls and cups from late V graves (opposite).

Fig.	Op.	Context	Ware	Type	Description	Dia.	Disposition
A	Dinkha B9a	Burial 27	—	Jar 3b	NR	10	—
B	Hajji Firuz K10	Burial 1	—	Jar 3b	NR	11	HF68-37
C	Dinkha B9a	Burial 26	—	HM 15	NR	9	—
D	Dinkha VII	Burial 1	—	Jar 3a	NR	10	—
E	Dinkha B9a	Burial 17	—	Jar 3b	NR	11.5	—
F	VIe Str. 5	Burial SK459	MBW Ib	HM 8	Buff, Reddish-Orange Slip	11.5	HAS64-91
G	Dinkha B9a	Burial 23	—	Jar 1a	NR	11	—
H	Dinkha B9a	Burial 17	—	Jar 3a	NR	10.5	—
I	Dinkha B10b	Burial 10	—	Jar 3a	NR	10.5	—
J	VIe Str. 5	Burial SK459	MBW	Jar 3a	Buff	8	HAS64-90, UPM 65-31-41

Holemouth jars make up a large part of the assemblage, but are not especially diagnostic of time period. There is likely a trend from true holemouth vessels to vessels with rim treatments that place them at the transition between holemouth vessels and jars. In the latter part of the period we see the growing popularity of mid-body carinated jars (Type 3). Jars with high necks and simple rims occur in Period VIa and V graves (Type 6), but are absent in occupation deposits. Type 1 and 2 jars typify occupation deposits and occur in graves. Bridgeless spouts are rarely attested in Hasanlu and Dinkha occupation deposits and Dinkha graves, and are absent in the Hasanlu mortuary assemblage. Such jars are common in the later Period V graves at Dinkha (Seriation). There is little decoration of MBW at Hasanlu in the LBA, save for occasional pattern burnishing and appliqués on holemouth jars and Type 6 jars.

Ceramics of Hasanlu IVc/Iron I (1250–1050 BC)

Operations RS22–23 and YZ27–29 are the most substantial assemblages of Hasanlu IVc and are bracketed by radiocarbon dates (Appendix II). RS22–23 provides the most carefully collected assemblage of Period IVc material as well as a group of late Period IVc–early Period IVb lots. A review of the excavation records indicates the YZ27–29 assemblage contains an admixture of material from late Period V and possibly small amounts of early Period IVb (see Chapter 3), but the vast majority of the assemblage belongs to the Iron I. Most other Period IVc assemblages at Hasanlu (see below) fall within the later part of the period and often likely contain substantial amounts of early Period IVb material. No occupation deposits at Dinkha date to Period IVc. Graves at Dinkha and Hasanlu can be assigned to the Iron I (see Chapter 5). A similar ceramic assemblage was recovered at Kordlar IV–III (see esp. Lippert 1979). Kordlar IV and III are dated to late Hasanlu V and IVc by radiocarbon and dendrochronology (Ehringhaus 1994:58–59). Overall in Hasanlu IVc vessels continue the developmental trends of the LBA, which exhibits close ties to northern Mesopotamia and the southern Caucasus, particularly Nakhichevan. Such connections are more difficult to trace for the Iron I given the paucity of well-dated material of the late 2nd millennium BC in northern Mesopotamia.

The RS22–23 and YZ27–29 sherds were left in Iran and are currently unavailable for analysis. Information on ware types was rarely recorded in the field but, given the predominance of MBW in other contexts of late Period V, Period IVc (see below), and Period IVb, we may safely assume MBW dominated the assemblage. Aside from tall tankards, all of the diagnostics previously attributed to "Period V" and the EWGW horizon by Dyson and Young are present in YZ27–29, including "worm bowls" (Fig. 4.44:C, F, H–I), short pedestal-base cups/tankards

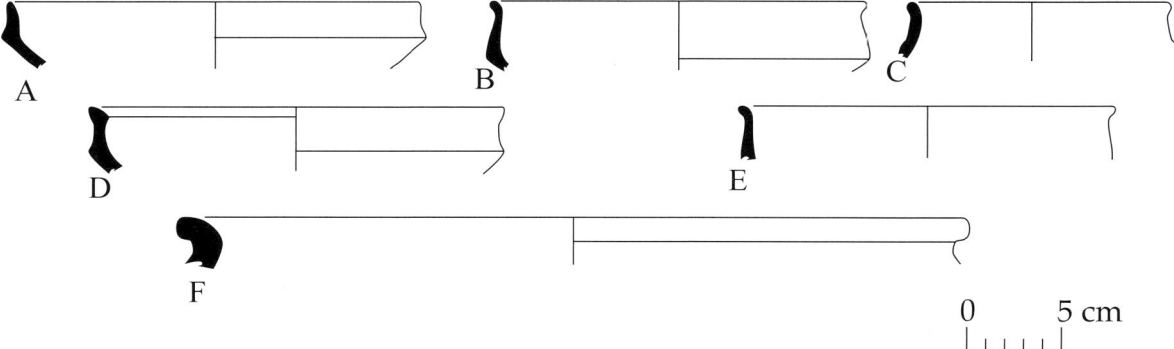

Fig. 4.37 Hasanlu Tepe: Period V ceramics from below the late Hasanlu V columned-hall structure of RS22–23.

Fig.	Op.	Context	Ware	Type	Description	Dia.	Disposition
A	S23E	3	NR	Bowl 3d	NR	22	Sherd Drawing
B	S23E	3	NR	Bowl 3d	NR	20	Sherd Drawing
C	S23E	3	NR	Cup 8?	NR	14	Sherd Drawing
D	S23E	3	NR	Bowl 3a	NR	22	Sherd Drawing
E	S23E	3	NR	Bowl 8	NR	20	Sherd Drawing
F	S23E	3	NR	HM 1	NR	42	Sherd Drawing

(Fig. 4.50:H–T), double-pierced lugs on carinated bowls (Fig. 4.45:M, T), double piercing and piercing of bowls (Figs. 4.45:AA, 4.46:N), bridgeless-spouted jars (Fig. 4.47:G–K), and pattern-burnishing on the upper bodies of holemouth jars in simple crosshatched patterns (Figs. 4.47:T, 4.48:M). A narrower range of forms was found in the Period IVc RS22–23 Building, which was likely a columned-hall structure. Such variation between the assemblages of RS22–23 and YZ27–29 can be attributed to functional differences in the use of space: an elite residence versus rooms associated with internal fortifications leading to ritual spaces such as BBII.

Bowls

Carinated bowls make up the larger part of the assemblage. Carination becomes more pronounced and vessels are frequently decorated with rilling and often have handles at the rim. These are trends that continue throughout the succeeding stages of the early Iron Age.

Type 1a, 2a, and 2c "Worm Bowls"

Only one Type 1a bowl was found in a Period IVc context at Hasanlu (Grave SK73, see Chapter 5) and no Type 2b bowls were found, but Type 2a bowls continue in Period IVc. Only one occurrence of a bowl resembling this entire class is currently known from an early Period IVb grave at Hasanlu (Seriation: Grave SK56). This Type 2c bowl shows the characteristic thinning of vessel walls typical of these bowls in the initial part of the early Iron Age. At Dinkha, a Type 1a bowl with double piercing was found in an early Iron II grave, B9b Burial 19 (Seriation; Muscarella 1974: fig. 27, no. 236). This bowl is noteworthy in that it represents a form typical of the early LBA with a stylistic attribute of the later LBA and Iron I. In RS22–23, two hemispherical bowls of Type 2c, albeit without the tripod bases characteristic of this type in graves, exhibit the early Iron Age trends towards thinner vessel walls, horizontal ribs, and thinned rims, which are especially diagnostic of the

Iron I at the site (Fig. 4.41:O–P). One Type 2a bowl with flat base and pattern-burnished interior (the design was not illustrated) is the only flaring, open bowl of the class from RS22–23 (Fig. 4.41:W). Conversely, the bowls from YZ27–29 are of Type 2a and two bear the double crescent motif (Fig. 4.44:C, F, H–I). One had three lug feet; two were present on the fragmentary vessel (Fig. 4.44:I). Such lugs are a developmental link to the tripod-footed bowls of Hasanlu IVc (Type 2c) and the higher tripod bowls and stands of Period IVb (Fig. 4.51:A–C). Type 2c appears in the graves of Dinkha at this time (Fig. 4.51:A–D). One bowl has double drilling (Fig. 4.51:B) and another has a crescent and drilled hole (Fig. 4.51:C). Nearly all of these hemispherical bowls with simple rims have short tripod legs. Higher tripod legs and full-fledged ceramic footed stands, attached to vessels or as separate objects, are well attested in the MBW ceramic assemblage of Period IVb at Hasanlu, Dinkha (only attached types), and other Iron II sites. Other "worm bowl" types occur with tripod feet, albeit rarely, and they seem to date to late Period IVc and early Period IVb. Muscarella assigns Grave B10a Burial 16 at Dinkha to early Period IVb (Seriation), but it could also be dated to late Period IVc on the basis of the ceramics, particularly a Type 1a bowl with tripod feet higher than those attested for Bowl Type 2c (Muscarella 1974: fig. 28, no. 230).

As previously mentioned, the "worm bowl" class *in toto* is broadly similar to the class of broad shallow bowls of northern Mesopotamia of the Mitanni and Middle Assyrian periods (Postgate, Oates, and Oates 1997: pls. 35–37; Starr 1939: pls. 85, 86:A, D, E, H–I, L–Q; pl. 87:A–M, Q; pl. 88:N; pl. 91:G). In northern Mesopotamia, tripod bowls resembling Type 2c are known from Mitanni occupations at Tell al-Rimah (Postgate, Oates, and Oates 1997: pl. 100 nos. 1201–2), Tell Brak, where they span the period from 1500–1200, and Nuzi, where they occur in burnished grey ware (Starr 1939:403, pl. 92:V–BB). At Brak, such bowls were found in the final Mitanni palace (HH Level 2), which was destroyed in the 13th century by Shalmaneser (Oates, Oates, and McDonald 1997:13–14, 35, table 1, fig. 205 nos. 525–27). Such a dating accords well with the late Period V–early IVc date for YZ27–29, and such bowls must also date even later at Hasanlu given the links between the form and vessels of the Iron II.

Type 3 Bowls

All variants of Type 3 bowls continue into Period IVc (Figs. 4.41:A–B, D, F, H–I, K–N, Q, Y, 4.44:A, B, 4.45:H, J–Q, S–Y, BB–DD, 4.51:G, H, K). Such bowls were occasionally provided with handles at the rim (Figs. 4.41:L, 4.45:V, DD, 4.51:H). Bowls of Type 3b and Type 3d occasionally have bi-lobed lugs with vertical double piercing (Figs. 4.45:M, T, 4.51:G). Type 3F with thinned rim is unique to the period (Fig. 4.45:S), but is attested in Geoy Tepe A (Burton-Brown 1951: fig. 39 no. 207). Bowl Type 3d of late Period V and Period IVc represents one of the best-attested Mitanni bowl forms of northern Mesopotamia in burnished grey ware (Oates et al. 1997:74). According to Oates, Oates, and McDonald (1997:74), "Many of the Brak grey ware vessels are precisely paralleled at Rimah and Nuzi, perhaps indicating a closely connected network of production centres." Type 3G, attested in Q24 and RS22–23, is a type new to Hasanlu in late Period V–IVc (Figs. 4.38:T, 4.41:V). The carinated form was achieved through the reduction of the vessel wall by excising, a technique seemingly related to the production of thinned rims on many vessel types by the same means in the Iron I.

Type 4 and 5 Bowls

Type 4 incurving bowls are represented (Fig. 4.46:O–Q), as are Type 5 incurving bowls with simple rims (Fig. 4.51:I). One has a channel spout at the rim (Fig. 4.46:S). No bowls of this class were found in RS22–23, where carinated forms predominate.

Type 6 Bowls

Type 6 incurving carinated bowls are well represented in both occupation deposits and graves, and the type often has double drilling below the rim (Figs. 4.41:X, Z, AA, 4.44:D, 4.45:AA, EE, 4.51:E, F, J). This bowl type and bowls of Type 3—particularly 3d, with handles—become the common types for inclusion in graves in Period IVc and especially Period IVb, apparently coinciding with the decline of "worm bowls." Rim treatments vary somewhat within Type 6, with simple, thickened, and channel rims—the latter apparently being diagnostic of the Iron I at Hasanlu (Fig. 4.41:AA, see below).

226

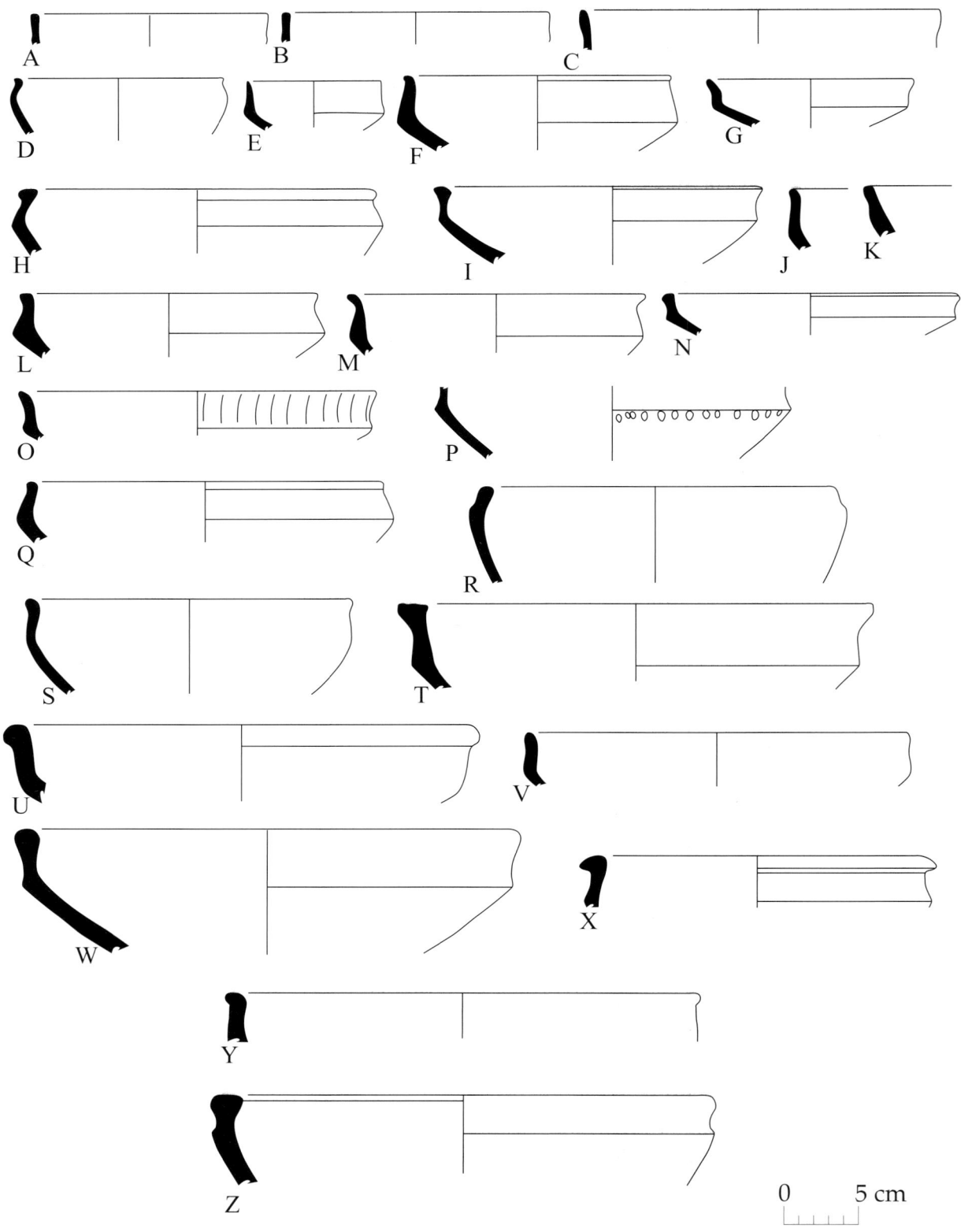

Fig. 4.38

Fig. 4.38 Hasanlu Tepe: ceramics from Q24 Stratum 10 (opposite).

Fig.	Op.	Context	Ware	Type	Description	Dia.	Disposition
A	Q24	10	NR	Bowl 3d?	NR	16	Sherd Drawing
B	Q24	10	NR	Bowl 3d?	NR	18	Sherd Drawing
C	Q24	10	NR	Bowl 3d?	NR	24	Sherd Drawing
D	Q24	10	NR	Bowl 5	NR	14	Sherd Drawing
E	Q24	10	NR	Bowl 3d	NR	9	Sherd Drawing
F	Q24	10	NR	Bowl 3d	NR	18	Sherd Drawing
G	Q24	10	NR	Bowl 9	NR	14	Sherd Drawing
H	Q24	10	NR	Bowl 6	NR	24	Sherd Drawing
I	Q24	10	NR	Bowl 3a	NR	22	Sherd Drawing
J	Q24	10	NR	Bowl 3c	NR	–	Sherd Drawing
K	Q24	10	NR	Bowl 8	NR	–	Sherd Drawing
L	Q24	10	NR	Bowl 3b	NR	20	Sherd Drawing
M	Q24	10	NR	Bowl 9	NR	20	Sherd Drawing
N	Q24	10	NR	Bowl 3b	NR	20	Sherd Drawing
O	Q24	10	NR	Bowl 9	Scraped/Excised	24	Sherd Drawing
P	Q24	10	NR	–	Impressed	–	Sherd Drawing
Q	Q24	10	NR	Bowl 3c	NR	24	Sherd Drawing
R	Q24	10	NR	Bowl 6	NR	24	Sherd Drawing
S	Q24	10	NR	Bowl 8	NR	22	Sherd Drawing
T	Q24	10	NR	Bowl 3g	NR	32	Sherd Drawing
U	Q24	10	NR	Bowl 3a	NR	32	Sherd Drawing
V	Q24	10	NR	Bowl 3d	NR	26	Sherd Drawing
W	Q24	10	NR	Bowl 3a	NR	34	Sherd Drawing
X	Q24	10	NR	Bowl 19	NR	24	Sherd Drawing
Y	Q24	10	NR	Bowl 8	NR	32	Sherd Drawing
Z	Q24	10	NR	Bowl 3b	NR	33.5	Sherd Drawing

Type 8 Bowls

Type 8 bowls with simple and thickened rims are quite common in occupation deposits (Figs. 4.41:C, R, T, 4.45:Z, 4.46:D–E, G–K, M, R).

Type 9 Carinated Bowls

The appearance of carinated bowls with a lower, more prominent point of carination and everted rim represents the introduction of a form common to the Iron II–IV (Fig. 4.45:A–F). Alternatively, since these bowls only occur in the stratigraphically lumped YZ27–29 assemblage (see Chapter 3), their presence might signal contamination of the Iron I deposit with early Iron II material. Similar bowls are attested at Geoy Tepe A (Burton-Brown 1951: fig. 36 no. 357).

Type 10 Bowls

This hemispherical bowl with squared rim is unique in Period IVc (Fig. 4.46:C).

Type 12 Bowls

Coarse bowls, as is the case with other utilitarian vessels, are fairly rare in the available assemblages and especially so in Period IVc (Fig. 4.46:F).

Type 13 Bowls

Hemispherical and carinated bowls of Type 13 with thickened or ledge rims are fairly well attested in this period (Figs. 4.41:S, 4.46:L, N). Another bowl of this type was found in the U22 Sounding (see below)

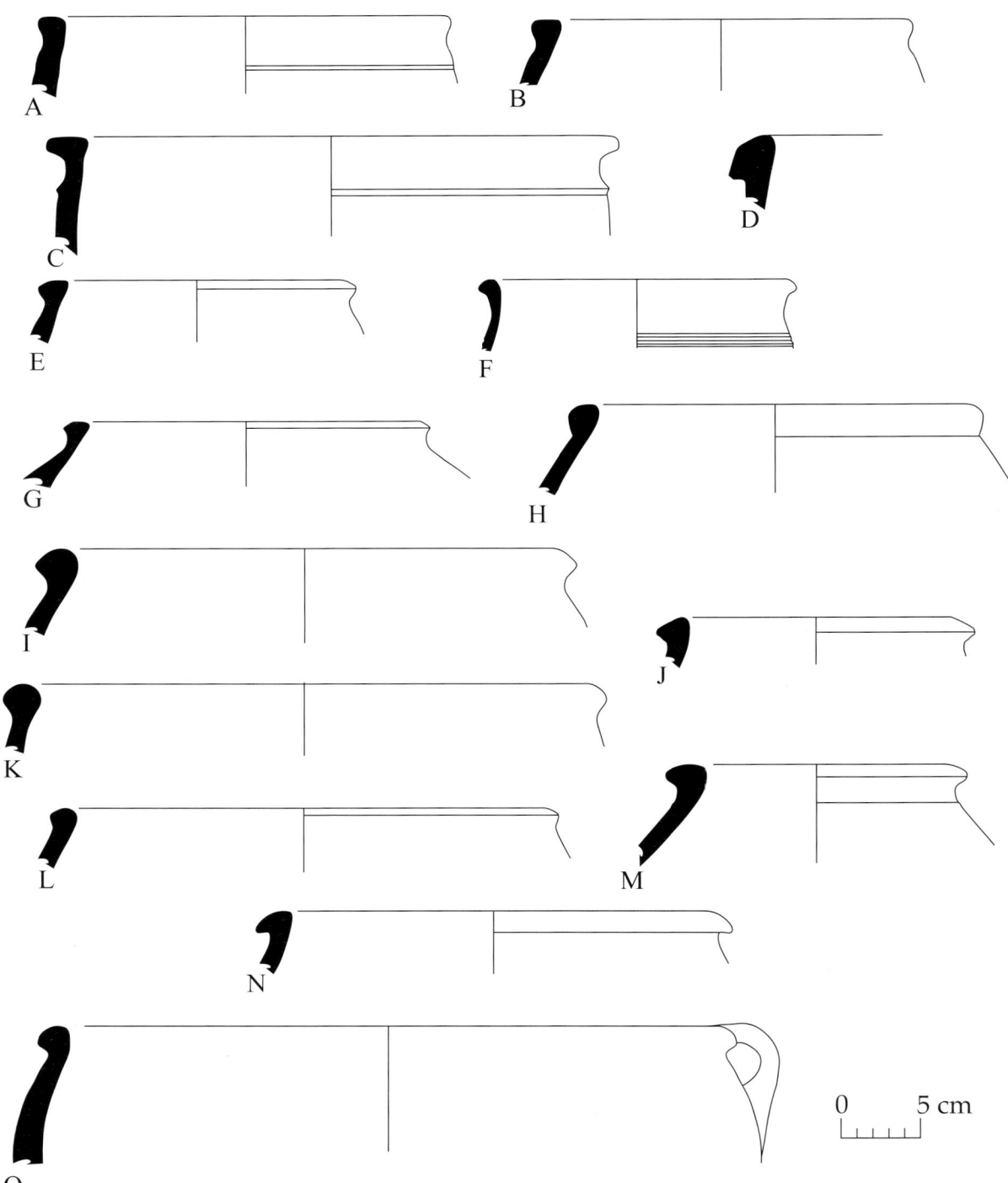

Fig. 4.39

Fig. 4.39 Hasanlu Tepe: ceramics from Q24 Stratum 10 (opposite).

Fig.	Op.	Context	Ware	Type	Description	Dia.	Disposition
A	Q24	10	NR	HM12	NR	26	Sherd Drawing
B	Q24	10	NR	HM3	NR	24	Sherd Drawing
C	Q24	10	NR	—	NR	36	Sherd Drawing
D	Q24	10	NR	HM3	NR	—	Sherd Drawing
E	Q24	10	NR	HM12	NR	20	Sherd Drawing
F	Q24	10	NR	HM5	NR, Rilling	20	Sherd Drawing
G	Q24	10	NR	HM5	NR	23	Sherd Drawing
H	Q24	10	NR	HM5	NR	26	Sherd Drawing
I	Q24	10	NR	HM5	NR	34	Sherd Drawing
J	Q24	10	NR	HM5	NR	20	Sherd Drawing
K	Q24	10	NR	HM4	NR	28	Sherd Drawing
L	Q24	10	NR	HM4	NR	32	Sherd Drawing
M	Q24	10	NR	HM5	NR	19	Sherd Drawing
N	Q24	10	NR	HM5	NR	30	Sherd Drawing
O	Q24	10	NR	HM5	NR, Loop Handle	43.5	Sherd Drawing

and the type seems to date to the late LBA and Iron I.

Type 15 Bowls/Trays

Crude trays are present in Period IVc (Figs. 4.43:M, 4.44:E). They are first attested in late Period V.

Type 19 Bowls

This deep bowl (Figs. 4.41:U, 4.45:R) is closely related to Type 3c, but taller with a rounder lower body.

Type 20 Bowls/Trays

Type 20 bowls or trays are new in this period and range markedly in size (Figs. 4.44:G, 4.46:A, B). Similar bowls, also varying markedly in size, occur in LBA Mesopotamia where they are described as Mitanni red-edged bowls (Oates, Oates, and McDonald 1997: fig. 188: nos. 153, 158). A bowl/tray of this type is known from Geoy Tepe A (Burton-Brown 1951: fig. 36 no. 290).

Type 21 Bowls

Also new to the period are short carinated bowls with out-turned or vertical rims (Figs. 4.41:E, G, 4.45:G, 4.46:T); the rims are thinned, a common treatment in the Iron I. These bowls are closely related to, and grade into, the pyxides that become increasingly more common in the Iron I and Iron II (see below). The type is known from Geoy Tepe A, where it also may have a thinned rim (Burton-Brown 1951: fig. 38 nos. 227, 228).

Holemouth Jars

As in the LBA, holemouth forms are ubiquitous, occurring in a range of sizes, body forms, and rim treatments. The increased evidence of bridgeless-spouted vessels at Hasanlu represents a significant development. The jars of RS22–23 tend to have incised horizontal lines just below the rim (rilling). Some vessels were decorated with pattern-burnish crosshatching and, more frequently, with cannelures (grooves).

Type 1 Holemouth Jars

Holemouth jars of Type 1 are abundant in Period IVc, continuing a long-established trend in the popularity of this simple utilitarian form (Figs. 4.42:A, E–F, H, J, 4.48:B–F, I, U). One jar from Hasanlu Burial SK24 has pattern burnish decoration (Fig. 4.52:I).

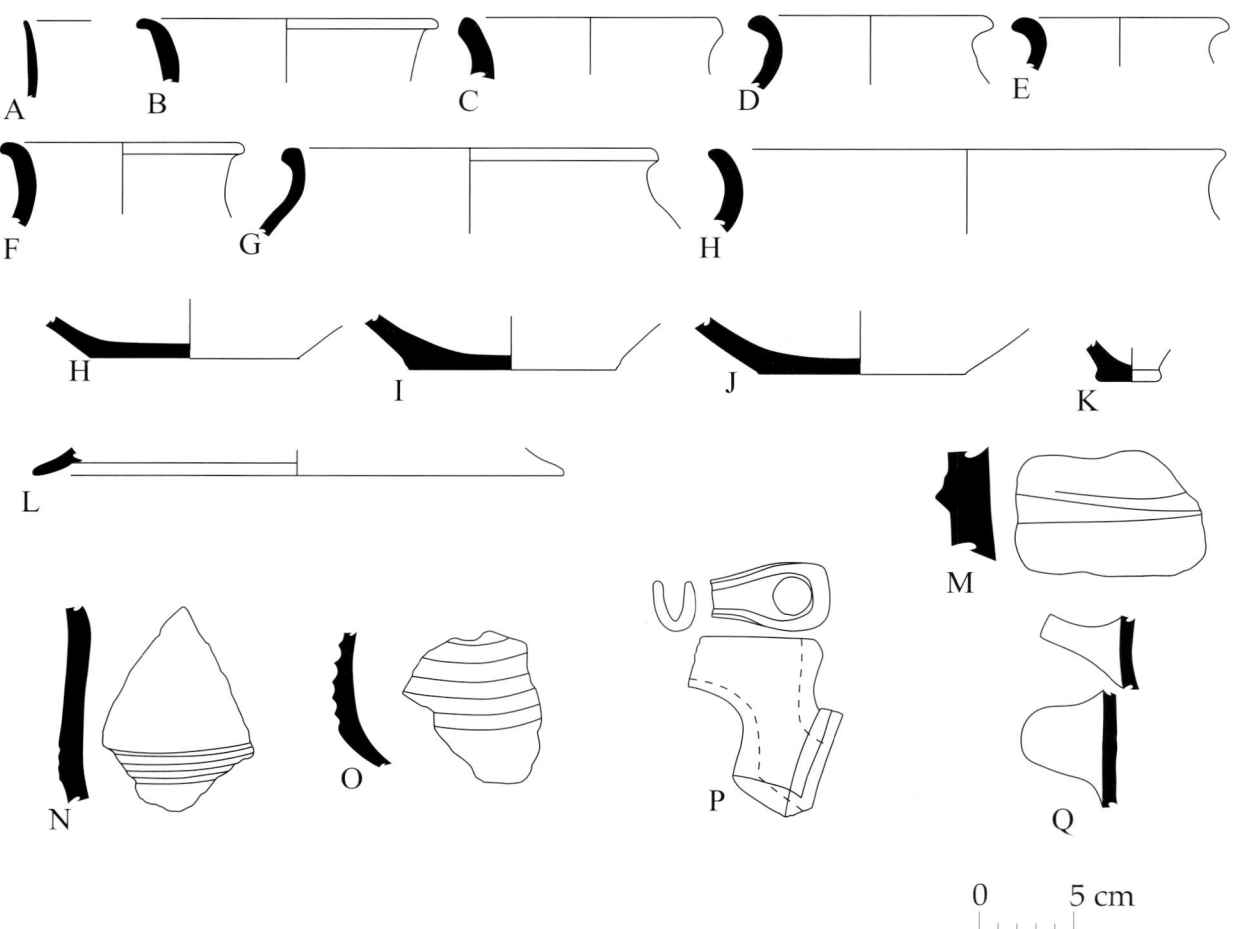

Fig. 4.40 Hasanlu Tepe: ceramics from Q24 Stratum 10.

Fig.	Op.	Context	Ware	Type	Description	Dia.	Disposition
A	Q24	10	NR	Cup 1 or 7	NR	—	Sherd Drawing
B	Q24	10	NR	Jar 2	NR	16	Sherd Drawing
C	Q24	10	NR	Jar 2	NR	14	Sherd Drawing
D	Q24	10	NR	Jar 2	NR	13	Sherd Drawing
E	Q24	10	NR	Jar 2	NR	11	Sherd Drawing
F	Q24	10	NR	Jar 2	NR	13	Sherd Drawing
G	Q24	10	NR	Jar 2	NR	20	Sherd Drawing
H	Q24	10	NR	Jar 2	NR	27	Sherd Drawing
I	Q24	10	NR	—	NR	11	Sherd Drawing
J	Q24	10	NR	—	NR	11	Sherd Drawing
K	Q24	10	NR	—	NR	11	Sherd Drawing
L	Q24	10	NR	—	NR	3.5	Sherd Drawing
M	Q24	10	NR	—	NR	—	Sherd Drawing
N	Q24	10	NR	—	NR, Rilling	—	Sherd Drawing
O	Q24	10	NR	—	NR, Rilling	—	Sherd Drawing
P	Q24	10	NR	—	NR, Bridgeless Spout	—	Sherd Drawing
Q	Q24	10	NR	—	NR, Tab Handle	—	Sherd Drawing

Type 2 Holemouth Jars

These vessels appear to be cooking pots; one was provided with upright tab handles (Figs. 4.47:V, 4.48:S).

Type 3 Holemouth Jars

The only Period IVc Type 3 jars were found in RS22–23 (Fig. 4.42:B, D, L) and are likely associated with domestic activities. One has a channel rim typical of Iron I Hasanlu (Fig. 4.42:L).

Type 4 Holemouth Jars

This type remains a popular storage vessel in the Iron I (Figs. 4.42:C, M, 4.47:O, R–U, 4.48:A, N–O) and one example is decorated with pattern-burnish crosshatching (Fig. 4.47:T).

Type 5 Holemouth Jars

These storage jars are fairly prevalent in Period IVc (Figs. 4.42:I, K, 4.47: Q, 4.48:G, J–M, Q, 4.50:HH). One example is decorated with pattern-burnish crosshatching (Fig. 4.48:M) and another nearly whole example in Buff IVa has vertical ribbing (Fig. 4.50:GG).

Type 8 Holemouth Jars

This jar is fairly rare in Period IVc with one attestation in YZ27–29 (Fig. 4.48:R) and another in the U22 Sounding (see below, Fig. 4.54:Q).

Type 9 Holemouth Jars

As in Period V, these small globular jars are relatively common (Fig. 4.47:A–F) and there is abundant evidence of tails, beards, and bridgeless spouts (Fig. 4.47:G–K). In the Iron I it seems that holemouth jars provided with bridgeless spouts tended toward globular forms, while the typical spouted jars of Dinkha in the later LBA and Iron I are bi-conical and generally were provided with a low-to-medium neck and rim (Fig. 4.52:F–H). One probable Type 9 jar was elaborately incised and was provided with a loop handle and has a mid-body carination (Fig. 4.42:N). One unusual jar of this type with a low pedestal base, bridgeless spout, and appliquéd horn motif tail comes from a grave at Dinkha Tepe (Fig. 4.52:G). This jar has the mid-body carinated form characteristic of Middle and Late MBW jars and was found with an inverted carinated bowl with drilling (Fig. 4.51:J, Seriation: Dinkha B9a Burial 24).

Type 17 Holemouth Jars

Only one Type 17 jar was found in a Period IVc context (Fig. 4.48:P). The distinguishing feature of the type is a pronounced channel rim, perhaps, as with other channel-rim vessels of the period, designed to facilitate the placement of a lid and/or sealing.

Type 18 Holemouth Jars

This small pot or cup is unique (Fig. 4.47:N). It may represent a large version of a Type 12 Cup (see below), but the thickened rim is inconsistent with that type.

Type 19 Holemouth Jars

This mid-body carinated holemouth vessel is preserved well enough to show the carination typical of holemouth and other jars of late Period V and IVc (Fig. 4.48:T).

Type 20 Holemouth Jars

This small holemouth jar with carination, medium neck, and simple everted rim is rare in Period IVc (Fig. 4.47:P), but its individual attributes certainly accord well with larger developmental trends of the late 2nd millennium BC toward the production of low carinated forms, classified as cups and pyxides (see below).

Type 22 Holemouth Jars

This interesting elliptical vessel with a hollow tubular lug is unique (Fig. 4.47:L).

Type 23 Holemouth Jars

This jar is similar to Jar Type 2 and lies in the area of overlap between bag-shaped jars and holemouth jars: since it lacks a distinct shoulder/neck I have categorized it as a holemouth form (Fig. 4.42:G). The

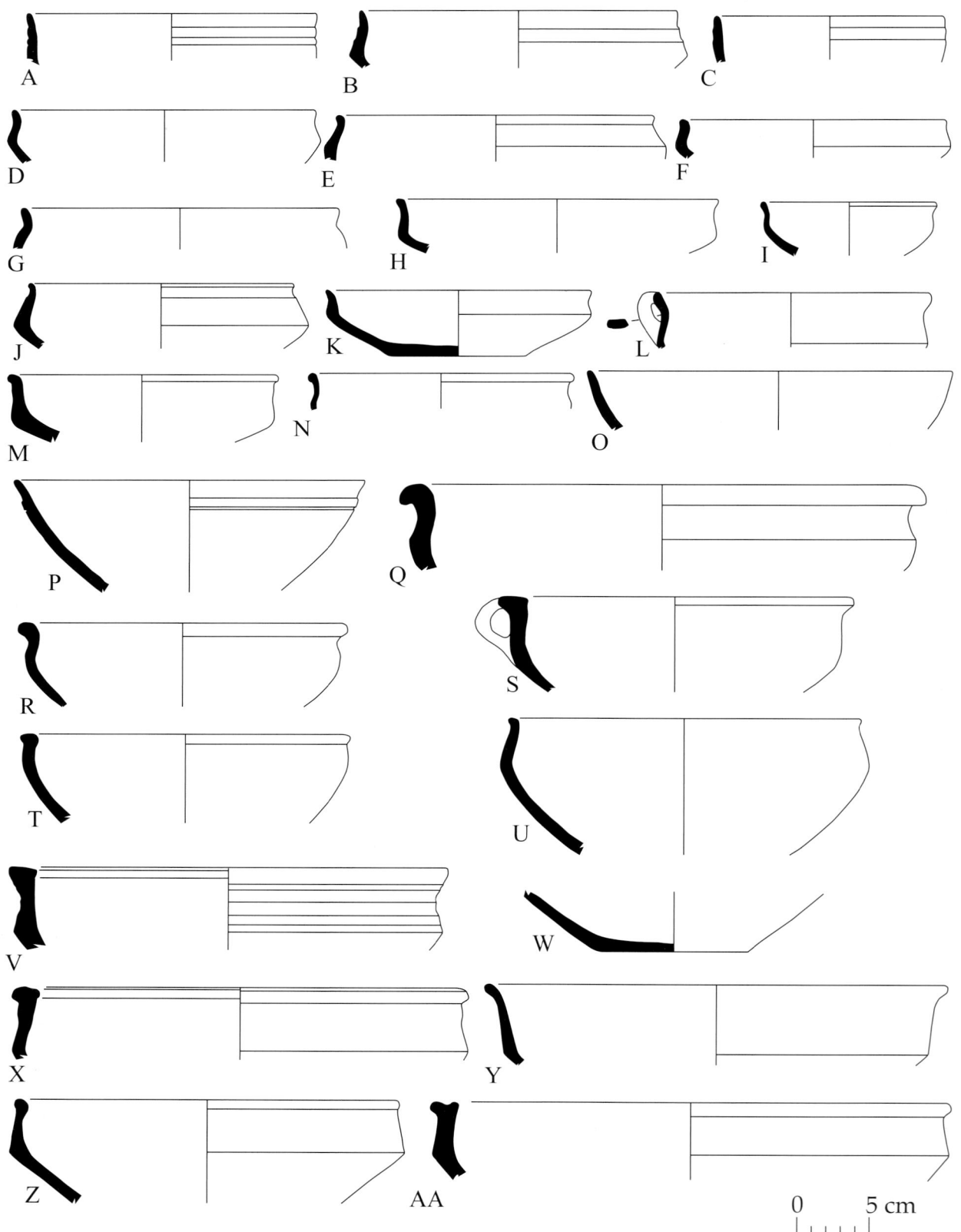

Fig. 4.41

Fig. 4.41 Hasanlu Tepe: Period IVc bowls from RS22-23 (opposite).

Fig.	Op.	Context	Ware	Type	Description	Dia.	Disposition
A	S23E	2	NR	Bowl 3d	NR, Rilling	20	Sherd Drawing
B	S23E	2	NR	Bowl 3d	NR, Rilling	22	Sherd Drawing
C	S23E	2	NR	Bowl 8	NR, Rilling	16	Sherd Drawing
D	S23E	2	NR	Bowl 3c	NR	21	Sherd Drawing
E	S23E	2	NR	Bowl 21	NR	22	Sherd Drawing
F	S22	Area 11 Str. 2	NR	Bowl 3c	NR	18.5	Sherd Drawing 408
G	S23E	2	NR	Bowl 21	NR	22	Sherd Drawing
H	S22	Area 11 Str. 10	NR	Bowl 3d	NR	22	Sherd Drawing 409
I	RS22-23	—	NR	Bowl 3c	NR	12	Sherd Drawing
J	S22	Area 12 Str. 9	NR	Bowl 21	NR	18.5	Sherd Drawing
K	RS22-23	6	NR	Bowl 3c	NR	18.5	Sherd Drawing 706
L	R23	Area 5 Str. 8	MBW IIIb	Bowl 3b	Orangish Buff	19	Sherd Drawing
M	RS22-23	6	NR	Bowl 3d	NR	19	Sherd Drawing 707
N	RS22-23	4	NR	Bowl 3c	NR	18	Sherd Drawing
O	R23	Area 5 Str. 8	MBW IIIc	Bowl 2c	Grey	25	Sherd Drawing
P	RS22-23	—	NR	Bowl 2c	NR, Raised Band	24.5	Sherd Drawing 700
Q	RS22-23	6	NR	Bowl 3b	NR	36	Sherd Drawing 704
R	RS22-23	6	NR	Bowl 8	NR	23	Sherd Drawing 705
S	S22	Area 11 Str. 10	NR	Bowl 13	NR	24.5	Sherd Drawing 405
T	RS22-23	6	NR	Bowl 8	NR	23	Sherd Drawing 703
U	S22	Area 12 Str. 9	NR	Bowl 19	NR	24.5	Sherd Drawing
V	RS22-23	Str. 6	NR	Bowl 3g	NR	30.5	Sherd Drawing 709
W	R23	Area 3-4 Str. 8	MBW IIIc	Bowl 2a	Black, Int. Pattern Burnish	10.5	Sherd Drawing
X	RS22-23	Area 5 Str. 8	NR	Bowl 6	NR	31.5	Sherd Drawing 695
Y	R23	Area 3-4 Str. 7	MBW IIIc	Bowl 3d	Buff, Ext. Smudged	31.5	Sherd Drawing
Z	S22	Area 13 Str. 8	NR	Bowl 6	NR	26.5	Sherd Drawing
AA	S23	Area 3-4 Str. 8	MBW IIIc	Bowl 6	Grey	36	Sherd Drawing

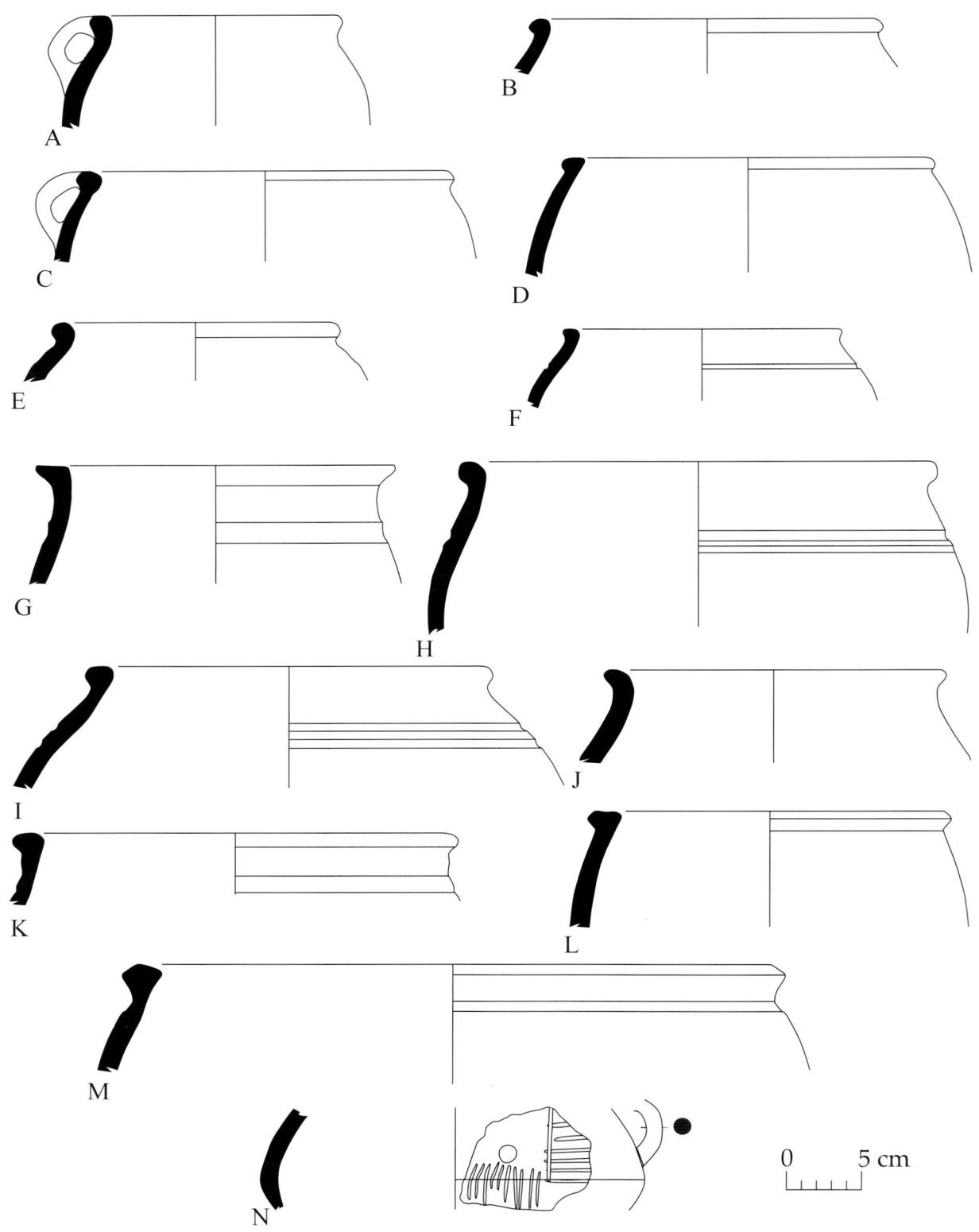

Fig. 4.42

Fig. 4.42 Hasanlu Tepe: Period IVc holemouth jars from RS22–23 (opposite).

Fig.	Op.	Context	Ware	Type	Description	Dia.	Disposition
A	S22	Area 11 Str. 10	NR	HM 1	NR, Strap Handle	17	Sherd Drawing 414
B	S22	Area 11 Str. 10	NR	HM 3	NR	24	Sherd Drawing 413
C	RS22-23	6	NR	HM 4	NR, Strap Handle	25	Sherd Drawing 712
D	S22	Area 11 Str. 10	NR	HM 3	NR	25	Sherd Drawing 416
E	RS22-23	6	NR	HM 1	NR	19	Sherd Drawing 708
F	S22	Area 12 Str. 9	NR	HM 1	NR, Cannelure	18.5	Sherd Drawing
G	R23	Area 5 Str. 8	MBW IIIc	HM 23	Orangish Buff, Ext. Raised Band, Int. Matte	24	Sherd Drawing
H	RS22-23	Period "IV-V"	NR	HM 1	NR, Cannelure	32	Sherd Drawing
I	RS22-23	4	NR	HM 5	NR, Cannelures	27	Sherd Drawing 698
J	S22	Area 11 Str. 10	NR	HM 1	NR	23	Sherd Drawing 415
K	RS22-23	6	NR	HM 5	NR, Raised Band	29.5	Sherd Drawing 711
L	R23	Area 5 Str. 8	CPW IIIa	HM 3	Buff	24	Sherd Drawing
M	S22	Area 11 Str. 10	NR	HM 4	NR	44	Sherd Drawing 417
N	S23E	Str. 1 "Below Pd. IV Surface"	NR	HM 9?	Ext. Excised Deco., Loop Handle	–	Sherd Drawing

ledge rim represents a trait revived in the Iron I—along with the related channel rim—and the horizontal band below the rim is typical of Hasanlu IVc.

Jars

The jars of Period IVc are, on the whole, in keeping with the broader developmental trends in style documented for Period V. Deep rilling on jar shoulders represents a highly diagnostic attribute that continues into the Iron II and is part of a larger trend toward increased ornamentation through the use of incising, excising, and appliqué.

Type 1 Jars

Rims from likely Type 1a (Fig. 4.49:C, E) and 1b (Figs. 4.43:H–I, 4.49:D, F–G, J) jars are attested in the occupation deposits of Hasanlu. A few whole examples were found in graves at Dinkha (Fig. 4.53:E, G).

Type 2 Jars

There are few jars of this type in Period IVc and early IVb relative to earlier periods (Figs. 4.43:J, L, 4.49:K).

Type 3 Jars

Type 3a mid-body carinated jars with simple everted rims and short-to-medium necks are common in the graves at Dinkha (Fig. 4.53:A–C). Rims from probable Type 3a jars were found in occupation deposits at Hasanlu (Figs. 4.43:K, 4.49:A–B, H–I). Type 3b short, squat jars with bridgeless spouts are decorated with excising and more elaborate appliquéd tails,

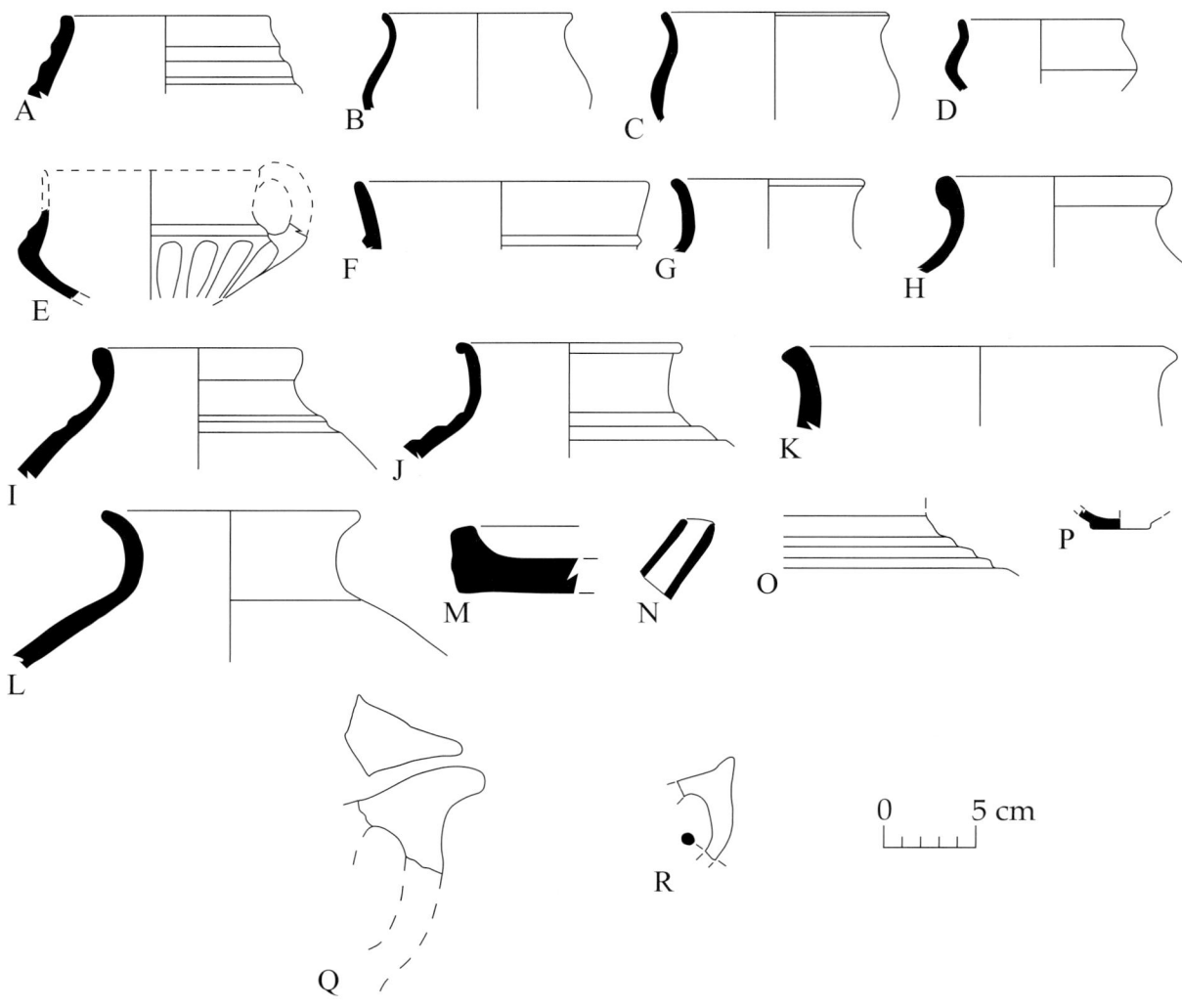

Fig. 4.43

and one occurrence has an excised "waffle base" (Fig. 4.52:F, H). This type of base is also attested on a late Period V Type 2a "worm bowl" from Hasanlu (Fig. 4.44:H).

Type 4 Jars

One jar of this type, unique to the Hasanlu assemblage, has a handle affixed at the rim (Fig. 4.49:R).

Type 9 Jars

This carinated jar with double handles, a feature common in the Iron II, is rare in the Period IVc assemblage but quite common in the Iron II (Fig. 4.49:N). The type, similar to a *kantharos*, often has high swung handles (see below) and also occurs in Geoy Tepe A (Burton-Brown 1951: fig. 41 no. 339).

Cups

As with jars, Period IVc cups continue LBA trends while incorporating new innovations. Cups are particularly diagnostic index fossils in the 2nd–early 1st millennia BC in Ušnu-Solduz. The series also exhibits many of the same stylistic treatments attested in other vessel categories, particularly in Period IVc, with a prevalent use of raised horizontal ribs and rilling.

Fig. 4.43 Hasanlu Tepe: Period IVc ceramics from RS22–23 (opposite).

Fig.	Op.	Context	Ware	Type	Description	Dia.	Disposition
A	S22	Area 12 Str. 9	NR	Cup 9	NR, Rilling		Sherd Drawing
B	R23	Area 5 Str. 8	MBW IIIb	Cup 8	Scraped, Orangish Buff		Sherd Drawing
C	R23	Area 3-4 Str. 8	MBW IIIb	Cup 8	Buff		Sherd Drawing
D	S23	Area 3-4 Str. 8	MBW IIIc	Cup 12	Buff		Sherd Drawing
E	S22	Area 11 Str. 10	NR	Cup 11b	NR, Gadrooning		Sherd Drawing 424
F	S23E	2	NR	Cup 8	NR, Raised Band		Sherd Drawing
G	RS22-23	6	NR	Cup 8	NR		Sherd Drawing 702
H	RS22-23	4	NR	Jar 1b	NR		Sherd Drawing 689
I	R23	Area 5 Str. 8	MBW IIIb	Jar 1b	Pale Buff, Cannelure		Sherd Drawing
J	R23	Area 5 Str. 8	MBW IIIc	Jar 2	L. Grey, Rilling		Sherd Drawing
K	S22	Area 11 Str. 10	NR	Jar 3a	NR		Sherd Drawing 421
L	S23	Area 3-4 Str. 8	MBW IIIc	Jar 2	Black		Sherd Drawing
M	RS22-23	4	NR	Bowl 15	NR		Sherd Drawing 696
N	R23	Area 3-4 Str. 8	MBW IIIc	—	Black		Sherd Drawing
O	R23	Area 11 Str. 8	NR	—	NR, Rilling	—	Sherd Drawing
P	S22	Area 11 Str. 10	NR	—	NR		Sherd Drawing 412
Q	RS22-23	"Pd. IV-V"	MBW Ic	—	Grey, High Swung Handle	—	Sherd Drawing
R	S22	Area 12 Str. 9	NR	—	NR, High Swung Handle	—	Sherd Drawing

Cup Type 7 Short Carinated Pedestal-base Cups

These cups occur in high numbers in the Period IVc deposit of Hasanlu YZ27–29 (Fig. 4.50:B–D, H–U) and in graves at both Hasanlu and Dinkha (Fig. 4.52:A–C), and are an important marker of the Iron I. In Dinkha graves (Seriation), these cups co-occur with tripod-base "worm bowls" (Bowl Type 2c). When these cups occur in graves they are, as a rule, associated with the burials of children. They also occur in the Iron I citadel, as attested by the sherdage from YZ27–29. The type is almost certainly related to the tall tankards of the LBA—Cup Type 1, with the trend toward shorter, broader vessels in the later LBA and Iron I—and are in turn likely the precursors of the carinated mugs and beakers of the later Iron I and Iron II (see esp. Cup Type 11). Type 7 cups also occur at Geoy Tepe A (Burton-Brown 1951: figs. 36 no. 102; 41 no. 27).

Cup Type 8 Fine Shouldered Beakers

Type 8b and 8c shouldered beakers first appear in large numbers in Period IVc and are especially common in the latter part of the period and in early Period IVb (Figs. 4.43:B–C, F–G, 4.49:O, 4.50:A). Whole examples of Type 8b beakers reveal they are ovoid and generally have a mid-body carination as opposed to a true shoulder (e.g., Fig. 4.49: O). Rims are simple and are straight or slightly everted. Beakers of Type 8c, an ovoid form with short neck, shoulder, simple everted or out-turned rim, and flat base, were included among the grave goods of SK73 at Hasanlu (Fig. 4.52:J–K) and among those in SK57 (Fig. 4.53:F), although this latter vessel is larger but nevertheless fine and of identical form. In the Iron II, these beakers and related miniature jars are often found in groups in graves and usually have a horizontal rib at the shoulder-neck transition.

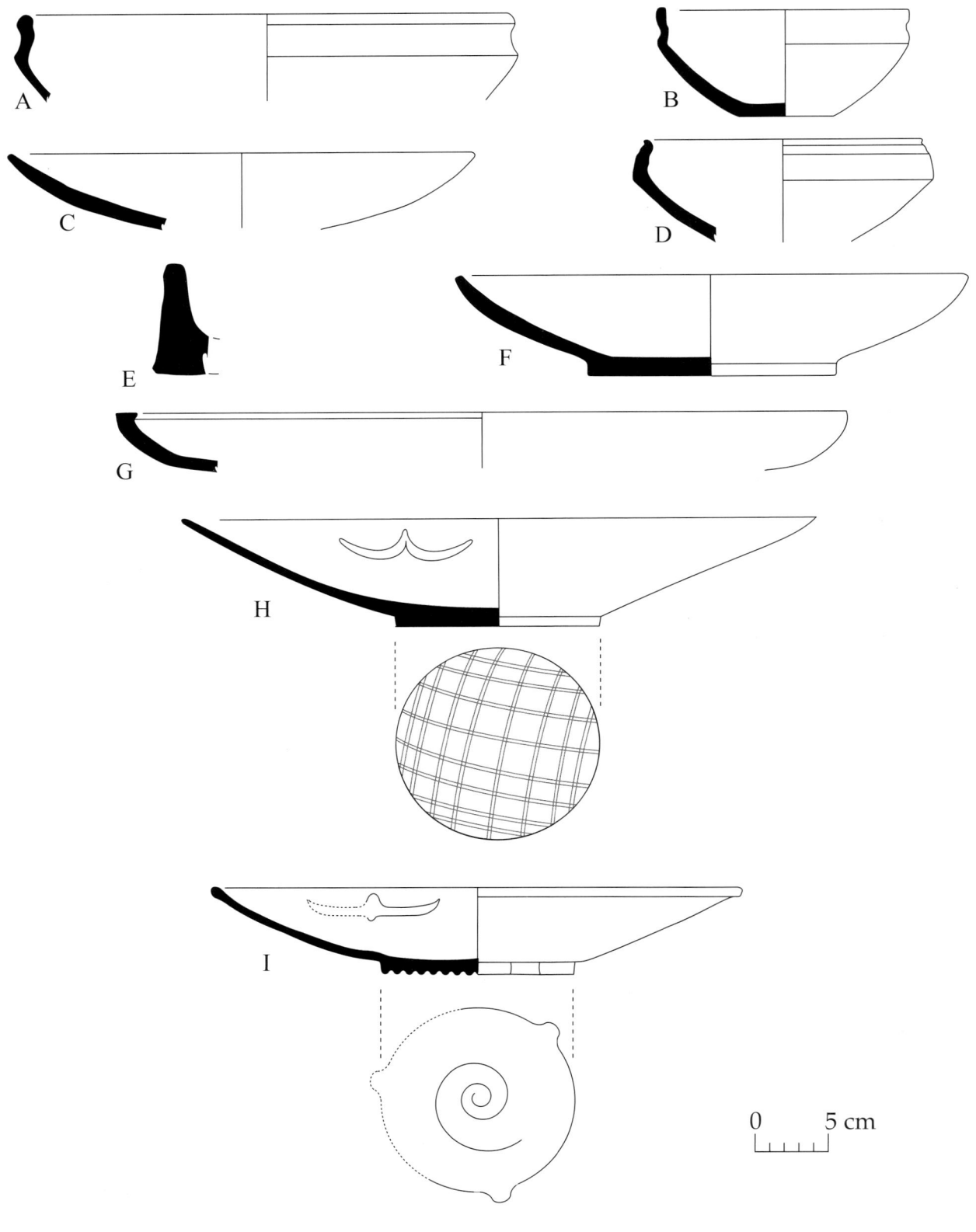

Fig. 4.44

Fig. 4.44 Hasanlu Tepe: Period IVc bowls from YZ27–29 (opposite).

Fig.	Op.	Context	Ware	Type	Description	Dia.	Disposition
A	Y28	Area 2	NR	Bowl 3b	NR	34	Sherd Drawing 31
B	X28	Area 10 Str. 4	MBW Ic	Bowl 3b	NR	18	HAS72N-173 UPM 73-5-135
C	Z28	Area 1 Str. 10/11	MBW IVc	Bowl 2a	NR	32	Sherd 54
D	Y28	Area 4	MBW IVb	Bowl 6	NR	19	Sherd 34
E	Z28	Area 1 Str. 11	NR	Bowl 15	NR	—	Sherd Drawing 04
F	Z28	Area 1 Str. 10	NR	Bowl 2a	NR	35	—
G	Y28	Area 4	NR	Bowl 20	NR	50+	Sherd Drawing 52
H	Z28	Area 1 Str. 10	MBW	Bowl 2a	Grey, Excised Waffle Base, Double Crescent Appliqué Only half the vessel extant	43	HAS72-99 UPM 73-5-131
I	Z28	Area 2 Str. 10	MBW	Bowl 2a	Grey, Lug Feet, Double Crescent Appliqué	36	HAS72-100

Cup Type 9

This cup type is only attested in sherds from Hasanlu Period IVc (Figs. 4.43:A, 4.50:E–F) and probably was a variant form of a beaker or tankard.

Cup Type 11 Low Carinated Mugs/Beakers

These vessels are an important marker of the Iron I and Iron II at Hasanlu and first appear in the earlier Iron I occupation deposits. Type 11a, low carinated mugs or beakers, have simple everted rims (Fig. 4.49:L, M). Type 11b beakers/mugs are similar to Type 11a in most respects (Figs. 4.43:E, 4.52:D), and are more common in late IVc and early IVb. As with other drinking vessels and jars, these vessels frequently have a raised horizontal rib. Gadrooning (fluting) becomes increasingly common on vessels over the course of the Iron I–II (Fig. 4.43:E). The type in several variants is well attested at Geoy Tepe A (Burton Brown 1951: figs. 37 no. 29; 38 nos. 111, 217, 227, 228, 399; 41 nos. 157, 158, 221, 223).

Cup Type 12

Two examples of this simple cup form occur in Period IVc (Figs. 4.43:D, 4.50:G) and an earlier occurrence is known from the Dinkha early Hasanlu V "trash deposit" in Incised and Impressed MBW (Fig. 4.18:J). Despite this similarity in form, an admittedly generic one, it is unlikely there is a connection between these disparate occurrences. These cups are typical of the late Iron I and early Iron II occupation deposits of Hasanlu—many were found in the terminal Period IVc deposit of BBV (see below). The type is also known at Geoy Tepe A (Burton-Brown 1951: fig. 37 no. 650).

Cup Type 14

This cup, from grave SK479 (see Chapter 5), is unique in the Ušnu-Solduz dataset (Fig. 4.52:E). Similar cups occur with and without pedestal bases at Giyan in, for example, Graves 61 and 62. Henrickson (1983–1984: table 4, fig. C) places Grave 61 in both his Late Giyan II and Carinated Pedestal Base Goblet classes, dated respectively to 1600–1400 BC (MBIII herein) and 1450–1200 (LBA and early Iron I herein). Based on the co-occurrence of a hemispherical "worm bowl" with this cup in grave SK479 at Hasanlu, I have dated Type 14 and this grave to the early Iron I. I would leave open the possibility of an earlier dating of late Hasanlu V, but an attribution to the MBIII seems doubtful.

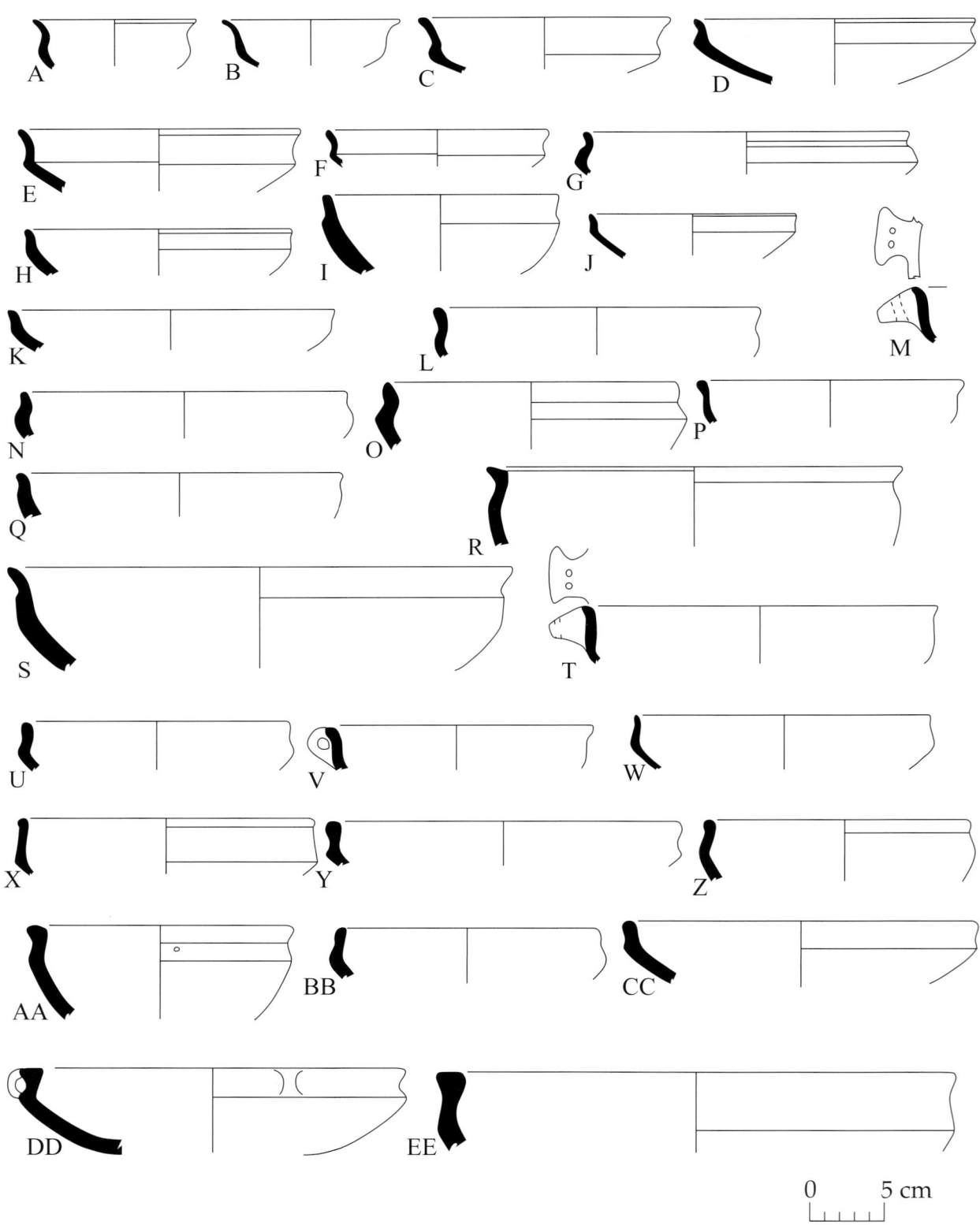

Fig. 4.45

Fig. 4.45 Hasanlu Tepe: Period IVc bowls from YZ27–29 (opposite).

Fig.	Op.	Context	Ware	Type	Description	Dia.	Disposition
A	Y28	Area 4	MBW Ic	Bowl 9	NR	11	Sherd Drawing 22
B	Y28	Area 4 Pit 2	NR	Bowl 9	NR	12	Sherd Drawing 23
C	Y28	Area 4	NR	Bowl 9	NR	17	Sherd Drawing 24
D	Y28	Area 2	NR	Bowl 9	NR	19	Sherd Drawing 25
E	Y28	Area 4	MBW IIIc	Bowl 9	NR	19	Sherd Drawing 26
F	Y28	Area 4	MBW IIIc	Bowl 9	NR	15	Sherd Drawing 21
G	Y27/Y28	Area 1	NR	Bowl 21	NR	22	Sherd Drawing 33
H	Z29	Area 3 Str. 10a	NR	Bowl 3c	NR	18	Sherd Drawing 07
I	Z29	Area 1-2 Str. 11	NR	Bowl 10	NR	16	Sherd Drawing 44
J	Y28	Area 4	NR	Bowl 3d	NR	14	Sherd Drawing 27
K	Z29	Area 3 Str. 10a	NR	Bowl 3c	NR	22	Sherd Drawing 08
L	Y27/Y28	Area 1	NR	Bowl 3c	NR	22	Sherd Drawing 18
M	Y28	Area 4	NR	Bowl 3d	NR, Bi-Lobed, Double-Pierced Lug	19	Sherd Drawing 13
N	Z28	Area 1-2 Str. 10/11	MBW IIIc	Bowl 3c	L. Grey	22	Sherd Drawing 10
O	Y28	Area 4	NR	Bowl 3d	NR	20	Sherd Drawing 29
P	Y29	"Floor and below"	MBW IIIc	Bowl 3c	NR	18	Sherd Drawing 05
Q	Z28	Area 1-2 Str. 10-11	MBW Ib	Bowl 3c	Ext. Orange Int. Grey	22	Sherd Drawing 09
R	Z28	Area 2 Str. 10	NR	Bowl 19	NR	28	Sherd Drawing 36
S	Z29	Area 1-2 Str. 11	NR	Bowl 3f	NR	34	Sherd Drawing 35
T	Z29	Area 4 Str. 10a	NR	Bowl 3d	NR	24	Sherd Drawing 15
U	Z29	Area 4 Str. 10a	NR	Bowl 3a	NR	18	Sherd Drawing 19
V	Z28	Area 1 Str. 10	Buff	Bowl 3c	Buff, Loop Handle	18	Sherd Drawing 11
W	Y29	Area 5	NR	Bowl 3c	NR	20	Sherd Drawing 17
X	Y28	Area 6	MBW IVb	Bowl 3d	Ext. L. Brown	20	Sherd Drawing 16
Y	Y28	Area 9 Str. 2	MBW IIIc	Bowl 3a	NR	24	Sherd Drawing 32
Z	Z29	Area 1-2 Str 11	NR	Bowl 8	NR	18	Sherd Drawing 20
AA	Z29	Area 1-2 Str. 11	NR	Bowl 6	NR, Drilled Hole	18	Sherd Drawing 28
BB	Z29	Area 4 Str. 10a	NR	Bowl 3a	NR	18	Sherd Drawing 04
CC	Z28	Area 1 Str. 10	NR	Bowl 3a	NR	24	Sherd Drawing 30
DD	Y28	Area 4 Pit 2	MBW Ic	Bowl 3a	Handmade, Loop Handle	26	Sherd Drawing 08
EE	Y28	Area 2	NR	Bowl 6	NR	35	Sherd Drawing 37

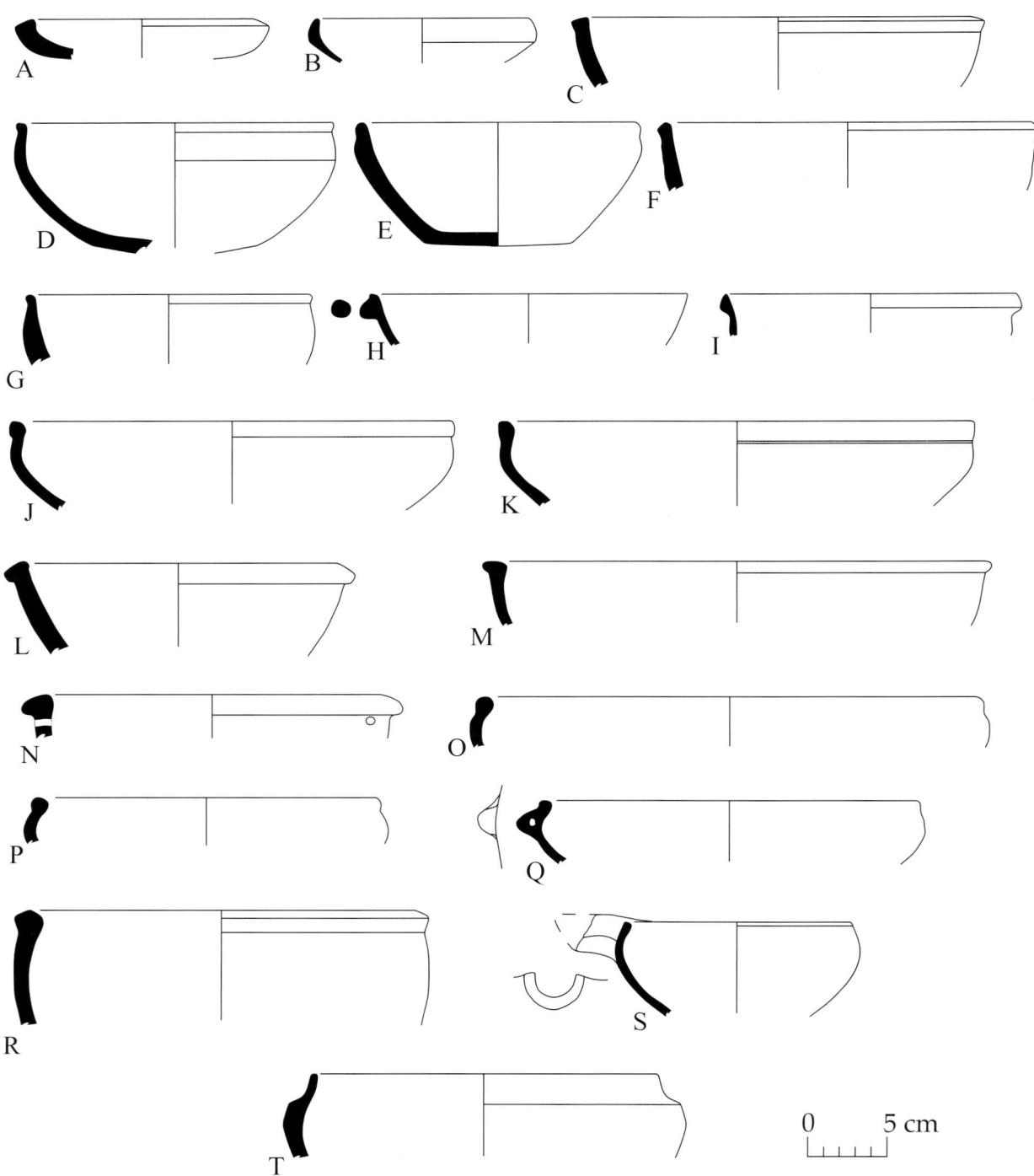

Fig. 4.46

Fig. 4.46 Hasanlu Tepe: Period IVc bowls from YZ27–29 (opposite).

Fig.	Op.	Context	Ware	Type	Description	Dia.	Disposition
A	Y28	Area 4 Pit 2	NR	Bowl 20	NR	16	Sherd Drawing 50
B	Y28	Area 4 Pit 2	NR	Bowl 20	NR	14	Sherd Drawing 51
C	Z28	Area 2 Str. 10	NR	Bowl 10	NR	26	Sherd Drawing 39
D	Z28	Area 1 Str. 11	NR	Bowl 8	NR	20	Sherd Drawing 46
E	Y28	Area 4 Pit 2	MBW Ic	Bowl 8	Ext. Orange	18	Sherd Drawing 45
F	Z29	Area 10	MBW Ib	Bowl 12	Ext. Orangish-Buff Int. Dark Orange	24	Sherd Drawing 40
G	Z28	Area 10	MBW Ib	Bowl 8	Ext. Orange Int. Fire Blackened	18	Sherd Drawing 47
H	Z28	Area 1 Str. 10	NR	Bowl 8	NR, Knob Lug	20	Sherd Drawing 12
I	Y28	Area 4	NR	Bowl 8	NR	19	Sherd Drawing 13
J	Z29	Area 4 Str. 10a	NR	Bowl 8	NR	28	Sherd Drawing 43
K	Z29	Area 4 Str. 10a	NR	Bowl 8	NR	30	Sherd Drawing 06
L	Z28	Area 2 Str. 10	NR	Bowl 13	NR	22	Sherd Drawing 41
M	Y28/Z28	Area 9 Str. 3	NR	Bowl 8	NR	32	Sherd Drawing 42
N	Z28	Area 1-2 Str. 10	MBW IIIc	Bowl 13	Ext. Brown, Drilled Hole	24	Sherd Drawing 14
O	Z28	Area 1 Str. 11	MBW Ic	Bowl 4	NR	32	Sherd Drawing 01
P	Z29	Area 10	MBW IIIc	Bowl 4	Ext. Red-Black Int. Black	22	Sherd Drawing 03
Q	Z29	Area 1-2 Str. 11	NR	Bowl 4	NR, Loop Handle	24	Sherd Drawing 02
R	Z29	Area 1-2 Str. 11	NR	Bowl 8	NR	26	Sherd Drawing 38
S	Z28	Area 1 Str. 11	MBW IIc	Bowl 5	Grey, Channel Spout	14	Sherd Drawing 49
T	Z28	Area 1-2 Str. 10	NR	Bowl 21	NR	12	Sherd Drawing 48

Miscellaneous Period IVc Ceramics

A few sherds from Period IVc contexts are likely extrusive from earlier periods, such as fragments of jars from YZ27–29 of Period VIb–c date (Fig. 4.49:P–Q). This is consistent with the fact that, in some small test excavations in the area of the Lower Court, MBII deposits were found just below Iron II surfaces (Dyson, pers. comm. 2001). Other vessels provide links to Period IVb, such as a medium globular jar with flat base and vertical handles at the sides (Fig. 4.49:S). This Type 1b jar is the earliest attested, conclusive example of a class/type typical of the Iron II, the so-called *hydriai*, which occur in the Iron II graves of Dinkha and Hasanlu as well as the occupation deposits of the Hasanlu citadel and Lower Town. Early *hydriai* of the Iron I and early Iron II tend to be Type 1b jars. In the latter part of the Iron II, these jars are teardrop-shaped with high, gradually constricting necks and narrow openings.

The Ceramics of Late Period IVc– Early IVb

Other exposures of the Iron I to early Iron II are included here to supplement the RS22–23 and YZ27–29 material and extend chronological coverage into the late Iron I and early Iron II. Six contexts were excavated from this time range, including RS22–23, U22 beneath BBVII, and in soundings in the storerooms of BBII (Rooms 13 and 14) and BBV (Rooms 4 and 6) (see Chapter 3). The Operation U22

244

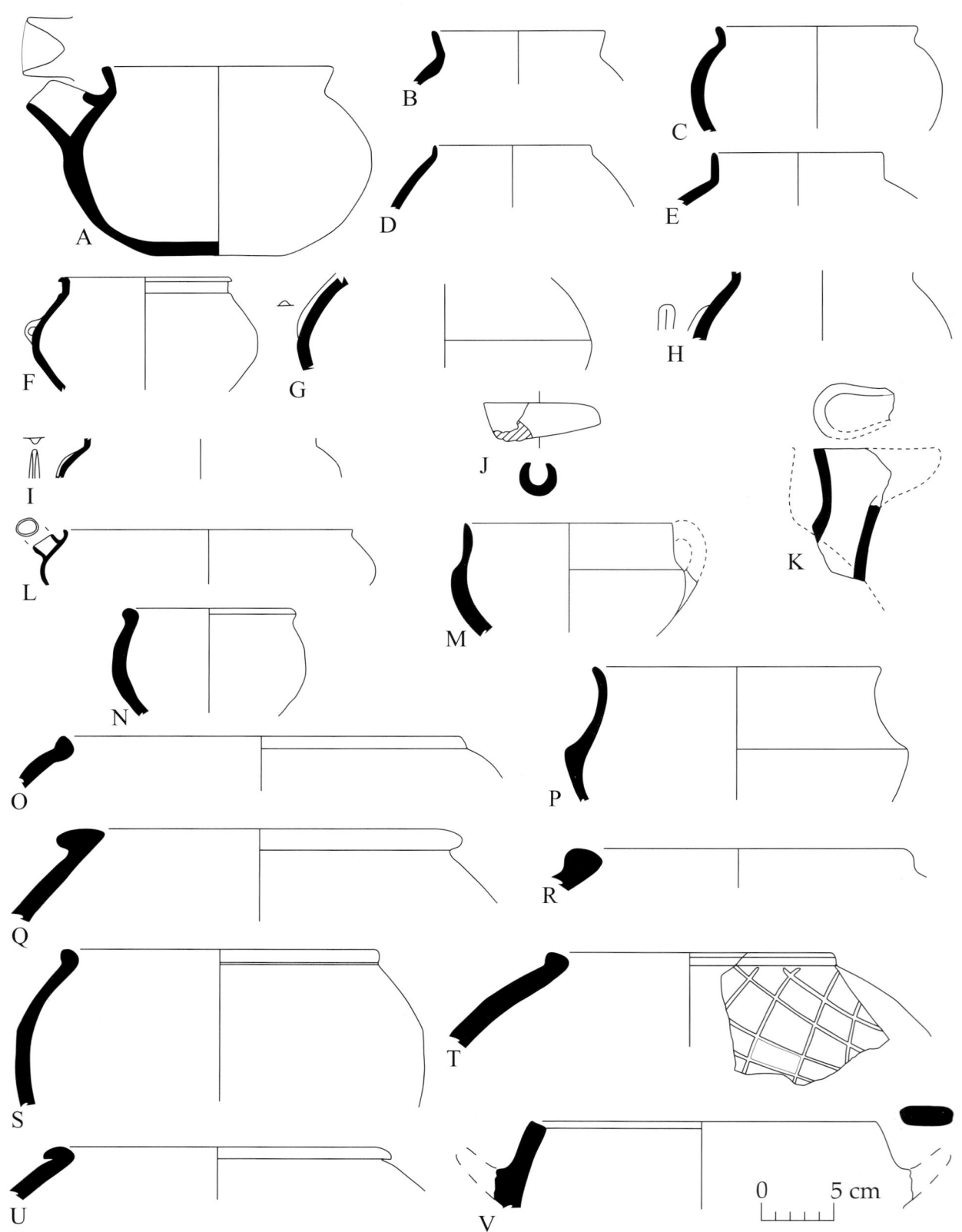

Fig. 4.47

Fig. 4.47 Hasanlu Tepe: Period IVc holemouth jars from YZ27–29 (opposite).

Fig.	Op.	Context	Ware	Type	Description	Dia.	Disposition
A	Z29	Area 1-2 Str. 11	NR	HM 9	NR, Tube Spout	16	Sherd Drawing 26
B	Z29	Area 4 Str. 10a	NR	HM 9	NR	12	Sherd Drawing 24
C	Y29	"Floor and below"	NR	HM 9	NR	14	Sherd Drawing 25
D	Y28	Area 9 Str. 2	NR	HM 9	NR	11	Sherd Drawing 22
E	Z29	Area 4 Str. 10a	NR	HM 9	NR	12	Sherd Drawing 23
F	Y28	Area 4 Pit 2	NR	HM 9	NR, Loop Handle Tail	12	Sherd Drawing 09
G	Y29	"Trash pit below floor"	NR	HM 9	NR, Appliqué Tail	—	Sherd Drawing 31
H	Y27/28	Area 1	NR	HM 9	NR, Appliqué Tail	13	Sherd Drawing 32
I	Z28	Area 1 Str. 11	NR	HM 9	NR, Appliqué Tail	16	Sherd Drawing 33
J	Y29	—	NR	—	NR, Bridgeless Spout	—	Sherd Drawing 14
K	Z29	Area 4 Str. 10a	NR	—	NR, Bridgeless Spout	—	Sherd Drawing 15
L	Y28	Area 4 Pit	NR	HM 22	NR, Tube Lug	20	Sherd Drawing 27
M	Z29	Below Floor of BBIE South Wall	NR	Cup 10	NR, Loop Handle	15	Sherd Drawing 29
N	Y28	Area 6	MBW IVb	HM 18	Ext. Brown	22	Sherd Drawing 48
O	Y28/Z28	Area 9 Str. 3	NR	HM 4	NR	28	Sherd Drawing 12
P	Z28	Area 14 Str. 10a	NR	HM 20	NR	20	Sherd Drawing 30
Q	Z28	Area 2 Str. 10	MBW IVb	HM 5	Ext. Brown	28	Sherd Drawing 08
R	Z28	Area 1 Str. 10	MBW Ib	HM 4	Ext. D. Brown	24	Sherd Drawing 15
S	Z29	Area 1-2 Str. 11	NR	HM 4	NR	22	Sherd Drawing 10
T	Z28	Area 1 Str. 10	NR	HM 4	NR, Pattern Burnish Deco.	20	Sherd Drawing 11
U	Z28	Area 1 Str. 11	MBW IIIc	HM 4	NR	24	Sherd Drawing 13
V	Y28	—	NR	HM 2	NR, Tab Handles	24	Sherd Drawing 18

Fig. 4.48

Fig. 4.48 Hasanlu Tepe: Period IVc holemouth jars from YZ27–29 (opposite).

Fig.	Op.	Context	Ware	Type	Description	Dia.	Disposition
A	Y29	"Floor and below"	MBW IIIc	HM 4	Ext. L. Grey	16	Sherd Drawing 04
B	Y29	"Trash pit below floor"	NR	HM 1	NR	18	Sherd Drawing 05
C	Z28	Area 1 Str. 10	MBW Ib	HM 1	Ext. Orangish Buff	20	Sherd Drawing 03
D	Z28	Area 1-2 Str. 10-11	NR	HM 1	NR	20	Sherd Drawing 07
E	Z28	Area 1-2 Str. 10-11	NR	HM 1	NR	26	Sherd Drawing 02
F	Y28	Area 2	MBW Ib	HM 1	Ext. L. Grey Int. D. Grey	22	Sherd Drawing 17
G	Y28	Area 2	NR	HM 5	NR	25	Sherd Drawing 01
H	Y29	Floor	NR	HM 8	NR	37	Sherd Drawing 04
I	Z28	Area 2 Str. 10	MBW IVc	HM 1	Ext. Brown Int. Black	18	Sherd Drawing 06
J	Y28	Area 6	NR	HM 5	NR	34	Sherd Drawing 03
K	Y28,	Area 9 Str. 2	NR	HM 5	NR	32	Sherd Drawing 02
L	Z29	Area 10	MBW IVb	HM 5	Ext. Orange	20	Sherd Drawing 01
M	Y28/Z28	—	MBW	HM 5	NR, Pattern Burnish	18	Sherd Drawing 16
N	Z29	Area 1-2 Str. 11	NR	HM 4	NR	15	Sherd Drawing 14
O	Z28	Area 2 Str. 10	MBW IIb	HM 4	Ext. Orangish Buff	22	Sherd Drawing 09
P	Z28	Area 2 Str. 10	MBW IIIc	HM 17	Ext. Grey	18	Sherd Drawing 07
Q	Y29	"Floor and below"	NR	HM 5	NR	18	Sherd Drawing 06
R	Z28	Area 1 Str. 11	MBW IVc	HM 8	NR	24	Sherd Drawing 20
S	Z29	Area 1-2 Str. 11	NR	HM 2	NR	30	Sherd Drawing 19
T	Y28	Area 2	MBW IVb	HM 19	NR	32	Sherd Drawing 05
U	Z28	Area 2 Str. 10	NR	HM 1	NR	26	Sherd Drawing 08

Sounding provided an exposure of buildings of probable late Period IVc–early IVb date beneath BBVII of Period IVb (see Chapter 3), although no radiocarbon dates were collected from the lower level (Fig. 4.54). A substantial assemblage of late IVc–early IVb pottery was also collected in the RS22–23 area lying below the Terminal Period IVb gate structure BBVIIE and above the destruction level of the Period IVc RS22–23 Building (Figs. 4.55, 4.56). Similarly dated exposures were achieved in soundings below the monumental Period IVb buildings of the Lower Court area. These buildings were first constructed during Period IVc and were destroyed by fire at the end of the Iron I and then rebuilt according to similar architectural plans and occupied throughout the Iron II. Sherds were collected from the lower Iron I–early Iron II levels of the western storerooms of BBII (Rooms 13 and 14) and the storerooms of BBV (Rooms 4 and 6) (Figs. 4.57–4.60). In some cases, these assemblages were partly mixed with material of late Period IVb date during excavation.

Contexts dating to the late Iron I and early Iron II reinforce our definition of Hasanlu IVc as developed from the assemblages of RS22–23 and YZ27–29

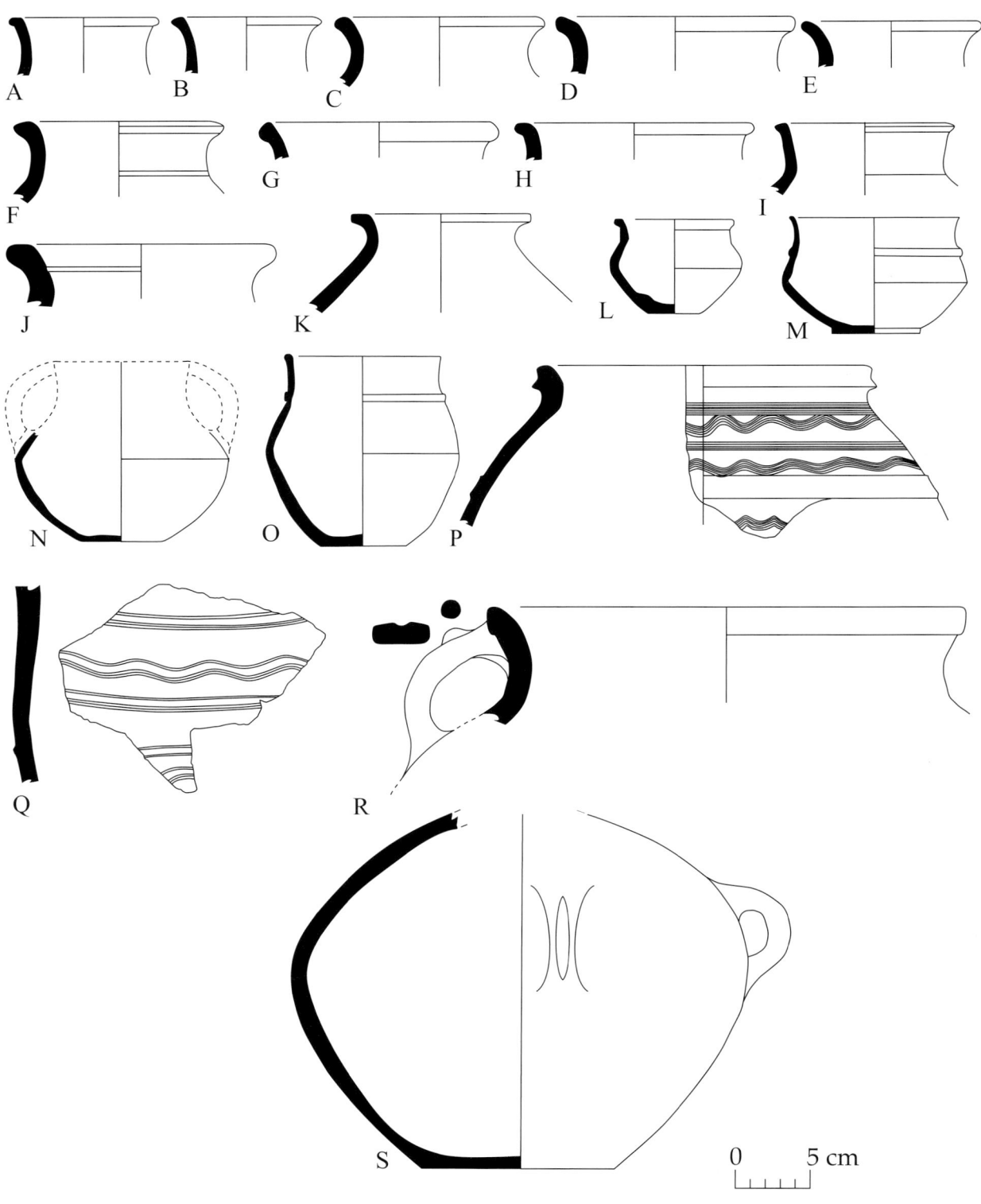

Fig. 4.49

Fig. 4.49 Hasanlu Tepe: Period IVc jars from YZ27–29 (opposite).

Fig.	Op.	Context	Ware	Type	Description	Dia.	Disposition
A	Z29	Area 4 Str. 10a	NR	Jar 3a	NR	10	Sherd Drawing 09
B	Z29	Area 4 Str. 10a	MBW Ic	Jar 3a	Ext. Grey/L. Brown	10	Sherd Drawing 17
C	Z29	Area 14 Str. 10a	NR	Jar 1a	NR	14	Sherd Drawing 14
D	Z29	Area 10	NR	Jar 1b	NR	16	Sherd Drawing 15
E	Z29	Area 10	NR	Jar 1a	NR	12	Sherd Drawing 18
F	Z29	Area 1-2 Str. 11	NR	Jar 1b	NR, Raised Band	14	Sherd Drawing 19
G	Y29	Area 9 Str. 2	NR	Jar 1b	NR	16	Sherd Drawing 11
H	Z28	Area 1-2 Str. 10-11	NR	Jar 3a	NR	16	Sherd Drawing 10
I	Z29	Area 1-2 Str. 11	NR	Jar 3a	NR	12	Sherd Drawing 16
J	Z28	Area 1-2 Str. 11	MBW Ib	Jar 1b	Ext. Orangish Buff	18	Sherd Drawing 20
K	Z29	Area 4 Str. 10a	MBW Ib	Jar 2	Ext. L. Grey	12	Sherd Drawing 13
L	Y28-29	Area 6 Str. 6	Unique	Cup 11a	Red fabric with whitish slip, sand and grit temper	8	HAS72-N175 UPM 73-5-150
M	X28	Area 10 Str. 4	MBW Ic	Cup 11a	Ext. Black, Raised Band	12	HAS72N-1727 UPM 73-5-165
N	Z29	Area 1-2 Str. 11	NR	Jar 9	NR, Two Missing High-Swung Handles	8–9	Sherd Drawing 35
O	X28	Area 10 Str. 4	MBW IIc	Cup 8b	NR, Raised Band	12	HAS72-N174 UPM 73-5-164
P	Z29	Area 4 Str. 10a	KW?	—	NR, Comb Incising	23	Sherd Drawing 16
Q	Y29	—	KW?	—	NR, Comb Incising	—	Sherd Drawing 17
R	Y28	Area 3	NR	Jar 4	NR, Loop Handle with Thumb Stop	32	Sherd Drawing 21
S	Z29	Area 4 Str. 10a	MBW Ic	—	Rim Missing, Three Loop Handles, Ext. Orangish Buff Int. Matte	—	HAS72-104

and further illustrate and extend our understanding of the developmental trends in ceramics of the later 2nd millennium.

Bowls

Bowls exhibit a great deal of variability in this time range with only Type 3 Bowls occurring with any frequency. Carinated forms are the norm.

Type 3 Bowls

Type 3 bowls of subtypes 3a–f are relatively common to this period, and four have handles (Figs. 4.54:B, E, K, X, 4.55:A–C, E–F, M, 4.58:D, E, 4.60:D). Two of these handles (Figs. 4.54:X, 4.55:C) are of the segmented variety, a style common in the Iron II, and one Type 3e bowl has gadrooning (Fig. 4.55:C).

Type 5 Bowls

Incurving bowls are rare in this period (Fig. 4.58:B). This pattern continued in the Iron II with the preference for carinated bowls, including inverted carinated bowls which seem to replace the class of incurving bowls.

Type 6 Bowls

Inverted carinated bowls are relatively rare in these occupation deposits despite the fact that they occur frequently in the graves of Period IVc and IVb and are ubiquitous in later Period IVb occupation deposits (Figs. 4.54:F, 4.55:D, G, I, 4.58:F).

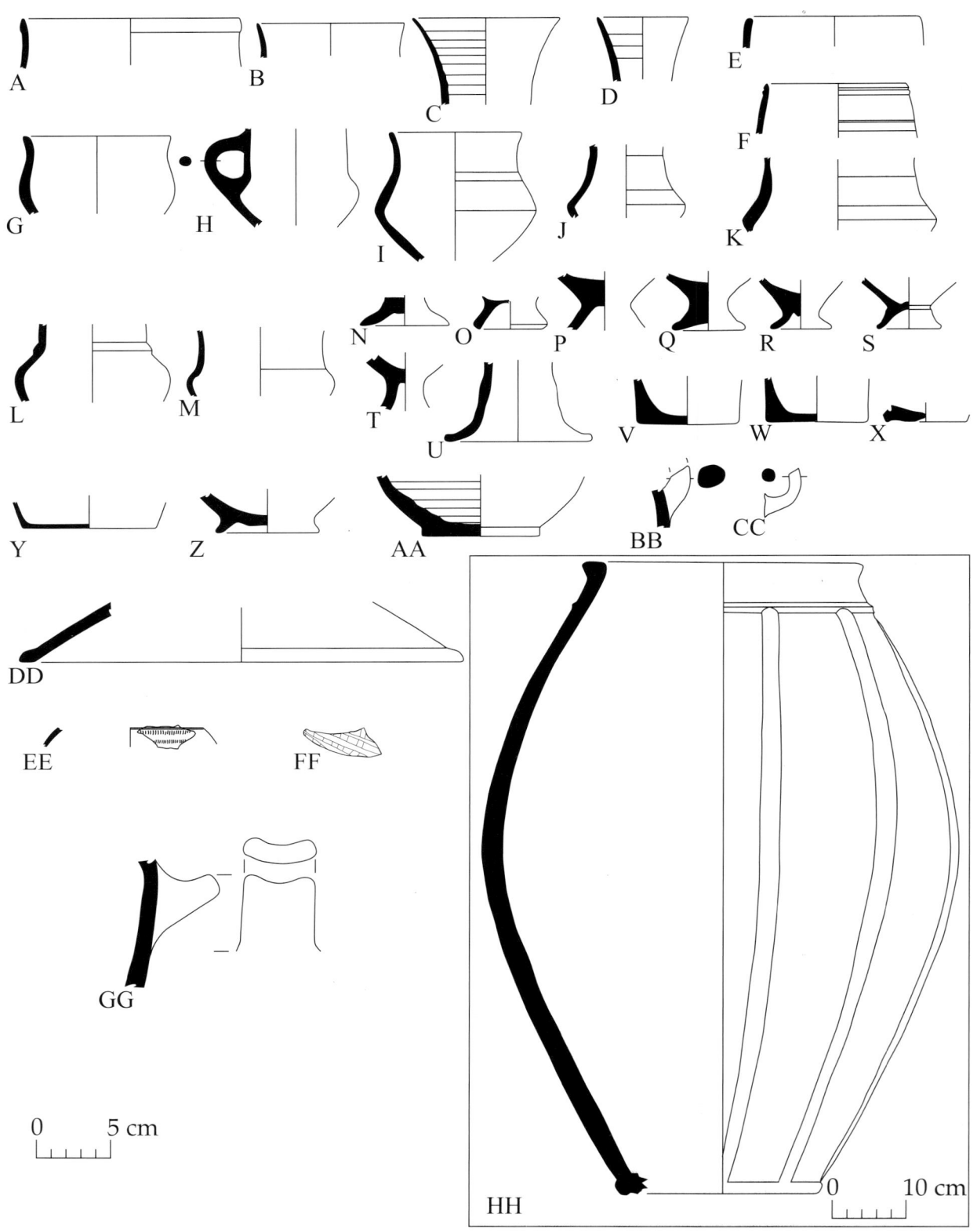

Fig. 4.50

Fig. 4.50 Hasanlu Tepe: Period IVc cups, holemouth jars, and jars from YZ27–29 (opposite).

Fig.	Op.	Context	Ware	Type	Description	Dia.	Disposition
A	Y28	Area 4	NR	Cup 8b	NR	15	Sherd Drawing 12
B	Z29	Area 10	NR	Cup 7	NR	10	Sherd Drawing 08
C	Z28	Area 1 Str. 10	NR	Cup 7	NR	10	Sherd Drawing 09
D	Z28	Area 1 Str. 10	NR	Cup 7	NR	6	Sherd Drawing 10
E	Z28	Area 2 Str. 10	NR	Cup 9	NR	12	Sherd Drawing 11
F	Y28	Area 9 Str. 2	MBW IIIb	Cup 9	Ext. L. Brown, Rilling	10	Sherd Drawing 12
G	Z28	Area 2 Str. 10	MBW Ib	Cup 12	Ext. Orangish Buff, Loop Handle	10	Sherd Drawing 01
H	Z28	Area 1-2 Str. 10-11	NR	Cup 7	NR	7	Sherd Drawing 07
I	Y28	Area 4 Pit 2	NR	Cup 7	NR, Raised Band	9	Sherd Drawing 02
J	Z29	Area 4 Str. 10a	NR	Cup 7	NR	8	Sherd Drawing 03
K	Z29	Area 4 Str. 10a	MBW IIc	Cup 7	NR	—	Sherd Drawing 04
L	Z28	Area 1-2 Str. 10-11	NR	Cup 7	NR, Raised Band	7	Sherd Drawing 05
M	Z28	Area 1 Str. 11	NR	Cup 7	NR	10	Sherd Drawing 06
N	Z28	Area 1 Str. 11	MBW IIIc	Cup 7	NR	6	Sherd Drawing 16
O	Y28	Area 5	NR	Cup 7	NR	5	Sherd Drawing 19
P	Z29	Area 4 Str. 10a	NR	Cup 7	NR	—	Sherd Drawing 17
Q	Z28	Area 2 Str. 10	MBW Ic	Cup 7	NR	5	Sherd Drawing 20
R	Y29	"Trash pit below floor"	NR	Cup 7	NR	4	Sherd Drawing 22
S	Z28	Area 1 Str. 11	MBWc III	Cup 7	NR	4	Sherd Drawing 21
T	Z29	Area 10	MBW IIIc	Cup 7	NR	—	Sherd Drawing 18
U	Z28	Area 1 Str. 10	NR	—	NR, Pedestal Base	10	Sherd Drawing 23
V	Z29	Area 4 Str. 10a	MBW Ib	—	NR, Cylinder Base	7	Sherd Drawing 14
W	Z29	Area 4 Str. 10a	NR	—	NR, Cylinder Base	7	Sherd Drawing 15
X	Z28	Area 2 Str. 10	NR	—	NR, Ring Base	6	Sherd Drawing 13
Y	Z29	Area 10	NR	—	NR, Flat Base	9	Sherd Drawing 6
Z	Z28	Area 1-2 Str/ 10	MBW Ic	—	NR, Ring Base	7	Sherd Drawing 3
AA	Z28	Area 1 Str. 11	MBW	—	Ext. Burnished Fine Grit Temper, Disc Base	8	Sherd Drawing 34
BB	Z28	Area 2 Str. 10	NR	—	NR, Loop Handle	—	Sherd Drawing 11
CC	Z28	Area 2 Str. 10	NR	—	Ext. L. Brown, Wet Smoothed Fine Grit Temper, Loop Handle	—	Sherd Drawing 12
DD	Z29	Area 4 Str. 10a	NR	—	NR, Pedestal Base	—	Sherd Drawing 13
EE	Z28	Area 1 Str. 11	NR	—	NR. Ext. Incised Decoration	—	Sherd Drawing 2
FF	Z28	Area 1-2 Str. 10/11	MBW IIc	—	NR.Ext. Pattern-Burnish Deco.	—	Sherd Drawing 01
GG	Z28	Area 1 Str. 10	NR	—	NR, Tab Handle	—	Sherd Drawing 10
HH	Y28	Area 6, Object 2	Buff IVa	HM 5	Orange	37	Drawing

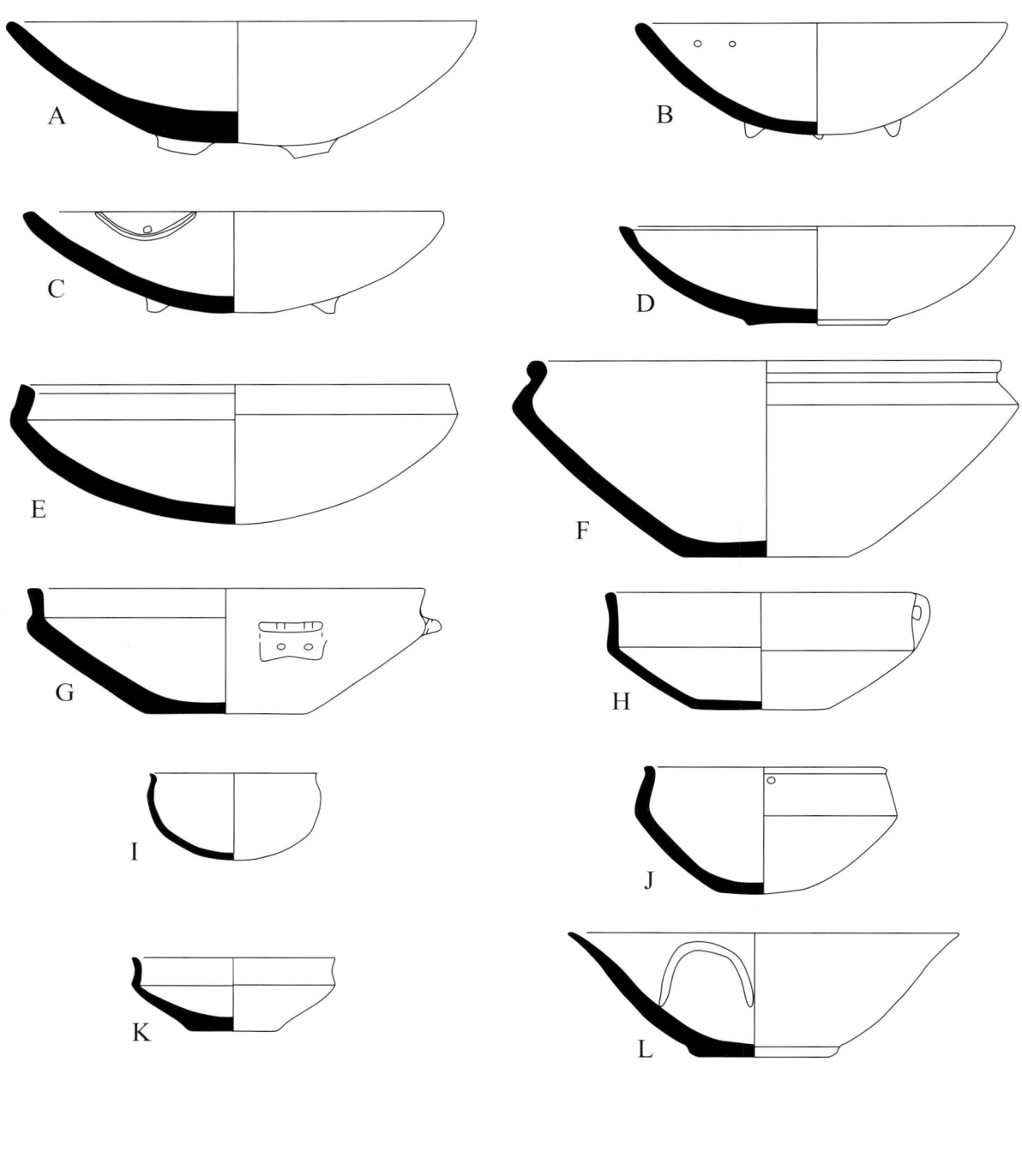

Fig. 4.51

Fig. 4.51 Hasanlu and Dinkha Tepe: Period IVc bowls from graves (opposite).

Fig.	Op.	Context	Ware	Type	Description	Dia.	Disposition
A	Dinkha B9a	Burial 19	NR	Bowl 2c	Three Broken Legs	29	—
B	Dinkha B9b	Burial 16	NR	Bowl 2c	Two Drilled Holes, Three Lug Feet	23	—
C	Dinkha B9b	Burial 12	NR	Bowl 2c	Crescent Appliqué, Drilled Hole, Three Lug Feet	26	—
D	VIf	Burial SK479	MBW	Bowl 2c	Grey	24.5	HAS64-175
E	Dinkha B9a	Burial 19	NR	Bowl 6	—	26.5	—
F	Dinkha B9b	Burial 11	NR	Bowl 6	—	29	—
G	VIa	Burial SK57	MBW	Bowl 3b	NR, Bi-Lobed, Double-Pierced Lug	25	HAS59-79
H	VIa	Burial SK62	MBW IIIb	Bowl 3d	Grey, Grooved Loop Handle	19	HAS59-118, TM
I	VIh	Burial SK494	CPW	Bowl 5	Ext. Smudged	10.5	HAS64-298, Disc.
J	Dinkha B9a	Burial 24	NW	Bowl 6	Drilled Hole	15	—
K	VIa	Burial SK73	MBW Ib	Bowl 3d	Buff	13.5	HAS59-188, Disc.
L	VIa	Burial SK73	MBW Ic	Bowl 1a	Grey, Ext. Burnished Int. Matte, Crescent Appliqué	24	HAS59-184, MET 60-20-19

Type 8 Bowls
Hemispherical bowls with simple or thickened rims occur with some frequency (Figs. 4.54:A, 4.55:H, J–K, 4.57a:A, 4.58:C). The trend seems to be toward thickened, slightly everted rims.

Type 9 Bowls
Small carinated bowls with everted rims are attested by a single occurrence (Fig. 4.54:I).

Type 13 Bowls
This bowl is one of the few examples of this distinctive type from Hasanlu (Fig. 4.54:G).

Type 15 Bowls/Trays
Crude trays continue to occur in the occupation deposits in low number (Figs. 4.54:L, 4.56:G, H).

Type 18 Bowls
This bowl or cup is unique within the period (Fig. 4.58:A).

Only one other occurrence from the Dinkha MBIII trash deposit is known and this early attestation is larger and coarser and doubtless developmentally unrelated.

Type 19 Bowls
This deep carinated bowl with simple everted rim is attested by a single example with a loop handle (Fig. 4.60:A). A nearly identical example comes from Geoy Tepe A (Burton-Brown 1951: fig. 38 no. 225) and the form is broadly attested there (Burton-Brown 1951: fig. 35 nos. 101, 108).

Type 21 Bowls
Although a unique occurrence, this type exhibits typical Iron I attributes, having a carinated form, a horizontal rib, and thinned rim (Fig. 4.54:C).

Type 23 Bowls
This large, coarse bowl with a rim diameter of 50 cm is unique (Fig. 4.58:G).

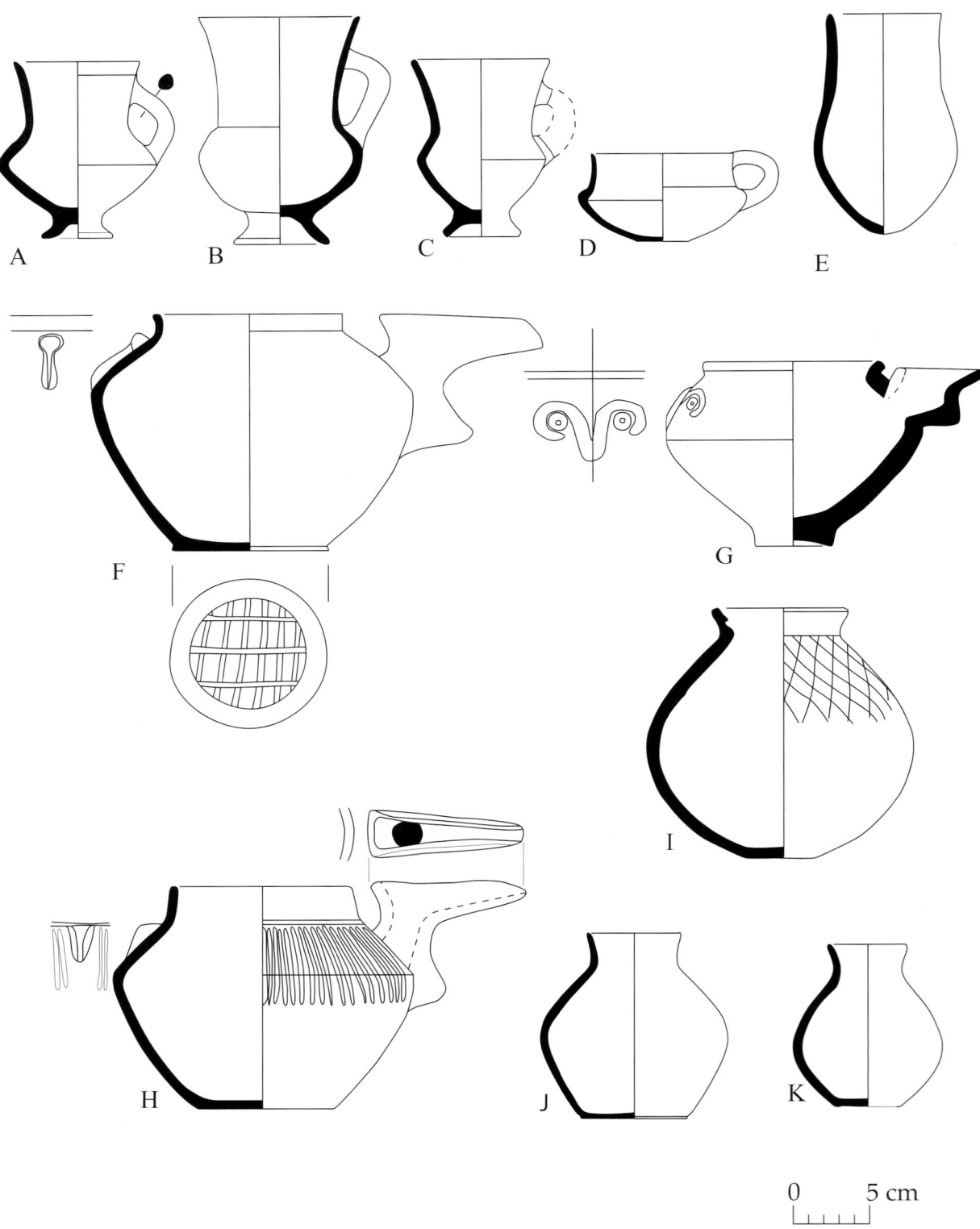

Fig. 4.52

Fig. 4.52 Hasanlu and Dinkha Tepe: Period IVc vessels from graves (opposite).

Fig.	Op.	Context	Ware	Type	Description	Dia.	Disposition
A	VIh	Burial SK494	MBW IIIc	Cup Type 7	Grey, Int. Matte	8	HAS64-299
B	Dinkha B9a	Burial 19	NR	Cup Type 7	Loop Handle	10.5	—
C	Dinkha B9b	Burial 12	NR	Cup Type 7	Loop Handle	9	—
D	VIa	Burial SK57	MBW Ic	Cup Type 11b	Buff, Red Slip, Loop Handle	9.5	HAS59-80, UPM 60-20-52
E	VIf	Burial SK479	MBW Ic	Cup Type 14	Grey	7.5	HAS64-176, NR
F	B9b	Burial 16	NR	Jar 3b	Excised Waffle Base, Appliqué Tail, Bridgeless Spout	12.5	—
G	B9a	Burial 24	NR	HM9	Appliqué Tail, Bridgeless Spout	11	—
H	B9b	Burial 11	NR	Jar 3b	Gadrooning, Appliqué Tail, Bridgeless Spout	12	—
I	VI	Burial SK24	MBW	HM1	Grey, Pattern Burnish Deco.	9	HAS57-121, UPM 58-4-47
J	VIa	Burial SK73	Buff Ia	Cup Type 8c	Orangish Buff	6.5	HAS59-183, Disc.
K	VIa	Burial SK73	Grey Ia	Cup Type 8c	Grey	5	HAS59-182, Disc.

Holemouth Jars

Holemouth jars continue to make up a large part of the assemblage of Hasanlu. Previous assessments of the MBW horizon have downplayed the sheer number of these jars and the variability within the series.

Type 1 Holemouth Jars
As in previous periods, jars of this type are fairly common (Figs. 4.54:N, R, 4.57b:B, 4.58:R, 4.60:N).

Types 3–5 Holemouth Jars
This class of holemouth vessel is relatively rare in late 2nd millennium BC assemblages as compared to previous periods (Figs. 4.54:O, P, 4.55:N–O, Q, S, 4.57a:C).

Type 6 Holemouth Jars
This type is relatively rare in the LBA and early Iron Age (Fig. 4.56:F) and likely represents a cooking pot.

Type 8 Holemouth Jars
True holemouth jars with simple rims are attested by a single example (Fig. 4.54:Q). The type, related to Type 9 Holemouth Jars, likely often had spouts.

Type 9 Holemouth Jars
As in previous periods, jars of this type are a common form and, when found whole, often have spouts (Figs. 4.55:P, R, 4.59:J–K, 4.60:K).

Type 11 Holemouth Jars Pyxides
Pyxides appear in the assemblage in the Iron I and become increasingly common in the latter part of the period and in the Iron II (Figs. 4.56:A, D, 4.58:T, V, 4.60:P). One unusually fine example has a double basket handle and was doubtless provided with a tube or channel spout (Fig. 4.56:A). The type is related to Type 20 Holemouth Jars.

Type 20 Holemouth Jars Pyxides
Such pyxides, particularly with basket handles and gadrooning, are known in Period IVc, as previously discussed, but are more common in the Iron II (Fig. 4.56:B).

Type 21 Holemouth Jars
This interesting small holemouth form with channel spout at the rim is unique, but such spouted vessels are known from the Iron II (Fig. 4.57b:A). The vessel walls were reduced by scraping away part of the outer surface.

256

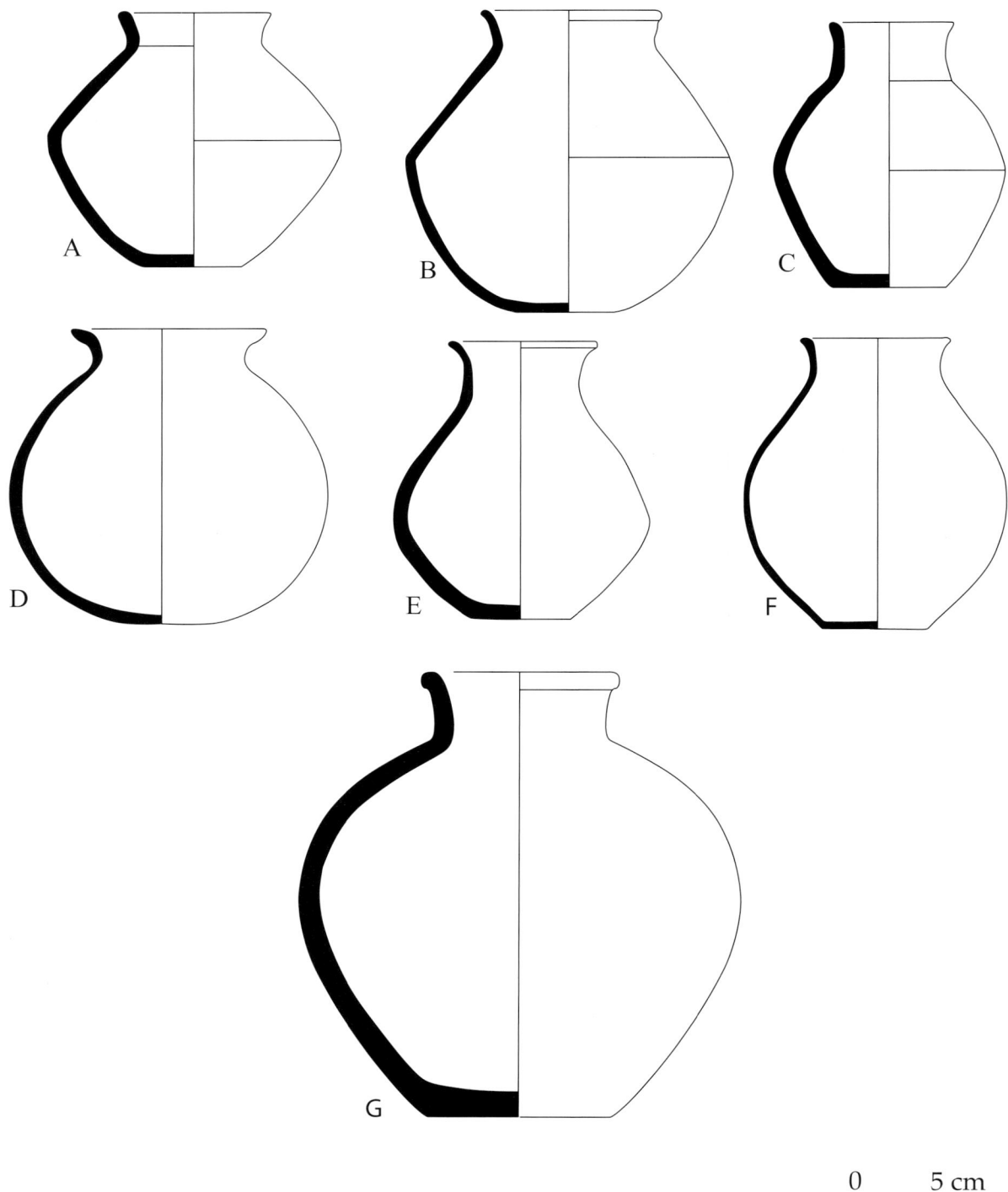

Fig. 4.53

Fig. 4.53 Hasanlu and Dinkha Tepe: Period IVc jars from graves (opposite).

Fig.	Op.	Context	Ware	Type	Description	Dia.	Disposition
A	Dinkha B9b	Burial 12	NR	Jar 3a	NR	9.5	—
B	Dinkha B9b	Burial 16	NR	Jar 3a	NR	11	—
C	Dinkha B9b	Burial 11	NR	Jar 3a	NR	7.5	—
D	VIf	Burial SK479	MBW Ic	Jar 1	Grey	12	HAS64-177, NR
E	Dinkha B9a	Burial 19	NR	Jar 1a	NR	9.5	—
F	VIa	Burial SK57	MBW IIIa	Cup Type 8c	Grey	9.5	HAS59-78, Disc.
G	VIa	Burial SK57	MBW IIa	Jar 1b	Grey	12	HAS59-77, Disc.

Jars

The best attested jar forms are *hydriai* or jar Type 1b; some Type 2 jars are also likely storage or water jars. Not surprisingly, bridge-spouted jars occur in these assemblages.

Type 1 Jars

Jars of Type 1 constitute a significant part of the late Period IVc/early Period IVb assemblage (Figs. 4.54:S–W, 4.59:F–G, N–O). These mostly represent *hydriai* or Type Ib. These vessels with constricted necks and narrow mouths are common to Hasanlu IVb.

Type 2 Jars

These medium-size jars with short neck and everted rim are not as widely attested in the available later 2nd–early 1st millennium BC assemblages as in previous periods (Figs. 4.55:L, T, 4.57b:D, 4.60:O).

Type 3 Jars

Jars of Type 3a make up a small part of the assemblage. One small example has a bridge spout, cannelure, and strap handle (Figs. 4.57b:E, 4.58:W).

Jar Type 9

These jars, akin to *kantharoi* and frequently provided with high-swung handles, are rare in late Period IVc–early IVb but presumably were on the rise in terms of popularity in light of their high frequency in the Iron II (Fig. 4.56:C). The gadrooning on this jar is in keeping with popular Iron II decorative styles. High-swung handles are also attested (Fig. 4.43:Q–R).

Type 10 Jars Pitchers

This pitcher is unique in the assemblage (Fig. 4.57a:B). The type is common to Period IVb.

Type 11 Jars

This bottle is only attested by two examples (Fig. 4.59:L–M), which could easily be sherds from the same vessel.

Type 12 Jars

This jar with broad shoulder, medium neck, and simple everted rim has multiple ribs/rills and vertical fluting on it shoulder (Fig. 4.59:I). While the form is only attested by this single example, the style of decoration is typical of Period IVc–IVb.

Cups

The most noticeable change in later Period IVc/early Period IVb deposits is the fall-off in the number of Type 7 cups. The most abundant cup type, by far, is the Type 8 fine, shouldered beaker. Type 11 beakers/mugs and Type 12 hemispherical cups are also well attested, and such vessels are common in later Iron II assemblages.

Type 7 Cups

Short carinated pedestal-base cups/tankards are not attested in late Period IVc and early Period IVb with the possible exception of a few rim sherds (Figs. 4.59:D, 4.60:Q). Rims listed below in Type 8 might also derive from Type 7 vessels.

Type 8 Cups / Fine Shouldered Beakers

These small, fine jars and beakers are abundant in later Period IVc and early Period IVb (Figs. 4.57b:C, 4.58:K–Q, 4.59:A–C, E, H, 4.60:G–J, L–M). One example, by definition a tankard, has a handle and may

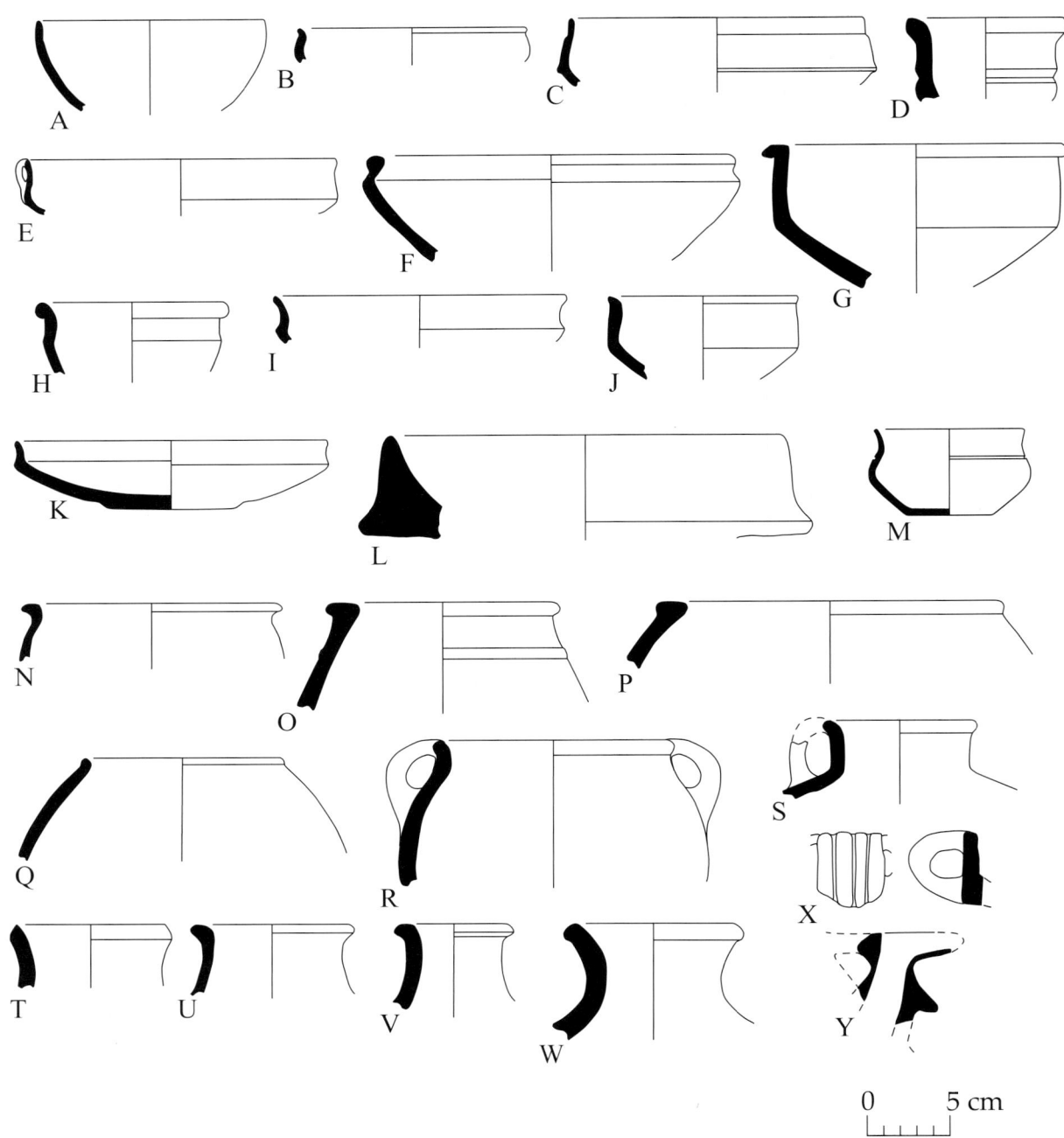

Fig. 4.54

Fig. 4.54 Hasanlu Tepe: Period IVc ceramics from U22 Stratum 5-6 (opposite).

Fig.	Op.	Context	Ware	Type	Description	Dia.	Disposition
A	U22	5-6	Buff - -	Bowl 8	Buff	14	UPM Sherd Coll.
B	U22	5-6	MBW -b	Bowl 3c	Buff	14	UPM Sherd Coll.
C	U22	5-6	MBW -c	Bowl 21	Grey, Raised Band	18	UPM Sherd Coll.
D	U22	5-6	MBW -b	Cup 13	Red Slip, Cannelure	9.5	UPM Sherd Coll.
E	U22	5-6	MBW -c	Bowl 3d	Grey, Loop Handle	19	UPM Sherd Coll.
F	U22	5-6	Buff - -	Bowl 6	Buff	22.5	UPM Sherd Coll.
G	U22	5-6	MBW -c	Bowl 13	Grey	18	UPM Sherd Coll.
H	U22	5-6	Buff - -	Cup 11a	Buff	11.5	UPM Sherd Coll.
I	U22	5-6	MBW -b	Bowl 9	Buff	17.5	UPM Sherd Coll.
J	U22	5-6	MBW -b	Cup 11a	Buff	11.5	UPM Sherd Coll.
K	U22	5-6	MBW -c	Bowl 3d	Grey	19	UPM Sherd Coll.
L	U22	5-6	NR	Bowl 15	NR	24	UPM Sherd Coll.
M	U22	5-6	NR	Cup 11a	NR, Cannelure	9	UPM Sherd Coll.
N	U22	5-6	Buff - -	HM 1	Buff	16	UPM Sherd Coll.
O	U22	5-6	MBW -c	HM 5	Grey, Raised Band	14	UPM Sherd Coll.
P	U22	5-6	CPW	HM 3	Buff, Smudged	21	UPM Sherd Coll.
Q	U22	5-6	MBW -c	HM 8	Buff	12	UPM Sherd Coll.
R	U22	5-6	CPW	HM 1	Smudged, Two Loop Handles	15.5	UPM Sherd Coll.
S	U22	5-6	MBW -c	Jar 1b	Grey, Loop Handle	9	UPM Sherd Coll.
T	U22	5-6	CPW	Jar 1a	Grey	10	UPM Sherd Coll.
U	U22	5-6	MBW -c	Jar 1b	Red Slip	10	UPM Sherd Coll.
V	U22	5-6	MBW -b	Jar 1b	Buff	7	UPM Sherd Coll.
W	U22	5-6	MBW -b	Jar 1b	Buff	11	UPM Sherd Coll.
X	U22	5-6	MBW -b	Bowl 3d	Buff, Segmented Handle	—	UPM Sherd Coll.
Y	U22	5-6	MBW -c	—	Grey, Bridgeless Spout	—	UPM Sherd Coll.

represent a late variety of Type 7 (Fig. 4.60:M). Single raised ribs are a common attribute (Figs. 4.57b:C, 4.58:K, N, P, 4.59:A–C, 4.60:M).

Type 11 Cups

Small, low carinated beakers/mugs are present in the assemblage, as in early Period IVc (Figs. 4.54:H, J, M, 4.58:U). These forms seem to be related to the preference for pyxides in the Iron I–II.

Type 12 Cups

These small, simple hemispherical cups with vertical or slightly everted rims are quite common in the late 2nd–early 1st millennia BC (Figs. 4.58:H–J, S, 4.60:B–C, E–F).

Cup Type 13

This occurrence is unique at Hasanlu within Period IVc (Fig. 4.54:D).

Miscellaneous Late Period IVc–Early IVb Ceramics

One of the more unusual ceramic finds from a transitional Iron I–II context is the flat base and lower portion of one corner of what was evidently a square stand or vessel with denticulated base and incised decoration (Fig. 4.56:E). The earliest attested bridge spout, the hallmark of the Iron II, was found in a late Period IVc, or possibly early IVb context at Hasanlu (Fig. 4.54:Y). Bridge-spouted vessels are typical of Iron

260

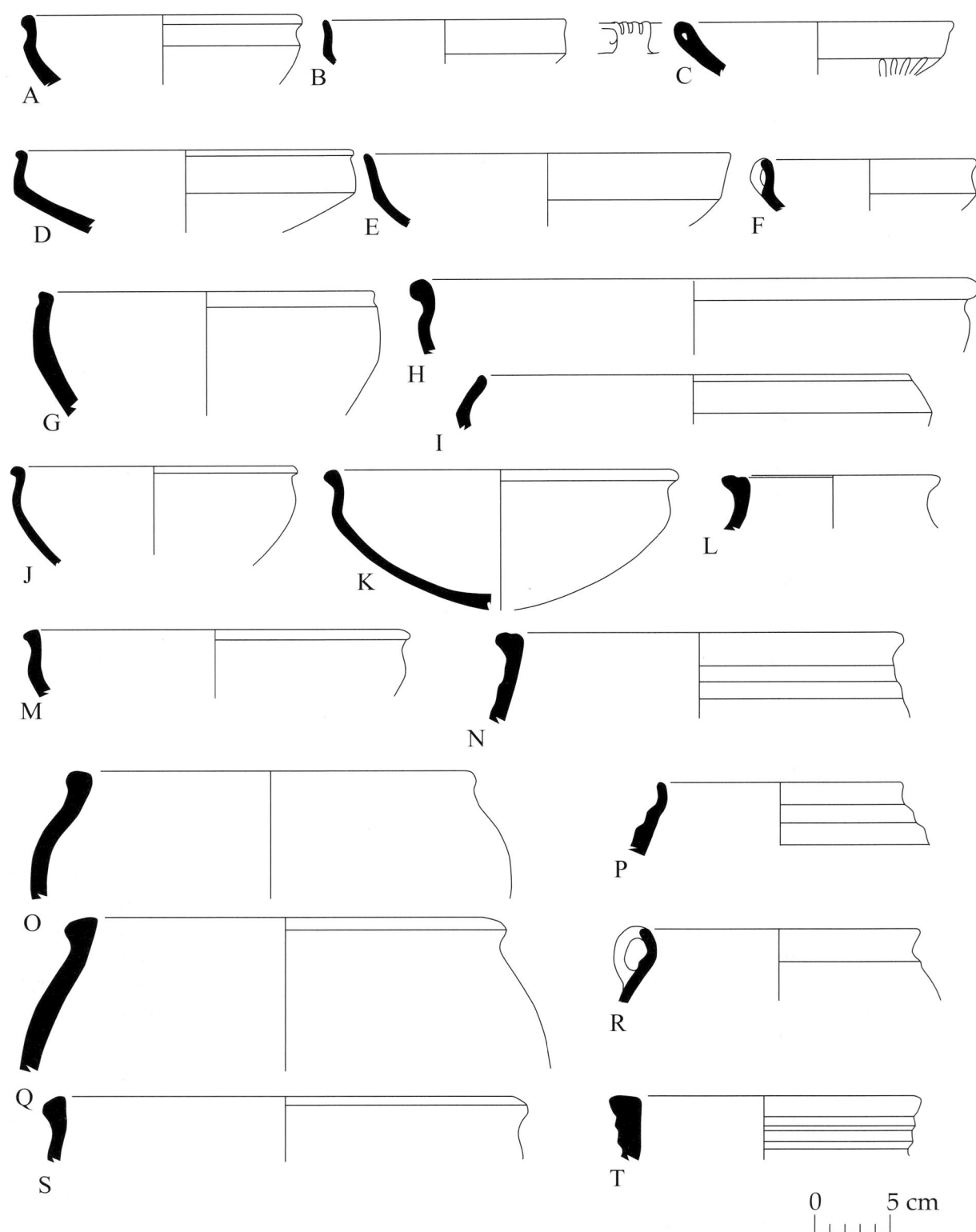

Fig. 4.55

Fig. 4.55 Hasanlu Tepe: late Period IVc–early Period IVb ceramics from RS22–23 (opposite).

Fig.	Op.	Context	Ware	Type	Description	Dia.	Disposition
A	S22	Area 11 Str. 8	NR	Bowl 3a	NR	18	Sherd Drawing 484a
B	S22	Area 11 Str. 8	NR	Bowl 3d	NR	16	Sherd Drawing 495
C	R22	South Balk	NR	Bowl 3e	Gadrooning, Segmented Handle	18	Sherd Drawing
D	S22	Area 11 Str. 8	NR	Bowl 6	NR	16.5	Sherd Drawing 476
E	S22	Area 11 Str. 8	NR	Bowl 3d	NR	24	Sherd Drawing 475
F	S22	Area 11 Str. 8	NR	Bowl 3c	NR	14	Sherd Drawing 481
G	S22	Area 11 Str. 8	NR	Bowl 6	NR	22	Sherd Drawing 484b
H	S22	Area 11 Str. 8	NR	Bowl 8	NR	27.5	Sherd Drawing 490
I	S22	Area 11 Str. 8	NR	Bowl 6	NR	28.5	Sherd Drawing 407
J	R22	–	MBW IIIc	Bowl 8	Pattern Burnish (not illustrated)	19	Sherd Drawing
K	R22	South Balk	NR	Bowl 8	NR	23	Sherd Drawing
L	S22	Area 11 Str. 8	NR	Jar 2a	NR	14.5	Sherd Drawing 492
M	S22	Area 11 Str. 8	NR	Bowl 3a	NR	25.5	Sherd Drawing 483
N	S22	Area 11 Str. 8	NR	HM 5	Rilling	27	Sherd Drawing 478
O	S22	Area 11 Str. 8	NR	HM 5		27	Sherd Drawing 493
P	S22	Area 11 Str. 8	NR	HM 9	Rilling	16	Sherd Drawing 474
Q	S22	Area 11 Str. 8	NR	HM 5	NR	29.5	Sherd Drawing 494
R	S22	Area 11 Str. 8	NR	HM 9	Loop Handle	18.5	Sherd Drawing 477
S	S22	Area 11 Str. 8	NR	HM 5	NR	32	Sherd Drawing 491
T	S22	Area 11 Str. 8	NR	Jar 2b	Rilling	20.5	Sherd Drawing 482

II graves at Hasanlu and Dinkha and never co-occur in such sealed contexts with bridgeless-spouted vessels. Tube spouts are also attested in the late 2nd–early 1st millennia BC (Fig. 4.56:I, J).

Period IVc Conclusions

Overall it is possible to distinguish Iron I assemblages and, to a lesser extent, individual Iron I vessels from the LBA and Iron II. The mixed nature of the YZ27–29 deposit puts us at a minor disadvantage since it contains some earlier and later sherdage, but the sequence from RS22–23 and late Period IVc–early Period IVb assemblages help us to reconstruct the developmental trends in most vessel classes, types, and stylistic and formal attributes. New vessel types and subtypes appear during this period, as do new formal and stylistic attributes distributed across a number of different vessel classes. Hallmarks of the period are short pedestal-base beakers and tankards (Cup Types 7) and fine shouldered beakers (Cup Type 8b/c), which develop out of the taller varieties of the LBA. These short tankards and beakers occur alongside a new class of mugs and beakers with flat bases (Cup Type 11) and with simple cups (Cup Type 12). Both types are common to Period IVb as well. Bridgeless-spouted jars continue from the LBA with some changes that may aid in distinguishing them from those of the LBA, although more attestations from controlled excavations are needed. Significantly, at Hasanlu and at Dinkha, vessels with bridgeless spouts never occur in grave groups with bridge-spouted vessels. Type 2a "worm bowls" continue into the Iron I, and hemispherical "worm bowls" (Bowl Type 2c), often with tripod bases, appear to be a new development. The "worm bowl" class of large bowls is almost never included in the graves of early Period IVb and is extremely rare in the occupation deposits of the period. Incurving-rim and everted-rim carinated bowls are the predominant bowl types in grave groups and occupation deposits of Period IVb;

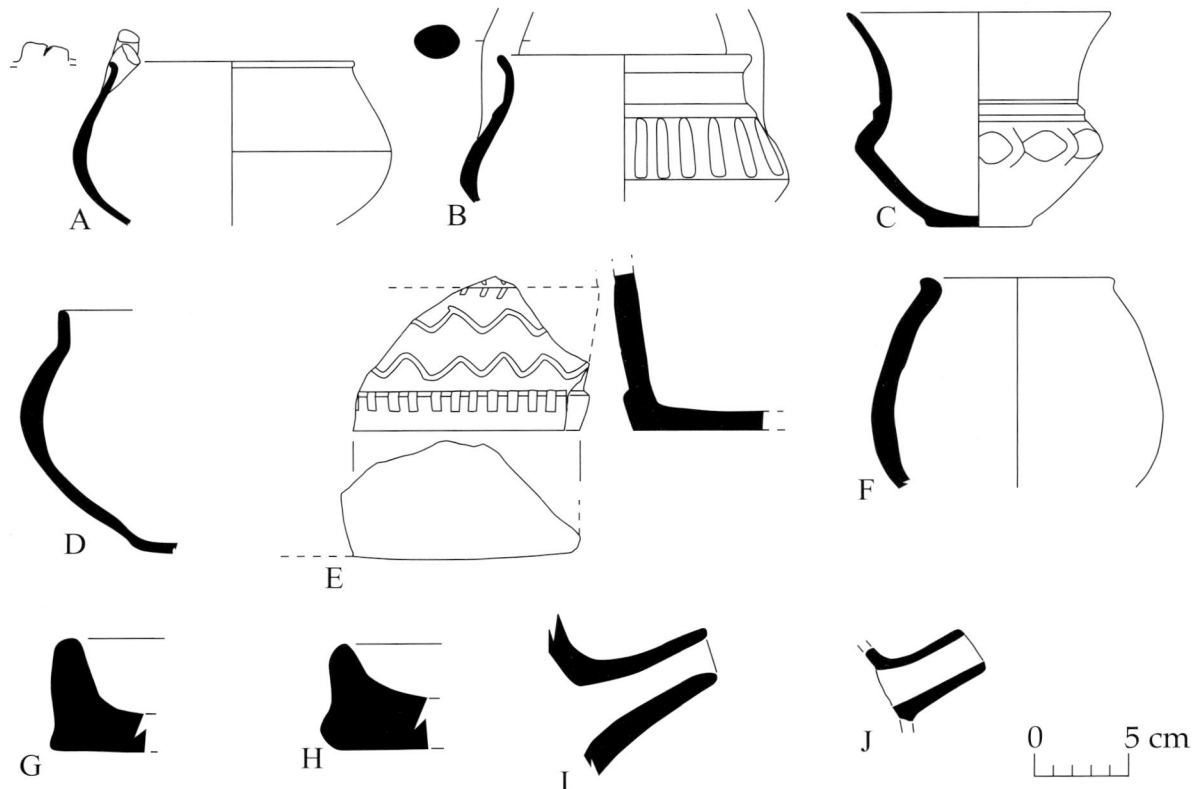

Fig. 4.56 Hasanlu Tepe: Late Period IVc–Early Period IVb ceramics from RS22–23.

Fig.	Op.	Context	Ware	Type	Description	Dia.	Disposition
A	R22	Balk	NR	HM 11	NR, Split Basket Handle	13	Sherd Drawing
B	S23	Area 9 Balk	MB IIc	HM 20	Grey, Basket Handle, Gadrooning, Raised Band	13.5	Sherd Drawing
C	R22	South Balk	MBW IIIc	Jar 9	Buff and Black, Gadrooning, Raised Band	14	Sherd Drawing
D	R22	South Balk	MBW IIIc	HM 11a	Black	—	Sherd Drawing
E	R23	Str. 6 South Balk	MBW IIc	Unique	Brown and Black, Excised and Incised	—	Sherd Drawing
F	S22	Area 11 Str. 8	NR	HM 6	NR	10	Sherd Drawing
G	S22	Area 11 Str. 8	NR	Bowl 15	NR	—	Sherd Drawing 486
H	S22	Area 11 Str. 8	NR	Bowl 15	NR	—	Sherd Drawing 406
I	S22	Area 11 Str. 8	NR	—	NR, Tube Spout	—	Sherd Drawing 479
J	S22	Area 11 Str. 8	NR	—	NR, Tube Spout	—	Sherd Drawing 480

in Period IVc we see the onset of this pattern and the development of new types of carinated bowls, especially markedly carinated bowls with higher, everted rims (Bowl Type 9), found only in occupation deposits in IVc. Mid-body carinated jars continue from late Period V, but ovoid jars with short necks and thickened rims of Type 1b typify the occupation deposits of IVc. In Period IVb this jar type, sometimes referred to as a *hydria*, often has three handles located at the sides. Such handles first appear in Period IVc. The double-handled *kantharos*-like jar/cup also may be a late Hasanlu IVc development and is typical of Hasanlu IVb, usually having high-swung handles with thumbstops.

As previously mentioned, certain formal attributes typify the ceramics of Period IVc. Bowls, cups, and holemouth jars with thinned rims appear to be unique to Period IVc Hasanlu (Figs. 4.41:B, J, P, 4.45:G, I, S, 4.46:E, G, T, 4.47:M, 4.54:C). Channel rims also stand out (Figs. 4.41:AA, 4.48:P–Q, 4.55:L, N). A variety of spouts occur at Hasanlu between late Period V and early Period IVb. Bridgeless spouts typify Period IVc at Hasanlu, although they are rare. They are first attested in late Period V and never occur in graves at the site—this is in contrast to Dinkha, where they are attested as early as the early LBA and are common in later LBA and Iron I graves. Bridged spouts appear in late Period IVc–early Period IVb (Figs. 4.54:Y, 4.58:W, 4.60:S) in Hasanlu occupation deposits and typify Iron II graves. Tube spouts are well attested in the later 2nd millennium BC; they are not in and of themselves diagnostic of a particular period. Channel spouts at the rims of bowls and holemouth jars seem to be a later development at Hasanlu, falling in the range of Period IVc–IVb (Figs. 4.46:S, 4.57a:D, 4.57b:A).

One of the most obvious and ubiquitous late Period V and especially Period IVc attributes is the narrow horizontal raised band on the upper shoulders or necks of jars and cups and, rarely, the sides of bowls (Figs. 4.41:P, 4.42:G, 4.43:F, 4.49:M, O, 4.50:I, L, 4.54:C, O, 4.57a:B, 4.57b:C, D, 4.58:K, M, N, 4.59:A–C, K, 4.60:O–P). Such bands continue in Period IVb but are a useful means for helping to distinguish later MBW from the MBIII and LBA. Thumbstops are frequently added to handles in late Period IVc–early Period IVb (Figs. 4.57a:B, 4.59:R, 4.60:Z) and are typical of the high-swung handles of the Iron II. High-swung handles appear in late Period IVc–early Period IVb (Fig. 4.43:Q–R). A profusion of lug and handle types were added to the vessels of Period IVc, including the segmented loop handle (Figs. 4.54:X, 4.55:C), the upright tabular lug (Figs. 4.47:V, 4.50:GG) and the bilobed, double-pierced lug (Figs. 4.45:M, T, 4.51:G). The segmented handle and upright tabular lug are typical of Period IVb. Often the walls of vessels are fluted in assemblages of late Period IVc–early Period IVb date—a type of decoration typical of the Iron II period (Figs. 4.58:D, 4.59:I, Q, 4.60:R). Gadrooning also emerges as a decorative technique (Fig. 4.43:E, 4.55:C, 4.56:C). Incised decoration becomes more common (Figs. 4.42:N, 4.56:E, 4.60:R) and there is liberal use of rilling (Figs. 4.41:A–C, 4.43:A, J, O, 4.55:N, P, T, 4.58:U, 4.59:I) and cannelures (Figs. 4.42:H–I, 4.43:I, 4.54:D, M, 4.56:C).

NOTES

4.1. The original coding used by Dyson, Young, and later Muscarella (1974) is maintained here alongside the new ware designations since many sherds were discarded in the field and, in most of the publication record touching on this dataset, ware information is absent.

4.2. Some key examples of this are revealing. The Iron Age typology focused on ceramics produced in dark colors since prevailing opinion traced the assemblage's origins back to the grey wares of northeastern Iran known primarily from Hissar. The MBW assemblage of Ušnu-Solduz likely originates from mid-2nd millennium BC burnished monochrome ware in a variety of colors, of which grey and black are but one component. The majority of such material was thus not considered with regard to the origins of the horizon because it was not grey. The MBA typology was developed to study the KW assemblage, and so alternative surface treatments such as burnishing and slipping were not as systematically recorded or quantified, again obscuring the early phases of MBW. This typology also inherited the "grey" bias from the already developed Iron Age typology. The period between the MBII and the Iron I at Dinkha was almost completely ignored because it lay outside the conceptual frameworks of the two predominant typologies.

4.3. Kramer analyzed 575 rim sherds, of which 79 were identified as KW (13%) (Hamlin 1971:136). Kramer provides some details on the overall assemblage from Dinkha, saying, "Though several thousand sherds were excavated at Dinkha, the sample on which my dissertation, and hence the following description, is based, comprises approximately 2,000 pieces (both sherds and vessels). At Dinkha, the information from three major excavation areas was supplemented by finds in wells, shallow connecting trenches, and small test trenches" (Hamlin 1974:125, n4).

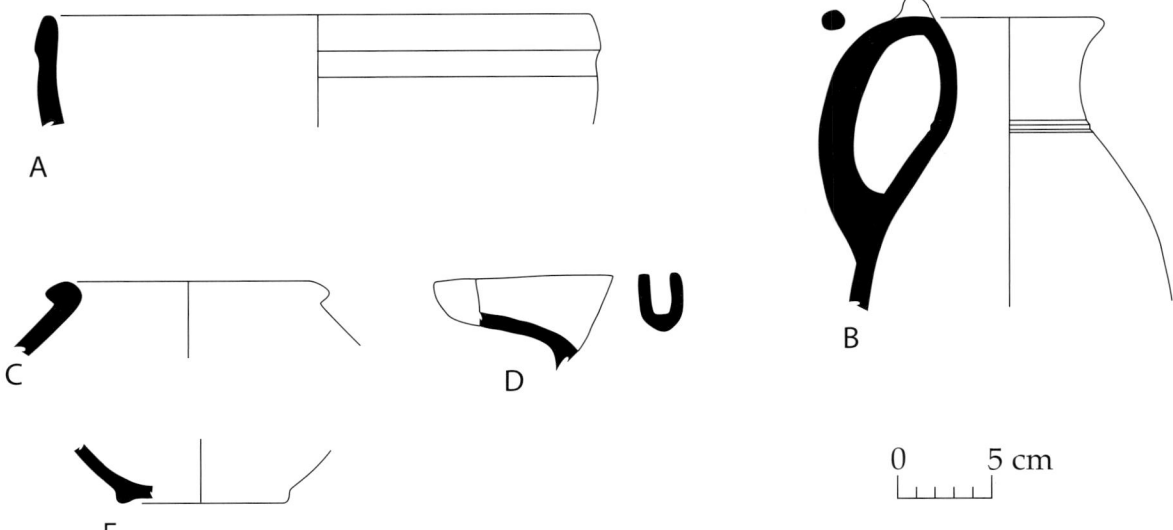

Fig. 4.57a

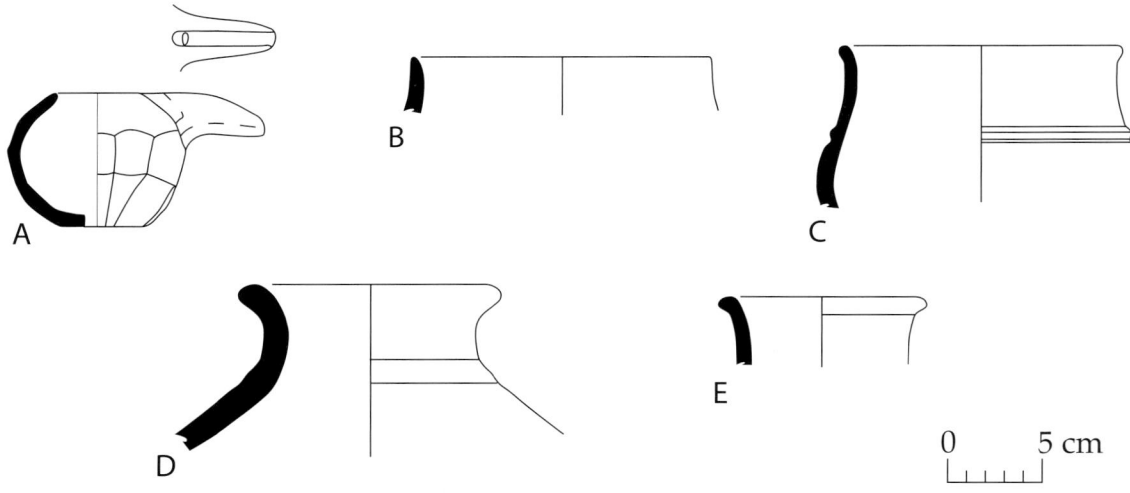

Fig. 4.57b

Fig. 4.57a Hasanlu Tepe: Period IVc ceramics from Test Trench A in the northwest storeroom (Room 13) of Burned Building II (Grid BB28) (opposite, top).

Fig.	Op.	Context	Ware	Type	Description	Dia.	Disposition
A	BB28	Test Trench A	NR	Bowl 8	NR	29	Sherd Drawing
B	BB28	Test Trench A	NR	Jar 10	NR, Strap Handle with Thumb Stop, Cannelures	9.5	Sherd Drawing
C	BB28	Test Trench A	NR	HM 4	NR	15	Sherd Drawing
D	BB28	Test Trench A	NR	—	NR, Channel Spout	—	Sherd Drawing
E	BB28	Test Trench A	NR	—	NR, Ring Base	9	Sherd Drawing

Fig. 4.57b Hasanlu Tepe: Period IVc ceramics from Test Trench A in the center west storeroom (Room 14) of Burned Building II (Grid BB28) (opposite, bottom).

Fig.	Op.	Context	Ware	Type	Description	Dia.	Disposition
A	BB28	Test Trench A	NR	HM 21	NR, Heavily Scraped, Channel Spout	8	Sherd Drawing
B	BB28	Test Trench A	NR	HM 1	NR	16	Sherd Drawing
C	BB28	Test Trench A	NR	Cup 8b	NR, Raised Band, Cannelure	15	Sherd Drawing
D	BB28	Test Trench A	NR	Jar 2	NR, Raised Band	14	Sherd Drawing
E	BB28	Test Trench A	NR	Jar 3a	NR	11	Sherd Drawing

4.4. This number does not include the few sherds found below the Phase A deposit which date to Hasanlu VIc or earlier.

4.5. This point is especially evident in Kramer's discussion of Grey Ware forms, as she states, "There are no jars made exclusively in grey ware [Ware V and VI]; some jars are represented by sherds of grey and buff color. Unfortunately, many of the types enumerated…are represented by only one specimen, so that it is not clear whether their grey color reflects controlled firing variation or represents one end of a generally buff range" (Hamlin 1971:137).

4.6. In the LBA and early Iron Age MBW of Hasanlu and Dinkha, any distinction made between "Grey Ware" and "Buff Ware" seems to be arbitrary.

4.7. Kramer mistakenly attributed some bowls to Phase D that belong to other phases, and other bowls that belong to Phase D were included in Phases A–C (Hamlin 1971: fig. 9). I have attributed 51 bowl attestations to Phase D.

4.8. Figure 4.8:C shows Kramer's Pot Type 17. Its similarity to Bowl Type 14b suggests that this vessel should be classified as a bowl.

4.9. Here Dyson is referencing a sherd of Hasanlu VIc–b type found in a Geoy C context (Burton-Brown 1951: pl. VIII:403), likely extrusive from Geoy Period G.

4.10. The study presented here involved the examination of sherd collections from Geoy Tepe in the University of Pennsylvania collections.

4.11. A grave at Hajji Firuz (Seriation) may be an exception, but the tankard and double-drilled Type 2 bowl appear, based on style, to be slightly later than early Period V, as does the jar with bridgeless spout.

4.12. On the dating of Sialk A to the 16th century, or the MBIII, see Dittmann 1990:127–35, Table I, and Tourovetz 1989. Dittmann provides a date range which spans the MBIII–LBA.

4.13. Hasanlu August 9, 1972 (Mohammad Nikkah, Excavation Supervisor) "Sherd of sheep head (two) and dog head." Notebook 56: 22, Hasanlu Publication Archive.

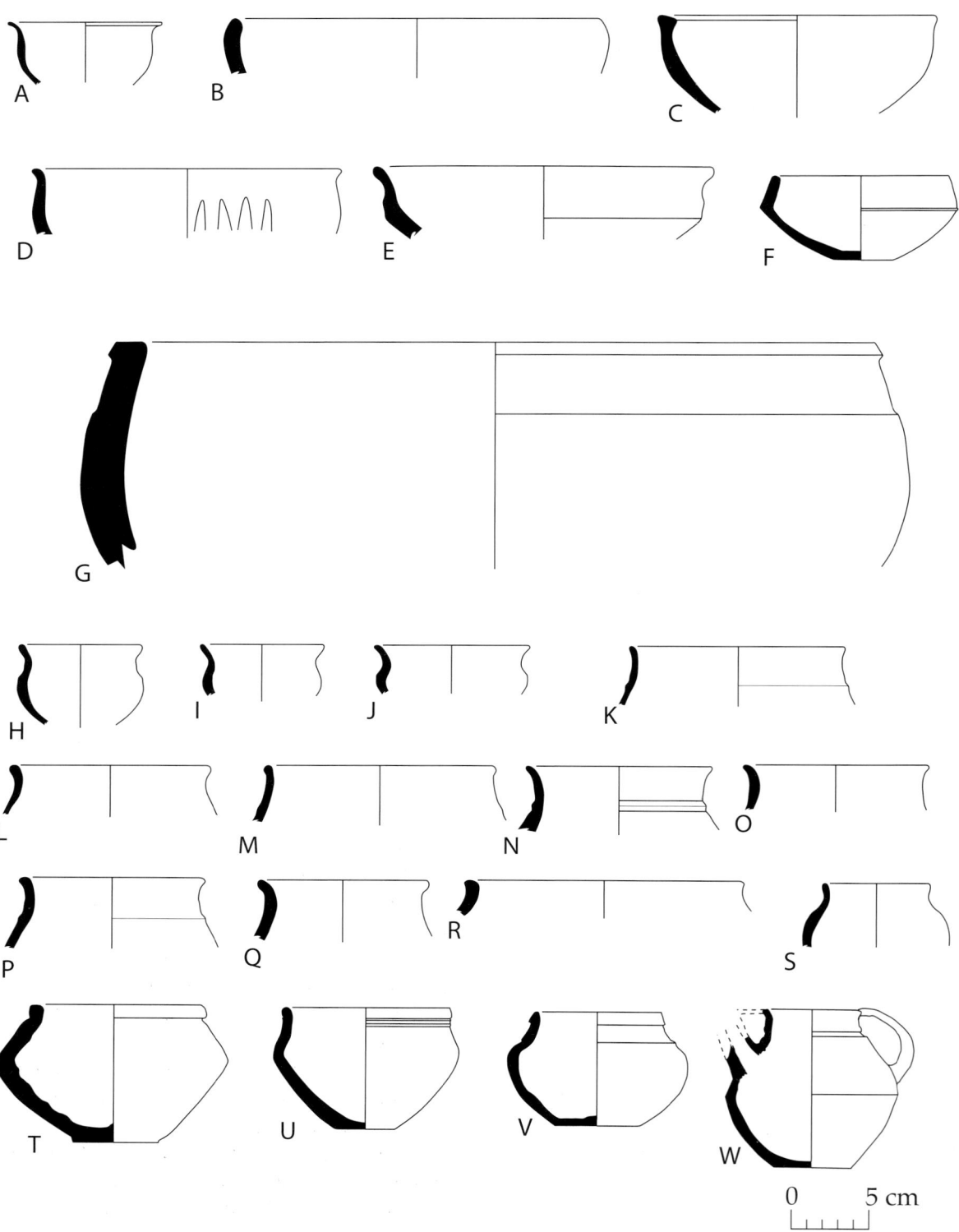

Fig. 4.58

Fig. 4.58 Hasanlu Tepe: Period IVc–IVb ceramics from the south storeroom (Room 6) of Burned Building V (opposite).

Fig.	Op.	Context	Ware	Type	Description	Dia.	Disposition
A	BBV	Room 6	NR	Bowl 18	NR	10	Sherd Drawing
B	BBV	Room 6	NR	Bowl 5	NR	24	Sherd Drawing
C	BBV	Room 6	NR	Bowl 8	NR	18	Sherd Drawing
D	BBV	Room 6	NR	Bowl 3c	NR, Gadrooning	20	Sherd Drawing
E	BBV	Room 6	NR	Bowl 3f	NR	22	Sherd Drawing
F	BBV	Room 6	NR	Bowl 6	NR	11.5	Sherd Drawing
G	BBV	Room 6	NR	Bowl 23	NR	49	Sherd Drawing
H	BBV	Room 6	NR	Cup 12	NR	8	Sherd Drawing
I	BBV	Room 6	NR	Cup 12	NR	8	Sherd Drawing
J	BBV	Room 6	NR	Cup 12	NR	10	Sherd Drawing
K	BBV	Room 6	NR	Cup 8b	NR, Raised Band	14	Sherd Drawing
L	BBV	Room 6	NR	Cup 8b	NR	13	Sherd Drawing
M	BBV	Room 6	NR	Cup 8b	NR, Raised Band	15	Sherd Drawing
N	BBV	Room 6	NR	Cup 8b	NR, Raised Band	12	Sherd Drawing
O	BBV	Room 6	NR	Cup 8c	NR	12	Sherd Drawing
P	BBV	Room 6	NR	Cup 8b	NR, Raised Band	12	Sherd Drawing
Q	BBV	Room 6	NR	Cup 8b	NR	11	Sherd Drawing
R	BBV	Room 6	NR	HM 1	NR	18	Sherd Drawing
S	BBV	Room 6	NR	Cup 12	NR	7	Sherd Drawing
T	BBV	Room 6	NR	HM 11a	NR	11	Sherd Drawing
U	BBV	Room 6	NR	Cup 11a	NR, Rilling	11	Sherd Drawing
V	BBV	Room 6	NR	HM 11b	NR	8	Sherd Drawing
W	BBV	Room 6	NR	Jar 3a	NR, Bridge Spout, Cannelure	6	Sherd Drawing

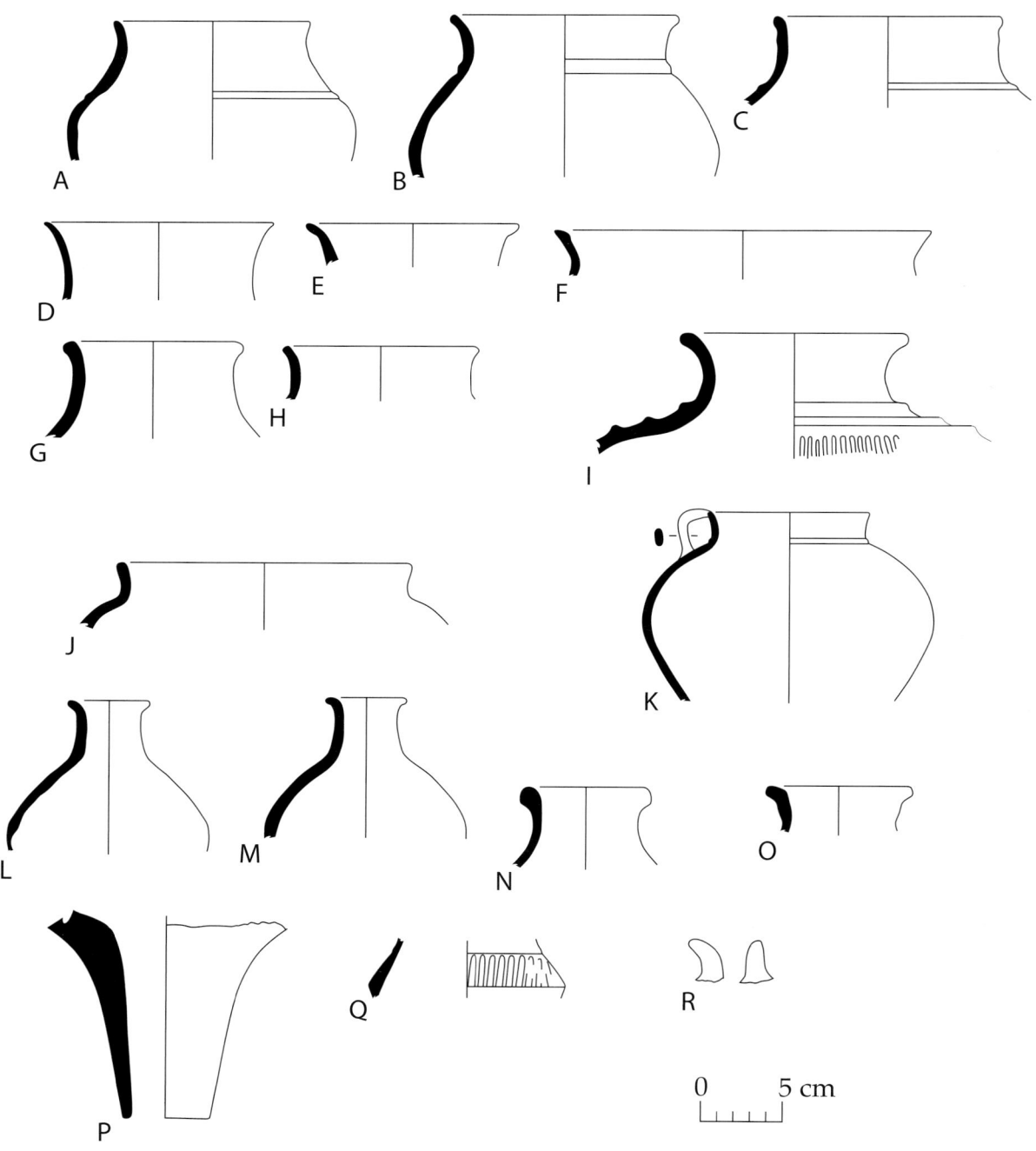

Fig. 4.59

Fig. 4.59 Hasanlu Tepe: Period IVc–IVb ceramics from the south storeroom (Room 6) of Burned Building V (opposite).

Fig.	Op.	Context	Ware	Type	Description	Dia.	Disposition
A	BBV	Room 6	NR	Cup 8c	NR, Raised Band	12	Sherd Drawing
B	BBV	Room 6	NR	Cup 8c	NR, Raised Band	14	Sherd Drawing
C	BBV	Room 6	NR	Cup 8c	NR, Raised Band	14	Sherd Drawing
D	BBV	Room 6	NR	Cup 7	NR	14	Sherd Drawing
E	BBV	Room 6	NR	Cup 8c	NR	13	Sherd Drawing
F	BBV	Room 6	NR	Jar 1a	NR	23	Sherd Drawing
G	BBV	Room 6	NR	Jar 1a	NR	11	Sherd Drawing
H	BBV	Room 6	NR	Cup 8c	NR	12	Sherd Drawing
I	BBV	Room 6	NR	Jar 12	NR, Rilling, Fluting	14	Sherd Drawing
J	BBV	Room 6	NR	HM 9	NR	18	Sherd Drawing
K	BBV	Room 6	NR	HM 9	NR, Raised Band, Loop Handle	10	Sherd Drawing
L	BBV	Room 6	NR	Jar 11	NR	7	Sherd Drawing
M	BBV	Room 6	NR	Jar 11	NR	5	Sherd Drawing
N	BBV	Room 6	NR	Jar 1b	NR	8	Sherd Drawing
O	BBV	Room 6	NR	Jar 1b	NR	9	Sherd Drawing
P	BBV	Room 6	NR	—	NR, Funnel	5	Sherd Drawing
Q	BBV	Room 6	NR	—	NR, Gadrooning	—	Sherd Drawing
R	BBV	Room 6	NR	—	NR, Thumb Stop	—	Sherd Drawing

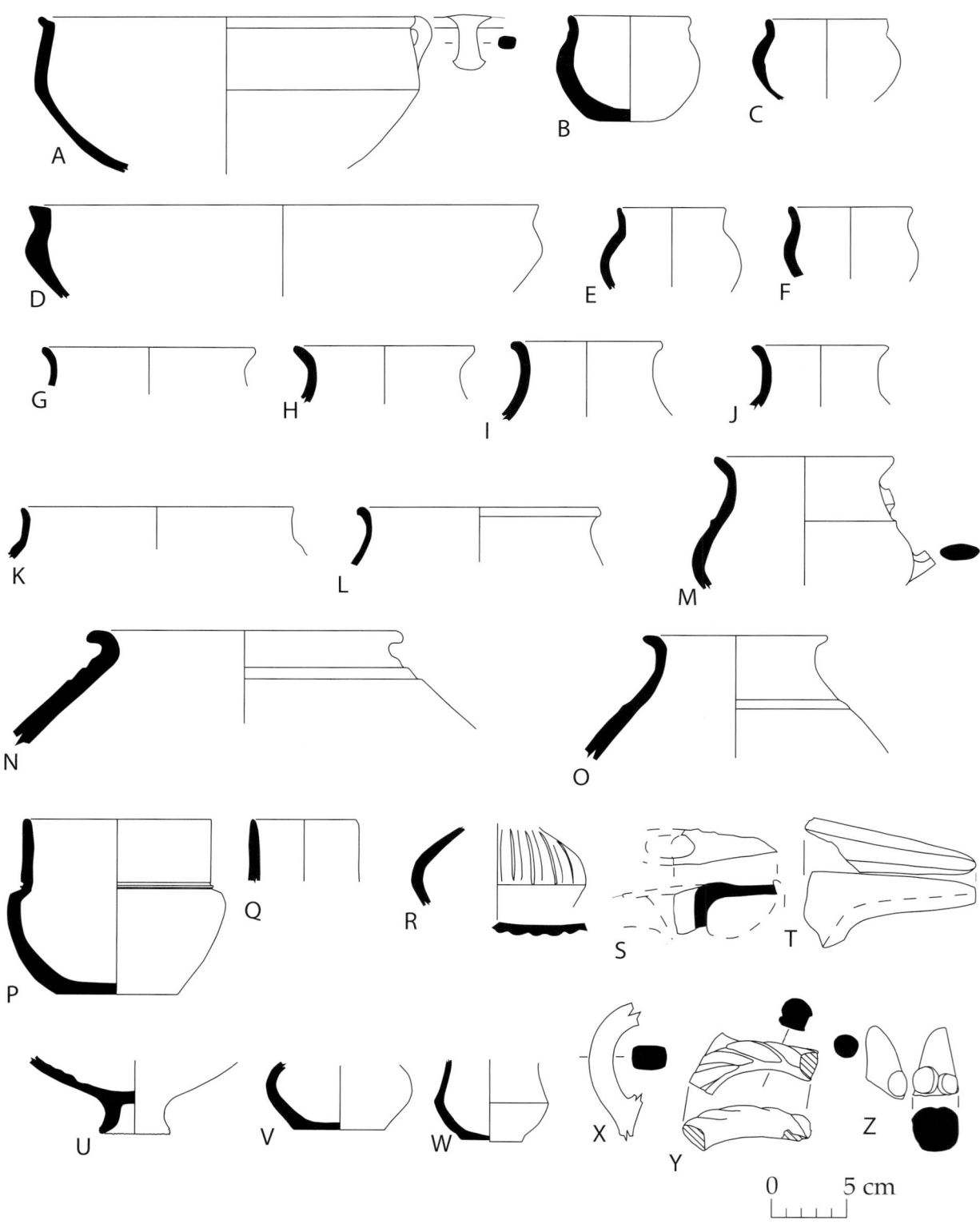

Fig. 4.60

Fig. 4.60 Hasanlu Tepe: Period IVc-early IVb ceramics from the west storeroom (Room 4) of Burned Building V (opposite).

Fig.	Op.	Context	Ware	Type	Description	Dia.	Disposition
A	BBV	Room 4	NR	Bowl 19	NR, Loop Handle	25	Sherd Drawing
B	BBV	Room 4	NR	Cup 12	NR	8	Sherd Drawing
C	BBV	Room 4	NR	Cup 12	NR	8	Sherd Drawing
D	BBV	Room 4	NR	Bowl 3b	NR	34	Sherd Drawing
E	BBV	Room 4	NR	Cup 12	NR	7	Sherd Drawing
F	BBV	Room 4	NR	Cup 12	NR	7	Sherd Drawing
G	BBV	Room 4	NR	Cup 8c	NR	14	Sherd Drawing
H	BBV	Room 4	NR	Cup 8c	NR	12	Sherd Drawing
I	BBV	Room 4	NR	Cup 8c	NR	10	Sherd Drawing
J	BBV	Room 4	NR	Cup 8c	NR	9	Sherd Drawing
K	BBV	Room 4	NR	HM 9	NR	18	Sherd Drawing
L	BBV	Room 4	NR	Cup 8c	NR	16	Sherd Drawing
M	BBV	Room 4	NR	Cup 8c	NR, Raised Band, Loop Handle	12	Sherd Drawing
N	BBV	Room 4	NR	HM 1	NR, Rilling	21	Sherd Drawing
O	BBV	Room 4	NR	Jar 2	NR, Raised Band	12	Sherd Drawing
P	BBV	Room 4	NR	HM 11c	NR, Cannelures	12.5	Sherd Drawing
Q	BBV	Room 4	NR	Cup 7	NR	7	Sherd Drawing
R	BBV	Room 4	NR	—	NR, Excised Deco.	—	Sherd Drawing
S	BBV	Room 4	NR	—	NR, Bridge Spout	—	Sherd Drawing
T	BBV	Room 4	NR	—	NR, Spout	—	Sherd Drawing
U	BBV	Room 4	NR	—	NR, Pedestal Base	5	Sherd Drawing
V	BBV	Room 4	NR	—	NR, Flat Base	6.5	Sherd Drawing
W	BBV	Room 4	NR	—	NR, Flat Base	4	Sherd Drawing
X	BBV	Room 4	NR	—	NR, Loop Handle	—	Sherd Drawing
Y	BBV	Room 4	NR	—	NR, Twisted Loop Handle	—	Sherd Drawing
Z	BBV	Room 4	NR	—	NR. Thumb Stop with Appliqué "Eyes"	—	Sherd Drawing

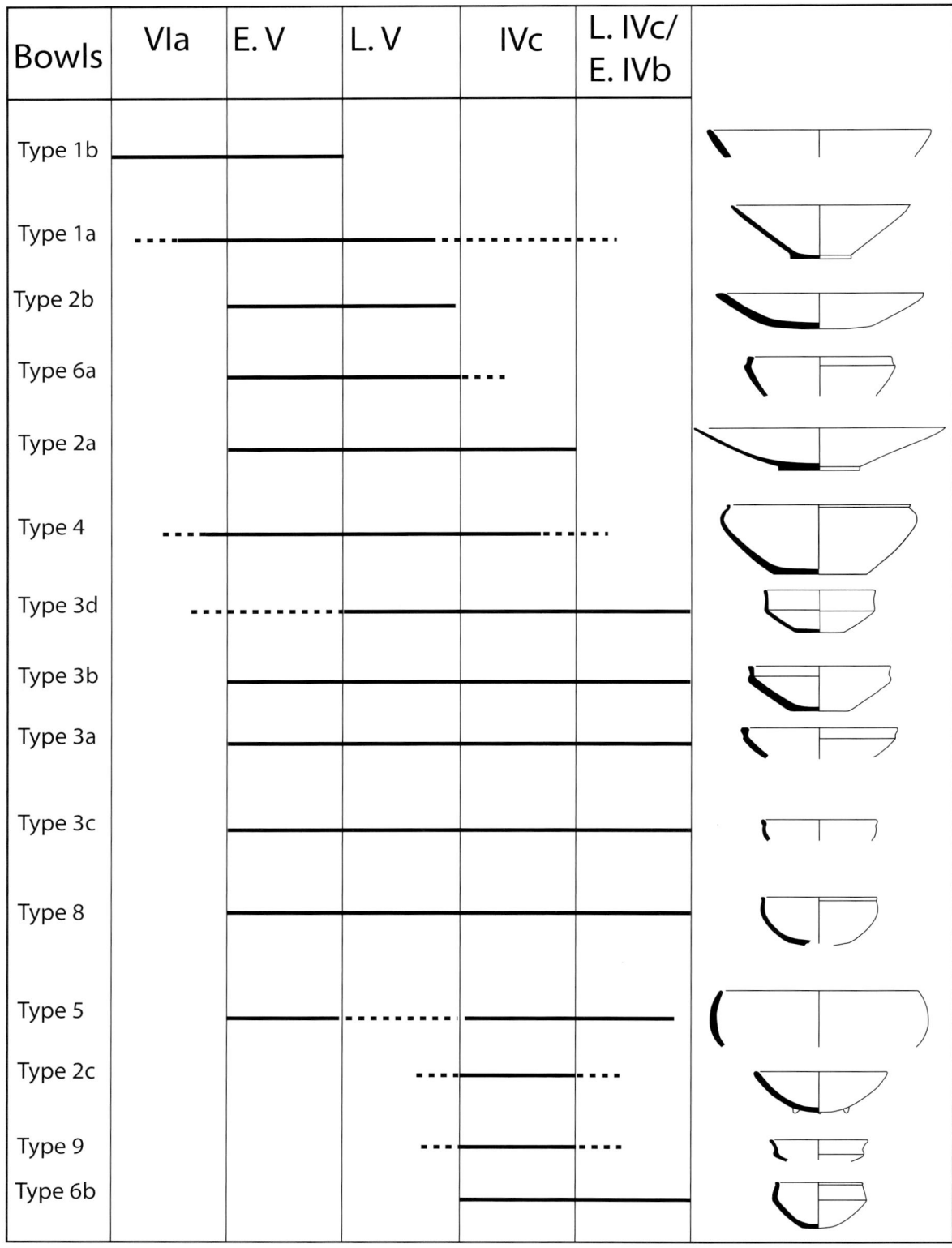

Fig. 4.61 Bowl types in Ušnu-Solduz over time.

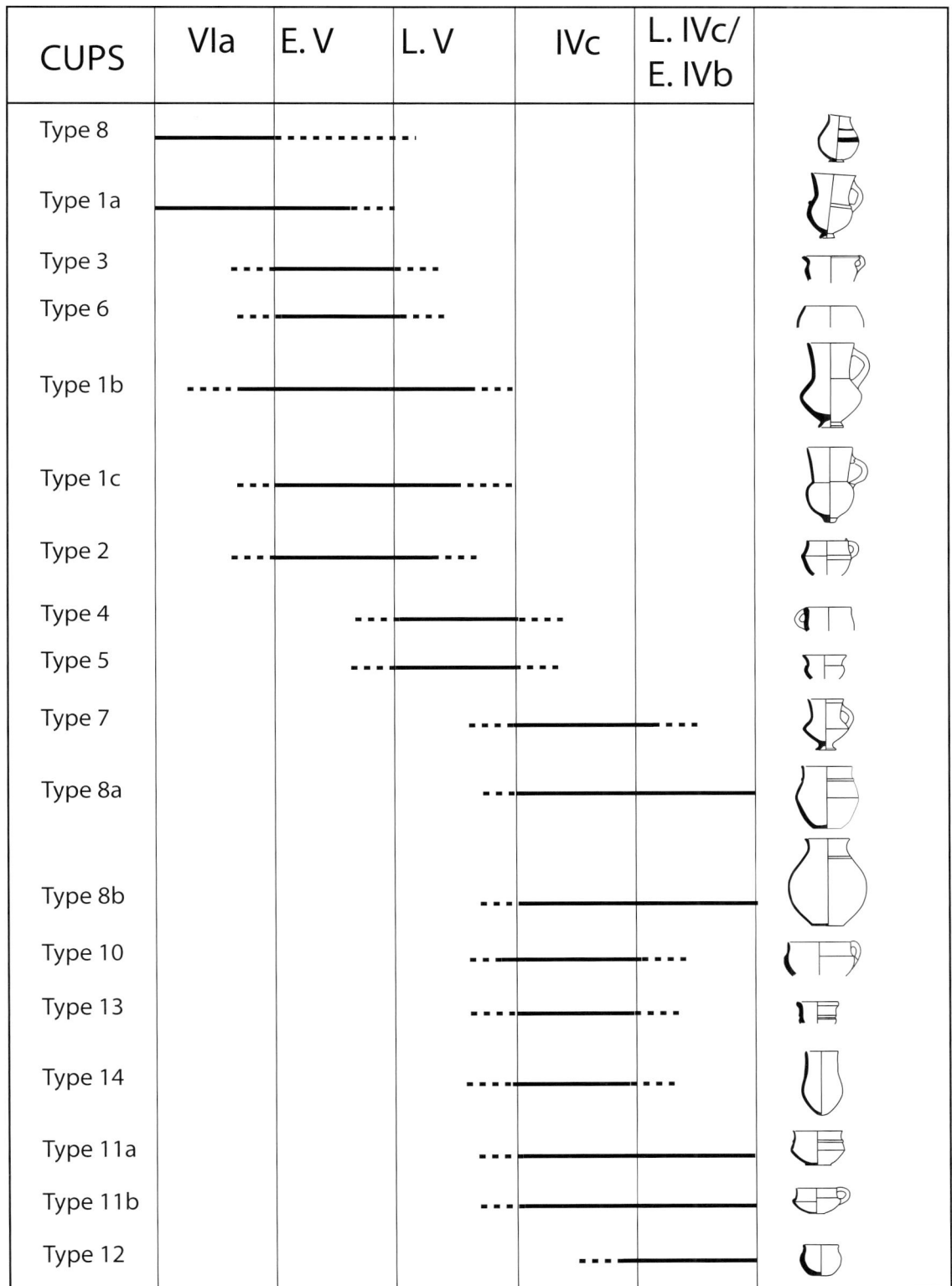

Fig. 4.62 Cup types in Ušnu-Solduz over time.

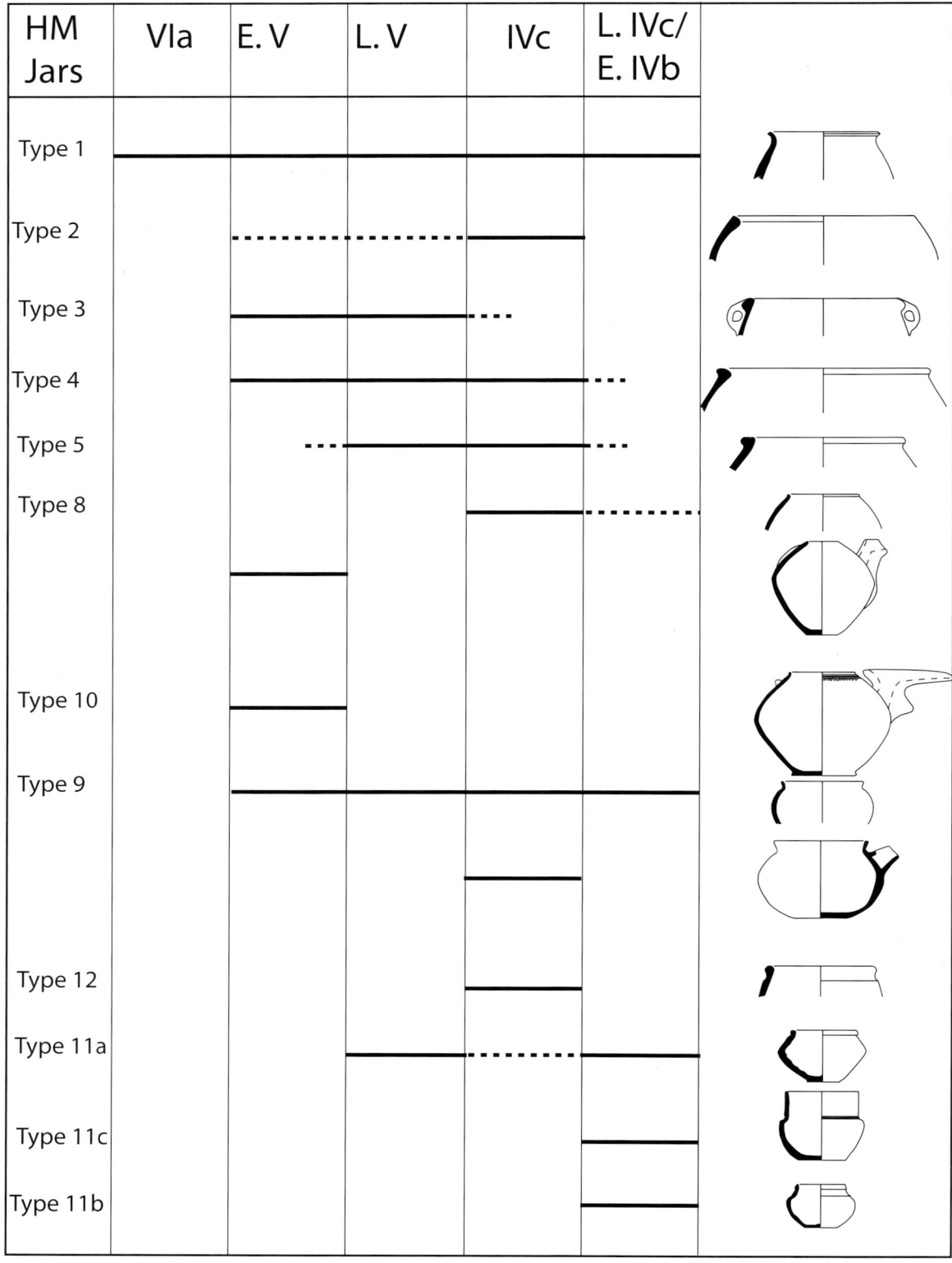

Fig. 4.63 Holemouth jar types in Ušnu-Solduz over time.

Jars	VIa	E. V	L. V	IVc	L. IVc/ E. IVb
Type 6a	⋯⋯——⋯⋯				
Type 6b		——			
Type 1a		——————————————————			
Type 1b			——————————⋯		
Type 2			——————————⋯		
Type 3b			——————————⋯		
Type 3a			—————————————		

Fig. 4.64 Jar types in Ušnu-Solduz over time.

5

The Middle Bronze, Late Bronze, and Iron I Graves of Hasanlu and Dinkha

Pulvis et umbra sumus.

The Hasanlu Project recovered graves of the 2nd millennium BC at Hasanlu, Dinkha Tepe, Dalma Tepe, and Hajji Firuz. Sir Aurel Stein had previously excavated graves at Hasanlu and Dinkha in 1936 (Stein 1940), and some graves had been excavated at Hasanlu on the Low Mound by Mahmoud Rad in 1947 and Ali Hakemi in 1949 (Hakemi and Rad 1950). Other Hasanlu graves were essentially plundered by the agents of commercial antiquities dealers in 1934–1935, with a small collection of finds later published by Ghirshman (1939:78–79, pl. c).

Having established a chronological framework for the MBIII, LBA, and Iron I of Hasanlu Tepe and Dinkha Tepe using stratified occupation deposits and radiocarbon dates, it is possible to place most of the graves excavated by the Hasanlu Project in a relative sequence using the ceramics in the grave groups and, to a lesser extent, other classes of grave goods and occasionally on stratigraphic relationships (Seriation). The graves of Dalma have yet to be analyzed. Appendix IVa provides a catalog of the graves of Periods VIb–IVc organized chronologically. Appendix IVb presents a listing of all Low Mound burials arranged by Skeleton Number.

The Graves of Dinkha Tepe: Overview

At least four graves were excavated by Stein at Dinkha (Stein 1940:373–4). These date to Hasanlu VIb–VIa and exhibit the wide range of burial practices typical of the periods with two inhumations, one pithos burial and a stone-built tomb (see also Chapter 4). The burials appear to have been within the area of the settlement. The Hasanlu Project discovered an unknown number of additional graves dating to the MBA in 1966 and 1968.[1] At least two inhumation graves of the MBII/Hasanlu VIb are mentioned by Muscarella and have yet to be fully published (Muscarella 1968:195).[2] Operation B10a uncovered stone-lined intramural tombs with multiple interments within the Dinkha IV Phase C and Phase D settlements—the MBII and Terminal MBII, respectively (Dyson 1973a; Hamlin 1974; Muscarella 1968:195; Rubinson 1991). The Phase C tomb was cut down from Stratum 9 and remains largely unpublished. The Phase D tomb—Operation B10a Burial 28—formed part of the Terminal MBII settlement and was cut down from Stratum 8. The objects from this tomb have been published in detail (McGovern, Fleming, and Swann 1991; Muscarella 1968:195, figs. 21–22; Rubinson 1991; see also Chapter 4).

Following the destruction of the final Phase D MBII settlement, trash deposits accumulated in the area of the northern mound, and graves of "Dinkha III," or Hasanlu VIa–IVc, were cut into this deposit and the Terminal MBII level. Most of the graves of these periods seem to have been concentrated on the northern part of the mound, although a few others were found in Operation B8e and Test Trenches IV, VII, IX, and XI. Muscarella identifies a total of 33 graves belonging to "Dinkha III" (1974:36, 83–85, table I). These graves exhibit less variability in terms of mortuary practices as compared to the preceding Dinkha IV/Hasanlu VIb sample collected by the Hasanlu Project and Stein. All burials were single inhumations with 23 simple cist graves and 10 mudbrick tombs (Muscarella 1974:37). Most such graves attributed to "Dinkha III" date to late Hasanlu V and IVc. Of the published graves, only one is potentially datable to Hasanlu VIa (B9a Burial 25), but it is more likely early Period V, and another 4 graves seem to be early Period V (see below). The chronological clustering of these graves could well be the result of sampling. Most of the "Dinkha III" graves (75%) were found in a single area of the mound, the so-called Control Sounding of B9/10a–b. The Hasanlu Project also excavated at least 68 graves of the Iron II (Muscarella 1974:58ff.).

Since many of the graves of the later 2nd millennium at Dinkha have been published in detail (Muscarella 1968, 1974; Rubinson 1991), in-depth descriptions are not repeated here. The important ceramic assemblages from these graves were included in this analysis drawing on the published results. Some stratigraphic information on the relationships of the Dinkha III graves can be gleaned from the publications. We know that Test Trench VII Burial 1 cut Strata 2–3 and lay above/sealed Burial 2, which cut Strata 4–6 (Muscarella 1974:38–40). Both graves date to the LBA/Hasanlu V (see below). More information is provided on Operation B9a: "In B9a a number of period III…burials were excavated in strata 5a and 6; six burials were also found below these in stratum 7" (Muscarella 1974:40). The ceramics and radiocarbon dates from the Control Sounding at Dinkha indicate that Stratum 7 dates to the MBIII (1600–1450 BC) or slightly later. This dating depends on the relationship between the ceramic assemblage—which contains polychrome Urmia Ware, Early MBW, and Incised and Impressed MBW—and a radiocarbon date from the final occupation of Dinkha Phase D Stratum 8 (Appendix II, P-1231) in the 16th century BC and a radiocarbon date for Stratum 7 (Appendix II, P-1449) in the late 15th–14th centuries BC. The ceramic assemblage of Strata 5–6 of the Control Sounding contains virtually no Urmia Ware and is characterized by Early MBW and Incised and Impressed MBW. The Strata 5–7 sequence is in lock-step with those of the southern Caucasus and northern Mesopotamia, and this later deposit of Strata 5–6 can be dated to the early LBA. The implications for the dating of the graves cut into this area are fairly straightforward. It is not clear from which stratum the graves were cut, but those cutting Stratum 7 are no earlier than the late MBIII (late Hasanlu VIa) and those cutting Strata 5a and 6 can be no earlier than the early LBA (early Hasanlu V). Most graves subject to these criteria have been dated on the basis of the seriation of their ceramic assemblages to late Hasanlu Period V and Hasanlu IVc (see below). Two of the graves thought by Muscarella to be early in the sequence on the basis of stratigraphy (1974:38–40) have been dated to early Period V using stylistic seriation (B9a Burial 25 and Test Trench VII Burial 2). Overall, the relative sequence obtained for the Dinkha graves from ceramic stylistic seriation and comparison with ceramic sequences from occupation deposits agrees well with the rudimentary sequence obtained from the published stratigraphic details.

The 2nd Millennium Graves of Hasanlu: Overview

Only a few details on the graves of Hasanlu have previously appeared in print. On the Low Mound the excavators recovered at least 145 graves. Another seven skeletons, identified as graves by the Hasanlu Project excavators, may represent burials or victims of an attack(s) on the Low Mound settlement(s). At least one victim of a Period IVb attack has been identified on the Low Mound in Burned Building XIII (Danti 2011). Burials of the Bronze Age (Hasanlu VII, VI, and V) and Iron I–II (Hasanlu IVc and IVb) were only located on the Low Mound. While Hasanlu has graves dating from Hasanlu VIb–IVc, most of these graves date to the LBA and few can be assigned to the Iron I period. Of the 2nd millennium BC graves excavated by the Hasanlu Project containing ceramics or datable by other means, five date to Period VIb, one dates to Terminal VIb, two date to Period VIa, five date to early Period V, and at least six may be assigned to Period IVc. A few graves can be dated to the later 2nd millennium BC but not to a specific period and have been included here separately, under the heading "Period V–IVc."

The Hasanlu graves of the 2nd millennium BC reinforce the interpretation gained from the High Mound excavations that the site was probably continuously occupied throughout the 2nd millennium BC. The chronological distribution of the graves reflects the time periods in which the northern Low Mound, part of the ever-shifting periphery of the settlement, offered open spaces for burials. The chronological distribution of the graves at Hasanlu suggests the northern Low Mound was open for use as a cemetery in Periods VIb, VIa, and early V. These graves were dug into the thick occupation deposits of the 3rd millennium BC, which in turn contained some graves of Period VIIa–b of the mid-3rd millennium BC. By late Period V and Period IVc little room was available for new graves. In the latter part of Period IVb, graves were once again dug in the area, as the memory or importance of the earlier graves had faded and deposition had raised the level of the Low Mound, possibly obscuring the location of earlier graves, as well. Iron II graves frequently cut into earlier graves of the 2nd millennium BC.

Although not covered in detail here, large numbers of Iron II burials were located on the Low Mound of Hasanlu. Around 97 graves can be tentatively assigned to the period based on ceramic assemblages, personal ornament, or stratigraphy. A selection of ceramics and some examples of the burials are referred to herein to contextualize the graves of Period IVc and to allow the presentation of an overview of burial practices in the early 1st millennium BC, since burial practices formed one important part of the definition of the "Grey Ware" horizon. In terms of the chronological sequence, where Hasanlu lacks evidence from burials Dinkha provides graves and vice-versa, providing a fairly continuous record of mortuary practices from the MBII to the Iron II.

A handful of other sites in the Lake Urmia region have provided graves—most are from "unattached" cemeteries cut into earlier mounds. Some "Iron I" graves, probably datable to Hasanlu Period V, were found at Dalma Tepe (Young 1962:707–8, fig. 8), and a late Period V grave was excavated at Hajji Firuz (see below). In the Urmia region, Burton-Brown found a stone-built tomb at Geoy Tepe dating to his Period B or Hasanlu Period V and other burials of likely Hasanlu IVc date (1951:141–45, figs. 28, 29, 32, 34). At Yanik Tepe in the eastern Lake Urmia Basin, Burney discovered "a cemetery containing inhumation burials all of one period (c. 1500–c. 1100 B.C.)" (Burney 1962:136). Only one of these eight graves, all of which are attributed to the "Iron I," has been published in any detail (Seriation; Burney 1962:136, 146–47, pl. XLIV, figs. 24–29).[3] Burney assigns another grave from Yanik Trench P a date of 1000 BC, although there seems to be little evidence for this Iron II attribution in light of the necklace and ceramic vessels (1964:60, pl. XV, nos. 14–19).

The Hasanlu Project: The Methodology of Mortuary Archaeology

The excavation of graves found in the Hasanlu Low Mound was typically carried out rapidly and with little recording by today's standards. I found it a difficult task to accurately locate the position of operations on the Low Mound, since little mapping was done in the early seasons of excavation. No standardized system for the recording of elevations was ever employed at Hasanlu, so one is reliant on relative elevations recorded above and below certain features within an operation, or on measurements below the surface. These points were not related to a fixed survey station, which then could have been used to determine universal elevations.

No standardized notebooks were kept during the early seasons of excavation at Hasanlu; rather a variety of loose-leaf notes and drawings, field journals, and diaries from the excavations were compiled into operation notebooks in the 1980s. This process has introduced errors since these various notes were often transcribed with a typewriter to form portions of the operation notebooks and the original archival material is not always available for comparison. My own experience has been that there are often significant discrepancies between these two separate sets of documents. Every effort has been made here to consult the original source material whenever possible.

In the notes on both the graves of the Low Mound and the remains of the victims of the Period IVb destruction level, one often reads that skeletal remains were, for instance, "wrecked during lunch." The rapid pace of excavation meant that not all graves and victims were drawn and photographed. Moreover, objects from graves were occasionally discarded without being drawn or photographed. Nearly all Low Mound excavations contained architecture, but only in rare cases were these features adequately mapped and drawn. Mudbrick walls typically appear only in sections and were almost universally cut through during excavation. Stone footings and pavings were more likely to be recorded. The end result is that it is often challenging to establish stratigraphic relationships between the burials and the deposits into which they were cut. Moreover, the excavators seldom recorded the levels from which graves were cut and usually did not include the pits cut for burials on plans, when such plans were completed.

When burials were found, they were assigned a Burial Number—for example "Burial 1," typically abbreviated "B1." Burial Numbers were only unique within a given operation and season. Sometime during the excavations, apparently in the late 1950s, Burial Sheets were introduced to the recordkeeping system to standardize recording, although large sections of these standardized forms were often left blank. Dyson later assigned a unique series of numbers—called Skeleton Numbers or SK Numbers—to every skeleton recovered from the site, both burials and the victims of the Period IVb attack. SK Numbers are used herein and a concordance of SK Numbers by Operation and Burial Number is provided in Appendix IV. The recording of stratigraphy, features, and grave objects followed typical excavation procedure, with Object Numbers assigned to finds by the operation supervisor (see Chapter 3). The registrar was responsible for later assigning a Hasanlu Number to these artifacts prior to the division of finds to sponsoring institutions or the discard of the item.

For the time, the Hasanlu Project completed a surprising amount of field photography, and quite a few of the burials were photographed prior to their removal. Skeletal remains were frequently not kept or were selectively sampled (Selinsky 2009:45–48, figs. 3.1, 3.2) and during the earliest seasons of excavation were especially prone to discard (Selinsky 2009). In the early 1960s, physical anthropologists George Bass and Ted Rathbun participated in the Hasanlu Project, and we thus have a great deal more information on skeletal remains, and skeletal materials were more likely to have been saved from that point forward (Rathbun 1972). Bass and Rathbun conducted extensive excavations on the northern Low Mound with the intention of recovering burials, and a large number were excavated in 1964. Skeletal remains that were saved and shipped to the US were eventually deposited in the University of Pennsylvania Museum and were given accession numbers (UPM Numbers, e.g., UPM65-31-773).

Method of Analysis

The total number of graves from the Low Mound excavations (n=145) was difficult to establish. Occasionally a single grave designation would in fact represent multiple interments, sometimes from different time periods since graves occasionally cut through earlier burials. In other cases, the Hasanlu Project would excavate part of a grave, which extended into a baulk, and would later excavate the remainder of the grave, unknowingly assigning different SK Numbers to different parts of the same skeleton. Records from all graves from the Low Mound at Hasanlu were examined as part of efforts to establish a relative chronology of the 2nd millennium BC burials, including the large number of Iron II graves of the late 2nd–early 1st millennium BC, to develop criteria by which to separate the early Iron II graves from those of the late Iron I. Prior to this study the graves had been assigned preliminary period designations that were recorded in various sets of records in the Hasanlu Project Archives. Along with information garnered from previous publications, this made it possible to reconstruct, to some extent, how the excavators' understanding of Hasanlu's chronology developed over time. It is important to bear in mind that the graves of the Low Mound played a critical role in the development of the Hasanlu chronological sequence.

The trends in ceramic production observed in the stratified assemblages from the occupation deposits from the Hasanlu High Mound—particularly those from the U22 Sounding and YZ27–29 supplemented by published information on Dinkha IV—aided me greatly in developing a relative chronological sequence for the contemporary graves of Hasanlu and Dinkha Tepe. The sequence of graves was subsequently refined through a stylistic seriation (Seriation). The most time-sensitive ceramic types for the later 2nd millennium BC graves, by far, were cups and bowls, although trends were also apparent in jars and holemouth vessels. Presentation of the graves from the Iron II and later is beyond the scope of the present work, but some examples of early Period IVb material are included here to facilitate comparisons. Toward this same end the graves of Hasanlu VI are presented here to illustrate the degree of continuity from the MBA and LBA.

On the whole, previous researchers had accurately assigned the graves of Hasanlu IVb/Iron II to this period. This is in large part due to the presence of the highly diagnostic and ubiquitous bridge-spouted jar, hallmark of the Iron II. The presence of this jar type along with other vessel forms distinctive of the Iron II allowed the excavators to securely assign a large number of graves to this period. They were also greatly assisted by the comparative potential of the Hasanlu IVb destruction level, which contained an enormous assemblage of whole ceramic vessels of the 9th century BC (cf. Muscarella 1974:59). The same accuracy is not the case, however, for earlier periods and Hasanlu "Period V," as previously defined, was to some extent a catchall for ambiguous or "older" looking "Grey Ware." The situation at Dinkha was more readily deducible for the excavators, since the earlier "Iron Age" graves tended to have bridgeless-spouted vessels—a hallmark of "Hasanlu V," "Dinkha III," "Iron I," and the "Early Western Grey Ware Horizon." As previously discussed, these spatio-temporal designations encompass the second half of the 2nd millennium BC. Other ceramic diagnostics purported by the original excavators to be characteristic of "Hasanlu V" were so-called worm bowls, button-base goblets (shouldered beakers), pedestal-base tankards/cups, jars and bowls with double piercing/drilling below the rim, vertically pierced lugs, and vessels bearing pattern-burnished decoration. A re-examination of the "Hasanlu V" graves supplemented by those from Dinkha III shows that we can currently discern at least four separate periods—Terminal Hasanlu VI/Dinkha IV, Hasanlu VIa, V, and IVc—all within the previously accepted "Hasanlu V"/Dinkha III designation.

The Intramural-Extramural Cemetery Dichotomy in the Lake Urmia Basin

As discussed above, scholars have long argued that an important marker of the "arrival" of the MBW horizon in northwest Iran is the shift from intramural burial, here defined as burials directly associated with residential architecture, to extramural burial, here meaning burial in cemeteries located either on the peripheries of settlements, in uninhabited parts of settlements, or unassociated with settlements. These distinctions have been ill defined, inconsistently applied, and are often difficult to establish. Excavation methods and recording were often too poor to establish associations between burials and residential structures and the spatial extent of residential areas and cemeteries naturally shifted over time. A review of the evidence for the Lake Urmia Basin shows that this supposed dichotomy in burial practices is virtually unattested and has often been employed indiscriminately in an *a priori* manner.

Dinkha Tepe allegedly has an extramural cemetery of the Late Bronze and Iron I periods, but no associated 'Iron I' settlement was ever identified (Muscarella 1974:37). The Dinkha III graves were cut into an erosional layer and trash deposit that sealed the remains of the Terminal MBII settlement. Muscarella dates this trash deposit to "Dinkha III"; the deposit cut by graves is itself a stratified sequence which spans the MBIII–LBA. This material continued to accumulate into the Iron II period (Dinkha II) and graves of that period were also found. In the same level as the Dinkha II graves (Iron II, Hasanlu IVb), the excavators found pottery kilns of Dinkha II date associated with domestic architecture. Muscarella supports the extramural position of the MBIII–Iron II cemetery stating, "the cemetery was abandoned before the end of period II. The settlement in existence at the time when the cemetery was in use seems to lie to the south, and fragments of walls apparently belonging to this period were excavated in a test trench" (1968:189). It is unclear why the walls and kilns in the cemetery area do not undermine the "extramural" designation or necessitate the redefinition of the term. Muscarella supports the use of extramural cemeteries as a defining characteristic of the earliest Iron Age, saying, "Culturally the break is equally clear and dramatic, notably in the pottery and in the burial customs, where single inhumations in an extramural cemetery replace intramural multiple burials" (1974:52–53). Yet there is no definitive proof regarding the location of the Dinkha III settlement. In Dinkha II, graves were found in potential association with Dinkha II architecture, but the extramural distinction is used, *prima facie*, to argue that the area was used as a cemetery and the settlement later expanded into the area. In fact, the situation at Dinkha seems identical to that of the Low Mound at Hasanlu, with areas used for LBA and early Iron Age burials interspersed with residential areas. The manner in which the Hasanlu Project excavators applied the definition rendered intramural Iron Age cemeteries a virtual logical impossibility and the presence of extramural cemeteries a foregone conclusion. Moreover, multiple burials of Iron II date were found at Dinkha and Hasanlu in rough stone-built tombs, brick tombs, and *hypogea* (Hakemi and Rad 1950; Muscarella 1974; Danti and Cifarelli n.d.). With the exception of Dinkha, these variations were glossed over or ignored.

"Iron I" burials were excavated by the Hasanlu Project at Dalma Tepe, south of Hasanlu (Young 1962:707–8, fig. 8). These graves were cut into the surface of this prehistoric mound. Muscarella (1974:49) suggests that, "an Iron I extramural cemetery existed here and that there may have been a settlement somewhere in the vicinity." No evidence of this settlement has yet been found.

An Iron I grave at Hajji Firuz, particularly notable since it contained all three diagnostic "Iron I" vessel forms, was discovered in 1968 (ibid.). The extramural distinction was not applied (ibid.). At Geoy Tepe, Tomb K of the early LBA is located on the high mound. The site may have Iron I trash deposits (ibid.) according to a post-excavation re-analysis conducted by Dyson. Muscarella concludes, "thus evidence of occupation from that period exists although never extensively excavated" (ibid.). The extramural distinction is implied; however, this tomb could equally be intramural. The subterranean stone-built tomb located on the southern fringe of the Geoy Tepe high mound likely had an entrance at the surface level and a pithos was found there—a black MBW holemouth jar with a crescent lug (Burton-Brown 1951:141, fig. 16 no. 48, pl. VI no. 48). This suggests the tomb was part of an actively used area. The possible defensive wall found in "Pit I" near the summit of the Geoy Tepe high mound provides additional evidence of occupation (Burton-Brown 1951:141), although it lies 180 m from the tomb. It is noteworthy that Tomb K has all three diagnostics of "Iron I" *but* is also a multiple interment in a stone-built tomb.

At Haftavan a grave of the Iron I was found in a cemetery immediately adjacent to the contemporary citadel (Burney 1970:170, fig. 8:1, 7, pl. III; 1973:155, 162–64; Burney and Lang 1972: fig. 40). Other stone-built tombs with overlying inhumations were found in "Pit III." These graves span the MBII–LBA and were not associated with architecture. One grave of an adult male was found on the high mound in Operation C2 Level 6 (Edwards 1983:11, figs. 6, 9), but is not directly associated with architecture. In Early Period VIB, two jar burials of children, both of which were sealed by stones, were found on the low mound in Y2 Phase 2 (Edwards 1983:62, figs. 35, 40) and in BB1/5 (Edwards 1983:66, fig. 46). They both cut through architecture. While the stones sealing these graves marked the surfaces from which they were cut, their direct association with the use-phase of an architectural level is unclear and they might easily belong to abandonment phases.

Other graves found in the Lake Urmia Basin datable to the MBW horizon, such as those at Yanik Tepe, seem to represent unattached cemeteries similar to Dalma Tepe. Overall, the intramural-extramural cemetery dichotomy as a distinctive marker between the MBA and the MBW horizon is at best equivocal. Second millennium BC burials at Haftavan, Geoy Tepe, and Hasanlu tend to be located on low mounds in areas with shifting patterns of use. The tombs of Dinkha IV are exceptional in this regard.

The Graves of Period VIb

This discussion of MBA graves is largely confined to Hasanlu Tepe. The intramural tomb of Dinkha IV Phase C remains unpublished, as do other MBII Dinkha graves (at least two are mentioned) excavated there in 1966 (Muscarella 1968:195). Stein excavated three graves of this period at Dinkha in 1936—the burials found in his section ii, section vi, and section viii (1940:373–74).

Graves of Hasanlu VIb are usually easily identified by their distinctive PKW and *istikhans*. The Hasanlu excavators occasionally misidentified Hasanlu VIb graves as "Hasanlu V" when they contained only MBA Grey Ware (e.g., see SK4–5, below). As at Dinkha, burial patterns in Hasanlu VIb exhibit significant variability, with stone-built tombs, simple inhumations, stone-covered inhumations, and multiple interments all attested in the small sample. The order in which the graves of Period VIb are presented below and in the seriation of graves (Seriation) is not indicative of a perceived relative sequence. I have detected no chronological subdivisions as yet in the mortuary ceramics of Hasanlu VIb/Dinkha Phases A–C: the graves of the period are presented by SK Number.

Hasanlu SK4–5
Multiple Inhumation, Adults, Undetermined Sex

Multiple inhumation grave SK4–5 of Operation IV was cut down from the base of the Period "V"/VI deposit (Strata 13 to 14) into Period VII strata and lay near SK6, which dates to Period IVc (see Chapter 3). Dyson initially dated all three graves in this area, SK4–6, to Hasanlu IVb, but he later reattributed them to "Period V" (1958:31; 1965:34–36, 39) citing (1) the small ceramic assemblage in SK4; (2) a sword/dagger in SK6 (see below, Dyson 1965:34–36, 39), and (3) similar beads allegedly found in SK4–6. SK4–5 lay exactly within the same grave cut, which was oriented east-west, but the excavators could not determine the positions of the bodies and did not note the intentional nature of this multiple interment. The skeletons were not drawn or photographed. SK4 lay a maximum of 30 cm above SK5 and the excavators remark on the difficulties they encountered in attempting to separate the bones and beads from the two individuals. Both graves were heavily disturbed, and it is questionable as to whether they constitute primary burials, although some skeletal elements were articulated. The situation is similar to that of SK45–47 in Operation X, which is datable to Period VIb (see below). With regard to the "Period V" attribution, the evidence of the beads is inconclusive. SK4 was accompanied by a bowl and a jar. The jar was a crude "Grey Ware" vessel and so the grave was eventually relegated to "Period V." This jar in fact belongs to Period VI. This misdating is one example of the difficulties the excavators had in distinguishing between MBA grey smoothed or burnished ceramics and the grey MBW of the MBIII and LBA. Both vessel types—bowl and jar—are attested in Dinkha IV (Hasanlu VIb). The bowl, HAS57-107/UPM58-4-10 (Fig. 5.1:A, Pl. 5.1a), can be compared to Kramer's Bowl 28 (Hamlin 1971:91, pl. III:28) and the jar, HAS57-108/TM10523 (Fig. 5.1:B, Pl. 5.1a), is similar to Kramer's Pot 2 (Hamlin 1971:103, pl. VI:2). Identical grey-black jars are attested in Sialk A in Tomb XIII (Ghirshman 1939: pl. XLV:659a–b), and therefore this grave might date as late as Hasanlu VIa. SK4 also contained a copper/bronze finger ring (HAS57-106), a bone handle (HAS57-44), and the aforementioned beads (HAS57-109) (Fig. 5.1:C–E, Pl. 5.1b). Burial SK5 contained beads (also HAS57-109), a copper/bronze knife blade (HAS57-129), two copper/bronze anklets (HAS57-130a, b), a fragmentary and broken copper/bronze pin (HAS57-131), and an animal skull of unspecified species, but likely sheep/goat (Fig. 5.1:F–I, Pl. 5.1b). Not only were the beads and skeletal remains of these two individuals difficult to separate, but it would appear that the blade of the dagger recorded as part of SK5 belongs to the handle "associated" with SK4 and listed in the registry as a cosmetic container. SK5 is thus likely a Hasanlu VIb multiple interment. The possibility that the grave might date to Terminal Hasanlu VIb or Hasanlu VIa remains open.

Hasanlu SK45–47
Multiple Stone-covered Inhumation, Adult ♀ (probably UPM49-4-104), Adult ♂, Child Indeterminate Sex
(Selinsky 2009)

Burial/Skeletons SK45, 46, and 47, a multiple stone-covered inhumation, was found in Operation X cut down from the base of Stratum 5 and cutting into Strata 6 and 7 (Fig. 3.63). The articulated primary burial of an adult female (SK45) was found with the partial secondary burials of a young male (SK46) and child (SK47) placed over her (Pls. 5.2a–b). The skeleton of SK45 was probably saved and later its identification was lost. Through a process of elimination it is likely UPM59-4-105, which is listed by Selinsky as a mature adult female coming from Operation X Stratum 6 but is listed with no SK Number or Burial Number (2009:208). SK45 lay in a flexed position with the body oriented east-west, with the skull to the west and facing south (Fig. 5.2). The skeletal elements from SK46 included unspecified skull fragments, an unspecified section of vertebrae, the disarticulated pelvis, right and left femurs, left tibia, and an unspecified humerus. SK47 was represented by a scapula, right humerus, radius, and ulna (sides were not determined on the bones unless specified). The grave was sealed by a large stone slab measuring 70 cm wide, 167 cm long, and 14 cm thick (not recorded).

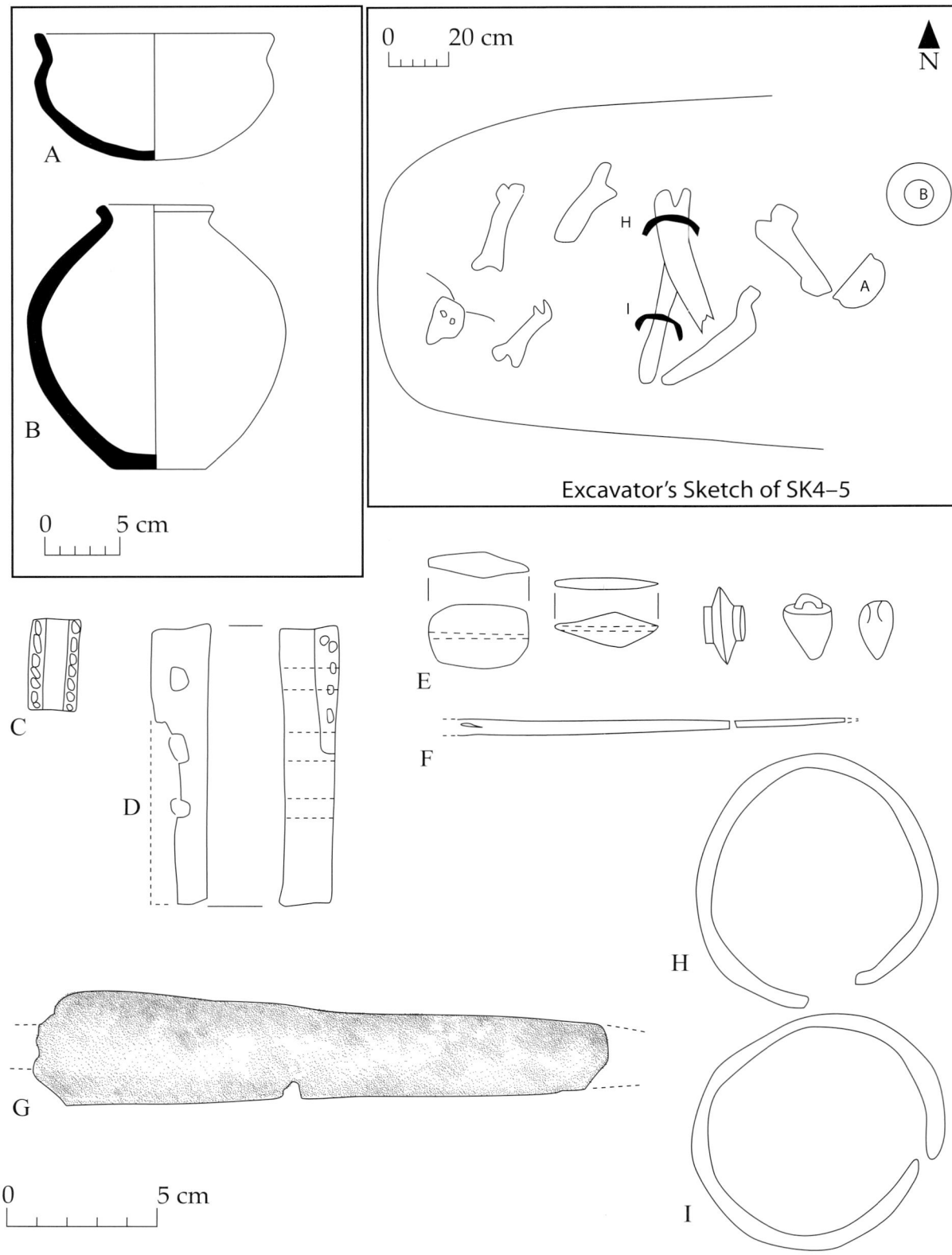

Fig. 5.1 Hasanlu Tepe: SK4-5, Operation IV.

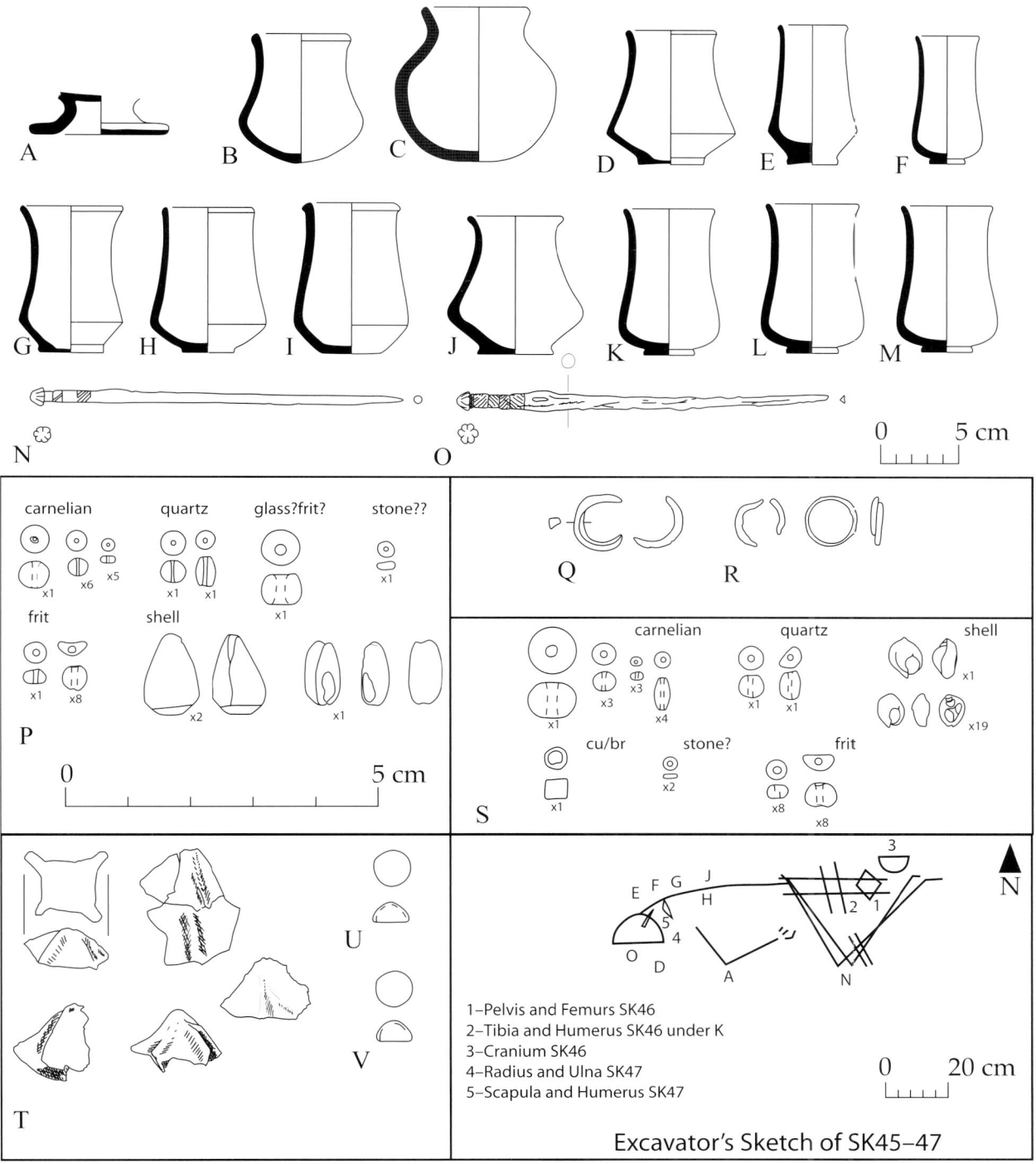

Fig. 5.2 Hasanlu Tepe: SK45, Operation X.

SK45 was accompanied by a large number of grave goods, most notably a number of cups of the so-called *istikhan* type (Fig. 5.2:D–M, Pls. 5.3a–b) and two small jars (Fig. 5.2:B–C). Five of the vessels lay in the fill just above the skull, one lay in front of the face and six were placed along the individual's back at various angles. The exact position of each vessel was not recorded, but the positioning of vessels in front of the face and along the back resembles SK66 of Period VIb (see below). A fragmentary low pedestal base of PKW lay at the left elbow and likely forms part of the intrusive burial fill from above (Fig. 5.2:A). The burial contained two copper/bronze toggle pins: one lay on the left side of the face (HAS58-132) and the other on the left shoulder (HAS58-133) (Fig. 5.2:N–O). Such pins with flaring heads and spiral designs are known from Dinkha Tomb B10a B27 (Rubinson 1991: fig. 22) and from another MBA grave at Hasanlu (cf. SK49 below). A coiled copper/bronze earring was found on the right side of the skull (Fig. 5.2:R; HAS58-135). A scatter of beads, interpreted by the excavators as a girdle, was found over the cups along the individual's back and atop the legs (Fig. 5.2:P; HAS58-136). Another group of beads was found around the neck (Fig. 5.2:S, Pl. 5.3c; HAS58-134). The largest carnelian bead was found in the mouth—the only case of an object similarly placed is a cylinder seal in a grave of late Period IVc (see below, SK57; Marcus 1994b). Two shell rings lay over the left elbow (Fig. 5.2:Q; HAS58-138, 139). A group of copper/bronze buttons and engraved sheeting was found in the grave (Fig. 5.2:T–V; HAS58-537, 140–5), which the excavators interpreted as the remains of harness ornamentation. These fragments have direct parallels at Giyan Tepe IV (Contenau and Ghirshman 1935: pl. 31, no. 107).

Hasanlu SK49
Stone-built Tomb, ♀ Mature Adult
(Selinsky 2009; Rathbun 1972:55)
UPM59-4-103

Burial/Skeleton SK49, a stone-built tomb similar to those of Dinkha IV found by Stein and the Hasanlu Project, was discovered in the southwest corner of Operation X near the aforementioned burials SK45–47 (Pl. 5.4). The burial was cut down from Stratum 5 (Figs. 3.62, 3.63) and the entrance was located a short distance from the southern baulk. The excavators tunneled into the baulk to enter the tomb. The tomb chamber, measuring 2.20 m east-west by 1.50 m north-south, contained an adult female in flexed position lying on the left side and oriented east-west with the head to the west, facing north (Fig. 5.3). While no ceramics were found in the tomb, food offerings were present near the deceased's knees in the form of a sheep/goat skull and four long bones, and in the northwest quadrant of the tomb, a sheep/goat pelvis and forelimbs were noted. A copper/bronze toggle pin of MBA type was found at the shoulder under the left arm (Fig. 5.3:A, Pl. 5.5a; HAS58-146). A copper/bronze blade (Fig. 5.3:C, Pl. 5.5a; HAS58-148) lay under the chin, point end toward the head; it resembles blades from Dinkha IV (Rubinson 1991: fig. 13; Stein 1940: pl. XXI no. 4). A "whetstone," more likely a stone archer's wrist-guard, lay just to the south of the dagger blade near an unspecified ulna or radius (Fig. 5.3:B, Pl. 5.5b; HAS58-149). An unspecified number of copper/bronze beads lay just west of the pin in the area of the neck (Fig. 5.3:D; HAS58-147). Joints of meat were laid around the capstones and parallel the earlier of the two MBA tombs at Dinkha IV. The absence of ceramics in this tomb and the paucity of other artifacts are puzzling and certainly atypical of other tombs of this type/period in the region. Hakemi (Hakemi and Rad 1950) had previously excavated in the area around Operation X, and one wonders whether he, earlier commercial antiquities agents, or looters might have excavated this tomb prior to the Hasanlu Project.

Hasanlu SK61
Artifacts Only

"Grave" SK61 was found in Operation VIb in Stratum 5 (Figs. 3.55, 3.58). No skeletal remains were present. Grave goods consisted of a small incised MBW jar (Fig. 5.4:A; HAS59-115), a PKW jar (Fig. 5.4:B, Pl. 5.5d; HAS59-116), and a PKW carinated bowl (Fig. 5.4:C, Pl. 5.5c; HAS59-91). The vessels lay at the east end of an alignment of flat stone slabs with a total dimension of 2.75 m x 1.25 m. Grave SK66 (see below) lay beneath the northwest end of these slabs and dates to Period VIb, thus the pots of SK61 were an offering associated with this stone-covered or stone-built tomb. During the MBA food offerings were left on the capstones of tombs at Dinkha Tepe and Hasan-

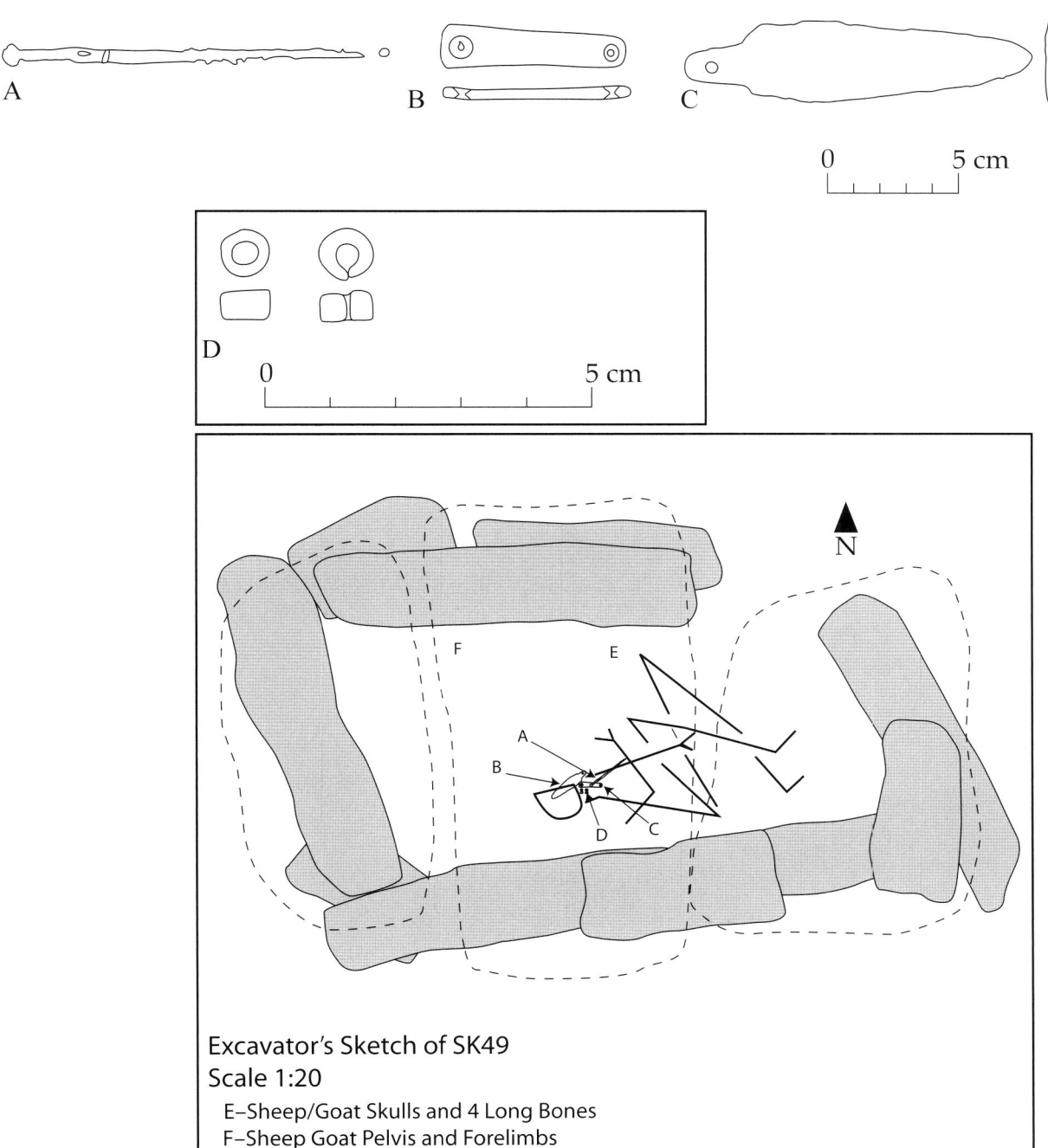

Fig. 5.3 Hasanlu Tepe: SK49, Operation X.

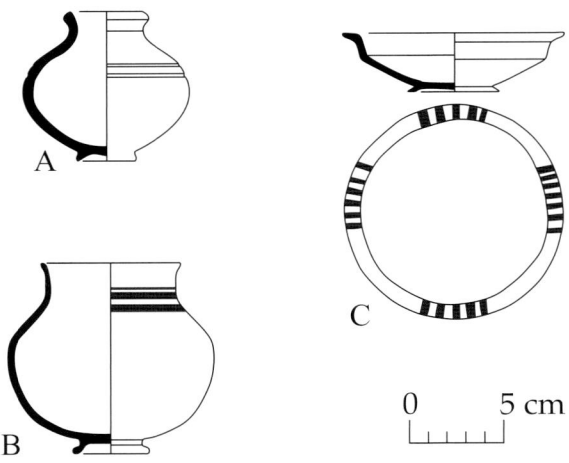

Fig. 5.4 Hasanlu Tepe: SK61, Operation VIa.

lu (see above, SK49). SK61 lay just north of grave SK68, of probable Period IVb date, and might also have been disturbed by it, providing an alternative, if less likely, explanation for the lack of a body in SK61.

Hasanlu SK66
Stone-covered
Inhumation, Child Indeterminate Sex

This grave of a child in Operation VIb lay directly under stone slabs (see above, SK61) in Area 2 Stratum 11. No burials seem to have been located at the southeast end of this stone alignment and it therefore seems SK66 was the primary interment.[4] The body lay in a flexed position with the head to the northwest facing northeast (Fig. 5.5). Sheep/goat bones were found near the head and two crossed sheep/goat bones lay under the pelvis. Possible offerings were placed on top of the stone slabs at their far southeast end (see above, SK61; Fig. 3.55). Two *istikhans* were placed along the back of the individual and another rested in front of the face (Fig. 5.5:A–C, Pl. 5.5e; HAS59-140–141). Two copper/bronze simple pins were found, in front of the face and near the sternum (Fig. 5.5:D–E; HAS59-133, 137). A shell or bone ring also lay in front of the face (Fig. 5.5:F; HAS59-138). Beads lay on the right (upper) temporal and near the neck (Fig. 5.5:G–H; HAS59-134, 136). A bronze ring was located near the right shoulder (Fig. 5.5:I; HAS59-135). The similarities to SK49 in tomb type, food offerings, and object placement indicate some uniformity in MBII burial patterns.

Hasanlu SK112
Simple Inhumation, Adult?

Burial/Skeleton SK112 was found in Operation LIVf, in "Stratum 4?," 2.70 m below the surface. The source of the ambiguity regarding the provenience is not elaborated on by the excavator, and in reality this grave was found at the base of Stratum 5, which was near or at the base level of a much-disturbed LBA occupation level (Danti and Cifarelli n.d.). This grave had been disturbed and possibly represents a secondary burial (Fig. 5.6). Burial goods included a red *istikhan* (Fig. 5.6:A; HAS59-223) and a PKW jar (Fig. 5.6:B, Pl. 5.6a; HAS59-224). The excavator noted that a relatively large number of sheep/goat bones were present and mixed with the human remains.

Graves of the Terminal MBII

As we have seen, the end of the MBA at Dinkha Tepe—the late 18th–17th centuries—represents a distinct subperiod, at least in terms of the ceramic assemblage (see Chapter 4). Those trends in ceramics that are discernable, particularly in Tomb B10a B27, anticipate developments of the MBIII and LBA; archaeological material equivalent to Dinkha IV Phase D, however, is not well attested at Hasanlu, with only one grave attributable to the subperiod. Stein excavated another grave likely dating to this period at Dinkha in his section iv (1940:373).

Hasanlu SK70
Simple Inhumation, Partial Skeleton

This grave, originally dated to "Period V" by the excavators, is one of the more interesting from Hasanlu and I have re-dated it to Terminal Period VIb. SK70 was uncovered in a small western extension of Operation VIa, just east of the pithos burial of an infant (SK72) of the same general time period, but was recorded as being slightly earlier by the excavators. SK70 was positioned on the right side facing

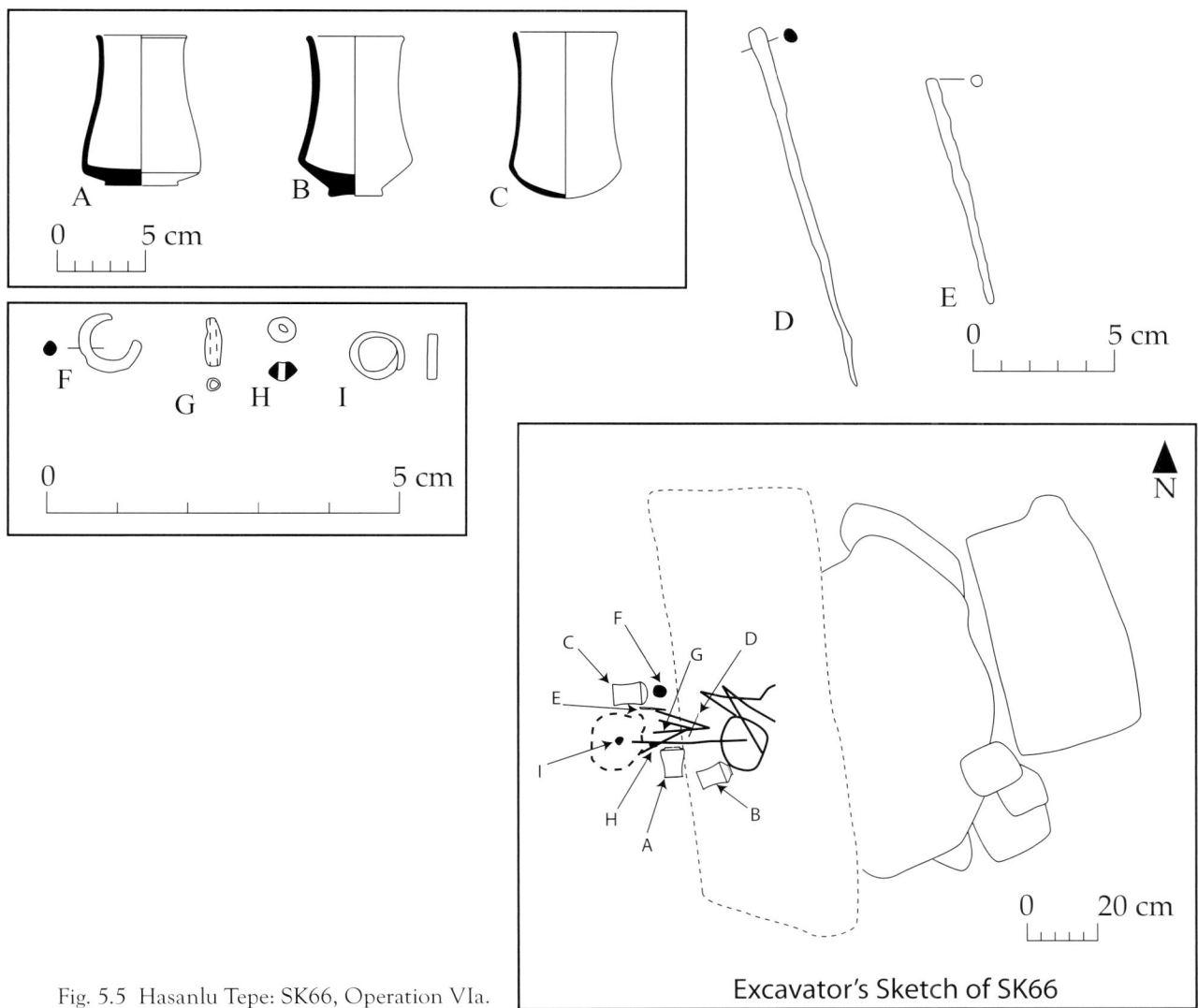

Fig. 5.5 Hasanlu Tepe: SK66, Operation VIa.

east with the head to the south. Traces of reed matting were found beneath the body, similar to the burial customs of the LBA and early Iron Age at Hasanlu. The left arm was situated in front of the face. The remainder of the skeleton was missing. The excavator recorded that the pelvis and legs evidently extended into operation, but were dug away and not noticed. In fact, the plotting of all graves in Operation VIa (Figs. 3.55, 5.7) reveals the lower post-cranial skeleton of SK70 lay within the burial cut of SK73 of Period IVc (see below), and thus was almost certainly cut away in antiquity. The jars included as burial goods in SK73 were found where the legs and feet of SK70 would

have been located, and SK73 lay at the same depth below the surface as SK70.

SK70 included two carinated jars made in a grey fabric, and a small buff cup with a loop handle at the rim lay just south of the cranium (Fig. 5.7:A–C, Pl. 5.6b–c; HAS59-169–71). While the jars are fairly generic, the cup is identical to one from Dinkha Tomb B10a B27 (Rubinson 1991: fig. 28b). Other grave goods include fragments of a copper/bronze ring on the left hand (Fig. 5.7:D; HAS59-172) and a copper/bronze earring in the vicinity of the left ear (Fig. 5.7:E; HAS59-173). Beneath the skull the excavators found another copper/bronze ring, possibly an earring (Fig.

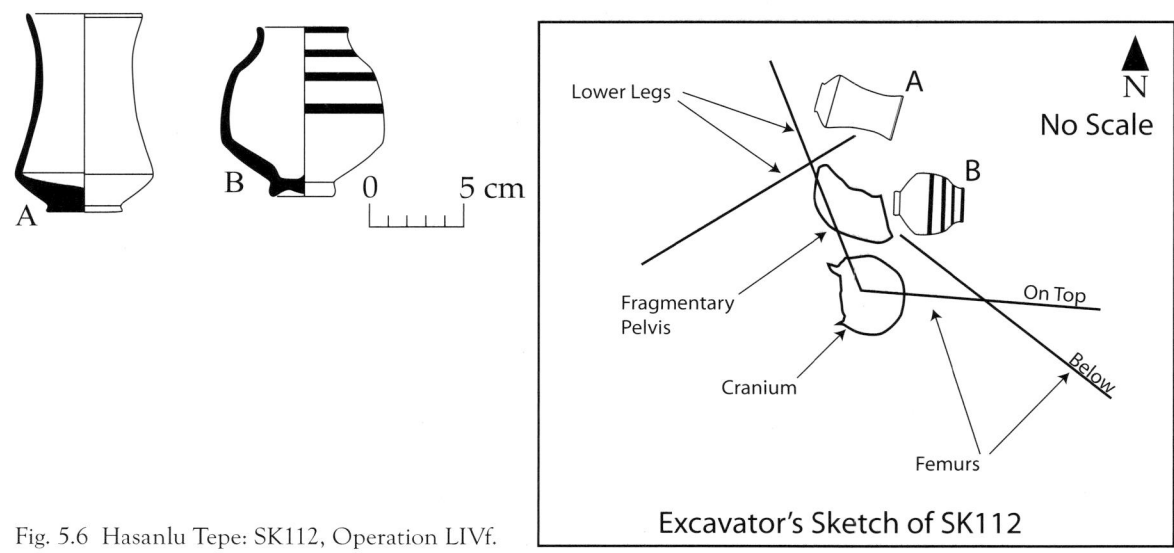

Fig. 5.6 Hasanlu Tepe: SK112, Operation LIVf.

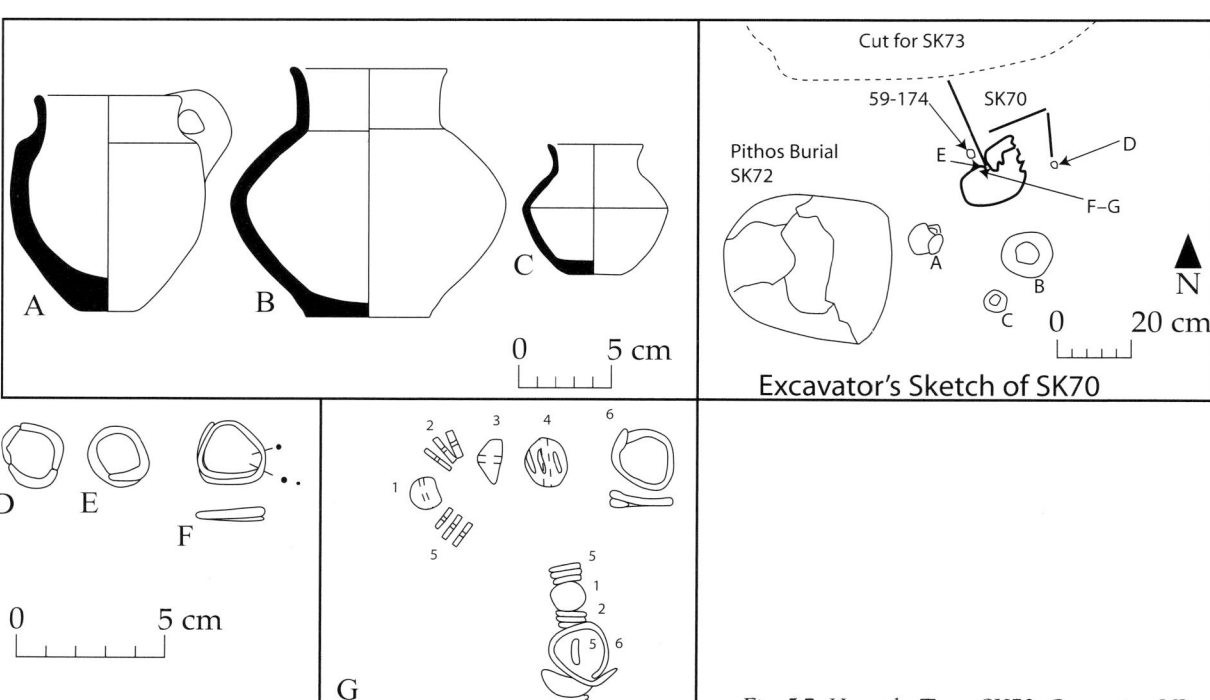

Fig. 5.7 Hasanlu Tepe: SK70, Operation VIa.

5.7:F; HAS59-175), and a similar wire ring with flattened ends attached to a bead and with other beads found in their original stringing order (Fig. 5.7:G; HAS59-176–7). This appears to be an elaborate earring. The order of the beads from the ring was: (1) a white frit incised disc; (2) a white frit dome; (3) three yellowish-white shell discs; (4) a dark grey domed bead of unidentified material; and (5) three yellowish-white shell discs. Disintegrated blue frit beads lay in the area of the neck (HAS59-174).

Graves of Hasanlu VIa

Three graves from Hasanlu can be tentatively dated to the MBIII. All are simple inhumations rather than stone-built tombs or stone-covered inhumations—styles of burial prevalent in the MBII in Ušnu-Solduz.

Hasanlu SK25
Simple Inhumation, ♀ Young Adult
(Selinsky 2009; Rathbun 1972:55)
UPM58-4-106

This simple inhumation grave of an adolescent female age 13–15 in Operation VI (Pl. 5.7a) contained a small PKW shouldered beaker (Fig. 5.8:A, Pl. 5.6d; HAS57-127) and a grey MBW button-base tankard (Fig. 5.8:B, Pl. 5.6d; HAS57-126). This combination of painted ware and "Iron Age Grey Ware" has received much attention in previous publications. The tankard, in an extremely "normalized" drawing, was included in a well-known illustration of diagnostic ceramics of "Period V" published by both Young and Dyson (Dyson 1965: fig. 3 no. 2; Young 1965: fig. 8 no. 2). The Type 1a tankard and the Type 8a PKW beaker could date as late as early Period V, but Period VIa seems likely for this small transitional ceramic assemblage. An identical tankard in Early MBW was found at Sialk A in Tomb XIV (Ghirshman 1939: pl. XLVI:670) and other similar tankards are well known there.

The body lay on the right side and was oriented southeast-northwest, in a flexed position facing north (Fig. 3.55). A copper/bronze bracelet was worn on each wrist (Fig. 5.8:C–D; HAS57-123a–b). A necklace of copper/bronze, stone, and blue frit beads was worn around the neck (Fig. 5.8:E; HAS57-124). Three simple copper/bronze pins were found near the

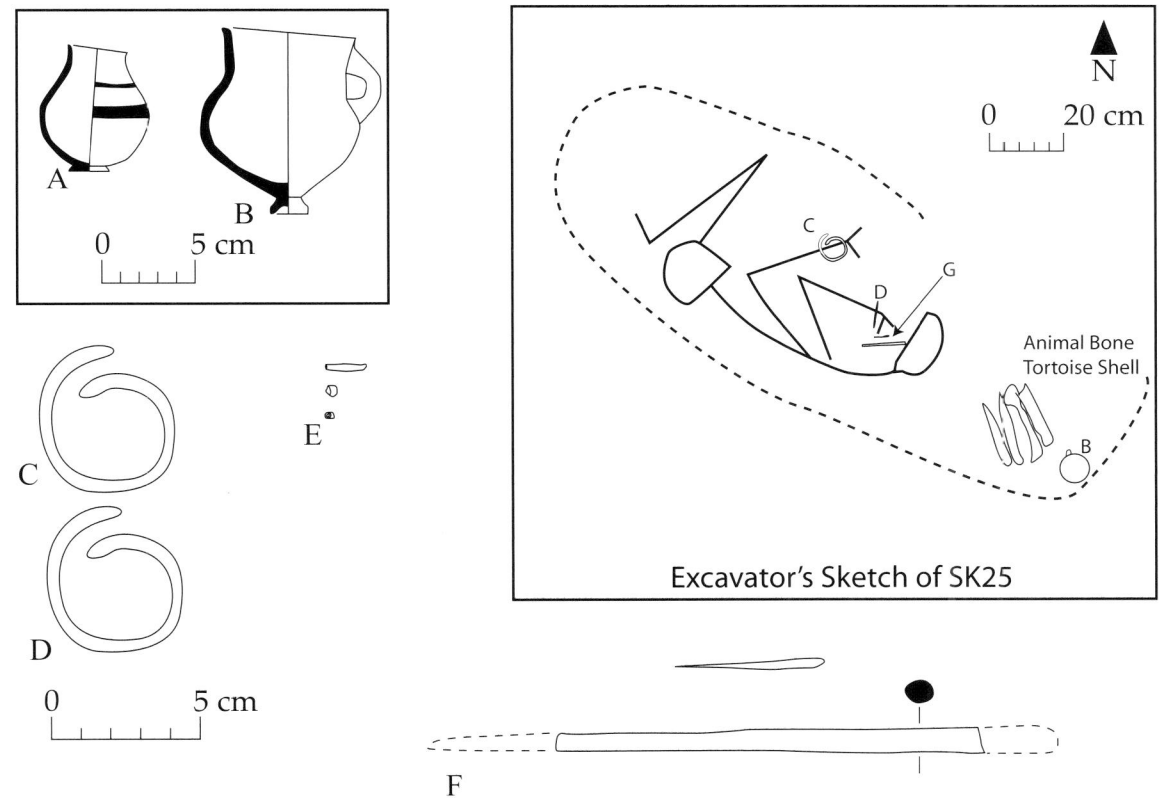

Fig. 5.8 Hasanlu Tepe: SK25, Operation VI.

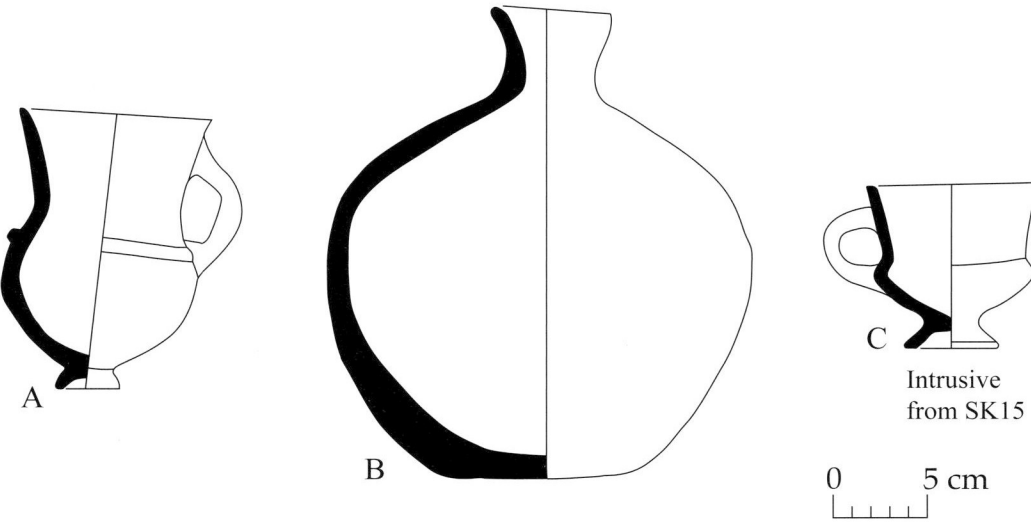

Fig. 5.9 Hasanlu Tepe: SK29, Operation VI.

neck (Fig. 5.8:F; HAS57-122a–c; one is not drawn or placed on the excavator's sketch), and the fragments of at least one copper/bronze finger ring were found in the fill (HAS57-125). A pile of sheep/goat bones and fragments of tortoise shell lay just southeast of the cranium and near the tankard. The excavator did not locate the PKW beaker on the plan of the burial (Fig. 5.8).

Hasanlu SK29
Simple Inhumation, ♂ 40 years
(Selinsky 2009; Rathbun 1972:53)
UPM58-4-109

Burial SK29 of Operation VI, the grave of a male approximately 40 years of age, was heavily disturbed by a later Iron II grave (SK15) (Figs. 3.55, 5.9, Pls. 5.7b, 5.8a). The burial contained an Early MBW button-base tankard of Type 1a (Fig. 5.9:A, Pl. 5.8b; HAS57-159) and a small Early MBW Type 6b jar with high narrow neck (Fig. 5.9:B, Pl. 5.8a–b; HAS57-187), both of Period VIa. Both vessels were coarse, handmade, and of grey fabric. The jar imitates Type 6a, which most commonly occurs in contemporary Urmia Ware and which is not attested after the early LBA (cf. Stein Grave Hasanlu Section XV, Dinkha Grave B9a Burial 25). This type is also attested in pattern-burnished MBW in a grave of late Period VIa or early Period V (see below, SK504). The excavators included a Type 7 pedestal-base carinated cup in MBW among the associated grave goods, but it is a highly diagnostic Iron I and early Iron II type and strongly suggests the mixing of grave goods with the overlying SK15 (Fig. 5.9:C, Pl. 5.8a; HAS57-188). The northeast corner of Operation VI contained many graves (Fig. 3.55) and it was clearly difficult to attribute some finds to their associated burials during excavation. The archival records contain some errors, and later edits were made to the object numbering. This cup, typical of Hasanlu IVc and early IVb, was included by Young and Dyson in their early chronological assessments of "Hasanlu V," as were the tankard and jar (Dyson 1965: fig. 3 nos. 7, 9–10; Young 1965: fig. 8 nos. 7, 9–10). There is other evidence of the mixing of finds between the two burials. Grave SK29 allegedly contained an iron finger ring (HAS57-184), which has often been cited as evidence for iron in "Hasanlu V." Given the likely 16th–early 15th centuries BC date of the grave, however, this seems highly suspect. The excavators recorded SK15 of early Period IVb as likely having disturbed SK29, and noted that finger rings associated with SK29 (three copper/bronze and one iron) were found "loose in the fill."

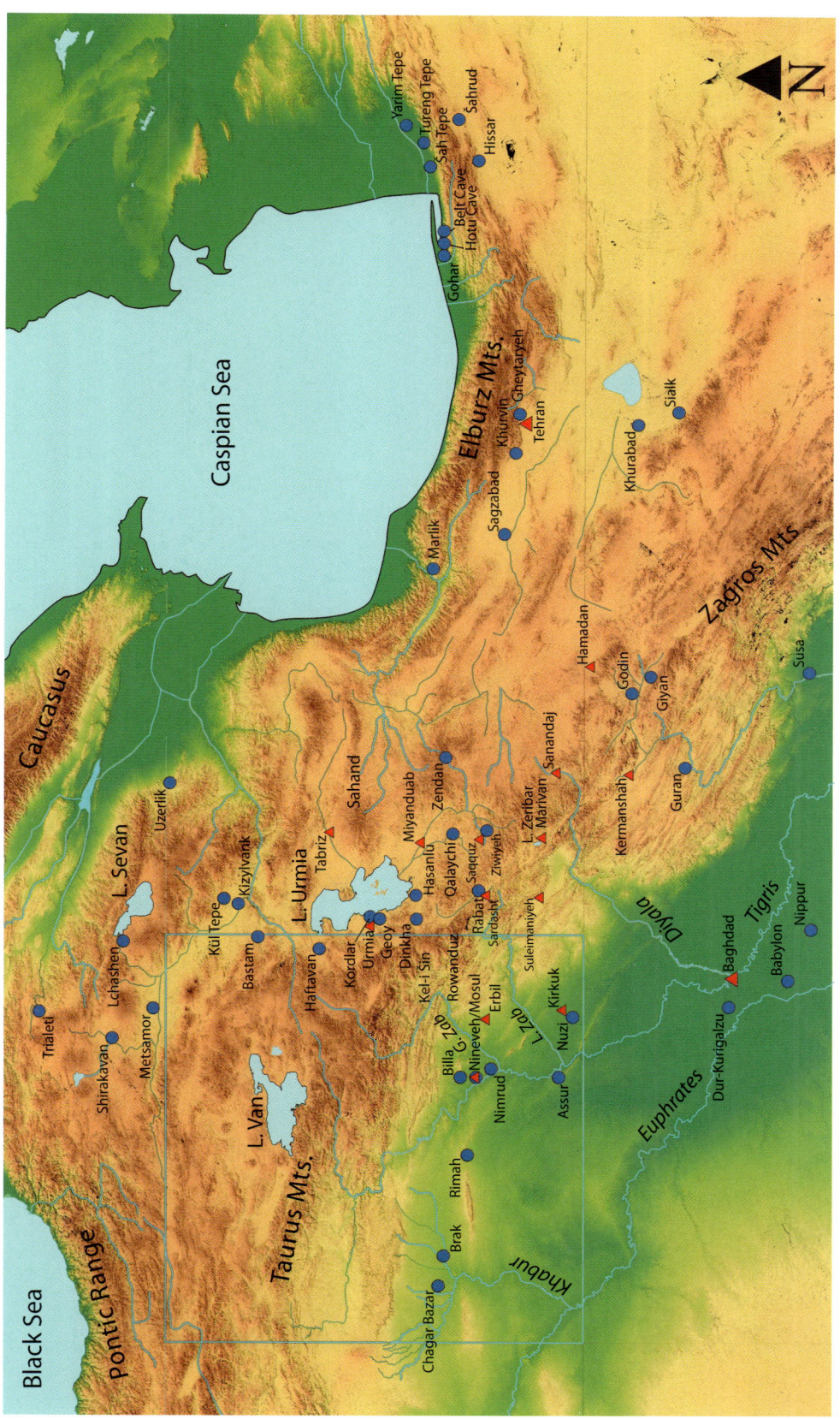

Fig. 1.1 Map of the Near East.

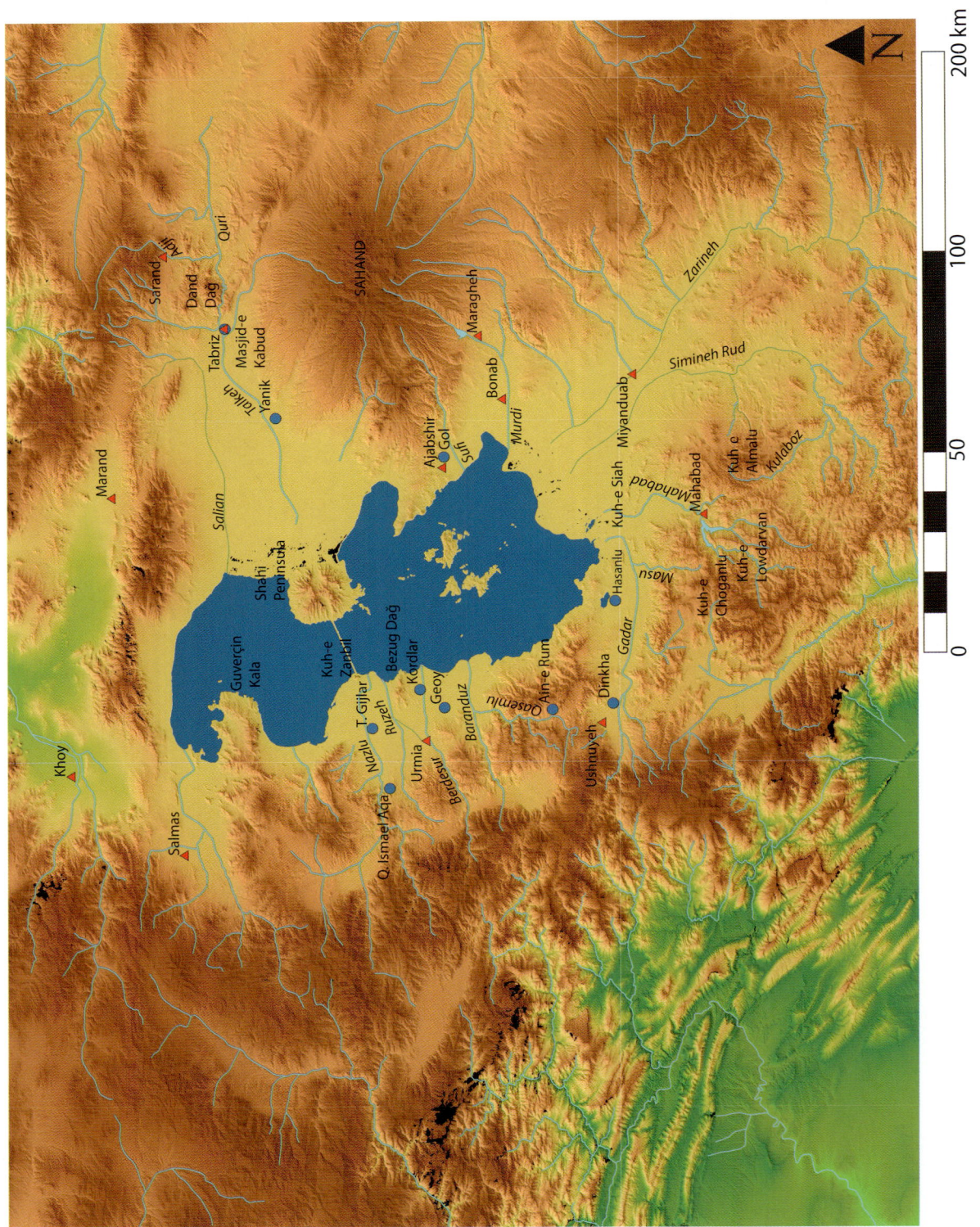

Fig. 1.2 The Lake Urmia Basin.

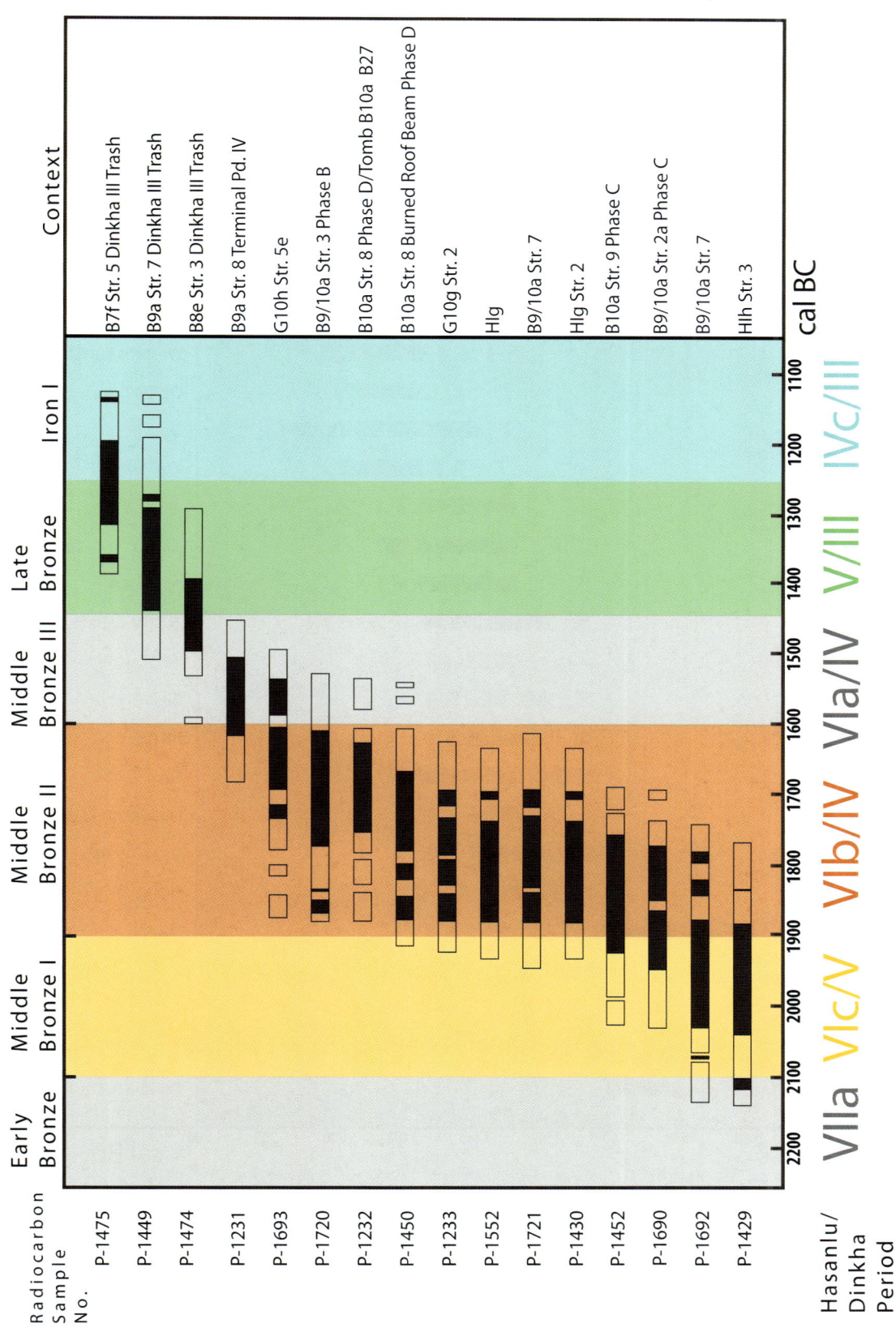

Fig. 2.3 Two-sigma radiocarbon date ranges for Hasanlu and Dinkha, Periods VII–IVc.

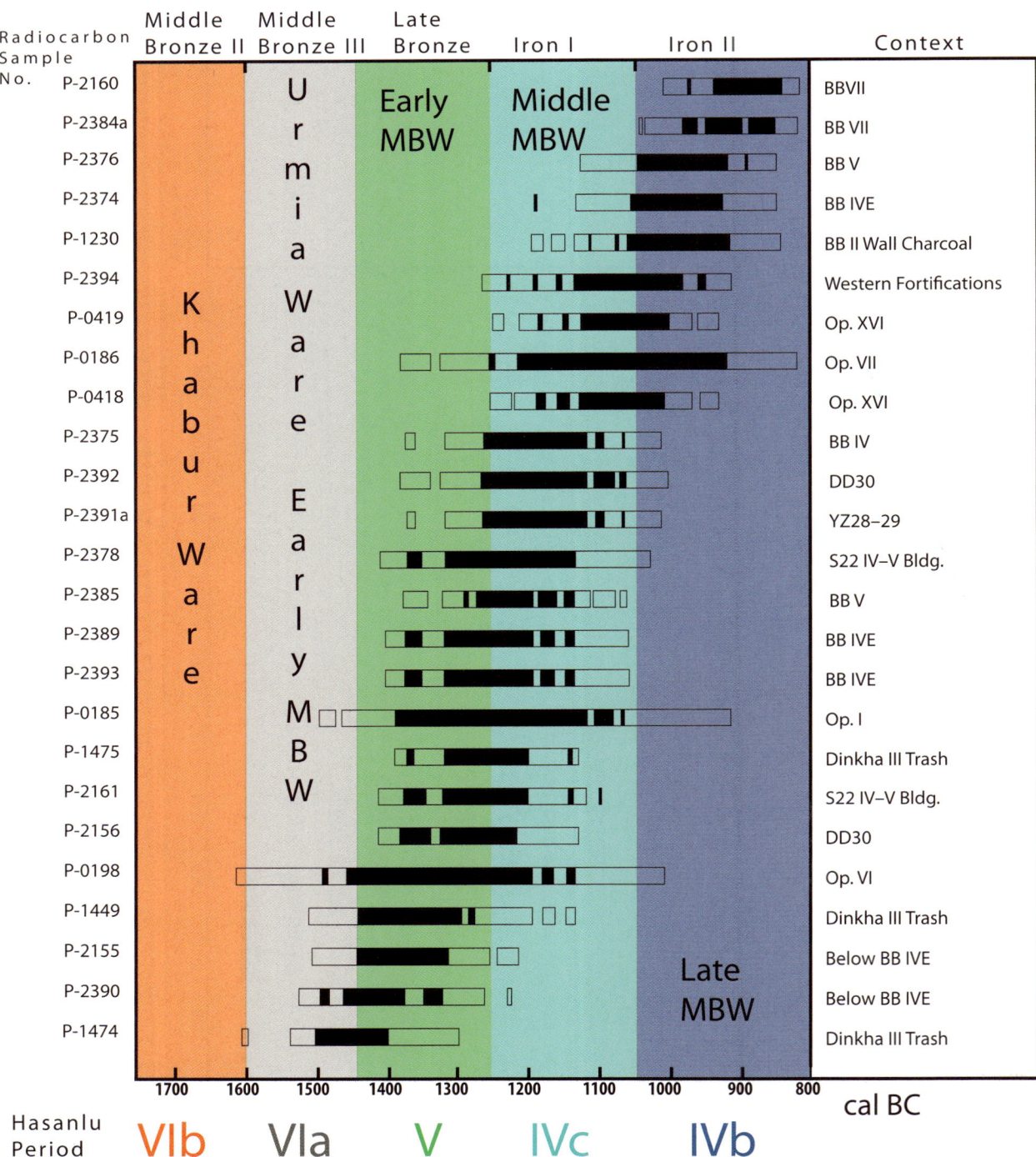

Fig. 2.4 Two-sigma radiocarbon date ranges for Hasanlu and Dinkha, Periods VIb–IVb.

C-5

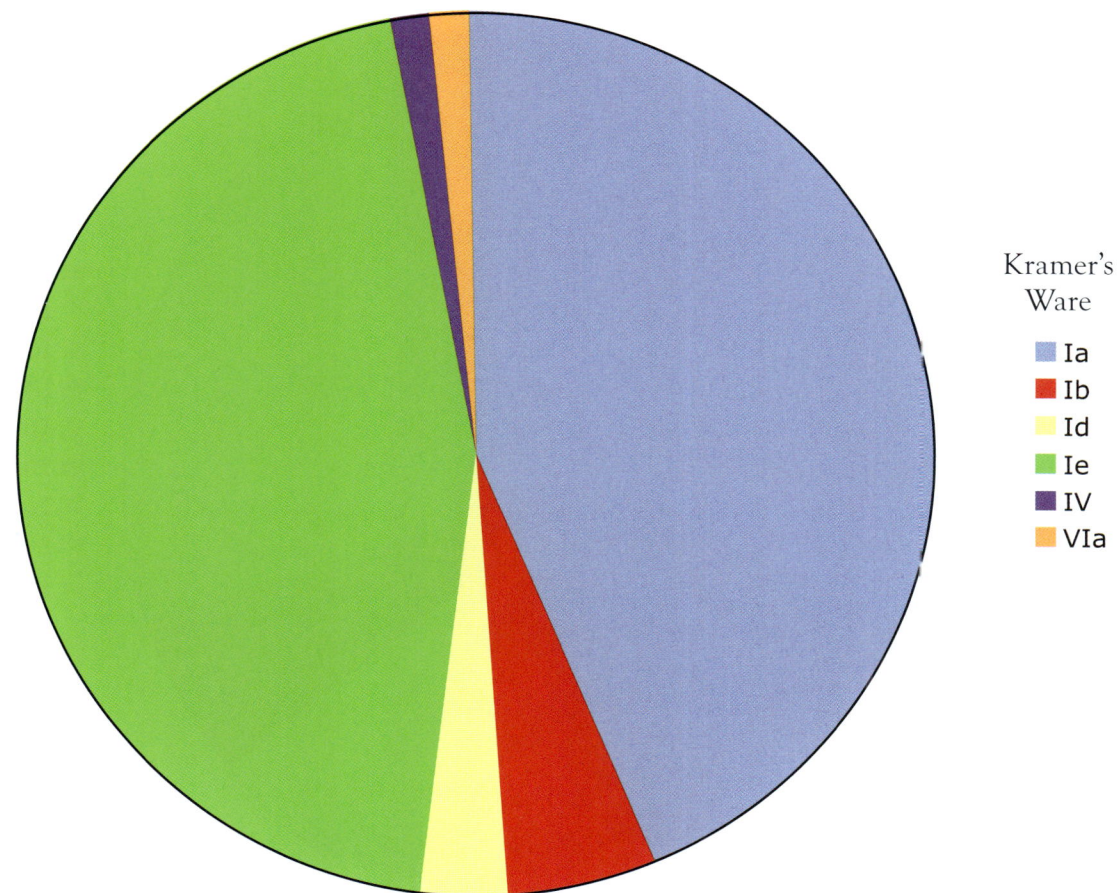

Fig. 4.3 Dinkha IV jars by Ware Types.

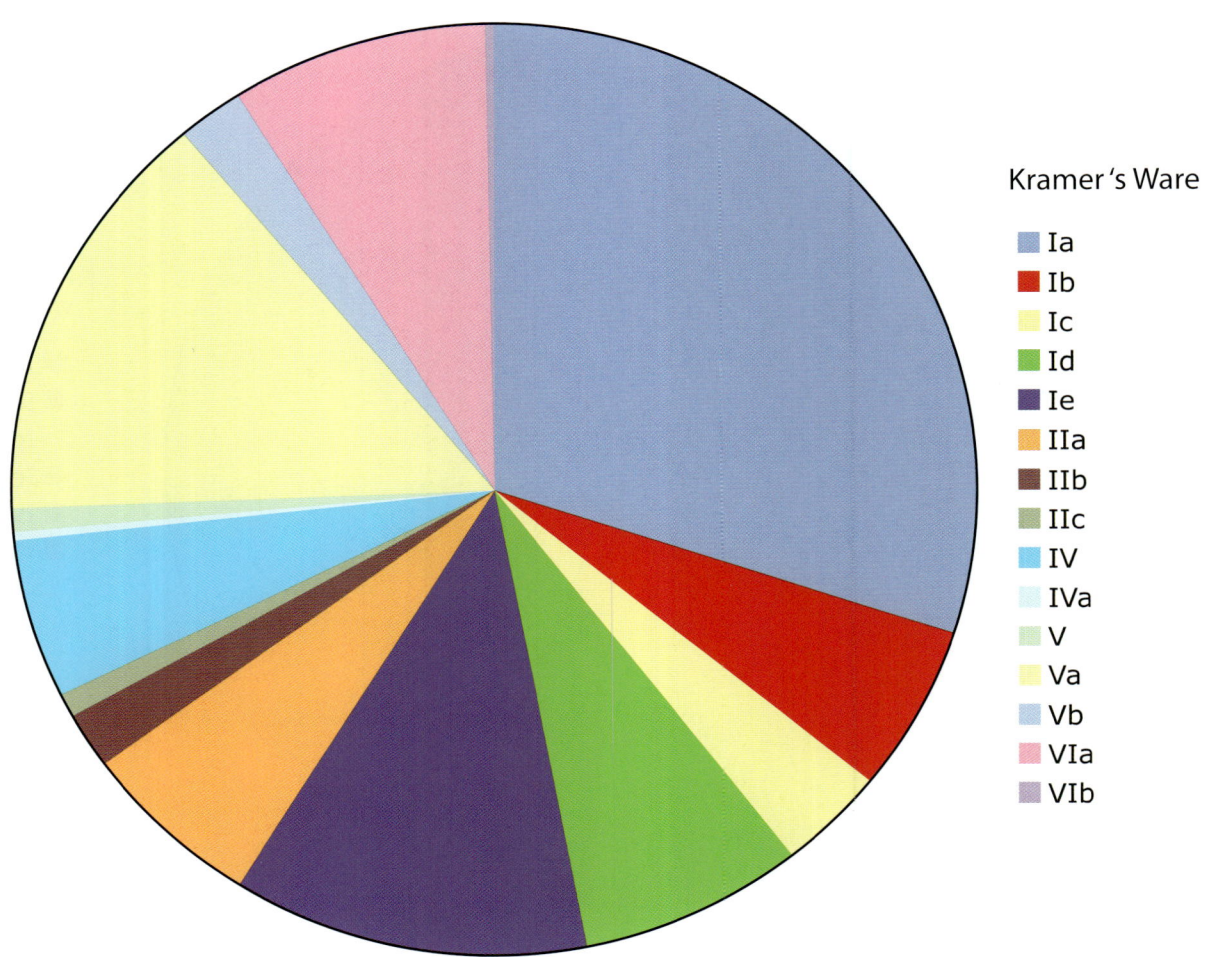

Fig. 4.4 Dinkha IV bowls by Ware Types.

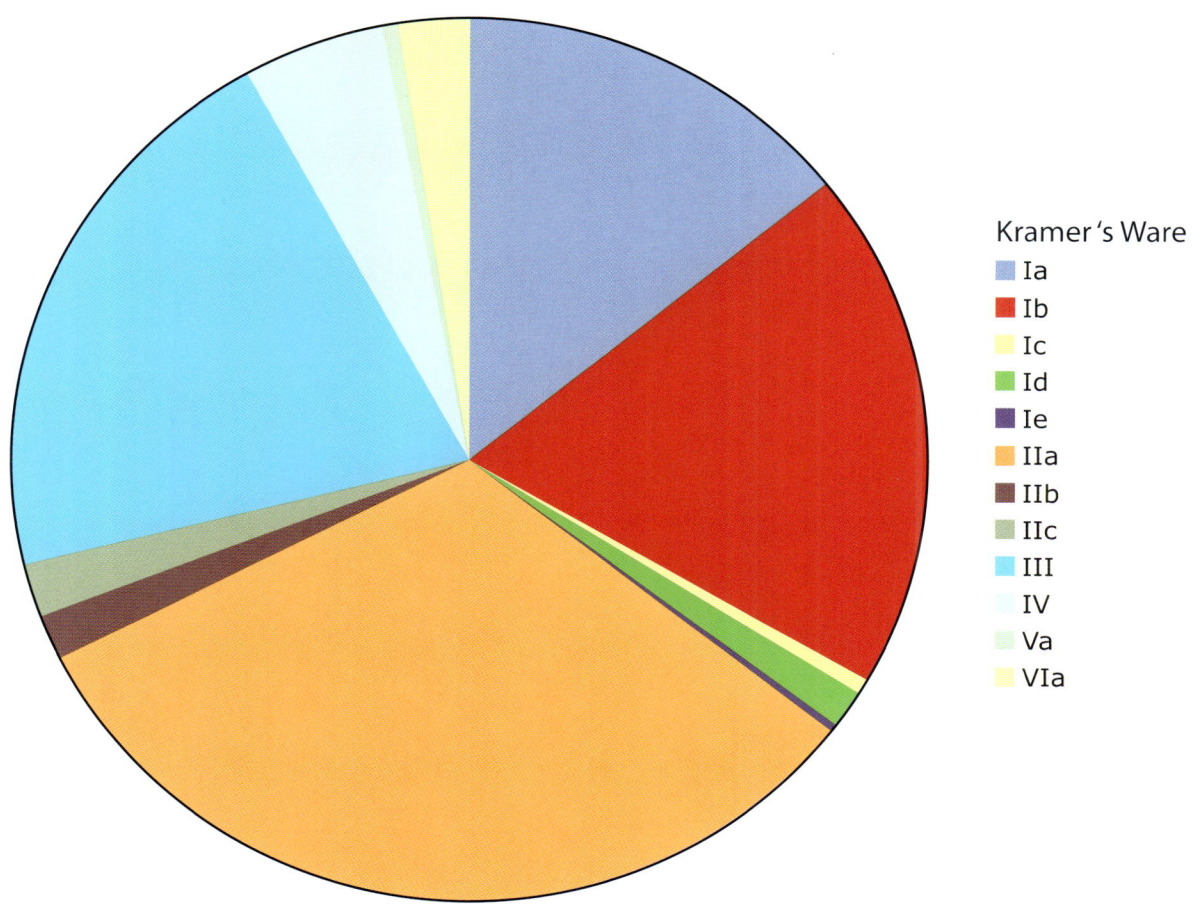

Fig. 4.5 Dinkha IV pots by Ware Types.

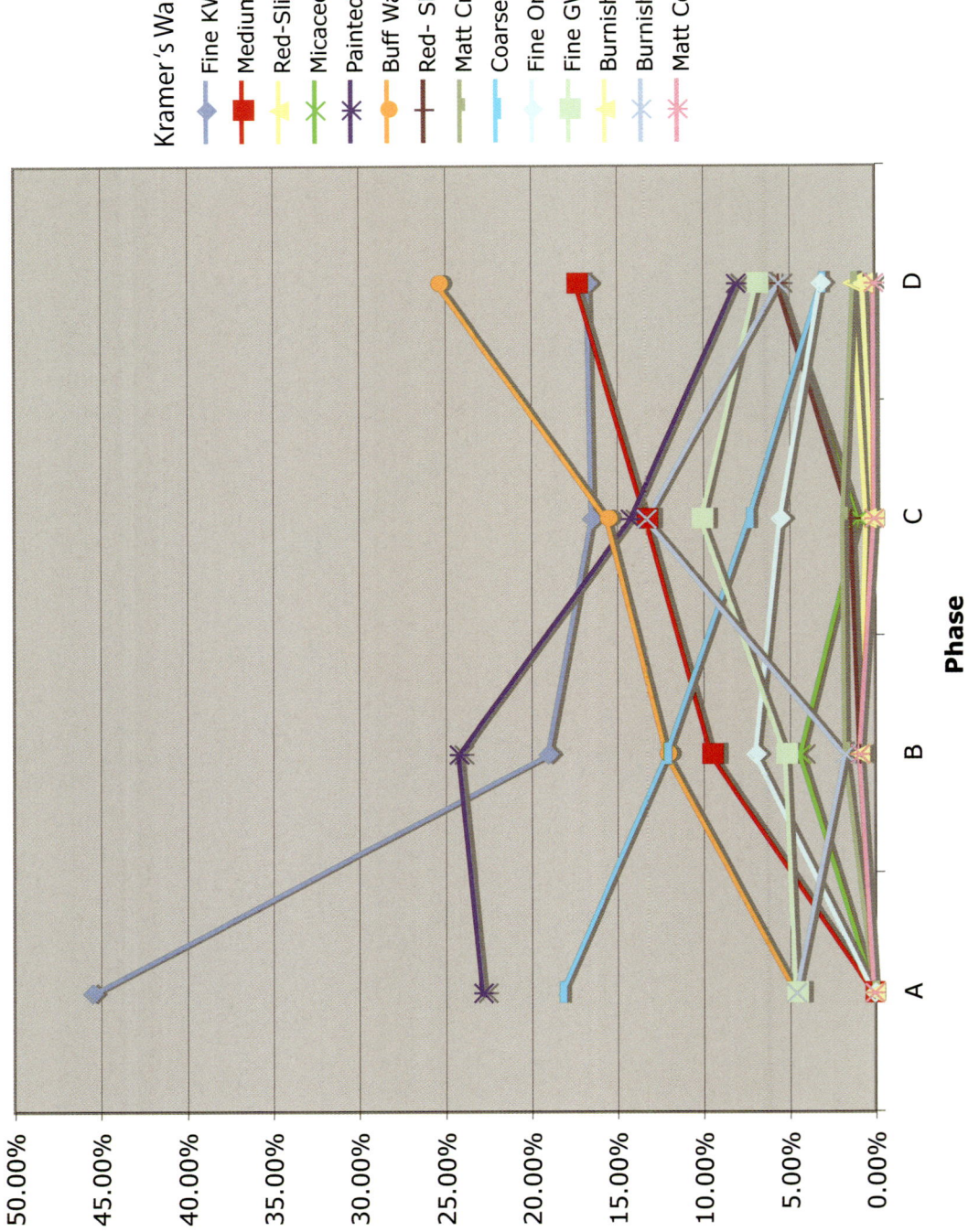

Fig. 4.6 Frequency of Dinkha IV wares by phases.

The overlying SK15 was associated with two copper/bronze rings in the area of the right hand (Pl. 5.9) and one copper/bronze ring on the left.[5] The excavation photo of SK15 shows that the right hand had been heavily disturbed (Pl. 5.9), probably during excavation. SK15's lower (left) hand would have been within the area of the disturbed SK29 and the iron ring and Type 7 cup were inadvertently attributed to the much earlier grave. Alternatively, given the later edits and contradictions in the excavation record, the objects may simply have been mixed during or following the excavation. I would attribute the rings found loose in the fill and the pedestal-base cup to the later SK15. Regardless, this demonstrates that this attribution of iron and a well-attested Iron I–early Iron II vessel form to a mid-2nd millennium BC context is far from secure. Ultimately, this later resulted in the mixing of highly diagnostic MBIII and Iron I attributes into "Hasanlu V" and contributed to the supposed mid-2nd millennium gap that is now filled by Hasanlu VIa.

Hasanlu Stein Section XV
Simple Inhumation, Probable ♂ Adult

Stein found this grave of Period VIa at the periphery of the northern Low Mound of Hasanlu, near the canal skirting its modern topographic edge in his Section xv (Stein 1940: Sketch Plan 25). The grave lay at an approximate depth of 3.70 m. The individual, presumably an adult male based on the grave goods, lay in a flexed position with the head to the north, facing east (Stein 1940:401). A polychrome Urmia Ware jar rested near the cranium (Stein 1940: pls. XXIV no. 3; XXXI) and beside it was a large incurving bowl with thickened rim "dressed red" (Seriation; Stein 1940: pl. XXXI, no.1). This bowl type is known from the Hasanlu U22 Sounding in Early MBW, where it is associated with button bases of the type typical of Period VIa and early Period V tankards found in graves. Items of personal ornament lay near the neck, including a pear-shaped white stone pendant, a carnelian "disc head," and a copper/bronze ring (Stein 1940:402, pl. XXV, nos. 21, 27, and 20). A copper/bronze socketed javelin head with a round-section blade was also found along with fragments of its wooden handle (Stein 1940: pl. XXVI no. 2).

Graves of Early Hasanlu V

Early LBA mortuary patterns at Hasanlu continue the MBIII trend of simple inhumation burial, although there is some evidence of possible secondary burials. At Dinkha, some individuals were buried in brick tombs, but little conclusive evidence of such structures was found at Hasanlu. At Geoy Tepe, Tomb K may be dated to this period and provides an example of mortuary architecture designed to accommodate multiple interments (Burton-Brown 1951:141–45, figs. 28, 29, 32, 34).

Grave goods are limited to ceramic vessels, relatively simple items of personal ornament, and food offerings, which are attested by sheep/goat bones stacked in the burial or contained in a large bowl. At the present time, the distinction between the end of the MBIII and the start of the LBA remains poorly defined due to the limited amount of evidence. The key ceramic diagnostics I use to identify graves of the early LBA are tall tankards with pedestal or pointed bases, bowls with vertically pierced lugs, Type 1 "worm bowls," and, at Dinkha, bridgeless-spouted holemouth jars. Some potential biases in the dataset ought to be addressed. First, all but one of the tall pedestal-base tankards of Types 1b–c were found in the graves of adult males with the possible exception of one from an adult grave of undetermined sex at Dinkha (Dinkha B10a Burial 23; see below). Moreover, the majority of the early Period V graves—that is, graves with tall tankards—are from Hasanlu. The possibility that such graves were found at Dalma, or are among the unpublished graves of Dinkha, is a topic to be investigated. Moreover, future research may demonstrate that the distinction between early Period V and late Period V posited here in the relative sequence of graves may be an effect of sampling and/or differences in the ceramic traditions and mortuary practices of Hasanlu and Dinkha in the LBA. In this vein, the Incised and Impressed MBW of the "trash deposit" at Dinkha, for example, certainly suggests some highly localized variability in the early LBA, as does the occurrence of mudbrick tombs there. Put another way, the late Period V graves of Dinkha (see below) with "worm bowls" and bridgeless-spouted vessels may in fact date to the early LBA; tall pedestal-base tankards simply may not have been a preferred grave good among the site's occupants. Tall pedestal-base tankards seldom co-occur with bridgeless-spouted jars. Most were found at Hasanlu, where bridgeless-spouted jars, an important marker of late Period V and IVc, were not included in graves even though they are attested, albeit rarely, in contemporary occupation deposits. While future research may support a degree of overlap between the early Period V graves, mainly found at Hasanlu, and those of late Period V as I have defined it, which are attested primarily at Dinkha, other lines of evidence strengthen this sequence—particularly trends noted in the stylistic development of large "worm bowls" and drinking vessels in both mortuary and occupation contexts. The absence of Incised and Impressed MBW, a key component of the earliest LBA at Dinkha, in the graves of Ušnu-Solduz may alternatively be used to support the conclusion that we in fact have few graves of early Period V from Dinkha. Although it seems less likely, it is also possible that Incised and Impressed MBW may not have been included as a grave good.

Dinkha B9a Burial 25
Simple Inhumation, ♂ Adult

This inhumation grave of a mature adult male in a flexed position was cut into Stratum 7. The body was lying on the back and oriented east-west with the head to the east (Muscarella 1974:40). Grave goods included a toggle pin similar to those of Hasanlu Period VI (Muscarella 1974: fig. 3, 473P), a necklace of paste beads, an Early MBW tankard (grey IIC, Muscarella 1974: fig. 3, 696T), and a polychrome Urmia Ware jar (Seriation, Muscarella 1974: fig. 3, 420T, fig. 5). Muscarella conditionally attributed this grave to early Dinkha III, the equivalent of Hasanlu VIa–early V, and noted it is "the only painted vessel from the Iron Age at Dinkha" (1974:40). The grave can be attributed to the 16th–15th centuries BC. Given the style of the tankard, I would provisionally date this grave to early Hasanlu V—the early LBA—given that it cuts *at least* Stratum 7 of the MBIII. The jar (Type 6a, see Chapter 4) could be somewhat earlier, and additional research is needed to clarify the issue of whether the association of these two vessels is in fact secure.

Hasanlu SK504
Secondary Inhumation, ♂ Mature Adult
(Selinsky 2009; Rathbun 1972:54–55)
UPM65-31-789

This grave in the northeast corner of Operation VIj (Fig. 3.61) was of a male aged 30–40 years (Rathbun 1972:54–55) and appeared to the excavators to resemble a secondary bundle burial (Fig. 5.10, Pl. 5.10a).

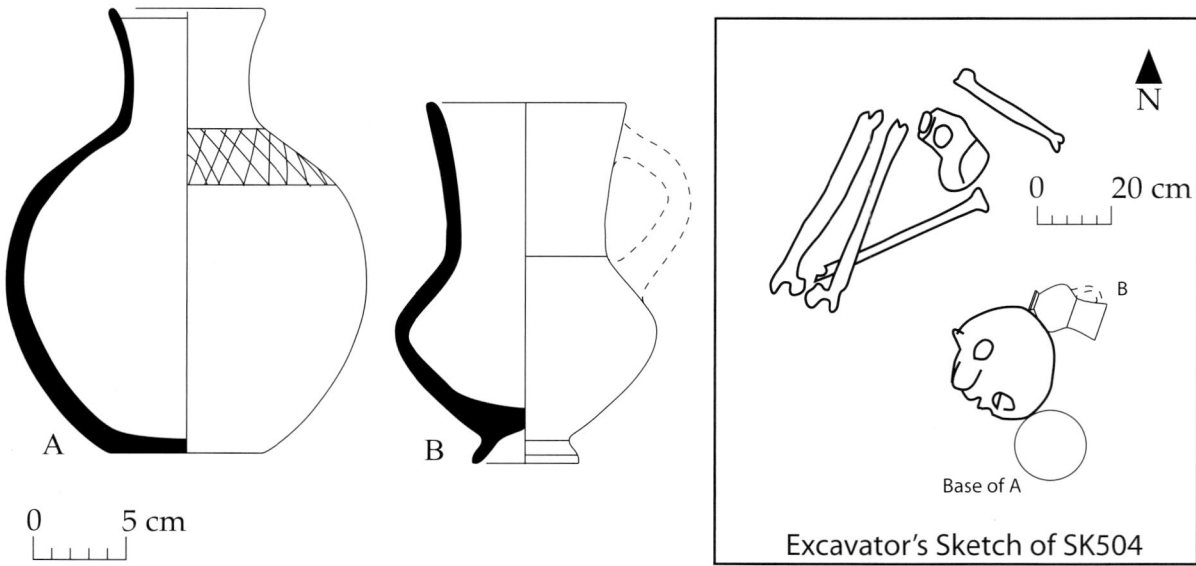

Fig. 5.10 Hasanlu Tepe: SK504, Operation VIj.

The major post-cranial bones lay in a pile and the skull was turned upside down, resting between two ceramic vessels, which constituted the only grave goods. The Type 6a jar (Fig. 5.10:A; HAS64-580) is also attested in Urmia Ware and Early MBW in Period VIa at Hasanlu and Dinkha Tepe. The shoulder of the jar was decorated with a band of pattern-burnished cross-hatching. The tall tankard, typical of Period V, has a button base verging on a pedestal base and is sharply carinated (Fig. 5.10:B; HAS64-579). This represents an important transitional form from small, low button-base tankards to taller tankards with pedestal bases.

Dinkha Test Trench VII Burial 2
Mudbrick Tomb, ♂ Young Adult

Muscarella attributed this grave in Test Trench VII Stratum 6 to the early part of Dinkha III, citing its stratigraphic position and the small ceramic assemblage (Muscarella 1974:38–39), which fits well with the LBA sequence from Hasanlu (Seriation). This young adult male in a mudbrick tomb lay in an extended position with legs slightly flexed. The body was oriented east-west with the head to the east. Grave goods included a copper/bronze bracelet, a tanged dagger, a solid-footed tankard in grey MBW (Ware IIb), and a holemouth jar with bridgeless spout in red-orange MBW (Ware IIb) (Muscarella 1974: fig. 3). The tall, solid-footed tankard, a unique narrow variant of Type 1 with straight sides, dates to Period V. The spouted jar represents an early example of this class of vessel, typical of the LBA and Iron I graves of Dinkha but absent in the contemporary graves of Hasanlu. Spouted jars appear to follow the same general developmental trends as non-spouted jars, with holemouth varieties dominating the assemblage early followed by the development of wider carinated jars with low flaring necks in late Period V and IVc. This early example has only a hint of a "beard" beneath the spout and a simple "tail." These features become more pronounced and are increasingly elaborately rendered over time. In later Period IVc and into Period IVb these vessels are often decorated with modeling/appliqué, incising, and excising. The earliest bridgeless spout from Hasanlu was found in the U22 Sounding in Stratum 10 (Fig. 4.27:FF). Most attestations were found in Period IVc contexts. Stratum 10 of U22 is likely a mixed deposit of mainly early Period V with Period VIa, late V, and IVc material; as such, the period in which this highly diagnostic attribute first appears remains an open question, but it certainly dates to at least the third quarter of the 2nd millennium BC.

Dinkha B10a Burial 23
Simple Inhumation, ?

This inhumation grave of an individual of undetermined sex was oriented east-west with the body positioned on the back with the head to the east and looking up (Muscarella 1974:85). The arms and legs were flexed. The grave goods consisted of a bracelet, pin, and a Type 1 pedestal-base tankard (Seriation; Muscarella 1994a: fig. 12.4.2, no. 716).

Hasanlu SK116
Simple Inhumation, ♂ Very Old Adult
(Selinsky 2009; Rathbun 1972:53–54)
UPM60-20-236

Operation LIII was the only Hasanlu Project sounding located in the area of the western Low Mound. There are almost no excavation records pertaining to it (Fig. 1.3). SK116 was cut down from Stratum 4 into occupation strata of Period VII (Fig. 3.64). A "large rugged hyperdolichocranic male" of 35–40 years of age (Rathbun 1972:53–54) was positioned on his right side in a flexed position with head to the northeast facing northwest (Fig. 5.11). Grave goods consisted of a Type 1b pedestal-base tankard, a large Type 3b carinated bowl with vertically pierced upturned lug, and a small jar/cup with a loop handle at the shoulder (Fig. 5.11:A–C, Pl. 5.6e–f; HAS59-323–325). All three vessels were grey MBW and date to early Period V. Similar Type 3a–c bowls occurs in Stratum 10 of U22 (e.g., Fig. 4.20:L).

Hasanlu SK67
Simple Inhumation, ♀ Very Old Adult
(Selinsky 2008; Rathbun 1972:56)
UPM60-20-228

The skeletal remains from SK67, catalogued as UPM60-20-228, are incorrectly listed in Rathbun (1972:56) as 60-20-288. This grave of a female aged

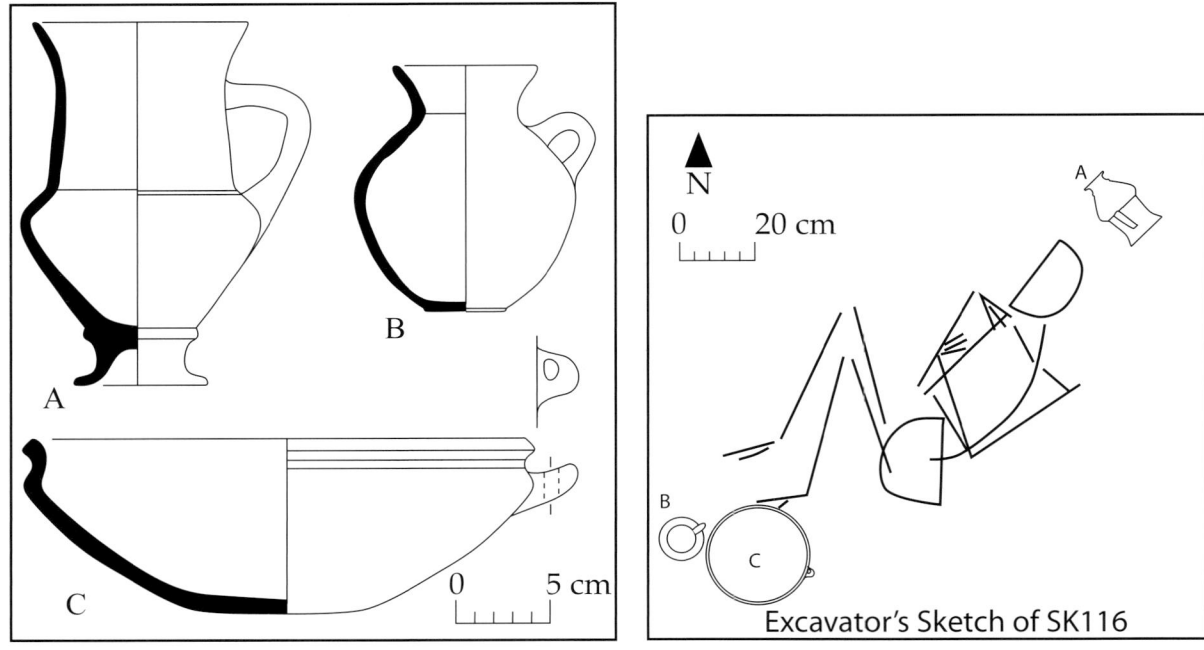

Fig. 5.11 Hasanlu Tepe: SK116, Operation LIII.

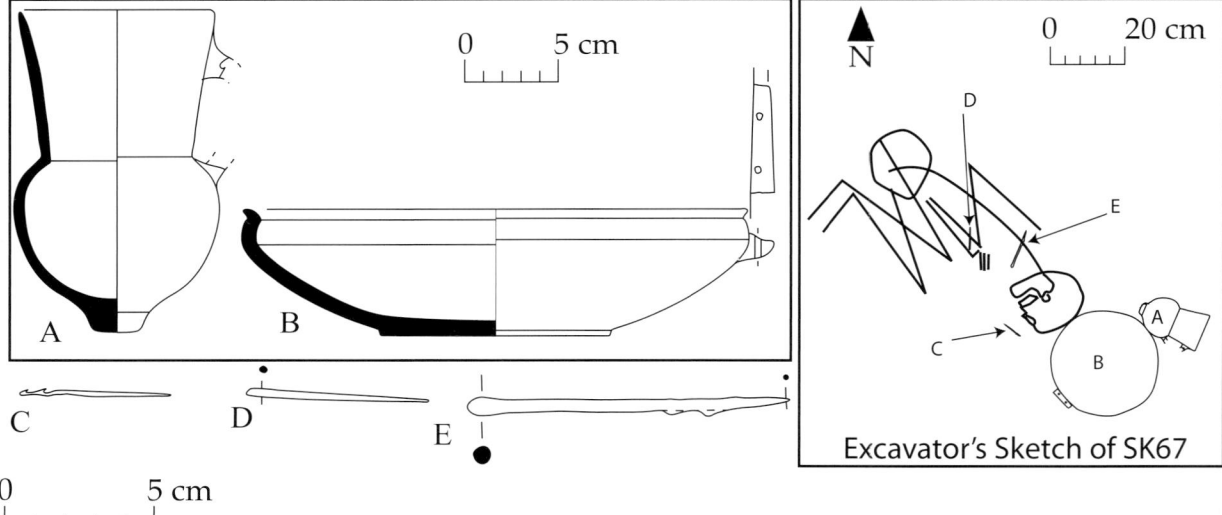

Fig. 5.12 Hasanlu Tepe: SK67, Operation VIb.

40+ (ibid.) lay in the southwest corner of Operation VIb in Area 2 Stratum 11 (Figs. 3.55, 5.12, Pl. 5.10b). The body was oriented northwest-southeast and lay on the left side in a tightly flexed position with the head to the southeast looking southwest. A MBW Type 1c tankard with a nipple base and a bowl similar to that found with SK116 with a lug vertically double-pierced, both grey in color, date the grave to early Period V (Fig. 5.12:A–B, Pl. 5.11a–b; HAS59-146–47). Copper/bronze pins were found placed in front of the

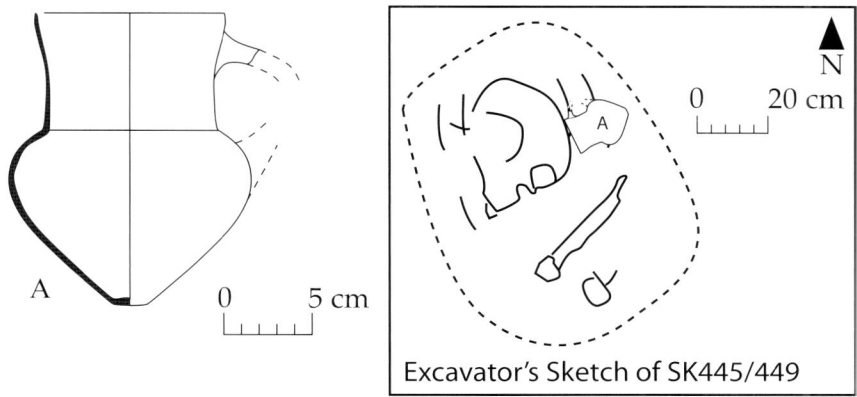

Fig. 5.13 Hasanlu Tepe: SK445/449, Operation VIc.

face (Fig. 5.12:C; HAS59-145), near the lower chest (Fig. 5.12:D; HAS59-144), and on the right shoulder (Fig. 5.12:E; HAS59-143).

Hasanlu SK445/449
Secondary Inhumation, ♂ Old Adult
(Selinsky 2009:211–12; UPM65-31-773, UPM65-31-749

SK445 was located in Operation VIc in Stratum 5 and consisted of a cranium without a mandible of a male, aged 30–40 years, and a Type 1c nipple-base tankard in grey MBW (Figs. 3.55, 5.13:A, Pl. 5.12a; HAS64-335) similar to that found in SK67. The skull rested on the left side facing south and the mouth of the tankard rested against the frontal and parietals. The tankard of SK67 supports a date in early Period V. At an unknown point later in the excavation campaign of the same year, 1964, SK449 was discovered in Stratum 5 in the exact same position as the cranium and tankard of SK445 but slightly lower, and it is obviously the missing portions of SK445. SK449 consisted of the jumbled post-cranial skeleton and mandible of a male, aged 30–40, with no skull or grave goods, and thus the grave was split and assigned two SK Numbers. The excavator noted that the body was "disturbed and jumbled…dug through when Burial 4 [SK448] was interred." SK448 dates to fairly late in Period IVb. There is little definitive evidence that SK448 disturbed SK445/449 and it seems certain that this is a secondary bundle burial.

Dinkha B10b Burial 13
Mudbrick Tomb, ♀?

This grave of an adult female lay in a mudbrick tomb oriented north-south with the body positioned on the left side in a flexed position with the head to the north facing east (Muscarella 1974:85; 1994: fig. 12.4.2). Grave goods included pins, earrings, a needle, and three ceramic vessels (Muscarella 1994: fig. 12.4.2). The ceramic assemblage (Seriation) dates to Hasanlu V and includes a "worm bowl," jar, and bridgeless-spouted vessel. The bowl is of the early, high-sided Type 1 with a characteristic Dinkha appliquéd crescent and drilled holes located near the rim. The spouted holemouth jar is also early in the range of this class of vessel but later than the spouted jar in Dinkha VII Burial 2 since it has a prominent "beard" beneath the spout, an appliquéd "tail," and incising under the rim. The other jar is an early example of the mid-body carinated type with flaring neck and simple rim, which becomes fairly common in Period IVc.

Dinkha B8e Burial 7
Mudbrick Tomb, Disturbed

This mudbrick tomb was disturbed, presumably in antiquity, and little can be said of it beyond its date in mid-Period V or possibly late Period V, which I would argue is fairly secure given the buff MBW IIc

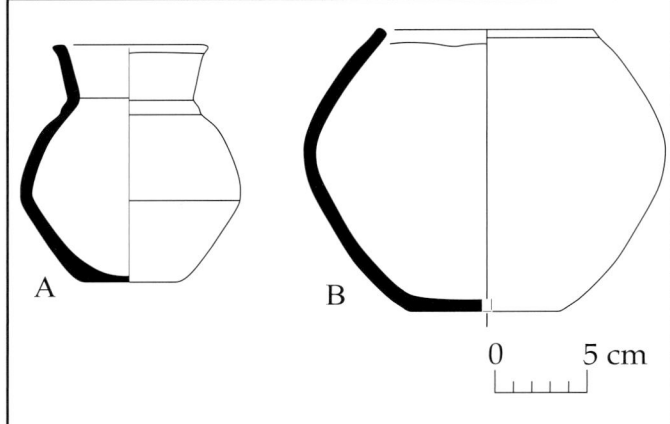
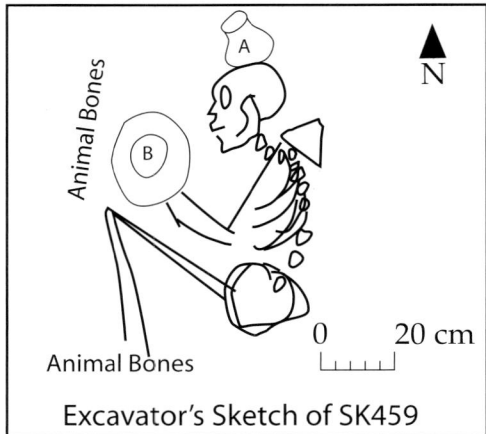

Fig. 5.14 Hasanlu Tepe: SK459, Operation VIe.

"worm bowl" of transitional form with lower, slightly curving sides, two crescents, and two drilled holes (Seriation; Muscarella 1974:47, fig. 17). The small orange matte "teapot" with basket handle and loop handle does not aid in the dating.

Graves of Late Hasanlu V

Graves of late Period V are known mainly from Dinkha Tepe with the exception of one grave from Hajji Firuz and one from Hasanlu. At Dinkha two of these graves, B9a Burial 17 and Test Trench VII Burial 1, were identified by Muscarella as stratigraphically later in the sequence of the Control Sounding—that is, occurring after early Period V/the early LBA (Muscarella 1974:40). An additional three burials were potentially earlier since they cut Stratum 7, a deposit containing MBIII ceramics; the relationship of the grave cuts to the overlying Strata 5 and 6 is not provided, however, and one may conclude only that the graves are post-MBIII. The bowls and bridgeless-spouted jars are all quite similar, forming a chronologically tight group. The "worm bowls" of Type 2a resemble those from the late Period V and Period IVc occupation deposits at Hasanlu (see Chapter 4).

Late Period V graves contain a wider range of mortuary offerings and suggest increased access to elite goods. Torques are included in graves, and a cylinder seal, *phiale mesomphalos*, weapons, and a large amount of personal ornament, especially glass beads, all suggest affluence in the later LBA.

Hasanlu SK459
Simple Inhumation, ♂ Mature Adult
(Selinsky 2009:212; Rathbun 1972:54)
UPM65-31-788

This grave in Operation VIe1 Stratum 6 is the only one from Hasanlu potentially dating to late Period V. This raises several possibilities regarding dating using ceramics from mortuary assemblages in identifying this period. Additional graves and occupation deposits of the late 14th–early 13th century BC are needed if we are to resolve this issue. In part, I may have included graves of later Period V at Hasanlu within early Period V and Period IVc. The absence of bridgeless-spouted jars at Hasanlu complicates dating given these jars are an important diagnostic of the period at Dinkha. Alternatively, our sample may be biased, with Dinkha providing the majority of our attestations.

This simple inhumation of a young adult male was positioned in a flexed position on the right side, oriented with the head to the north, facing west (Fig. 5.14, Pl. 5.13a–b). The grave lay near and under the western baulk of the operation, and the excavators extended the unit to recover the portions of the skeleton that extended beyond the baulk. I would argue for a late Period V date given the mid-body-carinated jar in Buff Ware with a relatively high neck and simple rim (Fig. 5.14:A, Pl. 5.13d; HAS64-90). The only other grave good is an unusual holemouth jar/deep bowl in reddish-orange slipped Buff Ware with simple rim and a hole (0.80 cm in diameter) through the center of the base (Fig. 5.14:B, Pl. 5.13d; HAS64-91). A large pile of animal bones that included sheep/goat was located to the west of the body in the grave cut and over the feet of SK459.. The jar rested against the top of the skull and the right hand lay beneath the holemouth jar.

The small mid-body-carinated jar could date to late Period V or Period IVc, although it most closely resembles jars of late Period V. The presence of a holemouth jar in a LBA grave at Hasanlu is interesting. The absence of bridgeless-spouted jars in mortuary assemblages at Hasanlu and their presence at Dinkha illustrate the distinct regional variations in mortuary traditions of the LBA. Perhaps the Type 8 holemouth jar from SK459, exhibiting the same size and proportions as bridgeless-spouted jars from Dinkha, served a similar function, although the hole in the base—not drilled but cut out prior to firing—is puzzling.

Hajji Firuz K10 Burial 1
Simple Inhumation, ?

As noted by Muscarella, this important grave contains all three major diagnostic vessel classes previously cited by scholars as typical of the former "Iron I" of northwestern Iran (Muscarella 1994:142). This inhumation burial of an adult was oriented north-northwest to south-southeast with the body positioned flexed on right side, head to the north-northwest, and facing southwest (Fig. 5.15; Voigt 1976:810–14, fig. 116, pls. LXI–LXII). A dog skeleton found nearby appeared to be associated with the grave, but later pitting in the area made tracing the burial cut difficult. The grave included a bridgeless-spouted jar in grey MBW (HF68-37), a ring-base cup/tankard in a light brown to grey smoothed coarse ware (HF68-47), and a bowl with flaring sides with two drilled holes (HF68-36) (Fig. 5.15:A–C). The bowl is a transitional type. It is lower in height than those I have assigned to early Period V and has slightly curving sides. It is similar to bowls from Dinkha Tepe, which provisionally mark the transition to late Period V (Seriation). The tankard is lower than the tankards of early Period V but has a base characteristic of some early Period V vessels, showing a close affinity to true button bases. It is only slightly carinated and is difficult to date. The jar also lies in the middle of the spectrum of Period V–IVc variation. The grave also contained spherical glass beads (HF68-41, 42)—such personal ornament is more common from late Period V onward.

Dinkha B9a Burial 17
Simple Inhumation, ? Adult

This inhumation of an adult of undetermined sex was oriented north-south, positioned on the left side with head to the north facing southeast. The left arm was flexed and the right arm was missing. This grave had a fairly high number of grave goods, including bracelets, anklets, a ring, toggle pins, beads, a needle, and a torque (Muscarella 1974:44, 84, figs. 10, 11). Ceramic vessels included a grey MBW IIb spouted jar, a grey MBW IIc bowl with two drilled holes, and a grey MBW IIc carinated jar (Seriation). The ceramics support a late Period V dating.

Dinkha B9a Burial 27
Simple Inhumation, ♂ Adult

This inhumation of an adult male was oriented north-south with the body positioned on the back partially flexed with the head to the south facing northeast (Muscarella 1974:43, 84, figs. 7 and 8). Grave goods included a copper/bronze bracelet, a stone "button," beads of faience and possibly glass, a copper/bronze socketed spearhead, a dark grey bridgeless-spouted jar similar to that in B10b Burial 10, and a grey MBW IIc bowl with two holes drilled in the side (Muscarella 1974: fig. 7; Seriation).[6] As noted by Muscarella, the spearhead resembles others of Dinkha II produced in iron (1974:43). This is the first securely attested bladed weapon of this type in the 2nd millennium BC graves of Hasanlu and Dinkha.

300

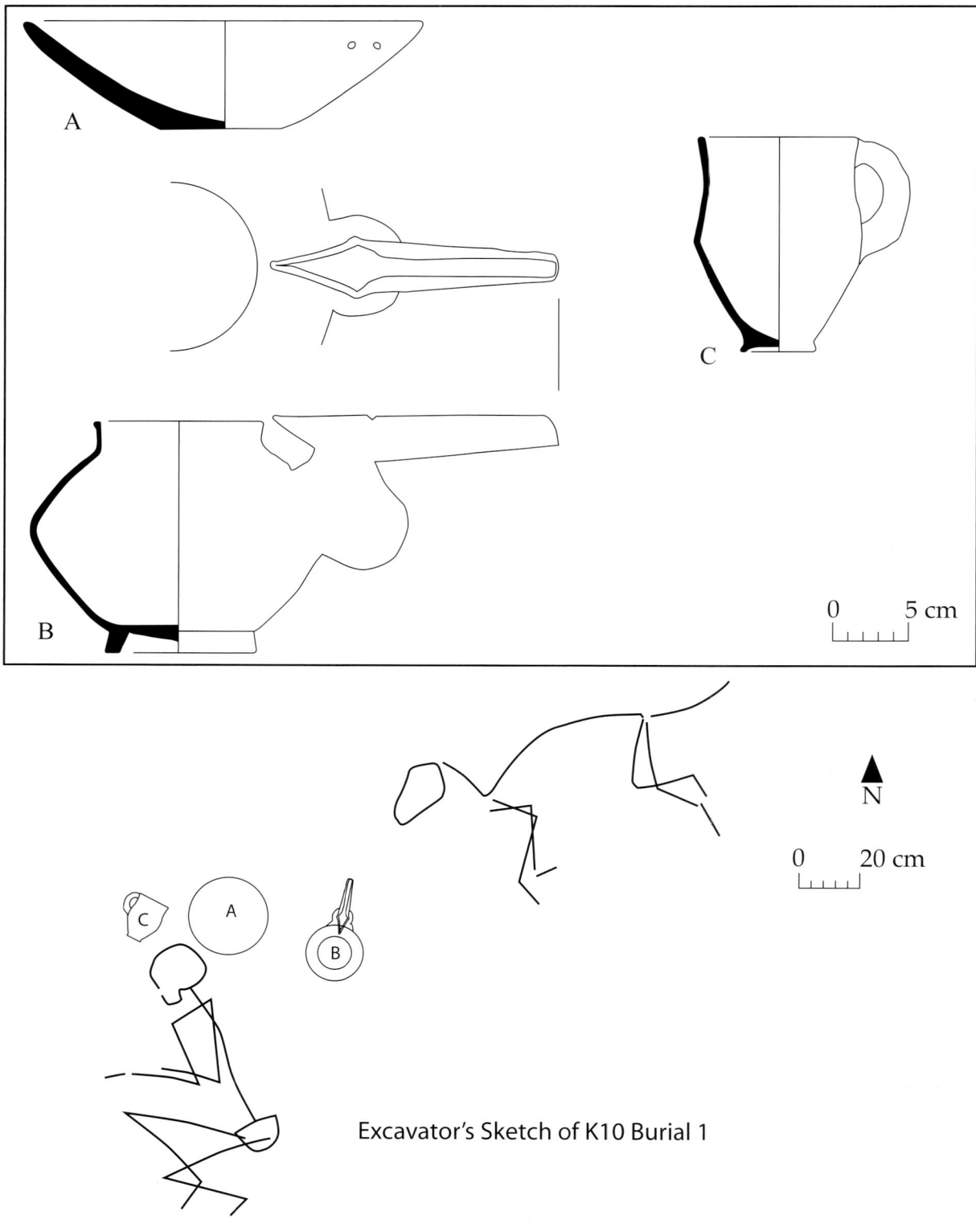

Fig. 5.15 Hajji Firuz Tepe: K10 Burial 1.

Dinkha B9a Burial 23
Simple Inhumation, ♂ Adult

This grave provided a rare cylinder seal in a 2nd millennium BC mortuary context (Seriation; see also SK57 of Period IVc).[7] Information on the location of the seal is not available (Muscarella 1974:40–43, fig. 6). The seal was made of blue faience and belongs to the Mitanni style, widespread in the 15th–14th centuries BC. The grave was an inhumation of an adult male oriented north-south with head to the south. Other grave goods included bracelets, a ring, a bone pendant, beads, and two daggers found in a jar. The ceramic vessels date the grave to late Period V and include a grey MBW IIc bridgeless-spouted vessel, a grey IIc jar, and a grey IIb low bowl with flaring sides with two drilled holes. The bowl accords well with the current ceramic definition of later Period V, while the bag-shaped jar exhibits affinities with early Period V.

Dinkha Test Trench VII Burial 1
Simple Inhumation, ♀ Young Adult

This inhumation of a young adult female was oriented north-south with the body positioned on the right side, head to the north (Muscarella 1974:39–40, fig. 3). The arms were extended at the sides. Grave goods included a torque, bracelets, a pin, and earrings. A bowl with flaring sides and two holes drilled in the side, a bridgeless-spouted jar similar to that from B10b Burial 10, and a mid-body-carinated jar provide a date of late Period V (Seriation).[8] All vessels were grey MBW IIc.

Dinkha B9a Burial 26
Child Indeterminate Sex

This inhumation of a child is noteworthy given its copious grave goods. The body was positioned north-south on the left side with head to the north facing northeast (Muscarella 1968: fig. 6; 1974:43, 84, fig. 7). The arms and legs were flexed. Grave goods included a torque, bracelets, anklets, pins, rings, earrings, needles, beads, a copper/bronze *phiale mesomphalos*, a grey MBW bowl, a smoothed Buff Ware basket-handle teapot, and a grey-brown MBW jar with bridgeless spout similar to that in B10b Burial 10 (Seriation).[9] The bowl is a small version of the "worm bowl" class typical of this period but without the characteristic holes drilled through the side. The pottery dates the grave to late Period V. The copper/bronze *mesomphalos* is especially intriguing: it is the earliest attestation of this metal vessel type in the region. It is atypical in the sense that in the Iron II, when copper/bronze *phiale* are slightly more common, they tend to occur in the graves of male warriors (Danti and Cifarelli n.d.).

Dinkha B10b Burial 10
Mudbrick Tomb, ♀ Adult

This burial consisted of an adult female interred in a mudbrick tomb. The body was positioned north-south on the left side with the head at the north, facing east (Muscarella 1968: fig. 2; 1974:46, figs. 15, 16). The arms and legs were tightly flexed. Grave goods included pins, earrings, rings, and beads. The pottery supports a date in late Period V. A grey burnished carinated jar with bridgeless spout shows little stylistic elaboration (Seriation). More important for dating is the red-slipped open bowl with flaring sides of the "worm bowl" class with two holes drilled through its sides.[10] This type is fairly common among the late Period V graves of Dinkha. The bowl contained animal bones. A mid-body-carinated jar with out-turned neck and simple rim rounds out the assemblage and is fairly common in later Period V and IVc graves.

The Graves of Period IVc

The distinction between late Period V and Period IVc is currently based primarily on ceramics from the occupation deposits of Hasanlu YZ27–29, RS22–23, and the U22 Sounding (see Chapter 4). There appear to be few graves of this period at Hasanlu. The predominant type of burial continued to be inhumation with one brick tomb at Dinkha.

The ceramic assemblage of this period attested in graves, as in occupation deposits, matches that previously defined for the EWGW horizon, with "worm bowls," bridgeless-spouted jars, and pedestal-base cups/goblets—the three basic vessel types of the previous "Hasanlu V"—but these are not found in the same graves. The cups are an important diagnostic in my definition of the period, as are changes in the form and stylistic attributes of the large open bowls broadly dubbed "worm bowls." While the pedestal-base carinated cups of Type 7 are well attested in the Iron I Hasanlu citadel, they are only found in the graves of children at Hasanlu and Dinkha. "Worm bowls" often have tripod feet, a trend continued in Period IVb in the form of higher feet or attached ceramic tripod stands imitating copper/bronze stands. The Period IVc bowls are more hemispherical in profile compared to those of late Period V. In early Period IVb, a few bowls of this class are known from Hasanlu and Dinkha Tepe (Seriation). Jars tend to be of the mid-body carinated type with flaring rims and higher necks, a trend seen in late Period V and Period IVb. Carinated bowls are typical of the period, foreshadowing developments of Period IVb—particularly incurving carinated bowls, occasionally with holes drilled though the vessel wall or lobed tabular lugs with single or double piercing. These lobed lugs are likely the antecedents of the animal head lugs and handles (ibex being especially popular) that appear early in Period IVb.

As in late Period V, the graves of Dinkha in particular suggest ready access to precious materials in the form of a torque, weapons, glass, "needles," and a cylinder seal. Graves generally have a high number of grave goods. This is especially noteworthy in the case of the burials of children (Dinkha B9a Burial 19 and B9b Burials 11 and 12), which certainly suggest the development of ascribed status. Iron is not attested in the graves of Dinkha or Hasanlu in the Iron I.

Dinkha B9a Burial 19
Simple Inhumation, Child Indeterminate Sex

Burial 19 was of a child oriented north-south, positioned on the right side, head to the south facing east (Muscarella 1974:44–45, 84, fig. 12). The body was in a semi-flexed position. Grave goods included a bracelet and ring. The ceramic vessels include a pedestal-base cup, still taller than those typical of later Period IVc and early Period IVb (Seriation). A tripod hemispherical bowl seems to be a coarser example of a type typical of the later range of large bowls of the "worm bowl" class. This bowl lacks appliqué or drilled holes. A large carinated bowl with incurving rim is a precursor to the bowls typical of late Period IVc and Period IVb, but the round base is an early attribute. The bag-shaped jar is fairly rare in this period (see also SK57).

Hasanlu SK479
Simple Inhumation, ♀ Young Adult
(Selinsky 2009; Rathbun 1972:56)
UPM65-31-775

This inhumation grave in Operation VIf Stratum 5 of an adult female was disturbed by SK480 of Period IVb (Fig. 5.16, Pl. 5.14a–b). The body lay in a flexed position on the left side, oriented northeast–southwest with the head to the northeast looking south. A number of grave goods were included in the burial. A grey MBW bowl of the later "worm bowl" class lay near the pelvis (Fig. 5.16:A; HAS64-175). The bowl had been broken by the later digging of grave SK480. The extant portions of the bowl bore no appliqué design or drilled holes, but the form is typical of Period IVc at Dinkha. A jar lay southwest of the feet (Fig. 5.16:B; HAS64-177) as did an unusual cup/goblet of unique form but known at Giyan (see Chapter 4, Fig. 5.16:C, Pl. 5.13e; HAS64-176), both in grey MBW. Animal bones, the remains of food offerings, were found in this same area. Copper/bronze pins were found at the right and left shoulders (Fig. 5.16:D–E; HAS64-171, -182). A copper/bronze bracelet was worn on the right wrist (Fig. 5.16:F; HAS64-172) and a copper/bronze ring was worn on the left hand (Fig. 5.16:G; HAS64-173). A copper/bronze band made of thin sheeting with two perforations (Fig. 5.16:H; HAS64-184) lay in the area of the forehead, suggesting the individual wore a headband. This interpretation is further supported by the presence of beads in the area of the cranium, including 12 cylindrical white paste beads colored dark blue at their ends, 7 rounded carnelian beads, and a lozenge-shaped bone bead with incised circles (Fig. 5.16:I; HAS64-174).

Dinkha B9b Burial 16
Simple Inhumation, ? Young Adult

This inhumation of a young adult of unknown sex was oriented north-south and positioned on the right side with the head at the south and facing

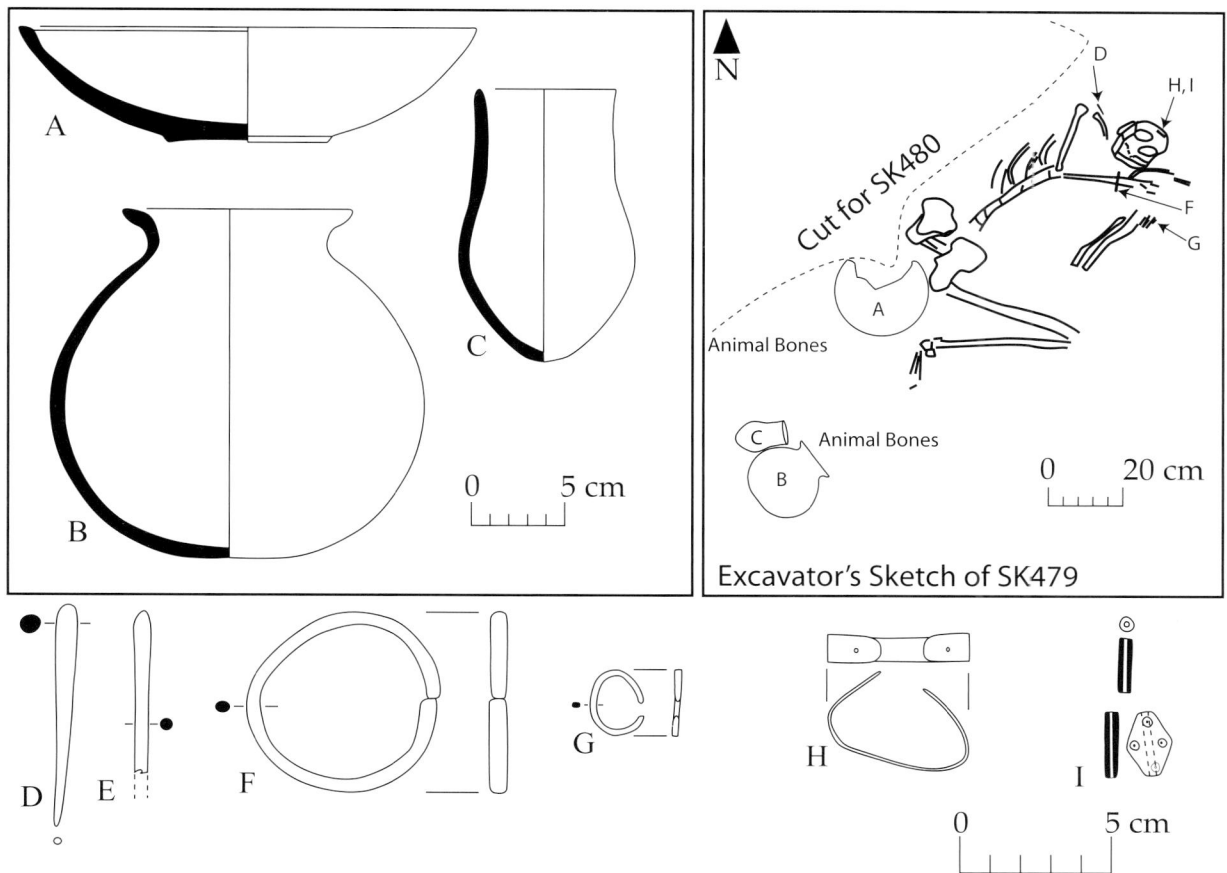

Fig. 5.16 Hasanlu Tepe: SK479, Operation VIf.

east. The body was in a flexed position (Muscarella 1974:46, figs. 2, 14). Grave goods include a bronze necklace, bone awl, bracelets, beads, and a dagger. The tripod bowl with two drilled holes, bridgeless-spouted jar with an incised pattern on the base, and mid-body carinated jar date the grave to Period IVc (Seriation).

Hasanlu SK494
Simple Inhumation, Infant Indeterminate Sex (Selinsky 2009:212; Rathbun 1972:57) UPM65-31-766

This inhumation grave is one of the few attributable to Period IVc from the Hasanlu North Cemetery (Fig. 5.17). It was located in Operation VIh Stratum 5 in an extension of the original excavated area located at the northwest corner. The size and dimensions of this extension were not recorded and it was evidently opened to recover SK494 and the nearby grave SK499 (Burial 9) of Period IVb. This Period IVc grave was thus presumably at or near the far periphery of the cemetery of the mid-to-late 2nd millennium BC. The body was positioned on the back and oriented northeast-southwest with head to the northeast looking southwest. The right arm was flexed with the hand lying on the left side of the abdomen. The legs were flexed and to the left. The grave goods include a sharply carinated pedestal-base cup of Type 7 (grey MBW IIc) resting against or near the left side of the skull. This vessel provides a date of Period IVc (Fig. 5.17:A, Pl. 5.13f; HAS64-299). A simple bowl of unspecified ware lay to the east of the skull (Fig. 5.17:B; HAS64-298). The deceased wore

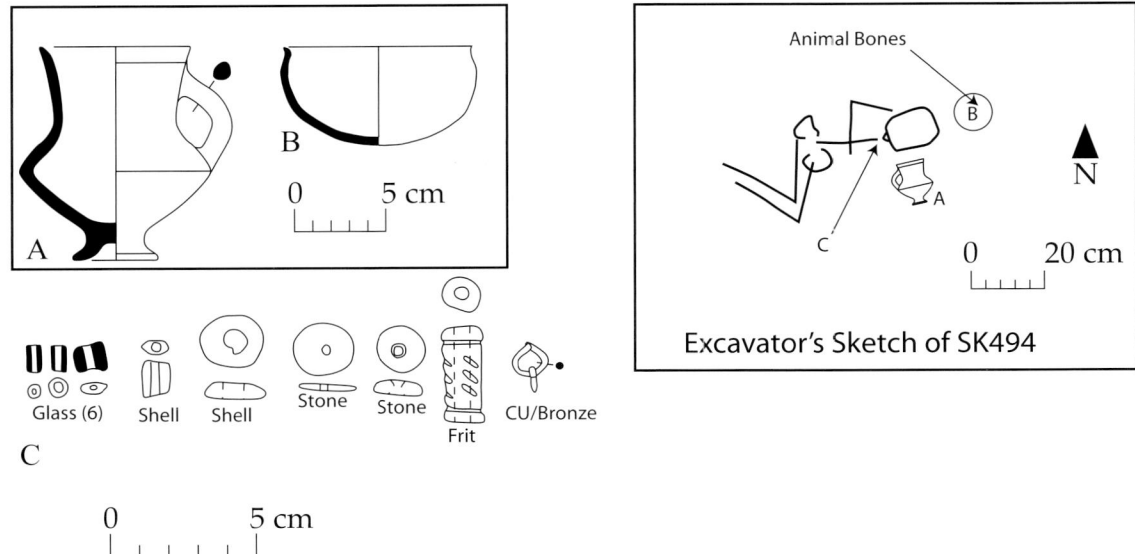

Fig. 5.17 Hasanlu Tepe: SK494, Operation VIh.

a necklace comprised of a large frit cylinder, carnelian spheres, shell discs, stone discs, and small glass cylinders with two copper/bronze wire rings linked together, possibly serving as a clasp (Fig. 5.17:C; HAS64-337).

Dinkha B9b Burial 12
Simple Inhumation, Child Indeterminate Sex

This inhumation grave of a child had few burial goods (Muscarella 1968: figs. 15, 17 right; 1974:45–46, 84, fig. 13). The body was oriented north-south and positioned on the back with the head south. The arms and legs were flexed. A copper/bronze bracelet was worn on the right wrist.[11] Three astragals were found in a hole dug near the head. A tripod "worm bowl" in grey MBW IIb was placed over the head (Seriation). The crescent motif appliqué is present in this case, and this is a late attestation of it. In late Period IVc and Period IVb the appliquéd crescent (possibly a lug) still appears on jars. A small Type 7 pedestal-base cup (grey MBW IIb) and a jar (orange Buff IIb) were placed near the feet. The jar and pedestal-base cup are both typical of Period IVc.

Dinkha B9a Burial 24
Simple Inhumation, ? Adult

This grave and others of Period IVc contain artifact attributes and types more common in early Period IVb. The replacement of the "worm bowl" class by types of carinated bowls represents the most obvious change. Bridgeless-spouted vessels, although poorly attested, begin to show a higher degree of stylistic elaboration, particularly in appliquéd design and incising/excising—this is typical of the bridge-spouted jars of Period IVb. Short pedestal-base cups become increasingly rare and are replaced by carinated flat-base mugs and beakers.

This inhumation of an adult of unknown sex was oriented north-south with head to the south and the body on the left side with arms and legs flexed. Grave goods include a bracelet, pins, rings, needles, and beads (Muscarella 1968: fig. 19; 1974:43, 84, fig. 6). An unusual Buff Ia bridgeless-spouted vessel with a foot and an appliquéd "horn" motif located at the tail provides support for a dating in late Period IVc, since the appliqué design and the development of a foot typify Period IVb (Seriation). The IVc dating is further supported by a Buff Ia carinated bowl of the incurving type with a single hole drilled below the rim. The bowl occurs in Period IVc occupation deposits at Hasanlu.

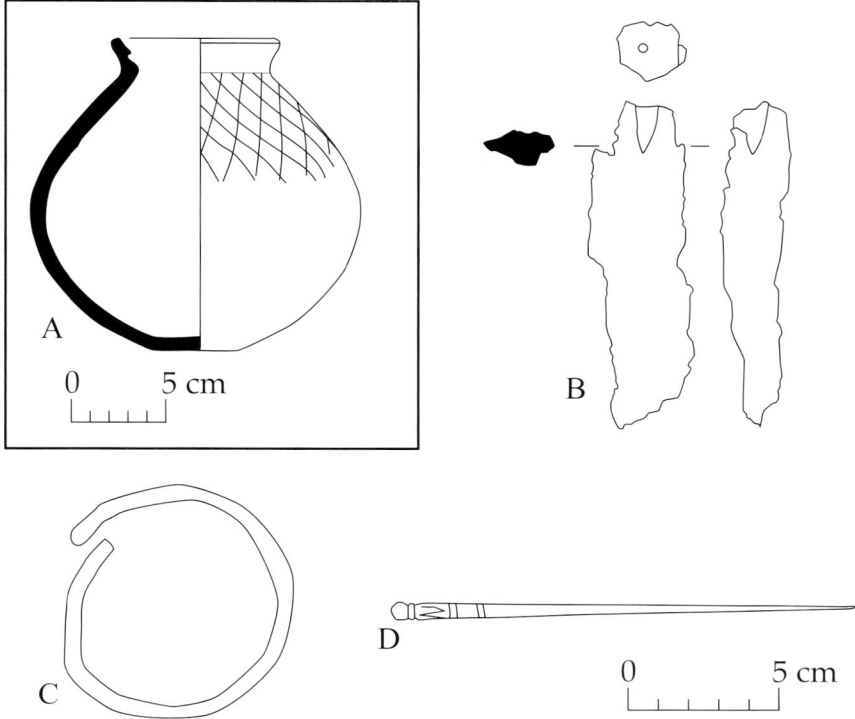

Hasanlu SK24
Simple Inhumation, ♀ Mature Adult
(Selinsky 2009; Rathbun 1972:55)
UPM58-4-105

This burial in Operation VI of a female, aged 30–40 (Rathbun 1972:55), lay at a depth of 2.60 m below the surface (Figs. 3.55, 5.18, Pl. 5.11c) in lower Stratum 3. The body was oriented northwest-southeast and was lying on the left side in a flexed position with head to the southeast looking south. A "red pot" (discarded and not drawn) and a grey MBW holemouth jar with pattern-burnish decoration (Fig. 5.18:A, Pl. 5.12b; HAS57-121) were the only ceramics—the latter likely dates to late Period V or IVc (cf. Lippert 1979: pl. 1). A piece of iron (unplaced) that resembles a socketed spear or similar weapon/implement was also listed for this grave (Fig. 5.18:B; HAS57-120). In the excavation photo, the iron appears to be lying in front of the chest (Pl. 5.11c). This represents one of the earliest occurrences of iron currently known from Ušnu-Solduz. Copper/bronze pins were found by the side of the neck, the back of the right arm, and at the

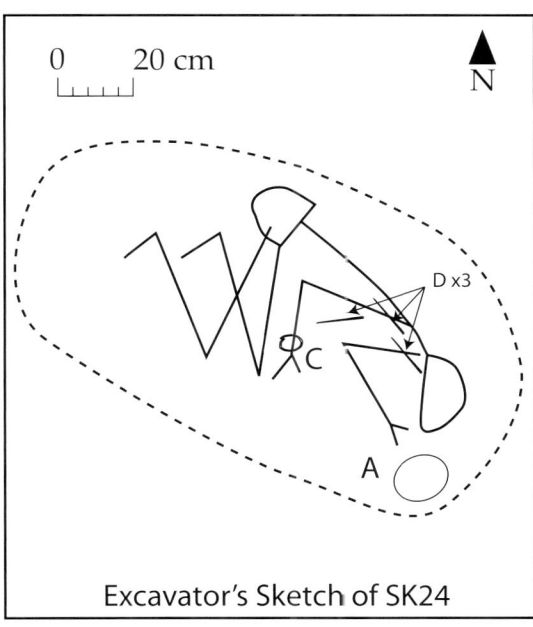

Fig. 5.18 Hasanlu Tepe: SK24, Operation VI.

sternum (Fig. 5.18:D; HAS57-118a–c). The incised decoration on these pins reinforces an early Iron Age date. A simple copper/bronze bracelet was worn on the right wrist (Fig. 5.18:C; HAS57-119).

Hasanlu SK73
Simple Inhumation, Child Indeterminate Sex

This grave of a child was located in the small western extension of Operation VIa Area 1 dug to expose SK72 of terminal Period VIb. The body lay on the right side in a flexed position oriented east-west with the head to the east looking north. The cut of this grave had removed the lower post-cranial skeleton of SK70 of terminal Period VIb. Just southeast of the cranium were a small jar/beaker, a beaker, and a Type 1 "worm bowl" with a smaller carinated bowl inside it (Fig. 5.19:A–D, Pl. 5.12c; HAS59-182–4, -188). The "worm bowl" provides an interesting, if unusual, late example of this highly diagnostic type and stylistic motif (Seriation). The appliquéd crescent on the interior from which the style derives its name is unusual in that the crescent is oriented in the opposite direction of all other examples. Identical copper/bronze coiled bracelets were worn on each wrist (Fig. 5.19:E–F; HAS59-186–187) and a bead necklace was found around the neck (Fig. 5.19:G; HAS59-185). This grave is difficult to date, and I have placed it in Period IVc based on the beaker and carinated bowl.

Dinkha B9b Burial 11
Mudbrick Tomb, Child Indeterminate Sex

This mudbrick tomb contained a child oriented north-south with the head to the north, facing east. The body was positioned on the left side in a flexed position. Grave goods were fairly numerous and elite in nature, similar to some earlier child burials of latest Period V and Period IVc, and include a plain torque, bracelets, anklets, earrings, and beads. The ceramic vessels support a date in the latter part of Period IVc. A grey MBW IIb bridgeless-spouted vessel has an appliquéd "tail" ornament consisting of a "V" framed by double parallel lines (Seriation). The shoulder and upper body were decorated with rows of vertical raised bands. The late Period IVc dating is reinforced by an incurving carinated bowl in orangish-red MBW IIb. The grave also contained an orange MBW IIb carinated jar of IVc type.

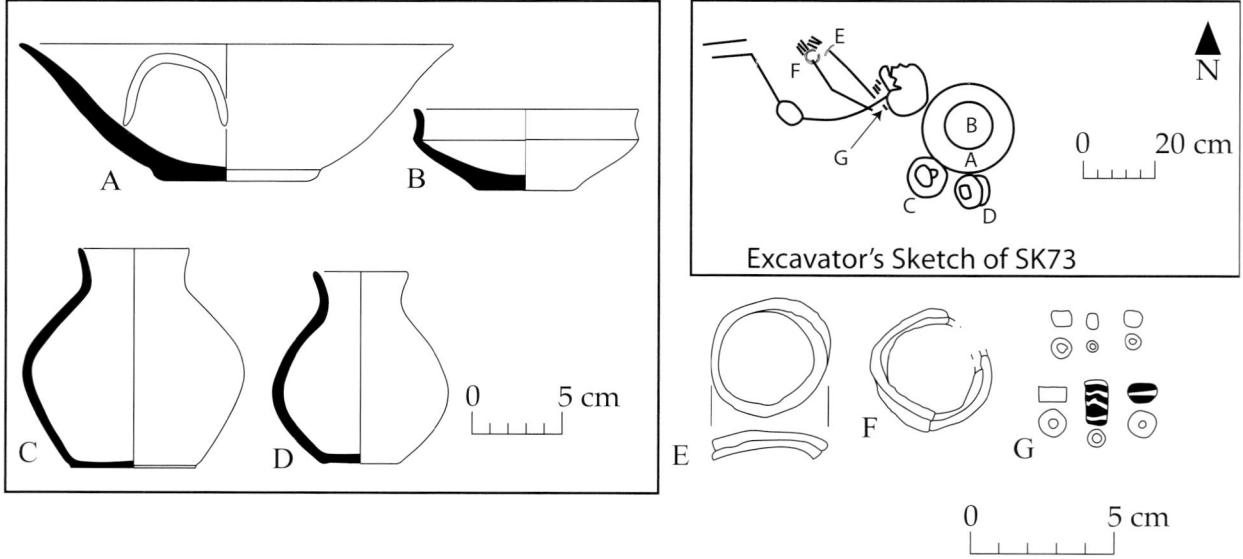

Fig. 5.19 Hasanlu Tepe: SK73, Operation VIa.

Hasanlu SK57
Simple Inhumation, ♂ Mature Adult
(Selinsky 2009; Rathbun 1972:53)
UPM60-20-223

This burial in Operation VIa of a "large, rugged, but hyperdolichocranic male" represents an especially interesting and rare grave of late Period IVc from the Hasanlu North Cemetery (Rathbun 1972:53). The ceramic assemblage associated with this grave lay beneath the feet of burial SK55 of Period IVb. SK57 was oriented southeast-northwest with the head to the southeast looking north (Fig. 5.20). The body was positioned on the right side in a loosely flexed position. The ceramic assemblage includes a grey carinated bowl with slightly flaring rim and a bi-lobed lug with double vertical piercing; ware specifics were not recorded (Fig. 5.20:A, Pl. 5.15d–e; HAS59-79). The form is typical of late IVc and especially Period IVb bowls. The lug form is attested in Period IVc and IVb at Dinkha and Hasanlu (Muscarella 1974: fig. 32, no. 401). A carinated "mug" in red-slipped Buff Ic is especially important for the dating of the grave and our understanding of the evolution of drinking vessels in the late 2nd millennium BC (Fig. 5.20:B, Pl. 5.13g; HAS59-80). The form differs from the mugs of secure Period IVb graves and occupation deposits. It is shorter and more sharply carinated and illustrates the transition from short pedestal-base tankards and cups to taller, gradually carinated mugs and beakers in the late 2nd–early 1st millennium BC. A jar and small jar/beaker in grey Ia of similar form but differing size and body thickness round out the assemblage (Fig. 5.20:C–D, Pl. 5.15c; HAS59-77–78). The ceramic assemblage may represent the early stages of the trend toward the inclusion of "drinking sets" in Iron II graves, that is, a jar (often a *hydria*), small-to-medium carinated bowl, a bridge-spouted jar, and groups of drinking vessels. Though it lacks the handles of typical Iron II *hydriai*, this jar resembles the earlier Iron II vessels with a flat base, ovoid form, and short neck with slightly thickened rim.

The body was adorned with a bead necklace (Fig. 5.20:E; HAS59-81) and a bronze finger ring (Fig. 5.20:F; HAS59-82). A cylinder seal fashioned from a light green composite material was clenched in the front teeth (Fig. 5.20:G, Pl. 5.15a–b; HAS59-83). Marcus assigns a date of manufacture for the seal sometime in the late 2nd millennium BC, citing Elamite and Middle Assyrian parallels (1996a:27, 143–44, fig. 115, pl. 48, no. C1).

Hasanlu SK6
Stone-covered Secondary Inhumation

SK6 of Operation IV was cut down from Stratum 6 (Period IVc or early Period IVb) into the Period VII deposit, the same level as SK4–5 of the MBII, but lay slightly deeper within the Period VII deposit. The grave was oriented northeast-southwest and contained paste beads (Fig. 5.21:B; HAS57-150, UPM58-4-12) and a tin/bronze lappet-flanged dagger with a Type IIA1b hilt fashioned to receive wood or bone inlay (Dyson 1965:34, fig. 2 no.1, pl. IX, 1; Thornton and Pigott 2011:163, fig. 6.31) (Fig. 5.21:A; HAS57-149). Similar hilts appear in Period IVb (Thornton and Pigott 2011:163). This dagger probably dates the grave to the late 2nd millennium BC or Hasanlu IVc or possibly early Period IVb, although a Period V date cannot be ruled out with regard to the dagger alone.[12] The large spherical beads are typical of the late 2nd–earliest 1st millennium BC and support a Period IVc attribution. The most convincing evidence for dating the grave to Period IVc to early Period IVb is its grave cut (see Chapter 3). The skeleton, not drawn, appeared to be a secondary interment and the cranium and feet were not present.

Graves of Probable V–IVc Date

Some graves from Hasanlu can be ascribed to the later 2nd millennium BC but, largely due to the absence of ceramics and other chronologically sensitive finds, cannot be placed within a specific period.

Hasanlu SK53
Simple Inhumation, Child Indeterminate
Sex? (Selinsky 2009; Rathbun 1972:55–56)
UPM60-20-220?

This inhumation grave of a child lay in the northwest corner of Operation VIa. The lower half of the body had been cut away by Burial SK54 of Period IVb (Fig. 5.22). The skeleton was likely in a flexed

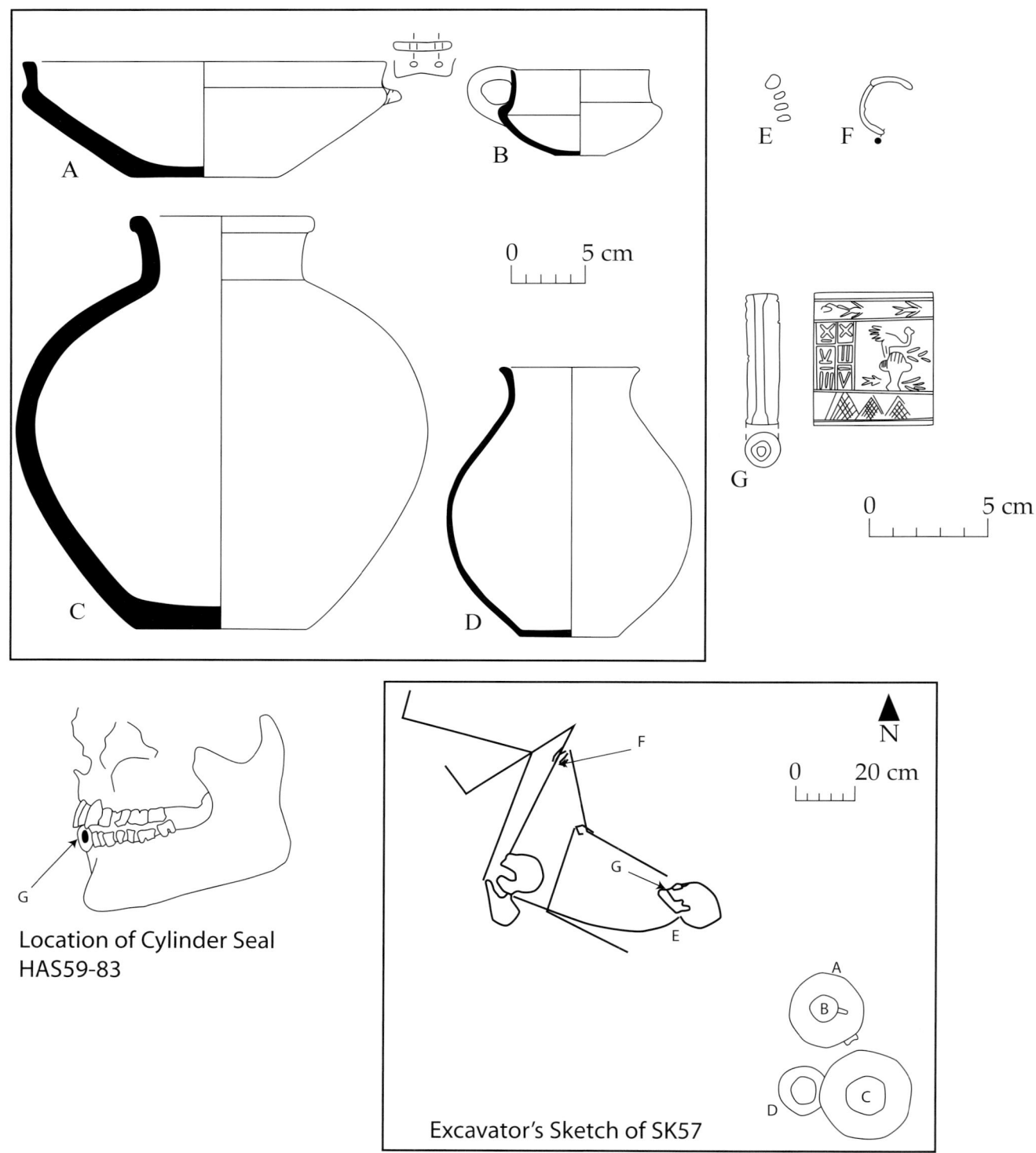

Fig. 5.20 Hasanlu Tepe: SK57, Operation VIa.

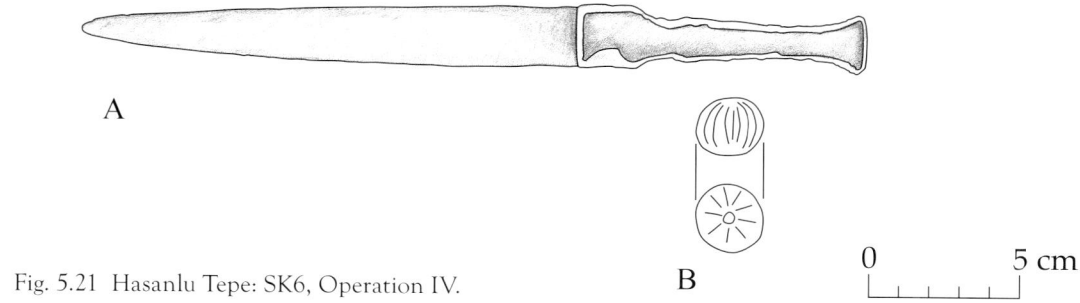

Fig. 5.21 Hasanlu Tepe: SK6, Operation IV.

position lying on the right side, head to the northeast facing north. Grave goods include a small copper/bronze finger ring found on the left hand (Fig. 5.22:A; HAS59-56)—a registrar's note from the field records the ring as being too small for an adult. A necklace consisting of 12 small white frit beads and a glass crescent-shaped amulet (Fig. 5.22:B, Pl. 5.13h; HAS59-57) were found around the neck.

Skeletal remains from SK53 were recorded as UPM60-20-220, but there is surely an error in the records/skeletal collections. The excavation photo, excavator's notes, and the finger ring indicate this disturbed burial was a young child or infant. Selinsky (2009:208) lists SK53 as a mature adult female, and the later SK54, which might potentially have been confused or mixed with SK53 during the collection of the skeletal remains, is also listed as a mature adult female (Selinsky 2009:208). The skeletons from the two graves were either mixed and the infant bones were lost, the recording was somehow transposed, or an additional unknown skeleton was listed as UPM60-20-220.

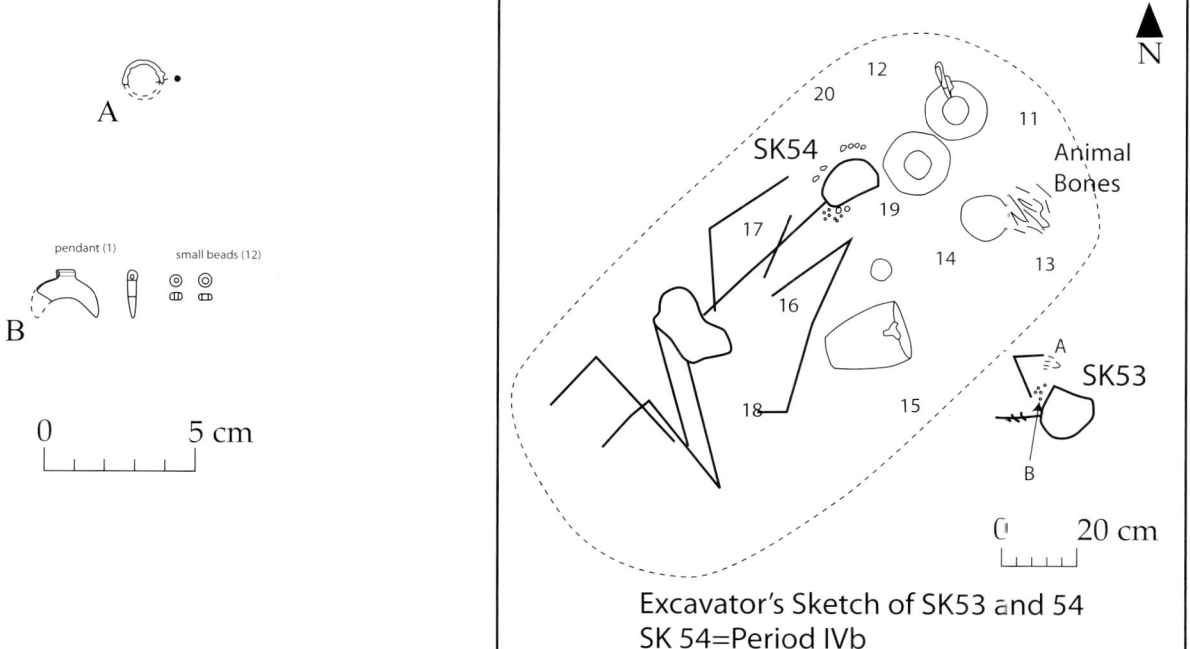

Fig. 5.22 Hasanlu Tepe: SK53, Operation VIa.

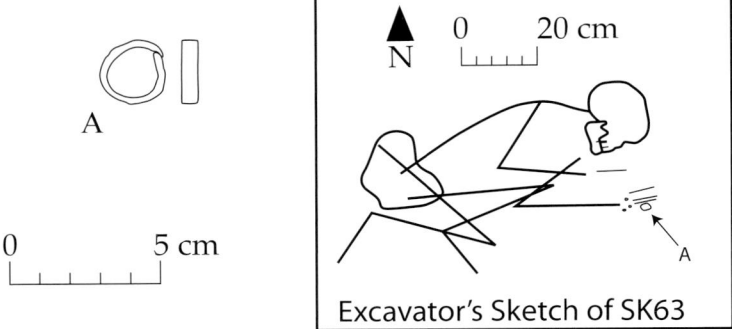

Fig. 5.23 Hasanlu Tepe: SK63, Operation VIb.

Hasanlu SK63
Simple Inhumation, ♀ Old Adult
(Selinsky 2009:208; Rathbun 1972:56)
UPM60-20-227

This inhumation grave of an old adult female lay in the southwest corner of Operation VIb in Stratum 7. The body was laid out in a flexed position on the left side with the head to the east, facing south (Fig. 5.23). The grave is difficult to date since the only grave good it contained was a copper/bronze finger ring (Fig. 5.23:A; HAS59-125).

Graves of Early Period IVb

A major obstacle to understanding the early Iron Age cultures of northwestern Iran has been the transition from the Iron I to the Iron II in the late 2nd millennium BC. This transition was encountered in the excavations of the High Mound of Hasanlu Tepe, but our chronological precision has suffered from a lack of detailed publication, poor stratigraphic control, and a lack of consistent, detailed recording. This chronological imprecision especially affects the dating of material collected from archaeological surveys or mortuary assemblages, the latter presenting a major obstacle since so much of our Late Bronze and early Iron Age dataset—the MBW horizon—comes from cemetery excavations. Ascribing an Iron I or Iron II designation often hinges on the fortuitous presence of one of the few well-known ceramic diagnostics dating exclusively to one of these periods—the paragons being bridge- and bridgeless-spouted vessels. The result has been that many archaeological sites and contexts have been assigned, perforce, an "Iron I–II" designation owing to indistinct "Grey Ware" sherds. As previously discussed, MBW may date as early as the MBIII and as late as the Iron III. This in effect is what the old "Iron I–II" designation could encompass. Moreover, there appears to be a marked degree of regional variation in northwestern Iran—as an example, consider the rarity of bridgeless-spouted vessels at Hasanlu and the absence of MBIII–early LBA Incised and Impressed MBW in Solduz. The graves of Hasanlu and Dinkha provide some clues on the transition from the Iron I to the Iron II ceramic assemblages. This transition seems sudden, and only a few graves may at present be dated to this timeframe.[13]

Graves of the Iron II (Hasanlu IVb/Dinkha II) were identified at Hasanlu and Dinkha first and foremost based on associated bridge-spouted vessels. While the bridgeless-spouted vessel was rare at Hasanlu in the LBA and Iron I, the bridge-spouted vessel is ubiquitous. No graves from Hasanlu and Dinkha have bridge-spouted and bridgeless-spouted vessels occurring together. At least 41 of the 77 definite Period IVb graves of Hasanlu contained at least one bridge-spouted vessel—approximately 53%. There are certainly other developments that mark the transition. Pedestal-base cups rapidly disappear and are replaced by carinated mugs, carinated beakers, and a range of other drinking vessels. These beakers, as well as small jars which probably also served as cups, often occur in "drinking sets" in Period IVb graves, sometimes found near a bridge-spouted jar and *hydria*. Tripod bowls and, especially, tripod stands occur in some graves, usually supporting a bridge-spouted jar. Vessels often sport animal-head lugs and handles—what appears to be an ibex is a popular motif. Carinated bowls, incurving types in particular, occur in high numbers to the exclusion of the earlier "worm bowl" class, which is present in rare transitional graves of the early Iron II at Hasanlu and Dinkha. Mid-body carinated jars continue in the Iron II and often have ribbing at the shoulder or neck. Small-to-medium ovoid and teardrop-shaped jars with vertical bar or loop handles on their sides, called *hydriai*, are frequently found in graves. Excising, incising, appliqué, modeling, fluting, cannelures, and gadrooning are all frequently employed to decorate vessels. Iron weapons and items of personal ornament often occur in the graves of Hasanlu and Dinkha. The transition to the Iron II is also apparent in the styles of personal ornament, with the appearance of new pin types such as breast plaques, "archer's" rings, and the popularity of new styles of beads—especially large spherical and dome-shaped beads in composite material decorated with incising. Finally, a few graves contain repoussé bronze belts.

Muscarella identifies four graves from Dinkha as potentially early Iron II based on relative depth but he claims this "does not seem to have independent support on typological grounds" (1974:59–60). These graves are B9a Burial 9, B9b Burial 19, B10a Burial 16, and B10b Burial 11. Of these, I would at least assign B9b Burial 19 to the early Iron II given the overall form and style of a double-pierced "worm bowl" (Seriation; Muscarella 1974: Fig. 27 no. 236). The grave also included a bridge-spouted vessel with animal-head handle, a mid-body carinated jar, a bronze torque, and two bronze groove-headed straight pins. B10a Burial 16 might also be dated to the early Iron II since it contained a tripod bowl (Seriation; Muscarella 1974:61, fig. 28). Such bowls probably represent the final stage in the development of the Type 2c footed "worm bowls" of Period IVc.

Similar to Dinkha, at Hasanlu we see that a crude "worm bowl" with double drilling occurs in at least one Period IVb grave, SK56, with a bridge-spouted vessel and other ceramics typical of Hasanlu IVc with IVb attributes such as torus molding and parallel cannelures and rills on jar shoulders and necks (Seriation). The mortuary assemblage from Hasanlu Grave SK62 may be dated to late Period IVc or early IVb (Seriation) since it contained a drinking set of four small jars or beakers, which is common in Iron II graves. The double-drilled mid-body-carinated jar, rather than the bridge-spouted jar that usually accompanies such sets of cups, would seem to reflect a date close to the end of the Iron I.

While only a few graves can currently be dated to early Period IVb, future research on Hasanlu IVb and related Iron II mortuary assemblages should improve our chronological resolution using the trends presented here for the graves of the LBA and Iron I.

NOTES

5.1. Muscarella alludes to the fact that "Bronze Age graves, simple inhumations rather than stone tombs, found in various parts of the mound as a result of our test trenches…contained pottery of the Khabur type" (1968:195).

5.2. These graves were found in Test Area IV. Burial 7 had "several buff vessels with painted designs of hatched lozenges enclosed in plain triangles" (Muscarella 1968:195, fig. 23). Burial 9 included *istikhans* (Muscarella 1968:195, fig. 24).

5.3. The scale specified on Burney 1962: pl. XLIV, nos. 26–27, 29 must be incorrect and is adjusted here by 200%. The other vessels shown on this same plate, nos. 24, 25 and 28, are shown here at the scale originally specified (1:2), but it is unclear whether this is correct.

5.4. The excavator of Operation VIb recorded the presence of a stone-built tomb but the plan was never labeled as to the burial in Operation VIb to which the feature belonged. On the plan of Operation VIb, the excavator recorded what are surely the capstones for a tomb as part of grave(s) SK61/66. Circumstantially, the capstones and stone-built tomb thus likely formed parts of SK61/66. This tomb resembles SK49 in construction technique, orientation, dimensions, and dating.

5.5. The excavator's notes contradict this information from the object record, citing "Bronze or copper ring on finger of left hand. 4 rings (co/bronze) on finger of right hand." Moreover, there were numerous fragments of iron found in SK15, including "iron club heads" [mace heads] (HAS57-72) and a fragment of an iron blade (lost).

5.6. In the seriation, the bridgeless-spouted vessel was copied from the example recovered in B10B Burial 10.

5.7. In the seriation, the bridgeless-spouted vessel was copied from the example recovered in B10B Burial 10.

5.8. In the seriation, the bridgeless-spouted vessel was copied from the example recovered in B10B Burial 10.

5.9. In the seriation, the bridgeless-spouted vessel was copied from the example recovered in B10B Burial 10.

5.10. In the seriation, this "worm bowl" was copied from grave Dinkha VII Burial 1.

5.11. The catalog lists a ring rather than a bracelet (Muscarella 1974:84).

5.12. I would like to thank John Curtis (pers. comm. 2012) for bringing to my attention the potential earlier dating—in the 14th century BC—of similar daggers from Ur and Nippur (Curtis 1983).

5.13. Muscarella was the first scholar to grapple with this problem, assigning mortuary assemblages to the early part of Period IVb (1974:59–60).

6

The Personal Ornaments of Hasanlu VIb–IVc

Megan Cifarelli

Analysis of the personal ornaments deposited in the burials in the Low Mound cemetery which date to Hasanlu VIb–IVc is fraught with the same difficulties one encounters when studying the site as a whole. The burials themselves were difficult to distinguish in the field, and they seem to have been hastily excavated, idiosyncratically recorded, and many of the finds discarded. Objects recorded as coming from a particular burial by the excavators in the field have occasionally been reassigned to another burial at a later date, and the placement and number of objects within the burial were not consistently recorded in the field.[1] To further complicate matters, examination of the objects in the University of Pennsylvania Museum's collection revealed occasional discrepancies between the physical objects and the recorded descriptions, drawings, and field photographs.[2] It is therefore impossible to consider any burial assemblage as complete, or as necessarily discrete. Given a dataset so small and compromised, any interpretive strategies have to be drawn with very broad strokes.

Methodology

This catalog of personal ornaments has been compiled from a number of sources. Michelle Marcus assembled a preliminary catalog of all of the personal ornaments at Hasanlu based on field notes, drawings, photographs, direct examination, and conversations with the excavation's Director. Her work, although unpublished, has formed the basis for this study.[3] Independently of Marcus, Michael Danti and his former graduate student, Laetitia Raiciulescu, assembled a catalog of all burial furnishings in preparation for this volume and as part of Ms. Raiciulescu's Master's Thesis (2011). These versions of the catalog have been reconciled with one another and with the field notes, drawings, and photographs. Finally, the objects themselves, which were distributed among the Tehran Museum in Iran, the Metropolitan Museum of Art in New York, and the University of Pennsylvania Museum, were examined directly whenever possible.

While every class of artifact that constitutes the material record of a particular time and place has much to reveal about that culture, and the cultural identity of any individuals, personal ornaments are unique in their ability to illuminate *individual* identity, precisely because they are *personal*—i.e., they are often individual possessions, worn close to or on the body. The significance of dress in general in constructing and communicating social and individual identity in ways that can shift over the life course has been amply documented and the point does not have to be belabored here (Marcus 1994a, 1995, 1996a, b; Rubinson and Marcus 2005:132).[4] Cemeteries such as that on the Low Mound at Hasanlu provide the opportunity to identify patterns of mortuary dress through the analysis of durable ornaments (Hodder 1987:6–7). One of course cannot assume that those ornaments deposited in burials reproduce those worn in daily life or that their meaning would be the same in both contexts.

The well-known destruction contexts from Hasanlu IVb, however, provide a unique opportunity to make some tentative comparisons between this earlier mortuary material and the personal ornaments found on the bodies of those accidentally buried in the Burned Buildings. Moreover, in addition to the victims of the assault and conflagration, the destruction contexts include what appear to have been elite, sealed storage rooms in the burned buildings on the citadel. Object types represented in these storerooms will be considered to be prestigious by association with their context: They had been intentionally collected, stored, and, in some cases, sealed, and can therefore be said to have been controlled by the elite of the site (Marcus 1990:179; 1991:539).

Two significant variables in the analysis of patterns of mortuary adornment and their significance within this group are the age and sex of the deceased. While the excavators sometimes noted the sex and age of the skeletons as they excavated, their criteria are not articulated and might rely on assumptions about gendered grave goods. Their conclusions may be warranted, but this study will rely instead and exclusively on Paige Selinsky's meticulous study of the skeletal remains from Hasanlu in the collections of the University of Pennsylvania Museum (Selinsky 2009).[5] Of the 15 burials dated to Hasanlu Periods VIb-IVc that contain articles of personal adornment, Selinsky has determined sex (in the case of post-adolescents) and approximate age for 8 skeletons. Based on the size of the human remains recorded in field drawings and photographs, at least 4 of the remaining 7 appear to be children; the remaining 3 appear to be adults. Again, this paucity of data presents an incomplete picture but a few observations regarding the distribution of personal ornament with respect to both sex and age will be hazarded on the strength of Selinsky's study.

Personal Ornaments in the Outer Town Cemetery

For this chapter, burials from Hasanlu Periods VIb–IVc will be divided into four groups corresponding to Danti's MBII (Hasanlu VIb)/1900–1600 BC), MBIII (Hasanlu VIa/1600–1450 BC), LBA (Hasanlu V/1450–1250 BC), and Iron I (1250–1050 BC).[6] Only those burials whose recorded contents include personal ornaments will be considered here.

Hasanlu VIb

Personal ornaments are recorded in a total of five of the seven burials now dated by Danti to Hasanlu Period VIb—SK4/5, 45–47, 49, 66, and 70 (see above, Chapter 5).[7] Burial SK45–47 is particularly well furnished. All of the personal ornaments in this burial are associated with SK45; SK46 and SK47 are fractional burials of a child and an adult. The excavators recorded SK45 as an adult female without providing any rationale, and the remains were included in Selinsky's study. The ornaments decorating SK45 include two copper/bronze pins, an earring, a button, six objects identified as "harness ornaments," as well as two mixed groups of beads of stone, shell, metal, and composite. The two garment pins found near the left shoulder and the left side of the head are relatively long, approximately 15 cm, with flaring heads shaped in six-lobed rosettes (Fig. 5.2:N-O; HAS58-132, -133). Both bear bands of incised diagonal lines, perhaps chevrons, around the shaft near the head. HAS58-132 is certainly a toggle pin. It was not possible to determine from the field photo if HAS58-133 is a straight pin or a toggle pin. While there are no known comparanda for the rosette form of the head, the overall flared shape of the head, its proportion to the shaft, and the placement and quality of the incised decoration are paralleled by pins from Dinkha Tomb 10a B27 (Rubinson 1991: fig. 21b, c) and less closely by examples excavated at Atsquri (Licheli and Rusishvili 2008: fig. 6:5, 21) and the Tsaghvli Necropolis (Ramishvili 2008:324, fig. 30:2, 3, 7) in Transcaucasia. The presence of these pins may substantiate the excavators' otherwise unexplained identification of the body as female, as pins appear to be associated with female burials at Hasanlu.[8]

The fragmentary ornament discovered on the right side of SK45's skull is almost certainly an S-shaped earring of a shape very common to this region and period (Fig. 5.2:R; HAS58-135).[9] While the form of this example is similar to local parallels found at Dinkha, Kordlar, Haftavan, and other sites, the manufacture seems to differ in that the wire constituting the earring is rectangular rather than round in section and the lower loop is lapped rather than open. A similar S-shaped earring (HAS59-175) appears in Period VIb

Burial SK70, also exhibiting the lapped lower loop (HAS59-175, UPM60-20-212). The S-shaped earring type continues to appear in burials at Hasanlu into Period IVb.[10]

Beads are the most abundant form of personal ornament in Burial SK45. At least two strands of beads decorated the body: One was found around the neck (Fig. 5.2:S, Pl. 5.3c; HAS58-146) and the other was found "over pots along back and scattered over legs" (Fig. 5.2:P; HAS58-136).[11] The former is likely to have been a necklace and, while the excavators later referred to the second bead group as a "girdle," it is equally likely to have been the type of body jewelry seen worn on terracotta figurines from Marlik (Negahban 1972: figs. 10, 11), for example, or another necklace placed in the grave on its own. In addition, bead-like ornaments in this grave include two shell rings found near the elbow of the deceased (HAS58-138, -139) and a large spheroid carnelian bead found in the skeleton's mouth (HAS58-134).

The bead strands featured a typically colorful mixture of well-polished carnelian, rock crystal, white frit (?), antimony (?), and short cylindrical bronze beads, as well as numerous perforated shells. All of these beads are of common types—spheroid, cylinder, short barrel, and oblate—well known from the burials at Dinkha and numerous sites in Iran and Mesopotamia (e.g., McGovern, Fleming, and Swann 1991; Rubinson 1991: figs. 18–20).

Similar groups of beads were found on a number of the bodies crushed by the destruction of BBII as well as in the collapse of storerooms on the upper story of BBII, confirming that bead strands such as these were not solely funerary in nature but were worn by elite individuals during their daily lives and were collected and held in public and religious buildings.[12] The shells in these bead groups have not been analyzed but, based on Reese's (1989) study of the Hasanlu IVb shells, they resemble most closely the *Arcularia* shells from the Mediterranean and not the more common *Engina* from the Persian Gulf (1989: figs. 3, 4). If this identification is confirmed by a study of these shells and *Arcularia* shells are indeed present at Hasanlu in these quantities in Period VIB, it would provide further evidence of the Ušnu-Solduz region's participation during this period in the western trade networks that were dominated by Mesopotamian superpowers.[13] Indeed, *Arcularia* shells have been found in large quantities in the 14th–12th century BC Middle Assyrian hoard at Khirbet Karhasan on the Tigris and in lesser quantities as far west as Mari, in southern Mesopotamia at Larsa and Nippur, and closer to Hasanlu, at Haftavan Tepe.[14] Further connections with Mesopotamia may also be evident in the *Conus* shell rings found near the elbow of SK45, which bring to mind the shell rings found by Woolley at the waists of attendants in the earlier Royal Cemetery at Ur, as well as those found in burials in the Early Dynastic cemetery at Khafajeh (Gensheimer 1984:67; Zettler and Horne 1998:94). The presence of these ornaments clearly indicates the high status of SK45, and the association of shell hoards with temple or votive contexts at Hasanlu and at other sites could suggest that she or he played a priestly role.[15]

While the bulk of the personal ornaments in Burial SK45 are useful for the analysis of cultural connections at Hasanlu at this time they offer little aid in reconstructing the rituals and beliefs attending to the transition from life to death in this culture. The existence of such beliefs and rituals is hinted at by the discovery of a relatively large, well-polished spheroid carnelian bead (HAS58-134) in the mouth of SK45. The placement of a large and valuable bead in the mouth of the deceased is even more remarkable because it is analogous to the placement of a cylinder seal in the mouth of SK57 in a burial that dates to Hasanlu IVc. Marcus has argued convincingly that the placement of the seal in the mouth of SK57 is a magical action, or ritual, that may function to "seal" the mouth of the deceased to prevent pollution of the living, or as an amulet to ensure the safe passage of the dead (1994b). An alternative explanation is that the mouth of the deceased is a "safe" place to deposit valuables that will be offered as gifts or payment to underworld guardians, as in the later Greek tradition of "Charon's obol" or the Chinese Shang and Zhou dynasties' practice of burying the deceased with cowrie shells in their mouths (Peng and Zhu 1995:7–8; Stevens 1991). The practice of placing valuables in the mouth of the deceased is undocumented elsewhere in Mesopotamia, Anatolia, or Iran prior to the Persian period.[16] It is impossible to know whether the bead in the mouth of SK45 was meant to function as an amulet or as a potential gift or payment to the guardians or gods of the underworld. If we tentatively posit that these two burials represent continuity of practice at Hasanlu, it is tempting to then suggest that the carnelian bead in the mouth of SK45 marks an earlier phase in this practice, prior to the introduction of seals and sealing technology to this region.

Ornaments similar to those found with SK45 were found in the other two adult burials from this period, SK49 and SK4–5. SK49 is a stone-built tomb with a single inhumation of a mature adult female, 36–49 years old (Selinsky 2009:208). Despite the large size and relative expense of the tomb architecture, remarkably few ornaments were recovered. The body was decorated with a single garment pin near the left shoulder (Fig. 5.3:A, Pl. 5.5a; HAS58-146), a copper/bronze dagger blade at the chin pointing toward the skull (Fig. 5.3:C, Pl. 5.5a; HAS58-148), and a group of short, cylindrical copper/bronze beads near the pin, west of the shoulder (Fig. 5.3:D, Pl. 5.5a; HAS58-147). Just below the tang of the dagger was a rectangular stone object with a perforation at each end, identified as a whetstone by the excavators although it shows no obvious signs of wear (Fig. 5.3:B, Pl. 5.5b; HAS58-149). Based on remarkably similar parallels from prehistoric Europe, Danti has tentatively identified this object as a type of wrist guard used by archers (Fig. 5.3:B, Pl. 5.5b; HAS58-149).[17] The garment pin appears to be of the same general size and form as those found in SK45. SK4–5, a multiple internment (not sexed), also contained a blade (Fig. 5.1:G, Pl. 5.1b; HAS57-129) as well as a fragmentary garment pin (Fig. 5.1:F, Pl. 5.1b; HAS57-131), simple penannular anklets (Fig. 5.1:H, I, Pl. 5.1b; HAS57-130a, b), a number of carnelian, shell, and composite beads (Fig. 5.1:E, Pl. 5.1b; HAS57-109), and a beautifully made copper/bronze finger ring decorated with two rows of raised bosses (Fig. 5.1:C, Pl. 5.1b; HAS57-106). These two burials are interesting in that they include objects that are gendered as female at Hasanlu (garment pins), as well as objects more typically associated with male burials, particularly in the case of the tanged dagger found with SK49.[18]

The remaining Period VIb burials with personal ornaments in Operations VIa and VIb in the Low Mound are, based on the size of the remains, those of very young children. SK66 is a single inhumation of a small child in a stone-built tomb. The personal ornaments associated with this burial include a pair of garment pins placed near the face and shoulder (Fig. 5.5:D–E; HAS59-133, -137), a copper/bronze ring on the skull (Fig. 5.5:I; HAS59-135), a shell ring in front of the face (Fig. 5.5: F; HAS59-138), and a pair of composite beads near the neck (Fig. 5.5:G–H; HAS59-134, -136). The smaller of the two garment pins is a club-headed toggle with incised chevrons on its upper shaft. The field drawings yielded little detail about the other pin, although it appears to be approximately the same size—13.5 cm—as those found in other graves of this period. The second child burial, SK70, was found nearby, adjacent to a pithos burial of an infant from the same era (SK72) and cut into by a later child burial of Period IVc (SK73). While half of the body of SK70 was cut away in antiquity, what remained was quite well appointed. The child wore a ring on its left hand (Fig. 5.7:D; HAS59-172), blue frit beads at the neck (HAS59-174), and the ornaments around the head included an earring at the right ear (Fig. 5.7:E; HAS59-173), an S-shaped earring under the skull on the left side (Fig. 5.7:F; HAS59-175), with an attached pendant consisting of a group of composite beads, the order of which was preserved, and a bronze hoop (Fig. 5.7:G; HAS59-176, -177). The beads included six flat frit disks, one spheroid fluted frit bead, one plain spheroid bead, possibly of glass, and one conical bead. Although the bead types are common there are no parallels for this group, nor is it possible to determine if this pendant was part of an earring or part of a headdress or hair ornament.

It is interesting to note that not only do these two burials of very small children contain the same types and quality of personal ornaments as do the contemporary adult burials, with the important exception of blades, they are also in close proximity to one another. The burials of children and the extent to which they are differentiated from adults and the elderly provide an opportunity to analyze social complexity.[19] While the role of gender in the distribution of grave goods has been studied more extensively, it appears that, in many cultures, children and/or the elderly are marginalized in mortuary contexts both with respect to the location and the furnishing of their burials.[20] The presence of even two incomplete but well-adorned children's burials in an "adult" cemetery can reasonably be interpreted as a signal of social stratification and complexity, as wealth associated with a child is a marker of family or group, rather than individual, status (Alekshin et al. 1983; Crawford 2000:175).[21] With only two child burials from this period, at least one of which is incomplete, it is impossible to determine at this time if the absence of blades and the clustering of burials represents a pattern of differential treatment for children's burials at Hasanlu.

Period VIa is represented by two burials in Operation VI of the Lower Mound, only one of which contained personal ornaments. SK25 is that of a young woman, 20–35 years old, and SK29 is that of an older man, 50–64 years old (see above, Chapter 5; Selinsky 2009:208). SK25 was decorated with three garment pins (Fig. 5.8:F; HAS57-122a–c), a finger ring (HAS57-125), a few beads of copper, stone, and composite materials (Fig. 5.8:E; HAS57-124), and a cast, lapped simple bracelet on each wrist (Fig. 5.8:C–D; HAS57-123a–b). SK29 contained no personal ornaments, perhaps an indication of differentiated treatment of the burials of the elderly.[22] In earlier publications an iron finger ring was associated with SK29 (HAS57-184), but closer analysis of the excavation records has revealed the ring to have been intrusive, perhaps from SK15, a Hasanlu IVb burial immediately above SK29.[23]

Of the five burials now assigned to Hasanlu V only one, SK67, contained personal ornaments, suggesting that Period V was a time of decreased prosperity at Hasanlu. SK116 and SK445/449 contained older adults and a secondary bundle burial (Selinsky 2009:209, 213), and SK504 and SK459 were poorly furnished burials of a mature and a young adult male, respectively (2009:214). SK67 is that of an elderly woman, 60+ years old, and her ornaments consisted of three garment pins found near her face, chest, and on her right shoulder (Selinsky 2009:209) (Fig. 5.12:C, D, E; HAS59-143–145). Two of the three pins were discarded; the third is club headed, perhaps with incised decoration on the head. While the paucity of ornaments may result from the lack of resources at Hasanlu in this period, it is also possible that the age of the deceased played a role. It is interesting to note that in the latter part of this period at Dinkha, grave goods include ornaments in greater quantities and of more elite types, such as torques, than are found at Hasanlu.[24]

Eight burials from the Lower Mound have been assigned to Hasanlu IVc, all of which contained personal ornaments—again indicating an uptick in prosperity at Hasanlu at this time. SK63 in Operation VIb is a poorly furnished burial of an older adult female, 50–64 years old (Selinsky 2009:209), adorned with a single bronze finger ring (Fig. 5.23:A; HAS59-125), reinforcing the notion that the elderly were buried with minimal adornment. SK6, a disturbed burial in Operation IV, probably of an adult, contained a well-preserved lappet-flanged tin/bronze dagger (Dyson 1965:34, fig. 2 no.1, pl. IX, 1; Thornton and Pigott 2011:163, fig. 6.31) (Fig. 5.21:A; HAS57-149) and a pair of fluted (melon), spheroid composite beads of a type well represented in Period IVb burials (Fig. 5.21:B; HAS57-150, UPM58-4-12).[25] It is worth noting that this burial was located less than 1.5 m from SK4–5, which also contained a dagger.

As was the case in Period VIb, the burials of adult women appear to contain the greatest number and most valuable of personal ornaments in Period IVc. SK24 in Operation VI is that of a mature adult female, 35–49 years old (Selinsky 2009:208). She was buried with three decorated garment pins near her chest and neck (Fig. 5.18:D; HAS57-118a–c)[26] and a copper/bronze bracelet with snake head terminals on her right wrist (Fig. 5.18:C; HAS57-119). Bracelets and armlets with snake head terminals occur with some frequency in Period IVb, with 6 examples buried with a single individual in the Lower Mound Cemetery and 29 found on bodies crushed in the destruction of BBII. These bracelets have been associated with examples excavated at Artik, in present-day Armenia, and Rubinson and Marcus have argued that these parallels indicate a strong connection between Hasanlu and the Southern Caucasus in Period IVb (Rubinson and Marcus 2005:131–38, esp. 136).[27] The presence of a snake-headed bracelet in a Period IVc burial both associates the individual in SK24 with the elite status of those who died in BBII and confirms that these Caucasian components are a consistent feature of the Hasanlu koiné.

SK479 is another well-furnished burial of a young woman, 20–34 years old, in Operation VIf (Selinsky 2009:213). Her ornaments include cast club-headed garment pins at the right and left shoulders (Fig. 5.16:D–E; HAS64-171, -182), a single penannular ring on her left hand (Fig. 5.16:G; HAS64-173), a plain bracelet on the right wrist (Fig. 5.16:F; HAS64-172), and what appears to be an elaborate headdress consisting of a bronze band and beads. This extremely fragile bronze band is approximately 11 cm long with a perforation at each end, perhaps for attachment to a leather band (Fig. 5.16:H; HAS64-184). It was accompanied by a group of beads which included five white composite cylinders, three crudely carved carnelian spheroids, and a single lozenge-shaped shell bead with incised circle-and-dot motifs (Fig. 5.16:I; HAS64-174). The placement of an elaborate beaded headband on a young woman is in keeping with burial assemblages in the Low Mound Cemetery from Hasanlu IVb, again indicating both cultural continuity between IVc and IVb, and likely marking the special status of these young women.[28] The elite and possibly sacral nature of this headdress is suggested by the presence of identical incised *Conus* shell beads among the contents of the second-story storeroom above Room 7 of BBII (Reese 1989: figs. 16, 17).

SK57 is the only anthropologically sexed male in the Low Mound cemetery from the periods in question who was interred with personal ornaments (Selinsky 2009:210). In addition to a group of 10 frit neck beads (Fig. 5.20:E; HAS59-81) and a bronze finger ring (Fig. 5.20:F; HAS59-82), this burial of a mature male, 35–49 years old, is best known because of the presence of a locally made frit cylinder seal placed in the mouth of the deceased (Fig. 5.20:G, Pl. 5.15a–b; HAS59-83), interpreted by Marcus as evidence of a magical or ritual action which "sealed" the mouth of the deceased, either for his protection or to protect the living from him (Marcus 1994b; 1996a:27, 143–44, fig. 115, pl. 48, no. 1). It is tempting to interpret this intentional "closing" of the mouth of the deceased as an example of a deviant burial practice but the lack of normative data for male burials in this period currently prohibits any such interpretation. Moreover, the parallel between this burial and the placement of a carnelian bead in the mouth of SK45 suggests that we are not looking at an isolated phenomenon.

The three remaining IVc burials were identified by the excavators as small children based on the size of the remains: SK73, SK53, and SK494. SK73 is immediately adjacent to two earlier child burials, SK70 and SK72. This child's body was decorated with coiled copper/bronze bracelets on each wrist (Fig. 5.19:E–F; HAS59-186–187), as well as neck beads in variegated glass and frit (Fig. 5.19:G; HAS59-185). Aside from a tiny finger ring (Fig. 5.22:A; HAS59-56), the only adornment on the body of SK53 is a necklace of very uniform, tiny frit beads and an inverted crescent-shaped pendant of frit or glass (Fig. 5.22:B, Pl. 5.13h; HAS59-57). Crescentic amulets in precious metals are well known from the early 2nd millennium BC throughout the Levant and Mesopotamia (Bass et al. 1989:2–5, fig. 6; Maxwell-Hyslop 1971:88–89, 149–50), as well as at Dinkha (Rubinson 1991). At least one exemplar, in gold, was found in a Period IVb burial in Operation VI at Hasanlu.[29] In Mesopotamian iconography the crescent is emblematic of the moon god (Black, Green, and Rickards 1992:54); it appears in the visual arts worn around the necks of kings,[30] and in the Biblical record as a type of ornament to be stripped from the "haughty daughters of Zion."[31] Divine emblems, even those made of humble materials, may not operate simply as amulets but as powerful manifestations of the presence of the deity (Bahrani 2003:127; Spaey 1993). The marking of this child's body with what may be a divine symbol is significant, whether it was intended to confer special protection or an affiliation with a lunar deity.

At what must have been the very edge of the cemetery in Period IVc was SK494, the burial of a child 2–3 years old (Selinsky 2009). This young child wore a necklace consisting of 13 highly varied elements, including beads of various shapes in carnelian, shell (*Conus* whorl), bone, white stone, and glass, two bronze rings, and a complete blue-green frit cylinder seal or seal bead (Fig. 5.17:C; HAS64-337). The *Conus* whorl and bone beads are closely paralleled by beads from Cave A4 of the Baq'ah Valley Project (McGovern 1986: pls. 26b, 28b). The geometric design on the cylinder seal or seal bead consists of vertical rows of short diagonal lines framed by a line at either end. Parallels for this seal are found at numerous late 2nd millennium BC sites in Iran, Mesopotamia, and as far west as the Baq'ah Valley.[32] It is nearly identical to a number of seals found in Period IVb contexts, including in the collapse of the upper-story storage rooms in BBII, and in a burial with beads near the skull of the deceased. Marcus has classified seals of this type as "Other Iranian Style," suggesting they were locally manufactured.[33] Again, the inclusion of objects of adornment of types similar to those found both on the deceased and in the storerooms in the monumental buildings on the citadel seems meant to mark the high status of this elaborately decorated infant.

Given the sparseness and quality of the data from the Low Mound cemetery at Hasanlu in Periods VIb–IVc, any conclusions offered here are highly speculative. Overall, the personal ornaments in these burials are modest, particularly in comparison to those found at Dinkha in the same periods (Muscarella 1974; Pizzorno 2011; Rubinson 1991) and to the finds of Hasanlu IVb. The Hasanlu Periods VIb–IVc assemblages contain no precious metals or particularly rare and valuable materials, suggesting that during these periods Hasanlu had less access than did Dinkha to the most prestigious goods and materials, such as those detailed by Rubinson (1991). Moreover, most of the objects or personal adornments are of "common" types—there is a dearth of distinctive forms or styles of decoration, as well as a lack of a uniquely local production along the lines of the "Hasanlu Local Style" which characterized some of the artistic production of Period IVb (Winter 1977).

Within the context of the Hasanlu Lower Mound cemetery, the limited data suggest some patterns of deposition and adornment, patterns which may relate to the construction and expression of social and individual identity. This cemetery generally seems to be the locus of burials of elite women, children, and perhaps older men, suggesting that the younger adult men were buried elsewhere on the mound.[34] The men who are buried in this cemetery are treated somewhat differently from the rest of the burials. Of the six definitively sexed male burials, five have no personal ornaments (SK57, 29, 504, 116, 445/9, and 459), and three of those are classified by Selinsky as "old" or "very old" (2009). The only male with personal ornaments has had his mouth "sealed" with a cylinder seal, a treatment which may relate to the carnelian bead placed in the mouth of SK45 from Period VIb.

Distinctions seem to exist among the women and children, as well. Elderly women are buried with the least valuable assemblages of personal ornaments and this relative exclusion from typical mortuary ritual may express the diminished social value of those no longer able to perform their primary social function, which was presumably childbearing. Younger adult women are accompanied by the most diverse and prestigious goods, including personal ornaments, and in at least one burial, SK49, and probably two more—SK4/5 and SK6—blades or weapons. The presence in numerous burials of ornaments of types and materials that were highly valued and collected at Hasanlu, as evidenced by their presence in the storerooms and on the bodies of those who died in the Burned Buildings on the citadel in the Period IVb destruction, is a clear indication of the elite status of those individuals.

Perhaps the most interesting patterns to emerge from this analysis are related to the burials of young children. These burials appear to be clustered and are largely surrounded by adult burials, an arrangement which could be related to a perceived need of children for adult care, even after death. While children's burials at many sites are furnished like those of the poorest adults (Alekshin et al. 1983; Crawford 2000), the children in the Low Mound cemetery at Hasanlu are buried with the same range of ornaments, including the most elite types, found in adult (female) burials. It is likely that the wealth and prestige of these burials indicates the elite status of the dead child's family and the unrealized potential of the child within "the community of lineage" (Mizoguchi 2000:146).

The personal ornaments at Hasanlu, while lacking in prestige and value, demonstrate cultural continuity over the periods studied, as well as an affinity with other sites in the Lake Urmia region. The style and materials of the artifacts themselves attest to a local koiné that is consistently inflected by Iranian, Syro-Mesopotamian, and Trans-Caucasian material culture. Evidence of cultural continuity and, more specifically, the clear identification of personal ornaments found in burials as early as MBII with the equivalent contents of the sealed storerooms of Iron II BBII raises some interesting questions about elite practices at Hasanlu. It seems possible that, as early as Period VIc, elites at Hasanlu were collecting prestige goods and that these heirloom collections were maintained over generations, perhaps in public or religious buildings.[35] The notion of a powerful local elite operating within a complex, hierarchical society during these periods is bolstered by the evidence for differential mortuary treatment for different segments of the community, expressed through patterns of distribution of significant ornaments as well as the geographic distribution of burials.

NOTES

6.1. For a very clear articulation of the extraordinary challenges posed to researchers working on the publication of the Hasanlu Expedition sites, see Danti Chapter 3 herein and Pizzorno 2011.

6.2. See specific notes in catalog, below.

6.3. Michelle Marcus undertook this work between 1990 and

1999. Her research was funded by a Collaborative Research Grant through the National Endowment for the Humanities and the Hasanlu Project.

6.4. Marcus has laid the foundation for the interpretation of personal ornament and dress at Hasanlu. For important perspectives from other sites, see Gansell 2007 and Golani 2010.

6.5. See above, Chapter 5, and Selinsky, 2009:39–41 for a discussion of earlier skeletal studies of the Hasanlu material by Bass and Rathbun.

6.6. For the sake of consistency, all of the dating criteria established by Danti in this volume will be adhered to for the dating of the burials and the analysis of personal ornament. The objects, of course, may have dates of manufacture which are prior to their deposition.

6.7. Burials will be referred to by Skeleton Numbers (SN), as these are the only unique designations at Hasanlu. Burial numbers were repeated across operations.

6.8. A total of eight skeletons from burials ranging between Periods VIb-IVc are accompanied by garment or toggle pins. Of these eight, five have been anthropologically sexed as female by Selinsky (2009), a sixth is a child, and the remaining two, including SK45, are undetermined. Conversely, the burials of two skeletons identified by Selinsky as male, SK29 and SK57, contained no pins. While these data are hardly sufficient, they bear witness to a trend that will continue through Hasanlu IVb despite the appearance of a bearded figure wearing garment pins on the Hasanlu Gold Bowl (Porada 1965:98–99, fig. 633:64).

6.9. This type of artifact has been variously identified as a hair or ear ornament, but at Hasanlu and at Dinkha Tepe it occurs exclusively in burials on either or both sides of the skull in the area of the ears (Pizzorno, pers. comm.). There is no reason to suppose it is anything other than an earring. With the exception of Muscarella (1974) and Rubinson (1991), the burials at Dinkha Tepe are largely unpublished. I am grateful to Gabriel Pizzorno for sharing with me the results of his unpublished analysis of the burials at Dinkha Tepe. Similar ornaments are found in burials from the Haftavan IV cemetery (Tala'i and Aliyari 2009: pl. 7); Kordlar Tepe (Lippert 1979: Abb. 15); and Sialk B (Ghirshman 1939: pl. L, Tomb 3; pl. LXXI:S.894d, Tomb 62; pl. LXXII:S.936e, Tomb 66; pl. XCIV:S.1715b).

6.10. A number of examples come from North Cemetery burials assigned to Hasanlu IVb, including HAS64-244, HAS64-245a, HAS64-239, HAS59-104, HAS50-105, HAS64-71, and HAS62-944.

6.11. Hasanlu Excavation Notebook 5, 1958, p. 10 (Burial Sheet).

6.12. At the north end of BBII, for example, in Room 5, SK136 was found with two strands of carnelian beads and shell (HAS58-532a) and SK255 was found with six strands of carnelian, shell, bronze, frit, and bone beads (HAS62-421). Most of the shells found in the destruction levels of Hasanlu IVb, however, were held in the storeroom above Room 7 in the upper level of BBII (Reese 1989:82–83, Table 1), a structure which Dyson identified as a temple (1989a:120–24). The ritual or religious significance of such shell collections is suggested by their appearance as offerings and in foundation deposits off religious structures at a range of Mesopotamian and Iranian sites (Reese 1989:83).

6.13. This position was argued convincingly by Rubinson (1991:398) with respect to the burial furnishings from Tomb B10a B27 at Dinkha.

6.14. See Tucker 1992:158–60, 168ff. For the distribution of Arcularia shells in the region, see Reese 1992: Appendix A, particularly Table 3.

6.15. Tucker states that Arcularia shells, for example, were found in a hoard in the later Ishtar Temple at Assur, as well as in a deposit on the acropolis at Nimrud (1992:168).

6.16. This practice is found in 6th century BC burials in the Levant (Wolff 2002:136), as well as in 5th century BC tombs at Pichnvari on the Black Sea in Georgia (Vickers and Kakhidze 2001:68). According to Stevens (1991:227), the Greek historian Hesychius believed that the practice of placing coins in the mouth of the deceased originated in Persian Asia Minor. The notion of presenting gifts or payment to underworld deities to ensure passage into the afterlife is also found in the Mesopotamian myth of the Descent of Ishtar, in which Ishtar must divest herself of articles of adornment in order to pass through the seven gates to the underworld (Wolkstein and Kramer 1983:51–90).

6.17. For examples of these objects and an analysis of their significance in a particular context, see Fokkens, Achterkamp, and Kuijpers 2008:109–40.

6.18. Gabe Pizzorno (pers. comm.) reports that numerous burials from Dinkha contain flat blades which curve up at the tip, similar to HAS57-129, and that the distribution of these objects appears to be unrelated to the gender of the interred.

6.19. The literature on the archaeology and material culture of childhood is rich and expanding (see in particular Derevenski 2000). According to Koji Mizoguchi, in his analysis of a cemetery in the Fukouka prefecture dating to the Yayoi period: "The terminated life of a child and the unrealized potential, unfulfilled predictions and expectations of parents and other adult members of the community made the dead child a uniquely powerful symbol. The mobilisation of the child as a symbol was enhanced by the sense of individual and communal loss and the way in which the death of a child problematised the self-identity of the parent and the other adult carers in a manner which life-course transitions of the living did not. Adults acquired their own self-identity with reference to children and by acknowledging the existence of children within society. The death of a child therefore required the resolution of adult identity through the situation of the dead child and the living adult within the community of lineage" (Mizoguchi 2000:149).

6.20. These phenomena are extraordinarily complex and manifest themselves in ways that are chronologically and culturally specific. In Turkmenistan during the late 3rd–early 2nd millennium BC, infants under the age of 1 and middle-aged and older women have the poorest burial assemblages, while men in their prime have the richest (Alekshin et al. 1983). In early Anglo-Saxon England, children are treated in burial rites as poor adults, albeit with notable exceptions (Crawford 2000). Separate burial areas for young children are found in Etruria (Becker 2007) and segregation by age and gender has been reported at Haftavan IV (Tala'i and Aliyari 2009:12ff.).

6.21. Schwartz and Curvers (1992:401) suggest that in the late 3rd millennium BC burials at Tell el-Raqā'I in northern Mesopotamia, "the distinction between simple unfurnished children's graves and relatively rich graves with mudbrick constructions may imply the existence of social stratification."

6.22. This phenomenon is attested in Alekshin et al. 1983.

6.23. The iron ring was embedded in a stack of four rings, the other three of which are bronze. Mentioned first by Dyson (1965:196), the ring is described by Pigott (1977:223) as "the only iron artifact presently known to have come from a well stratified Iron I context in Azerbaijan." Reassigning this ring to a Hasanlu IVb burial is warranted archaeologically; it makes sense in terms of the chronological distribution of iron artifacts in the region, and stacked rings do not generally appear at Hasanlu until Period IVb.

6.24. Gabriel Pizzorno (pers. comm.) reports that 12 torques were found in burials at Dinkha. Torques are entirely missing from the pre-IVb levels at Hasanlu.

6.25. E.g., SK100 and SK111 (Raiciulescu 2011:54).

6.26. Marcus (1993b) describes these three pins as follows: "A. Domed head, incised decoration (alternating bands of vertical and diagonal chevrons on upper shaft), cast, broken at tip; B. Domed head, three registers of vertical chevrons on upper shaft; C. Flat head, cast, bead and reel decoration on upper shaft." These pins unfortunately could not be located. A note in the file refers to UPM93-4-133, which does not match the above descriptions.

6.27. Bracelets found at Atsquri exhibit bulbous terminals that may indicate snake heads as well (Licheli and Rusishvili 2008: fig. 8:1).

6.28. Beaded headbands with metal elements are found in Period IVb Burials SK59, 455, and 503, all of which have been identified by Selinsky (2009) as young adult females. Possible headdresses are also associated with SK19, an older adult of indeterminate sex, and SK100, not sexed. More elaborate headdresses are found in graves identified as female at Haftavan IV (Tala'i and Aliyari 2007:100–102, pl. 3).

6.29. HAS57-132 (TM 10533) was found in SK26 in Operation VI.

6.30. E.g., the Stele of Ashurnasirpal from the Temple of Ninurta, Nimrud, at the British Museum (ME 118805).

6.31. Isaiah 3:18–23, as cited by Pulak (2008:351, catalog no. 217a, b).

6.32. For example, see Parker 1977: no. 41 (Tell al-Rimah); McGovern 1986: fig. 94:1 (Baq'ah); Burney 1972:135 (Haftavan); Negahban 1977: "Group 5," esp. fig. 11: no. 13, figs. 15–16: nos. 17, 18 (Marlik).

6.33. Based on contextual analysis, Marcus (1996a:16, 36–37, catalog nos. 33–42) concludes that these seals served primarily as beads rather than as seals.

6.34. There is, for example, a cluster of male burials from Period IVb in Operation VIh.

6.35. This suggestion is not unprecedented; for instance, Marcus' (1991) assignment of the Hasanlu mosaic glass vessels found in the destruction level of BBII to a mid-2nd millennium BC date of manufacture clearly identifies these objects as heirlooms. Although it is not known if these vessels spent the centuries between their manufacture and their deposition at Hasanlu, the evidence from these burials suggests that it is at least within the realm of possibility.

7

Conclusions

Ebenso unabdingbar ist eine Vorlage der Siedlungskeramik aus Hasanlu V, damit die Eisenzeit I nicht nur anhand von Grabkeramik aus Dinkha Tepe III definiert wird. Auch würde erst eine phasenspezifische Publikation der Keramik von Hasanlu VI bis IVC-A es erlauben, feinchronologisch enger benachbarte Komplexe aufeinander zu beziehen.

— Dittmann 1990:136–37

Following the approach cogently argued for by Dittmann, we see the later 2nd millennium BC at Hasanlu and Dinkha in a new light: MBW emerges no later than the mid-2nd millennium and is rooted in MBA traditions regardless of whether such traditions are viewed as indigenous to northwestern Iran or typical of northeastern Mesopotamia and the southern Caucasus. Previous scholars who have examined this phenomenon have cited changes in the MBW ceramic horizon, burial practices, and architecture in Ušnu-Solduz as the primary indicators of a major cultural disjunction/migration in the mid-2nd millennium BC. At the present time I see little evidence to support this. Earlier theories and the attendant spatio-temporal constructs underpinning them appear to be incoherent; in part this stems from biases inherent in the Hasanlu Project's methodologies and the available datasets. This situation was rooted in, and subsequently magnified by, the espousal of a migrationist theoretical stance, which has its genesis in the writings of Arne and Ghirshman. All too often, hypothetical long-range migration routes have speciously followed the spatio-temporal vagaries of pioneering archaeological research and the erratic publication record. Tenuous ties between northwestern Iran and the plateau were highlighted while broader similarities centered on the local MBA and, more generally, on northern Mesopotamia and the Caucasus received little attention. Regional archaeological sequences must be firmly established before grappling with these larger theoretical issues. As Dittmann has stressed with regard to the Grey Ware phenomenon writ large:

Der vermeintliche "genetsiche" Bezug der verschiedenen Manifestationen der diversen grauen Warenproduktionen ist kein inhärenter, sondern nur anhand weniger Formen festzumachen. Alle diese Manifestationen zeigen jedoch auch ein Fülle von Merkmalen, die auf Traditionen lokaler Art hinweisen. Die vermeintlichen Homogenität ist eine Chimäre und besteht nur in der Färbung der Ware und ist ein Konstrukt anhand weniger in den verschiedenen Regionen übereinstimmender oder ähnlicher Formtypen, die als typisch herausgestellt, ein "offensichtlichen," direkten Bezug vermitteln. Betrachtet man die bekannten Gesamtassemblages, so überwiegen, erwartungsgemäß, die Unterschiede zwischen den Regionen. Die lokale Tradition ist oftmals mangels Grabungen aufgrund von unbekannten spätbronzezeitlichen [herein Middle Bronze Age]

Aspekten nicht definiert. Dies bedeutet a priori jedoch nicht, daß sie potentiell nicht vorhanden sind. Grau polierte Ware als Produkt hat im Nordost-Iran eine lange tradition, und diese, vor allem thoreutisch beeinflußte Ware, hatte sicher einen hohen Stellenwert. Dies könnte ein Hinweis darauf sein, daß dieses Produkt langsam in Regionen, wo diese Tradition nicht bestand, aufgenommen, imitiert und weiter entwickelt wurde. (1990:134–35)

I would add only that, to an even greater extent, the same processes and time depth apply to northern Mesopotamian and Transcaucasian cultural influences in northwestern Iran.

The previous definition of the Iron I as applied to Ušnu-Solduz, a pastiche of material which spans 600 years, can no longer be maintained: it is in fact at least three periods. The newly defined MBIII (Hasanlu VIa) fills the gap that previously led researchers to interpret the appearance of the MBW horizon as a punctuated cultural replacement or as an abrupt cultural change. This gap or break is artificial and additional research is yet needed to improve the precision of our chronology. The Terminal MBII and MBIII form a transitional period, which saw the development of the Early MBW horizon in northwestern Iran, characterized by strong regional variations that were to some extent reduced over time. This effectively turns the previous interpretation of the development of the EWGW and LWGW horizons on its head—Young had originally argued for homogeneity, attendant on the arrival of a new population(s), followed by regional diversification. The material correlates posited for the EWGW horizon do not arrive fully developed at once; rather they appear gradually and specific forms and styles of ceramics and other artifact categories often can be linked to the Terminal MBII (17th century BC). Others develop later. A certain degree of uniformity and a distinct regional character gradually develop in the material culture of northwest Iran in the Iron I (Hasanlu IVc) and Iron II (Hasanlu IVb), in lock-step with increasing sociopolitical complexity.

The MBIII and LBA (Hasanlu V) represent the continuation of strong ties with northern Mesopotamia, especially the Hurro-Mitanni horizon/period in the north and particularly the northeast. Such connections seem far better documented than do links to the east. The LBA ceramic assemblage and other artifact categories largely fit within the LBI and LBII framework known from northeastern Mesopotamia with ties to the southern Caucasus as well, especially at Dinkha Tepe and sites in the northern Lake Urmia Basin. The Terminal MBII and MBIII may be characterized as a time of instability. Again, this parallels developments in northern Mesopotamia. The pattern is reversed by the later LBA, and a process of secondary state formation occurred in the later 15th–14th centuries BC. These patterns continue unabated in the Iron I (Hasanlu IVc), with increasing sociopolitical competition evidenced by the development of citadels and fortifications, destruction levels at Kordlar Tepe and Hasanlu, and heightened militarization attested by, for example, weapons appearing in grave assemblages. The material cultures of the later LBA and Iron I evince ascribed status, heightened social hierarchy, and heterarchy and increased access to precious goods such as glass, marine shell, semi-precious stone, and small amounts of iron. The architecture of the later LBA and Iron I at Hasanlu has its strongest parallels to the west in terms of building plans, niched and buttressed facades, and the use of portico rooms. In short, the later 2nd millennium BC continues patterns established in the early 2nd millennium BC or Hasanlu VIc–VIb and Dinkha V–IV.

To conclude, it is useful to review the findings of this study point by point with regard to the overall dataset, ceramics, architecture, graves and archaeological chronology and periodization, and cultural processes.

Biases and Weak Points in the Dataset

The strong Mesopotamian influences at Hasanlu and Dinkha exhibited in the material culture of the MBA and LBA complicate cross-sequence comparisons with neighboring regions, foremost in the list being the northern Lake Urmia Basin. This also suggests that the Hasanlu sequence—based almost entirely on materials from Hasanlu and Dinkha—might not be wholly representative of Ušnu-Solduz. We lack excavations at smaller sites and at sites further removed from important lines of communication.

The only large-scale excavation of an occupation deposit relevant to defining the MBIII and early LBA at Hasanlu is the U22 Sounding. Later 2nd millennium BC deposits were encountered in soundings on the Low Mound but were not adequately recorded.

The Control Sounding at Dinkha is the only stratified, seemingly continuous MBII to early LBA sequence we currently have for the southern Lake Urmia Basin.

The "trash deposit" of Dinkha, which represents stratified assemblages crucial to understanding the MBIII and early LBA, was selectively published and was not used in revising the Hasanlu sequence.

The Early MBW deposit at Hasanlu, Strata 9–10 of the U22 Sounding, was contaminated: a potential MBIII deposit was mixed with the early LBA assemblage along with later intrusive material in an unidentified pit(s) of the later LBA and Iron I.

The Hasanlu U22 Sounding shows no evidence of a Terminal MBII deposit, although such material is present at Dinkha and in a grave at Hasanlu. The MBII deposit in the U22 Sounding predates the Terminal MBII. Given the differences that are manifest in the ceramics of the early LBA at Dinkha as compared to Hasanlu, one might predict similar disparity between the two sites for the Terminal MBII and MBIII.

Terminal MBII and MBIII graves at Hasanlu were lumped together and described as "Hasanlu V." The researchers were unable to distinguish burnished grey ware in these assemblages from EWGW *sensu* Young (1963, 1965).

Material of Hasanlu IVc was lumped with "Hasanlu V". This had the detrimental effect of making "Hasanlu V," EWGW, and the "Iron I" appear to be far more developed (homogeneous) in terms of the putative ceramic assemblage when selectively published.

Hasanlu IVc, a later addition to the Hasanlu sequence, was first defined as a "universal" architectural phase in the monumental buildings of the Iron II citadel but was given an absolute timespan (i.e., a subperiod designation); the implications of doing so for "Hasanlu V" as originally defined, however, were not pursued. The result was a hollow subperiod, Period IVc, which obscured the late 2nd millennium BC.

Assemblages of isolatable late Period IVc and early Hasanlu IVb date were not analyzed to establish trends in the ceramic sequence.

"Early Western Grey Ware"

Wares

Painted Khabur Ware was already in sharp decline in the Terminal MBII (the 17th century BC). Painted ceramics were found in MBIII contexts; they drop out of assemblages in Ušnu-Solduz in the early LBA. Painted wares were still produced to the north, including Kordlar Painted Ware attested at Kordlar and Gijlar and the painted wares of the Salmas region and points further north.

INAA analysis of sherds from Dinkha reveals KW and Early MBW were produced using identical clay sources (Bedal et al. 1995). Khabur Ware seems to have been imported to Hasanlu from Dinkha.

Burnished monochrome ceramics are well attested in Terminal MBII deposits at Dinkha. This material is not MBA Grey Ware and likely represents the direct precursor of the Early MBW of the MBIII and LBA.

Burnished ceramics, especially grey ware, occur in LBA Mitanni and related assemblages in northern Mesopotamia. Future research should focus on analyzing possible connections.

Urmia Ware and late variations of KW occur with Early MBW and Incised and Impressed MBW at Dinkha and with Early MBW at Hasanlu. Nuzi Ware is completely absent in Ušnu-Solduz, as are other markers of the LBA in northern Mesopotamia such as red-rimmed bowls and animal motifs in the painted ware.

Varieties of impressed grey ware occur at Nuzi and other northern Mesopotamian sites. These wares may be related to similar material in northwestern Iran. Impressed grey ware with white in-filling occurs in Mitanni assemblages, especially at Nuzi. The ware is rare at Mitanni sites in the west.

Varieties of impressed monochrome smoothed and burnished ceramics with white in-filling similar to Incised and Impressed MBW at Dinkha Tepe occur in the southern Caucasus in the Lchashen-Metsamor horizon.

Vessel forms typical of Early MBW occur in Urmia Ware at Geoy Tepe and in the related painted wares of the southern Caucasus, particularly in Nakhichevan. There is some overlap between Urmia Ware forms and Early MBW and Incised and Impressed MBW forms at Dinkha in the MBIII.

Two incompatible ceramic typologies were developed to analyze the ceramics of the early and late 2nd millennium BC in Ušnu-Solduz, respectively, and intervening material was not subjected to rigorous analysis—in fact, some material seems never to have been analyzed at all. This magnified perceived differences between the "Bronze Age" and "Iron Age."

The ware typology used for the "Early Western Grey Ware" horizon at Hasanlu masked variations in firing color and surface treatments in burnished, smoothed, and slipped wares, creating a homogenous "Grey Ware" category and splitting related material into other ware types. One can discern a teleological bias here deriving from early findings at sites such as Sialk and Hissar. The assemblage, and concomitantly the EWGW horizon, was deemed fully developed and distinct upon "arrival" based on a perceived degree of homogeneity in ware type and the supposed ubiquity of certain type fossils. Biased taxonomic methods, a lack of chronological precision, the absence of discrete indicators of diachronic change, and artificial gaps in the sequence, however, all act to nullify these findings. Put another way, the resultant analytical unit was a 600-year pastiche—EWGW—spread across northern and western Iran, which permitted an unacceptable degree of interpretive latitude in discerning synchronic and diachronic/directional linkages in cross-sequence comparisons.

Monochrome Burnished Ware in northwestern Iran is contemporary to, or perhaps even earlier than, various grey wares found to the east, for instance at Khurvin (vanden Berghe 1964), Gheytaryeh (Curtis 1989; Kambaxsh-Fard 1969, 1970), and Sialk V (Ghirshman 1939; Tourovetz 1989).

Monochrome Burnished Ware develops out of local MBA ceramic traditions; additional research is needed, however, if we are to better understand the timing and geographic extent of the origins of this ceramic horizon. In this regard, we see a pattern similar to that noted by Piller (2003–2004) in north-central Iran in describing the interplay between Sagzabad Ware and Central Grey Ware. Broadly construed, Grey Ware assemblages in northern and western Iran develop gradually and evince links to local MBA traditions.

The ware typology developed for the MBA at Dinkha typologically split monochrome burnished ceramics that were not MBA "Grey Ware" into unrelated types. These types were not the focus of the analyses.

The Terminal MBII assemblage from Dinkha was excavated after the formal definition of EWGW had been established and little or no attempt was made to investigate connections between the two.

The researchers involved in the pioneering (and only) studies of ceramics in Ušnu-Solduz, Carol Kramer and T. Cuyler Young, moved to other research projects, leaving our understanding of the topic in stasis.

Vessel Forms

Terminal MBII vessel forms continued to exhibit connections to northern Mesopotamia, as well as connections with transitional assemblages known from Sialk A, the northern Lake Urmia Basin (e.g., at Haftavan Late VIB), and north-central Iran. The Terminal MBII and MBIII constitute a period of normative change/evolution in material culture, that is, there remains some measure of continuity and no punctuated break or replacement.

All types of so-called worm bowls, a large, open bowl form, are widely attested in LBA northern Mesopotamia, northwestern Iran, and the southern Caucasus. The addition of a crescent or double crescent is a western Iranian and southern Caucasian attribute.

In Ušnu-Solduz, LBA and early Iron Age drinking vessels can be traced to MBA forms that are also well attested in Mesopotamia. Middle Bronze III and LBA tankards and shouldered beakers are directly related to contemporary drinking vessels in northern Mesopotamia, and particularly to assemblages attributable to the late Old Babylonian, Kassite, and Mitanni periods. Middle Assyrian links are less common. The addition of handles and high pedestal bases to shouldered beakers in western Iranian assemblages represents a regional variation.

Bridgeless-spouts are not well attested until the later LBA and are extremely rare in occupation deposits and graves at Hasanlu. This serves as a cautionary tale regarding the use of the Dinkha III graves to explicate the so-called EWGW horizon. In comparison to Hasanlu, Dinkha exhibits more links to the northern Lake Urmia Basin and Nakhichevan in the MBIII, LBA, and Iron I.

Architecture and Urban Form

Columned-hall architecture is not attested at Hasanlu until the later LBA—centuries after the development of the MBW ceramic assemblage.

It is invalid to state that architectural forms typical of the MBW horizon at Hasanlu are significantly different from earlier periods since we have no meaningful, coherent architectural plans from earlier periods at Hasanlu—that is, from the MBA. The architecture of Dinkha IV cannot be assumed to be representative of northwest Iran.

Hasanlu was almost certainly fortified in the later LBA and certainly in the Iron I and Iron II.

Portico rooms form an integral part of the monumental structures of Hasanlu starting in the Iron I. Our dataset pertaining to the LBA is currently too limited to allow comment on the origins of these monumental entries.

The urban layout and basic architectural units of the Hasanlu citadel known so well from the Period IVb destruction level first appear in the later LBA.

Mortuary Practices

One may hardly speak of intramural burial as typical of the MBII given that Dinkha provides our only unequivocal evidence and the site can hardly be seen as typical of the period in northwestern Iran.

Extramural burial as a marker of the MBW horizon has been applied rather loosely. The known graves of the MBA, LBA, and early Iron Age at Hasanlu were *all* located on the Low Mound and were not directly associated with architecture, although LBA and Iron I architecture was present in some areas of the Low Mound, such as in Operation V. No conclusive evidence of Period VI occupation was found on the Low Mound. Evidence of MBW occupation was found in areas with MBW graves at Dinkha. In the various publications of the Hasanlu Project, despite a great deal of equivocal evidence, the importance and ubiquity of extramural cemeteries was stringently maintained through a pattern of circular logic: If there were MBW graves in an area with architecture, then that area was a cemetery and the contemporaneity of the architecture was dismissed since MBW graves were *a priori* extramural. Additional interpretive wiggle room was provided by the ambiguity inherent in the definition, or lack thereof, of "extramural." Evidence of LBA and early Iron Age architecture on the Hasanlu Low Mound was often missed, or it was ignored with regard to the "extramural" status of the contemporary burials. Moreover, the extramural status of Hasanlu's MBW graves is inconclusive since we do not know where the fringes of Hasanlu's lower settlements were located in any given period. The modern villages of Hasanlu and Aminlu along with modern agricultural activities have obscured the borders of the ancient settlement, and Dyson has frequently noted that occupation likely extended beyond the borders of the site as defined on the topographic map as the mounded area bounded by modern canals, villages, and roads.

Using the definition developed and employed by the excavators, the Period VI and VII cemeteries at Hasanlu are as "extramural" as those of Periods IV and V. No graves were found in direct association with architecture—that is, they were *cut into* earlier Period VII occupation deposits.

The extramural/intramural dichotomy (Dyson 1965:196) in burial patterns is dubious at best as a marker of the MBW horizon in Ušnu-Solduz and, I would argue, for northwestern Iran more broadly. The idea ultimately stems from Ghirshman's discovery of such cemeteries at Giyan and especially Sialk. Extramural cemeteries occur at Geoy Tepe and Khurvin—important sites from which the Hasanlu Project drew comparanda in its early years (Dyson 1958:32; Young 1965:70). The distinction seems to be imposed on Hasanlu and Dinkha and one again senses a teleological bias.

Isolated and "unattached" cemeteries—that is, cemeteries removed from settlements—are typical of the MBW horizon in the Lake Urmia region and northwest Iran in general. The existence of such unattached cemeteries, as well as new settlement patterns and urban forms typical of the MBW horizon—less densely occupied centers characterized by fortified citadels—may be indicative of the shift from Bronze Age economies with highly integrated agropastoralism to LBA and early Iron Age economies emphasizing higher degrees of transhumance. These early Iron Age economies were likely driven by the increasing importance of raising large numbers of horses, which had profound effects on patterns of seasonal transhumance, transport, and military tactics. Seen another way, the MBW horizon may evince the early stages of pastoral nomadism, as opposed to the shorter-range transhumance practiced in the Near East prior to this.

A wide range of burial practices is attested for the MBII in Ušnu-Solduz with a gradual shift to single inhumation burials in the MBIII and LBA and a consequent reduction in the variability of mortuary practices. Some regional differences are nevertheless exhibited within Ušnu-Solduz in the LBA and early Iron Age, as is evidenced by the use of tombs at Dinkha and Geoy Tepe.

Graves of the later LBA and Iron I contain more grave goods and a wider assortment of materials and object classes, suggesting increased access to prestige goods.

The graves of the later LBA and Iron I strongly suggest ascribed status and increased social hierarchy and heterarchy.

Stylistic and formal attributes typical of Iron II weaponry and personal ornament emerge in the later LBA and early Iron I.

Absolute Chronology and Periodization

The cultural affinities and time range of Hasanlu V (1450–1250 BC) and the post-excavation definition of Hasanlu IVc require a rethinking of the periodization currently applied to northwestern Iran. Hasanlu V should be equated with the LBA. Other scholars have expressed the view that this period is technically the LBA or that it should be completely redefined (Haerinck 1988:64n1; Kroll 1994a:116; Lippert 1979:134; Muscarella 1974:79; 1994a:140; 1994b:284; Overlaet 2003:6, fig. 3). Accordingly, Hasanlu IVc should be designated the Iron I. This redefinition of the Iron I designation is similar to the conclusion reached by Overlaet for Luristan (2003:6, fig. 3). Similar to this study, Overlaet's distinction between the Iron I and Late Bronze is based on ceramics (Overlaet 2003:1, 8, fig. 3, 236ff.); however, he detects a "clear breach with the earlier Bronze age cultures" (Overlaet 2003:1). This revised system corresponds to the use of chronological terminology in northeastern Mesopotamia, the region to which Hasanlu and the southern Lake Urmia Basin were most closely tied from Hasanlu X/Hajji Firuz Period (Hassuna) until the start of the Achaemenid period (Hasanlu IIIa). Concomitantly, Hasanlu VI should be called the MBA and Hasanlu VII the EBA. Kramer was well aware of the singular use of terminology employed by the Hasanlu Project for the "Bronze Age" and "Iron Age" and preferred the use of "Middle Bronze Age" for Dinkha IV and Hasanlu VI (Hamlin 1971:256–57).

We must still be cautious with regard to the absolute dating of Periods V and VI since this part of the Hasanlu sequence is based on the radiocarbon determinations from two sites of potentially different character. We have seen that the earliest radiocarbon dates from Hasanlu "Period V" derive from insecure contexts, but what do the radiocarbon dates from Dinkha tell us? *Hasanlu "Period V" was defined on the basis of ceramics from graves at Hasanlu and Dinkha, but was dated using radiocarbon determinations from loosely associated and unassociated occupation strata at both sites.* We have seen that the ceramics from the lower "trash deposit" at Dinkha belong to the MBIII and early LBA, and the bulk of the graves formerly designated as "Dinkha III," critical in verifying the archaeological definition of "Hasanlu V," are attributable to late Period V and Period IVc. The dating of the end of Hasanlu VI/Dinkha IV (and the start of Hasanlu V/Dinkha III, which is now Hasanlu Period VIa) was largely based on radiocarbon dates from the terminal occupation of Dinkha IV and the overlying trash levels, which contained Early MBW (MBIII and early LBA).

Cultural Processes

This re-designation of Hasanlu V and IVc is not simply a matter of semantics; it helps to refocus attention on northern Mesopotamia and Transcaucasia, and it highlights the southern Lake Urmia Basin's position on the peripheries of these areas, linking them. Scholars investigating MBW origins have previously strained themselves to find cultural affinities between northeastern and northwestern Iran indicative of migration patterns or cultural diffusion while neglecting all but the most obvious links to northeastern Mesopotamia and the Caucasus.

There is no conclusive evidence in the southern Lake Urmia Basin for a punctuated wave migration of newcomers ending the "Bronze Age" and initiating the MBW horizon and the Iron Age. From a theoretical standpoint, such an event would be wholly astonishing. As David Anthony succinctly observes, " 'Cultures' do not migrate" (1990:908). Migration is a selective, carefully planned, and goal-oriented process (ibid.). Nevertheless, I would caution that migration cannot simply be eschewed as a cultural mechanism operating in antiquity (Anthony 1990, 1997; Burmeister 2000). Migration is a common demographic force in most populations, but recent research has emphasized that it does not operate in the manner the Iranian Migrationist Paradigm envisioned—that is, as a punctuated, high magnitude, inexorable force driving sudden population/culture replacements. On the one hand, the textual record of Assyria makes clear that Iranian populations were in the Zagros no later than the reign of Shalmaneser III. On the other, we see that attempts to link their sudden arrival to the MBW horizon hinged on the initial and incorrect absolute dating of this horizon's inception in the late 2nd millennium BC and on an unproven break/gap in the archaeological sequence. The hunt for early Medes and Persians, as it were, should be adjusted accordingly. Whether northwestern Iran should even be a focus for such lines of research is well beyond the bounds of the current volume (Young 1985).

The gradual cultural changes of the mid 2nd millennium BC in the Lake Urmia Basin might be linked to migration streams—I would argue we should think in terms of the effects of both structured migration and return migration, emigration and immigration. Focusing on the contemporary cultural processes documented for northeastern Mesopotamia should provide new avenues of research. Nevertheless, we need a great deal more scientifically collected evidence from the mid 2nd millennium southern Lake Urmia Basin to begin to address these issues, as well as efforts to fill gaps in our understanding of northeastern Iraq, particularly the area of Rowanduz/Soran.

Hasanlu VIa –IVc lay at the periphery of the Hurro-Mitanni and, later, the Middle Assyrian kingdoms. For the sake of argument, if one chooses to seek migrationist or diffusionist causation for the shift from Hasanlu VI to V (*sensu* Dyson), why not first hypothesize that the gradual development of the MBW archaeological horizon was influenced by migration streams (Burmeister 2000) bringing select groups of Indo-Iranians to and from the Hurrian purlieu (Parpola 1999)? The anticipated answer with regard to the work of previous researchers would be that Nuzi Ware, the all-important marker of Mitanni influence, is unknown in the Lake Urmia Basin (pots not equating with people aside). At the same time, late Old Babylonian and LBA band-painted buff ware (late KW) is attested. Previously, this received some attention from Kramer using the source material available at the time. Hrouda, in his study of the painted wares of the MBA and LBA, dubbed such late band-painted jars as "younger" Khabur Ware (1957:23, 25, pl. 8); these vessels were without provenience. In pursuing the issue of Khabur Ware's end date and the nature of this "younger Khabur Ware," Kramer refers the reader to comparisons with Tell Billa 3 (Speiser 1933: pl. LX), Tell Aqrah (El-Amin and Mallowan 1950: pl. IX:8, 13, 14), Tell Fakhariyeh (McEwan et al. 1958), and her Dinkha jar types 1–3 (Hamlin 1971:165). All of these sites save Dinkha have Nuzi Ware occurring with KW: Kramer believed such assemblages were either transitional/ late KW or were simply the product of faulty methods (ibid.). Kramer sums up: "there are as yet no sites with good internal evidence for dating the end of Habur Ware. Perhaps the best dating indicator is the occurrence at several sites of Nuzi Ware overlying Habur Ware…Nuzi Ware dates to the 16th and 15th centuries" (Hamlin 1971:254).

The lack of Nuzi Ware in northwestern Iran surely influenced the Hasanlu researchers to interpret a gap in the Hasanlu sequence and to shift their attention away from Mesopotamia when interpreting "Hasanlu V." The MBIII now fills this gap, and it would appear to be a period characterized by closer ties with the northern Lake Urmia Basin and the southern Caucasus. Other elements of Hasanlu VIa and V, however, such as early MBW vessel forms and cylinder seals, attest to continuing connections with LBA northern Mesopotamia. Moreover, elite items from Hasanlu IVb contexts interpreted as heirlooms from "Period V," such as the famous gold bowl, a mosaic glass beaker, and a small number of inscribed objects, to name but a few, evince close ties to successive Hurrian- and Assyrian-dominated northeastern Mesopotamia, as well as Babylonia. As we continue to re-evaluate the Late Bronze and Iron I of northwestern Iran, we must look closely at recent work on these time periods in northern Mesopotamia and the Caucasus. We must not let "Grey Ware" cloud our thinking.

Appendix I

Archaeological Survey and Reconnaissance of Ušnu-Solduz

The following site catalog compiles the work of a number of different researchers who conducted archaeological reconnaissance and survey in the Gadar River Valley. The first fairly comprehensive work was that of Aurel Stein, who carried out reconnaissance and soundings in 1936 at a number of sites (Stein 1940). Following this pioneering work little survey was completed until the start of the Hasanlu Project in 1956. In that year, Robert Dyson traveled to Iran to search out a site for excavation and visited a number of locations, working with Sadegh Samimi and Jason Paige. He conducted a four-month survey, collecting a large amount of material, mostly surface sherds, for the UPM. This work began with daytrips made from Tehran with Colonel Pete Smith. The first phase of this survey focused on the areas east and west of Tehran in the vicinity of Chandar and points south. Dyson visited Tepe Sialk, Khorvin, Chandar, Cheshmeh Ali, Tepe Hissar, Tureng Tepe, Shah Tepe, Hotu and Belt Caves, Qaramini, and sites west of Gurgan around Gunbad, such as Chia Ganuz. The second phase of this project focused on the area from Hamadan west to Kermanshah and north to Saqquz (Ziwiyeh) to the southern shore of Lake Urmia and east to Tabriz. A total of 45 sites were visited. After a one-week mapping and section-drawing project in Hamadan, Dyson went on to Hasanlu, where he spent a short season conducting soundings (Dyson 1956, 1957).

In 1957, Dyson formally started the Hasanlu Project and excavations began at the site in earnest (Dyson 1958). He also carried out soundings at Pisdeli Tepe and visited and collected materials from sites in the southern Lake Urmia Basin (Dyson and Young 1960). Reconnaissance continued through the late 1950s. No systematic survey was completed until 1962, when T. Cuyler Young carried out a more thorough cataloging of sites in Ušnu-Solduz, but the results of this work were not published and, to my knowledge, there are virtually no notes. Young produced a map of Ušnu-Solduz and attributed general chronological periods to the sites based on an early version of the Hasanlu Sequence. Young fairly obviously revisited sites mentioned by Stein. In 1966, Regnar Kearton conducted a small survey of the Ušnu valley, but again this work was not published. His results were incorporated into another survey carried out in 1970 by William Sumner. Vincent Pigott completed some surveying in 1974 and finally, in 1977, Mary Voigt implemented a survey, some of the details of which were included in her dissertation and monograph on Hajji Firuz Tepe (Voigt 1976, 1983).

More systematic and scientific surveys were conducted by the Italians in Ušnu (Pecorella and Salvini 1984). Wolfram Kleiss and Stephan Kroll also conducted a long-term survey project in Ušnu-Solduz and surrounding regions (Kleiss and Kroll 1977, 1979, 1992).

Map of Solduz

The map of Solduz used in this volume (Fig. 1.3) was produced using the Russian Map Series Iran, Eastern and Western Azerbaijan, subset sheets J-38-103-4

(Hasanlu), J-38-104-3 (Yadgarlu), J-38-115-2 (Naqadeh), and J-38-116-1 (Qarakishlan). The scale of these maps is 1:50,000 and they were originally produced in 1944 and corrected in 1973–74. This map series captures conditions in the region in the period just following the sedentarization and settlement of various transhumant pastoralist groups. Information on these maps was cross-checked and updated using SPOT satellite images.

Site Catalog

This site catalog combines the results of all previous researchers. One objective is to establish a single numbering system for sites in the Ušnu-Solduz region and a standardized transliteration of names. To this end, the catalog follows the conventions established by Kroll for the Lake Urmia region (1994a).

The designation of chronological periods is complicated by a number of factors, chief among them the differences between the various periodization schema used by previous researchers. Another concern is the variability that can be glossed over with too general a system of period designations. Early Bronze Age sites in Ušnu-Solduz, for example, might be said to belong to the ETC tradition in the main, or might manifest the POW horizon, or some combination of both. Since Ušnu-Solduz truly was a crossroad of cultural influences in antiquity, contemporary sites might differ substantially in their archaeological cultures. The same holds to an even higher degree for the Lake Urmia Basin more broadly, as there are often pronounced differences between the various subregions, particularly between the northern and southern ends of the lake. To deal with such variability, period designations are often provided with subdesignations, e.g., "EBA (ETC)" to convey as precise an understanding as is possible as to how chronological assessments have been made. Sites are listed here alphabetically and a concordance of site names with site numbers is also provided.

Adgamlu I (Var. Ajamlu, Solduz Valley)

Location: probably 36°59' 13" N, 45°28' 31" E
Map Reference: U20
Periods: Young/Sumner I
Survey Number: Young/Sumner 8
Bibliography: —
Comments: Little data is available for this site, which lies somewhere along the road between the villages of Aqah Biglu and Hajji Firuz.

Adgamlu II (Var. Ajamlu, Solduz Valley)

Location: 36°58' 21" N, 45°26' 59" E
Map Reference: S22
Periods: Young/Sumner I
Survey Number: Young/Sumner 20
Bibliography: —
Comments: This site is located on the southeast side of the modern village of Adgamlu and the Dalma hill range and on the north side of the Gadar Çay. Its size could not be determined due to the modern occupation.

Adgamlu III (Var. Ajamlu, Solduz Valley)

Location: Approximately 36°58' 24" N, 45°25' 54" E
Map Reference: Q22
Periods: Sumner I/II, VIII
Survey Number: —
Bibliography: —
Comments: This small site was found by Sumner in 1970 but was not assigned a Survey Number. Sumner Survey Notes: "This is not TCY [T. Cuyler Young Site] 20. 40 paces in diameter, low rocky. Riverside road to Adgamlu crosses mound. Ca. 1 mile northwest of village, below hill fort–mound (which is above Dalma village)."

Agabaglu (Solduz Valley)

Location: Approximately 36°59' 30" N, 45°29' 18" E
Map Reference: V20
Periods: Sumner VIII
Survey Number: Sumner 42. Possibly Voigt 77-15 (Agha Bali)
Bibliography: —
Comments: Sumner Survey Notes: "Round, 75 paces diameter, very low, smooth contour (ca. 2 m high) with very little disturbance. Between Shonqar and T. Mohammadyar near Shonqar."

Agrab Tepe (Var. Dalma 2, Solduz Valley)

Location: 36°59' 2" N, 45°25' 37" E
Map Reference: Q21
Periods: Kroll Iron II–III, Iron III (Urartian), Sum-

ner IIIa-b
Survey Number: Kroll NQ 49, Young/Sumner 12
Bibliography: BIB-IRAN I:2163–2172; BIB-IRAN II; BIB-IRAN III; Kleiss 1976:31, fig. 8; Kroll 1994a, 2005:69; Muscarella 1973:47–63
Comments: This small fortress (roughly 0.50 ha) is located southwest of Hasanlu near the village of Dalma. Dyson Survey Notes (1957) with addenda: "Dalma village three small tepes, one suspected to be a tumulus mound, one later excavated (1964) and named Agrab Tepe [Dalma 2], third one excavated in 1961 and named Dalma Tepe. Young found no sherds in 1962." Kroll: "Small fort mainly from Iron III period. In Muscarella's publication Groovy Pottery is illustrated (Muscarella 1973: fig. 15, 10–11). He also speaks of of 'Burnished Grey Ware'" (2005:69). Muscarella divides the Iron III use of the site into three phases. Kroll has pointed out there are also Iron II ceramics from the site, both "Rillenkeramik" and Grey Ware (MBW), and thus the earliest period of occupation should be moved back to the 9th century BC (Kroll 1994a). Kleiss connected the site to the Urartians based on the architecture, which is not strongly supported by the ceramic evidence, which find its primary comparanda at Bastam (Kroll 1994a). Kroll notes strong connections to Ziwiyeh and Zendan-i Suleiman (1994a).

Ajam Tepe (Solduz Valley)

Location: Approximately 36°56' 59" N, 45°26' 21" E
Map Reference: R24
Periods: Sumner III or later
Survey Number: Sumner no number
Bibliography: —
Comments: This site was not plotted on any map. I have used compass bearings recorded by Sumner from the site to other points in the valley to determine its general location southeast of the modern village of Mehmandar. Sumner Survey Notes: "Double topped, low mound—almost sterile. Donut hole excavated in top. 80 paces diameter."

Aliabad (Ušnu Valley)

Location: —
Map Reference: —
Periods: Kroll Prehistoric, Medieval
Survey Number: Kroll NQ 25

Bibliography: Stein 1940:365
Comments: Small tepe around 3 m high located east or southeast of Ušnu and west of Sodja.

Aqah Biglu [South] (Var. Agah Baglu, Solduz Valley)

Location: 36°58' 25" N, 45°28' 19" E
Map Reference: U22
Periods: Young I–Chalcolithic, Sumner I, II?, VIII
Survey Number: Young/Sumner 7. Possibly Voigt 77-15 (Agha Bali)
Bibliography: —
Comments: Site size was estimated at ca. 1–1.50 ha using SPOT imagery. The tepe appears to consist of a high mound and low mound in satellite images, which matches Sumner's description. Sumner Survey Notes: "240 paces circumference. Rather tall (not as tall as Hajji Firuz). Yellow mound. Some earth removal (very little). Has graveyard on W, S, and E. Lower skirts with carved gravestones." See also Agabaglu for a similarly named site.

Asember (Ušnu Valley)

Location: —
Map Reference: —
Periods: Kroll Iron III (Urartian), Iron IV?
Survey Number: Kroll NQ 10, Pecorella and Salvini 122
Bibliography: Kleiss 1971:62–63, fig. 13, pl. 8 no.3; Kroll 1976:91–92; Pecorella and Salvini 1984:173, fig. 23 F9 No. 122
Comments: Small fortress 8 km northeast of Ušnu. The architecture and ceramic finds indicate a likely date of construction for this fortified enclosure in the Urartian period. There are hints of later use of the site as well, likely Achaemenid or Parthian.

Badr-ed Din, Tepe

See below, Nalus Tepe I

Bagan Gali (Var. Bigolun Qaleh, Beygimkale, Solduz Valley)

Location: 36°55' 45" N, 45°28' 41" E
Map Reference: U27

Periods: Young Islamic, Pre-Islamic Buff, Sumner I
Survey Number: Young/Sumner 28
Bibliography: —
Comments: Tepe measuring 5.1 ha and standing at least 7–9 m above the surrounding plain. The tepe lies just east of the village of the same name.

Balakchi Tepe (Var. Balakche Tepe, Balukhi, Qabrestan, Solduz Valley)

Location: 36°55' 22" N, 45°22' 48" E
Map Reference: L26
Periods: Dyson IX, Young IX, Sumner VIII, IX, Kroll Chalcolithic
Survey Number: Kroll NQ 48, Young/Sumner 32, Voigt 77-17
Bibliography: Mahdavi and Bovington 1972:148–51.
Comments: The toponym "Balakchi" was used for more than one site, which has led to some confusion in the survey data with at least three sites bearing the name. This has been resolved here by using compass bearings recorded by Sumner in 1970. This tepe lies just outside the southern limit of modern Naqadeh and northeast of modern Balakchi. Dyson (Survey Notes 1957): "Vicinity of Jal[a]van village at entrance to valley, Kurdish cemetery on tepe. Surface covered in painted Dalma Ware." Dyson (Survey Notes 1958): "South of Nagadeh. Dalma Impressed (Fingertip) Ware, Painted (Red/Orange) Dalma (Balakchi) Ware, Plain Dalma Red Ware, Obsidian." Mahdavi and Bovington analyzed 5 obsidian samples from the site and determined they came from Hassan Dagh in central Anatolia.

Balakchi South/Balakchi B (Solduz Valley)

Location: 36°56' 9" N, 45°22' 44" E
Map Reference: L26
Periods: Dyson I, Sumner III, VIII
Survey Number: Sumner 44
Bibliography: —
Comments: This small tepe was located using compass bearings recorded by Sumner in 1970. Dyson (Survey Notes 1957): "Low rectangular mound a little south of Balakche. Has Islamic plain ware and incised ware." Sumner: "Lower and smaller than TCY Balakchi (TCY [T. Cuyler Young Site] 32). 50 paces diameter."

Balakchi Hill Fort (Solduz Valley)

Location: 36°55' 3" N, 45°20' 59" E
Map Reference: J28
Periods: Hasanlu I
Survey Number: Dyson no number, Sumner no number
Bibliography: —
Comments: This hill fort is located at the center of the east-west stretch of the Balakchi Valley, on a hill at its southern edge. Dyson (Survey Notes 1957): "Islamic fort—Balakche Valley, at a point where the valley turns halfway along the valley. There is a pyramidal hill with the top flattened. Islamic fort has octagonal outer wall, plain ware and rare glazed sherds."

Balestan Tepe (north of Solduz Valley on route to Urmia)

Location: 37°9' 32" N, 45°22' 59" E
Map Reference: L1
Periods: Iron II–III, Medieval
Survey Number: Kroll NQ 54
Bibliography: Kroll 2005:69
Comments: Small tepe in the village of the same name on the Mahabad-Urmia road, 15 km northwest of Haidarabad. Kroll: "Settlement. Kleiss found here several sherds of Grey Ware" (2005:69).

Baranu Tepe (Var. Barani, Baranlu, Sayyid Hammadani, Solduz Valley)

Location: 37°0' 51" N, 45°29' 55" E
Map Reference: W17
Periods: Kroll Neolithic, Early Iron Age; Young I, X, Sumner I, X, Voigt X
Survey Number: Kroll NQ 52, Young/Sumner 5, Voigt 77-8 and 77-9
Bibliography: Kroll 2005:69; Stein 1940:405; Voigt 1983:269, fig. 120
Comments: Two small tepes located 5 km east of Hasanlu with a modern village on the southeast periphery. Kroll: "Settlement. Stein mentioned pottery identical to Hasanlu" (2005:69). Sumner Survey Notes: "Oval mound at North. 140 paces long. This is a very broad, rectangular mound. It is not clear where the prehistoric occupation was. Is this indeed the mound NQ-6 where [Frank] Hole got C14 sample for

[BLANK]? The 140 paces are just a small part, about 1/3, of whole mound and may be the early mound although prehistoric sherds are scattered elsewhere on South mound as well." Apparently there was confusion regarding the date of these sites stemming from two neighboring mounds of the same name being confused with one another. Based on satellite imagery the area of ancient occupation could be as large as 22 ha with multiple regions of interest suggesting a complex, multicomponent site and/or multiple mounds.

Böyük Tepe (Ušnu Valley)

Location: —
Map Reference: —
Periods: —
Survey Number: Kroll NQ21
Bibliography: Pecorella and Salvini 1984:173, fig. 23 F10 No. 123; Stein 1940:367
Comments: Tepe located 4 km west of Dinkha Tepe, measuring 55 m x 28 m, H. 10 m.

Caravansarai (Var. Karavanserai, Solduz Valley)

Location: Approximately 36°57' 53" N, 45°25' 31" E
Map Reference: P23
Periods: Young Chalcolithic, Hasanlu IV–III mixed, Sumner IIIA, IIIb, IV
Survey Number: Young/Sumner 30, Voigt 77-24
Bibliography: —
Comments: This site evidently lies under or near the modern villages of Caravansarai and Tazeh (Toppuzabad) on the right bank of the Gadar River just east of Naqadeh. Young and Sumner provide the general location and the date. On satellite images there are at least three potential tepes in this general area.

Çahrezak (Solduz Valley)

Location: 37°3' 16" N, 45°17' 58" E
Map Reference: E13
Periods: Sumner II
Survey Number: Sumner no number
Bibliography: —
Comments: This small tepe (0.60 ha) is located in the Dilançi Valley. Sumner: "Lot 70-20. Ca. 12 km northwest Hasanlu."

Çali (Solduz Valley)

Location: 37°0' 42" N, 45°27' 57" E
Map Reference: T17
Periods: Young/Sumner I
Survey Number: Young/Sumner 19
Bibliography: —
Comments: This site lies northeast of Hasanlu and is difficult to locate on satellite images due to damage. Sumner: "2 stumps of a mound, completely removed to fields." The site's area appears to have been approximately 0.75 ha.

Çiana

Location: 36°57' 24" N, 45°21' 14" E
Map Reference: J24
Periods: —
Survey Number: Young R, Kroll NQ 36
Bibliography: Stein 1940:363
Comments: This site lies in or near the village of the same name, 3 km west of Naqadeh. The site was plotted on Stein's map but not mentioned in the text (1940:363).

Çut Çandeh, Tepe (Solduz Valley)

Location: 36°58' 75" N, 45°25' 16" E
Map Reference: P22
Periods: Sumner I, prob. II
Survey Number: Sumner no number
Bibliography: —
Comments: This site of approximately 0.66 ha lies opposite Caravansarai on the north bank of the Gadar River. Sumner Survey Notes: "Not less than 80 paces diameter. Beside river. Almost completely destroyed by earth removal. Islamic Qaleh mound adjoins. Not sherded or measured."

Dalma Tepe (Solduz Valley)

Location: 36°59' 7" N, 45°25' 46" E
Map Reference: Q20
Periods: Hasanlu IX–X, Hasanlu V and later graves.
Survey Number: Young/Sumner 3, Kroll NQ 46
Bibliography: BIB-IRAN I:2132–40; BIB-IRAN II; BIB-IRAN III; Hamlin 1975:111–15; Kroll 2005:69; Stein 1940:390; Voigt 1983:268, fig. 120
Comments: Dalma is a small mound (Dia. 50 m) stand-

ing only 4 m high and located 4 km southwest of Hasanlu. The Hasanlu Project conducted excavations at the site 1958–61, uncovering a Chalcolithic village. Kramer mentioned 16 burials attributable to Hasanlu V and later (Hamlin 1975:113). Dyson (Survey Notes 1957): "Dalma village three small tepes, one suspected to be a tumulus mound, one later excavated (1964) and named Agrab Tepe [Dalma 2], third one excavated in 1961 and named Dalma Tepe." Dyson 1958: "South of Hasanlu, Painted and Plain Balakchi (Dalma) Ware." When I visited the site in 2004, it had been recently "excavated" with heavy machinery and little archaeological deposit remained.

Dalma 2 (Solduz Valley)

See above, Agrab Tepe.

Dalma 3 (Solduz Valley)

Location: 36°59' 2" N, 45°25' 23" E
Map Reference: P21
Periods: —
Survey Number: Young/Sumner 13
Bibliography: —
Comments: Apparently a tumulus (0.50 ha). Young found no sherds. Dyson (Survey Notes 1957): "Dalma village three small tepes, one suspected to be a tumulus mound, one later excavated (1964) and named Agrab Tepe [Dalma 2], third one excavated in 1961 and named Dalma Tepe." Sumner Survey Notes: "Sterile."

Dilançi Argheh (Solduz Valley, Var. Dilanchi)

Location: 37°1' 2" N, 45°17' 52" E
Map Reference: E17
Periods: Kroll Prehistoric?/Early Iron Age?
Survey Number: Young M, Kroll NQ 41
Bibliography: Stein 1940:385
Comments: Stein and others refer to this mound as Dilanchi, but it is more properly called Dilançi Argheh since there are two mounds in the modern village of Kulela referred to by local inhabitants as Tepe Kulela and Dilançi Tepe. After visiting Kulela, Stein traveled northeast to Dilançi Argheh. Dilançi Argheh is a small mound located 2 km northeast of Kulela. Stein found red polished ceramics here that could be either Chalcolithic or early Iron Age (Kroll 1994a). The exact location of the site is not provided on Stein's map (1940: Map VII), but it is easily located on SPOT imagery. The site covers 1.60 ha.

Dinkha Tepe (Ušnu Valley, Var. Denkha Tepe)

Location: —
Map Reference: —
Periods: Hasanlu VIc–a, Hasanlu V, Hasanlu IVc, Hasanlu IVb, Islamic
Survey Number: Young G, Kroll NQ 18
Bibliography: Dyson 1968:83–90; Hamlin 1974, 1975; Kramer 1977; Kroll 2005:68; Muscarella 1968, 1974; Rubinson 1991, 2004; Stein 1940:367–76
Comments: Dinkha Tepe, lying 10 km southeast of Ušnu, measures 360 m x 340 m and stands 15 m high. The site was once larger, the northern end of the tepe has been eroded away by the Gadar Çay. The Hasanlu Project excavated this site in 1966 and 1968, and it is described in the text herein.

Dosoq Kaleh (Ušnu Valley)

Location: —
Map Reference: —
Periods: Kroll Early Iron Age, Iron III (Urartian)
Survey Number: Kroll NQ 4
Bibliography: Kleiss and Kroll 1979:195–98, 230–33, figs. 4, 17–20; Pecorella and Salvini 1984:172, fig. 23 F8 No. 111.
Comments: Fortress measuring 50 m x 70 m located 5 km south of Ain-i Rum. Kleiss records an orthogonal structure with typical Urartian buttresses and corner towers attributable to the early Urartian period. Surface finds from the site indicate that the enclosure spans the Urartian period.

Durba Qal'eh (Ušnu Valley)

Location: —
Map Reference: —
Periods: Kroll Iron IV, Pecorella and Salvini Achaemenid
Survey Number: Kroll NQ9
Bibliography: Kleiss and Kroll 1979:213, 242, pl. 41; Pecorella and Salvini 1984:172, fig. 23 F9 No. 114
Comments: Small fortress at the village of Durba

southeast of Gerd-i Qalat (NQ8). The enclosure dates exclusively to the Iron IV.

Galavan (Var. Jalavan, Solduz Valley)

Location: 36°54' 51" N, 45°19' 19" E
Map Reference: G28–29
Periods: Young I, Sumner VIII, IX
Survey Number: Young/Sumner 34
Bibliography: —
Comments: The exact location of this site was not recorded. Young named it after the nearest village in the Balakchi Valley but Sumner, who later recorded a site in the same area, questioned whether it was the same site visited by Young at which he had found Islamic remains. A potential archaeological site appears on satellite imagery to the north of the modern village. Dyson Survey Notes (1957): "Jalvan (Galavan) Village Low Mound—terracotta figurine [neg. 73781:3, HAS57-173, UPM58-4-3]." Sumner Survey Notes: "Are [pottery] lots 70-15 and 19 from the same site listed by TCY?" I believe Young may have been calling the Islamic period Balakchi Hill Fort to the east "Galavan." Sumner obviously visited a Neolithic–Chalcolithic tepe.

Gandar Gah (Solduz Valley)

Location: 36°59' 35" N, 45°25' 43" E
Map Reference: Q20
Periods: —
Survey Number: Sumner no number
Bibliography: —
Comments: Sumner Survey Notes: "Sterile. Rectangle, 100+ m long. By main road from Naqadeh." The site lies in the seasonal lakebed north of Dalma village and measures 1.70 ha.

Garnah Tepe (Var. Qarna, Qarnat, Solduz Valley)

Location: 36°55' 31" N, 45°18' 36" E
Map Reference: F27
Periods: Early Iron Age
Survey Number: Kroll NQ 35
Bibliography: Kroll 2005:68
Comments: The site lies southwest of Naqadeh in the direction of Piranšahr in the Balakchi Valley, likely in the village of the same name. The layout and elevation of the modern village suggests it was founded on a tepe. Sumner Survey Notes: "Ca. 8 km SW Nagadeh." Sumner also mentions: "K[earton] 70-7" pottery collection lot and this site appears on Kearton's map of 1966. Kroll: "Settlement; surface finds of Grey Ware and Groovy Pottery by Kleiss" (2005:68).

Gerd Agi (Solduz Valley)

Location: 37°01' 5" N, 45°32' 12 E
Map Reference: Z17
Periods: VII?, VIII, IX
Survey Number: Sumner 41
Bibliography: —
Comments: This sites lies at the southernmost end/inlet of Lake Kheder Hajji. Sumner Survey Notes: "Round diameter 130 paces. Seems to have small square (5x5m) in top and other excavation that look archaeological. Radial spoil heaps or trenches. Beside small lake that lies to North and East of village of Gol. One obsidian fragment." These excavations are still visible on SPOT satellite images. The site area as estimated by Sumner would be 1.33 ha. The maximum site area estimated from satellite photos is 3.51 ha.

Gerd-i Ali

Location: —
Map Reference: —
Periods: —
Survey Number: Voigt 77-13
Bibliography: —
Comments: Same as Gerd-i Allah (see below)?

Gerd-i Durwani (Ušnu Valley)

Location: —
Map Reference: —
Periods: Sumner I, II/ IIIa
Survey Number: —
Bibliography: —
Comments: Sumner survey Lot 70-3

Gerd-i Gargaru (Ušnu Valley)

Location: —
Map Reference: —
Periods: Kroll Iron Age?, Late Medieval

Survey Number: Kroll NQ 17, Pecorella and Salvini 125
Bibliography: Kleiss 1977a:41, fig. 22; Pecorella and Salvini 1984:175, fig. 23 D11 No. 125
Comments: Castle measuring 100 m x 50 m located 13 km south of Ušnu and 7 km north of Sufiyan.

Gerd-i Gawra (Ušnu Valley)

Location: —
Map Reference: —
Periods: Sumner II/IIIa, V, VI, VII, VIII, IX
Survey Number: —
Bibliography: —
Comments: Sumner survey Lot 70-1

Gerd-i Hasan 'Ali, A and B (Ušnu Valley)

Location: —
Map Reference: —
Periods: Chalcolithic, early EBA (Hasan Ali), Early Iron Age?
Survey Number: Young J, Kroll NQ 33, Pecorella and Salvini 126
Bibliography: Kroll 1994a, 2004c; Nagel 1962:7, 10, fig. 43:1–3; Pecorella and Salvini 1984:174; Calmeyer 1957–1971:381–82; Stein 1940:377–81, fig. 24, pl. XXIII
Comments: These two sites are located 2 km south of the village of Dehšams and 7 km southeast of Dinkha Tepe. Tepe A, the larger of the two mounds, measures 120 m x 100 m and stands 12 m high. Tepe B covers an area of 100 m x 50 m and is 5 m high. In 1936, Stein conducted soundings in both mounds. Pecorella and Salvini show only one undatable mound here—evidently the second mound has since been destroyed.

Gerd-i Molla Ahmed (Ušnu Valley)

Location: —
Map Reference: —
Periods: Kroll Iron III, Pecorella and Salvini Iron III
Survey Number: Kroll NQ 12, Pecorella and Salvini 128
Bibliography: Kroll 1994a; Pecorella and Salvini 1984:175, fig. 23 E10 No. 128
Comments: Elliptical mound on the outskirts of the modern city of Ušnu measuring 100 m x 30 m and standing 18 m high with a small ridge at the top and a small eastern eminence (Pecorella and Salvini 1984:175). There is a modern canal along the northwest flank of the site, and a regular series of holes along the southern side that probably represents traces of a modern military encampment (Pecorella and Salvini 1984). The site could be a settlement or fortress (Kroll 1994a).

Gerd-i Mosa

See below, Sergis.

Gerd-i Qalat (Ušnu Valley)

Location: —
Map Reference: —
Periods: Kroll Early and Middle Iron Age, Pecorella and Salvini Iron I, III
Survey Number: Pecorella and Salvini 113, Kroll NQ8
Bibliography: Kleiss and Kroll 1979:213–14, 241–42, fig. 41; Kroll 2005:67; Pecorella and Salvini 1984:172, fig. 23 F9 No. 113
Comments: Small fort located on a mountain summit north of the village of Durba and southeast of Gerd-i Qalat with surface finds of MBW (Kroll 2005:67). Further down the slope Kleiss found another wall, which he dated to the later Urartian period on the basis of architectural criteria.

Gerd-i Qisal (Var. Kaniki Zar, Kaniki Sar, Shekhan, prob. Young's Shikan, Ušnu Valley)

Location: —
Map Reference: —
Periods: Kroll Iron I–III, Medieval Islamic, Pecorella and Salvini Iron III, Islamic
Survey Number: Young B, Pecorella and Salvini 127, Kroll NQ 14
Bibliography: Kleiss 1976:33, fig. 17, pl. 10 no. 3; Kroll 1976:110, 172, 182; 2005:67; Pecorella and Salvini 1984:174, fig. 23 E10 No. 127; Stein 1940:366
Comments: Kroll: "Small fort with surface finds of Groovy Pottery" (2005: 67). Pecorella and Salvini interpret the site as an Urartian control point or a small square fort sited to guard the route via the Kel-i Shin Pass and important routes within the valley, as well as the branch of the Ak Çay leading from the Gadar Çay. Traces of two fortification walls are visible on the surface on the south side of the tepe.

Gerd-i Siran (Ušnu Valley)

Location: —
Map Reference: —
Periods: Kroll Iron III, Islamic, Pecorella and Salvini Iron III, Islamic
Survey Number: Kroll NQ 13, Pecorella and Salvini 129
Bibliography: Pecorella and Salvini 1984:175, fig. 23 E10 No. 129
Comments: The remains of this fortress, a roughly triangular tepe measuring 140 m x 60 m, sit on a mountain spur that is separated into two levels and divided from the rest of the promontory by a fosse (Pecorella and Salvini 1984:175). The site is strategically located to guard the route to the Kel-i Shin Pass and lies just west of the confluence of the Gadar and the Ak Čay 6 km south of modern Ušnu (Pecorella and Salvini 1984).

Girdagun (Ušnu Valley)

Location: —
Map Reference: —
Periods: Kroll (1994) Early–Middle Iron Age?, Iron IV
Survey Number: Kroll NQ 3, Pecorella and Salvini 110
Bibliography: Kleiss 1977a:24–25, fig. 4 no. 28; Pecorella and Salvini 1984:172, fig. 23 F8 No. 110
Comments: Small fortified settlement 2 km south of Ain-i Rum.

Gird-i Allah (Ušnu Valley)

Location: —
Map Reference: —
Periods: Sumner II/IIIa, IV, VIII, IX, X, Kroll Neolithic
Survey Number: Kroll NQ 19
Bibliography: Kroll 1994a; Voigt 1983:269, fig. 120
Comments: This small tepe is located immediately west of Dinkha on the right bank of the Gadar Çay. Sumner survey Lot 70-2.

Goruq, Tepe (Solduz Valley)

Location: 36°57' 12" N, 45°24' 44" E
Map Reference: O24
Periods: Sumner III?, IV, VI
Survey Number: Sumner no number
Bibliography: —
Comments: This small tepe (0.65 ha) lies on the outskirts of modern Naqadeh. Sumner Survey Notes: "200 x 80 paces. Low smooth contour."

Gundavela Tepe (Var. Gundavileh, Gun-Dakela, etc., Ušnu Valley)

Location: —
Map Reference: —
Periods: Kroll Chalcolithic, MBA (KW), Pecorella and Salvini Iron I, Iron II?
Survey Number: Kroll NQ 30, Pecorella and Salvini 130
Bibliography: Kleiss 1977a:27, fig. 8; Pecorella and Salvini 1984:175 fig. 23 F10 No. 130
Comments: Ovoid tepe (Dia. 25 m, H. 15 m) that probably had a stone block defensive wall and a gate of the 2nd millennium BC (Kleiss 1977a:27, fig. 8; Pecorella and Salvini 1984:175). The site lies 3 km west of Qalatgah at the foot of the mountain.

Gur-khaneh (Var. Gor Khaneh, Solduz Valley)

Location: 36°55' 27" N, 45°34' 28" E
Map Reference: DD27
Periods: Kroll Early Iron Age; Young Islamic, Buff Iron Age, Grey Ware, Sumner I, IIIa
Survey Number: Young/Sumner 21, Kroll NQ 64
Bibliography: Kroll 2005:71; Stein 1940:407
Comments: The site (8.75 ha), an occupation mound and cemetery, is located in southeastern Solduz, 4 km north of Mohammadšah beneath the modern village of Gur Khaneh. Stein: "At the hamlet of Gur Khaneh ('Place of Graves')…a small mound is completely covered with dwellings and graves. Its antiquity is proved by two vessels of grey-black burnished ware which had recently been found in a pit dug for clay to make bricks with; one of them was a long-spouted jug of the type frequent at Hasanlu" (1940:407).

Gurdji Cemetery (Var. Gurji, Ušnu Valley)

Location: —
Map Reference: —
Periods: Kroll Early Iron Age
Survey Number: Kroll NQ 34
Bibliography: Kroll 2005:68; Stein 1940:381
Comments: Kroll: "A Grey Ware jar of grey-black col-

or with a bridged spout, given to Stein by the Khan of the village of Gurdji, is kept in the collection of the BM (ANE 136185)" (1994a; 2005:68). The site's size is unknown.

Gurnabad (Solduz Valley)

Location: 36°58' 24" N, 45°19' 25" E
Map Reference: I G–H22
Periods: —
Survey Number: Young Q, Kroll NQ 27
Bibliography: Stein 1940:363
Comments: Stein placed this site on his map (1940: 363) as north of the village of Gurnabad and around 6 km west of Naqadeh, but does not mention it in the text. This site is probably the tepe visible on satellite images lying northwest of the village of Gurnabad-Kaze.

Hajji Firuz Tepe (Solduz Valley)

Location: 36°59' 40" N, 45°28' 28" E
Map Reference: U19
Periods: Hasanlu I, II, IV, V, VI, VII–X
Survey Number: Young/Sumner 2, Kroll NQ 45
Bibliography: BIB-IRAN I:2120–28; BIB-IRAN II:4266–67; BIB-IRAN III:5227–30; Hamlin 1971:32; Stein 1940:388; Voigt 1976, 1983
Comments: Stein noted "burnished red ware" when he visited the site briefly in 1936, as well as sherds "painted with annular lines in darker red" (1940:388). Hajji Firuz lies 2 km southeast of Hasanlu Tepe. The mound covers 2.3 ha and is 9 m high. The site was excavated by the Hasanlu Project and detailed information is available for the Neolithic and Chalcolithic remains; however, graves of the EBA and LBA have not been published in detail. A sherd of polychrome Urmia Ware was found in a wash layer with sherds of "Hasanlu V" (Hamlin 1971:32). The site also yielded material of Parthian-Sasanian date and trash pits of Seljuk date.

Hasanabad Tepe (Var. Hasanawa, Ušnu Valley)

Location: —
Map Reference: —
Periods: Kroll Neolithic, Chalcolithic, EBA, Iron I, Parthian, Late Medieval
Survey Number: Young C, Kroll NQ 15, Pecorella and Salvini 131
Bibliography: Kroll 1994a, 2005:68; Pecorella and Salvini 1984:176, Plan, fig. 23 F10 No. 131; Stein 1940:366–67
Comments: Small settlement 6 km southeast of Ušnu with surface finds of Grey Ware as well as earlier and later periods (Kroll 1994a, 2005:68). The site is located in the village of the same name and measures 120 m x 50 m, and is 10 m high.

Hasanlu Tepe (Solduz Valley)

Location: 37°0' 16" N, 45°27' 31" E
Map Reference: S–T18
Periods: Hasanlu I–IX and probably X
Survey Number: Young/Sumner 1, Kroll NQ 44
Bibliography: See esp. Dyson and Voigt 1989
Comments: See text.

Hasanlu Islamic (Solduz Valley)

Location: —
Map Reference: —
Periods: Dyson I, Sumner I
Survey Number: Dyson no number, Sumner no number
Bibliography: —
Comments: Dyson collected this site. Sumner Survey Notes: "60 paces diameter (could be larger)."

Hasanlu Islamic II (Solduz Valley)

Location: —
Map Reference: —
Periods: Sumner I
Survey Number: Sumner no number
Bibliography: —
Comments: Sumner Survey Notes: "35 paces diameter."

Hasanlu Islamic III (Solduz Valley)

Location: —
Map Reference: —
Periods: Sumner I
Survey Number: Sumner no number
Bibliography: —
Comments: —

Hasanlu Islamic IV (Solduz Valley)

Location: —
Map Reference: —
Periods: Sumner I
Survey Number: Sumner no number
Bibliography: —
Comments: Sumner Survey Notes: "60 paces."

Hasanlu Islamic V (Solduz Valley)

Location: —
Map Reference: —
Periods: Sumner I
Survey Number: Sumner no number
Bibliography: —
Comments: Sumner Survey Notes: "Very low mound by road between Hajji Firuz and Agha Baglu [Agabaglu]. Badly cut up."

Hasanlu Islamic VI (Solduz Valley)

Location: —
Map Reference: —
Periods: Sumner I
Survey Number: Sumner no number
Bibliography: —
Comments: Sumner Survey Notes: "Badly cut up. Remnant, low and jumbly."

Hasanlu Islamic VII (Solduz Valley)

Location: —
Map Reference:
Periods: Sumner I
Survey Number: Sumner no number
Bibliography: —
Comments: Sumner Survey Notes: "By road to Sonqar just a couple hundred meters from Hajji Firuz. Estimated 100+ m long."

Hasanlu Islamic VIII (Solduz Valley)

Location: —
Map Reference: —
Periods: Sumner I
Survey Number: Sumner no number
Bibliography: —
Comments: Sumner Survey Notes: "Round, 80 paces diameter. On road (literally under road) midway between Gol and Baranu. Very low (1–2 m) rather jumbly mound with some earth mining digs."

Hasanlu Islamic IX (Solduz Valley)

Location: —
Map Reference: —
Periods: Sumner I
Survey Number: Sumner no number
Bibliography: —
Comments: Sumner Survey Notes: "Less than 2m height. Nebulous shape but not more than 60 paces diameter."

Haykh Ahmed

Location: —
Map Reference: —
Periods: —
Survey Number: Voigt 77-10
Bibliography: —
Comments: —

Hill Fort (Var. Dalma Dark Mound, Dalmeh Qaleh, Solduz Valley)

Location: 36°58' 33" N, 45°25' 44" E
Map Reference: Q22
Periods: Islamic and probably later Iron Age
Survey Number: Dyson no number, Sumner no number, probably Voigt 77-20
Bibliography: —
Comments: Dyson Survey Notes 1957 "'Dark Mound'—on ridge behind Dalma Tepe. Plain buff and red-slipped buff ware, and light green Islamic glazed. Local tradition connected this place to Nadir Shah." Sumner Survey Notes: "Small rectangular mound, 33 x 18 paces." Sumner frequently used this prominence for compass bearings when conducting survey in the southern Solduz valley.

Hosain, Tepe (Solduz Valley)

Location: Approximately 36°57' 30" N, 45°25' 9" E
Map Reference: P23
Periods: —
Survey Number: Sumner no number.

Bibliography: —
Comments: Sumner Survey Notes: "Dinkha type baked hearth fragment. Small mound, mostly sterile. Twin mounds: 50 and 30 paces diameter. Badly destroyed—center removed."

Imam 'Ali (Var. Mamaleh, Mamalu, Solduz Valley)

Location: 36°54' 5" N, 45°33' 54" E
Map Reference: BB27
Periods: Kroll Early Iron Age, Late Medieval, Young Islamic, Buff Iron Age, Grey, Sumner I, IIIa
Survey Number: Young/Sumner 23, Kroll NQ 65
Bibliography: Kroll 2005:71; Stein 1940:407
Comments: Located at the south edge of the village of the same name, this tepe measures 200 m x 250 m (5 ha) and is 9 m high. It lies 4 km north of Mohammadšah at the entrance to the Masu Çay valley. Kroll (2005:71): "Settlement. Stein noted 'sherds of grey-black burnished ware dating from the Hasanlu period.'"

Kalifan (Solduz Valley)

Location: 36°55' 30" N, 45°25' 51" E
Map Reference: Q27
Periods: Young V?, VIII, IX, Sumner I, VIII, IX
Survey Number: Young/Sumner 29, Voigt 77-19
Bibliography: —
Comments: Sumner: "57 paces in diameter." Estimated size from satellite photos is 0.70 ha. Located 1.25 km northwest of the modern village of the same name.

Kamos (Solduz Valley)

Location: 36°59' 30" N, 45°16' 57" E
Map Reference: D20
Periods: Kroll Early Iron Age
Survey Number: Young K, Kroll NQ 39
Bibliography: Kroll 2005:68; Stein 1940:385
Comments: Kroll: "Cemetery? Stein mentions 'black burnished pot of Hasanlu type' (Grey Ware)" (2005:68). Thirteen km northwest of Naqadeh on the right bank of the Gadar Çay.

Kara Bala, Tepe (Solduz Valley)

Location: 37°1' 9" N, 45°28' 58" E
Map Reference: U–V17
Periods: Sumner I
Survey Number: Sumner no number, Voigt 77-10?
Bibliography: —
Comments: This tepe covers 3.25 ha. Sumner: "Oval 190x80 paces. Low jumbly mound on lake shore with sub-rectangular excavation in the East end."

Kečik Tepe (Ušnu Valley)

Location: —
Map Reference: —
Periods: Kroll Prehistoric
Survey Number: Kroll NQ20, Pecorella and Salvini 132
Bibliography: Pecorella and Salvini 1984:176, fig. 23 F10 No. 132; Stein 1940:367
Comments: Small tepe (30 m x 20 m, H. 4 m) located north of the Gadar River 4 km northwest of Dinkha Tepe near Khaledabad, 0.5 km north of Böyük Tepe (Kroll 1994a; Pecorella and Salvini 1984:131).

Kel-i Shin (Var. Kelišin)

Location: —
Map Reference: —
Periods: Iron III (Urartian)
Survey Number: Kroll NQ1
Bibliography: BIB-IRAN I:2167–72; BIB-IRAN II:4270; König 1955:41–50; Pecorella and Salvini 1984:63–64; RLA 5 (1976–80):568–69
Comments: The location of an inscribed stele 150 m east of the border between Iraq and Iran in the high pass of the same name along the main route between Rowanduz and Ušnu. The stele bears an inscription of the Urartian kings Išpuini and Menua in Urartian and Assyrian.

Kojast

See below, Rock Fort

Kuh-i Çorblah (Var. Kuh-e Chörblach, Solduz Valley)

Location: 37°5' 53" N, 45°32' 16" E
Map Reference: Z8
Periods: Iron II, Parthian-Sasanian

Survey Number: Kroll NQ 59
Bibliography: Kleiss 1973:29–30, fig. 26, pl. 4 no. 2; Kleiss and Kroll 1977:78, fig. 29; Kroll 2005:69, fig. 4.
Comments: Large fortress east of the Mahabad-Urmia road, 10 km southeast of Haidarabad, not far from the shore of Lake Urmia. Kroll: "Fortress. In this large site, near the shore of Lake Urmia, Kleiss could map the system of the Early Iron Age fortification walls. He also collected a good number of Grey Ware sherds" (2005:69).

Kulela (Solduz Valley)

Location: 37°00' 21" N, 45°17' 14" E
Map Reference: D18
Periods: Early Iron Age, Hasanlu VI
Survey Number: Young L, Kroll NQ 40
Bibliography: Kroll 2005:68; Stein 1940:385, pl. XXIV, 26
Comments: A mound with a diameter of approximately 200 m and a height of 10 m located 14 km northwest of Naqadeh on the left bank of the Gadar Çay. Kroll: "Settlement with black polished sherds (Grey Ware) like Kamos" (2005:68; Stein 1940:385). Stein noted some painted sherds of Khabur Ware (BM WA 129941a).

Kurvech Tepe (Solduz Valley)

Location: 37°4' 50" N, 45°17' 42" E
Map Reference: E10
Periods: Sumner I, II
Survey Number: —
Bibliography: —
Comments: Sumner visited this site, located at the southern end of the village of Konech in the Dilançi Valley, but did not record it in detail. It appears to be a small, conical tepe of 1.70 ha with the remains of a circular structure on its summit. Sumner Survey Notes: "Lot 70-14, Ca. 12 km northwest Hasanlu."

Mahuradlu, Tepe (Solduz Valley)

Location: —
Map Reference: —
Periods: —
Survey Number: Voigt 77-25
Bibliography: —
Comments: —

Mamaleh/Mamalu

See above, Imam 'Ali

Mamiani (Solduz Valley)

Location: 36°58' 44" N, 45°36' 32" E
Map Reference: approximately KK20
Periods: Kroll Prehistoric
Survey Number: Kroll NQ 66
Bibliography: Kroll 1994a, Stein 1940:408
Comments: Small tepe on the lower reaches of the Gadar Çay north of the village of Mohammadšah. Mentioned but not visited by Stein, nor is it located on his regional map. Allegedly, ancient ceramics had been coming from the site for the last 30 years (thus starting around 1900). The modern village of Mamiani sits at the base of a mountain spur in the far southeastern part of the Solduz valley, not far from the neighboring Mahabad Valley.

Mavaran (Var. Mavalan, Solduz Valley)

Location: 37°0' 50" N, 45°28' 50" E
Map Reference: U17
Periods: Young/Sumner I, VIII, IX
Survey Number: Young/Sumner 17, Voigt 77-7
Bibliography: —
Comments: This site lies northeast of Hasanlu near the southern shore of Šur Gol. Its size as measured from satellite imagery is 1.20 ha. A possible low mound to the south would raise this estimate to 4.25 ha. Sumner Survey Notes: "Circular 190 paces circumference (possibly larger). Dirt removed around edges. A fairly high, rather flat-topped mound."

Mehmandar (Solduz Valley)

Location: 36°57' 6" N, 45°25' 52" E
Map Reference: Q24
Periods: Hasanlu III
Survey Number: No number
Bibliography: —
Comments: Small tepe (0.30 ha) located at the south edge of the village of Mehmandar east of Naqadeh. Sumner Survey Notes: "30 paces dia."

Mergeh Karvan (Ušnu Valley)

Location: —
Map Reference: —
Periods: Iron III (Urartian)
Survey Number: Kroll NQ 2
Bibliography: Kleiss and Kroll 1977:81–82, fig. 33; Pecorella and Salvini 1984:79–96; RLA 5 (1976–80):568–69
Comments: Stone stele of the Urartian king Rusa I located between the Kel-i Shin Pass and Ušnu, approximately 7 km east of Kelišin (NQ 1).

Mirabad Tepe I (Solduz Valley)

Location: 36°59' 11" N, 45°18' 28" E
Map Reference: F20
Periods: Early Iron Age, Medieval
Survey Number: Young N, Kroll NQ 38
Bibliography: Kroll 2005:68; Stein 1940:384–85
Comments: This tepe, measuring 8.5 ha and 10–12 m high, has a mudbrick fortress on top it. The site is 10 km northwest of Naqadeh in the village of Mirabad. Stein notes a collapsed mudbrick fortification, Dia. 275 m, with gates on the north and south sides. Within the fortified area Stein found a lower mound. These features are visible on SPOT images. Kroll: "Stein found 'many burnished red and dark-grey potsherds, also fragments of ribbed ware.' 2 sherds from Mirabad are kept in the BM (ANE 150181–182: Grey Ware and Groovy Pottery)" (2005:68). Dyson (Survey Notes 1957): "Medieval (lustre ware), Hasanlu IV Grey Ware, Red Ware, some black/white painted ware (Hasanlu VI?)."

Mohammad Šah Tepe (Var. Mahamadshah, Mohammadšah, Tepe Mehmed Shah, Solduz Valley)

Location: 36°54' 4" N, 45°33' 54" E
Map Reference: CC30
Periods: Kroll Chalcolithic, EBA (ETC, POW), MBA (HAB), Early Iron Age, Parthian, Late Medieval; , Young Islamic, Buff Iron Age, Grey, Sumner I, II, IIIb (likely IIIa), IV, V, VIII, IX
Survey Number: Young/Sumner 22, Kroll NQ 63, Voigt 77-26?
Bibliography: Kroll 2005:71; Stein 1940:406–7
Comments: This important tepe is located on the left bank of the Masu Çay, "half a mile north of the village" of the same name (Stein 1940:407). Stein 1940:Map VII, however, shows it on the right bank in the location of the modern village. The Masu Çay is a tributary of the Gadar, which forms a north-south-running side valley in southeastern Solduz. The tepe is an oval measuring 345 m north-south and 170 m east-west and stands 17 m high. Its size on satellite imagery is 5.4 ha. Kroll: "This site is one of the largest in the region, occupied from the Chalcolithic to the Iron Age. It was probably surveyed by lots of people. Stein mentioned pottery like Hasanlu. Kleiss collected many sherds, among them good grey ware" (2005:71). In addition, Sumner mentions the presence of an "unknown painted ware."

Mohammadyar Tepe (Solduz Valley)

Location: 36°59' 22" N, 45°30' 42" E
Map Reference: X19
Periods: Kroll Prehistoric, Early Iron Age, Late Medieval, Sumner I, IV, Young I–Chalcolithic
Survey Number: Young/Sumner 6, Kroll NQ 62, Voigt 77-14
Bibliography: Kroll 2005:71; Mahdavi and Bovington 1972:148–51; Stein 1940:388
Comments: Mohammadyar is located 2 km north of the village of the same name, 4.85 km east-southeast of Hasanlu, with an occupied area of 1.45 ha and standing 10 m high. Kroll: "Settlement. Stein noted 'fragments of burnished dark-grey and buff ware.' Mahdavi and Bovington mention a site Mohammair with Iron Age occupation, which could be Mohammadyar" (2005:71). Sumner Survey Notes: "Oval-round, 260 paces circle. Just beside main Shaikhahmad-Mohammadyar road just North of latter extensive earth mining on the SE side (roadside) and some 'archaeological' excavation on top (5x5), trench on NE side. Much human and animal bone scattered about. Steep, tall mound with flat on SE."

Nalivan (Ušnu Valley)

Location: —
Map Reference: —
Periods: Kroll Chalcolithic, EBA? (ETC), MBA (KW), Iron III, Pecorella and Salvini Iron III (7th century)
Survey Number: Kroll NQ11, Pecorella and Salvini 133
Bibliography: Pecorella and Salvini 1984:176, fig. 23

F9 No. 133
Comments: Pecorella and Salvini (1984:176) located this site north of the modern village of Nalivan and near two abandoned military camps. The ancient fortress was strategically located on a natural rise and was elliptical in form, measuring 70 m x 30 m. The remains of dry masonry were found on the surface.

Nalus, Tepe 1 (Var. Tell Badr-ed Din, Ušnu Valley)

Location: —
Map Reference: —
Periods: Pecorella and Salvini Iron III
Survey Number: Kroll NQ22, Pecorella and Salvini 134
Bibliography: Kleiss and Kroll 1977:77, 115, fig. 27; Pecorella and Salvini 1984:177, fig. 23 F10 No. 134
Comments: Kleiss and Kroll (1977: fig. 27) and Pecorella and Salvini (1984:177) locate this site, a small, circular mound (Dia. 8 m) in the southern part of the Ušnu valley, 3 km southwest of Dinkha Tepe in a strategic location near the outlet of the Qalatian Çay on the route to Sufian. The tepe is ovoid, measuring 50 m x 40 m and standing ca. 7 m high (Pecorella and Salvini 1984). The northwest side of the site is cut by a modern canal and part of the site is covered by a modern village.

Nalus, Tepe 2 (Ušnu Valley)

Location: —
Map Reference: —
Periods: —
Survey Number: Kroll NQ23, Pecorella and Salvini 135
Bibliography: Pecorella and Salvini 1984:177, fig. 23 F10 No. 135
Comments: Small site (8 m x 8 m, H. 8 m) just east of Tepe Nalus 1 and 3 km south of Dinkha Tepe.

Nameless (1957)—between Hasanlu and Shaytanabad villages.

Nameless (1957)—between Hasanlu and Shaytanabad villages.

Obsidian and Dalma Ware sherds overlain by Islamic.

Nameless 77-1 (1977) —

Nameless 77-2 (1977) —

Nameless 77-3 (1977) —

Nameless 77-4 (1977) —

Nameless 77-5 (1977) —

Nameless 77-12 (1977)—near Yadegardlu

Nameless 77-18 (1977) —

Nameless a and b 77-21 (1977) —

Nameless 77-22 (1977) —

Nameless a and b 77-23 (1977) —

Nameless

Location: —
Map Reference: —
Periods: Sumner III
Survey Number: Sumner no number
Bibliography: —
Comments: Sumner: "30 paces diameter."

Naqadeh (Solduz Valley)

Location: 36°57' 19" N, 45°23' 16" E
Map Reference: M24
Periods: Kroll Early Iron Age, Sasanian, Late Medieval, Young Grey and Buff Ware, Sumner IIIa, IV, V, VI
Survey Number: Young/Sumner 33, Kroll NQ 43
Bibliography: Dyson and Young 1960:20; Kleiss 1981:115–16, Fig. 20; Kroll 2005:69; Rawlinson 1840:14; Stein 1940:383–84; Schmidt 1940: pl. 85b
Comments: Naqadeh is a fairly large mound, probably larger than Hasanlu and exhibiting identical mound morphology. This is most obvious in aerial photos taken by Schmidt in 1937 (1940:AE 631, 653). The site consists of a central high mound surrounded by a

low mound. The modern town has obscured the low mound somewhat, but its contours can still be traced and the total site size is estimated at 22 ha, minimally. The high mound stands 15 m and covers approximately 6.75 ha. Rawlinson passed through Naqadeh in 1838 and noted "a quadrangular fort, with eight bastions, the strong place of the district. Here Mehdi Khan…resides." The fortress appears in Schmidt aerial photo AE 653, which shows an octagonal structure with round towers at each corner. Kroll: "Cemetery? Stein describes 'superior burnished ware, both red and dark grey.' A Grey Ware jar with ibex-handles (Stein 1940:384) is in the collection of the BM (ANE 136184). Dyson and Young mention Grey Ware" (2005:69). Sumner Survey Notes: "The size and configuration are like Hasanlu. There is every reason to assume that essentially the same sequence of periods occurs here under the town." Dyson noted that the site appeared to have been burned in the early Iron Age based on an exposed section (pers. comm., 1999). In 1959 Dyson documented a looted hypogeum at the site similar to one excavated by Hakemi and Rad (1950:30–31, fig. 12) and the Hasanlu Project in 1959 (Danti and Cifarelli n.d.). Given the site's location at the approximate center of the Solduz valley, its size, and its control of local transportation routes, it is likely to have served as a regional center of some importance in antiquity.

Naqadeh Cemetery (Solduz Valley)

Location: 36°57' 11" N, 45°23' 48" E
Map Reference: N24
Periods: Young Grey, Buff [Iron Age], Pisdeli, and other painted wares, Sumner IIIa, VIII
Survey Number: Young/Sumner 31
Bibliography: —
Comments: Dyson 1957: "Small tepe with a tomb on it on the north side of the road from vicinity of Mirabad to Naghadeh." This mound appears on the Soviet-era map of the region.

Nerziwa (Ušnu Valley)

Location: —
Map Reference: —
Periods: —
Survey Number: Young D
Bibliography: —
Comments: —

Nizamabad (Solduz Valley)

Location: 36°57' 12" N, 45°31' 28" E
Map Reference: Y24
Periods: Kroll Prehistoric
Survey Number: Kroll NQ 61
Bibliography: Stein 1940:387
Comments: Tepe with a diameter of 100 m and standing 8 m high located in the village of the same name 14 km east of Naqadeh and 4 km south of Muhammadyar. Stein mentions "sherds of burnished ware painted with annular bands of red or brown" (1940:387). These could be Hasanlu VIb KW or Hasanlu VIIa-b POW.

Nizamad (Solduz Valley)

Location: approximately 36°55' 41" N, 45°31' 41" E
Map Reference: X27
Periods: Young Buff Iron Age, Islamic; Sumner I, IIIa
Survey Number: Young/Sumner 24
Bibliography: —
Comments: Young located this site on his map at the southern edge of the Solduz valley on the south side of a marsh not far from the village of Sakse Tepe and due south of Nizamabad on an outwash fan. In the records of the Hasanlu Project the site of this name is occasionally confused with the site of Nizamabad. Nizamabad appears on the Young-Kearton map, but the site is not named and no information is provided in the notes, nor is information provided on Nizamad save the periods of occupation.

Pisdeli (Solduz Valley)

Location: 37°1' 11" N, 45°30' 30" E
Map Reference: X17
Periods: Hasanlu Medieval, V?, VI?, VII–IX
Survey Number: Young/Sumner 4, Kroll NQ 47
Bibliography: BIB-IRAN I:2129–31; Dyson and Young 1960:19–28
Comments: Pisdeli is a small tepe, just over 1 ha in area, which lies northeast of Hasanlu near a small freshwater lake. The site was sounded by the Hasanlu Project in 1957 (Dyson and Young 1960).

Qaladjaq (Var. Qal'a Jukh, Qalajuk, Solduz Valley)

Location: 36°58' 48" N, 45°20' 31" E
Map Reference: I21
Periods: —
Survey Number: Young P, Kroll NQ 42
Bibliography: Stein 1940:386
Comments: This site is located 5 km northwest of Naqadeh on the right side of the Gadar, just west of the village of Qaladjaq. Stein noted some painted sherds here. The tepe covers 1.23 ha and is 4 m high.

Qalateh Qal'eh (Ušnu Valley) (Var. Qaleh Qalaleh)

Location: —
Map Reference: —
Periods: Kroll Iron IV?, Pecorella and Salvini Achaemenid, Parthian/Sassanian
Survey Number: Kroll NQ 5, Pecorella and Salvini 112
Bibliography: Kleiss 1978:18, fig. 7; Pecorella and Salvini 1984:172, fig. 23 F8 No. 112
Comments: Small orthogonal fortress located 12 km east of Ain-i Rum.

Qalatgah (Ušnu Valley)

Location: —
Map Reference: —
Periods: Iron III (Urartian), Iron IV
Survey Number: Kroll NQ 28, Pecorella and Salvini 136
Bibliography: BIB IRAN I:2149–53; Dyson 1969:179–81; Kleiss 1971:63–64, fig. 14, pl. 8 no. 4; 1976:31, n49; Kleiss and Kroll 1977:70–72, 109, figs. 22–23; Kroll 1976:92–96, figs. 39–40; Muscarella 1971b:44–49; Pecorella and Salvini 1984:177, fig. 23 G10 No. 136; van Loon 1975:201–7
Comments: This Urartian fortress lies 15 km east of Ušnu and 22 km northwest of Naqadeh. It measures at least 500 m x 200 m and lies at an elevation of 80–100 m above the surrounding plain. The site is located on a prominent rise, which juts into the Ušnu valley from the north, at the bottleneck between the Ušnu and Solduz valleys. The site has a commanding view of the valley and the mountain passes leading into it to the west and thus served as an important watch-point for the Urartian military in the region. The site also has a perennial spring-fed lake at its base, Çešme Gol. Architectural remains include a watchtower, walls, and terraces. An inscribed stele of the Urartian rulers Išpuini and Menua was found at the site.

Qalatgah II (Ušnu Valley)

Location: —
Map Reference: —
Periods: Iron I–II, Iron III (Urartian)
Survey Number: Kroll NQ 29
Bibliography: Kleiss and Kroll 1977:70–72, 109, figs. 22–23; Kroll 1976:94–8, fig. 41; Kroll 2005:68
Comments: This small settlement lies northwest of Qalatgah fortress and has surface finds of Grey Ware and Groovy pottery.

Qalat (Solduz Valley)

Location: 36°55' 23" N, 45°30' 51" E
Map Reference: X27
Periods: Young Islamic, Iron Age?, Sumner I
Survey Number: Young/Sumner 26
Bibliography: —
Comments: This rather generically named site is located in the southern Solduz valley near or under the modern village of Kopakly. The site sits at the mouth of a wadi on an outwash fan. A marsh is located to the north of the site. Sumner and Young provide only the general location and dates.

Qal'eh Qalaleh (Ušnu Valley)

Location: —
Map Reference: —
Periods: Kroll Iron IV?
Survey Number: Kroll NQ 6
Bibliography: Kleiss 1978:17–18, fig. 7
Comments: A round structure or tumulus with a diameter of 45 m with an orthogonal structure inside of it located on the high pass east of Qalateh Qal'eh. Few pottery diagnostics were found and the material dates no earlier than the Iron IV.

Qarasaqqal Tepe (Ušnu Valley)

Location: —
Map Reference: —

Periods: —
Survey Number: Kroll NQ 27, Pecorella and Salvini 137
Bibliography: Pecorella and Salvini 1984:178, fig. 23 F10 No. 137
Comments: Pecorella and Salvini (1984:178) describe this site, which measures 65 m x 60 m and is 7 m high, as elliptical in shape and locate it at the center of the Ušnu valley, enclosed by two arms of the river. There was too little surface material to date the site. It is located 4 km southeast of Dinkha Tepe.

Qaveh Khaneh (Solduz Valley)

Location: Approximately 36°55' 29" N, 45°30' 39" E
Map Reference: X27
Periods: Young/Sumner I
Survey Number: Young/Sumner 25
Bibliography: —
Comments: This site is located on the south edge of the Solduz valley, on an outwash fan just north of the modern village of Kopakly. Young and Sumner provide only its general location and date.

Rock Fortress (Solduz Valley)

Location: —
Map Reference: —
Periods: Sumner I, II
Survey Number: Sumner no number
Bibliography: —
Comments: Virtually no information was provided on this site. Sumner Survey Notes: "Kojast? Lot 70-16."

Sakse Tepe (Solduz Valley)

Location: 36°56' 05" N, 45°30' 30" E
Map Reference: X26
Periods: Kroll Chalcolithic?, Early Iron Age, Late Medieval, Young III, IV, VII, possibly Chalcolithic (cf. Stein), Sumner I, III, IV–V
Survey Number: Young/Sumner 27, Kroll NQ 60
Bibliography: Kroll 2005:71; Stein 1940:386–87
Comments: The morphology of this tepe is quite similar to Hasanlu, with a high mound (Dia. 220 m) covering 3.6 ha surrounded by a low mound taking in an additional 9.4 ha. The flat-topped citadel mound stands 10 m high and has been used as a cemetery, while the low mound now has a village on it. The site lies 12 km east of Naqadeh and 5 km south of the village of Muhammadyar. Kroll: "Settlement. Stein found here polished Grey Ware" (2005:71). Stein saw a trench 2 m deep and 4 m wide around the mound. Sumner Survey Notes: "Flat top citadel. Top is 75 x 50 paces. Whole mound probably 1/3 longer in each dimension." Sumner Survey Lot 70-12 IV-V? The site is located on the north side of a marsh that is now dry.

Salaman Tepe (Var. Salman, Solduz Valley)

Location: 37°0' 30" N, 45°28' 26" E
Map Reference: U18
Periods: Kroll Neolithic, Young/Sumner I, X
Survey Number: Kroll NQ 51, Young/Sumner 18, Voigt 77-6
Bibliography: Voigt 1983:269, fig. 120
Comments: Sumner Survey Notes: "Oblong, 75 paces long. Two shallow holes excavated in top." Estimated site size based on satellite imagery is 1.20 ha. The site is located 2 km east of Hasanlu. Sumner found Hajji Firuz ceramics here, as did Voigt on a later visit.

Sangan, Tepe (Var. Singhan, Singa, Sanjan, Ušnu Valley)

Location: —
Map Reference: —
Periods: —
Survey Number: Young A, Kroll NQ 16, Pecorella and Salvini 138
Bibliography: Lehmann-Haupt 1910:247; Pecorella and Salvini 1984:178, fig. 23 E10 No. 138; Stein 1940:366
Comments: The site, a small settlement and fortress, is located on the north slopes of the western end of the Ušnu valley, 5 km southwest of Ušnu. Pecorella and Salvini (1984:178) describe the site as having been almost completely obliterated by modern occupation. Stein describes it as a large mound (H. 12 m).

Sé Girdan (Var. Seh Girdan, Seh Gird, Ušnu Valley)

Location: —
Map Reference: —
Periods: Kroll Early Iron Age

Survey Number: Kroll NQ 32, Pecorella and Salvini 139
Bibliography: BIB IRAN I: 2154–62; Deshayes 1973:176–78; Dyson 1969:179–81; Muscarella 1969:5–25, 1971d:5–28, 1971c:169–70, 1973a:178–80; Pecorella and Salvini 1984:178, fig. 23 G10 No. 139; Stein 1940:376–77
Comments: Eleven tumuli located 5 km east of Dinkha Tepe and measuring from 15 m to 60 m in diameter and between 0.5–8.0 m high. Some of these tumuli were excavated by the Hasanlu Project. Some had burial chambers. Muscarella has redated the tumuli to the Maikop Period.

Sergis (Var. Gerd-i Mosa, Gird-i Moza, Sarghis, Sarjis, Serjis, Ušnu Valley)

Location: —
Map Reference: —
Periods: Sumner II/IIIa, IIIb, V, VI, VII?, IX, Pecorella and Salvini/Kroll Iron I?
Survey Number: Young H, Kroll NQ 26, Pecorella and Salvini 140
Bibliography: Pecorella and Salvini 1984:178, fig. 23 F10 No. 140; Stein 1940:365–66
Comments: Sumner survey Lot 70-5. The site is located on the right bank of the Gadar, southeast of Dinkha. Pecorella and Salvini (1984:178) describe the site as elliptical in plan (35 m x 18 m, H. 15 m) with steep sides. The site is located near a modern canal east-southeast of Dinkha in the southern Ušnu valley (Pecorella and Salvini 1984).

Shaykh Maruf (Solduz Valley)

Location: 36°55' 18" N, 45°35' 30" E
Map Reference: EE27
Periods: —
Survey Number: Voigt 77-16
Bibliography: —
Comments: No information is currently available for this site. The coordinates are for the modern village of the same name in southeastern Solduz.

Shetanabad (Solduz Valley)

Location: 36°59' 47" N, 45°26' 19" E
Map Reference: R19

Periods: Young/Sumner I
Survey Number: Young/Sumner 11
Bibliography: —
Comments: Sumner Survey Notes: "To W[est] of Shaitanabad and probably under village [of same name]." Located on satellite images using the position of the modern village. Estimated size is 3.2 ha.

Sodja, Tepe (Var. Sauja Tepe, Sowja(h) Tappeh, Ušnu Valley)

Location: —
Map Reference: —
Periods: Sumner II/IIIa, IV, VI, Pecorella and Salvini/Kroll Iron III, Islamic
Survey Number: Young E, Kroll NQ24, Pecorella and Salvini 141
Bibliography: Pecorella and Salvini 1984:178, fig. 23 F10 No. 141; Stein 1940:365
Comments: Sumner survey Lot 70-4. Pecorella and Salvini (1984:178) describe the tepe as elliptical (65 m x 60 m, H. 20 m) with a modern village of the same name at its south side and a modern canal to the north and west. The remains of military fortifications were noted at the summit, dated by local informants to 1947. The site is located at the center of the Ušnu valley north of the Gadar River.

Tabiyeh East (Var. Tabia, Tabieh, Solduz Valley)

Location: 36°59' 35" N, 45°27' 5" E
Map Reference: S19–20
Periods: Sumner I, II, IIIa, VIII, IX?, X, Young Islamic, Grey Ware, Voigt X
Survey Number: Young/Sumner 9, Kroll NQ 53, Voigt 77-27
Bibliography: Voigt 1983:269, fig. 120
Comments: Sumner Survey Notes: "Low, even contour, some earth removed but mostly undisturbed. This is the larger of the two mounds [called Tabiyeh, see Tabiyeh West] side by side." I have estimated site size from satellite imagery as 1.68 ha.

Tabiyeh West (Var. Tabia, Solduz Valley)

Location: 36°59' 41" N, 45°26' 54" E
Map Reference: R–S19

Periods: Dyson Grey Ware, Sumner I, VIII, IX, Young Islamic, Grey Ware
Survey Number: Young/Sumner 10, Voigt 77-28
Bibliography:
Comments: Dyson: "Low mound with Grey Ware." Sumner Survey Notes: "Round, 50 paces dia." Site size estimated from satellite photos as 0.40 ha.

Tazakand (Solduz Valley)

Location: 37°2' 25" N, 45°24' 1" E
Map Reference: N14
Periods: Young/Sumner I
Survey Number: Young/Sumner 16
Bibliography: —
Comments: The probable location of this site on the west side of Lake Urmia was recorded by Young and a potential site was identified using satellite photos, although recent industrial activity in this area has changed conditions since the 1960s. The site appears to be 6.25 ha.

Tikkan Tepe (Ušnu Valley)

Location: —
Map Reference: —
Periods: —
Survey Number: Young F
Bibliography: —
Comments: —

Ugh Qal'eh (Solduz Valley)

Location: 37°0' 21" N, 45°26' 43" E
Map Reference: R18
Periods: Young/Sumner I
Survey Number: Young/Sumner 14
Bibliography: —
Comments: Site size as estimated using satellite imagery is 0.50–1.25 ha. On the south side of the site lies the village of Hajji Baglu, and the site likely extends beneath it. Young placed the site on his map but provided no other information beyond the date. Sumner did not visit the site.

Umuru (Var. Umuru, Solduz Valley)

Location: 37°2' 3" N, 45°26' 24" E
Map Reference: R15
Periods: I, VIII, IX
Survey Number: Young/Sumner 15
Bibliography: —
Comments: This mound was located using the general position recorded on Young's survey map. Today the site is surrounded by water, sitting amid the outflow of the Hasanlu Dam located on the southwest corner of Šur Gol. The site area is 2.1 ha. Dyson Survey Notes 1957: "West shore of gol. Pisdeli Ware, Dalma Ware, Impressed (Fingertip) Ware, obsidian, compact burnished ware with brown paint, white slipped ware like Ziwiyeh." Sumner Survey Notes: "An island in winter with heavy runoff of melt waters and rain. In July 1970 a dry salty flat. Badly potted and trenched (it is said by the landlord). Masses of small square foundation stones like those currently being used. Slope to east is fine ash and clamshells of Islamic period. Central mound full of stones. Slope to southwest yields Pisdeli and 10 years ago Dalma. Site now picked clean."

Unknown (Solduz Valley)

Location: southeast of Agrab Tepe
Map Reference: Q21
Periods: Chalcolithic, Iron III
Survey Number: Kroll NQ 50
Bibliography: Kleiss and Kroll 1979:221, 243
Comments: Small tepe southeast of Agrab Tepe with rectilinear architectural remains of an indeterminate nature.

Unknown (Solduz Valley)

Location: Approximately 37°6' 2" N, 45°30' 6" E
Map Reference: W7
Periods: Iron II–III
Survey Number: Kroll NQ 56
Bibliography: Kleiss and Kroll 1977:78, 116, fig. 29, pl. 17 no. 1
Comments: Area of ruins measuring 20 m x 25 m located 5 km east of Haidarabad on the shore of Lake Urmia.

Unknown (Solduz Valley)

Location: Approximately 37°5' 54" N, 45°31' 37" E
Map Reference: Y8
Periods: Iron II

Survey Number: Kroll NQ 58
Bibliography: Kroll 2005:69
Comments: Small tepe 44 km north of Mahabad on the road to Urmia at the base of the small Derbeser Peninsula. Kroll: "Kleiss found here several sherds of Grey Ware" (2005:69).

Wardawi (Ušnu Valley)

Location: —
Map Reference: —
Periods: Iron I–II, Late Medieval
Survey Number: Kroll NQ 31
Bibliography: Kroll 2005:68; Stein 1940:377
Comments: Kroll: "Cemetery on a low hill situated along a side branch of the Gadar a half mile south of Qalatgah. A Grey Ware jar with bridged spout from Wardawi is kept in the collection of the BM (ANE 136186)" (2005:68).

Yediar

Location: Approximately 37°5' 56" N, 45°30' 40" E
Map Reference: X8
Periods: Iron III (Urartian)
Survey Number: Kroll NQ 57
Bibliography: Kleiss 1976:32–33, fig. 16, pl. 10 1–2; Kroll 1976:102–4, fig. 44
Comments: Small stone fortress 5 km east of Haidarabad and 45 km north of Mahabad on the road to Urmia.

Yolbar Tepe (Var. Jolbar)

Location: north of Balestan Tepe
Map Reference: —
Periods: Hasanlu X
Survey Number: Kroll NQ 55
Bibliography: Lippert 1978:49, fig. 1
Comments: Yolbar is a small tepe 15 km north of the village of Haidarabad on the road to Urmia. Lippert shows sherds of Hajji Firuz Ware from the site (1978: fig. 1, right).

Ziavan (Ušnu Valley)

Location: —
Map Reference: —
Periods: —
Survey Number: NQ 7
Bibliography: Kleiss 1978:18, fig. 7, upper left
Comments: Rectangular entrenchment located south of the village of the same name, between Qal'eh Qalateh and Ain-i Rum.

Listing of Sites in Ušnu-Solduz by Site Number
(see Kroll 1994a)

NQ1 Kelišin
NQ2 Mergeh Karvan
NQ3 Girdagun
NQ4 Dosoq Qalah
NQ5 Qalateh Qal'eh
NQ6 Qalaleh Qal'eh
NQ7 Ziavan
NQ8 Gerd-i Qalat
NQ9 Durba Qal'eh
NQ10 Asember
NQ11 Nalivan
NQ12 Gerd-i Mollah Ahmed
NQ13 Gerd-i Siran
NQ14 Gerd-i Qisal
NQ15 Hasanabad Tepe
NQ16 Sangan
NQ17 Gerd-i Gargaru
NQ18 Dinkha Tepe
NQ19 Gird-i Allah
NQ20 Kečik Tepe
NQ21 Böyük Tepe
NQ22 Nalus 1
NQ23 Nalus 2
NQ24 Sodja
NQ25 Aliabad
NQ26 Sergis Tepe
NQ27 Qarasaqqal Tepe
NQ28 Qalatgah
NQ29 Qalatgah II
NQ30 Gundavela Tepe
NQ31 Wardawi
NQ32 Sé Girdan
NQ33 Gerd-i Hasan Ali
NQ34 Gurdji Tepe
NQ35 Garnah Tepe
NQ36 Çiana

NQ37 Gurnabad
NQ38 Mirabad
NQ39 Kamos
NQ40 Kulela
NQ41 Dilançi
NQ42 Qaladjaq
NQ43 Naqadeh Tepe
NQ44 Hasanlu Tepe
NQ45 Hajji Firuz Tepe
NQ46 Dalma Tepe
NQ47 Pisdeli Tepe
NQ48 Balukhi
NQ49 Agrab Tepe
NQ50 Unknown
NQ51 Salman Tepe

NQ52 Baranu Tepe
NQ53 Tabiyeh
NQ54 Balestan Tepe
NQ55 Yolbar Tepe
NQ56 Unknown
NQ57 Yediar
NQ58 Unknown
NQ59 Kuh-i Çorblah
NQ60 Sakse Tepe
NQ61 Nizamabad
NQ62 Mohammadyar
NQ63 Mohammad Šah Tepe
NQ64 Gur-khaneh
NQ65 Imam 'Ali
NQ66 Mamian

Appendix IIa–e

Appendix IIa: Radiocarbon Dates of Hasanlu IVb Relevant to Periods IVc–V

Sample Number	BP	Recalibration BC	Context	Previously Reported
P-0250	2740±54	One Sigma [cal BC 967: cal BC 965] 0.006344 [cal BC 928: cal BC 823] 0.993656 Two Sigma [cal BC 1003: cal BC 806] 1.	Charcoal from roof beam in BBIW, Op. XXV, Str. 3, Area 2.	Dyson and Muscarella 1989:6
P-0323	2858±34	One Sigma [cal BC 1111: cal BC 1103] 0.050031 [cal BC 1081: cal BC 1065] 0.104843 [cal BC 1056: cal BC 975] 0.773238 [cal BC 954: cal BC 943] 0.071888 Two Sigma Ranges [cal BC 1127: cal BC 921] 1	Charcoal from burned post in east column of south wall of main columned-hall room of BBIW, Op. XXII, Str. 3, Area 2.	Dyson and Muscarella 1989:6
P-0421	2913±56	One Sigma [cal BC 1208: cal BC 1201] 0.02748 [cal BC 1196: cal BC 1139] 0.291451 [cal BC 1135: cal BC 1016] 0.681069 Two Sigma [cal BC 1292: cal BC 971] 0.973012 [cal BC 960: cal BC 934] 0.026988	Charred wooden beam from floor of Northwest Storeroom (Room 13) of BB II, Op. XLVI, Str. 3.	963 BC Dyson 1962:643, Fig. 6; Stuckenrath 1963:86
P-0423	2892±51	One Sigma [cal BC 1192: cal BC 1176] 0.065645 [cal BC 1162: cal BC 1143] 0.083463 [cal BC 1132: cal BC 1001] 0.850892 Two Sigma [cal BC 1258: cal BC 1231] 0.03859 [cal BC 1218: cal BC 967] 0.904331 [cal BC 965: cal BC 928] 0.057078	Charred wood, beam fragments from door in east wall of main room, BBIE, Op. XLIV, Str. 3, Area 8.	Dyson and Muscarella 1989:6

(cont'd.)

APPENDIX IIA: RADIOCARBON DATES OF HASANLU IVB RELEVANT TO PERIODS IVC–V

Sample Number	BP	Recalibration BC	Context	Previously Reported
P-0424	2816±55	One Sigma [cal BC 1046: cal BC 904] 1. Two Sigma [cal BC 1126: cal BC 835] 1.	Charcoal from structural timber, BBIW, Op. XXIV, Str. 3, Area 1.	Dyson and Muscarella 1989:6
P-0425	2871±74	One Sigma [cal BC 1189: cal BC 1180] 0.031117 [cal BC 1157: cal BC 1145] 0.04171 [cal BC 1130: cal BC 968] 0.791421 [cal BC 964: cal BC 929] 0.135753 Two Sigma [cal BC 1287: cal BC 1285] 0.000583 [cal BC 1268: cal BC 890] 0.973854 [cal BC 881: cal BC 844] 0.025562	Charcoal from structural timber, BBIW, Op. XXV, Str. 2, Area 3.	Dyson and Muscarella 1989:6
P-0437	2841±56	One Sigma [cal BC 1111: cal BC 1103] 0.037357 [cal BC 1076: cal BC 1065] 0.051102 [cal BC 1056: cal BC 919] 0.911542 Two Sigma [cal BC 1194: cal BC 1141] 0.054046 [cal BC 1133: cal BC 890] 0.912536 [cal BC 880: cal BC 845] 0.033417	Large pieces of charcoal from the columned hall (Room 5) of BBII, Op. X.XXVII, Str. 5.	891 BC Stuckenrath 1963:87
P-0439	2812±56	One Sigma [cal BC 1045: cal BC 901] 1. Two Sigma [cal BC 1124: cal BC 833] 1	Charcoal, BBIW, Op. XXV, Str. 3, Area 1	Dyson and Muscarella 1989:6
P-0440	2864±64	One Sigma [cal BC 1126: cal BC 969] 0.859729 [cal BC 962: cal BC 931] 0.140271 Two Sigma [cal BC 1260: cal BC 1226] 0.03187 [cal BC 1223: cal BC 895] 0.961665 [cal BC 867: cal BC 857] 0.006465	Charcoal and charred wood from large wooden beam on the bench of the kitchen (western Room 2) next to the stairway of BBII, Op. XL, Str. 4.	914 BC Stuckenrath 1963:86
P-0576	2681±69	One Sigma [cal BC 902: cal BC 798] 1. Two Sigma [cal BC 1012: cal BC 756] 0.989757 [cal BC 684: cal BC 669] 0.009151 [cal BC 606: cal BC 603] 0.001092	Charred wheat from R23 Str. 3, Floor 3. The context of this sample was not recorded during excavation.	731 BC Stuckenrath 1963:88

(cont'd.)

APPENDIX IIA: RADIOCARBON DATES OF HASANLU IVB RELEVANT TO PERIODS IVC–V

Sample Number	BP	Recalibration BC	Context	Previously Reported
P-0577	2767±54	One Sigma [cal BC 975: cal BC 954] 0.165151 [cal BC 944: cal BC 840] 0.834849 Two Sigma [cal BC 1041: cal BC 811] 1.	"Dried" grapes from R24 Str. 3 Area 2 inside Container 8.	829 BC Stuckenrath 1963:88
P-0860	2718±55	One Sigma [cal BC 907: cal BC 815] 1. Two Sigma [cal BC 995: cal BC 988] 0.010063 [cal BC 980: cal BC 798] 0.989937	Charred grain mixed with charred reeds on the floor south of the oven in BBIII, Room 4.	768 BC Stuckenrath et al. 1966:349
P-0861	2627±53	One Sigma [cal BC 888: cal BC 883] 0.024974 [cal BC 842: cal BC 767] 0.975026 Two Sigma [cal BC 910: cal BC 748] 0.89396 [cal BC 687: cal BC 666] 0.042788 [cal BC 643: cal BC 590] 0.050843 [cal BC 579: cal BC 560] 0.012408	Charred grain on floor BBIII Room 4.	677 BC Stuckenrath et al. 1966:350
P-0863	2604±55	One Sigma [cal BC 835: cal BC 754] 0.854058 [cal BC 685: cal BC 668] 0.09958 [cal BC 610: cal BC 598] 0.046362 Two Sigma [cal BC 898: cal BC 731] 0.713422 [cal BC 691: cal BC 660] 0.091099 [cal BC 651: cal BC 544] 0.19548	Charred grain mixed with charred reeds on floor east of grindstone BBIII Room 4.	654 BC Stuckenrath et al. 1966:350
P-0865	2529±53	One Sigma [cal BC 791: cal BC 742] 0.299064 [cal BC 689: cal BC 663] 0.160684 [cal BC 647: cal BC 549] 0.540252 Two Sigma [cal BC 803: cal BC 505] 0.96993 [cal BC 491: cal BC 490] 0.000778 [cal BC 462: cal BC 450] 0.009008 [cal BC 440: cal BC 418] 0.020285	Charred wheat from R23 Floor 3 of citadel. *This sample is from an insecure context and was undersized. It represents the remainder of sample P-0576 and therefore should not be used for the dating of the Terminal Hasanlu IVb destruction.*	579 BC Stuckenrath et al. 1966:350
P-0905	2700±54	One Sigma [cal BC 896: cal BC 811] 1. Two Sigma [cal BC 975: cal BC 953] 0.035809 [cal BC 945: cal BC 792] 0.964191	Charred barley from floor of gate building (Room 4) of BBIII.	750 BC Stuckenrath et al. 1966:349

(cont'd.)

APPENDIX IIA: RADIOCARBON DATES OF HASANLU IVB RELEVANT TO PERIODS IVC–V

Sample Number	BP	Recalibration BC	Context	Previously Reported
P-0906	2648±54	One Sigma [cal BC 893: cal BC 875] 0.139262 [cal BC 847: cal BC 787] 0.860738 Two Sigma [cal BC 967: cal BC 965] 0.000889 [cal BC 929: cal BC 754] 0.976632 [cal BC 685: cal BC 668] 0.016407 [cal BC 610: cal BC 598] 0.006072	Charred grain on floor of gate building (Room 4) of BBIII.	698 BC Stuckenrath et al. 1966:349
P-0907	2699±53	One Sigma [cal BC 896: cal BC 863] 0.382658 [cal BC 861: cal BC 811] 0.617342 Two Sigma [cal BC 974: cal BC 955] 0.030388 [cal BC 942: cal BC 792] 0.969612	"Dried" grapes from jar on "floor" of BBIII, Room 5. This jar was in fill above the floor and probably fell from the building's upper story. See also P-0577 for other grapes sampled from jar HAS62-209.	749 BC Stuckenrath et al. 1966:350
P-1230	2830±60	One Sigma [cal BC 1110: cal BC 1103] 0.023404 [cal BC 1074: cal BC 1065] 0.03485 [cal BC 1056: cal BC 906] 0.941746 Two Sigma [cal BC 1192: cal BC 1174] 0.016639 [cal BC 1164: cal BC 1143] 0.020498 [cal BC 1132: cal BC 836] 0.962863	Charcoal from north wall of the Anteroom (Room 2) of BBII sealed in the layer between the first and second courses of brick during the reconstruction of the building, Op. AA30, Wall H.	1100–1030 ±60 BC Fishman and Lawn 1978:221
P-2384	2770±50	One Sigma [cal BC 975: cal BC 953] 0.182525 [cal BC 945: cal BC 887] 0.497227 [cal BC 884: cal BC 843] 0.320247 Two Sigma [cal BC 1038: cal BC 1034] 0.003184 [cal BC 1028: cal BC 813] 0.996816	Charcoal from V22W Str. 3 Area 5. This sample is from the south end of BBVII.	Fishman and Lawn 1978:221

Appendix IIb: Radiocarbon Dates from "Hasanlu V" and Dinkha III—now Hasanlu IVc and Hasanlu V

Sample Number	BP	Recalibration BC	Context	Previously Reported
P-0185	2990±120	One Sigma [cal BC 1386: cal BC 1110] 0.894802 [cal BC 1103: cal BC 1075] 0.078303 [cal BC 1065: cal BC 1056] 0.026896 Two Sigma [cal BC 1494: cal BC 1473] 0.011434 [cal BC 1464: cal BC 912] 0.988566	Operation I Str. 5d ash.	1132±124 Dyson 1962:643, Fig. 6; Ralph 1959:50
P-0186	2873±119	One Sigma [cal BC 1252: cal BC 1241] 0.030852 [cal BC 1213: cal BC 913] 0.969148 Two Sigma [cal BC 1494: cal BC 1473] 0.011434 [cal BC 1464: cal BC 912] 0.988566	Operation VII ash.	1009±123 Dyson 1962:643, Fig. 6; Ralph 1959:49
P-0187	2765±117	One Sigma [cal BC 1108: cal BC 1105] 0.009575 [cal BC 1056: cal BC 803] 0.990425 Two Sigma [cal BC 1306: cal BC 751] 0.984971 [cal BC 686: cal BC 667] 0.00669 [cal BC 636: cal BC 622] 0.003228 [cal BC 613: cal BC 595] 0.005111	"Grey Ware Phase" from the Low Mound in Operation IV, Str. 3, near the top of the south baulk.	Dyson 1962:643, Fig. 6; Ralph 1959:49–50
P-0198	3075±120	One Sigma [cal BC 1491: cal BC 1480] 0.02607 [cal BC 1456: cal BC 1191] 0.903777 [cal BC 1177: cal BC 1160] 0.040224 [cal BC 1144: cal BC 1131] 0.029929 Two Sigma [cal BC 1610: cal BC 1003] 1.	East baulk above Burial 13 of early Period IVB, Op. VI, Str. 3, charcoal and ash.	1217±126 BC Dyson 1962:643, Fig. 6; Ralph 1959:50
P-0418	2898 ±49	One Sigma [cal BC 1192: cal BC 1176] 0.077552 [cal BC 1163: cal BC 1143] 0.093007 [cal BC 1132: cal BC 1008] 0.829441 Two Sigma [cal BC 1260: cal BC 1227] 0.050492 [cal BC 1222: cal BC 971] 0.917676 [cal BC 960: cal BC 935] 0.031832	Hasanlu Op. XVI, Str. 5 Area 1 under Wall A, charcoal	949 BC 1036±51 BC 1314–1190 BC Dyson 1962:643, Fig. 6; Stuckenrath 1963:86

(cont'd.)

Sample Number	BP	Recalibration BC	Context	Previously Reported
P-0419	2889 ±45	One Sigma [cal BC 1128: cal BC 994] 0.966289 [cal BC 988: cal BC 980] 0.033711 Two Sigma [cal BC 1211: cal BC 925] 1.	Hasanlu Op. XVI, Str. 5 Area 1 under Wall A, charcoal	930 BC 1016±47 BC Dyson 1962:643, Fig. 6; Stuckenrath 1963:86
P-1230	2830±60	One Sigma [cal BC 1110: cal BC 1103] 0.023404 [cal BC 1074: cal BC 1065] 0.03485 [cal BC 1056: cal BC 906] 0.941746 Two Sigma [cal BC 1192: cal BC 1174] 0.016639 [cal BC 1164: cal BC 1143] 0.020498 [cal BC 1132: cal BC 836] 0.962863	Charcoal from AA30 Wall H of BBII anteroom North Wall sealed in 1st and 2nd courses of brick.	1100–1030±60 BC Fishman and Lawn 1978:221
P-1449	3099±70	One Sigma [cal BC 1439: cal BC 1290] 0.952693 [cal BC 1281: cal BC 1270] 0.047307 Two Sigma [cal BC 1510: cal BC 1191] 0.979034 [cal BC 1177: cal BC 1160] 0.011416 [cal BC 1143: cal BC 1131] 0.00955	Dinkha III charcoal from Test Trench 3, immediately above and resting on the Bronze Age deposit (Str. 8) at base of Dinkha III fill, Area B9 at north edge of the central mound. Stratigraphically close to P-1474.	1149 BC Lawn 1970:578
P-1474	3157±55	One Sigma [cal BC 1497: cal BC 1392] 1. Two Sigma [cal BC 1601: cal BC 1592] 0.006493 [cal BC 1532: cal BC 1294] 0.993507	Dinkha III charcoal from pit over stone foundation of Wall E, Area B8, summit of mound. This sample is stratigraphically earlier that P-1474.	1207 BC Lawn 1970:578
P-1475	3005±40	One Sigma [cal BC 1370: cal BC 1356] 0.06996 [cal BC 1316: cal BC 1194] 0.891855 [cal BC 1141: cal BC 1134] 0.038185 Two Sigma [cal BC 1386: cal BC 1127] 1.	Dinkha III, charcoal immediately over Wall A, Area B7, summit of mound.	1055 BC Lawn 1970:577
P-2155	3110±60	One Sigma [cal BC 1442: cal BC 1309] 1. Two Sigma [cal BC 1505: cal BC 1252] 0.974418 [cal BC 1241: cal BC 1213] 0.025582	Charcoal, V31 Str. 5 BBIVE debris of Period V sealed in bench, south side of columned hall.	1480–1460 ±60 BC Fishman and Lawn 1978:222
P-2156	3020±50	One Sigma Ranges [cal BC 1381: cal BC 1334] 0.271636 [cal BC 1323: cal BC 1211] 0.728364 Two Sigma Ranges [cal BC 1409: cal BC 1125] 1.	DD30 Area 1 Str. 5. From structure against the south end of BBII, which Dyson believed to date to late Period V. The structure survived until Period IVb.	1360–1310 ±50 BC Fishman and Lawn 1978:222

(cont'd.)

APPENDIX IIB: RADIOCARBON DATES FROM...HASANLU IVC AND HASANLU V

Sample Number	BP	Recalibration BC	Context	Previously Reported
P-2160	2750±50	One Sigma [cal BC 969: cal BC 962] 0.049475 [cal BC 931: cal BC 832] 0.950525 Two Sigma [cal BC 1004: cal BC 810] 1.	Building cut by BBVII's north end and post-dating U22–23. S22 Area 13, Str. 10. Sample from posthole penetrating the floor of "Building II" in Period V. Dyson notes that the sample was probably intrusive from overlying Period IVb (Fishman and Lawn 1978:221).	990–940 BC Fishman and Lawn 1978:221
P-2161	3010±50	One Sigma [cal BC 1374: cal BC 1340] 0.181008 [cal BC 1319: cal BC 1194] 0.780712 [cal BC 1141: cal BC 1134] 0.03828 Two Sigma [cal BC 1409: cal BC 1114] 0.998671 [cal BC 1096: cal BC 1095] 0.001329	Charcoal S22 Area 11, Str. 8a, Sample 6. From stratum overlying Period V Building II [RS22–23 Period V Building], and underlying Period IVB level.	1360–1300 ±50 BC Fishman and Lawn 1978:222
P-2374	2830±50	One Sigma [cal BC 1050: cal BC 916] 1. Two Sigma [cal BC 1186: cal BC 1185] 0.000658 [cal BC 1129: cal BC 843] 0.999342	Charcoal V31W Area 4, Str. 2, upper collapse of BBIVe columned hall. The building was rebuilt following the Period IVc fire (the beginning of Period IVb).	1100–1030±50 BC) Fishman and Lawn 1978:221
P-2375	2950±50	One Sigma [cal BC 1262: cal BC 1112] 0.910924 [cal BC 1101: cal BC 1086] 0.06288 [cal BC 1063: cal BC 1058] 0.026196 Two Sigma [cal BC 1369: cal BC 1358] 0.009138 [cal BC 1315: cal BC 1009] 0.990862	Charred wood W30 part of a column from the east portico of BBIV. Portico was built at start of Period IVb; based on the early date, Dyson believed it was an older tree or a recycled column from Period IVc (Fishman and Lawn 1978:221). Recalibration provides a range which overlaps the start of Period IVb.	1270–1240 ±50 BC Fishman and Lawn 1978:221
P-2376	2820±50	One Sigma [cal BC 1040: cal BC 910] 1. Two Sigma [cal BC 1122: cal BC 887] 0.938279 [cal BC 884: cal BC 843] 0.061721	Charcoal Y31 Area 3, Str. 3, upper collapse of BBV	1080–1030 ±50 BC Fishman and Lawn 1978:221
P-2378	2990±70	One Sigma [cal BC 1370: cal BC 1346] 0.089935 [cal BC 1316: cal BC 1126] 0.910065 Two Sigma [cal BC 1407: cal BC 1024] 1.	Charcoal S22, Period IV-V Building, Area 11, Str. 8	1290±170 BC Fishman and Lawn 1978:222

(cont'd.)

Sample Number	BP	Recalibration BC	Context	Previously Reported
P-2384A	2770±50	One Sigma [cal BC 975: cal BC 953] 0.182525 [cal BC 945: cal BC 887] 0.497227 [cal BC 884: cal BC 843] 0.320247 Two Sigma [cal BC 1038: cal BC 1034] 0.003184 [cal BC 1028: cal BC 813] 0.996816	Charcoal V22W Area 5, Str. 3, south end of BB VII	2770 ±50 Fishman and Lawn 1978:222
P-2385	2980±40	One Sigma [cal BC 1289: cal BC 1282] 0.033824 [cal BC 1269: cal BC 1187] 0.643274 [cal BC 1184: cal BC 1153] 0.198247 [cal BC 1147: cal BC 1129] 0.124655 Two Sigma [cal BC 1374: cal BC 1340] 0.049431 [cal BC 1319: cal BC 1110] 0.904878 [cal BC 1103: cal BC 1072] 0.033901 [cal BC 1067: cal BC 1056] 0.011791	Charred wood from X32 Area 3, Str. 5. Part of doorframe of north door BBV. Dyson believed it might have belonged to the original Period IVc building (Fishman and Lawn 1978:222).	1300–1270 ±50 BC Fishman and Lawn 1978:222
P-2389	3000±60	One Sigma [cal BC 1371: cal BC 1345] 0.118605 [cal BC 1317: cal BC 1189] 0.710752 [cal BC 1180: cal BC 1157] 0.102998 [cal BC 1145: cal BC 1130] 0.067645 Two Sigma [cal BC 1401: cal BC 1055] 1.	Charred wood V31E Area 2, Str. 3, BBIVE roof beam. Dyson believed this was a Period IVc beam reused in a Period IVB structure.	1300 ±60 BC Fishman and Lawn 1978:222
P-2390	3130±60	One Sigma [cal BC 1492: cal BC 1476] 0.088074 [cal BC 1460: cal BC 1371] 0.727428 [cal BC 1346: cal BC 1316] 0.184498 Two Sigma [cal BC 1523: cal BC 1260] 0.996788 [cal BC 1227: cal BC 1222] 0.003212	Below BBIVE, between Floor 3 and floor of BBIVE Room 3 (V31E TTI Str. 5, Area 7). Structure below the columned hall of BBIVE.	1500 ±60 BC Fishman and Lawn 1978:222
P-2391A	2950±50	One Sigma [cal BC 1262: cal BC 1112] 0.910924 [cal BC 1101: cal BC 1086] 0.06288 [cal BC 1063: cal BC 1058] 0.026196 Two Sigma [cal BC 1369: cal BC 1358] 0.009138 [cal BC 1315: cal BC 1009] 0.990862	Charcoal Z29 Areas 1 and 4, Str. 10a, from structure beneath BBIE and its underlying foundation between Wall J and s. baulk of Z29. Dyson states that the pottery associated with this sample was "Period V" (Fishman and Lawn 1978:223).	1260–1220 ±50 BC Fishman and Lawn 1978:223

(cont'd.)

APPENDIX IIB: RADIOCARBON DATES FROM...HASANLU IVC AND HASANLU V

Sample Number	BP	Recalibration BC	Context	Previously Reported
P-2392	2950±60	One Sigma Ranges [cal BC 1262: cal BC 1109] 0.821473 [cal BC 1104: cal BC 1072] 0.1362 [cal BC 1066: cal BC 1056] 0.042327 Two Sigma Ranges [cal BC 1379: cal BC 1336] 0.042051 [cal BC 1322: cal BC 999] 0.957949	DD30 Area 4, Str. 5. Charred wood from structure at the south end of BBII. According to Dyson this structure was probably built in "Period V."	1260–1220 ±60 BC Fishman and Lawn 1978:223
P-2393	3000±60	One Sigma [cal BC 1371: cal BC 1345] 0.118605 [cal BC 1317: cal BC 1189] 0.710752 [cal BC 1180: cal BC 1157] 0.102998 [cal BC 1145: cal BC 1130] 0.067645 Two Sigma [cal BC 1401: cal BC 1055] 1.	Charcoal V31 TT1 Area 8, Str. 5, Lot 32 below BBIVE Room 3 (columned hall) between Floors 2 and 3 and Walls C and E.	1300 ±60 BC Fishman and Lawn 1978:223
P-2394	2880±60	One Sigma [cal BC 1189: cal BC 1180] 0.030859 [cal BC 1156: cal BC 1145] 0.04647 [cal BC 1130: cal BC 975] 0.876502 [cal BC 955: cal BC 943] 0.046169 Two Sigma [cal BC 1260: cal BC 1226] 0.041565 [cal BC 1223: cal BC 909] 0.958435	Charcoal V19 Area 2, fill between Walls J and K. West slope of tepe. Wall K overlain by Period IVb road system.	1110 ±60 BC Fishman and Lawn 1978:221

Appendix IIc. Radiocarbon Dates from Hasanlu VIb/Dinkha IVa–c

Sample Number	BP	Recalibration BC	Context	Previously Reported
P-1231	3285±50	One Sigma [cal BC 1618: cal BC 1503] 1. Two Sigma [cal BC 1684: cal BC 1452] 1.	Dinkha IV Phase D, charcoal Charcoal in B9a from terminal Bronze Age deposit, Str. 8, directly underlying Iron Age fill Str. 7 (cf. P-1449). From above the burned building of P-1232. Sample came from the last floor of the short period of reoccupation following the fire (Str. 8) underlying Bronze Age fill (Str. 7), Test Trench 3, Area B9, north edge of central mound. Cf. P-1449.	1335 BC 1434 BC Dyson 1973:705; Lawn 1970:578
P-1232	3402±50	One Sigma [cal BC 1753: cal BC 1626] 1. Two Sigma [cal BC 1878: cal BC 1839] 0.073208 [cal BC 1828: cal BC 1792] 0.048428 [cal BC 1785: cal BC 1605] 0.832079 [cal BC 1579: cal BC 1536] 0.046285	Dinkha IV Phase D, Charcoal From the floor debris of one of the last major buildings of the period (Area B10a, Stratum 8), which was burned. North edge of central mound.	1452 BC 1555 BC Dyson 1973:705; Lawn 1970:578
P-1233	3458±59	One Sigma [cal BC 1878: cal BC 1839] 0.264807 [cal BC 1829: cal BC 1791] 0.226368 [cal BC 1786: cal BC 1733] 0.362338 [cal BC 1717: cal BC 1693] 0.146486 Two Sigma [cal BC 1922: cal BC 1626] 1.	Dinkha IV, charcoal from ashy fill of Str. 2 under floor. Str. IA and Walls G and F in Area G10g at east edge of central mound. Ceramics equivalent to B10a Stratum 9 = P-1452.	1508 BC Lawn 1970:578
P-1429/1431	3598±66	One Sigma [cal BC 2115: cal BC 2099] 0.05709 [cal BC 2038: cal BC 1880] 0.933499 [cal BC 1837: cal BC 1834] 0.009411 Two Sigma [cal BC 2137: cal BC 1768] 1.	Dinkha IV, charcoal from floor north of Wall F and from pit cut into Wall G from Str. 3 in Area H1h. East end of mound. Walls F and G abut top of earlier massive Wall H1h-E of the earlier half of the Bronze Age occupation.	1648 BC Lawn 1970:579
P-1430	3468±59	One Sigma [cal BC 1880: cal BC 1738] 0.937748 [cal BC 1708: cal BC 1696] 0.062252 Two Sigma [cal BC 1932: cal BC 1635] 1.	Dinkha IV, charcoal from floor associated with Wall D in Area H1g. East end of central mound. Stratigraphically equivalent to P-1233.	1518 BC Lawn 1970:578

(cont'd.)

APPENDIX IIC: RADIOCARBON DATES FROM HASANLU VIB/DINKHA IVA–C 363

Sample Number	BP	Recalibration BC	Context	Previously Reported
P-1450	3434±61	One Sigma [cal BC 1876: cal BC 1842] 0.184559 [cal BC 1820: cal BC 1797] 0.111367 [cal BC 1781: cal BC 1668] 0.704074 Two Sigma [cal BC 1912: cal BC 1607] 0.989405 [cal BC 1571: cal BC 1560] 0.006364 [cal BC 1547: cal BC 1540] 0.004231	Dinkha IV Phase D, charcoal Charcoal from burned structural beams in fill near floor of final major structure of the Bronze Age, Area B10a, Area 1, Str. 8. North edge of central mound. Cf. P-1232.	1484 BC Lawn 1970:578
P-1452	3522±63	One Sigma [cal BC 1924: cal BC 1757] 1. Two Sigma [cal BC 2023: cal BC 1989] 0.041729 [cal BC 1985: cal BC 1727] 0.91762 [cal BC 1723: cal BC 1691] 0.040651	Dinkha IV, charcoal from trashy-fill layer, Area B10a, Str. 9. North edge of mound. Cf. P-1232 and P-1450. Tombs B27 and B28 cut this level.	1572 BC Lawn 1970:578
P-1552	3468±59	One Sigma [cal BC 1880: cal BC 1738] 0.937748 [cal BC 1708: cal BC 1696] 0.062252 Two Sigma [cal BC 1932: cal BC 1635] 1.	Dinkha IV, charcoal from room fill of big wall, Area H1G, east edge of central mound.	1518 BC Lawn 1970:579
P-1690	3539±59	One Sigma [cal BC 1948: cal BC 1863] 0.535122 [cal BC 1850: cal BC 1772] 0.464878 Two Sigma [cal BC 2030: cal BC 1737] 0.98756 [cal BC 1709: cal BC 1696] 0.01244	Dinkha IV, charcoal from Op. B9/10a Str. 2a, Area 5. North edge of central mound.	1589 BC Lawn 1973:374
P-1693	3353±65	One Sigma [cal BC 1735: cal BC 1714] 0.1111 [cal BC 1694: cal BC 1603] 0.609524 [cal BC 1588: cal BC 1534] 0.279376 Two Sigma [cal BC 1873: cal BC 1844] 0.024327 [cal BC 1815: cal BC 1800] 0.008984 [cal BC 1778: cal BC 1494] 0.966689	Dinkha IV, charcoal and soil from Op. G10h, Str. 5e, Area 2, sealed by Wall O. East edge of central mound.	1403 BC Lawn 1973:375
P-1720	3395±68	One Sigma [cal BC 1867: cal BC 1848] 0.064102 [cal BC 1774: cal BC 1609] 0.935898 Two Sigma [cal BC 1880: cal BC 1837] 0.086461 [cal BC 1834: cal BC 1528] 0.913539	Dinkha IV, charcoal from Op. B9/10a, Str. 3, Area 4. North edge of central mound.	1445 BC Lawn 1973:375

Appendix IId. Radiocarbon Dates from Hasanlu VIC/Dinkha V

Sample Number	BP	Recalibration BC	Context	Previously Reported
P-1692	3576±70	One Sigma [cal BC 2028: cal BC 1875] 0.833835 [cal BC 1842: cal BC 1818] 0.095917 [cal BC 1798: cal BC 1780] 0.070247 Two Sigma [cal BC 2134: cal BC 2077] 0.07194 [cal BC 2072: cal BC 2070] 0.002105 [cal BC 2064: cal BC 1743] 0.925955	Charcoal from Dinkha Op. B9/10a, Str. 7 at level of Wall K and hearth of Area 11. North edge of central mound.	1626 BC Lawn 1973:375
P-1721	3458±66	One Sigma [cal BC 1879: cal BC 1837] 0.25249 [cal BC 1832: cal BC 1730] 0.596153 [cal BC 1719: cal BC 1692] 0.151356 Two Sigma [cal BC 1945: cal BC 1614] 1	Two samples of charcoal from Dinkha Op. B9/10a, Str. 7. In SW corner of Wall K at the level of Wall K and hearth of Area 11. North edge of central mound. According to Dyson, "these two combined samples [P-1721 and P-1692] represent deepest stratified carbon above virgin soil at site" (Lawn 1973:375).	1508 BC Lawn 1973:375

Appendix IIe. Radiocarbon Dates from Hasanlu VII

Sample Number	BP	Recalibration BC	Context	Previously Reported
P-0188	3970±140	One Sigma [cal BC 2835: cal BC 2816] 0.036722 [cal BC 2667: cal BC 2282] 0.927466 [cal BC 2249: cal BC 2231] 0.029157 [cal BC 2218: cal BC 2213] 0.006655 Two Sigma [cal BC 2883: cal BC 2133] 0.991591 [cal BC 2081: cal BC 2060] 0.008409	Hasanlu Operation IV, Str. 16	Danti, Voigt, and Dyson 2004:587, table 1
P-0189	3950±130	One Sigma [cal BC 2623: cal BC 2275] 0.916764 [cal BC 2255: cal BC 2208] 0.083236 Two Sigma [cal BC 2873: cal BC 2134] 0.992411 [cal BC 2079: cal BC 2062] 0.007589	Hasanlu Operation V, Str. 21	Danti, Voigt, and Dyson 2004:587, table 1
P-0190	3950±130	One Sigma [cal BC 2623: cal BC 2275] 0.916764 [cal BC 2255: cal BC 2208] 0.083236 Two Sigma [cal BC 2873: cal BC 2134] 0.992411 [cal BC 2079: cal BC 2062] 0.007589	Hasanlu Operation V, Str. 34	Danti, Voigt, and Dyson 2004:587, table 1
P-0191	4010±130	One Sigma [cal BC 2854: cal BC 2812] 0.09057 [cal BC 2746: cal BC 2725] 0.041352 [cal BC 2697: cal BC 2396] 0.785326 [cal BC 2385: cal BC 2346] 0.082752 Two Sigma [cal BC 2889: cal BC 2199] 0.997416 [cal BC 2159: cal BC 2154] 0.002584	Hasanlu Operation VI, Str. 4	Danti, Voigt, and Dyson 2004:587, table 1
P-0194	4110±140	One Sigma [cal BC 2878: cal BC 2564] 0.903747 [cal BC 2532: cal BC 2495] 0.096253 Two Sigma [cal BC 3022: cal BC 2282] 0.994329 [cal BC 2249: cal BC 2232] 0.004641 [cal BC 2218: cal BC 2214] 0.001029	Hasanlu Operation VI, Str. 6	Danti, Voigt, and Dyson 2004:587, table 1

(cont'd.)

APPENDIX IIE: RADIOCARBON DATES FROM HASANLU VII

Sample Number	BP	Recalibration BC	Context	Previously Reported
P-0199	4390±140	One Sigma [cal BC 3331: cal BC 3214] 0.280204 [cal BC 3186: cal BC 3156] 0.065405 [cal BC 3127: cal BC 2895] 0.654391 Two Sigma [cal BC 3498: cal BC 3437] 0.022596 [cal BC 3378: cal BC 2832] 0.885492 [cal BC 2820: cal BC 2658] 0.085173 [cal BC 2653: cal BC 2633] 0.00674	Geoy Tepe K1, Pit 1, 432–56 in hearth at left of west section.	Danti, Voigt, and Dyson 2004:587, table 1
P-2163	3970±50	One Sigma [cal BC 2573: cal BC 2457] 0.923578 [cal BC 2418: cal BC 2408] 0.047636 [cal BC 2374: cal BC 2368] 0.028786 Two Sigma [cal BC 2619: cal BC 2607] 0.010477 [cal BC 2599: cal BC 2593] 0.004269 [cal BC 2585: cal BC 2332] 0.959681 [cal BC 2326: cal BC 2299] 0.025573	Hasanlu U22 Str. 20.	Danti, Voigt, and Dyson 2004:587, table 1

Appendix III

Concordance of Section Numbers and Stratum Descriptions

Figure 3.3. North Section of Operation I (T28)

Stratum	Original No.	Description
1a	—	Topsoil, turf
1b	1a	Grey-brown, pebbly, bricky
2a	3a	Pebbles, brick, sand
2e	—	Sand
4b	—	Unspecified, probably brick collapse
4c	3a [!]	Pebbles, brick collapse
5a	5a	Clay and brick
5b	5b	Clay and brick
5c	5c	Clay and brick
5d	5d	—
6a	6	Grey ash, brown soil
6c	—	—

Figure 3.4. East Section of Operation I (T28)

Stratum	Original No.	Description
1a	—	Topsoil, turf
1b	1a	Grey-brown, pebbly, bricky
2a	1b	Pebbles, brick, sand
2b	1c	—
2c	4a	Brick collapse
2d	4	Brick collapse. pit missed during excavation
2f	4d	Brick collapse
4g	4c	Brick collapse
4h	—	—
4i	4	Pebbles, brick collapse
5a–c	5a–c	"Broken brick"
5d	5d	Pebbles, brick collapse
5e	—	Ash, radiocarbon sample
6a	6	Grey ash, brown soil
6b	—	Ash
6c	—	—

Figure 3.6. North Section of Operation QR20

Stratum	Original No.	Description
1	—	Silt
2	—	Loose wash
3	—	Bricky collapse
4	—	Bricky
5a	—	Wash
5b	—	Robbed
5c	—	Robbed
5d	—	Brick wash on floor
6	—	Bricky
7	—	—
8	—	Wash
9	—	Mudbrick collapse

Figure 3.7. Operation II West Section

Stratum	Original No.	Description
1	2	Topsoil, turf
2	3	Compacted mudbrick collapse
3	—	Pit
4	3	Compacted mudbrick collapse
5	4	Ash
6	5	—
7	6	—
8	7	Ash and charcoal lenses
9	—	—

Figure 3.11. North Section of the U22 Sounding

Stratum	Original No.	Description
1	1962: 1	Topsoil, turf
2	1962: 2	Loose earth
2a	1962: 2a	Hard earth
3	1962: 3	Loose earth, mudbrick fragments
3a	1962: 3a	Pit
4	1962: 4	Loose earth
4a	1962: 4a	Mudbrick collapse, charcoal and ash layers
4b	1962: 4b	Soft plaster wash
4c	1962: 4c	Hard mudbrick collapse
4d	1962: 4d	Mudbrick wash, small pieces of charcoal
4f	1962: 4f	Pit, burned mudbrick fragments, wash
4g	1962: 4g	Powdery earth
4h	1962: 4h	Soft earth, layer of animal bones on bottom, lime [degraded plaster]
4i	1962: 4a	Burned, hard mudbrick collapse; charcoal
4j	1962: 4b	Soft plaster wash
4k	1962: 4e	Hard mudbrick wash, hard surface/ floor
4l	1962: 4i/4f (strata designations and descriptions vary between north and east sections)	Hard grey, soft grey ash
4m	1962: 4b	Soft plaster wash
5	1962: 5	Unspecified fill
6	1962: 6	Floor at base mentioned in notes
6a	1962: 8	Pit
6b	1962: 8	Pit
7	1962: 7 1	Light brown clay
8	1962: 8 2	Light brown clay

(cont'd.)

APPENDIX III: CONCORDANCE OF SECTION NUMBERS AND STRATUM DESCRIPTIONS

Stratum	Original No.	Description
8a	1962: 9	—
8b	1962: 9 / 4	Light brown clay
8c	1962: 9	Brick collapse
9e	1962: 10 / 6	Ash
9f	1962: 10 / 5	Brick collapse
10	1962: 10 / 7	Brown-grey ash, clay
10a	1962: 10 / 8	Bricky collapse, clay
10b	1962: 10 / 9	Brown-grey ash, clay
10c	1962: 10 / 10	Brown-grey ash
10d	11	
10e	1962: 10	Pit. missed in excavation
10f	1962: 10	Pit. missed in excavation
10g	1962: 10	Pit. missed in excavation
10h	1962: 10–11	Pit. missed in excavation
10i	1962: 10	Animal burrow
10j	1962: 10	—
10k	1962: 10	Clay
11	1962: 11/12 (numbering inconsistency between contiguous north and east sections) 1972: 12	Ash, brick fragments, pebbles
11a	1962: 11/12 (numbering inconsistency between contiguous north and east sections) 1972: 12	—
11b	1962: 11/12 (numbering inconsistency between contiguous north and east sections) 1972: 12	Red clay, brick fragments
11c	1962: 11/12 (numbering inconsistency between contiguous north and east sections) 1972: 12	Clay

(cont'd.)

Figure 3.11 (cont'd.). North Section of the U22 Sounding

Stratum	Original No.	Description
11d	1962: 11/12 (numbering inconsistency between contiguous north and east sections) 1972: 12	Ash, red clay, brick fragments
12	1962: 12/13 (numbering inconsistency between contiguous north and east sections) 1972: 13	Bricky striated with ash and clay
13	1962: 12/13 (numbering inconsistency between contiguous north and east sections) 1972: 13	1962: Striated alternating strata of ash and clay 1972: Layered clayey occupation debris
14	1972: 14	Layered occupation debris below "Green Brick Melt"
15	1972: 15	"Green Brick Melt" on brick floor labeled at base of stratum
16	1972: 16	Ash
17a	1972: 17	Brown soil, lime
17b	1972: 17	Brown Fill, Lime

Figure 3.12. East Section of the U22 Sounding

Stratum	Original No.	Description
1	1962: 1	Topsoil, turf
2	1962: 2	Loose earth
2a	1962: 2a	Hard earth
3	1962: 3	Loose earth
3b	1962: 3a	Pit, loose ashy fill
3c	1962: 4	Pit, missed in excavation
4	1962: 4	Loose earth
4a	1962: 4a	Hard mudbrick wash [description inconsistent with Stratum 4a of North Section]
4i	1962: 4a	Burned, hard mudbrick collapse; charcoal
4k	1962: 4e	Hard mudbrick wash, hard surface/floor

(cont'd.)

APPENDIX III: CONCORDANCE OF SECTION NUMBERS AND STRATUM DESCRIPTIONS

Stratum	Original No.	Description
4l	1962: 4i/4f [strata designations and descriptions vary between north and east sections]	Hard grey, soft grey ash
4m	1962: 4b	Soft plaster wash
4o	1962: 4c	Soft plaster wash
4p	1962: 4a	Burned, hard mudbrick collapse; charcoal [likely continuation of Stratum 4i]
4q	1962: 4d	Loose brown earth with small pieces of charcoal and burned barley
4r	1962: 4a	Hard mudbrick wash
4s	1962: 4e	Very hard mudbrick between floors
4t	1962: 4i	Burned mudbrick collapse with pieces of charcoal
5	1962: 5	Unspecified fill
6	1962: 6	Floor labeled at base of stratum
7	1962: 7 [not numbered on section]	Bricky
8	9 [mislabeled on section]	Bricky, ashy
9	1962: 9 [not numbered on section]	Bricky
9a	1962: 9 [not numbered on section]	Ash
9b	1962: 9 [not numbered on section]	Ash
9c	1962: 9	Ash
9d	1962: 9 [not numbered on section]	Bricky, floor labeled at base of stratum
10d	1962: 10	Bricky
11	1962: 11/12 (numbering inconsistency between contiguous north and east sections)	Ash, brick fragments, pebbles
12	1962: 12/13 (numbering inconsistency between contiguous north and east sections)	Bricky, striated with ash and clay

Figure 3.13. East Section of T22

Stratum	Original No.	Description
1	1	Topsoil, turf
2	2	Hard earth, partly mudbrick collapse
3	3	Loose earth and mudbrick collapse
3a	3d	Red burned earth and ash, fill of a fireplace
3c	3b	Loose ashy earth
3d	3c	Pit, grey ash Pit 4, grey and white ash layers
3e	Pit missed in excavation. Excavated as Strata 1–4	"Loose Undefinite [SIC] Fill"
3f	3f	Mudbrick wash
4	4b	Mudbrick wash
4a	4c	Loose, burnt brick collapse with charcoal
4b	4d	Hard, red burnt earth with charcoal
5	Multiple floors of Period IV BB VII	Multiple floors of period IV BB VII
5b	Unlabeled. Excavated as Stratum 5	—
5c	5	Hard packed wash, some ash layers
6	6	Bricky fill
7	7	Bricky fill
8	—	—

Figure 3.15. East Section of S22

Stratum	Original No.	Description
1	1962: 1	Topsoil, turf
2	1962: 2	"Loose Grey Dust"
3	Excavated as 1962: 2a (Upper) and Stratum 2b (Lower)	Stratum 2a: Very compact brown clay Stratum 2b: As Stratum 2a, looser consistency Floor B at base of stratum
3e	Excavated as 1962: Stratum 2	Pit
4	1962: 3	Buff colored earth with some flecks of charcoal and hard surface
4a	1962: 3 1972: 6–8a	1962: Buff colored earth with some flecks of charcoal and hard surface 1972: Green [this stratum specifically]
4b	1962: 3a, Pit 3 1972: 6–11	1962: "Powdery dust with layers of ash on both sides of pit and in pit 1972: Pit missed
4c	1962: 3 1972: 6–8a	1962: Buff colored earth with some flecks of charcoal and hard surface 1972: Green
4d	1962: 3–3a 1972: 6–8a	"Powdery Dust with Layers of Grey Ash" 1972: Hard, black, charcoal, burnt
4e	1962: 3–3a 1972: 6–8a	"Powdery Dust with Layers of Grey Ash" 1972: Hard, black, charcoal, burnt
5	1962: 3a 1972: 8	—
5a	1962: 3b (Upper Portion) 1972: 8–9	1962: Harder, partly eroded wash with some horizontal streaks of ash and fragments of burnt brick
5b	1972: 10–11	1972: "Brick Mixed Soil"
5c	1962: 3b (Upper Portion) 1972: "Pit 10" (Lower Portion) 1972: 8–10	1962: Harder, partly eroded wash with some horizontal streaks of ash and fragments of burnt brick
5d	1972: 10–11	—
6	1972: 8–9	—
7	1972: 8–9	—

Figure 3.18. East Section of R22

Stratum	Original No.	Description
1	1962: 1	Topsoil, sod
2	1962: 2	Wash, brick fragments
3a	—	Pit
3b	1962: 3	Hard pack, brick fragments, ash
3f	Pit	—
4a	1962: 4	—
4b	1962: 4	—
4d	1962: 3c	Soft ash, charcoal, brick collapse
4e	1962: 3d	Soft wash
5	1972: 11	Brown soil
5c	1972: 11	As Operation S22 Stratum 5c

Figure 3.26. West and North Sections below BB IE Room 3 of Period IVb

Stratum	Original No.	Description
10a	10	Hard brown clay
10b	10	Grey-brown occupation debris wash
10c	10	Yellow-brown hard matrix with pebbles and brick fragments
10d	10	Light brown wash with pebbles
10e	10	Grey-brown occupation debris wash
10f	10	Grey-brown bricky and occupation debris
10g	10	Yellow-brown bricky occupation debris with mudbrick fragments
10j	10	Yellow-brown bricky occupation debris with mudbrick fragments
10k	11	Brown bricky fill
10l	11	Light brown/yellow occupation debris wash and mudbrick collapse
10q	11	Grey-brown occupation debris with brick fragments and ash
10r	11	Brown bricky fill and occupation debris
10t	11	Light brown/yellow occupation debris wash and mudbrick collapse

Figure 3.27. East Section below BB IE Room 6

Stratum	Original No.	Description
10a	10	Occupation debris and bricky matrix
10b	10	Bricky layer
10d	10	Light brown occupation debris and bricky matrix
10o	10	Occupation debris layer

Figure 3.28. North Section below BB IE Room 6

Stratum	Original No.	Description
10a	10	Ash, occupation debris, and mudbrick collapse on original Period IVb floor
10b	10	Light brown occupation debris and bricky matrix
10d	10	Light brown occupation debris and bricky matrix
10f	Brick Floor	Brick floor

APPENDIX III: CONCORDANCE OF SECTION NUMBERS AND STRATUM DESCRIPTIONS

Figure 3.29. South Section below BB IE Room 6

Stratum	Original No.	Description
10a	10a	Light yellowish-brown hard bricky layer
10c	10a	Tan hard bricky layer
10e	10a	Dark brown
10f	10a	Dark brown clay, occupation debris, charcoal
10i	10a	Grey ash and occupation debris layer, excavator noted signs of disturbance, lower part dark brown to orange
10j	10a	Ash
10k	10a	—
10l	10a	Greenish-brown occupation debris layers
10m	10a	Greenish-brown occupation debris layers
10n	10a	Surface of packed dark brown and green matrix with some burned mudbrick particles and ash

Figure 3.30. West Section below BB IE Room 6

Stratum	Original No.	Description
10a	10/10a	Hard bricky layer
10c	10/10a	Light brown packed bricky matrix
10d	Area 2 Stratum 10	Brownish-yellow bricky matrix
10e	Area 4 10a	Brown occupation debris
10f	Area 2 Stratum 11	Brick floor
10g	Area 4 Stratum 10a	Dark brown/orange bricky matrix
10h	Areas 2 Stratum 11 Area 4 Stratum 10a	Grey ash
10i	Areas 2 Stratum 11 Area 4 Stratum 10a	Grey-brown occupation debris
10p	Area 4 Str. 10a	Dark brown occupation debris

Figure 3.31. East Section below BB IE Room 5

Stratum	Original No.	Description
10a	10	Brown bricky
10b	10	Brown occupation debris
10d	10	Ash
10k	10	Yellow clay
10l	10	Yellow bricky
10m	10	Brownish-yellow bricky
10n	10	Ash
10o	10	Brownish-yellow bricky
10p	10	Brownish-yellow bricky
10q	10	Ash
10r	10	Yellowish bricky
10s	10	Ash
10t	10	Brownish bricky
10u	10	Ash
10v	10	Greyish-yellow ash and occupation debris
10x	10	Yellow clay
10z	10	Brown hard packed occupation debris and brick fragments
10b1	10	Brick floor

Figure 3.32. West Section below BB IE Room 5

Stratum	Original No.	Description
10a	10	Brown bricky
10c	10	Grey-brown bricky
10g	10	Grey-brown ash and occupation debris
10h	10	Yellowish clay
10i	10	Ash
10j	10	Yellowish-grey
10y	10	Ash and occupation debris
10z	10	Brown hard-packed occupation debris and brick fragments
10a1	10	Occupation debris
10b1	10	Brick floor
10c1	10	Yellowish-brown bricky matrix

Figure 3.33. North Section below BB IE Room 5

Stratum	Original No.	Description
10a	10	Brown bricky
10b	10	Brown occupation debris
10c	10	Grey-brown bricky
10g	10	Grey-brown ash and occupation debris
10h	10	Yellowish clay
10l	10	Yellow bricky
10q	10	Ash
10r	10	Yellowish bricky
10s	10	Ash
10t	10	Brownish bricky
10u	10	Ash
10v	10	Greyish-yellow ash and occupation debris
10w	10	Loose fill and occupation debris
10x	10	Yellow clay
10y	10	Ash and occupation debris
10z	10	Brown hard-packed occupation debris and brick fragments
10b1	10	Brick floor

Figure 3.34. South Section below BB IE Room 5

Stratum	Original No.	Description
10a	10	Brown bricky
10b	10	Brown occupation debris
10c	10	Grey-brown bricky
10d	10	Ash
10e	10	Yellow clay, surface
10f	10	Orange burned bricky
10h	10	Yellowish clay
10d1	10	Brown hard-packed occupation debris and brick fragments
10e1	10	Grey occupation debris
10f1	10	Brick floor
10g1	10	Hard clay
10h1	10	Unspecified

Figure 3.40. Y27 West Section below BB IW

Stratum	Original No.	Description
1	Area 2	Brown surface, wash
2	Area 2	Light brown hard-packed matrix
2b	Area 2	Undifferentiated grey-brown wash layers
2c	Area 2	Brown hard-packed
3	Area 2	Dark brown occupation debris, wash, mud-brick fragments
4	Area 2	Ash, occupation debris
5	Area 2	Light brown occupation debris, wash, mud-brick fragments
6	Area 2	Brown hard-packed matrix with pebbles
7	Area 2	Greyish-yellow occupation debris, wash
8	Area 2	Light brown hard-packed matrix
9	Area 2	Yellow clay-like hard-packed matrix
10	Area 2	Greyish-yellow occupation debris and wash
11	Area 2	Greyish wash
12	Area 2	Greyish-yellow occupation debris
13	Area 2	Yellow clay and hard-packed matrix
14	Area 2	Fine grey silt with ash
15	Area 2	Greyish-yellow occupation debris
16	Area 2	Brownish-yellow bricky wash with burned granules
17	Area 2	Greyish-yellow occupation debris
18	Area 2	Brown hard-packed matrix
19	Area 2	Ash
20	Area 2	Yellow-grey wash with pebbles
21	Area 2	Brown hard-packed matrix
22	Area 2	Grey-brown wash
23	Area 2	Hard grey-brown wash

Figure 3.45. North Section of CC27

Stratum	Original No.	Description
1	1	Turf, topsoil
2	2	Loose brown wash
2a	2a	Loose brown wash
2b	2b	Ash
2c	2c	Occupation debris
2d	Unspecified	Heavy ash
2e	2e	Mudbrick collapse
2f	2f	Surface
2g	2e	Mudbrick collapse with underlying undifferentiated laid mudbrick
3	3	Mudbrick collapse
3a	3a	Bricky wash
3b	3b	Bricky wash
3c	3c	Compact bricky wash
3d	3d	Unspecified pit
3e	3e	Unspecified pit
3f	3f	Ash
3g	3g	Ash
3h	3h	Compact bricky wash
3i	3i	Ash
4	4	Compact bricky wash
4a	4a	Light grey ash
4b	4b	Ash
4c	4c	Unspecified

Figure 3.46. South Section of BB28–29

Stratum	Original No.	Description
1	1	Topsoil, turf
2	2	Loose grey-brown wash, mudbrick fragments
3	3	Loose grey-brown wash
3a	3a	Floor, Period II/IIIa
3b	3b	Bricky wash
3c	Unspecified	Unspecified pit
3d	Unspecified	Unspecified pit
4	Unspecified	Mudbrick collapse, brick bats, charcoal
5	4	Mudbrick collapse
6	4b	Heavy striated ash and burnt material atop burned floor
6a	6	"Burnt Floor, Grey Ware II" (Dyson Field Notes 1959), compact brick = Terminal Period IVb Destruction
7	4c	"Solid clean bricky material (brown) in local area. Gives impression of being a platform of some sort, but did not appear in horizontal as such" (T. Cuyler Young Field Notes, 1959).
8	Unspecified	Unspecified ash?
9	Unspecified	Pit, ash?
10	Unspecified	Compact bricky matrix
10a	Unspecified	Ash
10b	Unspecified	"3rd Floor, Grey Ware I" (R.H. Dyson Field Notes, 1959), compact brick
11	Unspecified	Compact bricky matrix
11a	Unspecified	Ash
11b	Unspecified	"2nd Floor, Grey Ware I" (R.H. Dyson Field Notes, 1959), compact brick
12	Unspecified	Compact bricky matrix
12a	Unspecified	"Original Floor, Grey Ware I" (R.H. Dyson Field Notes, 1959), compact brick

Figure 3.50. South Section of Operation IV

Stratum	Original No.	Description
1	1	Loose matrix with straw
1a	1a	Hard clay (tauf or mudbrick)
1b	1b	Hard clay (tauf or mudbrick)
2	2	Compact brown matrix
3	3	Compact brown matrix
5	5	Hard clay, occupation debris
6	6	Compact matrix, mudbrick fragments
7	7	Compact matrix, mudbrick fragments, charcoal
8	8	Compact matrix, mudbrick fragments, on Floor V
9	9	Compact matrix, mudbrick fragments
10	10	Compact matrix, mudbrick fragments
15	15	Soft brown matrix
15a	15a	Ash and charcoal
15b	15b	Hard light grey clay with ash
15c	15c	Hard very light grey clay with ash
15d	15d	Medium dark grey clay with ash
15e	15e	Brown compact matrix with ash
16	16	Hard green clay
17	17	Black ash
18a	18a	Hard green clay
18b	18b	Hard green clay
18f	18f	Brown clay
18g	18g	Charcoal
18h	18h	Charcoal and ash
19	19	Brown clay mudbricks
19a	19a	Light brown matrix and clay
19b	19b	Brown clay

(cont'd.)

Figure 3.50 (cont'd.). South Section of Operation IV

Stratum	Original No.	Description
20	20	Brown clay, streaks of charcoal
21	21	Lumpy brown clay
23	23	Brown clay with mudbrick fragments
25	25	Brown clay with mudbrick fragments
26	26	Brown clay with mudbrick fragments
27	27	Brown clay with streaks of dark brown clay
27a	27a	Charcoal
28	28	Brown clay
29	29	Brown clay with streaks of charcoal
30	30	Light brown clay
30a	30a	Brown compact matrix
30b	30b	Charcoal
31	31	Dark brown clay
31a	31a	Charcoal
33	33	Dark brown clay, much charcoal
34	34	Sterile sand

Figure 3.51. West Section of Operation IV

Stratum	Original No.	Description
1	1	Loose matrix with straw
2	2	Compact brown matrix
3	3	Compact brown matrix
4	4	Mudbrick collapse of Wall A
5	5	Hard clay, occupation debris
6	6	Compact matrix, mudbrick fragments

(cont'd.)

APPENDIX III: CONCORDANCE OF SECTION NUMBERS AND STRATUM DESCRIPTIONS

Stratum	Original No.	Description
7	7	Compact matrix, mudbrick fragments, charcoal
8	8	Compact matrix, mudbrick fragments, on Floor V
9	9	Compact matrix, mudbrick fragments
10	10	Compact matrix, mudbrick fragments
11	11	Ash
12		Soft bricky matrix
13	13	Ash lenses on Floor VII with Wall G
14	14	"Brick Foundation for Wall G"
15	15	Soft brown matrix
16	16	Hard green clay
17	17	Black ash
18a	18a	Hard green clay
18b	18b	Hard green clay
19	19	Brown clay bricks
20	20	Brown clay, streaks of charcoal
21	21	Lumpy brown clay
23	23	Brown clay with mudbrick fragments
24	24	Brown clay
25	25	Brown clay with mudbrick fragments
26	26	Brown clay with mudbrick fragments
27	27	Brown clay with streaks of dark brown clay
28	28	Brown clay
29	29	Brown clay with streaks of charcoal
30	30	Light brown clay
31	31	Dark brown clay
31a	31a	Charcoal
32	32	Light brown clay
33	33	Dark brown clay, much charcoal
34	34	Sterile sand

Figure 3.56. East and North Section of Operation VI

Stratum	Original No.	Description
1	1	Topsoil/turf
2	2	Loose grey wash
3	3	Soft grey-brown matrix
3b	3b	Mudbrick collapse
3c	3c	Mudbrick collapse
4	4	Ash and occupation debris
4a	4a	Bricky matrix
4b	4b	Soft brown matrix, ash
5	5	Soft brown matrix

Figure 3.57. South and West Section of Operation VI

Stratum	Original No.	Description
1	1	Topsoil/turf
2	2	Loose grey wash
3	3	Soft grey-brown matrix
3c	3c	Mudbrick collapse
4	4	Ash and occupation debris
4a	4a	Bricky matrix
4b	4b	Soft brown matrix, ash
5	5	Soft brown matrix

Figure 3.58. North and West Sections of Operation VIa

Stratum	Original No.	Description
1	1	Topsoil, turf
2	2	Powdery brown loose fill
2a	2a	Mudbrick collapse
2b	2b	Compact bricky
2c	2c	Loose matrix
3	3	Compact brown clay with mudbrick fragments
3a	4	Ash
3b	5	Compact brown and brick fragments (and cut for Burial SK57)
3c	5a	Loose fill (cut for Burials SK50 and SK55)
3d	No Designation	Cut for Burial SK70
4	7	Striated ash, compact matrix, and loose matrix
4a	8	Loose pit fill
4b	7	Striated ash, compact matrix, and loose matrix
5	5	Reeds
6	6	Ash, loose matrix
7	No Designation	Cut for Burial SK57 and tunnel excavated into balk to recover grave
8a	9	Red burnt surface
8b	10	Soft brown
8c	11	Compact yellow bricky
9	12	Striated Ash
10	11	Compact Yellow Bricky
11	11a	Ash and clay striations
12	13a	Ash
13	13	Compact greenish
14	14	Striated ash
15	15	Mudbrick collapse
16	16	Soft powdery grey

(cont'd.)

Figure 3.58 (cont'd.). North and West Sections of Operation VIa

Stratum	Original No.	Description
17	17	Burnt brown
18	18	Soft red-brown burnt
19	13	Ash
20	14	Mudbrick collapse
21	15	Soft brown with charcoal

Figure 3.60. South Section of Operation VIb

Stratum	Original No.	Description
1	1	Turf, topsoil
2	2	Loose pebbly wash
3	3	Ash
4	4	Compact light brown clay
5	5	Loose fill with mudbrick bats
6	6	Loose fill with mudbrick bats
7	7	Ash
8	8	Powdery brown matrix
9	9	Ash
10	10	Compact yellowish matrix
10a	10a	"Pit Fill"
10b	10b	Compact Yellowish Clay
11	11	Compact yellowish matrix
12	12	Ash
13	13	Compact clay
14	14	Loose clay

(cont'd.)

Stratum	Original No.	Description
15	15	Striated ash
16	16	Compact yellowish-green matrix
17	17	Pebbly brown clay
18	18	Reddish-brown clay
19	19	Compact pebbly greenish matrix
20	20	Pebbly brown clay

Figure 3.62. South Section of Operation X

Stratum	Original No.	Description
1a	1a	Displaced topsoil
1	1	Turf, topsoil
2	2	Wash
3	3	Stone pavement and bricky compact surface
4a	4a	Loose fill and sherds
4b	4b	Compact bricky material
4c	4c	Ash and mudbrick collapse
5	5	Clean, soft brown matrix
5a	5a	Clean loose matrix, cut for SK49
6b	6b	Mudbrick collapse

Figure 3.63. West Section of Operation X

Stratum	Original No.	Description
1	1	Turf, topsoil
2	2	Wash
3	3	Stone pavement and bricky compact surface
4a	4a	4a
4b	4b	4b
4c	4c	4c
4e	4e	Brown matrix
4f	4f	Yellowish mudbrick collapse
4g	4g	Soft dark brown matrix
5	5	Clean, soft brown matrix
5a	5a	Clean loose matrix, cut for SK49
6	6	Powdery brown matrix with sherds
6a	6a	Mudbrick collapse
6b	6b	Mudbrick collapse
7	7	Ash and green clay
7a	7a	Floor
8	8	Mudbrick collapse
8a	8a	Mudbrick collapse
9	9	Ash
9a	9a	Ash
9b	9b	Floor
9c	9c	Floor
10	10	Mudbrick collapse
10a	10a	Mudbrick collapse
11	11	Ash
11a	11a	Floor
11b	11b	Ash

(cont'd.)

APPENDIX III: CONCORDANCE OF SECTION NUMBERS AND STRATUM DESCRIPTIONS 395

Stratum	Original No.	Description
12	12	Mudbrick collapse
13	13	Grey Ashy wash
14	14	Mudbrick collapse
15	15	Ash and occupation debris
16	16	Mudbrick collapse
17	17	Ash and occupation debris
18	18	Mudbrick collapse
19	19	Ash and occupation debris
20	20	Mudbrick collapse
21	21	Ash and occupation debris
22	22	Heavily burned material, ash
23	23	Loose brown matrix
24	24	Ash
25	25	Sterile sand, water table

Figure 3.64. South Section Operation LIII

Stratum	Original No.	Description
1	1	Loose grey pebbly wash
2	2	Ash and burned material
3	3	Compact clay
3a	3a	Cut for Burial SK115 (Period IVb), loose fill
4	4	Soft pebbly grey
4a	4a	Dark brown
4b	4b	Loose fill
5	5	Compact pebbly grey
6	6	Compact clay

(cont'd.)

Figure 3.64 (cont'd.). South Section Operation LIII

Stratum	Original No.	Description
7	7	Compact clay
8a	8a	Striated clay
8b	8b	Striated clay
8c	8c	Striated clay
8d	8d	Striated Clay
8e	8e	Striated clay
9a	9a	Compact pebbly brown, ash, occupation debris
9b	9b	Compact pebbly brown, ash, occupation debris
9c	9c	Compact pebbly brown, ash, occupation debris
9d	9d	Compact pebbly brown, ash, occupation debris
9e	9e	Compact pebbly brown, ash, occupation debris
10	10	Compact brown bricky
11	11	Compact brown, ash, occupation debris
12	12	Compact grey-brown bricky
13	13	Compact grey clay
14	14	Sterile sand

Appendix IVa

Catalog of Hasanlu Burials of Periods VIb–IVc by Periods

This appendix presents the Period VIb–IVc burials by periods and SK number and lists pertinent information on all of the associated finds by Hasanlu Number with accompanying Object Type, Photo Negative Number, Museum Number (Disposition), and Dimensions. All measurements are in centimeters unless otherwise noted.

Period VIb

Skeletons 4, 5
Operation IV, Burials 4 and 5, Stratum 13

HAS57-44	Bone Handle	—	TM10497	L. 9.7, W. 0.2
HAS57-106	Finger Ring, Copper/Bronze	—	UPM58-4-9	Dia. 1
HAS57-107	Bowl (GW)	73779: 13	UPM58-4-10	Dia. 16
HAS57-108	Jar (GW)	73779: 13	TM10523	Dia. 8
HAS57-109	Bead Necklace: Carnelian, Shell, Paste, Granite (Black and White)	78186: 4	TM10505 Note: Cylindrical bead lost.	—
HAS57-129	Dagger, Copper/Bronze	78186: 4	TM10536	—
HAS57-130a, b	Anklets, Copper/Bronze	78186: 4	TM10535	Dia. 8
HAS57-131	Pin, Copper/Bronze	78186: 4	TM10537	L. 6.5

Skeletons 45, 46, 47
Photo Negatives: 78081: 18–19
Operation X, Stratum 7, Burials 2–4

HAS58-120	Cup (Buff IA, yellowish slip)	78094: 5–6	UPM59-4-12	Dia. 7
HAS58-121	Jar (Buff IA, yellowish slip)	78094: 5–6	UPM59-4-13/ ROM964.223.21	Dia. 7
HAS58-122	Cup (Buff IA, yellowish slip)	78094: 5–6	TM10596	Dia. 7
HAS58-123	Cup (Buff IA, yellowish slip)	78094: 5–6	UPM59-4-14	Dia. 6
HAS58-124	Cup (Buff IA, yellowish slip)	78094: 5–6	TM10596	Dia. 6
HAS58-125	Cup (Buff IA, yellowish slip)	78094: 5–6	UPM59-4-15	Dia. 6
HAS58-126	Cup (Buff IA, yellowish slip)	78094: 5–6	UPM59-4-16	Dia. 7
HAS58-127	Cup (Reddish Buff IA, slipped)	78094: 5–6		
58SL83			TM10596	Dia. 6
HAS58-128	Cup (Buff IA, slipped)	78094: 5–658SL83	TM10596	Dia. 6
HAS58-129	Cup (Buff IA, slipped)	78094: 5–658SL83	TM10596	Dia. 6
HAS58-130	Cup (Buff IA, slipped)	78094: 5–658SL83	UPM59-4-17	Dia. 5
HAS58-131	Cup (Buff IA, slipped)	78094: 5–658SL83	TM10596	Dia. 4
HAS58-132	Pin, Copper/Bronze	78094: 13	UPM59-4-119	L. 14.9, W. 0.5, Dia. Head 0.8
HAS58-133	Pin, Copper/Bronze	78094: 13	TM10614	L. 15, W. 0.5, Dia. Head 0.8
HAS58-134	Bead Necklace	78094: 20	UPM59-4-78	—
HAS58-135	Earring, Copper/Bronze	—	UPM59-4-131	Dia. 2.4
HAS58-136	Shell Beads	78094: 21	TM10671 and UPM59-4-79	—
HAS58-137	Khabur Ware Base (Buff IA)	—	UPM59-4-39	—

(cont'd.)

HAS58-138	Shell Ring	—	UPM59-4-80	—
HAS58-139	Shell Ring	—	UPM59-4-81	—
HAS58-140	Bronze Button	—	No Museum Number	Dia. 1.5, Th. 0.7
HAS58-141	Bronze Harness Ornament	—	Discarded	—
HAS58-142	Bronze Harness Ornament	—	Discarded	—
HAS58-143	Bronze Harness Ornament	—	Discarded	—
HAS58-144	Bronze Harness Ornament	—	Discarded	—
HAS58-145	Bronze Harness Ornament	—	Discarded	—
HAS58-537	Bronze Harness Ornament	—	No field card	—

Skeleton 49
Photo Negatives: 78081: 20–24
Operation X, Burial 5 Tomb

HAS58-146	Pin, Copper/Bronze	78094: 14	TM10677	L. 13.9, W. 0.8
HAS58-147	Beads, 2, Copper/Bronze	—	UPM58-4-169	—
HAS58-148	Dagger Blade, Copper/Bronze	78094: 14	TM10642	L. 13.3, W. 3.2
HAS58-149	Archer's Wrist Guard, stone	78094: 18	TM10670	L. 7.1, W. 1.8, Th. 0.5

Skeleton 61
Operation VIa, Stratum 5, Burial 12

HAS59-91	PKW Bowl (Buff IIB, black paint)	78104: 22–24	UPM60-20-53	Dia. 12
HAS59-115	Buff Ware Jar (Buff Ic)	—	Discarded	Dia. 9
HAS59-116	PKW Jar (Buff IIB, red paint)	78103: 17	TM?	Dia. 7

Skeleton 66
Operation VIa, Stratum 11 Area 2, Burial 17

HAS59-133	Pin, Copper/Bronze	—	UPM60-20-151	L. 8.4, Dia. 0.4
HAS59-134	Frit Bead	—	UPM60-20-152	H. 0.7, Dia. 0.1
HAS59-135	Ring, Copper/Bronze	—	Discarded	Th. 0.4, Dia. 2
HAS59-136	Frit Bead	—	UPM60-20-153	L. 1.8, Dia. 0.5
HAS59-137	Pin, Copper/Bronze	—	TM10972	L. 13.5, Dia. 0.5
HAS59-138	Bone Ring	—	Discarded	Th. 0.5, Dia. 2.3
HAS59-139	Cup (Orangish Buff IA)	—	Discarded	—
HAS59-140	Cup (Buff IB, yellowish slip)	78103: 32	MMA60-20-12	Dia. 5
HAS59-141	Cup (Buff IB, yellowish slip)	78103: 31, 78104: 21	TM10911	Dia. 6

Skeleton 112
Operation LIVf, Burial 4

HAS59-223	Cup (Buff Ia, whitish slip)	—	Discarded	Dia. 4
HAS59-224	PKW Jar (Buff Ia, whitish slip, red paint)	78107: 7–8	UPM60-20-57	Dia. 6

Terminal Period VIb

Skeleton 70
Operation VIa, Burial 21

HAS59-169	Jar (MBA Grey Ware Ib)	78103: 10, 11	Discarded	Dia. 9
HAS59-170	Jar (MBA Grey Ware Ia)	—	MMA60-20-17	Dia. 5
HAS59-171	Cup/Tankard (Buff Ware Ib)	78104: 19–20	UPM60-20-91	Dia. 8
HAS59-172	Ring, Copper/Bronze	—	Discarded	—
HAS59-173	Earring, Copper/Bronze	—	Discarded	—
HAS59-174	Beads, Blue Frit	—	Discarded	—
HAS59-175	Earring, Copper/Bronze	—	UPM60-20-212	W. 1.9, Th. 0.2
HAS59-176–77	Earring? with Copper/Bronze Ring and Beads	—	UPM60-20-156	—

Period VIa

Skeleton 25
Photo Negatives: 73783: 33
Operation VI, Burial 15

HAS57-122	Pins (3), Copper/Bronze	—	TM10540	—
HAS57-123	Bracelets (2), Copper/Bronze	—	TM10539	Dia. 6
HAS57-124	Bead Necklace	—	TM10541	—
HAS57-125	Finger Ring, Copper/Bronze	—	TM10515	—
HAS57-126	Tankard (Grey MBW)	73779: 19	TM10538	Dia. 8
HAS57-127	Cup (PKW)	73779: 19	TM10534	Dia. 4

Skeleton 29
Photo Negatives: 73783: 33
Operation VI, Burial 19

HAS57-159	Tankard (Grey MBW)	73781: 10	UPM58-4-52	Dia. 11
HAS57-184	Finger Ring, Iron	—	UPM58-4-53	Dia. 2
HAS57-187	Jar (Grey MBW)	73781: 10	Discarded	Dia. 6
HAS57-188	Cup (Grey MBW)	73781: 10	—	Dia. 9

Early Period V

Skeleton 504
Photo Negatives: 95244
Operation VIj, Burial 5

| HAS64-579 | Tankard | — | MMA65-163-75 | Dia. 11 |
| HAS64-580 | Jar (MBW, Pattern Burnish) | — | ? | Dia. 9 |

Skeleton 116
Operation LIII, Burial 2

HAS59-323	Tankard (Grey MBW Ib)	78102: 32	UPM60-20-58	Dia. 12
HAS59-324	Bowl (Grey MBW Ic)	—	UPM60-20-76	Dia. 27
HAS59-325	Jar (Grey MBW Ic)	78112: 15–16	TM	Dia. 8

Skeleton 67
Photo Negatives: 78097: 15
Operation VIa, Burial 18

HAS59-143	Pin, Copper/Bronze	—	UPM60-20-154	L. 10.8
HAS59-144	Pin, Copper/Bronze	—	Discarded	L. 6.1, Th. 0.3
HAS59-145	Pin, Copper/Bronze	—	Discarded	—
HAS59-146	Bowl (Grey MBW IIIc)	78107: 0–1	TM	—
HAS59-147	Tankard (Grey MBW Ia)	78103: 27	TM10915	—

Skeleton 445/449
Operation VIc, Burial 1/5, Stratum 5

| HAS64-335 | Tankard (Grey MBW) | 78162: 14 | UPM65-31-88 | Dia. 11 |

Late Period V

Skeleton 459
Photo Negatives: 78175: 7–8
Operation VIe, Burial 10, Stratum 6

HAS64-90	Jar (Buff)	78185: 32	UPM65-31-41	Dia. 8
HAS64-91	Holemouth Jar (Buff Ware, reddish-orange slip)	78162: 5–6	?	Dia. 12

Period IVc

Skeleton 479
Photo Negatives: 78176: 1–2
Operation VIf, Burial 8, Stratum 5

HAS64-171	Pin, Copper/Bronze	—	—	L. 8.1, Dia. 0.6
HAS64-172	Bracelet, Copper/Bronze	—	—	Th. 0.4, Dia. 6.7
HAS64-173	Finger Ring, Copper/Bronze	—	—	2.3 x 1.8, Th. 0.2
HAS64-174	Bead Headband: 12 Paste Cylindrical, 7 Carnelian Spherical, and 1 Incised Bone (see also HAS64-184)	—	UPM65-31-259	—
HAS64-175	Bowl (Grey MBW)	—	—	Dia. 25
HAS64-176	Goblet (Grey MBW Ic)	78162:11	TM	Dia. 7
HAS64-177	Jar (Grey MBW Ic)	—	—	Dia. 12
HAS64-182	Pin, Copper/Bronze	—	—	L. 5.8, Dia. 0.6
HAS64-184	Band, Copper/Bronze (see also HAS64-174)	—	UPM65-31-129	4.9 x 2.9, W. 0.9, Th. 0.1

APPENDIX IVA: CATALOG OF HASANLU BURIALS OF PERIODS VIB–IVC BY PERIODS 405

Skeleton 494
Operation VIh, Burial 4, Stratum 5

HAS64-298	Bowl	—	—	Dia. 10
HAS64-299	Cup	78162: 13	TM	Dia. 8
HAS64-337	Bead Necklace: Glass, Bone, Shell	—	—	—

Skeleton 24
Photo Negatives: 73783: 31
Operation VI, Burial 14

HAS57-118a	Pins (3), Copper/Bronze	—	UPM58-4-44a–c	L. 12.2, 11, 11.5
HAS57-119	Bracelet, Copper/Bronze	—	UPM58-4-45	Th. 0.5
HAS57-120	Iron Fragments (intrusive)	—	UPM58-4-46	L. 11, W. 3
HAS57-121	Jar (MBW, Pattern Burnish)	73779: 14	UPM58-4-47	Dia. 9

Skeleton 73
Operation VIa, Burial 24

HAS59-182	Jar (Grey MBW Ia)	—	Discarded	Dia. 5
HAS59-183	Jar (Orangish-buff Buff Ia)	—	Discarded	
HAS59-184	Bowl (Grey MBW Ic)	78104: 26	Discarded	Dia. 23
HAS59-185	Bead Necklace	—	MMA60-20-19	
HAS59-186	Bracelet, Copper/Bronze	—	Discarded	
HAS59-187	Bracelet, Copper/Bronze	—	TM10945	Th. 0.4, Dia. 4
HAS59-188	Bowl (Buff Ib)	—	Discarded	Dia. 13

Skeleton 57
Operation VIa, Burial 8

HAS59-77	Jar (Grey MBW Ib)	—	Discarded	Dia. 12
HAS59-78	Jar (Grey MBW Ia)	78106: 20	Discarded	Dia. 10
HAS59-79	Bowl (Grey MBW)	78102: 25–26	?	Dia. 25
HAS59-80	Cup (Buff Ic, red slip)	78106: 20, 78102: 27–28	UPM60-20-52	Dia. 9
HAS59-81	Bead Necklace, Frit	—	TM	—
HAS59-82	Finger Ring, Copper/Bronze	—	Discarded	—
HAS59-83	Cylinder Seal, Blue to Greenish-White Frit	78106: 20, 78109: 21–22	MMA60-20-5	L. 5.7, Dia. 1.6

Skeleton 6
Operation IV, Burial 6, Stratum 13

HAS 57-149	Dagger, Tin/Bronze	70320	UPM58-4-11	L. 35
HAS57-150	Beads (2), Paste	—	UPM58-4-12	H. 0.8, Dia. 1.1

Other Burials Likely of Period V–IVc

Skeleton 53
Operation VIa, Burial 4

HAS59-56	Finger Ring	—	Discarded	Th. 0.2, Dia. 1.3
HAS59-57	Bead Necklace: White, Frit? (12), with Crescent Glass Amulet	78108: 17–18	UPM60-20-147	W. 2, Th. 0.3,

Skeleton 63
Operation VIb, Burial 14, Stratum 7

HAS59-125	Finger Ring, Copper/Bronze	—	UPM60-20-149	2.1 x 2, Th. 0.5

Appendix IVb

Catalog of Hasanlu Low Mound Burials

This appendix presents the burials from the Hasanlu Low Mound by SK Number. University of Pennsylvania Museum Accession Numbers are provided for skeletons that were collected rather than discarded. Age and sex abbreviations are from Selinsky 2009:207 and are as follows: "FE – fetal (preterm), IN – infant (birth–3 years), CH – child (4–11 years), SA – subadult (12–19 years), YA – young adult (20–34 years), MA – middle adult (35–49 years), OA – old adult (50–64 years), VOA – very old adult (65+ years). Sex estimates abbreviations are: I (juv) – indeterminate juvenile, I – indeterminate (adult), F – female, M – male."

Skeleton No.	UPM No.	Operation	Burial No.	Stratum	Period	Comments	Selinsky (2009) Age Estimate and Sex
No #	Disc.	VI	10b		IVb		—
No #	59-4-104	X	6		V?		MA, F
1	Disc.	IV	1	1	-		—
2	Disc.	IV	2	1-2	-		—
3	Disc.	IV	3	4e-6b	IVb		—
4	Disc.	IV	4	13-15	VIb	Multiple Burial SK4-5	—
5	Disc.	IV	5	15	VIb	Multiple Burial SK4-5	—
6	Disc.	IV	6	15	IVc		—
7	58-4-95	V	1	2	III		MA, F
8	Disc.	V	2	12	VII		—
9	Disc.	V	3	12	VII		—
10	Disc.	V	4	12	VII		—

Skeleton No.	UPM No.	Operation	Burial No.	Stratum	Period	Comments	Selinsky (2009) Age Estimate and Sex
11	Disc.	VI	1	3	IVb		—
12	Disc.	VI	2	3	IVb		—
13	58-4-96	VI	3	3	IVb		MA, I
14	58-4-97	VI	4	3	IVb		MA, I
15	Disc.	VI	5	3	IVb		—
16	58-4-98	VI	6	3	IVb		CH, I (juv)
17	58-4-99	VI	7	3	IVb		YA, M
18	58-4-100	VI	8	3	IVb		SA, I (juv)
19	58-4-101	VI	9	3	IVb		OA, I
20	58-4-102	VI	10	3	IVb		MA, F
21	Disc.	VI	11	3	IVb	Cut by SK18	—
22/52	58-4-103	VI	12	3	IVb	Same as SK52	YA, F
23	58-4-104	VI	13	3	IVb		OA, I
24	58-4-105	VI	14	3	V?		MA, F
25	58-4-106	VI	15	3	VIa		YA, F
26	58-4-107	VI	16	3	IVb		VOA, M
27	58-4-108	VI	17	3	IVb		YA, M
28	Disc.	VI	18	3	IVb		—
29	58-4-109	VI	19	4	VIa	Below SK15	OA, M
30	58-4-110	VI	20	4	IVb		SA, I (juv)
31	58-4-111	VI	21	5	VII	Below SK29	SA, I (juv)
32	58-4-112	VI	22	3c	IVb		OA, M
34	Disc.	VI	23	3/3c	IVb		—
45, 46, 47	Disc.	X	2	6	VIb	Multiple Burial SK45–47	—
46, 45, 47	Disc.	X	3	6	VIb	Multiple Burial SK45–47	—
47, 45, 46	Disc.	X	4	6	VIb	Multiple Burial SK45–47	—

APPENDIX IVB: CATALOG OF HASANLU LOW MOUND BURIALS

Skeleton No.	UPM No.	Operation	Burial No.	Stratum	Period	Comments	Selinsky (2009) Age Estimate and Sex
48	Disc.	X	1	6	–		–
49	59-4-103	X	5	6	VIb	Stone-built Tomb	MA, F
50	Disc.	VIa	1	3	IVb or later	Seals SK55	–
51	Disc.	VIa	2		–		–
52 (22)	–	VIa	3		IVb	Same Grave as SK22	–
53	60-20-220	VIa	4		V?	Cut by SK53	MA, F
54	60-20-221	VIa	5		IVb		MA, F
55	Disc.	VIa	6		IVb	Sealed by SK50	–
56	60-20-222	VIa	7		IVb		MA, F
57	60-20-223	VIa	8		IVc		MA, M
58	60-20-224	VIa	9	6	IVb		MA, F
59	60-20-225	VIa	10		IVb		YA, F
60/74	–	VIb	11	5	IVb	Part of SK74	–
61/66	No Skeleton; Grave Goods	VIb	12	11 Area 2	VIb	Grave Goods atop Stone Slabs SK66	–
62	60-20-226	VIb	13	5	IVb		CH, I (juv)
63	60-20-227	VIb	14	7	V?		OA, F
64	Disc.	VIa	15		?		–
65	Not recovered/ Disc.	VIb	16		IVb	Partly in baulk	–
66/61	Disc.	VIb	17	11 Area 2	VIb	Stone Slab Burial	–
67	60-20-228	VIb	18	11 Area 2	V		VOA, F
68	Disc.	VIb	19	11	IVb		–
69	Disc.	VIb	20	11 Area 2	IVb		–
70	Disc.	Terminal VIb	21	Area 1	Terminal MBA		–
71	60-20-229	VIb	22	2? Area 1	IVb		YA, I
72	Disc.	VIa	23	Area 1	Terminal MBA	Pithos Infant Burial	–

Skeleton No.	UPM No.	Operation	Burial No.	Stratum	Period	Comments	Selinsky (2009) Age Estimate and Sex
73	Disc.	VIa	24	Area 1	IVc		—
74/60	Disc.	VIb	25	Area 2	IVb	SK60 part of this grave	—
75	Disc.	VIb	26	Area 2	IVb		—
76	Disc.	VIb	27	11 Area 2	?		—
98	Disc.	LIc	1	5	?		—
99	Disc.	LId	1	5	IVb		—
100	Disc.	LId	2	5	IVb		—
101	Disc.	LId	3	5	IVb		—
102	No Skeleton	LId	4	6	IVb	This grave consisted only of objects and was located along a baulk.	—
103	Disc.	LIe	1	4	IVb		—
104	Disc.	LIe	2	4	IVb?		—
105	Disc.	LIe	3	4	IVb	Stone Tomb with SK106, Secondary Burial	—
106	Disc.	LIe	4	4	IVb	Stone Tomb with SK105, Secondary Burial	—
107	60-20-233	LIe	5	5	IVb	Possible Stone Tomb	MA, M
108	Disc.	LIVe	1	4?	IVb		—
109	Disc.	LIVf	1	4?	IVb		—
110	Disc.	LIVf	2	4?	IVb		—
111	Disc.	LIVf	3	4?	IVb		—
112	Disc.	LIfV	4	4?	VIb		—
114	Disc.	LIe	6	5	IVb?	Smith? Mold and Iron Ingots	—
115	60-20-235	LIII	1	–	IVb		SA, I (juv)
116	60-20-236	LIII	2	4b	V		VOA, M
445/449	65-31-773	VIc	1	5	V	Same Grave as SK449	OA, M

APPENDIX IVB: CATALOG OF HASANLU LOW MOUND BURIALS 411

Skeleton No.	UPM No.	Operation	Burial No.	Stratum	Period	Comments	Selinsky (2009) Age Estimate and Sex
446	65-31-791	VIc	2?	2	IVb		OA, F
447	65-31-753	VIc	3	5	IVb or V		OA, M
448	65-31-732	VIc	4	5	IVb		MA, F
449/445	65-31-749	VIc	5	5	V	Same Grave as SK445	MA, M
450	65-31-739	VIe	1	4	IVb	Child	CH, I (juv)
451	Disc.	VIe	2	5	IVb		—
452	Disc.	VIe	3	5	IVb	Infant	—
453	65-31-727	VIe	4	5	IVb	Infant	IN, I (juv)
454	65-31-784	VIe	5	5	IVb		IN, I (juv)
455	65-31-742	VIe	6	5	IVb		YA, F
456	Disc.	VIe	7	5	IVb	Infant	—
457	Disc.	VIe	8	5	IVb?		—
458	65-31-755	VIe	9	5	VII		MA, I
459	65-31-788	VIe	10	6	V		MA, M
460	65-31-758	VIe	11	4	-		YA, F
461	65-31-783	VIe	12	5	IVb		CH, I (juv)
462	65-31-768	VIe	13	5	IVb		YA, F
463	65-31-735	VIe	14	5	IVb		IN, I (juv)
464	65-31-799	VIe	15	5	III?		MA, I
465	65-31-778	VIe	16	5	IVb		CH, I (juv)
466	65-31-750	VIe	17	5	-	Infant assoc. with SK467	CH, I (juv)
467	65-31-780	VIe	18	5	-	Infant assoc. with SK466	IN, I (juv)
468	65-31-728	VIe	19	5	IVb		CH, I (juv)
469	65-31-745	VIe	20	5	IV?		YA, M
470	65-31-774	VIe	21	5	IVb	Bundle Burial	MA, F
471	65-31-744	VIe	22	5	IVb		MA, M

Skeleton No.	UPM No.	Operation	Burial No.	Stratum	Period	Comments	Selinsky (2009) Age Estimate and Sex
472a	65-31-470a	VIf	1	2	IV?	Scattered, with SK472b	YA, M
472b	65-31-740b	VIf	1	2	IV?	Scattered, with SK472a	MA, M
473	65-31-786	VIf	2	3	IVb		CH, I (juv)
474a	65-31-805a	VIf	3	3	IV?		OA, M
474b	65-31-805b	VIf	3	3	IV?		YA, M
474c	65-31-805c	VIf	3	3	IV?		SA, I (juv)
475	65-31-736	VIf	4	3	IVb	Infant	IN, I (juv)
476	65-31-794	VIf	5	5	IVb		SA, I (juv)
477	65-31-770	VIf	6	5	IVb?	Infant	CH, I (juv)
478	65-31-751	VIf	7	5	IVb		OA, M
479	65-31-775	VIf	8	5	IVc		YA, F
480	65-31-734	VIf	9	5	IVb		MA, M
481	65-31-733, 65-31-801	VIf	10	5	IVb		MA, F
482	65-31-761	VIf	11	5	IVb?		CH, I (juv)
483	65-31-790	VIf	12	5	IVb		MA, F
484	65-31-796	VIf	13	5	IVb		MA, F
485	65-31-752	VIf	14	5	IVb		YA, M
486	65-31-795	VIg	1	5	IVb		MA, F
487	Disc.	VIg	2	5	IVb?	Skull Only	—
488	65-31-729	VIg	3	5	IVb		IN, I (juv)
489	65-31-782	VIg	4	5	IVb		IN, I (juv)
490	65-31-730	VIg	5	5	–	Infant	IN, I (juv)
491	65-31-764, 65-31-803	VIh	1	5	IVb		YA, M
492	65-31-767	VIh	2	5	IVb		IN, I (juv)
493a	65-31-792a	VIh	3	5	IVb		YA, M
493b	65-31-792b	VIh	3	5	VIh		OA, I

APPENDIX IVB: CATALOG OF HASANLU LOW MOUND BURIALS

Skeleton No.	UPM No.	Operation	Burial No.	Stratum	Period	Comments	Selinsky (2009) Age Estimate and Sex
494	65-31-766	VIh	4	5	IVc		IN, I (juv)
495	65-31-762	VIh	5	5	IVb		SA, I (juv)
496	65-31-756	VIh	6	5	IVb		MA, M
497	65-31-754	VIh	7	5	IVb		OA, M
498	65-31-760	VIh	8	5	IVb		CH, I (juv)
499	65-31-747	VIh	9	5	IVb		YA, M
500	Disc.	VIj	1	3	–	Infant	–
501a	65-31-765a	VIj	2	4	IVb?		IN, I (juv)
501b	65-31-765b	VIj	2	4	IVb?		CH, I (juv)
502a	65-31-737a	VIj	3	4	IVb	Multiple Grave?	SA, I (juv)
502b	65-31-737b	VIj	3	4	IVb	Multiple Grave?	MA, I
503	65-31-806	VIj	4	5	IVb		YA, F
504	65-31-789	VIj	5	5	V		MA, M
505	65-31-776	VIj	6	5	IVb		OA, M
506	65-31-771	VIj	7	5	IVb?	Fragmentary	YA, F
507	65-31-743	VIj	8	5	IVb		VOA, F
508	65-31-741	VIj	9	5	VII?		YA, F
509	65-31-748	VIj	10	5	VII		MA, M

Appendix V

Architectural Dimensions

Architectural Dimensions of the RS22–23 Building of Period V

Anteroom (RS22–23 Room 11/12)

Room Dimensions	L. 260 cm, W. 920 cm
North Wall	W. 95 cm
South Wall	W. 95 cm
Southern Pilaster	L. 30–40 cm, W. 100 cm
Main Entrance Stone Sill	Single Limestone Slab, L. 100 cm, W. 130 cm, Step Up (Exterior) 15 cm, Step Down (Interior) 18 cm

Columned Hall (RS22–23 Room 14)

Central Raised Hearth	L. 165 cm, W. 130 cm, Ht. 20 cm (above floor), Opening W. 28 cm
Central Hearth Curb Wall	H. 18 cm, Made of "Half Bricks," brick dimensions not provided
North Column Base, Stone Inset	68 cm N–S, 66 cm E–W, H. —
North Column Base, Plaster Base	58–65 cm N–S, 25–36 cm E–W, H. 25 cm
South Column Base, Stone Inset	55 cm N–S, 74 cm E–W, H. 15 cm
South Column Base, Plaster Base	104 cm N–S, 125 cm E–W, H. 25 cm
Column Base Mudbrick Wall	L. —, W. 55 cm, H. 23+ cm
Side Benches	W. 35 cm, H. 30 cm
Platform ("Throne Seat")	L. 100 cm, W. 150 cm, H. 10+ cm
Northeast Bench	L. 520 cm, W. 85 cm, H. 10+ cm
Paving	L. 90 cm, W. 75 cm
Northwest Doorway	W. 80 cm, no sill
North Wall	Th. 110 cm, no plaster
South Wall	Th. 110 cm, no plaster
East Wall	Th. 120 cm, no plaster

North Storerooms (RS22–23 Rooms 15–16)

East Wall	W. 95 cm
Dividing Wall	W. 75 cm

Appendix VI

Catalog of Personal Ornaments, Cemetery, Outer Town, Hasanlu Periods VIb–IVc

Period VIb Burial SK4/5, sex unknown

- 57-44 and 57-129. Dagger and bone handle (or cosmetic container?), L. 9.7 cm, W. 0.2 cm. TM10497 and TM10536.
- 57-106. Copper/bronze finger ring, annular, decorated with three bands, a plain band flanked by bands with raised dots. Dia. 2 cm, W. 1 cm. UPM58-4-9.
- 57-109. Beads: carnelian, shell, composite, and stone. Biconoid, collared, vase, and cylindrical. TM10505.
- 57-130a, b. Copper/bronze anklets, plain. Dia. 8 cm. TM10535.
- 57-131. Copper/bronze pin in four fragments with no head. L. 6.5 cm. TM10537.
- 57-128. Beads: composite. TM 10536 (same TM# as dagger blade). (See drawing from Excavation Notebook 1957 2:15b)

Period VIb SK45–47, possible female

- 58-132. Copper/bronze toggle pin with flaring six-lobed rosette head and four rows of hatched incised decoration in alternating directions at top of shaft. L. 14.9 cm, W. 0.5 cm, Dia. head 0.8 cm. UPM59-4-119.
- 58-133. Copper/bronze pin with flaring six-lobed rosette head. L. 15 cm, W. 0.5 cm, Dia. head 0.8 cm. TM10614.
- 58-134. Beads: 1 large spheroid carnelian (incorrectly marked 60.20.152), 1.9 cm by 1.4 cm; 3 medium carnelian spheroids, Dia. 0.8–0.9 cm; 3 small carnelian spheroids, Dia. 0.3–0.4 cm; 8 long carnelian barrels. L. 1.0–1.3 cm, W. 0.4 cm; 1 short copper/bronze barrel; 2 small antimony (?) donuts, Dia. outer 0.5 cm, Dia. inner 0.3 cm; 1 rock crystal spheroid, Dia. 0.8 cm; 1 rock crystal ellipsoid, L. 1.0 cm, W. 0.6 cm; 20 perforated shells (*arcularia*?), max. L. 1.5 cm; 18 composite/frit "beans," rock crystal: 8–10 mm, shell: max. 15 mm, paste/frit. UPM59-4-78.
- 58-135. Copper/bronze S-shaped earring. Dia. of each loop 2.4 cm, reconstructed earring is 5.0 cm. UPM59-4-131.
- 58-136. Beads: quantity unknown. Perforated shells, stone, copper/bronze. No dimensions recorded. TM10671 and UPM59-4-79.
- 58-138. *Conus* (?) shell ring, fragment. Ext. Dia. 2.3 cm, Int. Dia. 1.5 cm, Th. 0.3 cm. UPM59-4-80.
- 58-139. *Conus* (?) shell ring, fragment. Ext. Dia. 2.6 cm, Int. Dia. 1.7 cm, Th. 0.3 cm. UPM59-4-81.
- 58-140. Copper/bronze "button." Dia. 1.5 cm, H. 0.7 cm. No museum number.
- 58-141-145. Copper/bronze "harness ornaments." Discarded.

Period VIb SK49, female

- 58-146. Copper/bronze toggle (?) pin with flared head. L. 13.9 cm, W. 0.4 cm, Dia. head 0.8 cm. TM10677.
- 58-147. Copper/bronze short cylinder beads (2 recorded on burial sheet, 8 found under accession number in UPM). Dia. 1.0 cm, Th. 0.2 cm. UPM59-4-169.

- 58-148. Copper/bronze blade, flat in section with a short, wide tang with a single rivet hole. L. 13.3 cm, W. 3.2 cm. TM10642.
- 58-149. Grey stone archer's wristguard (?) or whetstone (?), perforated at both ends. L. 7.1 cm, W. 1.8 cm. TM10670.

Period VIb SK66, child

- 59-133. Copper/bronze toggle pin in two fragments. Club-headed, with possible incised decoration near head. L. 8.4 cm, Dia. 0.4 cm. UPM60-20-151.
- 59-134. Beads: 2 biconoid frit. Dia. 0.9 cm, Th. 0.2 cm. UPM60-20-152.
- 59-135. Copper/bronze finger (?) ring, lapped. Th. 0.4 cm, Dia. 2 cm. Discarded.
- 59-136. Bead: long barrel, frit. L. 1.8 cm, Dia. 0.5 cm. UPM60-20-153.
- 59-137. Copper/bronze club-headed pin. L. 13.5 cm, Dia. 0.5 cm. TM10972.
- 59-138. Shell ring. Dia. 2.3 cm, Th. 0.5 cm. Discarded.

Terminal Period VIb SK70, child

- 59-173. Copper/bronze earring, probably S-shaped, perhaps related to 59-176–177. No measurements recorded. Discarded..
- 59-174. Beads: blue frit. Unknown quantity. No measurements recorded. Discarded.
- 59-175. Copper/bronze S-shaped earring, tapers to a point. Dia. largest loop, 1.9 cm, Th. 0.2 cm, reconstructed length 4.0 cm. UPM60-20-212.
- 59-176-7. Beads: perhaps suspended from a copper/bronze coiled hoop, in order: 1 white frit incised disc, 1 white frit plano-convex bead, 3 flat frit or shell discs, 1 white fluted frit bead, 1 dark grey glass (?) spheroid, 3 flat frit or shell discs. Dia. largest fluted bead, 1.2 cm. UPM60-20-156.
- 59-172. Copper/bronze finger ring, fragmentary. Discarded.

Period VIa SK25, female young adult

- 57-123. Copper/bronze bracelets (2), lapped. Dia. 6 cm. TM10539.
- 57-122. Copper/bronze club-headed plain pins (3). Max L. 10 cm. TM10540.
- 57-124. Beads: 1 small composite barrel, stone barrel, and short copper/bronze barrel. No measurements recorded. TM10541.
- 57-125. Copper/bronze finger ring fragment. No measurements recorded. TM10515.

Early Period IVc SK67, female very old

- 59-143. Copper/bronze club-headed pin, perhaps with incised decoration near head. L. 7 cm. UPM60-20-154.
- 59-144. Copper/bronze flat-headed, plain pin. L. 6.1 cm, W. 0.3 cm. Discarded.
- 59-145. Copper/bronze pin in three fragments. Measurements not recorded. Discarded.

Period IVc SK24, female mature adult

- 57-118a. Copper/bronze pin, incised decoration, domed head with three bands of vertical chevrons on upper shaft. L. 12.2 cm, UPM58-4-44a-c. Missing.
- 57-119. Copper/bronze bracelet, penannular with snake-headed terminals (?). Dia. 6.3 cm, Th. 0.5 cm. UPM58-4-45. (Fleming, Nash, and Swann 2011:26, pl. 5.28)

Period IVc SK73, child

- 59-185. Beads: 20 disc and ball beads of various shades of glass/frit. No measurements recorded. TM unknown.
- 59-186. Copper/bronze bracelet, lapped, tapering ends. No measurements recorded. Discarded.
- 59-187. Copper/bronze bracelet, lapped, tapering ends. Dia. 4 cm, Th. 0.4 cm. TM10945.

Period IVc SK479, female young adult

- 64-171. Club-headed copper/bronze pin, plain. L. 8.1 cm, D. 0.6 cm. Discarded?
- 64-172. Copper/bronze bracelet, penannular, plain, ends meet. Dia. 6.7 cm, Th. 0.4 cm. Discarded?
- 64-173. Copper/bronze penannular finger ring. Dia. 2.3 cm, Th. 0.2 cm. Discarded?
- 64-174. Headdress beads (see also 64-184); 5 cylindrical white frit (glass?) beads, L. 2.0 cm, Dia. 0.3 cm; 3 carnelian small spheroids, Dia. 0.7 cm; 1 lozenge-shaped *Conus* shell bead with circle-dot incised decoration, L.

2.2 cm, W. 1.2 cm, H. 0.3 cm. UPM65-31-259.
• 64-182. Copper/bronze club-headed pin. L. 5.8 cm, Dia. 0.6 cm. Discarded?
• 64-184. Copper/bronze headband, in fragments, perforated at each end. L. 11 cm, W. 1 cm. UPM65-31-129.

Period IVc SK494, infant

• 64-337. Beads and cylinder seal: 1 round carnelian bead, Dia. 1.0 cm; 1 shell disc bead, Dia. 2.0 cm, Th. 0.7 cm; 1 oblate bone disc bead, Dia. 2.0 cm, Th. 0.4 cm; 1 oblate white stone disc bead, Dia. 1.7 cm, Th. 0.2 cm; 1 pillow-shaped shell bead, L. 1.4 cm, W. 0.9 cm; 6 glass beads (3 blue/black spheroids, Dia. 1.3 cm; 2 whitish coils, Dia. 1.0 cm; 1 yellowish glass [?] cylinder, Dia. 0.7 cm); 1 large blue-green frit cylinder seal with diagonal hatch marks, L. 3.3 cm, Dia. 1 cm; 1 copper/bronze ring with attached small copper/bronze ring, perhaps a clasp, Dia. 1.1 cm. UPM65-31-267.

Period IVc SK57, male mature adult

• 59-81. Beads: 10 composite disc-shaped. No measurements recorded. TM unknown.
• 59-82. Fragmentary copper/bronze finger ring. No measurements recorded. Discarded.
• 59-83. Cylinder seal, blue green frit. Main field divided into seven decorated panels: one large square flanked by two columns of three squares each. The largest unit shows a bird, facing right, perched over a tree with a thick trunk supporting a hemispherical cluster of branches. L. 5.7 cm, Dia. 1.6 cm. MMA60-20-5. (Marcus 1994b; Marcus 1996a:27, 143–44, fig. 115, pl. 48, no. 1)

Period IVc SK6, sex unknown

• 57-149. Lappet-flanged dagger with a handle fashioned to receive wood inlay. L. 35 cm. UPM59-4-112. (Thornton and Piggot 2011: fig. 6.31)
• 57-150. Beads: 2 fluted spheroid (melon) composite. H. 0.8 cm, Dia. 1.1 cm. UPM58-4-12.

(Likely) Period V–IVc SK53, child

• 59-56. Copper/bronze finger ring. Dia. 1.3 cm, H. 0.2 cm. Discarded.
• 59-57. Bead necklace: 12 small white frit round beads, 0.4 cm by 0.2 cm; 1 flat, inverted crescentic pendant of composite material, recon. L. 2.4 cm, recon. H. 1.6 cm. UPM60-20-147.

(Likely) Period V–IVc SK63, female older adult

• 59-125. Copper/bronze finger ring, lapped with an undecorated bezel. Dia. 2 cm, bezel 2.1 cm by 2 cm. UPM60-20-149.

Bibliography

Abdi, K. 2001. Nationalism, Politics, and the Development of Archaeology in Iran. *American Journal of Archaeology* 105:51–76.

Alavi, M. 1994. Tectonics of the Zagros Orogenic Belt of Iran: New Data and Interpretations. *Tectonophysics* 229:211–38.

Alekshin, V., B. Bartel, A. Dolitsky, A. Gilman, P. Kohl, D. Liversage, and C. Masset. 1983. Burial Customs as an Archaeological Source. *Current Anthropology* 24:137–49.

al-Janabi, K. 1961. The Excavations at Tell Shamlu. (In Arabic.) *Sumer* 17:174–92.

Anthony, D. 1990. Migration in Archeology: The Baby and the Bathwater. *American Anthropologist* 92:895–914.

———. 1992. The Bath Refilled: Migration in Archeology Again. *American Anthropologist* 94:174–76.

———. 1997. Prehistoric Migration as Social Process. In *Migrations and Invasions in Archaeological Explanation*, ed. J. Chapman and H. Hamerow, pp. 21–32. British Archaeological Reports International Series 664. Oxford: BAR.

Areshian, G., V. Oganesyan, F. Muradyan, P. Avetisyan, and L. Petrosyan. 1990. The End of the Middle Bronze Age between the Arax and Kura. (In Russian.) *Istoriko-filologicheskiy Zhurnal* 128:53–74.

Arne, T. 1935. The Swedish Archaeological Expedition to Iran 1932–1933. *Acta Iranica* 6:1–48.

———. 1945. *Excavations at Shah Tepé, Iran*. Stockholm: Elanders boktryekeri aktiebolag.

Asri, Y., and M. Ghorbanli. 1997. The Halophilous Vegetation of the Orumieh Lake Salt Marshes, NW. Iran. *Plant Ecology* 132:155–70.

Bahrani, Z. 2003. *The Graven Image: Representation in Babylonia and Assyria*. Philadelphia: University of Pennsylvania Press.

Bass, G., C. Pulak, D. Collon, and J. Weinstein. 1989. The Bronze Age Shipwreck at Ulu Burun: 1986 Campaign. *American Journal of Archaeology* 93:1–29.

Becker, M. 2007. Childhood among the Etruscans: Mortuary Programs at Tarquinia as Indicators of the Transition to Adult Status. *Hesperia Supplements* 41:281–92.

Bedal, L., S. Fleming, M. de Schauensee, and R. Hancock. 1995. Second Millennium B.C. Pottery at Hasanlu Tepe and Dinkha Tepe: INAA and Petrographic Studies. In *Material Issues in Art and Archaeology IV*, ed. P. Vandiver, J. Druzik, J. Galván Madrid, I. Freestone, and G. Wheeler, pp. 453–67. Philadelphia: Materials Research Society.

Berberian, M., and S. Arshadi. 1975. On the Evidence of the Youngest Activity of the North Tabriz Fault and Seismicity of Tabriz City. *Geological Survey of Iran, Internal Report* 39:397–414.

Biscione, R. 2003. Pre-Urartian and Urartian Settlement Patterns in the Caucasus, Two Case Studies: The Urmia Plain, Iran, and the Southern Sevan Basin, Armenia. In *Archaeology in the Borderlands*, ed. A. Smith and K. Rubinson, pp. 167–84. Los Angeles: Cotsen Institute of Archaeology.

———. 2009. The Distribution of Pre- and Protohistoric Hillforts in Iran. *Studi micenei ed egeo-anatolici* 51:123–43.

Black, J., A. Green, and T. Rickards. 1992. *Gods, Demons, and Symbols of Ancient Mesopotamia: An Illustrated Dictionary*. Austin: University of Texas Press.

Bobek, Hans. 1968. Vegetation. In *The Cambridge History of Iran*. Vol. I, *The Land of Iran*, ed. W. Fisher, pp. 280–93. Cambridge: Cambridge University Press.

Bobokhyan, A. 2008. *Kommunikation und Austausch im Hochland zwischen Kaukasus und Taurus: ca. 2500–1500 v. Chr*. Oxford: Archaeopress.

Boehmer, R. 1961. Die Keramikfunde vom Zindan-i Suleiman. In Takht-i Suleiman. *Vorläufiger Bericht über die Ausgrabungen 1959. Tehraner Forschungen* 1, ed. H. von der Osten and R. Naumann, pp. 82–86. Berlin.

———. 1964. Volkstum und Städte der Mannäer. *Baghdader Mitteilungen* 3:11–24.

———. 1967. Forschungen am Zendan-i Suleiman in Persisch-Aserbeidschan 1958–1964. *Archäologischer Anzeiger*, Supplement:573–85.

———. 1973. Zur Lage von Muṣaṣir. *Baghdader Mitteilungen* 6:31–40.

———. 1979. Zur Stele von Topzawā. *Baghdader Mitteilungen* 10:50–51, pls. 12–13.

———. 1986. Ritzverzierte Keramik aus dem mannäischen (?) Bereich. *Archäologische Mitteilungen aus Iran* 19:95–115.

———. 1993–1997. Muṣaṣir. *Reallexikon der Assyriologie und vorderasiatischen Archäologie*, ed. E. Ebeling, B. Meissner, E. Weidner, W. von Soden, D. Edzard, M. Streck, G. Frantz-Szabo, M. Krebernik, D. Morandi Bonacossi, J. Postgate, U. Seidl, M. Stol, G. Wilhelm, S. Ecklin, and S. Pfaffinger, pp. 444–450. Germany: Walter de Gruyter.

Boehmer, R., and H. Fenner. 1973. Forschungen in und um Mudjesir (Irakisch-Kurdistan). *Archäologischer Anzeiger* 88:479–521.

Bottema, S. 1986. A Late Quaternary Pollen Diagram from Lake Urmia (Northwestern Iran). *Review of Palaeobotany and Palynology* 47:241–61.

Braidwood, R., and L. Braidwood. 1960. *Excavations in the Plain of Antioch 1: The Earlier Assemblages Phases A-J*. Oriental Institute Publications 61. Chicago: University of Chicago Press.

Burmeister, S. 2000. Archaeology and Migration: Approaches to an Archaeological Proof of Migration. *Current Anthropology* 41:539–67.

Burney, C. 1961. Excavations at Yanik Tepe, North-West Iran. *Iraq* 23:138–53.

———. 1962. The Excavations at Yanik Tepe, Azerbaijan, 1961 Second Preliminary Report. *Iraq* 24:134–52.

———. 1964. The Excavations at Yanik Tepe, Azerbaijan, 1962: Third Preliminary Report. *Iraq* 26:54–61.

———. 1970. Excavations at Haftavān Tepe 1968: First Preliminary Report. *Iran* 8:157–71.

———. 1972. Excavations at Haftavān Tepe 1969: Second Preliminary Report. *Iran* 10:127–42.

———. 1973. Excavations at Haftavān Tepe 1971: Third Preliminary Report. *Iran* 11:153–72.

———. 1975. Excavations at Haftavān Tepe 1973: Fourth Preliminary Report. *Iran* 13:149–64.

———. 1977. The Economic Basis of Settled Communities in North-Western Iran. In *Mountains and Lowlands*, ed. L. Levine and T.C. Young, Jr., pp. 1–7. Malibu: Undena Publications.

Burney, C., and D. Lang. 1971. *The Peoples of the Hills: Ancient Ararat and Caucasus*. New York: Praeger Publishers.

Burton-Brown, T. 1951. *Excavations in Azerbaijan, 1948*. London: John Murray.

Calmeyer, P. 1957–1971. Gird-i Hassan 'Ali. *Reallexikon der Assyriologie* Vol. 3, ed. E. Weidner and W. von Soden, pp. 381–82. Berlin: Walter de Gruyter.

Chisholm, Michael. 1970. *Rural Settlement and Land Use: An Essay in Location*. Chicago: Aldine.

Çilingiroğlu, A. and D. French, eds. 1994. *Anatolian Iron Ages 3: The Proceedings of the Third Anatolian Iron Ages Colloquium Held at Van, 6–12 August 1990*. Ankara: The British Institute of Archaeology.

Contenau, G., and R. Ghirshman. 1935. *Fouilles du Tépé Giyan près de Néhavend 1931 et 1932*. Paris: Paul Geuthner.

Crawford, S. 2000. Children, Grave Goods and Social Status in Early Anglo-Saxon England. In *Children and Material Culture*, ed. J. Derevenski, pp. 169–79. London: Routledge.

Curtis, J. 1983. Some Axe-Heads from Chagar Bazar and Nimrud. *Iraq* 45:73–81, Pls. VII–VIII.

———. 1989. A Grave-Group from Qeytariyeh near

Tehran (?). In *Archaeologia Iranica et Orientalis miscellanea in honorem Louis Vanden Berghe*, ed. L. De Meyer and E. Haerinck, pp. 323–33. Gent: Peeters.

Curtis, J., ed. 1988. *Bronze-working Centres of Western Asia c. 1000–539 B.C.* New York: Kegan Paul.

Dandamaev, M., and V. Lukonin. 1989. *The Culture and Social Institutions of Ancient Iran.* Cambridge: Cambridge University Press.

Danti, M. 2004. *The Ilkhanid Heartland: Hasanlu Tepe (Iran) Period I.* Hasanlu Excavation Reports 2. Philadelphia: University of Pennsylvania Museum.

———. 2011. The Artisan's House of Hasanlu Tepe, Iran. *Iran* 49:11–54.

———. In Press. Hasanlu VI–IV: Overview and Recent Revisions. In *Der archäologische Befund und seine Historisierung. Dokumentation und ihre Interpretationsspielräume, Tagung Innsbruck 2009.*

Danti, M., and M. Cifarelli. n.d. Iron II Warrior Burials at Hasanlu Tepe, Iran. Forthcoming.

Danti, M., M. Voigt, and R. Dyson, Jr. 2004. The Search for the Late Chalcolithic/Early Bronze Age Transition in the Ushnu-Solduz Valley, Iran. In *A View from the Highlands*, ed. A. Sagona, pp. 583–616. Louvain: Peeters Press.

Delougaz, P. 1952. *Pottery from the Diyala Region.* Oriental Institute Publications 63. Chicago: University of Chicago Press.

de Morgan, J. 1905. Recherches au Talyche persan. *Mémoires de la Délégation en Perse* 8:251–341.

De Planhol, X. 1968. Geography and Settlement. In *The Cambridge History of Iran.* Vol. I, *The Land of Iran*, ed. W. Fisher, pp. 406–67. Cambridge: Cambridge University Press.

Derevenski, J. 2000. *Children and Material Culture.* London: Routledge.

de Schauensee, M. 1989. Horse Gear from Hasanlu. *Expedition* 31(2-3): 37–52.

———, ed. 2011. *Peoples and Crafts in Period IVB at Hasanlu Tepe, Iran.* Hasanlu Special Studies 4. Philadelphia: University of Pennsylvania Museum.

de Schauensee, M., and R. Dyson, Jr. 1983. Hasanlu Horse Trappings and Assyrian Reliefs. In *Essays on Near Eastern Art and Archaeology in Honor of Charles Kyrle Wilkinson*, ed. P. Harper and H. Pittman, pp. 59–77. New York: The Metropolitan Museum of Art

Deshayes, J. 1969. New Evidence for the Indo-Europeans from Tureng Tepe, Iran. *Archaeology* 22:10–17.

———. 1972. Tureng Tépé et la Période Hissar IIIC. In *The Memorial Volume of the Vth International Congress on Iranian Art and Archaeology*, pp. 34–38. Tehran: Offset Press.

———. 1973. La Date des Tumuli de Sé Girdan. *Iran* 11:176–78.

DeVries, K., P. Kuniholm, G.K. Sams, and M. Voigt. 2003. New Dates for Iron Age Gordion. *Antiquity* 77(296) Project Gallery. http://antiquity.ac.uk/ProjGall/devries296

DeVries, K., G.K. Sams, and M. Voigt. 2005. Gordion Re-dating. In *Anatolian Iron Ages* 5, ed. A. Çilingiroğlu and G. Darbyshire, pp. 45–46. London: British Institute at Ankara.

Diakonoff, I. 1956. *Istoriya Midii ot drevneishikh vremen do kontsa IV veka do n.e.* Moscow: Izd-vo Akademii nauk SSSR.

———. 1967. *Iazyki drevnei Perednei Azii.* Moscow: Nakua.

———. 1971. Vostochnyj Iran do Kira. In *Istoriya Iranskogo gosudarstva i kul'tury*, pp. 122–54. Moscow.

Diakonoff, I., and S. Kashkai. 1979. *Geographical Names According to Urartian Texts.* Répertoire Géographique des Textes Cunéiformes 9. Wiesbaden: L. Reichert.

Dittmann, R. 1990. Eisenzeit I und II in West- und Nordwest-Iran zeitgleich zur Karum-Zeit Anatoliens? *Archäologische Mitteilungen aus Iran* 23:105–38.

Djamali, M., J.-L. de Beaulieu, M. Shah-Hosseini, V. Andrieu-Ponel, P. Ponel, A. Amini, H. Akhini, S. Leroy, L. Stevens, H. Lahijani, and S. Brewer. 2008. A Late Pleistocene Long Pollen Record from Lake Urmia, NW Iran. *Quaternary Research* 69:413–20.

Dornemann, R. 1979. Tell Hadidi: A Millennium of Bronze Age City Occupation. In *Archaeological Reports from the Tabqa Dam Project—Euphrates Valley, Syria*, ed. D. Freedman, pp. 113–51. Cambridge: American Schools of Oriental Research

Dorner, J., K. Kromer, and A. Lippert. 1974. Die zweite Kampagne der österreichischen Ausgrabungen am Kordlar-tepe, Aserbaidschan. *Mitteilungen der Anthropologischen Gesellschaft in Wien* 104:111–36.

Dyson, R., Jr. 1956. Pennsylvania Survey in Iran. *Archaeology* 9(4): 284–85.

———. 1957. Iran, 1956. *University Museum Bulletin* 21:27–39.

———. 1958. Iron Age Hasanlu. *University Museum Bulletin* 22:25–32.

———. 1959. Digging in Iran: Hasanlu 1958. *Expedition* 1:4–18.

———. 1960a. Hasanlu and Early Iran. *Archaeology* 13:118–29.

———. 1960b. Where the Golden Bowl of Hasanlu Was Found: Excavations near Lake Urmia which Throw New Light on the Little-Known Mannaeans: Pt. I. *Illustrated London News* 236:132–34.

———. 1961a. Excavating the Mannaean Citadel of Hasanlu; and New Light on Several Millennia of Persian Azerbaijan. *Illustrated London News* 239:534–37.

———. 1961b. Hasanlu 1960 Campaign. *Archaeology* 14:63–64.

———. 1962. The Hasanlu Project. *Science* 135:637–47.

———. 1963a. Expedition News. Hasanlu. *Expedition* 5:33.

———. 1963b. Hasanlu Discoveries, 1962. *Archaeology* 16:131–33.

———. 1963c. Archaeological Scrap—Glimpses of History at Ziwiye. *Expedition* 5:32–37.

———. 1964a. Ninth Century Men in Western Iran. *Archaeology* 17:3–11.

———. 1964b. Notes on Weapons and Chronology in Northern Iran around 1000 B. C. In *Dark Ages and Nomads c. 1000 B. C.*, ed. M. Mellink, pp. 32–45. Istanbul: Historisch-Archaeologisch Instituut.

———. 1965. Problems of Protohistoric Iran as Seen from Hasanlu. *Journal of Near Eastern Studies* 24:193–217.

———. 1967a. Archaeological Activity in Iran (F); Early Cultures of Solduz, Azerbaijan. In *A Survey of Persian Art* 14, ed. A. Pope, assisted by P. Ackerman, pp. 2951–70. New York: Oxford University Press.

———. 1967b. Dinkha Tepe. *Iran* 5:136–37.

———. 1967c. Early Cultures of Solduz, Azerbaijan. In *Survey of Persian Art*, ed. Arthur Upham Pope pp. 2951–70. New York: Oxford University Press.

———. 1968. The Archaeological Evidence of the Second Millennium B.C. on the Persian Plateau. *The Cambridge Ancient History*, Fasc. 66. Vol. II, Chapter XVI, pp. 1–36. Cambridge: Cambridge University Press.

———. 1969. A Decade in Iran. *Expedition* 11:39–47.

———. 1971. Iran: Eleven Thousand Years of Cultural History." *Expedition* 13:4–5.

———. 1973a. The Archaeological Evidence of the Second Millennium B.C. on the Persian Plateau. [Revised fascicle 66 1968]. In *Cambridge Ancient History*, 3rd ed. Vol. II, Pt. 1, pp. 686–715. Cambridge: Cambridge University Press.

———. 1973b. Further Excavations at Tepe Hasanlu, Iran. *Archaeology* 26:303–4.

———. 1973c. Survey of Excavations: Hasanlu. *Iran* 11:195–96.

———. 1975. Hasanlu, 1974: The Ninth Century B.C. Gateway. In *Proceedings of the IIIrd Annual Symposium on Archaeological Research in Iran, 2nd–7th November, 1974*, ed. F. Bagherzadeh, pp. 179–88. Tehran: Iranian Center for Archaeological Research.

———. 1977a. The Architecture of Hasanlu: Periods I to IV. *American Journal of Archaeology* 81(4): 548–52.

———. 1977b. Architecture of the Iron I Period at Hasanlu in Western Iran and Its Implications for Theories of Migration on the Iranian Plateau. In *Le Plateau Iranien et l'Asie centrale des origines à la conquête Islamique*, Colloques 567, ed. J. Deshayes, pp. 155–69. Paris: CNRS.

———. 1989a. The Iron Age Architecture at Hasanlu: An Essay. *Expedition* 31(2-3): 107–27.

———. 1989b. Rediscovering Hasanlu. *Expedition* 31(2-3): 3–11.

———. 1999a. The Achaemenid Painted Pottery of Hasanlu IIIA. *Anatolian Studies* 49:101–10.

———. 1999b. Triangle-Festoon Ware Reconsidered. *Iranica Antiqua* 34:115–44.

Dyson, R., Jr., and O. Muscarella. 1989. Constructing the Chronology and Historical Implications of Hasanlu IV. *Iran* 27:1–27.

Dyson, R., and V. Pigott. 1975. Hasanlu. *Iran* 13:182–85.

Dyson, R., Jr., and M. Voigt. 2003. A Temple at Hasanlu. In *Yeki Bud, Yeki Nabud*, ed. N. Miller and K. Abdi, pp. 219–36. Cotsen Institute of Archaeology Monograph 48. Los Angeles: Cotsen Institute of Archaeology.

Dyson, R., Jr., and M. Voigt, eds. 1989. East of Assyria: The Highland Settlement of Hasanlu. *Expedition* 31(2–3), special issue.

Dyson, R., Jr., and T.C. Young, Jr. 1960. The Solduz

Valley, Iran: Pisdeli Tepe. *Antiquity* 34:19–28.

Edwards, M. 1981. The Pottery of Haftavan VIB (Urmia Ware). *Iran* 19:101–40.

———. 1983. *Excavations in Azerbaijan (North-western Iran): Haftavan, Period VI*. British Archaeological Reports International Series 182. Oxford: BAR.

———. 1986. "Urmia Ware" and Its Distribution in North-Western Iran in the Second Millennium B.C.: A Review of the Results of Excavations and Surveys. *Iran* 24:57–77.

Egami, N. 1972. The Connection between Sakzabad and Kansu Painted Pottery. In *The Memorial Volume of the VIth International Congress of Iranian Art & Archaeology*, ed. M. Kiani and A. Tajvidi, pp. 296–305. Tehran: Iranian Centre for Archaeological Research.

Egami, N., S. Fukai, and S. Masuda. 1965. *Dailaman I: The Excavations at Ghalekuti and Lasulkan, 1960*. Tokyo: Institute for Oriental Culture.

Ehringhaus, H. 1994. Gedanken zur Rekonstruction des Gebaudes Kordlar Tepe IV in Iranisch West-Azerbaidjan. *Archaeologische Mitteilungen aus Iran* 27:49–65.

El-Amin, M., and M. Mallowan. 1950. Soundings in the Makhmur Plain. *Sumer* 6:55–90.

Eph'al, I. 1999. The Bukan Aramaic Inscription: Historical Considerations. *Israel Exploration Journal* 49:116–21.

Fales, F. 2003. Evidence for West-East Contacts in the 8th c. BC: The Bukan Stele. In *Continuity of Empire (?): Assyria, Media, Persia*, ed. G. Lanfranchi, R. Rollinger, and M. Roaf, pp. 131–48. Padova: Sargon.

Felber, H. 1979. Vienna Radium Institute Radiocarbon Dates VIII. *Radiocarbon* 21:113–19.

Fisher, W. 1968. Physical Geography. In *The Cambridge History of Iran*. Vol. I, *The Land of Iran*, ed. W. Fisher, pp. 3–110. Cambridge: Cambridge University Press.

———. 1971. *The Middle East: A Physical, Social, and Regional Geography*. London: Methuen.

Fishman, B. and B. Lawn. 1978. University of Pennsylvania Radiocarbon Dates XX. *Radiocarbon* 20:210–33.

Fleming, S., S. Nash, and C. Swann. 2011. The Archaeometallurgy of Period IVB Bronzes at Hasanlu. In *Peoples and Crafts in Period IVB at Hasanlu Tepe, Iran*, ed. M. de Schauensee, pp. 103–34. Hasanlu Special Studies 4. Philadelphia: University of Pennsylvania Museum.

Fokkens, H, Y. Achterkamp, and M. Kuijpers. 2008. Bracers or Bracelets? About the Functionality and Meaning of Bell Beaker Wrist-Guards. *Proceedings of the Prehistoric Society* 74:109–40.

Frane, J. 1996. The Tell Leilan Period I Habur Ware Assemblage. PhD diss., University of North Carolina, Chapel Hill.

Fuchs, Andreas. 2004. Bis hin zum Berg Bikni. Zur Topographie und Geschichte des Zagrosraumes in altorientalischer Zeit (Tübingen, unpublished Habilitation).

———. 2012. Urartu in der Zeit. In *Biainili-Urartu*, ed. S. Kroll, C. Gruber, U. Hellwag, M. Roaf, and P. Zimansky, pp. 135–61. Acta Iranica 51. Leuven: Peeters.

Ganji, M. 1968. Climate. In *The Cambridge History of Iran*. Vol. I, *The Land of Iran*, ed. W. Fisher, pp. 212–49. Cambridge: Cambridge University Press.

Gansell, A. 2007. Identity and Adornment in the Third-Millennium BC Mesopotamian "Royal Cemetery" at Ur. *Cambridge Archaeological Journal* 17:29–40.

Gensheimer, T. 1984. The Role of Shell in Mesopotamia: Evidence for Trade Exchange with Oman and the Indus Valley. *Paleorient* 10:65–73.

Ghirshman, R. 1935. Rapport préliminaire sur les fouilles de Tépé- Sialk. *Syria* 16:229–46.

———. 1938. *Fouilles de Sialk I*. Paris: Paul Geuthner.

———. 1939. *Fouilles de Sialk, prés de Kashan, 1933, 1934, 1937*, Vol. II. Paris: P. Geuthner.

———. 1954. *Iran, from the Earliest Times to the Islamic Conquest*. Baltimore: Penguin Books.

———. 1964. *The Art of Ancient Iran*. New York: Golden Press.

———. 1977. *L'Iran et la migration des Indo-aryens et des Iraniens*. Leiden: E. J. Brill.

Gilbert, A., and P. Steinfeld. 1977. Faunal Remains from Dinkha Tepe, Northwestern Iran. *Journal of Field Archaeology* 4:329–51.

Godard, A. 1950. *Le Trésor de Ziwiyè*. Haarlem: H. Enschedel.

Goff, C. 1977. Excavations at Baba Jan: The Architecture of the East Mound, Levels II and III. *Iran* 15:103–40.

———. 1978. Excavations at Baba Jan: The Pottery and Metal from Levels III and II. *Iran* 16:29–65.

———. 1985. Excavations at Baba Jan: The Architecture and Pottery of Level I. *Iran* 23:1–20.

Golani, A. 2010. Jewelry as a Cultural Marker in the Archaeological Record: The Case of Basket Pendant Earrings. In *Proceedings of the Sixth International Congress of the Archaeology of the Near East*, Vol. 1, ed. P. Matthiae, L. Romano, et al., pp. 751–62. Wiesbaden: Harrassowitz Verlag.

Gopnik, H., and M. Rothman. 2011. *On the High Road: The History of Godin Tepe, Iran*. Costa Mesa, CA: Mazda.

Grantovsky, E. 1970, *Rannyaya Istoriya Iranskikh Plemen Peredney Azii*. Moscow.

———. 1998. *Iran i Irancy do Akhemenidov*. Moscow.

Günther, R. 1899. Contributions to the Geography of Lake Urmi and Its Neighbourhood. *The Geographical Journal* 14:504–23.

Haerinck, E. 1988. The Iron Age in Guilan: Proposal for a Chronology. In *Bronze-working Centres of Western Asia c. 1000–539 B.C.*, ed. John Curtis, pp. 63–78. New York: Kegan Paul International.

Hakemi, A. and Mahmud R. 1950. Rapport et resultats de fouilles scientifiques à Hasanlu, Solduz. *Guzarishha-yi bastan-shinasi* 1:87–103.

Hamlin [née Kramer], C. 1971. The Habur Ware Ceramic Assemblage of Northern Mesopotamia: An Analysis of Its Distribution. PhD diss. University of Pennsylvania, Dept. of Anthropology. Philadelphia.

———. 1974 .The Early Second Millennium Ceramic Assemblage of Dinkha Tepe. *Iran* 12:125–53.

———. 1975. Dalma Tepe. *Iran* 13:111–28.

Harris, M.V. 1989. Glimpses of an Iron Age Landscape: Plants at Hasanlu. *Expedition* 31(2-3): 12–23.

Harrison, J. 1968. Geology. In *The Cambridge History of Iran*. Vol. I, *The Land of Iran*, ed. W. Fisher, pp. 111–85. Cambridge: Cambridge University Press.

Hassanzadeh, Y. 2009. Qalʻe Bardine, a Mannaean Local Chiefdom in the Bukan Area, North-Western Iran. *Archäologische Mitteilungen aus Iran und Turan* 41:269–82.

Heinsch, S. 2004. Korldar Tepe. Stratigraphie und Keramik. Unpublished MA thesis, University of Innsbruck.

Helwing, B. 2005. Tappeh Sialk South Mound: Operation 3. In *The Fishermen of Sialk. Report of the Sialk Reconsideration Project* 4, ed. S. Shahmirzadi, pp. 27–66. Tehran.

Henrickson, E. 1985. The Early Development of Pastoralism in the Central Zagros Highlands (Luristan). *Iranica Antiqua* 20:1–42.

———. 1986. Ceramic Evidence for Cultural Interaction between Chalcolithic Mesopotamia and Western Iran. In *Technology and Style. Ceramics and Civilization* 2, ed. W. Kingery, pp. 87–133. Columbus: American Ceramic Society.

Henrickson, R. 1983–1984. Giyan I and II Reconsidered. *Mesopotamia* 18-19:195–220.

———. 1987a. The Godin III Revised Chronology for Central Western Iran, ca. 2600–1400 BC. *Iranica Antiqua* 22:33–115.

———. 1987b. Godin III and the Chronology of Central Western Iran ca. 2600–1400 BC. In *The Archaeology of Western Iran. Settlement and Society from Prehistory to the Islamic Conquest*, ed. Frank Hole, pp. 205–27. Smithsonian Series in Archaeological Inquiry. Washington, DC: Smithsonian Institution Press.

———. 2011. The Godin Period III Town. In *On the High Road. The History of Godin Tepe, Iran*, ed. H. Gopnik and M. Rothman, pp. 209–82. Costa Mesa, CA: Mazda.

Hepper, F. 1996. Timber Trees of Western Asia." In *The Furniture of Western Asia, Ancient and Traditional*, ed. G. Herrmann, pp. 1–12. Mainz: Philipp von Zabern.

Heydari, R. 2007. The Results of Second Season of Archaeological Projects at Rabat, Sardasht. (In Farsi.) *Archaeological Reports on the Occasion of the 9th Annual Symposium on Iranian Archaeology* 7, pp. 201–29.

Hodder, I. 1987. *The Archaeology of Contextual Meaning*. Cambridge: Cambridge University Press.

Hojabri Nobari, A. 2004. Excavations of Masjed-e Kabud in Tabriz: Its Place among Contemporaneous Iranian Iron Age Sites. (In Farsi.) In *Proceedings of the International Symposium on Iranian Archaeology: Northwestern Region*, ed. M. Azarnoush, pp. 265–76. Tehran: Iranian Center for Archaeological Research.

Hole, F., ed. 1987. *The Archaeology of Western Iran. Settlement and Society from Prehistory to the Islamic Conquest*. Washington, DC: Smithsonian Institution Press.

Hrouda, B. 1957. *Die bemalte Keramik des zweiten Jahrtausends in Nordmesopotamien und Nordsyrien.* Berlin: Mann.

Innocenti, F., P. Manetti, R. Mazzuoli, G. Pasquare, and L. Villari. 1982. Anatolia and North-western Iran. In *Andesites*, ed. R.S. Thorpe, pp. 327–49. New York: John Wiley.

Kambaxsh-Fard, S. 1969. Fouilles dans les tombes anciennes de Gheytaryeh. *Bastan Chenassi* 2:26.

———. 1970. Gheytaryeh. *Iran* 8:180.

Karakhanian, A., R. Djrbashian, V. Trifonov, H. Philip, S. Arakelian, and A. Avagian. 2002. Holocene-Historical Volcanism and Active Faults as Natural Risk Factors for Armenia and Adjacent Countries. *Journal of Volcanology and Geothermal Research* 113:319–44.

Kargar, B. 2004. Ghalaichi, Zirtu: Mannaean Capital. In *Proceedings of the International Symposium on Iranian Archaeology: Northwestern Region*, ed. M. Azarnoush, pp. 229–45. Tehran: Iranian Center for Archaeological Research.

Kargar, B., and A. Binandeh. 2009. A Preliminary Report of Excavations at Rabat Tepe, Northwestern Iran. *Iranica Antiqua* 44:113–29.

Kearton, R. 1969. Survey in Azerbaijan. *Iran* 7:186–87.

———. n.d. [1970]. Settlement Patterns in Western Azerbaijan, Iran. Unpublished manuscript, Hasanlu Publication Archive, University of Pennsylvania Museum.

Kelts, K., and M. Shahrabi. 1986. Holocene Sedimentology of Hypersaline Lake Urmia, Northwestern Iran. *Palaeography, Palaeoclimatology, Palaeoecology* 54:105–30.

Khatib Shahidi, H. 2006. Recent Investigations at Hasanlu and Reconsideration of its Upper Strata. *The International Journal of Humanities of the Islamic Republic of Iran* 13:17–29.

Khatib Shahidi, H., and R. Biscione. 2007. Iranian-Italian Archaeological Survey in Eastern Azerbaijan: Provisional Report on the 2006-1385 Season. *Gozaresha-ye Bastan Shenasi 7-Archaeological Reports* 7:25–34.

Kleiss, W. 1969. Bericht über zwei Erkundungsfahrten in Nordwest-Iran. *Archäologische Mitteilungen aus Iran* 2:7–119.

———. 1970. Bericht über Erkundungsfahrten in Nord-West-Iran im Jahre 1969, urartaische bis vorachämenidische Plätze. *Archäologische Mitteilungen aus Iran* 3:107–32.

———. 1971. *Zendan-i Suleiman: Die Bauwerk.* Wiesbaden: F. Steiner.

———. 1973. Bericht über Erkundungsfahrten in Iran im Jahre 1972. *Archäologische Mitteilungen aus Iran* 6:7–80.

———. 1974. Planaufnahmen urartäischer Burgen und Neufunde urartäischer Anlagen in Iranisch-Azerbaidjan im Jahre 1973. *Archäologische Mitteilungen aus Iran* 7:79–106.

———. 1975. Siedlungen und Burgen in Azerbaidjan. *Archäologische Mitteilungen aus Iran* 8:27–42.

———. 1976. Urartäische Plätze im Iran (Stand der Forschung Herbst 1975). *Archäologische Mitteilungen aus Iran* 9:19–43.

———. 1977a. Burganlagen und Befestigungen in Iran. *Archäologische Mitteilungen aus Iran* 10:23–52.

———. 1977b. Alte Wege in West-Iran. *Archäologische Mitteilungen aus Iran* 10:137–51.

———. 1978. Hügelgräber in Nordwest-Azerbaidjan. *Archäologische Mitteilungen aus Iran* 11:13–18.

———. 1981. Mittelalterliche Burgen im Zentraliranischen Hochland. *Archäologische Mitteilungen aus Iran* 14:95–116.

Kleiss, W., ed. 1979. *Bastam: Ausgrabungen in den urartäischen Anlagen.* Tehraner Forschungen 4–5. Berlin: Mann.

Kleiss, W., and S. Kroll. 1977. Urartäische Plätze in Iran. *Archäologische Mitteilungen aus Iran* 10:53–118.

———. 1979. Vermessene urartäische Plätze in Iran (West-Azerbaidjan) und Neufunde (Stand der Forschung 1978). *Archäologische Mitteilungen aus Iran* 12:183–243.

———. 1992. Survey in Ost-Azerbaidjan 1991: A. Architektur. Befunde aus vorgeschichtlicher bis hochmittelalterlicher Zeit. B. Vorgeschichtliche Keramik und Steinfunde. *Archäologische Mitteilungen aus Iran* 25:1–46.

König, F. 1955. *Handbuch der chaldischen Inschriften.* Archiv der Orientforschung, Beiheft 8. Graz: E. Weidner.

Kramer, C. 1977. Pots and People. In *Mountains and Lowlands: Essays in the Archaeology of Greater Mesopotamia*, ed. L. Levine and T.C. Young, Jr., pp. 91–112. Malibu: Undena Publications.

Kroll, S. 1970. Die Keramik aus der Ausgrabung Bastam 1969. *Archaeologische Mitteilungen aus Iran* 3:67–92.

———. 1976. *Keramik Urartäischer Festungen in Iran: Ein Beitrag zur Expansion Urartus in Iranisch-Azerbaidjan*. Archaeologische Mitteilungen aus Iran, Ergängzungsband 2. Berlin: Reimer.

———. 1979. Die urartäische Keramik aus Bastam. In *Bastam. Ausgrabungen in den urartäischen Anlagen*, ed. W. Kleiss, pp. 203–20. Berlin: Mann.

———. 1984. Archäologische Fundplätze in Iranisch-Ost-Azarbaidjan. *Archaeologische Mitteilungen aus Iran* 17:13–133.

———. 1992. Ein "Triple Road System" oder "Stallbauten" in Hasanlu IV B? *Archäologische Mitteilungen aus Iran* 25:65–72.

———. 1994a. Festungen und Siedlungen in Iranisch-Azarbaidjan. Untersuchungen zur Siedlungs- und Territorialgeschichte des Urmia-See-Gebiets in vorislamischer Zeit. Unpublished Habilitation, Ludwig-Maximilians-Universität.

———. 1994b. Habur-Ware im Osten oder: Der TAVO auf Irrwegen im Iranischen Hochland. In *Beiträge zur Altorientalischen Archäologie und Altertumskunde*, ed. P. Calmeyer, K. Hecker, L. Jakob-Rost, and C. Walker, pp. 159–66. Wiesbaden: Harrassowitz.

———. 2000. Nordwest Iran in achaimenidischer Zeit: Zur Verbreitung der Classic Triangle Ware. *Archäologische Mitteilungen aus Iran und Turan* 32:131–38.

———. 2004a. Bastam and Iron Age in North-western Iran. In *Persiens Antike Pracht*, ed. T. Stoellner, R. Slotta, and A. Vatandoust, pp. 360–69. Bochum: Deutschen Bergbau-Museum.

———. 2004b. Prehistoric Settlement Patterns in the Maku and Khoy Regions of Iranian Western Azerbaijan. In *Proceedings of the International Symposium on Iranian Archaeology: Northwestern Region*, ed. M. Azarnoush, pp. 45–53. Tehran: Iranian Center for Archaeological Research.

———. 2004c. Aurel Stein in Hasan Ali: Bemalte frühbronzezeitliche Keramik im Gebiet des Urmia-Sees: "Hasan Ali Ware." In *A View from the Highlands*, ed. A. Sagona, pp. 677–92. Louvain: Peeters Press.

———. 2005. The Southern Urmia Basin in the Early Iron Age. *Iranica Antiqua* 40:65–85.

———. 2010. Urartu and Hasanlu. In *Urartu and Its Neighbors. Aramazd*, Vol. 2, ed. A. Kosyan, A. Petrosyan, and Y. Grekyan, pp. 21–35. Yerevan: Association for Near Eastern and Caucasian Studies.

———. 2011. Urartian Cities in Iran. In *Urartu/Biainili: Transformation in the East*, ed. K. Köroğlu and E. Konyar, pp. 150–69. Istanbul: Yapı Kredi Yayınları.

———. 2012. Salmanassar III und das frühe Urartu. In *Biainili-Urartu*, Acta Iranica 51, ed. S. Kroll, C. Gruber, U. Hellwag, M. Roaf, and P. Zimansky, pp. 163–68. Leuven: Peeters.

———. In Press a. *On the Road(s) to Nowhere: A Reanalysis of the Hasanlu "Tripartite Road System" in Light of the Excavated Evidence*. Münster: Ugarit Verlag.

———. In Press b. Hasanlu III und die stratigraphische Evidenz der Triangle Ware. In *Der archäologische Befund und seine Historisierung. Dokumentation und ihre Interpretationsspielräume*, Tagung Innsbruck 2009.

Kromer, K. and A. Lippert. 1976. Die österreichischen Ausgrabungen am Kordlar-Tepe in Aserbaidschan. *Mitteilungen der Anthropologischen Gesellschaft in Wien* 106:65–82.

Kushnareva, K. 1997. *The Southern Caucasus in Prehistory: Stages of Cultural and Socioeconomic Development from the Eighth to the Second Millennium B.C.* Philadelphia: University of Pennsylvania Museum.

Kuz'mina, E. 2007. *The Origin of the Indo-Iranians*. Leiden: Brill.

Lalande, P. 1969. *Carte du tapis végétal de la région mediterrannéenne Feuille Est*. UNESCO-FAO.

Lanfranchi, G. 2003. The Assyrian Expansion in the Zagros and the Local Ruling Elites. In *Continuity of Empires (?): Assyria, Media, Persia*, ed. G. Lanfranchi, R. Rollinger, and M. Roaf, pp. 79–118. Padova: Sargon.

Lawn, B. 1970. University of Pennsylvania Radiocarbon Date List XIII. *Radiocarbon* 12:577–89.

———. 1973. University of Pennsylvania Radiocarbon Date List XV. *Radiocarbon* 15:367–81.

———. 1974. University of Pennsylvania Radiocarbon Dates XVII. *Radiocarbon* 16:219–37.

Lay, D. 1967. A Study of the Mammals of Iran Resulting from the Street Expedition of 1962–1963. *Fieldiana: Zoology* 54:1–282.

Lehmann-Haupt, C. 1910. *Armenien, einst und jetzt; reisen und forschungen von C. F. Lehmann-Haupt*. Berlin: B. Behr.

Lemaire, A. 1998. Une inscription araméenne du VIIIe siecle av. J.-C. trouvée à Bukan. (Azerbaidjan Iranien). *Studia Iranica* 27:15–30.

Levine, L. 1973. Geographical Studies in the Neo-Assyrian Zagros: I. *Iran* 11:1–27.

———. 1974a. Geographical Studies in the Neo-Assyrian Zagros: II. *Iran* 12:99–124.

———. 1974b. Archaeological Investigations in the Mahidasht, Western Iran—1975. *Paléorient* 2:487–90.

———. 1976. The Mahidasht Project. *Iran* 14:160–61.

———. 1977. Sargon's Eighth Campaign. In *Mountains and Lowlands*, ed. L. Levine and T.C. Young, Jr., pp. 135–51. Malibu: Undena.

———. 1987. The Iron Age. In *The Archaeology of Western Iran*, ed. F. Hole, pp. 229–50. Washington, DC: Smithsonian Institution Press.

Levine, L., and T.C. Young, Jr., eds. 1977. *Mountains and Lowlands: Essays in the Archaeology of Greater Mesopotamia*. Malibu: Undena.

Licheli, V., and R. Rusishvili. 2008. A Middle Bronze Burial at Atsquiri. In *Archaeology in Southern Caucasus*, ed. A. Sagona and M. Abramishvili, pp. 205–28. Louvain: Peeters Press.

Lippert, A. 1975. Ausgrabungen am Kordlar Tepe (Persisch-Westaserbeidschan). *Antike Welt* 6:298–99.

———. 1976. Vorbericht der österreichischen Ausgrabungen am Kordlar-Tepe in Persisch-Aserbaidschan: Kampagne 1974. *Mitteilungen der Anthropologischen Gesellschaft in Wien* 106:83–112.

———. 1977. Kordlar-Tepe. *Iran* 15:174–77.

———. 1978. Ausgrabungen am Kordlar Tepe in Persisch-Aserbaidschan. *Antike Welt* 9:49–57.

———. 1979. Die österreichischen Ausgrabungen am Kordlar-Tepe in Persisch-Westaserbeidschan (1971–1978). *Archäologische Mitteilungen aus Iran* 12:103–53.

Lippert, A., and H.-J. Hundt. 1978. Drei mittelalterliche Bestattungen am Kordlar Tepe. *Archäologische Mitteilungen aus Iran* 11:167–74.

Love, N. 2011. The Analysis and Conservation of the Hasanlu IVB Textiles. In *Peoples and Crafts in Period IVB at Hasanlu Tepe, Iran*, ed. M. de Schauensee, pp. 43–56. Hasanlu Special Studies 4. Philadelphia: University of Pennsylvania Museum.

Magee, P. 2008. Deconstructing the Destruction of Hasanlu: Archaeology, Imperialism and the Chronology of the Iranian Iron Age. *Iranica Antiqua* 43:89–106.

Mahdavi, A., and C. Bovington. 1972. Neutron Activation Analysis of Some Obsidian Samples from Geological and Archaeological Sites. *Iran* 10:148–51.

Malek Shahmirzadi, S. 1977. The Excavation of Sagzabad Mound, Qazvin Plain, Iran, 1970–71. *Marlik* 2, pp. 67–79. Tehran: Institute of Archaeology.

Mallory, J. 1989. *In Search of the Indo-Europeans*. London: Thames and Hudson.

Marcus, M. 1990. Glyptic Style and Seal Function: The Hasanlu Connection In *Aegean Seals, Sealings and Administration: Proceedings of the NEH-Dickson Conference, University of Texas, Austin, 1989*, ed. T. Palaima, pp. 175–93. Liège: Université de Liège.

———. 1991. The Mosaic Glass Vessels from Hasanlu, Iran: A Study in Large-Scale Stylistic Trait Distribution. *Art Bulletin* 73:536–60.

———. 1993a. Incorporating the Body: Adornment, Gender, and Social Identity in Ancient Iran. *Cambridge Archaeological Journal* 3:157–78.

———. 1993b. Preliminary Catalogue of Personal Ornaments from Hasanlu, Iran. Unpublished manuscript, courtesy of Michelle I. Marcus.

———. 1994a. Dressed to Kill: Women and Pins in Early Iran. *Oxford Art Journal* 17:3–15.

———. 1994b. In His Lips He Held a Spell. *Source* 13:9–14.

———. 1995. Art and Ideology in Ancient Western Asia. In *Civilizations of the Ancient Near East*, ed. J. Sasson, pp. 2487–505. New York: Scribner.

———. 1996a. *Emblems of Identity and Prestige: The Seals and Sealings from Hasanlu, Iran*. Hasanlu Special Studies 3. Philadelphia: University of Pennsylvania Museum.

———. 1996b. Sex and the Politics of Female Adornment in Pre-Achaemenid Iran (1000–800 B.C.E.). In *Sexuality in Ancient Art*, ed. N. Kampen, pp. 41–54. Cambridge: Cambridge University Press.

Maxwell-Hyslop, K. 1971. *Western Asiatic Jewellery c. 3000–612 B.C.* London: Methuen.

McEwan, C., L. Braidwood, H. Frankfort, and H. Guterbock. 1958. *Soundings at Tell Fakhariyah*.

Oriental Institute Publication 79. Chicago: University of Chicago Press.

McGovern, P. 1986. *The Late Bronze and Early Iron Ages of Central Transjordan: The Baq'ah Valley Project 1977–1981*. Philadelphia: University of Pennsylvania Museum.

McGovern, P., S. Fleming, and C. Swann. 1991. The Beads from Tomb B10a B27 at Dinkha Tepe and the Beginnings of Glassmaking in the Ancient Near East. *American Journal of Archaeology* 95:395–402.

McKenzie, D. 1972. Active Tectonics of the Mediterranean Region. *Geophysical Journal of the Royal Astronomical Society* 30:109–85.

———. 1976. The East Anatolian Fault: A Major Structure in Eastern Turkey. *Earth Planetary Science Letters* 29:98–109.

Medvedskaya, I. 1977. On the "Iranian" Association of the Grey Ceramics of the Early Iron Age. (In Russian.) *Vestnik Drevnej Istorii* 2:93–105.

———. 1982. *Iran: Iron Age I*. BAR International Series 126. Oxford.

———. 1983. Horse Harness from the Sialk B Cemetery. *Iranica Antiqua* 18:59–79.

———. 1988. Who Destroyed Hasanlu IV? *Iran* 26:1–15.

———. 1991. Once More on the Destruction of Hasanlu IV: Problems of Dating. *Iranica Antiqua* 26:149–61.

Mizoguchi, K. 2000. The Child as a Node of Past, Present and Future. In *Children and Material Culture*, ed. J. Derevenski, pp. 141–50. London: Routledge.

Mollazadeh, K. 2008. The Pottery from the Mannaean Site of Qalaichi, Bukan (NW-Iran). *Iranica Antiqua* 43:107–25.

Moorey, P. 1971. *Catalogue of the Ancient Persian Bronzes in the Ashmolean Museum*. Oxford: Clarendon Press.

———. 1999. *Ancient Mesopotamian Materials and Industries: The Archaeological Evidence*. Winona Lake: Eisenbrauns.

Motamedi, N. 1997a. Ziwiye: A Mannaean-Median Fortress. (In Farsi.) In *Proceedings of Iranian Architecture and City Building Congress*, ed. B. Shiraz, pp. 320–57. Tehran: ICHO.

———. 1997b. Excavation at Ziwiyeh, 1995: Architecture and Ceramics. (In Farsi.) *Archaeological Reports* 1:143–70.

Mousavi, A. 2005. Comments on the Early Iron Age in Iran. *Iranica Antiqua* 40:87–99.

———. 2008. Late Bronze Age in North-Eastern Iran: An alternative approach to persisting problems. *Iran* 46:105–20.

Muscarella, O. 1968. Excavations at Dinkha Tepe, 1966. *Bulletin of the Metropolitan Museum of Art* 27:187–96.

———. 1969. The Tumuli at Sé Girdan: A Preliminary Report. *Metropolitan Museum Journal* 2:5–25.

———. 1971a. Hasanlu in the Ninth Century B.C. and Its Relations with Other Cultural Centers of the Near East. *American Journal of Archaeology* 75:263–66.

———. 1971b. Qalatgah: An Urartian Site in Northwestern Iran. *Expedition* 13:44–49.

———. 1971c. Sé Girdan. *Iran* 9:169–70.

———. 1971d. The Tumuli at Sé Girdan: Second Report. *Metropolitan Museum Journal* 4:5–28.

———. 1973a. The Date of the Tumuli at Sé Girdan. *Iran* 11:178–80.

———. 1973b. Excavations at Agrab Tepe, Iran. *Metropolitan Museum Journal* 8:47–76.

———. 1974. The Iron Age at Dinkha Tepe, Iran. *Metropolitan Museum Journal* 9:35–90.

———. 1980. *The Catalogue of Ivories from Hasanlu, Iran*. Hasanlu Special Studies 2. Philadelphia: University of Pennsylvania Museum.

———. 1986. The Location of Ulhu and Uiše in Sargon II's Eighth Campaign, 714 B.C. *Journal of Field Archaeology* 13:465–75.

———. 1994a. North-western Iran: Bronze Age to Iron Age. In *Anatolian Iron Ages* 3, ed. A. Çilingiroğlu and D. French, pp. 139–54. Ankara: The British Institute of Archaeology.

———. 1994b. Denkha (Dinkha) Tepe. *Encyclopaedia Iranica*, Vol. VII, Fascicle 3, pp. 283–84. Costa Mesa, CA: Mazda.

———. 2004. The Hasanlu Lion Pins Again. In *A View from the Highlands*, ed. A. Sagona, pp. 693–710. Louvain: Peeters Press.

———. 2005. Review of *Luristan Excavations Documents, Volume 4. The Early Iron Age in the Pusht-i-Kuh, Luristan*, B. Overlaet. *Bulletin of the Asia Institute* 15:199–201.

———. 2006. The Excavations of Hasanlu: An Archaeological Evaluation. *Bulletin of the American Schools of Oriental Research* 342:69–94.

———. 2012. Hasanlu and Urartu. In *Biainili-Urartu*, ed. S. Kroll, C. Gruber, U. Hellwag, M. Roaf, and P. Zimansky, pp. 265–79. Leuven: Peeters.

Musche, B. 1988. *Vorderasiatischer Schmuck zur Zeit der Arsakiden und der Sasaniden*. Leiden: Brill.

Nagel, W. 1962. Zum neuen Bild des vordynastischen Keramikums in Vorderasien—II. *Berliner Jahrbuch für Vor- und Frühgeschichte* 2:1–83.

Naumann, R. 1977. *Die Ruinen von Tacht-e Suleiman und Zendan-e Suleiman und Umgebung*, Führer zu archäologischen Plätzen in Iran 2. Berlin: Reimer.

Negahban, E. 1964. *A Preliminary Report on Marlik Excavation. Gohar Rud Expedition, Rudbar 1961–1962*. Tehran: Offset Press.

———. 1972. Pottery Figurines from Marlik. In *The Memorial Volume of the 5th International Congress of Iranian Art and Archaeology*, pp. 142–52. Tehran: Ministry of Culture and the Arts.

———. 1973. Preliminary Report of the Excavation of Sagzabad. *Marlik* 1, pp. 1–9. Tehran: Tehran University Press.

———. 1977. Preliminary Report of Qazvin Expedition: Excavation of Zaghe, Qabristan, Sagzabad, 1971–1972. *Marlik* 2, pp. 26–44. Tehran: Institute of Archaeology.

———. 1996. *Marlik. The Complete Excavation Report*. Philadelphia: University of Pennsylvania Museum.

———. 2005. Sagzabad Excavations: 1970–71. In *A Survey of Persian Art XVII*, ed. A. Daneshvari and J. Gluck, pp. 115–26. Costa Mesa: Mazda.

Oates, D., J. Oates, and H. McDonald. 1997. *Excavations at Tell Brak*. Vol. 1, *The Mitanni and Old Babylonian Periods*. London: McDonald Institute for Archaeological Research.

Oguchi, H. 1997. A Reassessment of the Distribution of Khabur Ware: An Approach from an Aspect of Its Main Phase. *Al-Rafidan* 18:195–224.

———. 1998. Notes on Khabur Ware from Sites Outside Its Main Distribution. *Al-Rafidan* 19:119–33.

———. 2006. The Date of the Beginning of Khabur Ware Period 3: Evidence from the Palace of Qarni-Lim at Tell Leilan. *Al-Rafidan* 27:45–58.

Orton, N., and G. Stein. n.d. [1979] Hasanlu Faunal Report, April 22, 1979. Hasanlu Publication Archive, University of Pennsylvania Museum.

Overlaet, B. 2003. *Luristan Excavation Documents 4. The Early Iron Age in the Pusht-i Kuh, Luristan*. Acta Iranica 26. Louvain: Peeters.

Parker, B. 1977. Middle Assyrian Seal Impressions from Tell al Rimah. *Iraq* 39:257–68.

Parpola, A. 1999. The Formation of the Aryan Branch of Indo-European. In *Archaeology and Language III*, ed. R. Blench and M. Spriggs, pp. 180–208. London: Routledge.

Pecorella, P., and M. Salvini. 1984. *Tra lo Zagros e L'Urmia: Ricerche Storiche ed Archeologiche nell'Azerbaigian Iraniano*, Incunabula Graeca 78. Roma: Edizioni dell 'Ateneo.

Peng, K., and Y. Zhu. 1995. New Research on the Origin of Cowries in Ancient China. *Sino-Platonic Papers* 68:7–8.

Pigott, V. 1977. The Question of the Presence of Iron in the Iron I Period in Western Iran. In *Mountains and Lowlands*, ed. L. Levine and T.C. Young, Jr., pp. 209–34. Malibu: Undena.

———. 1981. The Adoption of Iron in Western Iran in the Early First Millennium B.C.: An Archaeometallurgical Study. PhD diss., University of Pennsylvania, Dept. of Anthropology. Philadelphia.

———. 1989. The Emergence of Iron Use at Hasanlu. *Expedition* 31(2-3): 67–79.

———. 2004. Hasanlu und das Auftreten des Eisens in Westiran im frühen 1. Jahrtausends v. Chr. In *Persiens Antiche Pracht*, ed. T. Stöllner, R. Slotta, and A. Vatandoust, pp. 350–57. Bochum: Deutsches Bergbau-Museum.

Piller, C. 2003–2004. Zur Mittelbronzezeit im nördlichen Zentraliran: Die Zentraliranische Graue Ware (Central Grey Ware) als mögliche Verbindung zwischen Eastern und Western Grey Ware. *Archäologische Mitteilungen aus Iran und Turan* 35–36:143–73.

———. 2004. The Iranian Highlands in the 2nd and 3rd Millennium BC: The Period of Early History. In *Persiens Antiche Pracht*, ed. T. Stöllner, R. Slotta, and A. Vatandoust, pp. 310–27. Bochum: Deutsches Bergbau-Museum.

———. 2008. Untersuchungen zur relativen Chronologie der Nekropole von Marlik. PhD diss., Ludwig-Mazimilians-Universität, Fakultät für Kulturwissenschaften.

———. 2010. Northern Iran in the Iron Age II and III: A Neighbor of Urartu? In *Urartu and Its Neighbors. Aramazd*, Vol. 2, ed. A. Kosyan, A. Petrosyan, and Y. Grekyan, pp. 53–75. Yerevan: Association for Near Eastern and Caucasian Studies.

———. 2012. Bewaffnung und Tracht urartäischer und nordwestiranischer Krieger des 9. Jahrhunderts v. Chr.: Ein Beitrag zur historischen Geographie des frühen Urartu. In *Biainili-Urartu*, Acta Iranica 51, ed. S. Kroll, C. Gruber, U. Hellwag, M. Roaf, and P. Zimansky, pp. 379–90. Leuven: Peeters.

Pizzorno, G. 2011. Dinkha Tepe Revisited: A Critical Evaluation and Stratigraphic Analysis of the Hasanlu Project Excavations. PhD diss., University of Pennsylvania. Philadelphia.

Popper, K. 1957. *The Poverty of Historicism*. 2nd ed. London: Routledge.

———. 1976. *Unended Quest: An Intellectual Autobiography*. LaSalle: Open Court.

Porada, E. 1959. The Hasanlu Bowl. *Expedition* 1:18–22.

———. 1965. *Ancient Iran*. London: Methuen.

———. 1967. Notes on the Gold Bowl and Silver Beaker from Hasanlu. In *A Survey of Persian Art*, 14, ed. A. Pope, 2971–78. New York: Oxford University Press.

Postgate, C., D. Oates, and J. Oates. 1997. *The Excavations at Tell al-Rimah: The Pottery*. Warminster: British School of Archaeology in Iraq.

Postgate, N. 1989. Männäer. *Reallexikon der Assyriologie* 7:340–42.

Pulak, C. 2008. The Uluburun Shipwreck and Late Bronze Age Trade. In *Beyond Babylon*, ed. J. Aruz, K. Benzel, and J. Evans, pp. 288–305. New York: Metropolitan Museum of Art.

Radner, K. 2012. Between a Rock and a Hard Place: Musasir, Kumme, Ukku and Šubria—The Buffer States between Assyria and Urartu. In *Biainili-Urartu*, ed. S. Kroll, C. Gruber, U. Hellwag, M. Roaf, and P. Zimansky, pp. 243–64. Leuven: Peeters.

Raiciulescu, L. 2011. Taken to the Grave: Personal Ornament from the Iron Age North Cemetery Burials at Hasanlu, Iran. MA thesis, Boston University, Dept. of Archaeology.

Ralph, E. 1959. University of Pennsylvania Radiocarbon Date List III. *Radiocarbon* 1:49–51.

Ralph, E., H. Michael, and C. Han. 1973. Radiocarbon Dates and Reality. *MASCA Newsletter* 9:1–20.

Ramishvili, A. 2008. The Tsaghvli Necropolis. In *Archaeology in Southern Caucasus*, ed. A. Sagona and M. Abramishvili, pp. 292–325. Louvain: Peeters Press.

Rathbun, T. 1972. *A Study of the Physical Characteristics of the Ancient Inhabitants of Hasanlu, Iran*. Miami: Field Research Projects.

Rawlinson, H. 1840. Notes on a Journey from Tabríz, Through Persian Kurdistán, to the Ruins of Takhti-Soleïmán, and from Thence by Zenján and Tárom, to Gílán, in October and November, 1838; With a Memoir on the Site of the Atropatenian Ecbatana. *Journal of the Royal Geographical Society of London* 10:1–64.

Reade, J. 1979. Hasanlu, Gilzanu and Related Considerations. *Archaeologische Mitteilungen aus Iran* 12:175–72.

———. 1995. Iran in the Neo-Assyrian Period. In *Neo-Assyrian Geography*, ed. M. Liverani, pp. 31–42. Rome: Istituto di studi del Vicino Oriente.

Reese, D. 1989. Treasures from the Sea: Shells and Shell Ornaments from Hasanlu. *Expedition* 31(2-3): 80–86.

———. 1992. Shells from the Hoard at Khirbet Karhasan (IRAQ). Appendix A, in A Middle Assyrian Hoard from Khirbet Karhasan, Iraq, D. Tucker. *Iraq* 54:178–81.

Rezvani, H. 2004. Kul Tarikeh Cemetery. In *Proceedings of the International Symposium on Iranian Archaeology: Northwestern Region*, ed. M. Azarnoush, pp. 81–110. Tehran.

Rezvani, H., and K. Roustaei. 2007. Preliminary Report on Two Seasons of Excavations at Kul Tarike Cemetery, Kurdestan, Iran. *Iranica Antiqua* 42:139–84.

Rivas-Martinez, S., D. Sánchez-Mata, and M. Costa. 1999. North American Boreal and Western Temperate Forest Vegetation. *Itinera Geobotanica* 12:5–316.

Rubinson, K. 1991. A Mid-Second Millennium Tomb at Dinkha Tepe. *American Journal of Archaeology* 95:373–94.

———. 2004. Dinkha Tepe, Iran and So-Called Urmia Ware. In *A View from the Highlands*, ed. A. Sagona, pp. 661–76. Louvain: Peeters Press.

Rubinson, K., and M. Marcus. 2005. Hasanlu IVB and Caucasia: Explorations and Implications of Context. In *Anatolian Iron Ages* 5, ed. A. Çilingiroğlu and G. Darbyshire, pp. 131–38. London: British Institute at Ankara.

Sagona, A., and M. Abramishvili, eds. 2008. *Archaeology in the Southern Caucasus: Perspectives from Georgia*. Leuven: Peeters.

Sayce, A. 1882. The Cuneiform Inscriptions of Van, Deciphered and Translated. *Journal of the Royal Asiatic Society* 14:377–732.

Schaeffer, C. 1948. *Stratigraphie Comparée et Chronologie de l'Asie Occidentale*. London: Oxford University Press.

Schmidt, E. 1933. The Tepe Hissar Excavations 1931. *Museum Journal of Philadelphia* 23:322–485.

———. 1937. *Excavations at Tepe Hissar, Damghan*. Philadelphia: University of Pennsylvania Museum.

———. 1940. *Flights over Ancient Cities of Iran*. Chicago: University of Chicago Press.

Schwartz, G., and H. Curvers. 1992. Tell al-Raqā'i 1989 and 1990: Further Investigations at a Small Rural Site of Early Urban Northern Mesopotamia. *American Journal of Archaeology* 96:397–419.

Selinsky, P. 2009. Death a Necessary End: Perspectives on Paleodemography and Aging from Hasanlu, Iran. PhD diss., University of Pennsylvania, Dept. of Anthropology. Philadelphia.

Seyidov, A. 2003. *Naxçivan e. ə. VII–II minilliklərdə*. (In Azeri.) Baku: ELM.

Sharifi, A. 2002. Factors Controlling the Sedimentological and Geochemical Characteristics of the Lake Urmia. (In Persian.) *Iranian National Centre for Oceanography, Internal Report*. Tehran.

Smith, A., R. Badalyan, and P. Avetisyan. 2009. *The Foundations of Research and Regional Survey in the Tsaghkahovit Plain, Armenia*, The Archaeology and Geography of Ancient Transcaucasian Societies 1. Oriental Institute Publications 134. Chicago: The Oriental Institute.

Sokoloff, M. 1999. The Old Aramaic Inscription from Bukan: A Revised Interpretation. *Israel Exploration Journal* 49:105–15.

Solecki, R.S. 1969. Survey in Western Azarbaijan. *Iran* 7:189–90.

Solecki, R.L., and R. S. Solecki. 1973. Tepe Seavan: A Dalma Period Site in the Margavar Valley, Azerbaijan, Iran. *Asia Institute of Pahlavi University, Bulletin* 3:98–117.

Spaey, J. 1993. Emblems in Rituals in the Old Babylonian Period. In *Ritual and Sacrifice in the Ancient Near East*, ed. J. Quaegebeur, pp. 411–20. Leuven: Peeters.

Speiser, E. 1933. The Pottery of Tell Billa. *The Museum Journal* 23:249–83.

Stapleton, C. 2011. Glass and Glaze Analysis and Technology from Hasanlu, Period IVB. In *Peoples and Crafts in Period IVB at Hasanlu Iran*, ed. M. de Schauensee, pp. 87–102. Hasanlu Special Studies 4. Philadelphia: University of Pennsylvania Museum.

Starr, R. 1937. *Nuzi: Plates and Plans*. Cambridge: Harvard University Press.

———. 1939. *Nuzi: Text*, Volume 1. Cambridge: Harvard University Press.

Stein, D. 1984. *Khabur Ware and Nuzi Ware: Their Origin, Relationships and Significance*. Assur 4. Malibu: Undena.

Stein, G., and N. Orton. n.d. [1979] Butchery Practices at Hasanlu Tepe, Iran. Hasanlu Publication Archive. Philadelphia: University of Pennsylvania Museum.

Stein, M.A. 1940. *Old Routes of Western Iran*. London: MacMillan.

Stevens, S. 1991. Charon's Obol and Other Coins in Ancient Funerary Practice. *Phoenix* 45:215–29.

Stöcklin, J., and A. Setudinia. 1972. Lexique Stratigraphique International III ASIE. Centre National de al Récherche Scientifique.

Stöllner, T., R. Slotta, and A. Vatandoust, eds. 2004. *Persiens Antike Pracht: Bergbau, Handwerk, Archäologie: Katalog der Ausstellung des Deutschen Bergbau-Museums Bochum vom 28. November 2004 bis 29. Mai 2005*. Bochum: Deutsches Bergbau-Museum.

Stronach, D., and M. Roaf. 2007. *Nush-i Jan I: The Major Buildings of the Median Settlement*. Leuven: Peeters.

Stuckenrath, R. 1963. University of Pennsylvania Radiocarbon Dates VI. *Radiocarbon* 5:82–103.

Stuckenrath, R., Jr., W. Coe, and E. Ralph. 1966. University of Pennsylvania Radiocarbon Dates IX. *Radiocarbon* 8:348–85.

Swiny, S. 1975. Survey in North-West Iran, 1971. *East and West* 25:77–96.

Tala'i, H. 1984. Notes on New Pottery Evidence from the Eastern Urmia Basin: Gol Tepe. *Iran* 22:151–56.

———. 2007. The Iron II (ca. 1200–800 B.C.) Pottery Assemblage at Haftavan IV, NW Iran. *Iranica Antiqua* 42:105–23.

Tala'i, H., and A. Aliyari. 2009. Haftavan IV (Iron

II) Settlement Cemetery, NW Iran, Azerbaijan. *Iranica Antiqua* 44:89–112.

Taylor, W. 1948. *A Study of Archaeology*. Memoir Series of the American Anthropological Association 69. Menasha, WI: American Anthropological Association.

Thomalsky, J. 2006. Die Eisenzeitliche Keramik von Zendan-e Suleiman in Iranisch Azarbaijan. *Archäologische Mitteilungen aus Iran und Turan* 38:219–89.

Thornton, C., and V. Pigott. 2011. Blade-type Weaponry of Hasanlu Period IVB. In *Peoples and Crafts in Period IVB at Hasanlu, Iran*, ed. M. de Schauensee, pp. 135–82. Hasanlu Special Studies 4. Philadelphia: University of Pennsylvania Museum.

Thrane, H. 2001. *Excavations at Tepe Guran in Luristan*. Jutland Archaeological Society 28. Moesgaard [Denmark].

Tosi, M. 1975. Hasanlu Project 1974: Paleobotanical Survey. *Iran* 13:185–86.

Tourovetz, A. 1989. Observations concernant le matériel archéologiques des nécropolis A et B de Sialk. *Iranica Antiqua* 24:209–44.

Tucker, D. 1992. A Middle Assyrian Hoard from Khirbet Karhasan, Iraq. *Iraq* 54:157–82.

vanden Berghe, L. 1964. *La Nécropole de Khurvin*. Leiden: Nederlands Instituut voor het Nabije Oosten.

vanden Berghe, L., and E. Haerinck. 1976. *Bibliographie analytique de l'archéologie de l'Iran ancien*. Tehran.

van Loon, M. 1975. The Inscriptions of Ishpuini and Meinua at Qalatgah, Iran. *Journal of Near Eastern Studies* 34:201–7.

van Zeist, W. 1967. Late Quaternary Vegetation History of Western Iran. *Review of Palaeobotany and Palynology* 2:301–11.

Vickers, M., and A. Kakhidze. 2001. The British-Georgian Excavation at Pichvnari 1998: The "Greek" and "Colchian" Cemeteries. *Anatolian Studies* 51:65–90.

Vita-Finzi, C. 1969. Late Quaternary Alluvial Chronology of Iran. *Geologische Rundschau* 58:951–73.

Voigt, M. 1976. Hajji Firuz Tepe: An Economic Reconstruction of a Sixth Millennium Community in Western Iran. PhD diss., University of Pennsylvania, Dept. of Anthropology. Philadelphia..

———. 1977. The Subsistence Economy of a Sixth Millennium Village in the Ushnu-Solduz Valley. In *Mountains and Lowlands,* ed. L. Levine and T.C. Young, Jr., pp. 307–46. Malibu: Undena.

———. 1983. *Hajji Firuz Tepe, Iran: The Neolithic Settlement*. Hasanlu Excavation Reports 1. Philadelphia: University of Pennsylvania Museum.

———. 2011. Foreword. In *Peoples and Crafts in Period IVB at Hasanlu Tepe, Iran*, ed. M. de Schauensee, pp. xxix–xxxiv. Hasanlu Special Studies 4. Philadelphia: University of Pennsylvania Museum.

Voigt, M., and R. Dyson, Jr. 1992. The Chronology of Iran, ca. 8000–2000 B.C. In *Chronologies in Old World Archaeology*, ed. R. Ehrich, pp. 122–78. 3rd ed. Chicago: University of Chicago Press.

Waters, M. 1999. The Earliest Persians in Southwestern Iran: The Textual Evidence. *Iranian Studies* 32:99–107.

Winter, I. 1977. Perspective on the "Local Style" of Hasanlu IVb: A Study in Receptivity. In *Mountains and Lowlands*, ed. L. Levine and T.C. Young, Jr., pp. 371–86. Malibu: Undena.

———. 1980. *A Decorated Breastplate from Hasanlu, Iran*. Hasanlu Special Studies 1. Philadelphia: University of Pennsylvania Museum.

———. 1989. The "Hasanlu Gold Bowl": Thirty Years Later. *Expedition* 31(2-3): 87–106.

Wolff, S. 2002. Mortuary Practices in the Persian Period of the Levant. *Near Eastern Archaeology* 65:131–37.

Wolkstein, D., and S. Kramer. 1983. *Inanna, Queen of Heaven and Earth: Her Stories and Hymns from Sumer*. New York: Harper and Row.

Woosley, A., and F. Hole. 1978. Pollen Evidence of Subsistence and Environment in Ancient Iran. *Paléorient* 4:59–70.

Wright, H. 1980. Cores of Soft Lake Sediments. *Boreas* 9:107–14.

Wulsin, F. 1932. *Excavations at Tureng Tappeh near Asterabad*. Supplement to the Bulletin of the American Institute for Persian Art and Archaeology 2. New York.

Young, T.C., Jr. 1959. Excavations at Hasanlu: The 1958 Season. *Bulletin of the Philadelphia Anthropological Society* 12:5–8.

———. 1962. Taking the History of the Hasanlu Area Back Another Five Thousand Years: Sixth- and Fifth-Millennium Settlements in the Solduz Valley, Persia. *Illustrated London News* 241:707–9.

———. 1963. Proto-Historic Western Iran, an Archaeological and Historical Review: Problems and Possible Interpretations. PhD diss., University of Pennsylvania, Dept. of Anthropology. Philadelphia.

———. 1965. A Comparative Ceramic Chronology for Western Iran, 1500–500 B.C. *Iran* 3:53–85.

———. 1966. Thoughts on the Architecture of Hasanlu IV. *Iranica Antiqua* 6:48–71.

———. 1967. The Iranian Migration into the Zagros. *Iran* 5:11–34.

———. 1969. *Excavations at Godin Tepe: First Progress Report.* Royal Ontario Museum Art and Archaeology Occasional Paper 17. Toronto.

———. 1971. The Search for Understanding: Excavating the Second Millennium. *Expedition* 13:22–27.

———. 1985. Early Iron Age Iran Revisited: Preliminary Suggestions for the Re-analysis of Old Constructs. In *De l'Indus aux Balkans. Recueil à la Mémoire de Jean Deshayes*, ed. J.-L. Huot, M. Yon, and Y. Calvet, pp. 361–78. Paris: CNRS.

———. 2002. Syria and Iran: Further Thoughts on the Architecture of Hasanlu. In *On Pots and Plans,* ed. L. al-Gailani Werr, J. Curtis, H. Martin, A. McMahon, J. Oates, and J. Reade, pp. 386–98. London: NABU Publications.

———. 2003. Parsua, Parsa, and Potsherds. In *Yeki Bud, Yeki Nabud,* ed. N. Miller and K. Abdi, pp. 242–48. Los Angeles: Cotsen Institute of Archaeology.

Young, T.C., Jr., and L. Levine. 1974. *Excavations of the Godin Project: Second Progress Report.* Royal Ontario Museum Art and Archaeology Occasional Paper 26. Toronto.

Zadok, R. 2002. The Ethno-Linguistic Character of Northwestern Iran and Kurdistan in the Neo-Assyrian Period. *Iran* 40:89–151.

Zehzad, B. 1989. Flora and Vegetation of Ashk Island (Urmia Lake National Park). *Journal of Science, University of Tehran* 18:57–64.

Zettler, R., and L. Horne, eds. 1998. *Treasures from the Royal Tombs of Ur.* Philadelphia: University of Pennsylvania Museum.

Zimansky, P. 1985. *Ecology and Empire: The Structure of the Urartian State.* Chicago: The Oriental Institute.

———. 1990. Urartian Geography and Sargon's Eighth Campaign. *Journal of Near Eastern Studies* 49:1–21.

Zohary, M. 1973. *Geobotanical Foundations of the Middle East.* Amsterdam: Gustav Fischer.

Plates

Plate 3.1 Hasanlu Tepe: The Well Trench and Well Sounding looking east in 1960.

Plate 3.2a Hasanlu Tepe: The Operation I area in the central depression of the High Mound in 1956, looking southwest.

Plate 3.2b Hasanlu Tepe: Operation I in 1956 showing the central depression of the High Mound.

Plate 3.3a Hasanlu Tepe: R24. Victims SK197, SK199, and SK200 of Terminal Period IVb in the court of Burned Building III in 1962.

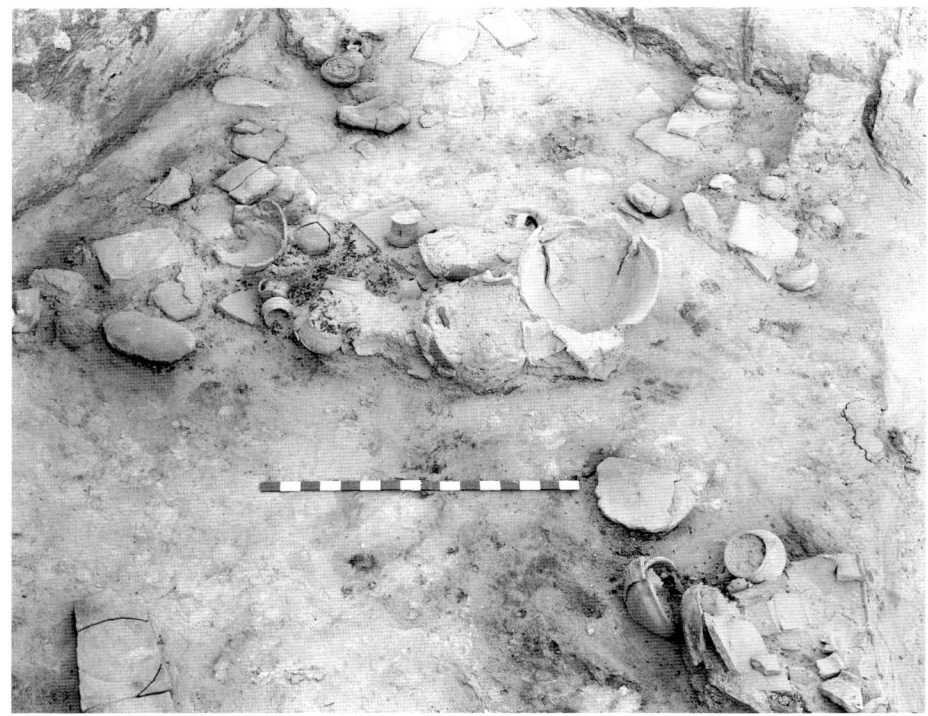

Plate 3.3b Hasanlu Tepe: S24. Distribution of objects in the BBIII Room 4 kitchen in 1962.

Plate 3.4 Hasanlu Tepe: S24 and R24. The BBIII Room 4 kitchen in 1962 looking south.

Plate 3.5 Hasanlu Tepe: R24. The north end of the Room 4 kitchen of BBIII in 1962 looking northwest to the doorway of Room 5.

Plate 3.6a Hasanlu Tepe: S24. The BBIII Room 4 kitchen in 1962 looking southeast.

Plate 3.6b Hasanlu Tepe: S24. Artifacts in the Room 4 kitchen of BBIII in 1962 looking southeast.

Plate 3.7 Hasanlu Tepe: R24. The interior of BBIII Room 5 showing the level of the floor and the upper portion of the burned deposit in 1962. Bronze in storage jar not *in situ*.

Plate 3.8a Hasanlu Tepe. Right foreground: Period IVc U22 Building Room 1. Center background: the eastern wall of Period IVB BBVII. Right background: Operation T23. Looking northeast in 1962.

Plate 3.8b Hasanlu Tepe. Foreground: U22 Stratum 6, U22 IVc Building Room 2. Center middle: U22 IVc Building Room 3. Left background: T23 Stratum 4. Looking north in 1962.

Plate 3.9a Hasanlu Tepe: The cleaning of the "U22 Period VI test pit" in 1970 looking southeast.

Plate 3.9b Hasanlu Tepe: U22 Deep Sounding looking north in 1972. The stone footings of the Period V structure are visible in the foreground (Rooms 1 and 2).

Plate 3.10 Hasanlu Tepe: U22 Deep Sounding Area 7 Stratum 15 looking northwest in 1972.

Plate 3.11a Hasanlu Tepe: U22 Deep Sounding Strata 37–42 from the west in 1974.

Plate 3.11b Hasanlu Tepe: U22 Deep Sounding Strata 37–42 from the southwest in 1974.

Plate 3.12a Hasanlu Tepe: S22 Wall D and Wall E in 1972 from the west.

Plate 3.12b Hasanlu Tepe: S22 stairwell in 1972 from the southwest.

Plate 3.13 Hasanlu Tepe: S22 stairwell in 1972 looking northwest.

Plate 3.14 Hasanlu Tepe: RS22–23 Period V structure, looking northwest in 1972.

Plate 3.15 Hasanlu Tepe: RS22–23 Period V columned hall, looking northeast in 1972.

Plate 3.16 Hasanlu Tepe: RS22–23 Period V columned hall, looking southeast in 1972.

Plate 3.17 Hasanlu Tepe: RS22 Stratum 11 column base and raised hearth, looking northeast in 1972.

Plate 3.18 Hasanlu Tepe: S22 Wall D looking southeast in 1972.

Plate 3.19 Hasanlu Tepe: S22 Area 15 Stratum 11 reed impressions under Wall D in 1972.

Plate 3.20 Hasanlu Tepe: Burned Building III portico room (Room 6) looking northwest in 1962.

Plate 3.21 Hasanlu Tepe: Burned Building III's main entrance looking northwest in 1962.

Plate 3.22 Hasanlu Tepe: Burned Building III buttresses in Q24 looking northwest in 1962.

Plate 3.23a Hasanlu Tepe: YZ28 Area 4 and Wall 22, Room 5 on the left and Room 2 on the right; looking west in 1972.

Plate 3.23b Hasanlu Tepe: Y28 Area 6 and Wall 22, Room 4 on the left and Room 2 on the right; looking west in 1972.

Plate 3.24a Hasanlu Tepe: Z29 Wall 26 and Area 4 on the right and Area 1/Room 4 on the left; looking east in 1972.

Plate 3.24b Hasanlu Tepe: Z29 Area 1/Room 4 on the right and Area 4 on the left; looking west in 1972.

Plate 3.25a Hasanlu Tepe: Y28 Area 6 and Wall 22 looking east in 1972. Stone footings of Walls 21 and 24 in the background; Room 2 on the left and Room 4 on the right.

Plate 3.25b Hasanlu Tepe: Y28 Area 6 from the north in 1972. Room 4 in the background, Room 2 in the foreground. Stone footings of Walls 21 and 24 on the left.

Plate 3.26a Hasanlu Tepe: Y28 Area 6/Room 2 looking north in 1972.

Plate 3.26b Hasanlu Tepe: Y28–29 Area 6/Room 2 looking northwest in 1972.

Plate 3.27a Hasanlu Tepe: Burned Building II northeast corner of Room 13.

Plate 3.27b Hasanlu Tepe: Burned Building II northeast corner of Room 14.

Plate 3.28 Hasanlu Tepe: The "Bead House" on the left and Burned Building II northwestern storeroom on the right in 1960.

Plate 3.29 Hasanlu Tepe: CC27/Operation XVI from the east in 1960.

Plate 3.30 The area of the North Cemetery from the northern perimeter of the Low Mound, looking southeast.

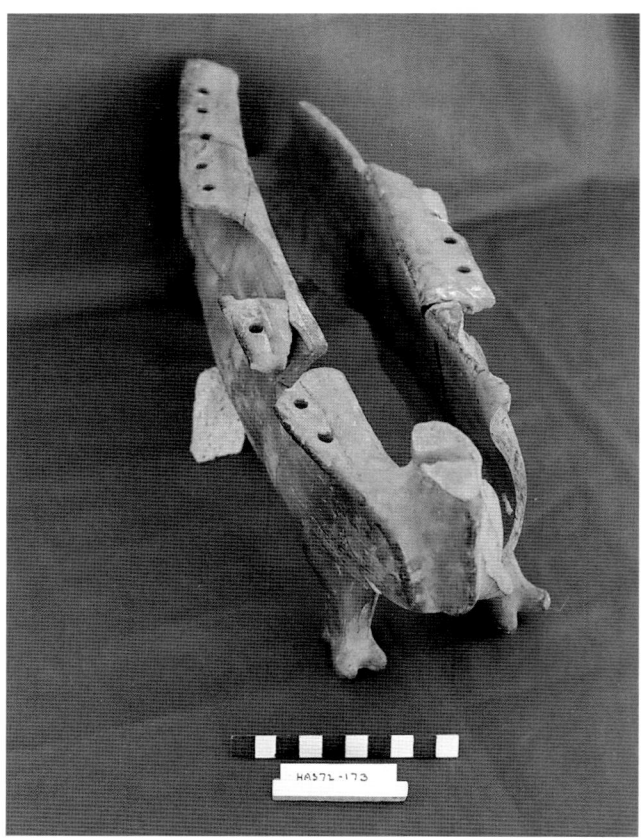
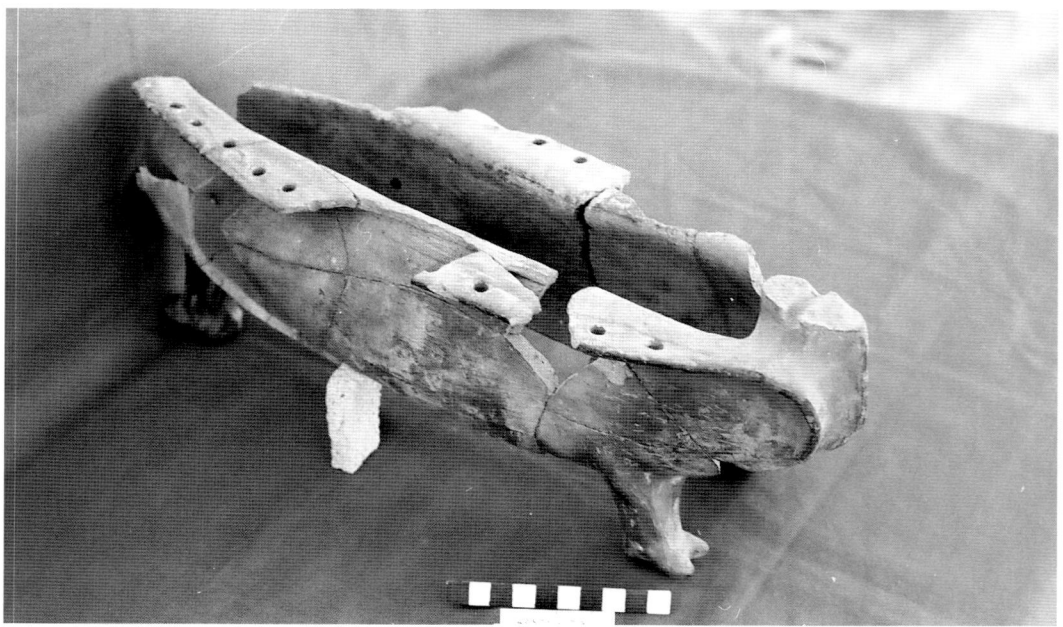

Plate 4.1 Hasanlu Tepe: Two views of the Theriomorphic Vessel from the Period V RS22–23 Building.

Plate 5.1a SK4–5 objects HAS57-107, -108.

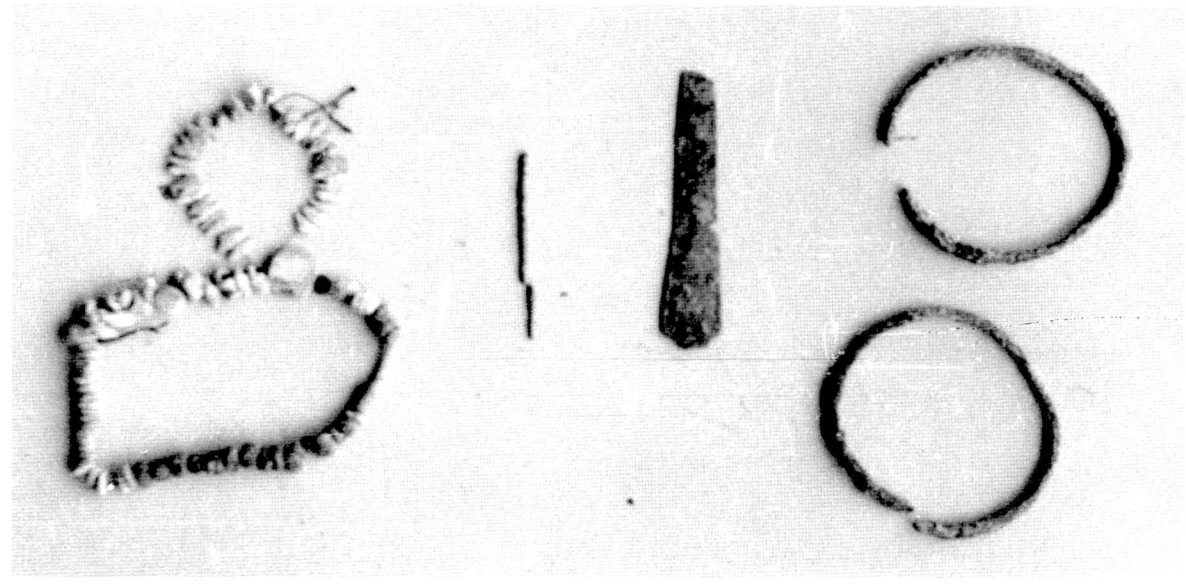

Plate 5.1b SK4–5 HAS57-109, -219, -130a–b, -131.

Plate 5.2a SK45-47 Operation X.

Plate 5.2b SK45-47 Operation X.

Plate 5.3a SK45–47 objects HAS58-120, -131.

Plate 5.3b SK45–47 Objects HAS58-121, -125, -126, -131.

Plate 5.3c SK45–47 Object HAS58-134.

Plate 5.4 Robert H. Dyson at the entrance to stone tomb SK49 in Operation X (1958).

473

Plate 5.5a (left) SK49 objects HAS58-146, -148.

Plate 5.5b SK49 object HAS58-149.

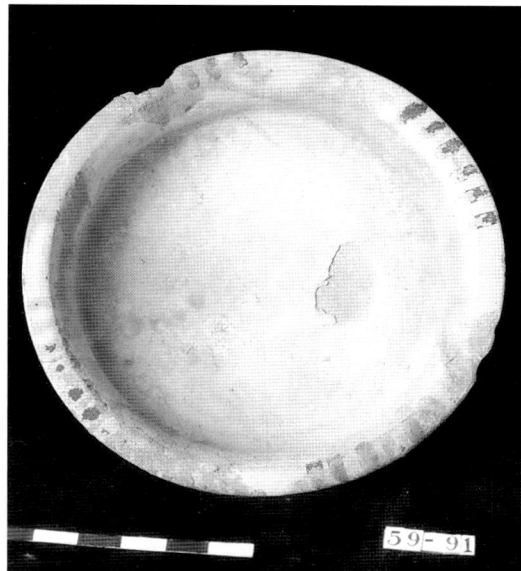

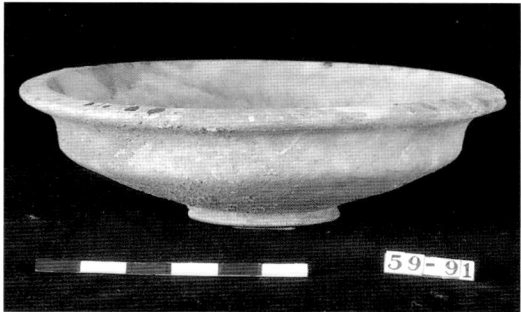

Plate 5.5c SK61 object HAS59-91.

Plate 5.5d SK61 object HAS69-116.

Plate 5.5e SK66 object HAS59-140, -141.

474

Plate 5.6a   SK112 object HAS59-224.

Plate 5.6b   SK70 object HAS59-169.

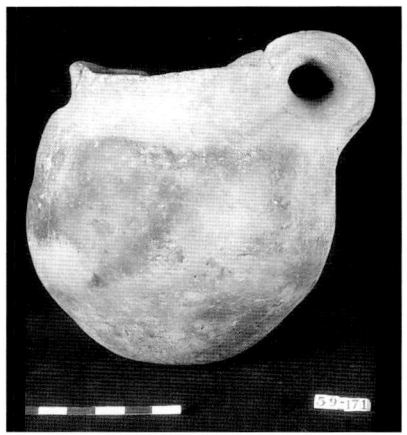

Plate 5.6d   SK25 objects HAS57-126, -127.

Plate 5.6c   SK70 object HAS59-171.

Plate 5.6e   SK116 object HAS59-323.

Plate 5.6f   SK116 object HAS59-325.

Plate 5.7a SK25 Operation VI Burial 15.

Plate 5.7b SK29 Operation VI Burial 19.

Plate 5.8a SK29 Operation VI Burial 19.

Plate 5.8b SK29 objects HAS57-159 (M), -187(L), -188 (R, intrusive).

Plate 5.9 SK15 of Operation VI dating to early Period IVb.

Plate 5.10a SK504 Operation VIj Burial 5.

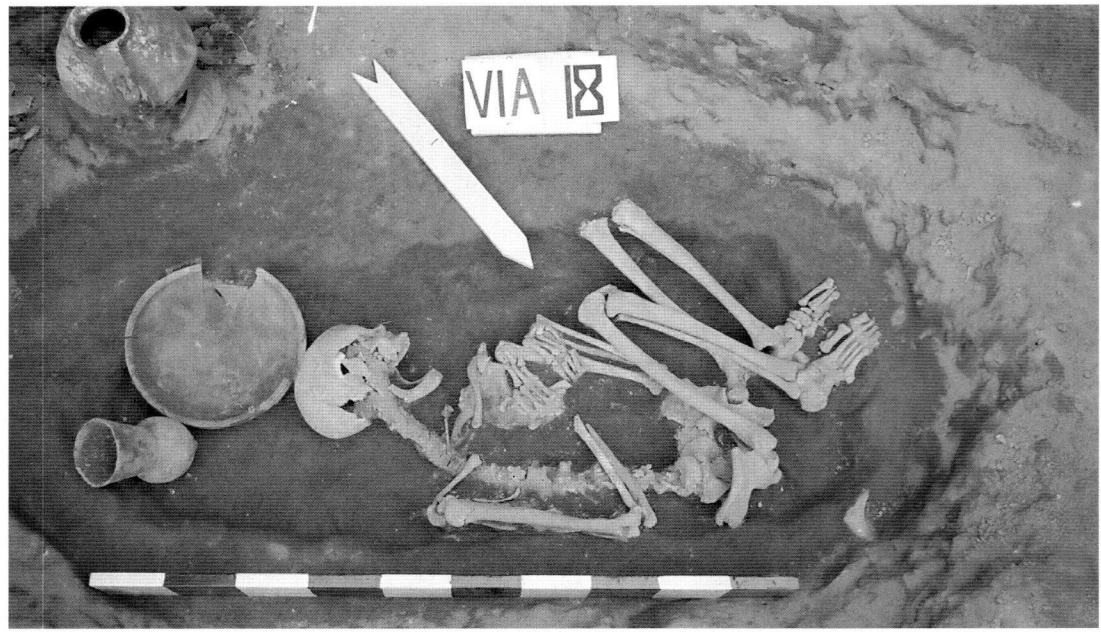

Plate 5.10b SK67 Operation VIa Burial 18.

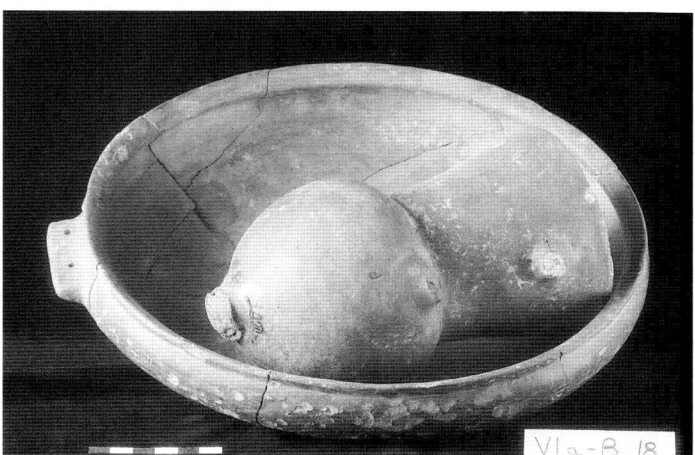

Plate 5.11a SK67 object HAS59-146, -147.

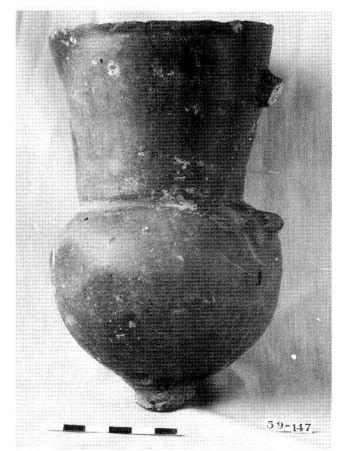

Plate 5.11b SK67 object HAS59-147.

Plate 5.11c SK24 Operation VI Burial 14.

Plate 5.12a SK445/449 object HAS64-335.

Plate 5.12b SK24 object HAS57-121.

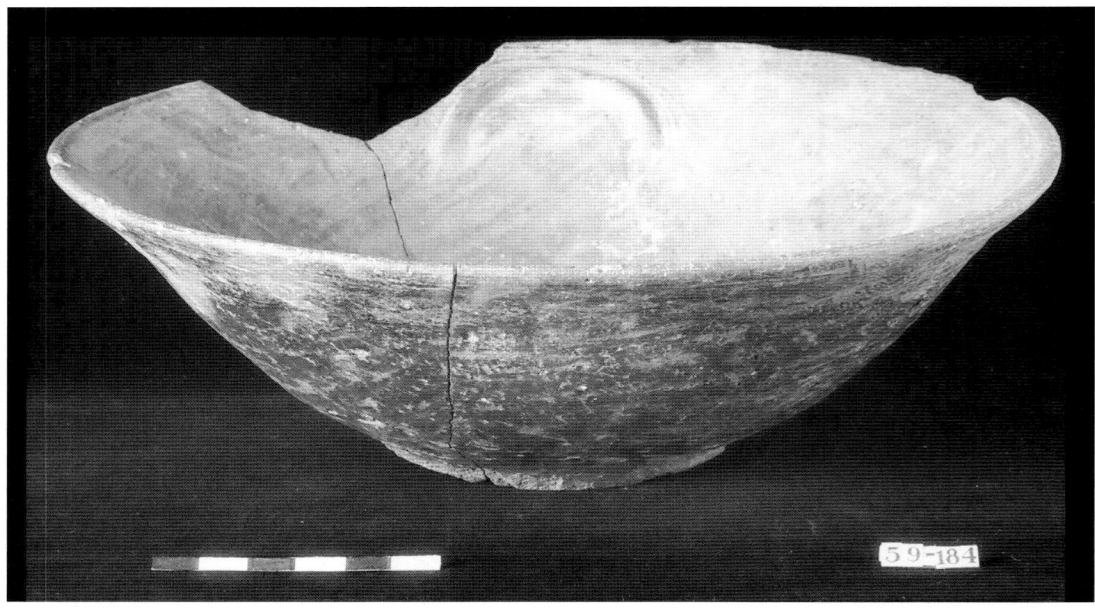

Plate 5.12c SK73 object HAS59-184.

Plate 5.13a SK459 Operation VIe Burial 10.

Plate 5.13b SK459 Operation VIe Burial 10.

Plate 5.13c SK459 object HAS64-90.

Plate 5.13d SK459 object HAS64-91.

Plate 5.13e SK479 object HAS64-176.

Plate 5.13f SK494 object HAS64-299.

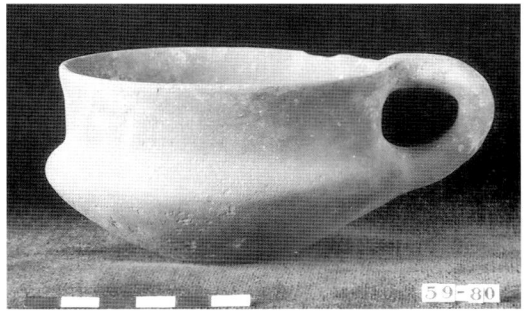

Plate 5.13g SK57 object HAS59-80.

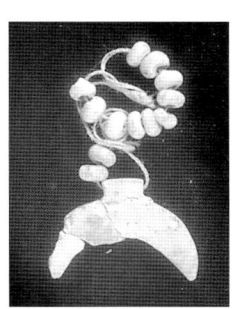

Plate 5.13h SK53 object HAS59-57.

Plate 5.14a SK479 Operation VIf Burial 8.

Plate 5.14b SK479 Operation VIf Burial 8.

Plate 5.15a SK57 object HAS59-83.

Plate 5.15b SK57 object HAS59-83.

Plate 5.15c SK57 object HAS59-77–80, -83.

Plate 5.15d SK57 object HAS59-79.

Plate 5.15e SK57 object HAS59-79.